"Willis Barnstone has a problem: he's too g
his invaluable *The Other Bible*, a compendiu... ... . .hould
be without, to his brilliant translations and beautiful poems, is a breathtaking
achievement."   —Carolyn Kizer, Pulitzer Prize–winning poet

"Willis Barnstone has been appointed a special angel to bring the 'other' to
our attention, to show how it is done. He illuminates the spirit for us and
clarifies the unclarifiable. . . . I think he does it by beating his wings."
                                    —Gerald Stern, National Book Award–winning poet

"Barnstone succeeds extremely well in making his readers approach the New
Testament with fresh eyes, shifting attention from points of doctrine and historicity, on to what is common to great religious poetry all over the world: its
power to inspire feelings of hope and joy, and at the same time to convey a
sense of the mystery of human existence. This is a superb achievement."
                                    —Alvar Ellegard, professor, Goteborg University, Sweden

"Such determination to restore the Semitic origins of the New Testament is
refreshing, and Barnstone doubles the fun by following the Gospels not with
Acts, as would be traditional, but with the Apocalypse, the Book of
Revelation. Here is where Barnstone's literary skill shines most clearly. . . . "
                                    —*Publishers Weekly*

"Barnstone's achievement will win plaudits from literary critics and textual
scholars: his gifts as a poet confer a graceful elegance on idiomatic directness,
while his talents as a scholar open up many historical and linguistic questions."   —*Booklist*

"Barnstone's feel for poetry lends [*The New Covenant*] a unique elegance and
power. . . . An important addition . . . "   —*Library Journal*

"It's a salutary turn of events, when someone comes up with a translation of
the New Testament that very explicitly—not in the footnotes, but in the warp
and weft of the translation itself—emphasizes the historical context. The
Hebrew and Aramaic names, for example, just keep hitting you, page after
page, conveying the sense that events didn't happen in Cedar Rapids."
                                    —George W. E. Nickelsburg,
                Distinguished Professor Emeritus of Religion, University of Iowa,
                                    from *The Chronicle of Higher Education*

ALSO BY WILLIS BARNSTONE

POETRY

From This White Island, 1960
Antijournal, 1969
A Day in the Country, 1971
China Poems, 1976
A Snow Salmon Reached the Andes Lake, 1980
Five A.M. in Beijing, 1987
Funny Ways of Staying Alive, 1993
The Secret Reader: 501 Sonnets, 1996
Algebra of Night: New and Selected Poems, 1999

TRANSLATIONS

The Other Alexander, 1959
(with Helle Tzalopoulou Barnstone)
Eighty Poems of Antonio Machado, 1959
Greek Lyric Poetry, 1961
Physiologus Theobaldi Episcopi—Bishop Theobald's Bestiary, 1964
Sappho: Poems in Greek with a Translation, 1967
The Poems of Saint John of the Cross, 1968
The Poems of Mao Zedong (with Go Jingbo), 1972
The Unknown Light: Poems of Fray Luis de Leon, 1976
Laughing Lost in the Mountains: Poems of Wang Wei
(with Tony Barnstone), 1991
Six Masters of the Spanish Sonnet, 1993
To Touch the Sky: Poems of Mystical, Spiritual, & Metaphysical Light, 1999

MEMOIRS

With Borges on an Ordinary Evening in Buenos Aires, 1993
Sunday Morning in Fascist Spain, 1995

LITERARY CRITICISM

The Poetics of Ecstasy: From Sappho to Borges, 1983
The Poetics of Translation: History, Theory, Practice, 1993

EDITIONS/ANTHOLOGIES

Modern European Poetry, 1967
Spanish Poetry from Its Beginnings Through the Nineteenth Century, 1970
Eighteen Texts: Writings by Contemporary Greek Authors
(with Edmund Keeley), 1973
Concrete Poetry: A World View
(with Mary Ellen Solt), 1974
A Book of Women Poets from Antiquity to Now
(with Aliki Barnstone), 1980
Borges at Eighty: Conversations, 1982
The Other Bible: Ancient Alternative Scriptures, 1984
The Literatures of Africa, Asia, and Latin America
(with Tony Barnstone), 1999

WILLIS
BARNSTONE

NEWLY TRANSLATED FROM
THE GREEK AND INFORMED
BY SEMITIC SOURCES

RIVERHEAD BOOKS
NEW YORK

THE NEW COVENANT

COMMONLY CALLED
THE NEW TESTAMENT

VOLUME I

THE FOUR GOSPELS AND APOCALYPSE

RIVERHEAD BOOKS
Published by The Berkley Publishing Group
A division of Penguin Putnam Inc.
375 Hudson Street
New York, New York 10014

An excerpt from Mark appeared in *The Ryder Magazine*, 1997; excerpts from Mark, Matthew, Luke, and John were in *Literatures of Asia, Africa, and Latin America*, ed. Tony Barnstone and Willis Barnstone (Prentice-Hall, 1999); poems attributed to Yeshua ben Yosef from Matthew and Luke, and The Apocalypse appeared in *To Touch the Sky: Spiritual, Mystical, and Metaphysical Poems in Translation* (New Directions, 1999); Apocalypse came out as *Apocalypse: A New Translation* (New Directions, 2000); and "Three Invisible Poets: Yeshua, Yohanan, and John of the Apocalypse" was published in *The Southwest Review*, 2001.

Copyright © 2002 by Willis Barnstone
Book design by Deborah Kerner/Dancing Bears Design
Cover design by Honi Werner
Cover art: Frans Pourbus the Younger, *The Last Supper* © Musée du Louvre, Paris/ET Archive, London/SuperStock

First Riverhead hardcover edition: April 2002
First Riverhead trade paperback edition: December 2002
Riverhead trade paperback ISBN: 1-57322-936-9

Visit our website at
www.penguinputnam.com

The Library of Congress has catalogued the
Riverhead hardcover edition as follows:

Bible. N.T. Gospels. English. Barnstone. 2002.
The New Covenant, commonly called the New Testament : the four
Gospels and Apocalypse / Willis Barnstone, newly translated from
the Greek and informed by Semitic sources.
p.   cm.
Includes bibliographical references.
ISBN 1-57322-182-1
I. Title: New Covenant, commonly called the New Testament. The four
Gospels and Apocalypse.   II. Title: Four Gospels and Apocalypse.
III. Barnstone, Willis, date.   IV. Bible. N.T. Revelation. English.
Barnstone. 2002.   V. Title.

BS25532B33   2002   2001019102
                225.5'209—dc21

Printed in the United States of America

10   9   8   7   6   5   4   3   2   1

CONTENTS

AFTERWORD: TRANSLATION HISTORY, ANTI-JUDAISM, AUTHORS AND SOURCES, YESHUA TO JESUS, PASSOVER DEATH AND ROME, AND YESHUA THE VOICE OF SPIRIT 429

APPENDICES 561

ACKNOWLEDGMENTS

In biblical work, mortals begin with error. So I want to express warmth to friends who have heartened and helped me immensely in this venture yet in no way do I wish to indict them for its mishaps. I thank Helle Tzalopoulou Barnstone, who led me to all things Greek: demotic, Byzantine, classical, and Koine, in that order. Tony Barnstone went through the Introduction and Afterword with tenacious brilliance and nudged me through a narrow gate of clarity. Sarah Handler read and encouraged the whole book, page by page, as it developed. For the gauche problems of consistency in transcribing proper nouns from Hebrew into English, I thank professors James Ackerman and Steven Katz at Indiana University and Robert Alter and Ruth Adler at UC Berkeley for their crucial scrutiny of the texts. Professor George Nickelsburg at the University of Iowa, whose own work in first-century Judaism and Christianity has for years instructed me, advised and carefully went over the Introduction and Afterword. David Trobisch, Professor of New Testament Language and Literature at Bangor Theological Seminary in Maine, has given us *The First Edition of the New Testament* (2000), which convincingly alters traditional notions of the redaction and dating of the first canonical New Testament. His new book and word came late and providentially. Professor Brenda Schildgen at the University of California at Davis has long informed me personally and through her books. To colleagues and collaborators in earlier projects, professors Marvin Meyer, Marc Hofstadter, and Harry Geduld, I am grateful for all their critical wisdom. And the poets Ruth Stone, Gerald Stern, Yusef Komunyakaa, and Stanley Moss because they are poets. At Riverhead Books I had the fortune of wonderful editors: Laura Matthews, Timothy Meyer, Nancy McKinley, who read the proofs with care and insight, and Cindy Spiegel, who deftly reshaped, offered ways, and many times saved this endeavor. In the end I also thank the indifferent ghost of time, who has let me enjoy years of reading and plotting and held me to the ways of composition, the spiritual loneliness.

I dedicate this essay at translation to Robert Alter, whose *Genesis* was the model.

PREFACE

YESHUA AND
THE POOR

YESHUA AND THE POOR

In those days again there was a great crowd who had nothing to eat, and
calling his students together he said to them,
>   I have pity for the crowd,
>   for they have already been with me three days
>   and have nothing to eat.
>   If I send them hungry to their homes,
>   they will collapse on the road
>   and some have come from far away.[1]

—MARK 8.1–3

The book of the canonical gospels, which treats the life and death of a
rabbi named Yeshua,[2] speaks many notes. It sounds danger, hope, amazement, suffering, a bit of joy, all elaborated with occasional irony and no scant
humor. It is at once riveting and repetitious, since it retells four versions of the
same events. It is grave and tragic, since it ends in the terrible torture-death
of the crucifixion, which the Romans devised for seditionists and criminals. In
the crucifixion, the human body is spiked through and left hanging in torment
until death gives it over to the vultures and dogs. There is an epilogue with a
glad resurrection that provides public hope to the rich in faith. But persisting
is the personal human agony of a few days earlier when a rabbi nailed to a
T-cross calls out in forsaken despair as he gives up the ghost on a Friday afternoon. In response the earth quakes and the sky blackens and cracks.

Beyond the public event of the crucifixion, the doctrine and the metaphysic,
beyond the gathering of followers who will become legion and inform the
world-dominating religious movement of Christianity,[3] the gospels speak to
the human condition of peasants in an occupied country in times of mean
opportunity.

---

[1] Citations are from this new translation unless otherwise noted.

[2] The name Jesus comes from the Greek Ἰησοῦς (Iesous), from the Aramaic and Hebrew יֵשׁוּעַ
(yeshua), which was probably Jesus' name in his lifetime. See pages 459–464 for the journey of Jesus
through Hebrew, Aramaic, Greek, and Latin into English.

[3] Christianity or messianism means "those who follow the Christ" or "the anointed." "Christ" is a
translation of the Hebrew word for messiah, which also means "the anointed." Christ comes from
the Greek Χρστός (Hristos), from the Hebrew מָשִׁיחַ (mashiah).

At the heart of the gospels is the wandering and compassionate rabbi Yeshua. He teaches and feeds the poor. He cures the leper and demoniac, the bleeding woman and a paralyzed on the floor. He restores life to a dead boy and a dead man. He is with Jew and foreigner, children of the carpenter and rich man, official or soldier—all who come to him for medical miracles and spiritual food. There are terrified students,[4] who fear for their lives on a boat in a windstorm on the Sea of Galilee[5] until Yeshua tells the winds to fall; and there are the masses whom Yeshua feeds with a few loaves and fishes to satisfy them. The primal physical needs of people living close to the edge of life and death show on virtually every page. The book of the gospels is a brief epic of hunger and humility and sicknesses. As such, it stands in black-and-white contrast to Homer's prosperous gods and soldiers and islanders, whose sensuality and adventure, rather than an impoverished human condition, excite us in resounding hexameters. The gospel figures, described in rudimentary Near Eastern Greek,[6] incite the reader's deep compassion.

That Yeshua comes as an earthly savior to the poor is poignant for us to observe. A woman falls to her knees begging the savior to touch her or her child and enact a cure. The man living in the tombs, possessed by demons, asks Yeshua whether he, too, has come to torment him, and then, cured by Yeshua, begs, unsuccessfully, to accompany him on his wanderings. The unclean are cleansed, the leper is washed, the hungry receive bread, the prostitute is not scorned, the woman (one of the Miryams,[7] wandering in the garden) discovers a resurrected crucified who touches her with hope—all these are the figures of the human landscape which the New Covenant[8] delivers without makeup or guise.

No authority other than Yeshua appeals to us in these pages. But there is a price which the poor must pay for Yeshua's powers, which is a heart-rending fear and degradation. Some call it humility and modesty. There is the shepherd and the sheep, and the sheep are beasts of the field who bend their heads to graze. In that allegorical surrender and humiliation is the pathos, which makes

---

4 Disciples—in other translations—from the Greek μαθητής (mathetes). The plain meaning of Greek *mathetes* is "pupil" or "student," which is lost in the ecclesiastical inflation to disciple.

5 Lake of the Galil. Also Lake Tiberius (after the Roman emperor). In modern Hebrew it is Lake Kinnerert, Lake Chinnereth (Num. 34.11, Matt. 4.18). The land around the lake is called Gennesaret (Matt. 14.34).

6 We lack the original Aramaic or late Hebrew source text or Aramaic oral witness accounts from which derive the existing texts in Greek. Aramaic, not Greek, was the spoken language of the Galilean Yeshua of Nazareth and his followers in Israel.

7 Marys. Mary is from the Greek Μαρία (Maria), from the Hebrew מִרְיָם (miryam), often Anglicized in English as Miriam.

8 New Testament is a mistranslation from the Greek διαθήκη (diatheke). In Jerome's Vulgata version of the Hebrew Bible, the Hebrew בְּרִית (berit *or* brit), meaning "new covenant," is translated as *Novum Testamentum,* meaning "New Testament."

this picaresque, episodic book perhaps the most evenly powerful work about the poor in body, soul, and hope. All politic, doctrine, even the beautiful poetry, parables, aphorisms, and ultimate drama of the agony of crucifixion pale before the constancy of the common person, who is the human everywhere and in all time. Therein lies the ordinary art and the plain great passion of the people in the gospels. That picture of primal nakedness covered by a colorless mean cloth, of hurting bodies that speak with need from a primal poverty, ensures that the gospels, independent of faith, doctrine, commandment, fearful warnings, and metaphysic, will always reach those with eyes to hear and feel the human condition of the spirited body waiting on the earth.

INTRODUCTION:
A REFORMATION
OF OPENNESS

*A New Translation, Three Invisible
Poets: Yeshua Ben Yosef,
Yohanan the Evangelist, and
John of The Apocalypse*

A REFORMATION OF OPENNESS

Reformations bring change, and historically have been informed with and been resisted with a sword. But to break the tradition of change that dresses in compulsion and death, a reformation of openness means only openness. No sword, no sin, no guilt, no infidel, no punishment. Truth has a small *t,* and heart a big *H,* and so one truth does not impose. A reformation of openness has silence to mediate controversy, understanding to mediate sectarian wrath, and peace to mediate the stranger. The heart of openness is love (another sweet tautology), which is a better key to the world than bitter closure. There is no end to openness. Imperfection in this temporary life is a good to be open to, so that the incorruptible Maximilien Robespierre does not arrest and execute the suspected traitor who has strayed from truth. Better is an itinerant who is open to the poor. A book need not end, nor a heart, nor a spirit roaming in the blur inside. The day and night of life need not end but stay open to vision, maybe the vision of the blind and crippled. So reformation is openness, and carries in its intellectual passion a small *r.*

In this introduction, we may first look at the efforts, seldom loved, often greeted not with openness but fire, of the translator's way.

A NEW TRANSLATION

Why a new translation of a biblical text? Why the King James Version in 1611, only eighty-some years after the masterful Tyndale translation, which is as austerely plain and beautiful as a field of wheat? The most obvious answer is that language changes and so, too, do literary conventions for making speech contemporary and natural. There may also be the call for a new approach, since translation is not only style and period, but way and purpose. The earliest versions in English by John Wyclif in 1380 and William Tyndale in 1525 were created to bring Latin scripture into the English vernacular. For their daring acts of replacing Jerome's fourth-century Latin (the authorized Christian Bible in the West) with their English vulgate, Wyclif's bones were dug up and burned and Tyndale was strangled and burned at the stake. Wyclif's and Tyndale's purpose had been to bring scriptures to the people. Tyndale, citing the aims of his model, the Dutch humanist Erasmus, wrote that the word of the gospels should reach the eyes of all women, Scots and Irishmen, even Turks and Saracens, and especially the farm worker at the plow and the weaver at the loom. Then in the early seventeenth century, the Tyndale and later versions were revised into the monumental King James Version, whose stated purpose by King James I's forty and seven translator scholars was to bring forth an authorized version for the Protestant peoples of the Church of England. The King James also had a literary and didactic aim, which appears in the first line of the prefatory "Translators to the Reader": "Translation it is that openeth the window, to let in the light."

I undertook a new translation of the New Covenant, commonly called the New Testament,[9] to give a chastely modern, literary version of a major world text. In the introduction, annotation, and text itself, I have some specific aims.

---

[9] New Covenant is an exact translation of the Greek *kaine diatheke* (καινή διαθήκη) found in the Septuagint and in Paul's Corinthians 11.25 and Hebrews 8.8–13, meaning "new covenant." The title New Testament derives from *Novum Testamentum*, a mistranslation of καινή διαθῆκη, appearing in the Vulgata (Vulgate), the fourth-century Latin translation attributed to Jerome. In English and the languages of Western Europe, the term *Novum Testamentum* has been rendered "New Testament." In recent translations and also in the new editions of the NRSV (New Revised Standard Version) and other standard modern versions, New Covenant is the preferred title and presented (as here on the title page) as "The New Covenant, commonly called The New Testament." Please see pages 513–516 for further discussion. If one wished to preserve the fact that the New Covenant is a post-Torah scripture composed by, addressed to, and about, Jews of Yeshua's day (including Peter [Kefa], James [Yaakov] and Paul [Shaul]), one might speak of the New Torah or New Tanak.

First, I wish to restore the probable Hebrew and Aramaic names and so frame the Jewish identity of the main figures of the covenant, including that of Yeshua (Jesus), his family, and followers. Second, I would like to clarify the origin of Christianity as one of the Jewish messianic sects of the day vying for dominion. Third, I wish to translate as verse what is verse in the New Covenant as in Yeshua's speech and the epic poem of Apocalypse, following a practice which, since the nineteenth-century Revised, has prevailed in rendering Hebrew verse as in Song of Songs, Psalms, and Job. On all questions of faith versus history, I take a neutral stance, and I minimally address the frequent and important conflicts of historical event and religious faith. As far as possible, I limit these matters to indicating a historical context of biblical happenings, always with the awareness that more is unknown than known.[10] In her brilliant *Jesus of Nazareth, King of the Jews* (New York: Knopf, 1999, 8), Paula Fredriksen presents the first fact, from which all historical speculation must radiate: "The single most solid fact about Jesus' life is his death: he was executed by the Roman prefect Pilate, on or around Passover, in the manner Rome reserved particularly for political insurrectionists, namely, crucifixion. Constructions of Jesus primarily as a Jewish religious figure, one who challenged the authority of Jerusalem's priests, thus sit uncomfortably on his very political, Imperial death: Pilate would have known little and cared less about Jewish religious beliefs and intra-Jewish religious controversy."

With regard to ascertainable fact and religious belief, while respecting all views, I have no pitch for any side. There is no more polemic or proselytizing here than were this book a new version of the *Odyssey* or of Sappho's fragments, yet I hope that my love for these extraordinary world scriptures will show through. My wish is also that the covenant will be read by all, and that the text and annotation will be a source of pleasure, and information, while giving some awareness of the background from which Yeshua ben Yosef, Jesus son of Joseph, came.

A number of new translations have changed the word "Jew" in their versions in order to diminish the accusations of villainy and guilt against Yeshua's coreligionists for their supposed judgment concerning the charismatic rabbi as the foretold messiah of Isaiah. So Jew is written as "opponent" or "Judean" or some other euphemism to spare the Jew abuse and to change the fact that the

---

[10] Events recounted in the gospels are essentially theologically framed accounts confined to the gospels themselves. External references to Yeshua tell us little. Suetonius (Nero 16.2) mentions the existence of *Christiani* and of Jesus; Tacitus (*Annales* 15.44) mentions Christians and Jesus, who was sentenced to death by Pontius Pilate; Pliny the Younger has a brief reference to Jesus. The main external source is the Jewish historian Josephus, who wrote in Greek and lived later in Rome, and there are problems with what is authentic and what may be a later emendation.

foundation of anti-Judaism[11] was and remains the New Covenant. Such changes are inaccurate to the texts as we have them, and actually reinforce a much more significant misconception, which is that Yeshua and family and followers were somehow *not* Jews, that Yeshua was not a rabbi (though in the Greek gospels[12] he is addressed as rabbi frequently). By a tradition of using largely Greek names for the Hebrew and Aramaic names of covenant figures, those who represent what is sometimes called "primitive Christianity" lose their Jewish identity, thereby making it possible for Christians to hate Jews, yet not hate Yeshua as a Jew, nor his mother Miryam and father Yosef, nor all his followers. The hostility to Jews is selective and occurs without awareness of the anomaly of loving Yeshua and hating his people and the religion he practiced. The disappearance of Yeshua's Jewish identity dumbfounds common sense and history, but, alas, this illusion has remained dominantly at the center of Christian reception of the New Covenant. Contemporary scholars and some readers know better, but the anachronistic portrayal of Yeshua and his circle as later Christians among enemy Jews permits an unquestioned antipathy to the Jew, and is a logical, understandable, and inevitable reading of the New Covenant as we have it. Yet the reader need not be a biblical scholar to notice something awry when Yeshua, a Jew, speaks in the voice of a later gentile admonishing Jews of terrible punishment when Rome will destroy Jerusalem. Such anomalies lead contemporary theologians to make corrective comments. The Christian theologian Marcus J. Borg corrects at all levels:

> Jesus was deeply Jewish. It is important to emphasize this obvious fact. Not only was he Jewish by birth and socialization, but he remained a Jew all of his life. His Scripture was the Jewish Bible. He did not intend to establish a new religion, but saw himself as having a mission within Judaism. He spoke as Jew to other Jews. His early followers were Jewish. All of the authors of the New Testament (with the possible exception of the author of Luke-Acts) were Jewish.

---

[11] Anti-Judaism is a religious term based on a theological contempt for Judaism and by extension for Jews. The actual term anti-Semitism was coined in 1879 by the German agitator Wilhelm Marr to designate anti-Jewish campaigns then underway in central Europe. Anti-Semitism had its beginnings during the first-century Roman Empire when Jews were often segregated for their refusal to participate in emperor worship and, by emerging Christians, for the Jews' failure to accept Jesus as their messiah. Many scholars argue that anti-Judaism is a more accurate term, since Jews are only one among Semitic peoples, and anti-Judaism means hostility only to religion, not to people. But faith and people are inevitably synonymous. In Northern Ireland, the anti-Catholicism, while not against Irish ethnicity, is directed against Irish people who hold Catholic beliefs. I have used both anti-Judaism and anti-Semitism, depending on whether the hostility is toward the religion or people or both.

[12] In the Introduction and Afterword I examine mainly the gospels and Apocalypse, which are the books contained in volume 1 of this edition of the New Covenant.

Though I find it hard to believe, some Christians are apparently unaware of the Jewishness of Jesus, or, if they are aware, do not give it much weight. Moreover, Christians have frequently been guilty of conscious or unconscious anti-Semitism, identifying Jesus with Christianity and his opponents with Judaism, and thereby seeing Jesus and the early Christian movement as anti-Jewish. . . . The separation of Jesus from Judaism has had tragic consequences for Jews throughout the centuries. The separation is also historically incorrect, and any faithful image of Jesus must take with utmost seriousness his rooted-ness in Judaism.[13]

I address this dire and central question of disenfranchising Yeshua of his religious identity in two ways: by restoring the probable Hebrew or Aramaic names to biblical figures and by framing some fiercely anti-Semitic passages in a historic context in the Introduction and the textual annotation. It should first be understood that although the extant gospels are only in Greek, and Yeshua speaks Greek in the gospels, Yeshua did not use Greek, if indeed he had any knowledge of it. In his daily life and on the cross when he cried in agony to God, Yeshua spoke in Aramaic, a Semitic language close to Hebrew, which had by and large become the spoken language of the Jews after their return to Israel from the Babylonian defeat (586 B.C.E.).[14] Hebrew remained the language of the Temple and religion. Yet we have Greek names for Yohanan (John—although the Germans retain the Hebrew in Yohan, as in Johann Sebastian Bach). Somehow Yaakov or Jacob in the Hebrew Bible becomes James in English, and Miryam becomes the Greek Maria. By recovering what are the Hebrew and Aramaic names of covenant personages, I believe that the Semitic origin and climate will at last persuade in the gospels. In the same way that the Homeric names Zeus, Athena, and Artemis are finally heard in twentieth-century translations and no longer romanized as Jupiter, Minerva, and Diana, so, too, the Jewish names of Yaakov, Yeshua, Yosef, and Yohanan are used here rather than their irrelevant and misleading Greek or Anglicized forms.

In introducing or restoring names, I balance the urgency of restoration with familiarizing the reader with new referents. Hence, in the introduction and annotation, the evangelists are still called Mark, Matthew, Luke, and John for

---

[13] Marcus J. Borg, *Meeting Jesus for the First Time* (San Francisco: HarperSan Francisco, 1994), 22.

[14] From the seventh century B.C.E. until the rise of Islam in the seventh century C.E., when Aramaic yielded to Arabic, Aramaic was the lingua franca of the Fertile Crescent and the greater Mesopotamian region and competed with Greek after the coming of Alexander the Great, who conquered the region. The Syrian Christian Church used their dialect of Aramaic, but as Aramaic became associated with pagans, they spoke of it as Syriac and developed an altered alphabet.

easy reference, while in the texts biblical restorations rather than standard Hellenizations are used for most names and places. In the annotation, where other texts are cited, conventional spelling is followed. Any change in standard orthography takes a while, but, like becoming used to new jargon or currency, it is often quickly absorbed and accepted.

"Jesus Christ" is a Greek formulation and not recognizably a biblical Semitic name. If the name in English were chosen in keeping with other traditional English versions of biblical Hebrew names, he could also be "Joshua the Messiah," "Joshua the Anointed," "Yeshua ben Yosef," "Yeshua bar Yosef,"[15] or "Yeshua of Nazareth," and all these names have been given him by diverse commentators and scholars.

This restoration of Semitic names does wonders to afford a truthful perception of the identity of New Covenant peoples. It will help us recall, as Bishop John Shelby Spong has observed, that the New Covenant was written by Jews about Jews for Jews. The New Covenant—though largely unread by Jews and when read may be perceived with deep fear—is the last major Jewish text of biblical Judaism, the parent religion of Christianity and Islam.

The second way of handling traditional anti-Judaism is through the introduction and annotations in the texts where I attempt to place these remarks in a historical perspective. There was, of course, the inevitable inflated rhetoric of interfamily rival sects within Judaism, each seeking dominion during Yeshua's life. However, the texts were not fashioned in Greek until late in the first and early in the second centuries, with many unknown hands copying, redacting, and emending the stories and re-creating conversations, even of secret deliberations that allegedly took place behind the walls of the Sanhedrin.[16] By the time these texts were finally accepted by religious councils in the fourth century, what had been a first-century controversy between Jewish groups, allegedly between Pharisees and messianics, was now seen ahistorically as a conflict between Jews and later Christians. By then, in name and thought,

---

[15] *Bar* is Aramaic for *ben,* "son of."

[16] Sanhedrin from the Greek συνέδριον (synedrion). Sanhedrin is a council or court of the Jews in Jerusalem. It is a Hebraized form of the Greek *synedrion,* meaning a council or assembly. In the Mishnah, a collection of rabbinic oral traditions set down as writing (ca. 200 C.E.), the first use of Sanhedrin occurs. Therefore "Sanhedrin" in New Covenant translations to mean "court" is, as here, anachronistic. In the New Covenant, Sanhedrin refers to judicial courts presided over by the high priest. Its usage is imprecise and the Sanhedrin may be connected to the council of elders in Israel. Sanhedrin may also mean just a "gathering" or "assembly." In Acts 22.5, Paul refers to the *presbyterion* (elders) as the authority that gave orders to arrest Yeshua. In Mark 15.1, it is called the *symboulion* (council). The use of a Greek word derived from a beginning-of-the-third century C.E. Hebraized version of it indicates both an anachronism, and textually the presence of a late hand in the composition or emending of the gospels, which are said to have been set down in the late first century.

Christianity was politically separated from Judaism, though it retained the Jewish Bible (Old Testament) as its own Bible, to which it added the Jewish scripture of the New Covenant.

There is enormous, sad irony in these separations and conflicts, based on misunderstandings and contentions of power. Jews and Christians share one Hebrew Bible, and Christians read the last great biblical document of the Jews, the New Covenant. With so much vitally in common and believers sharing the same invisible God, why such division and history of hostility? Yet this initial rivalry between Jew and Christian Jew, and in the next century between Jew and Christian, was to be repeated again and again in the schisms now within Christianity. Rome broke away from Constantinople, with equal consequences of fury and death, and there began nearly two millennia of contending Orthodox and Roman Catholics. After the Reformation, the Protestants broke with Catholics and more blood battles ensued. There were the Western crusades against Catharist France, Byzantium, and Islam. Each year, under changing names and banners, these blood schisms stain parts of the globe.

In the end, all people are people, and any marker of sect and theology that distinguishes people adversely is human error. So the gospels and Apocalypse can be read not for conflicts between believers and infidels but for a universality of spirit in a world desperately poor in coming to terms with human consciousness within the perishable body. The covenant is a book of the mind, and is infused with compassion and courage. It treats the great questions of being, death, time, and eternity. For the perceptive reader, spirit eludes name, dogma, and even word to reside in the silence of transcendence.

HOW OLD VERSIONS OF THE BIBLE SHAPED
SECULAR LITERATURE AND HOW NEW VERSIONS HAVE NOT

Historically, the single book most deeply affecting the writers in the English language has been the Bible. Imagine John Donne, George Herbert, John Milton, William Blake, Emily Dickinson, Walt Whitman, Gerard Manley Hopkins, T. S. Eliot, H. D., and Dylan Thomas without it. But little of this flame—the fires of poetry—came from the New Covenant, as they knew it, or from contemporary versions of the Hebrew Bible. Most of the biblical language and tale that entered English literature was found in early translations, those made in that short period between and including the Tyndale publications in the 1520s and 1530s and the King James Version in 1611. Not only was the language of the English Bible established during that period, but English itself, through word inventions in the Bible, became immensely expanded and enriched. In the nineteenth century, there were major scholarly and literary revisions, and in our time, especially in the last decades, there has been an opening and candor in religious studies as never before, permitting all to be said or speculated, doctrinaire and radical. But while theology and history have experienced liberation, in both studies and permissible translation, literary artistry has not done well. Perhaps because the need for intellectual freedom has been so imperative, art and the quality of the word have suffered by neglect in Bible translation.

Early in the twentieth century, T. S. Eliot pitilessly attacked Gilbert Murray's old-fashioned, wooden, Swinburnean translations of the Greek tragedians and called for a renovation of Greek and Latin classics in English. Robert Fitzgerald, Dudley Fitts, and William Arrowsmith answered his plea with consummate renditions. In our time, ancient and modern texts, from the Chinese to the Italian, Spanish, and Russian, have enjoyed a renaissance of excellent translations and translators. Yet despite academic interest in using reliable Greek sources to translate more accurately, no imperious Eliot has shown up to rebuke, in the name of art, contemporary translations of holy scripture. We have not the accomplishment of philosopher-theologian Martin Buber, who gave the modern German Bible a flowing, poetic, etymologically keyed alternative to Luther's famous sixteenth-century version. During the past century, we were given variations of the nineteenth-century English and American Revised Versions editions (1898–1990), of which the best was the recent NRSV (New Revised Standard Version, 1990). The NRSV aims for accuracy and softening the male-oriented articulation, yet retains the essential archaizing, proper, and pious tone of biblical language. As is often the case with literature deemed sacred, the Bible has been held to criteria alien to the art of literary translation. Reform has often come under the emblem of objectivity where "information transfer," as in technical translation of business and science, is the measure. There are also, for the sake of reader comprehension, interpretive translations and dumbed-down versions of the Bible, yet not in the manner of Mark's plain Greek, but as chatty or off-key street-talk renderings.

The Bible in English deserves what our foremost writers can bring to it. It is a richly complex document, with many levels of expressive meaning. Translation that fails to bring over the maximum semantic load, that slights poetic language, abuses the hope of true equivalence. The Bible is a volume charged with immense connotative meanings, as are all our religious classics, including the *Dao De Jing, Bhagavad-Gita,* and *Odyssey.* A version in our day that scarcely goes beyond a word-for-word transfer between tongues signifies that again our age has failed to provide a classical work in English as Tyndale did and the Authorized did. The latter became for many, right or wrong, "an authorized original."

Today's Bible should inspire the devout and the secular reader as the King

James Bible once did. Yet unseen are inspiring new versions. Hence, outside classrooms and religious institutions, the readers of "the great books" are not interested in contending with the Authorized or prosaic updates.

Abandoned by our best-known writer-translators and generations of readers, we have lacked even those who dedicated themselves to turning one great book of the Bible into a masterpiece, as Sir Philip Sidney and Lady Herbert from Elizabethan London did to give us a new rendition of the Psalms.[17] We have had no contemporary English or American equal to Poland's Nobel laureate in literature, Czeslaw Milosz (who learned Hebrew specifically to translate the Songs of Songs into Polish), who might render distinguished books of the Bible in English. Perhaps it is an unfair burden to ask our leading contemporary religious scholars to become the Luthers and Dantes for our time and refresh the English language. In days of territorial specialization, literature and art are not their terrain. The consequences are clear.

Old versions are remote and contemporary ones do not sing. In contrast to the King James, whose scholars helped establish literary tradition, in the new Bibles, after the corrections and recorrections, the seminarian translators have kept repetition of seminal clichés intact in pedestrian speech sullenly remote from literature. So a great literature is captive to neglect. It is imperative to remember that these holy books from the coastal strip of Western Asia contain the most intense concentration of the arts of narration, drama, and poetry the world has assembled.

Apart from the gloom, there are areas of light. If there are not new resplendent Bibles, there are writers infused with Bible light, with a magnificence of language and spirit whose source remains the King James Version. Consider T. S. Eliot's "Ash Wednesday," *Murder in the Cathedral,* and *The Four Quartets.* For all his cranky urbane anti-Semitism, Eliot is probably the last major poet in the English language who has produced enduring pieces deriving directly from the two covenants. Eliot's competitor might be James Baldwin of *Go Tell It on the Mountain,* who uses the full rhetoric of biblical speech preserved in the African-American church. Martin Luther King spoke the rhetoric of the Bible in his dream speech. Of course, these examples mirror the mighty King James Version and not the readable and more accurate Revised and New Revised and New Revised Standard Versions.

One could wish that in the last twenty years of his life, when his own creative well went dry, Eliot had, in the grand tradition, turned his hand to creat-

---

[17] *The Psalms of Sir Philip Sidney and the Countess of Pembroke,* ed. J. C. A. Rathmell (Garden City, NY: Doubleday, 1963). First published in 1823 under the title *The Psalmes of David translated into divers and sundry kindes of verse.*

ing the Bible in English. The task fell to the American classical scholar Richmond Lattimore. Trained in the fullness of the Greek tongue, Lattimore had spent his life turning Homer, Aeschylus, and Pindar into powerful English poetry. In his last years he turned his gaze to the New Covenant and gave us a catholic, impeccably smooth version, with dignity, freshness, and a touch of beautiful ancient rhetoric. And although his 1962 publication went largely unnoticed, it remains by far the finest version we have of the words of the Covenant scriptures in English.[18] In translating the New Covenant, Lattimore (the first of the Lattimore-Fitzgerald-Fagles triad of splendid Homer translators) is the exception, but his work proves that it is possible to marry scholarship and art in translating the Bible, as was done by his contemporaries in giving us Homer, Sappho, and Virgil. What is to be done? At the very least, one should be aware that the larger, once fertile plain is arid. And then, with a hint from the scriptures, one can hope the day of a Hebrew Bible and New Covenant scriptures resurrected in English is near.[19]

YESHUA SPEAKING VERSE

Much of the two covenants is verse. Historically, if there are words in the canonical gospels that were uttered by an identifiable speaker, they are probably wisdom sayings in verse attributed to Yeshua the Messiah, commonly called in English Jesus Christ or Jesus the Christ.

---

[18] Even Richmond Lattimore follows the earlier sacred tradition of blurring Yeshua's identity as a Jew through selectively false translation. After Yeshua praises Nathanael for being "truly a Jew," Nathanael says to Yeshua, "Rabbi, you are the son of God. You are the king of Israel" (John 1.49). In Greek we have *Rabbi*, but Lattimore, the most just literary scholar translator of his day, here as elsewhere, still renders *Rabbi* in Greek as "Master" in English. More recent translators, however, reflecting the present mood, uniformly translate *Rabbi* as "Rabbi," including the New King James Version (1979), which corrects the King James Version (1611) "Master" to read "Rabbi."

[19] In 1996 Reynolds Price published *Three Gospels* (New York: Scribners, 1996), which includes Mark, Matthew, and John, a revision from an earlier version of the four canonical gospels. It is of the same literary quality throughout as the Lattimore, less lofty and more modern, and very close to the Greek. It has no extra words and is a literary breakthrough. Price uses "wrong" rather than "sin" as one way of reducing what he calls the "puritan" practice in translating from the koine. As pure observation and no reproach, I note that he comes closer than others, but makes no essential break with a strongly Christianizing bias in converting Greek into English and doesn't move the text from a Hellenization of name, place, and spirit back to its Hebrew Bible base. He does mitigate, where he can without stylistic contortions, the domination of male gender words.

A major change from the pedestrian Hebrew Bible translations that our century has sponsored has been the 1996 publication of Genesis in versions by Robert Alter and by Stephen Mitchell and the 1999 translation of Alter's *David*. Alter and Mitchell are both literary, the Alter rhythmically rhetorical and austerely beautiful, with significant annotation; the Mitchell more contemporary, clean, and, like the Alter, at once close to both the King James and to modern speech. Like the Everett Fox lineated translation of *The Five Books of Moses*, the first lines of Genesis in the Alter version have orchestral power and balance, although Alter does so in prose rather than verse.

As for these wisdom poems attributed to Yeshua, they are of extreme importance, indeed at the heart of the gospels, and are more likely than the narrations
to have claims to historicity. Yet these sayings, too, though they may have been
uttered by Yeshua, also have a source in the preserved wisdom sayings of earlier
figures, since it is natural and expected that a charismatic sage will repeat the
famous traditional wisdom phrases of the past. With respect to their prosodic
form, the sayings, like Psalms, Song of Songs, and most of the words of Isaiah
and Jeremiah in the Hebrew Bible, may be read and lineated as poetry, even
though the monumentally poetic King James Version cast them in prose. In
the gnostic Gospel of Thomas,[20] which has no narration and is exclusively
Yeshua's sayings, Yeshua's words are also preserved in traditional aphorism that
may be read as verse. Here in this version, Yeshua's words are lineated as poetry,
just as most of Yeshua's words, especially in John, are lineated in the French
and English editions of the New Covenant in the Catholic Jerusalem Bible
(1990). To most of us it is a secret that Yeshua's speech takes the form of poems.
Even more obscure is the notion that the authentic core of the gospels stands
in verse. This translation will introduce the Jewish messiah of the Christians[21]
as the great oral poet of the first century C.E., who heretofore has been our invisible poet.

MARK, THE VERNACULAR STORY TELLER

When the writer or writers of Mark assembled the earliest of the canonized
gospels, its story was of an itinerant rabbi who talked, healed miraculously, and
walked the hills of Yehuda (Judea) and alleys of the holy city of Yerushalayim
(Jerusalem); who mesmerized his followers with his word, at once wise, evasive,
lyrical, and surreal; and who suffered, if the story of the Roman crucifixion is
accurate, the most dramatic and meaningful death in history. He was a wandering preacher. Recently, theologians compare him to a Greek Cynic philosopher,
a late Diogenes looking with a lantern in bright daylight for an honest man.
Not only were his followers about to have in letters a document describing a
new, small sect of first-century Jews, a new Judaism—that would eventually
take on its own identity and name, Christianity[22]—but the book would, in

---

[20] The Gospel of Thomas was discovered in 1945, in Coptic translation from the Greek, among the
Nag Hammadi texts in Egypt. The dating is problematic. Some scholars suggest 50 or 55 C.E., while
others suggest it may be the late second century or even the third. Its translation from Greek into
Coptic was probably third century. There also exists fragments of Thomas in Syriac.

[21] Christian is from the Greek *Hristianos* (χριστιανός), meaning "messianic" or "anointed."

[22] For further discussion of the complexity of the emerging development of the Yeshua movement, see
George W. E. Nickelsburg, "Revealed Wisdom as a Criterion for Inclusion and Exclusion: From
Jewish Sectarianism to Early Christianity," in Jacob Neusner and Ernest S. Frerichs, eds., *To See*

plainest speech, detail Jewish and Greek thought concerning time and eternity, body and spirit, and the life of a skygod residing on earth who dies on a Roman cross and returns to the sky. These assumptions and events will in the next two thousand years spread around the globe as Christian theology.

The narrative means employed in the gospels would also alter the use of language. The Greek resting point at which the New Covenant exists found its lexicon and style in both the Hebrew Bible and the diverse postbiblical scriptures that make up the noncanonical apocrypha and pseudepigrapha of the period. In Mark there was something else: the perfection of the ordinary, the pure, the rude,[23] and the popular. It is spare. A raconteur could say or dream it, but Aeschylus or even the great Shakespeare of Lear might not notice it as art. Or, if they did, their version, as Shakespeare's borrowings from Plutarch, would be fleshed out beyond recognition. Yet in its lucid minimalism, Mark prefigured a formal revolution in style of two thousand years later when Hemingway, in gnomic works like *The Old Man and the Sea,* came upon a speech that made the novelists of America and Europe go plain. In the opening picture in the wilderness are Mark's direct rhythmic words and bright plainness:

Yohanan the Dipper appeared in the desert and preaching an immersion of repentance for the remission of sin. The whole land of Yehuda[24] and all the people of Yerushalayim[25] came out to him and were being immersed by him in the Yarden River,[26] and confessing their sins. Clothed in camel hair, Yohanan wore a belt of hide around his waist, and he ate locusts and wild honey.

The author of Mark wrote in Koine, a form of demotic or spoken Greek, and his voice is a spoken tale—not a learned written report in elegantly difficult syntax. It is a teller's story, one largely repeated by Matthew and Luke, each of whose version varies as a teller's account will. Here the Hebrew Bible and the gospels share the medium of talk. Nothing is plainer than the talk-narration of Genesis, which is to be heard as speech or chanted as song. One

---

Ourselves as Others See Us: Christians, Jews, "Others" in Late Antiquity (Chico, CA: Scholars Press, 1985), and Wayne Meeks, *The First Urban Christians: The Social World of the Apostle Paul* (New Haven: Yale University Press, 1983).

[23] It is frequently speculated that the author's rudimentary Greek, a language probably foreign to the author or translator of a Semitic source text, accounts for the book's primitive force. Unfamiliarity is not, however, a key to literary innovation, though limited linguistic means may be a factor in determining the strong direct speech.

[24] Judea.

[25] Jerusalem.

[26] Jordan River.

must remember that God did not write but "spoke" creation through the word; his feats on those six days of labor were dictated into the Torah. Mark's gospel story of the days of Yeshua turned out to be divine talk for later Christians. His tone also reflects the unknown sources of his specific tale which, whether written, oral, or both, certainly carried the same character of common speech.

Given the spontaneity and plain tuning of the gospels, the concern for finding and keeping the fixed word, the exact letter of the Bible, seems almost an impertinence. The reader is always dealing with translation and a text that itself is a translation from an unknown written text or witness report that is sometimes called "oral gospeling." Many layers stand between the reader and exact, documentary speech. Talk may be fixed by a playwright or scribe or digital recorder, but, with regard to biblical witnessing, such reports are obscure, and their next expression will be different and contain new revelations. This uncertainty pertains to versions of most ancient texts, especially to religious texts, and has its own virtues. The salient virtue of unfixed scripture is its liveliness, its imitation of convincing speech. Plato cast his writings in the form of *The Dialogues,* philosophical talk, precisely to preserve the spontaneous live speech, which, he argued, holds meanings that the written word cannot capture. Speech comes from live persons. Writing becomes dry ink. Through Socrates' voice, Plato said that "to write with pen and ink is to write in water, since the words cannot defend themselves. The spoken word—the living word of knowledge, which has a soul—is thus superior to the written word, which is nothing more than its image" (Plato, *Phaedrus,* 278b). So at the heart of the gospels is the living, heard voice of Yeshua, usually in the form of a platonic dialogue. The letters (epistles), too, are a form of live speech, the voice of one person speaking to others. By contrast, the thinkers Descartes and Hume are master stylists, but unlike the gospels they reason abstractly, never dialogically, nor through the voice of an author intimately addressing the reader. Their texts are eloquent and convincing, but they never sing.

Each of the gospels has its own genius of style and preserves its authoritative way through discussion. Unlike the intimate tale of the gospels, the Apocalypse (Revelation)[27] takes us elsewhere. Although also in Koine, Apocalypse, like the many extant apocalypses of the era—Jewish and Christian-Jewish—is one long breath of Hebrew Bible prophecy of the end. Like the primeval tales

---

[27] Apocalypses may be found in James H. Charlesworth, *The Old Testament Pseudepigrapha* (Garden City, NY: Doubleday, 1983–1985) and in Willis Barnstone, *The Other Bible* (San Francisco: Harper-San Francisco, 1984). All the other apocalypses are called "apocalypses," but the Apocalypse in the New Covenant in most translations into English is "Revelation." In other languages, especially in those where Greek Orthodoxy is followed, the Greek word "apocalypse" is transliterated as apocalypse rather than translated as revelation.

of creation and destruction in Genesis and the grotesque sky beasts in Daniel, its immediate source, the primal grandeur of Apocalypse carries us in vision all over the heavens and under the earth.[28] The gospels of healing, poetry, parabolic wisdom, and the culminating passion along with the angelic vision of Revelation make the New Covenant the ultimate Christian-Jewish book.

The "ultimate Christian-Jewish book" refers to the fact that although the gospels are Jewish books composed by Jews about Jews, as is each book in the Hebrew Bible, the gospels can also be seen as Christian-Jewish books. The later Christians received the gospels as Christian scripture, where Christian carries the meaning of messianic. Yeshua's followers saw him as the messiah, the foretold Jewish messiah, there being not yet a separate religion one could call Christianity. An increasingly prevalent understanding holds that the gospels are Jewish books written by Christian Jews, which were ultimately appropriated and shaped by later Christians who had lost their Jewish centrality and who saw intra-Jewish rivalry in the New Covenant as a struggle between gentile Christians and demonized Jews. In John Shelby Spong's *Liberating the Gospels: Reading the Bible with Jewish Eyes* (San Francisco: HarperSan Francisco, 1996), the Episcopal bishop asserts that "The Gospels are Jewish Books" (title of chapter 2). He notes that although Christians have been educated to deny that the New Testament is a Jewish book, "the Gospels are Jewish attempts to interpret the life of a Jewish man" (20) and "in a deep and significant way, we are now able to see that all of the Gospels are Jewish books, profoundly Jewish books" (36). He observes that the gospels were written by four Jews (Mark, Matthew, John, and Luke, a convert) about Jews. The bishop goes on to confess his own worldwide, Christian-prejudiced education with regard to the gospels: "How was it that one whose name was Yeshuah or Joshua of Nazareth, whose mother's name was Miriam, could come to be thought of in history as anything but a Jew? . . . Not only did I not understand that Jesus was Jewish, but it never occurred to me to assume that his disciples were Jewish either. I could not imagine Peter, James, John, and Andrew as Jews, to say nothing of Mary Magdalene and Paul" (24–25). In his extensive study of the New Covenant, he tells us, "We are beginning to recognize the Gospels as Jewish books" (33), but as for their historicity, he notes that the dark Judas, the dark "anti-hero of the Christian tradition" (258), was "a later Christian invention. . . . Judas never existed but was a fictional scapegoat created to shift the

---

[28] In *Omens of Millennium* (New York: Riverhead Books, 1996), Harold Bloom reminds us that apocalyptic tradition, so widespread in intertestimental times and especially in the diverse noncanonical books of Enoch, has a long tradition from Zoroaster to Islam: "From Zoroaster on, apocalyptic expectations flourished and made their way into Judaism and its heretical child, early Christianity, and then into Islam, which sprang forth from Jewish Christianity" (41).

blame for Jesus's death from the Romans to the Jews." Please see last paragraphs of "On Historicity" for more information on Judas.

It is sad and hopeful that one must reiterate what is or should be obvious to scholars and eventually to the general readership, which is the centrality of the New Covenant as Jewish scripture. It should be as obvious as believing that Plato's *Republic* is Greek philosophy with a Greek cast and author. But Yeshua's Jewishness is not clear. Moreover, in the extant Greek form, it is not meant to be clear. This version, which at least restores the home geography and Semitic identity of the characters, has the fancy that it may incite a journey of understanding.

In a grand book—problematic, imperfect as grand books of all faiths must be since these are the writings of humans, not of God—there is a page behind the page. On the underpage lies the good news of the Jewish teacher, rabbi Yeshua ben Yosef. But on other uncertain pages in the New Covenant are words reflecting persuasions of later churchmen that have fashioned Yeshua as an alien Galilean denouncing his coreligionists and sending them to a punishment worse than that found in Sodom and Gomorrah. These outbursts should be understood as perfectly implausible and unworthy of Yeshua's nature and mission. Then begins understanding and good feelings. Then Matthew of the lovely Sermon and the empathetic Beatitudes, "Blessed are the gentle / for they will inherit the earth" (5.5), reaches us and not Yeshua militant, "who comes not to bring peace on earth but a sword" (10.34). That battle-sword anger should not, with a positive twist, be explained away hermenutically but rejected outright as alien noises of sectarian rivalry penned by later anonymous hands. Then, released from stains of anger, Yeshua's voice speaks an innocence of light in the heart, of "light filling the whole body." It is a covenant of the noblest and kindest love, enveloping us in a firmament of soul. And the Christian believer—or reader of any faith or joy—is released from negations to read the book of concordance.

PRINCIPLES OF PERSUASION

Having known the scarlet T of translation much of my life, along with some other letters of sin, academic and creative, and having written a book about translation's history, which centered in part on Bible conversion, I'd rather say nothing about the way taken here. Rather than defend, repeat, or assert notions of translation which many, including myself, have made thin by repetition, I would prefer to guard silence and let the reader read with no excuses from me. It would be better. But for reasons I think clear, it is not fair (and not the practice) to be silent about linguistic methods of converting a book of holy scripture.

PRINCIPLES OF PRESENTATION

So after speaking with some passion about the New Covenant and of the equally deep need for windows to see it through, I offer some principles that have helped me to attempt this translation.

1. The English text should read with the plain grace of the Greek page.
2. The invisible Hebrew Bible and Aramaic sources are in part refreshed by giving in most instances the Hebrew Bible and Aramaic names of person and place rather than the misleading Hellenizing Greek versions of the names, where the apparent intention of Greek mediation is to remove the book from its Semitic sources. The book should read not as a Greek book in English but as a Semitic book about Semites, which has passed through Greek in reaching us.
3. The names of prophets or titles of books of the Hebrew Bible cited in the text are identified and mentioned by name. Where in the Greek it says "and it is written" or "and the prophet says," it is normal practice in annotated translations to identify these names solely in minuscule reference name initials, along with chapter and verse numbers, in the margin or at the bottom of the page.[29] Matthew might have expected his informed readers to know which Jewish prophet spoke a specific passage and where that passage occurred, as in the famous first reference to the messiah in Matthew 2.5–6. In the New Revised Standard Version, in answer to the question "Where the messiah was to be born" it reads,

> In Bethlehem of Judea; for so it is has been written by the prophet.

In this translation it reads,

> In Beit Lehem in Yehuda, for so it is written by the prophet Malaci.

The name of the prophet Micah is spelled out. In the excellent *The New Annotated Oxford Bible* of the NRSV (1997), the prophet's name may be guessed from a note that reads "Mic. 5.2," embedded in an eight-line note on "the wise men" (Magi). However, it is unlikely that a reader will seek out this reference. It should be said that the prophet's names are normally, but

---

[29] The 1993 *Harper Study Bible* uses bottom-of-the-page references to Torah texts. It also has the most annotations of contemporary translations. Its annotations are historical, which is becoming the practice in most study Bible annotations.

not always, omitted from the Greek scripture, as we see in the first line of Mark,

> As it is written in Yeshayah the prophet:
> "Look, I send my messenger ahead of you,
> and he will prepare your road."
>
> *Mark 1.2*

Here Isaiah is in the Greek text and it is not necessary to search elsewhere for the name.

Unless the specific information of the prophet's name or source book is made known in the English text, the translation is incomplete, since the present audience in English, including scholars, will not identify the intended reference that has been cited to give ancient authority to the text. If one must look to the margin or bottom of page to find this specific name, the page becomes unreadable. In summary, most readers do not search out name references that an ancient reader might have understood, and unless such information informs the English translation, the translation fails to inform the English reader.

4. With respect to certain offensive gender-biased language, solutions are at best tentative. In the same way that anti-Semitism cannot be glossed over by euphemism or alteration of the text, so, too, the intentional male language, reflecting habits of bigotry toward women, cannot also be eliminated without falsifying these unfriendly intentions in the text. I have diminished the preponderance of male-gender speech where the Greek does not demand a male interpretation. An example of misleading male-biased translation is to confuse *anthropos* (ἄνθρωπος), "human being" or "person," with *aner, andros* (ἀνήρ, ἀνδρός), the normal word for "man." *Anthropos* means human being in Greek without reference to gender (though in Greek, too, some people assume that all human beings are men). Yet *anthropos* is normally translated into English as "mankind." Gender-free "people" or "person" is preferred to the more abstract or sociological "humanity" or the hybrid "humankind." Yet Robert Alter in his *Genesis* (1996) uses "human" and "humankind" naturally and with easy authority—which has helped to establish them in some moments as the right and apparently only right words. In the past, men and women alike accepted "man" synecdochically to mean "man and woman," but that meaning of man and woman never fully worked.

The word *anthropos* also brings us to a key theological and literary word problems of the New Covenant. What do we do with the phrase Son of Man? In Greek, the phrase *ho huios tou anthropou* (ὁ υἱὸς τοῦ ἀνθρώπου) (Matt. 12.8) was not a negation of women, since it actually means "son of a human being," probably as opposed to a divine being. *Ho huios tou anthropou* definitely does not and cannot mean "Son of Man," its prevalent translation, for that mistranslates the word *anthropou*, which, as said, means a human being, a person, humanity, and not restrictively a man. If one insists on one gender, "son of woman" would be a more logical translation in order to indicate, as apparently intended, that Yeshua is a human being born of a mother as opposed to a god or God. What "man," or more reverently "Man," means is a favorite theological discourse. The capitalization in English (not in Greek) adds another mystery to the English translation. I have a few solutions, none satisfactory, since as in all translation of multivalent words, one choice of meaning excludes another.

Given that the primary meaning of *ho huios tou anthropou* is "the son of a person who is human," a human being, as opposed to a divine essence, it is probable that the Greek phrase came, as Geza Vermes suggests in *Jesus the Jew* (Philadelphia: Fortress Press, 1981), 163–168, either from Jewish Aramaic *bar nasha*, "son of a person," or *hahu gabra*, "that man," as a simple circumlocution or expression for "an Israelite from Palestine." Or *huios tou anthropou* could carry its full messianic title, as in the famous source passage in Daniel 7.13. In the King James Version we have:

> I saw in the night visions, and, behold, one like the Son of man came
>   with the clouds of heaven.

and in the New Revised Standard Version:

> I saw one like a human being
>   coming with the clouds
>   of heaven.

As for where the meaning belongs in every appearance—between a simple synecdoche for "son of man and woman," where the one represents the whole, or whether it has its more mysterious meaning of the forecast messiah as found in Daniel, Enoch, the Dead Sea Scrolls, and elsewhere—that is the provenance of secondary writing. The problem is to find a solution for the text here that is not stylistically crude and that rejects the unacceptable "son of man." "Son of a human" is awkward, and "son of the people" may evoke a political coloring of Red Square. While translation of connotative material is and should be as imperfect as it is rich, here the imperfection of the translation is especially troubling, since the phrase in question is key. I have settled on changing the adjectival genitive *tou anthropou* (τοῦ ἀνθρώπου), "son of people," to a simple preceding adjective. "Earthly son" seems a good way of indicating that Yeshua is a human being (which is the literal meaning of *anthropou*) as opposed to a "heavenly son" or "divine son."

5. This is an unbiased version. It does not proselytize by inflation, sectarian piety in the lexicon, or use any strategy to promote or demote one religious position or denomination over another, or to affirm or deny religious faith and rightness.

6. With respect to speech, I wish the English to come alive in a version close in meaning to the original, without tampering with the extraordinary metaphors by redoing them through equivalent metaphors or paraphrasing them abstractly. Similarly, images are as far as possible not changed or replaced by dubiously "equivalent" images. In this sense, the translation attempts to convey art and magic by remaining as close as possible to the Greek, discovering great freedom, essential information, and every mystery in the literal. The authors should speak, not the translator or what the translator may represent. The version should be simple and modern, without dropping into basic English. While it avoids churchy and pompous speech, it is happy, as the King James Version was, to exploit the range of the English language.

7. With respect to etymology and the Greek language in its koine form, I interpret words not only in their traditionally New Testament dictionary interpretation, which are often puffed up with a later religious rhetoric, but in their classical Greek usage, which was the base of the Koine-writing authors. Hence, while respecting the tradition and scholarship of earlier versions, this translation is done directly from the Greek, rather than from other English versions with a mere nod to the Greek and the Latin Vulgata. Consequently, it tries to ignore erroneous "habits," to use Jorge Luis Borges's preferred polite word for traditional practices of pious speech that have become frozen by custom. This means the translation seeks the better word, not the sanctified one. Many words and phrases have been sanctified in the course of centuries of translation from scripture. These clichés are often inaccurate and help enforce traditional misunderstandings of the Greek.

Although I have followed the principle of looking at each word freshly and meticulously, the effort, I wish to think, is not pedantic. My joy of discovery has been constant. An example of a minor, but perhaps representative, translation opportunity occurs in Matthew 28.8. After the crucifixion, the two Miryams are rushing off, full of fear and happiness from the place of internment of the body of the messiah, to spread the good news of the resurrection. Up to this moment in Matthew, each reference to the burial site is to Yeshua's *taphos* (τάφος), his tomb or grave. Now *taphos* is replaced in Greek by *mnemeion* (μνημεῖον), which like *mnemia* means commonly a tomb or grave, but it is literally "a token of remembrance" and so carries the meaning of a memorial, and is given in Liddell and Scott the meaning in Latin of *monimentum*, which stresses the aspect of a "memory tomb." Following the etymology as well as a pertinent ordinary meaning of the word, I have translated *mnemeion* as "memorial place," retaining the implication that the messiah's burial place has already become a memorial, that is, a place to remember the dead, which fits this moment in the drama.

8. As for the sound of the Greek and the English, I have found a way that helps me hear, which I hope is transferred to the reader. Before seeking an English equivalent of the text, I read each few lines aloud to myself, and when the Koine resonates smoothly, I look for English words. I approach the Koine as both written text and as speech and chant still heard in Greek Orthodox chapels and monasteries. The gospels would be very poor if they did not live in the ear in Greek.

9. Yeshua's specific voice, which expresses itself in the tradition of the chanted Jewish Bible and which he alludes to and cites, should come through in English with overheard poetic rhythm.

By these means—modest yet significantly new, which neither alter, interpret, paraphrase, nor clarify scripture—I hope that these concluding books of the Bible will be seen as late narratives about Jews, a rabbi, his family and his followers, who were to be the essential figures of Christianity.

The Jewish Bible has bequeathed us Christianity and Islam. By restoration of Aramaic and Hebrew biblical names in the New Covenant, these books will at last also look like Jewish, not Greek, scripture, and be read as such. Then perhaps the New Covenant, which has for millennia been the main source of the demonization of the Jews, will no longer serve that pitiful end, and both Jews and Christians can read the uplifting, tragic, and mysterious voyage of the New Covenant for its spiritual firmaments and literary marvels.

THREE INVISIBLE POETS:
YESHUA BEN YOSEF,
YOHANAN THE EVANGELIST,
AND YOHANAN OF THE APOCALYPSE[30]

WHITMAN OR ISAIAH

William Blake and Walt Whitman, whose main source for their renovation of poetry into free verse was the Bible, saw, without reference to the verse typography found in the revised versions, that the Bible was an endless fountain of poetry:

> The carpenter measures with a line and makes an outline with a marker;
> he roughs it out with chisels and marks it with compasses.
> He shapes it in the form of man, of man in all his glory, that it may dwell
>   in a shrine.
> He cut down cedars, or perhaps took a cypress or oak.
> He let it grow among the trees of the forest, or planted a pine, and the rain
>   made it grow.
> It is man's fuel for burning; some of it he takes and warms himself,
> he kindles a fire and bakes bread.

No, this is not a passage from Walt Whitman's "Song of the Broad-Axe" or "Song for Occupations" but from the New International Version (1973) of Isaiah 44.12–15. These are words translated from the Hebrew of a Jewish poet who wrote in the mid-sixth century B.C.E. Although when Whitman was reading the Bible, the versions of translated Bible were not yet lineated in verse, he knew what poetry was locked up in its prose typography. Recently, the Jerusalem Bible and John Dominic Crossan have taken New Covenant sayings by Yeshua and put them into verse. And Everett Fox's translation of the Torah is pioneer in highlighting new areas of chanted verse.[31] In that grand

---

[30] Yohanan of the Apocalypse rather than John because, whoever he was, he is generally considered a Hellenized Jew, who spoke and wrote in Greek and may have used his public Greek name rather than his Hebrew name. His given name in the synagogue could, like all the authors of the New Covenant, have been Yohanan or any other Hebrew or Aramaic name.

[31] Everett Fox followed his German model, the translation of the Hebrew Bible into German, *Die Schrift*, by Martin Buber and Franz Rosenzweig, who held that the Bible is oral literature written down and that a good translation should reproduce the Hebraic voice.

gesture, he completed the task begun in the nineteenth century when sections of the diverse "Revised" editions of the Hebrew Bible began to be lineated in verse, including the Song of Songs, Psalms, Job, and large segments of the prophets.

YESHUA BEN YOSEF

There are and always will be many tones and ways, from Milton to Cole Porter, of making poems and writing down words. I prescribe no single way but hope, in my own attempts, for plainness and lyrical clarity. Despite the dissuasions of missing line breaks, it is clear that one of the world's major poets is and has been for two millennia Yeshua the Messiah. His pen was in the hands of others who recorded and translated his words into Greek.

We are accustomed to believe that poetry resides in the Hebrew Bible and that the New Covenant is a story and a play, a fabling narration and a drama, but that the only poetry in it are snatches from the Hebrew Bible, unassigned to a specific prophet, which are essentially cited in Greek from the Septuagint translation of the Bible. Yet Matthew, the gospel with the most dialogue, anthologizes the diverse wisdom talk and prayers of Yeshua from the other gospels into the Sermon on the Mount, a string of poems that includes the psalm of the Lord's Prayer. Matthew is mainly poetry.

The poet of the New Covenant is invisible, obscured in prose. And we do not know the voice and identity of the recorder or recorders. Yet hear that voice and hear a poet. Few have recognized the poet, because they were not led, by the shape of the print on the page, to use their ears, although Yeshua's voice (except in brief dialogue) came uniformly and sonorously in verse sayings. The poems remained confined to lucent and fluent English prose of the sixteenth and seventeenth centuries, but no matter. So were Job and the Song of Songs until their release into verse in the English Revised Version (1885). Once released, the tradition of verse rendition began for the Hebrew Bible, and we analyzed its prosody. The question of verse was settled. Now there is a sound of poetry in the air for the Greek scriptures. It has been slow and irregular in coming, but with new versions the sound will prevail. It is time to hear the poet.

The concentration of poetry in the New Covenant is commonly called "Jesus' sayings," a phrase that ignores or fails to recognize the poetry. The Jerusalem Bible, a Catholic translation, translates much of John and most of Yeshua into verse. Curiously, it does not render Apocalypse into verse, which is the single long, indisputable poem of the New Covenant. Where the Jerusalem version found poetry, however, is not astonishing. And yet, the translators failed to make it sing. By contrast, the Tyndale and King James prose renditions of these passages are charged with poetry. Other standard modern versions of the poetic speech in the New Covenant, with the marked exception of the Lattimore, are largely without brightness of word.

The poems in the gospels are clean and incomplete and their endings elusively open. Even the most gnomic couplets are concentrated wisdom sayings, which, though proverbial, do not limit by finality. They are not conclusions but a hint for further meditation. Some longer ones ramble magnificently in the form of parable narrations. Some aphoristically take a moment of nature, using only images and shunning abstraction, to give the metaphysics of life on earth and of eternity:

> You are the salt of the earth.
> But if the salt has lost its taste, how will it recover its salt?
> Its powers are for nothing except to be thrown away
>   and trampled underfoot by others.
>
> *Matt. 5.13*

With multiple ambiguities, the question is asked about the salt that has lost its taste and its powers. The salt can only be picked up and thrown away, obliterated. Or is the recovery of the salt—humankind's redemption on earth—to be attained precisely through its loss and awareness of loss? Similarly through image alone, the Greek poet Sappho speaks of love, loss, and the beginning of knowledge in her fragment about the hyacinth trampled by others into the earth, yet which blooms:

> Like a hyacinth crushed in the mountains
> by shepherds; lying trampled on the earth
> yet blooming purple.
>
> *Sappho, 168*

In the verses that follow, Yeshua goes from salt to light, from the element in the earth to the spiritual light inside the "you," his listener. And that light is so strong that it expands, by its example, as good news to the world. It appears blatantly as a city on a mountain and then returns to the privacy of the house where there, too, it glows on everyone near it.

> You are the light of the world.
> A city cannot be hidden when it is set on a mountain.
> Nor do they light a lamp and place it under a basket, but on a stand,
> and it glows on everyone in the house.
>
> *Matt. 5.14–15*

Continuing the image of light, the poet says,

> The lamp of the body is the eye.
> If your eye is clear, your whole body is filled with light,
> but if your eye is clouded, your whole body will inhabit darkness.
> And if the light in your whole body is darkness,
> how dark it is!
>
> *Matt. 6.22–23*

The poet in Matthew has many moods and voices, largely but not always spoken by Yeshua, including explosions of invective, admonishing survival,

> Do not give the holy to the dogs
> or cast your pearls before the pigs.
> They will probably trample them underfoot
> and turn and tear you to pieces.
>
> *Matt. 7.6*

And there is an abundance of wisdom poetry, maybe the best we have from Asia that has entered the West, and later the world,

> Go in through the narrow gate,
> since wide is the gate and spacious the road
> that leads to destruction,
> and there are many who go in through it.
> But how narrow is the gate and cramped is the road
> that leads to life,
> and there are few who find it.
>
> *Matt. 7.13–14*

Among the great passages of poetry are the birds of the sky and lilies of the field verses in Matthew 6.26–30. The temporal splendor of flower, clothing, and grass is what we live by. It is here today, yet tomorrow it is all ominously "cast into the oven" to die by fire, a phrase that cannot help but evoke the terrors of the twentieth century. The poet Yeshua in Matthew, evoking the image of emptiness promised to those of little faith, asks the listener to consider what raiment God will offer when those coverings of field and body have disappeared,

> Consider the birds of the sky.
> They do not sow or reap or collect for their granaries,
> yet your heavenly father feeds them.

Are you not more valuable than they?
Who among you by brooding can add one more hour
to your life?
And why care about clothing?
Consider the lilies of the field, how they grow.
They do not labor or spin,
but I tell you not even Shlomoh in all his splendor
was clothed like one of these lilies.
And if the grass of the field is there today
and tomorrow is cast into the oven
and in these ways God has dressed the earth,
will he not clothe you in a more stunning raiment,
you who suffer from poor faith?

Matt. 6.26–30

YOHANAN THE EVANGELIST

In the prologue to John, the invisible poet bears another unknown name, and the voice is philosophical, making the word an instrument of creation, miming the Genesis phenomenon. This is the poet we call Yohanan the Evangelist, author of the fourth gospel, who explores spirit and body, eternity and temporal residence. In the great beginning of the Gospel of John, the author blends voices of sundry currents of a period palpitating with philosophy and new religious divisions, especially gnosticism and early Kabbalah. The beginning is a mirror of Genesis's creation command, "Let there be light." It argues syllogistically about the word in the fashion of the Greek sophists. And influenced by gnosticism, John elaborates on the light of the soul. His word takes us not only to Greek notions of the *logos* as the mind of the world, but to the Kabbalists' notion of the word and creation. In the Kabbalah, before creation is the word to speak creation (and before even the word are the letters to create a word with which God speaks the creation). The great scholar of the Kabbalah Gershom Scholem places the beginnings of the Kabbalist word and letters together with the emergence of Jewish gnosticism[32] in Palestinian Judaism, stating that "[t]he growth of Merkabah mysticism among the rabbis constitutes an inner Jewish concomitant to Gnosis, and it may be termed 'Jewish and rabbinic Gnosticism'" (*Kabbalah*, Scholem, 13). Like the Kabbalists' word, John's word precedes creation, and his word is all things: God, beginning, life,

---

[32] In the second and third centuries, the classical Christian gnostics of Alexandria took John as their principal text to exegete in proof of their dualistic message.

and light which the darkness cannot *apprehend*—neither physically seize nor spiritually understand,

> In the beginning was the word
> and the word was with God,
> and God was the word.
> The word was in the beginning with God.
> Through it everything came about
> and without it not a thing came about.
> What came to be in the word was life
> and the life was the light of people
> and the light in the darkness shines
> and the darkness could not apprehend it.

In the Gospel of John, the light, the first entity to be created in Genesis, immediately takes on a spiritual opposition to the uncomprehending darkness, and the notion of light as knowledge, light as the ultimate principle of knowledge, which is confirmed throughout the Nag Hammadi scriptures and, in particular, in "The Creation of the Earth."

The poems in John stand alone, or connect in strings, sometimes in strings of three- and four-line-related but separate poems (like strings of Japanese tankas), or they inform a dramatic dialogue. In John 4.21–26, Yeshua tells the Samaritan woman that salvation is from the Jews and the hour is coming. Now we can hear Yeshua and the woman as poets, and so distinguish between the opening authorial voice of John and the recorded voice of Yeshua. Because we know no one's name for certain, we have the absolute problem, an impossible but pleasant problem of distinguishing between the unnamed authorial voice and his created or recorded lines of the poet Yeshua. Where one starts and the other ends is the instant where a drop joins the sea.

With an Asian simplicity reminiscent of the Asian poets, Yeshua declares himself the savior:

> Yeshua said to her,
> > Believe me, woman, the hour is coming
> > when not on this mountain
> > nor in Yerushalayim will you worship the father.
> > You worship what you do not know.
> > We worship what we know
> > since salvation is from the Jews.
> > But the hour is coming and it is now

when the true worshipers will worship the father
in spirit and truth,
for the father seeks such people to worship him.
God is spirit
and those worshiping must worship him
in spirit and truth.
The woman said to him,
I know a mashiah[33] is coming who is called the anointed. When he
comes he will declare all things to us.
Yeshua said to her,
I am he,
talking to you.

Finally, punning with the double meaning of *pneuma,* which is "breath" or "wind over the earth" and, by its metaphorical abstraction and later ecclesiastical and Latin usage, God's "spirit," Yeshua again carries on the metaphysic of the temporal and what exists beyond the temporal:

Unless you are born from water and the wind of God
you cannot enter the kingdom of God.
What is born from the flesh is flesh,
what is born from the wind is wind.
Do not wonder that I told you
that you must be born again from above.
The wind blows where it wants to
and you hear its sound
but you don't know where it comes from
and where it goes.
So it is for everyone born from the wind of God.
John 3.5–8

For those who don't believe or understand his statement, he tells us plainly,

The breath keeps us alive.
The flesh is of no help.
The words I spoke to you
are the breath of spirit and are life.
John 6.63

So speaks the invisible poet in the gospels.

---

[33] Messiah.

The voice revealed through translation of his words into the Greek, and now into English, is a world poet. To call an unidentified poet Yeshua of the gospels or John the Evangelist or John of the Apocalypse is a shadowy name and distinction, since in each case there is a poet or recorder of the poet behind that voice: the evangelists in the case of Yeshua, and John and a Greek Jew, said to be from Patmos or Efesos—though his origin is quite dubious—behind the great revelation in the Apocalypse. The voices, of uncertain name and of distinctive mystery of origin, must be perceived so we may hear them as we have heard other ancient wisdom poets of Asia, of a religious and metaphysical cast, from China's Laozi tradition, India's Mahadevi, Sumeria's Enheduanna, and Israel's many-voiced prophets. Isaiah and Laozi are respectively the great poets of the Hebrew Bible and the Chinese Daoist Daode jing, yet in each case what is held together under each name are several voices. We speak of Isaiah 1, Isaiah 2, Isaiah 3. We speak of Laozi as the author of the Daode jing or Confucius as the author of the Confucian odes. But in each instance we know it is many songs under a single name. In short, under each name is a tradition. In the New Covenant, the most distinctive voices are Yeshua and the two Johns (of gospel and Apocalypse). Following the tradition of retelling the gospel story in different voices, in each gospel the poems take distinctive wordings as they are retold.

YOHANAN OF THE APOCALYPSE

The poet of the Apocalypse has given us a single book by the last invisible poet of the New Covenant. He is the one of epic breath, whom John Milton seems to have invented as his primary precursor for his paradises lost and found. We speak of John of the white island of Patmos or of the marble city of Efesos, the author of the apocalpytic narration purportedly done in a cave near the port in Patmos. The monastery and cave are there, and you can see the rock where John, during a two-year retreat, is said to have written Apocalypse. His identity and actual location, as with all figures in the New Covenant with the exception of Paul, are similarly clouded. But we see his markings when his lamb opens the seals, the cosmos shudders, and the sun becomes black like sackcloth of hair:

When the lamb opened the sixth seal I looked
and there took place a great earthquake
and the sun became black like sackcloth of hair
and the full moon became like blood.

And the stars of the sky fell to the earth
as the fig tree drops its unripe fruit
shaken by a great wind. And the sky
vanished like a scroll rolling up
and every mountain and island of the earth
was torn up from its place and moved.

6.12–14

We are in an *Inferno* when we see the beasts of the Apocalypse, appropriated from Daniel, and we soon know where Dante, Milton, and Blake found the tradition of their bestial apocalyptic visions:

Then I saw a beast coming up from the sea,
with ten horns and seven heads and on his horns
ten diadems, and on his heads were the names
of blasphemy. The beast I saw was like a leopard,
his feet like a bear and his mouth like the mouth
of a lion. And the dragon gave him his power
and his throne and fierce power of dominion.
One of his heads seemed to be stricken to death
but the wound causing his death was healed
and the whole world marveled after the beast

13.1–3

These three poets, Yeshua ben Yosef, Yohanan the Evangelist, and Yohanan of the Apocalypse (it could be Yohanan of Revelation or Yohanan of Patmos or Yohanan of Efesos), are the poetic constellations of the New Covenant—a book unjustly in shadow to the poetic grandeur of the Hebrew Bible. We have felt them, heard them, but failed to identify their poetic profile, and that very failure of identification, of assigning an identity card, has preserved their nameless solitudes as poets. Yet only from the collaboration of a single poetic solitude and a rich tradition could such poetry have emerged. Homer also is invisible and unknown, but whatever the preceding tradition, the editing, the assemblage by others, the poems did not happen without a single creating hand behind them or two hands and male or female, if there were a Homer for each epic.

The three principal New Covenant poets have been concealed in unfriendly prose typography. They are orphans of uncertain name, of dubious pedigree, and yet these poets from Asia's Mediterranean lands were filled with rabbinic light from a millennium of prophetic verse. On their own, despite the enigma concerning their identity, their light has glowed over into Coptic Egypt, down to Ethiopic Africa, east through Armenia of Persia, north crossing the Syriac bridge up to Byzantium, Old Slavonic principalities, on their way to Latin Europe, and then into the entire world.

We also know very little about Shakespeare and Homer, but texts carrying their names exist. In the instance of the gospels and Apocalypse, we have not had the habit of detecting poems or assigning them authorship. The names assigned to the gospels and the Apocalypse authors are almost certainly pseudepigraphical, and whether John the Evangelist is the same person as John of Patmos and all these unknowns of name is secondary. What counts is the existence of the texts. Yet at least as uncertainly as we attribute the gospels to the evangelists, we can also assign the poems within the gospels and Apocalypse to their speakers. So we have the good names of the poets, Yeshua ben Yosef, Yohanan the Evangelist, and Yohanan of the Apocalypse. But more important than names, we have their many fixed words, bright words, in verses that sing deep in four compassionate narrations and one amazing apocalyptic vision.

GOSPELS AND APOCALYPSE

A NOTE ON
NEW COVENANT SCRIPTURE

THE NEW COVENANT IS A COLLECTION OF GOSPELS, ACTS (A SEQUEL LUKE), AND LETTERS, AND, LIKE THE HEBREW BIBLE, AN ANTHOLogy of distinct literary genres. Specifically, the New Covenant consists of the canonical gospels, Acts of the Apostles, Letters, and Apocalypse (Revelation). A gospel (meaning, a book of "good news") tells the life, teachings, and death by crucifixion of Yeshua the Mashiah (Jesus Christ) and is also an account of the followers of Yeshua (Jesus). The followers included his students (disciples) and the crowds that traveled with this itinerant rabbi and healer around the hills of Upper and Lower Galilee, the fields of Yehuda, and the streets of Yerushalayim.

Yeshua ben Yosef was born in turbulent times of rebellion against the Roman occupiers of Israel in about 3–7 B.C.E. It may seem strange to say that Christ was born before Christ, but it is now generally accepted among scholars that the date set for Yeshua's birth, by Dionysius Exiguus, the creator of the Christian calendar, was off by several years.

The earliest texts of the New Covenant we have are written in Greek. Although Paul's letters were written in Greek, the gospels of Matthew, Mark, Luke, and John are later Greek versions of earlier lost accounts, both oral or written, from Aramaic and probably Hebrew sources. The scriptures of the Christian New Covenant concern the lives of Jews who followed Yeshua and Paul and Peter, who reflected one sect among other revolutionary Jewish sects, which included the Pharisees, Zealots, Essenes, Hasidim, and early gnostics. The gospels of the New Covenant were written by or ascribed to Matthew, Mark, Luke, and John, who are called the evangelists. They are traditionally thought to be three Jews, and a convert to Judaism (Luke), though any knowledge of the evangelists outside of the texts ascribed to them does not have a scholarly or historical basis. Like the Hebrew Bible, the Greek scriptures of Christianity underwent countless modifications and radical restructuring as they moved from oral history to a fixed place in the canon. As for the extent to which the narration itself has a historical base, again we have essentially no source outside the gospels themselves. We do not know what scribal hands copied, redacted, and fashioned the gospels into their present narration. In a few documents, in Tacitus, Philo, and Josephus, it is noted that there was a man named Jesus who was crucified by the Romans.

In the first years after the crucifixion, the Christian Jews (those who followed Yeshua) were in contention with other Jews in the synagogues for dominance. Paul wrote letters to the congregations of the synagogues in Rome, Corinth, Thessaloniki, Antioch, and Athens to persuade his coreligionists to follow Christ. By the time of the destruction of Jerusalem by Titus in 70 C.E. and the subsequent diaspora of the inhabitants of the city, the division between Christian Jews and those who did not receive Yeshua as the mashiah became more decisive; by the second century the separation between Jew and Christian was irreversible. But the new Christians had no scripture of their own. The Pauline letters were not then considered holy documents. The Hebrew Bible was the sole Christian Bible, which most of the "primitive Christians" read in its Greek Septuagint translation or in later Christianized versions of the Septuagint. The New Covenant gradually was assembled, with an initial edition around 150. Through the next centuries its contents were debated fiercely by the Church fathers until the end of the fourth century when there was a consensus. Athanasios (293–373) is nominally credited with setting the twenty-seven books in the order we have them today in 367, but in all probability *The First Edition* was published around 150, and it already established the selection, if not the final order or wording. Then, after the councils of Laodicea (363), Hippo (393), and Carthage (397), the Athanasian collection was accepted as canon. With his revision of earlier Latin translations of the Hebrew Bible, and from the Greek New Covenant, followed by his own new translation of Hebrew texts, which he studied in Israel and available Greek texts found elsewhere, Saint Jerome (347–420) produced in about 405 the Latin Bible of the Catholic Church. For the first time, the Christians who depended on Rome at last had a complete Bible in Latin, the famous Vulgate (*editio vulgata*). In 1546, the Council of Trent declared Jerome's version to be the exclusive Latin authority for the Bible.

A NOTE ON
THE GREEK SOURCE TEXTS

THE SOURCE TEXT FOR THIS TRANSLATION IS *THE GREEK NEW TES-TAMENT*, 4TH EDITION (1993), PUBLISHED BY THE UNITED BIBLE Societies, which is a unified edition of the United Bible Societies (the UBS) text, and the twenty-sixth edition of *Novum Testamentum Graece*, edited by Eberhard and Erwin Nestle, based on an earlier edition by Kurt Aland (1979). An earlier but still available Greek text from which translations have been made is the Majority Text, which is based on a consensus of manuscripts that includes some passages generally omitted in the UBS and other available editions, including the Alexandrian Text. The UBS and Alexandrian Text consult manuscripts discovered in the late nineteenth and early twentieth centuries, in particular, the Codex Vaticanus and Codex Sinaiticus, both from the fourth century. In some instances, I have noted the Majority Text reading, where it differs from the prevailing UBS text used in this translation. In one crucial instance, in the Lord's Prayer, in Matthew 6.9–13, I include, in brackets indicating interpolation, the last lines of the model prayer: "For yours is the kingdom and the power and the glory forever. Amen." The UBS and other modern Greek texts and translations such as the NRSV (New Revised Standard Version) exclude this famous ending. It was added by the early church as an appropriate concluding doxology to Yeshua's prayer in keeping with David's prayer in 1 Chronicles 29.11–13. The extraordinary but uncertain ending is, however, found in Tyndale (1534), which used the best Greek texts available at the time and in the King James Version (1611), based on the *Textus Receptus* (1516), which derives from few manuscripts and not the better or older ones that we now have in our possession.

Although more than five thousand manuscripts exist in Greek, and many more in Latin translation from the Greek, it is unlikely that there will be a final correct edition of the Greek text, much less a true Aramaic or Hebrew source text for the gospels. The most engaging possibility of an earlier textual source for the gospels is the Gospel of Thomas, limited to wisdom sayings of Yeshua, found in 1945 at Nag Hammadi, Egypt, along with classical gnostic scriptures, all translated into Coptic (the language of non-Greek Egyptians). Some, though not most, scholars suggest that Thomas may precede Mark (ca. 70 C.E.) by twenty years, and hence presents us with the earliest extant translated words of Yeshua.

In its presentation, brackets signify that a translation has been made from a Greek word or phrase that appears in the earlier Majority Text, but not in the UBS Fourth (the source of this translation), and indicates that such a word or phrase does not appear in our earliest extant, full ancient texts.

The brief subtitles before passages throughout, which most translations into English since the Revised add, generally follow their placement in other versions. The titles help locate each distinct segment and show the episodical nature of the short pieces that comprise the narration. The titles reveal but do not scoop the story. They do not interpret, nor say so much as to replace or lessen the reading experience.

Annotation is light and generally explanatory or linguistic. Though not a study Bible, the linguistic resource gives derivations from Greek, Aramaic, and Hebrew so that the interested reader may pursue that course of inquiry. The etymology of changing names provides a historical key to sectarian and ethnic politics of the New Covenant.

MARKOS
(MARK)

MARKOS (MARK)

A S IN THE OTHER GOSPELS, THERE IS NO INTERNAL EVIDENCE OF THE AU-
THORSHIP OF THE BOOK OF MARK. AN EARLY CHURCH FIGURE, BISHOP
Papias (ca. 130–140 C.E.), states that Mark was John Mark, a close associate of
Peter, and that the Gospel of Mark is essentiallly an arrangement of Peter's
preachings in Rome. The second-century bishop Iraeneus also places Mark in
Rome. Another tradition claims Alexandria as the place of origin. Others assume that because the Markan gospel is probably the earliest that it was composed in Israel. Mark was written at least thirty to forty years after Yeshua's
death, and the gospel authors' names were appended to the gospels more than
a hundred years after Yeshua's death. The traditions that assert authorship of
the gospels frequently deny each other, and here, as elsewhere, none has a
strong historical probability. Authorship in the New Covenant remains an
enigma.

Like Luke 1.1, Mark 1.1 begins with the presentation of "the good news"
about Yeshua the Mashiah. Mark stresses Yeshua's miracles and his powers of
healing, the drama and mystery of his death. The first verses quote the prophet
Isaiah to prove that Yeshua is "the voice crying out in the wilderness" and that
he is therefore God's messenger. But after this initial declaration, Mark
plunges directly into the stories of John the Baptist and of Yeshua tempted for
forty days in the desert by Satan (which parallels Moses' forty years in the
desert tempted by Baal). It follows his wanderings through the land of Israel,
where he takes on disciples and crowds of followers, who accompany him in
his ministry. Mark gives us a series of miracles, teachings through parables,
and finally the "passion week" of Yeshua's arrest, trial, death, burial, and disappearance from the tomb. Here the gospel ends. This so-called "abrupt ending"
has bothered theologians and has caused some to speculate that we have a
truncated or unfinished gospel. Most disturbing is that there is no mention of
Christ risen, and since Mark is the source of Matthew and Luke, the absence
of a resurrected Yeshua is not desirable. As a probable result of this discomfort
with the present ending, two appended endings have been appended to Mark,
the so-called "Shorter Ending of Mark" and the "Longer Ending of Mark."
The very short one has Yeshua send word of eternal salvation out from east to
west. The longer one has Yeshua appear resurrected before Mary Magdalene

and the disciples and then describes Yeshua ascending into heaven. The shorter ending may have been added in the fourth century, the longer one as early as the third or second. Both endings are termed "orphans," because they are spurious, and do not exist in the earliest manuscripts, which are the Vaticanus and Sinaiticus codexes.

Mark is most often characterized as an author whose Greek is crude and rudimentary in contrast especially to Luke, who is more classical, and John, who is clearly influenced by Greek philosophical and gnostic models. But Mark is in many ways the greatest stylist among the evangelists. Mark writes with plain clarity, concision, with dramatic power, minimal and striking diction. The original ending of the Gospel of Mark may be less satisfying as theology, but it is overwhelmingly dramatic and mysterious in its understatement of the sublime terror of Yeshua's disappearance from the tomb. When the two Marys enter the tomb and find that Yeshua is not there, Mark writes, "So they went out and fled from the tomb, seized by trembling and ecstasy. And they said nothing to anyone. They were afraid" (16.8).

❖ C H A P T E R 1

Good news

₁ The beginning of the gospel[1] of Yeshua the mashiah,[2] son of God.

₂ As it is written in Yeshayah[3] the prophet:

Look, I send my messenger ahead of you,[4]

and he will prepare your road;

₃ a voice of one crying out in the desert:

"Prepare the way of Adonai[5]

and make his paths straight."[6]

Yohanan the Dipper in the desert

₄ Yohanan the Dipper[7] appeared in the desert, preaching an immersion of repentance for the remission of sin.[8] ₅ The whole land of Yehuda[9] and all the people of Yerushalayim[10] came out to him and were being immersed by him in the Yarden[11] river and confessing their sins. ₆ Clothed in camel hair, Yohanan wore a belt of hide around his waist, and he ate locusts and wild honey. ₇ He preached, saying,

After me will come one more powerful than I am

of whom I am not fit to stoop down and untie the strap

of his sandals.

---

[1] Gospel from the Greek εὐαγγέλιον (euangelion), meaning "good news" or "good tidings" as well as "gospel." "The beginning" in Mark is parallel to "In the beginning," the first words in Genesis.

[2] Jesus the Messiah. Jesus is from the Greek Ἰησοῦ (Iesous), from the Hebrew יֵשׁוּעַ (yeshua), from the Hebrew יְהוֹשֻׁעַ (yehoshua); and messiah is a translation of Christ (the Greek word for 'the anointed," from the Greek Χριστός (Hristos) translated from the Hebrew מָשִׁיחַ (mashiah). Messiah is a free transliteration of the Hebrew mashiah.

[3] Isaiah from the Greek Ἡσαΐας (Esaias), from the Hebrew יְשַׁעְיָה (yeshayah).

[4] "Before your face" in the Greek.

[5] "Lord" or "Adonai" from the Greek κύριος (kyrios or kurios). When referring to the divine lord, the Greek κύριος may be translated as "lord" or "Adonai" (אֲדֹנָי) as here in the Hebrew text cited from Isaiah; when referring to Jesus, *kyrios* may be translated as "sir," "master," "teacher," or "rabbi," when the implicit Hebrew source is רַבִּי (rabbi).

[6] Isa. 40.3.

[7] John the Baptist. John from the Greek Ἰωάννης (Ioannes), from the Hebrew יוֹחָנָן (yohanan). The Dipper is from the Greek ὁ βαπτίζων (ho baptizon), meaning "one who dips, washes, or immerses" as in Jewish ritual washings.

[8] Sin from the Greek ἁμαρτία (hamartia), also translated literally as "missing the mark," "wrong," "wrongdoing," or "error."

[9] Judea from the Greek Ἰουδαία (Ioudaia), from the Hebrew יְהוּדָה (yehuda). Also is the name Yehuda.

[10] Jerusalem from the Greek Ἱερουσαλήμ (Yerousalem), from the Hebrew יְרוּשָׁלַיִם (yerushalayim).

[11] Jordan from the Greek Ἰορδάνης (Iordanes), from the Hebrew יַרְדֵּן (yarden).

8I immersed you in water,
but he will immerse you in holy spirit.[12]

Yeshua immersed

9And it happened in those days that Yeshua came from Natzeret[13] in the Galil[14] and was immersed in the Yarden by Yohanan. 10And as soon as he came out of the water, he saw the skies torn open and the spirit like a dove descending on him. 11And there came a voice out of the skies:

You are my son whom I love.
With you I am well pleased.

Temptation in the desert

12And at once the spirit drove him out into the desert. 13He was in the desert forty days, tested by Satan, and he was among the wild beasts, and the angels attended him.

Preaching in the Galil and first students

14After Yohanan was arrested, Yeshua came into the Galil preaching the gospel of God,[15] 15and saying,

---

[12] Johanan the Dipper is introduced competitively with Yeshua, for Yohanan baptizes in water while Yeshua baptizes in the spirit. Joseph Campbell's *The Masks of God: Occidental Mythology* (New York: Penguin Arkana, 1991) and David Fideler's *Jesus Christ, Son of God* (Wheaton, IL: Quest Books, 1993) trace Yohanan back to the traditional Sumerian god of water and Yeshua to the god of sun. For more than two centuries there was serious rivalry, in both Orthodox Christian and gnostic Christian sects, between those who favored Yeshua and those who favored Yohanan as the true foretold messiah.

[13] Nazareth from the Greek Ναζαρέτ (Natzaret), from unknown village in Galilee probably spelled Natzeret.

[14] Galilee from the Greek Γαλιλαία (Galilaia), from the Hebrew גָּלִיל (galil). Galil is a "circle," "district," or "province." It is often used in the phrase גְּלִיל הַגּוֹיִם (galil hagoyim), meaning "province of the goyim (Gentiles)."

[15] God in the New Covenant may be more properly translated "El," "Eloah," "Elohim" (plural or plural of majesty of El) or "Yahweh" or "YHWH" (which is closest to the un-voweled Hebrew consonants), or "Adonai." In Matthew 27.46, where he addresses God in the Aramaic/Hebrew rather than in the Greek, Yeshua cries out in Greek transcription, ἠλι ἠλι λεμα σαβαχθανι; (*eli eli lema sabachthani?*), "My God, my God, why have you forsaken me?" repeating "My God," the first line of Hebrew Psalm 22, "My God, my God, why have you forsaken me?" So in Matthew 27.46 in recent translations from the Hebrew Bible, as in Everett Fox's *The Five Books of Moses* (New York: Schocken Books, 1995) and now elsewhere, God is translated YHWH. God in English is derived from Middle English and Germanic *god*. Please see page 562.

Yeshua in the New Covenant is called diversely "rabbi," "teacher," "master," and "lord." "Rabbi," from Hebrew רַבִּי *rabbi*, master + -*i*, my, and "rabboni" appear many times in the gospels (Mark 9.5, 10.51, 11.21; Matt. 23.7, 23.8; John 1.39, 1.49, 3.2, 3.26, 6.25, 20.16). In the synoptic versions of Matthew in Mark and Luke "rabbi" usually becomes in Greek "teacher" (διδάσκαλος), "master" (ἐπιστάτης), or "lord" (κύριος), suggesting that the word "rabbi" in these Greek texts and other instances of address has been changed in order to dissociate Yeshua from the Jews. These changes of address from "rabbi" to "master," "lord," and "teacher" occur not only in going from one Greek text to another, from Mark to Matthew and Luke, but when "rabbi" in the Greek text is translated into English. So the

The hour is fulfilled and the kingdom[16] of God
   is near.
Repent and believe in the good news.[17]

16And as Yeshua went by the Sea of the Galil, he saw Shimon[18] and his brother Andreas[19] casting nets into the sea, for they were fishermen, 17and Yeshua said to them,

Come follow me,
   and I will make you fishers of people.

18And at once they dropped their nets and followed him.

19And going on a little farther he saw Yaakov[20] the son of Zavdai[21] and his brother Yohanan in their boat mending their nets. 20And at once he called them, and leaving their father Zavdai in the boat with the hired hands, they followed him.

An unclean spirit

21They came into Kfar Nahum[22] and just on Shabbat[23] he went into the synagogue and taught.

22The people were in wonder at his teaching, for he taught them as one who has authority and not like the scholars.[24] 23Suddenly in their synagogue there was a man

---

King James Version (1611) of Mark 9.5, "Rabbi, it is good for us to be here," becomes "Master, it is good for us to be here." Other early English Bibles—Tyndale (1525), Great (1539), Geneva (1562), Bishops' (1568)—similarly change "rabbi" in Mark 9.5 to "master" or "teacher." Only the Rheims-Douai (1582), a Catholic Bible translated into English by persecuted English exiles in France, renders Greek "rabbi" of Mark 9.5 (as most versions do today) as "rabbi." Please see Afterword.

[16] In the Oxford *New Testament and Psalms,* each instance of "kingdom" is replaced by "dominion," since "kingdom," βασιλεία (basileia), contains the word "king," βασιλεύς (basileus). "Kingdom" is not gender free, and "dominion" is a rich alternative, but to use "dominion" would mask the intended meaning, which is "to evoke the dominion of a king."

[17] See note 1, p. 47.

[18] Simon from the Greek Σίμων (Simon), from the Hebrew שִׁמְעוֹן (shimon).

[19] Andrew from the Greek Ἀνδρέας (Andreas). Andreas, like Markos and Lukas, are Greek names used by Jews in Israel.

[20] James (Jacob) from the Greek Ἰάκωβος (Iakobos), from the Hebrew יַעֲקֹב (yaakov). When referring to New Testament followers of Yeshua, Iakobos is given a Greek ending; when the same Hebrew name refers to the Old Testament patriarch Jacob, it is undeclined in the Greek as Ἰακώβ (Iakob), thereby distinguishing Old Testament from New Testament personages. James is an English name derived freely from the Greek, which does not suggest Jacob. In French it is Jacques, in Spanish Jaime, Diego, or Santiago (St. James). In German and other languages, Iakobos is usually rendered in a way to suggest Jacob, thereby referring it back to the Hebrew Bible name.

[21] Zebedee from the Greek Ζεβεδαῖος (Zebedaios), from the Hebrew זַבְדִּי (zavdai).

[22] Capernaum. Latin *Capernaum* from the Greek Καφαρναούμ (Kafarnaoum), from the Hebrew כְּפַר נָחוּם (kfar nahum), meaning "village of Nahum."

[23] Sabbath from the Greek σάββατον (sabbaton), from the Hebrew שַׁבָּת (shabbat).

[24] From the Greek γραμματεύς (grammateus), traditionally translated as "scribe" is in more recent translations rendered as "scholar."

with an unclean spirit and he screamed, 24"What are you to us, Yeshua the Natzrati?25 Did you come to destroy us? I know you, who you are. God's holy one!"

25Yeshua rebuked him, saying,

Be silent and come out of him!

26And convulsing him and crying out in a great voice, the unclean spirit came out of him.

27Everyone was so amazed they started to ask each other, "What is this? A new teaching? What authority does he possess?" And he commanded the unclean spirits and they obeyed him. 28Word of him at once went out everywhere through all the surrounding countryside of the Galil.

Healing at Shimon's house

29As soon as they left the synagogue they went into the house of Shimon and Andreas with Yaakov and Yohanan. 30Shimon's mother-in-law was lying in bed with a fever and right away they told Yeshua about her.

31He came to her, and holding her hand he raised her.

The fever left her and she served them.

32When dusk came and the sun set, they brought him all the sick and those possessed by demons.[26] 33And the whole city gathered together at the door. 34He cured many who were sick with various diseases and expelled many demons, and would not let them speak, because they knew him.

In a desolate place

35Early in the morning while it was still like night, he got up and went to a desolate place, and there he prayed. 36Shimon and those with him searched for him, 37found him, and said to him, "Everyone is looking for you."

38He said to them,

Let us go elsewhere into the neighboring towns

so I may preach there also. For this I came.

39And he went all over the Galil, preaching in the synagogues, and cast out demons.

With a leper

40A leper came to him begging on his knees,[27] and said to him, "If you wish to, you can make me clean."

---

[25] Nazarene from the Greek Ναζαρηνός (Nazarenos), from Natzeret, that is, a Natzrati.

[26] From the Greek δαιμονιζομένους (daimonizomenous), meaning "possessed by demons" or "demonized." The King James Version translates "demons" as "devils," suggesting hell's evil and Satan. The ancient Greek word demon, as dark and evil as it is, carries no Jewish or later Christian reference to the devil. Contemporary translations render "demon."

[27] "On his knees" or "kneeling" is omitted in more recent Greek texts.

₄₁And filled with pity, he stretched out his hand and touched him and said,

> I wish to. Now be clean.

₄₂At once the leprosy went from him, and he was made clean. ₄₃Then warning him sternly, he sent him away at once. ₄₄And he said to him,

> See that you say nothing to anyone,
>
> but go and show yourself to a priest
>
> and give your cleansing prescribed by Mosheh[28]
>
> as a testimony to others.

₄₅But the man went out and began to proclaim many things and to spread the word, so that Yeshua could no longer go into a city openly, and kept to desolate places.

And they came to him from everywhere.

CHAPTER 2

A paralytic

After a few days Yeshua went back to Kfar Nahum[29] and it was heard that he was in a house. ₂And many gathered so there was no room, not even at the door, and he spoke the word to them. ₃They came, bringing him a paralytic carried by four men. ₄But when because of the crowd they could not reach him, they uncovered the roof above Yeshua, and when they had made an opening in it they lowered the bed on which the paralytic lay.

₅When Yeshua saw their faith, he said to the paralyzed man,

> My child, your wrongs are forgiven.

₆But there were some scholars sitting there, debating these things in their hearts. ₇"Why is he speaking like this? He blasphemes. Who can forgive sins, but God alone?"

₈Yeshua immediately knew in his soul what they were saying to each other, and he told them,

> Why do you argue these things in your heart?
>
> ₉What is easier to say to the paralytic,
>
> "Your wrongs are forgiven" or to say,
>
> "Stand, pick up your bed, and walk"?
>
> ₁₀But so you know that the earthly son[30]
>
> has the powers to forgive wrongs on earth,

---

[28] Moses from the Greek Μωϋσῆς (Moyses), from the Hebrew מֹשֶׁה (mosheh).

[29] Capernaum.

[30] "Son of Man" or "son of man" is the usual translation from the Greek ὁ υἱὸ τοῦ ἀνθρώπου (*ho huios tou*

he said to the paralytic,

11I tell you, "Stand up, take your bed,

and go to your house."

12And he stood up, and immediately took his bed and went outside in front of everyone so that all were astonished and glorified God, saying, "We have never seen anything like this!"

Calling on Levi the tax collector

13Yeshua went out again by the sea, and the whole crowd came to him and he taught them. 14And passing by he saw Levi[31] the son of Halfai[32] sitting in the tax office, and he said to him,

Follow me.

And he stood up and followed him.

15As he sat in Levi's house, many tax collectors and sinners lay back with Yeshua and his students.[33] There were many who followed him.

16When the Prushim scholars[34] saw that he was eating with sinners and tax collectors, they said to his students, "Does he eat with sinners and tax collectors?"

---

anthropou), which literally means "son of a person" or "son of people." The Greek ἀνθρώπου is not "man" but without gender, like "person." In the Hebrew Bible, "son of people" was an idiomatic way of saying "human being." In the gospels it may also suggest the son on earth as opposed to the son in heaven. Hence, "earthly son," rather than "son of man," "son of people," or "human being," may work better poetically and theologically.

[31] Levi, from the Greek Λευί, (Levi), from the Hebrew לֵוִי (levi), the tax collector in scripture, is usually identified as Matthew, which later, probably in the second century, became the evangelist's apostolic name: Matthew from the Greek Μαθθαιοσ (Maththaios), from the Hebrew מַתִּתְיָה (mattityah).

[32] Alphaeus from the Greek Ἀλφαῖος (Halfaios), from the Hebrew חַלְפִי (halfi).

[33] "Lay back" suggests lying or leaning back on a couch, which was the customary way of sitting in a house, alone or at a table, whether for talk or eating. "Student" is from the Greek μαθητής (mathetes), meaning "student" or "pupil." In Latin, student is discipulus, from which "disciple" comes. Through usage the more formal "disciple" has become a standard translation of the New Covenant Greek mathetis. Here "student" or "disciple" is used, depending on context.

[34] Pharisees from the Greek Φαρισαῖος (Farisaisos), from the Hebrew פְּרוּשִׁים (prushim). Pharisee (s.) is Parush. Historically, Pharisees, like Yeshua and Paul, reflect an open, oral interpretation of law, messiahship, and afterlife. In this first mention in the gospels of the Pharisees, the group is here and elsewhere depicted as a body of religious hypocrites and legalists, who are enemies of Yeshua, plotting his downfall and death. The reader is instructed to hate the Pharisees, who embody the soul of the Jews. Some modern scholars view the historical Yeshua as a rabbi of the Pharisees, placing him, therefore, with those who strongly opposed Roman occupation of Israel. Pharisees were a principal opponent of Rome, and it is commonly assumed that Yeshua was crucified as a seditionist. Since Jews and emerging Christians were persecuted and frequently slaughtered by the Romans in the first centuries of the Common Era, they were not likely to have been sympathetic to Rome in Israel. Consequently, the depiction of Yeshua in the gospels as an enemy of Pharisees and apologist for Rome—in "Give unto Caesar what is Caesar's"—is hard to reconcile with historical probability. Extreme examples of the gospels as an apologia for Rome appear when the Roman centurion, who has carried out the execution, becomes, with his soldiers, the first to gaze "with awe" on the crucified Yeshua and declares him innocent, God, and risen. These words, declaring Yeshua's innocence,

17When Yeshua heard, he said to them,

> The strong ones have no need of a doctor,
> but the sick do.
> I came to call not on the just but on the wrongdoers.

Fasting

18Then Yohanan's students and the Prushim were fasting, and people came to him and said, "Why are the students of Yohanan and the students of the Prushim fasting, but your students do not fast?"

19And Yeshua said to them,

> Can the attendants of the bridegroom fast
> while the bridegroom is with them?
> As long as they have the bridegroom with them,
> they cannot fast. 20But days will come
> when the bridegroom is taken away from them.
> Then on that day they will fast.
> 21No one sews an unshrunk patch of cloth
> on an old garment
> since the new pulls the patch away from the old
> and the tear becomes worse.
> 22No one pours new wine in old skins,
> since the wine splits the skins
> and both wine and skins are lost.
> No, put new wine in new skins.

Hunger on Shabbat[35]

23It happened on Shabbat that he was walking through the grain fields, and as his students made their way they were pulling ears of wheat.

24The Prushim said to him, "Look, why are you doing what is forbidden on Shabbat?"

25He said to them,

> Have you never read what David did when he had need
>   and hungered,
> he and those with him?
> 26How in the days of the high priest Evyatar[36]

---

divinity, and resurrection, are uttered implausibly by the Roman officer, who has just killed Yeshua. So Rome becomes the first to recognize Yeshua's divinity.

[35] Sabbath.

[36] Avyatar from the Greek Ἀβιαθάρ (Abiathar), from the Hebrew אֶבְיָתָר (evyatar).

he went into the house of God and ate the loaves
    of consecrated bread,
which only priests are allowed to eat,
and gave it also to those with him?

27And he said to them,
    Shabbat was made for a man and woman,
    not a man and woman for Shabbat.
    28So the earthly son is rabbi even of Shabbat.

CHAPTER 3

Man with a shriveled hand

Once again he entered the synagogue and there was a man who had a shriveled hand. 2They were watching him to see if he would heal on Shabbat so they might accuse him.

3He said to the man with the shriveled hand,
    Stand here in the middle.

4And he said to them,
    Is it right on Shabbat to do good or do harm,
    to save life or to destroy?

But they were silent.

5He looked around at them with anger, and grieved at the hardness of their heart. He said to the man,
    Stretch out your hand.

He stretched it out and his hand was restored.

6Then the Prushim left and at once began to plot against him with the Herodians as to how to destroy him.

At the sea and on the mountain with his twelve students

7Then Yeshua with his students withdrew to the sea. 8On hearing what he did, a great multitude from the Galil followed him, and they came also from Yehuda and from Yerushalayim and from Edom[37] and from beyond the Yarden and the region around Tzor[38] and Tzidon.[39] 9And he told his students to have a

---

[37] Edom. Idumea in its Latin version from the Greek Ἰδουμαία (Idoumaia), from the Hebrew אֱדוֹם (edom). Here it refers to an area south of Yehuda.

[38] Tyre from the Greek Τύρος (Tyros), from Hebrew צוֹר or צֹר (tzor), meaning "hard quartz" or "a flint knife," from the Aramaic טור (tur), meaning "a rock."

[39] Sidon from the Greek Σιδών (Sidon), from the Hebrew צִדוֹן (tzidon).

boat[40] ready for him, because of the crowd, so they would not crush him. 10He had healed many, and those who were in torment pushed forward that he might touch them. 11When the unclean spirits saw him they fell down before him and cried out, saying, "You are the son of God!"

12He warned them forcefully not to make him known.

13Then he went up on the mountain and called to those whom he wanted, and they came to him. 14He appointed twelve, whom he named messengers,[41] to be with him so he might send them out to preach 15and have the right to cast out demons.[42] 16He gave Shimon[43] the name Kefa.[44] 17And Yaakov[45] son of Zavdai and Yohanan brother of Yaakov he named Benei Regesh,[46] which means "Sons of Thunder." 18And Andreas and Filippos[47] and Bartalmai[48] and Mattai and Toma[49] and Yaakov son of Halfai and Taddai and Shimon the Cananean,[50] 19Yehuda of Keriot,[51] who betrayed him.

---

[40] From the Greek πλοιάριον (ploiarion), "a small ship" or "boat." "Boat" is often favored, since "ship" implies a larger vessel as in πλοῖον (ploion), which, depending on context, as in Mark 4.1, where the vessel is obviously a small one, may also be translated as "boat."

[41] "Whom he named messengers" is omitted in many Greek texts. "Messenger" or "envoy" rather than "apostle" is the common meaning of *apostolos*. *Apostolos* (in most translations "apostle") means "one from Yeshua's inner circle who is sent out on a mission." Another classical Greek word for "messenger" is ἄγγελος (angelos), whose New Covenant meaning is "angel" or "God's messenger." So there is an earthly messenger, ἀπόστολς, and a heavenly messenger, ἄγγελος. "Angel" has its lexical source in the earlier Septuagint Bible (the second-century B.C.E. Hebrew Bible in Greek translation for Jews of Alexandria). New Covenant Greek words that differ in meaning from their classical Greek source, by having acquired a religious and ethical dimension, usually are taken from the Septuagint.

[42] In other texts the phrase "he appointed the twelve" is repeated.

[43] Simon.

[44] Peter. The name *Petros* from the Greek Πέτρος (Petros) means "rock" or "stone" and is a translation of the Aramaic כֵּיפָא (kefa), also meaning "rock" or "stone." However, in John 1.42 and in three letters of Paul, Peter is called by his Aramaic name Kefa, which has been transliterated into the Greek and given a Greek ending to make it Κηφᾶς (Kefas), which is then romanized into English to read as Cephas. Shimon Kefa would be a fully Aramaic/Hebrew equivalent to the English Simon Peter. Peter's Semitic name Kefa is far removed from English, being a translation and not a transliteration, and hence cannot, without a glossary, be recognized as Peter by the English reader, unlike Yosef, which is readily seen to be Joseph.

[45] James from the Greek Ἰάκωβος (Iakobos), from the Hebrew יַעֲקֹב (yaakov).

[46] Boanerges from the Greek Βοανηργές, from the Hebrew בְּנֵי רֶגֶשׁ (benei regesh), meaning "sons of anger" or "thunder."

[47] Philip from the Greek Φίλιππος (Filippos).

[48] Bartholomew from the Greek Βαρθολομαῖος (Bartholmaios), from the Hebrew בַּר חַלְמִי (bar talmai). Bartalmai means "son of Talmai." Talmai may be Ptolemy, an Egyptian king.

[49] Thomas from the Greek Θωμᾶς (Thomas), from the Hebrew תָּאוֹמָא (toma). Thomas elsewhere in the gospels is called Θωμᾶς Δίδυμος (Thomas Didumos), meaning "Thomas the Twin."

[50] In Matthew 10.4 in the list of the twelve messengers or apostles it is "Simon the Zealot."

[51] Iscariot from the Greek Ἰσκαριώθ (Iskarioth), from the Hebrew אִישׁ קְרִיּוֹת (ish keriot), meaning "man of Keriot." In English, "Keriot" is also transcribed "Kerioth." Keriot is a village or town some twenty miles south of Jerusalem. Yehuda of Keriot, or more fully, Yehuda ben Shimon ish Keriot, Yehuda son of Shimon, man of Keriot, John 6.71, which is normally anglicized as Judas son of Simon Iscariot.

If a house is divided

20He came into a house, and the crowd gathered again so they could not even eat their bread. 21On hearing this, his family went out to restrain him, for they said, "He has lost his mind."[52] 22And the scholars who came down from Yerushalayim said, "He has Baal Zevul[53] in him, and it was through the prince of the demons that he drove out demons."

23Gathering them together, he spoke to them in parables,

How can Satan cast out Satan?
24If a kingdom is divided against itself
that kingdom cannot stand.
25If a house is divided against itself
that house cannot stand.
26And if Satan rises against himself and is divided
he cannot stand but comes to an end.
27No one can enter the house of the strong man
to plunder his possessions
unless he first ties up the strong man,
and then he will plunder his house.

28Truly I tell you,
the children of man and woman will be forgiven
for everything, their wrongs and blasphemies
as much as they blaspheme.
29But whoever blasphemes against the holy spirit
will be unforgiven everlastingly
and be guilty of everlasting wrong,
30 for they had said "his spirit is unclean."

---

[52] The family of Yeshua and especially his mother Miryam are portrayed negatively through the gospel of Mark, in contrast to Luke's positive portrayal. Here the family accepts the crowd's view that Yeshua "has lost his mind" and may be demonized, and seize him to restrain him. Yeshua resentfully rejects his family for their lack of faith in his powers, stating that his true mother and brothers are those out in the fields (Mark 3.33–35) and that a prophet is without honor in his own house and in his own family (Mark 6.4).

[53] Baal Zevul is Beelzebul, Satan, and originally a Philistine diety worshiped at Ekron, twenty-two miles west of Yerushalayim (2 Kings 1.2–18). Beelzebul is from Greek Βεελζεβούλ (Beelzeboul), from the Hebrew בַּעַל זְבוּל (Baal Zebul). Elsewhere we find Baal Zevuv, who is Beelzebub, from Greek Βεελζεβούβ (Beelzeboub), from Hebrew בַּעַל זְבוּב (Baal Zevuv). Baal Zevul may mean "Lord of Dung," and Baal Zevuv may mean "Lord of the Flies." In John Milton's *Paradise Lost* Beelezebub is the prince of evil spirits and Satan's chief lieutenant.

Yeshua rejects his mother and brothers

31Then his mother came and his brothers, and standing outside they sent someone in to call him. 32A crowd sat round him and said to him, "Look, your mother and your brothers[54] are outside looking for you."[55]

33He answered them, saying,

> Who is my mother and who are my brothers?

34And looking at those sitting around him in a circle, he said,

> 35Whoever does the will of God,
> that one is my brother and sister and mother.[56]

CHAPTER 4

Sower parable

Again he began to teach beside the sea, and a great crowd was gathered near him so he got into a boat and sat on the sea, and all the crowd near the lake was on the land. 2He taught them much in parables, and told them in his teaching,

> 3Listen.
> Look, the sower went out to sow
> 4and it happened that as he sowed
> some seed fell on the road
> and birds came and ate it.
> 5Another fell on stony ground
> where there was little soil,
> and at once it sprang up
> because it had no deep soil.
> 6And when the sun rose
> it was burnt, and because
> it had no roots it dried away.
> 7Another fell among the thorns
> and the thorns came up

---

[54] Other texts add "and your sisters."

[55] The reference to Yeshua's brothers indicates Mark's ignorance of the later doctrine of Mary's perpetual virginity. The brothers are mentioned later as James, Joseph, Judas, and Simon.

[56] In Mark and the other gospels there is a thread of resentment against his mother and brothers (and sisters) who are always elsewhere, outside when he is inside, inside when he is preaching in the meadows. See note 52, p. 56.

and choked the sprouts
and it bore no fruit.
8But some fell into good soil
and it bore fruit, shooting up
and increasing and it bore
thirty and sixty and one hundredfold,
9and he said,
Who has ears to hear, hear.

Secret of the kingdom

10When he was alone, those who were around him asked him about the parables. 11He said to them,
You have been given the mystery of the kingdom
of God.
For those outside, everything comes in parables
12so that, as in the words of Yeshayah,
"Looking they might look and not see,
hearing they might hear and not understand,
lest they might turn and be forgiven."[57]
13And he said to them,
Do you not know the parable
and how will you know all the parables?
14The sower sows the word.
15And these are the ones by the road
where the word is sown.
When they hear it, at once Satan comes
and takes the word sown in them.
16These are ones sown on stony ground,
and when they hear the word
at once they receive it happily
17and have no root in themselves
but are people of the moment.
When trouble or persecution comes
because of the word's sake,
at once they are shaky and fall.
18Others are those sown among thorns.
These are ones who heard the word,
19but cares of age and lure of wealth

---

[57] Isa. 8.16.

and desires for other things come in
and choke the word and it turns barren.
20And there are ones sown on good earth,
who hear the word, receive it, and bear fruit
thirty and sixty and one hundredfold.

Lamp on a stand

21Then he said to them,
Is a lamp brought inside to be placed
under a basket or under a couch
rather than set on a lampstand?
22So nothing is hidden except to be disclosed
or secret except to come into the open.
23If someone has ears to hear, hear.

Measure

24He was saying to them,
Consider what you hear. The measure
by which you measure will measure you,
and more will be added for you.
25Whoever has, more will be given,
and whoever has nothing, even that nothing
which he has will be taken from him.

Seed on the earth

26And he was saying,
The kingdom of God is as if a man threw seed on the earth,
27and would sleep and rise night and day
and the seed sprouts and grows big
in a way he does not perceive.
28On its own the earth bears fruit,
first grass then a stalk then the full grain in the ear.
29But when the grain is ripe, immediately
he takes out his sickle. The harvest has come.

The mustard seed and the kingdom of God

30And he said,
To what can we compare the kingdom of God
or in what parable shall we place it?
31Like a mustard seed which is sown on the earth,

smaller than all the seeds on the earth,
32yet when it is sown it grows and becomes greater
than all garden plants,
and makes branches so big that under its shade
the birds of the sky
may find there a place to nest in its shade.

33With many such parables he spoke the word to them insofar as they could understand, as far as they were able to hear. 34He spoke to them only in parable, but to his own students privately he explained all.

Calming the storm and the sea

35And on that day, as dusk took over, he said to them,

Let us cross over to the other side.

36And leaving the crowd behind, they took him with them into the small ship, just as he was. Other vessels were with him. 37There arose a furious wind storm and the waves were crashing against the boat so that it was beginning to fill. 38He was in the stern, sleeping on a pillow.

They woke him and said to him, "Rabbi, don't you care that we are perishing?"

39He got up and scolded the wind and spoke to the sea,

Silence, be still.

The wind died down and there was a dead calm.

40And he said to them,

Why are you cowards? Do you not have faith?

41They feared with great dread and said to one another, "Who is this that even the wind and the sea obey him?"

CHAPTER 5

Demoniac and the pigs

They came to the other side of the lake to the county of the Gerasenes. 2When Yeshua got out of the ship, at once a man with an unclean spirit came out of the tombs and met him. 3He lived in the tombs, and not even a chain could hold him back. 4He had often been bound with shackles and chains and he tore the chains apart and smashed the shackles. No one was strong enough to subdue him. 5Night and day in the tombs and in the mountains, constantly he was screaming and smashing himself with stones. 6Seeing Yeshua from a distance, he ran and fell to his knees before him 7and screaming in a great voice, he said, "What am I to you, Yeshua son of the highest God? I beg you, don't torment me."

8Yeshua was saying to him,

Foul[58] spirit, come out of this man!

9He asked him,

What is your name?

The man said to him, "My name is Legion, for we are many." 10And he implored him again and again not to send him out of the country.

11Now near the mountain was a big herd of pigs feeding. 12The demons begged Yeshua, "Send us to the pigs so we can go into them."

13And he consented.

The foul spirits came out and went into the pigs. And the herd rushed down the steep slope into the sea, about two thousand, and they drowned in the sea.

14Those feeding the pigs fled and reported it in the city and on the farms. And people came to see what happened. 15They came to Yeshua and saw the man who had been possessed by the legion of demons, seated, dressed, and of sound mind. And they were afraid. 16Those who saw what happened to the demoniac and the pigs reported it. 17And they began to plead with Yeshua to leave their district.

18As he was boarding the ship, the demoniac begged Yeshua to take him with him.

19He would not take him, but he said to him,

Go to your house and to those who are yours

and say how much Adonai has done for you

and how much he has pitied you.

20And the man left and spread word in Dekapolis[59] of how much Yeshua did for him.

Everyone wondered.

Girl near death and a woman bleeding

21When Yeshua crossed over again in the ship to the other side, a big crowd gathered around him beside the lake. 22One of the synagogue leaders named Yair[60] came, and seeing him, fell to his knees 23and begged him intensely, say-

---

58 Foul from the Greek ἀκάθαρτον (akatharton). Literally, "unclean."
59 Dekapolis from the Greek Δεκαπόλει, translated as "Ten Towns."
60 Jairus, from the Greek Ἰάϊρος (Iairos), from the Hebrew יָאִיר (yair).

ing, "My daughter is at the point of death. Come and put your hand on her so she may be healed and live."

He went with him. 24And a great crowd went with him and pressed against him. 25There was a woman who for twelve years had a flow of blood. 26She suffered much under many doctors, and spent all she had but she was no better. Rather she got worse. 27She had heard about Yeshua, and coming up behind him in the crowd she touched his garment. 28She was saying, "If I can even touch his garments, I will be healed."

29At once the source of her blood dried up and she knew in her body that she had been healed of her terrible disease.

30Immediately aware in himself that power had gone out from him, Yeshua turned around in the crowd and said,

Who touched my clothing?

31His students said to him, "You see the crowd pressing against you, and you say, 'Who touched me?'"

32He looked around to see who had done it.

33Then the woman—in fear and trembling, knowing what had happened to her—came and fell before him and told him the whole truth.

34He said to her,

Daughter, your faith has healed you.

Go in peace

and be cured of your affliction.

35While he was speaking, some people came from the house of the leader of the synagogue. "Your daughter died," they said. "Why are you still bothering the rabbi?"

36But ignoring what they said, Yeshua said to the leader of the synagogue,

Do not fear. Only believe.

37And he let no one follow him except Kefa[61] and Yaakov and Yohanan, brother of Yaakov.[62]

38They came to the house of the leader of the synagogue and saw a commotion and people weeping and wailing loudly. 39On going inside, he said to them,

Why this commotion and weeping?

The child didn't die. No, she is sleeping.

40But they laughed at him.

Then he put everyone outside, and took the child's father, mother, and those with him, and went inside where the child was. 41He took the child's hand and said to her,

---

[61] Peter.
[62] James and John, brother of James.

Talitha koum,[63]

which translated from Aramaic means, "Little girl, I say to you, Awake!"

42And at once the girl got up and walked around. She was twelve years old. They were amazed with great ecstasy.

43He gave them repeated orders that no one should know this and said to give her something to eat.

CHAPTER 6

Rejected in his town and by his family

Yeshua left that place and went to his home town,[64] and his students followed him. 2When Shabbat came, he began to teach in the synagogue and many who heard him were amazed, saying, "Where did he learn all these things, and what is this wisdom given to him, and how is it that such powers[65] have come into his hands? 3Isn't he the carpenter, the son of Miryam[66] and brother of Yaakov and Yosef[67] and Yehuda and Shimon? And are his sisters not here with us?"

They were offended by him.

4Yeshua said to them,

> A prophet is not without honor
> except in his own country,
> in his own family, and in his own house.

---

[63] An Aramaic expression. Aramaic was the lingua franca of the region from Canaan to Phoenicia and was the language Yeshua would have commonly spoken. Hebrew by his time was the language of the book and the synagogue.

[64] From the Greek πατρίς, ίδος (patris, idos), meaning "hometown," "native land," "fatherland," or "country." Since Nazareth was surely a small village yet is referred to as a *polis* (πόλις), a "city," it is difficult to find one word that fairly represents *patrida* (πατρίδα, dative).

[65] From the Greek δύναμις (dynamis). From *dynamis*, "power" or "strength," as in dynamism. *Dynamis* is translated as "miracles" in NIV (New International Version), New American Standard Bible, and Annotated Scholars. In NRSV (New Revised Standard Version), it is "deeds of power." Lattimore gives "powers," Reynolds Price "acts of power." In Tyndale, we have "virtues," in KJV "mighty works," in the New American Bible "mighty deeds." Although New Covenant lexicons accommodate "explanatory" ecclesiastical meanings, in the standard Liddell and Scott's *Greek-English Lexicon*, "miracle" is not given as a meaning for the Greek δύναμις (dynamis). The miracle is essential to the figure of the messiah, who with transcendental powers operates in disregard of laws of nature. In other instances I have used "miraculous powers" to suggest the clear intention of miracle, but Tyndale, James and most modern translations of this crucial word have resisted endowing their versions with the heresy of explanation and give us only what the Greek states.

[66] Mary from the Greek Μαρία (Maria), from the Hebrew מִרְיָם (miryam), often Anglicized in English as Miriam.

[67] Joseph from the Greek Ἰωσήφ (Iosef), from the Hebrew יוֹסֵף (yosef).

5He could not perform any powers except on a few sick people, laying hands on them, and healing them. 6He was astonished by their disbelief.

Shake the dust off from under your feet

7Then he went around the villages, teaching. And he called the twelve and began to send them out two by two, and he gave them authority over unclean spirits, 8and ordered them to take nothing on the road except a staff, but no bread, bag, no copper coins in their belts. 9To wear sandals and not to wear two tunics. 10He told them,

> Wherever you go into a house,
> stay there until you leave there.
> 11And when a place will not receive or hear you,
> as you leave there, shake the dust off from under your feet
> as a testimony against them.[68]

12They went out and preached the message of repentance. 13They cast out many demons, rubbed olive oil[69] on many who were sick, and healed them.

Herod and Yohanan's head

14At that time King Herod[70] heard about Yeshua, for his name had become well known, and people were saying that "Yohanan the Dipper had been raised from the dead which is why those powers are at work through him." 15But others were saying, "It is Eliyah";[71] and others said, "It is a prophet." 16But when Herod heard, he said, "It is Yohanan whom I beheaded. He has been raised."

17Herod himself had sent to have him arrested and bound in prison because of Herodias, the wife of his brother Filippos. Herod had married her. 18Yohanan told Herod, "It is not lawful for you to take the wife of your brother." 19So

---

[68] The King James Version continues Mark 6.11: "Verily I say unto you, it shall be more tolerable for Sodom and Gomorrah [Sedom and Amorah] in the day of judgment, than for that city." The vindictive response of "shake the dust off from under your feet as a testimony against them" becomes more specifically destruction and intolerable punishment if the apostles' ministry is refused. The Greek text is disputed and not translated in modern versions other than the Amplified Bible (1958), which puts it in italics. The older Rheims Bible (1588) also omits this passage.

[69] "Rubbing olive oil" has the religious meaning of "anointing," from the Greek ἀλείφω (aleifo), from the Hebrew מָשִׁיחַ (mashiah), "the anointed one," giving us the word "messiah." Another Greek word, also for anointing, gives us the word "Christ": χρίω (Chrio or Hrio), from which comes Χριστός (Christos or Hristos). In Greece and the Near East the people anointed with oil (usually olive oil) and spice (often myrrh). Olive oil was used as a medicine to rub on as a balm and also for athletes.

[70] The Greek title for Herod Antipas, son of Herod the Great, who was tetrarch of Galilee. Mark calls him King.

[71] Elijah or Elias from the Greek Ἠλίας (Elias), from the Hebrew אֵלִיָה (eliyah).

Herodias bore a grudge against him and wanted to kill him, but she was unable to. 20Herod feared Yohanan, knowing that he was a just and holy man, and he protected him. When he heard him, he was greatly disturbed, yet gladly he listened to him.

21Then came an opportune day when Herod on his birthday had a banquet for the great courtiers and military commanders and foremost people of the Galil. 22When his daughter Herodias came in and danced, she delighted Herod and those reclining at the table. And the king said to the girl, "Ask me whatever you want and I will give it to you." 23He swore to her, "Whatever you ask of me, I will give you up to half my kingdom."

24She went out and said to her mother, "What must I ask?"

And she said, "The head of Yohanan the Dipper."

25At once she rushed back eagerly to the king and made her request: "I want you to give me right now on a platter the head of Yohanan the Dipper."

26The king was despondent because of his oaths and those reclining at the table and he didn't wish to refuse her. 27At once the king sent an executioner and commanded him to bring the head of Yohanan.

The guard left and beheaded him in the prison, 28and brought his head in on a platter, and the girl gave it to her mother. 29Hearing about this, his students came and took his corpse and placed it in a tomb.[72]

Bread for the five thousand on the green grass

30The messengers[73] rejoined Yeshua and reported to him everything they had done and taught. 31He said to them,

> Come yourselves alone to a deserted place
> and rest a while.

For many of them were coming and going and they had no chance even to eat. 32And they went off in a ship to a deserted place by themselves.

33Now many saw them going and had heard of them, and from all the towns they ran there on foot and got there ahead of them.

---

[72] The story of Herod the Great's son Herod Antipas and his daughter Salome (not Herodias, as in Mark and Matthew) is the legendary subject of gospel, play, and opera. However, the historian Josephus tells us that John was imprisoned and executed by Herod, not in his palace but in his grim fortress of Machaeros, and identifies Herod's daughter as Salome and her mother as Herodias. In this incident, as told in Mark and Matthew, the villain is the wife, and her daughter who is obeying her mother's orders. Herod, like Pontius Pilate, respects and admires the prisoner but is unhappily fulfilling a trick promise. In both incidents, the rulers, Herod and Pilate, strong repressive figures loyal to the Romans, are exonerated from the unpleasant act of executing major Christian heroes, which thereby reduces Rome's responsibility for wrongdoing in the drama of emerging Christianity.

[73] See note 41, p. 55.

34On coming ashore, Yeshua saw a great crowd and he pitied them, for they were like sheep without a shepherd, and he began to teach them many things.

35When it was already late the students came to him, saying, "This is a deserted place and it is already late. 36Send them off so they can go into the surrounding farms and villages and buy themselves something to eat."

37But he answered, saying to them,

> You give them something to eat.

They said to him, "Shall we go and buy two hundred denarii[74] worth of loaves and give them that to eat?"

38And he said to them,

> How many loaves do you have?
> Go and see.

When they found out, they said, "Five, and two fish."

39He told them all to sit down in groups on the green grass. 40They sat down in groups of hundreds and fifties.

41He took the five loaves of bread and the two fish, and looking up into the sky he blessed and broke the loaves and gave them to his students to set before the people, and the two fish he divided among them all. 42Everyone ate and they were filled. 43And they picked up twelve full baskets of crumbs and fish. 44Those who had eaten were five thousand men.[75]

Walking on the sea

45Immediately Yeshua had his students climb into the ship and go ahead to the other side, to Beit Tzaida,[76] while he dismissed the crowd. 46And after saying goodbye to them he went off to the mountain to pray.

47When dusk came the ship was in the middle of the sea and he was alone on the land. 48Seeing the students straining at the oars—the wind was against them—about the fourth watch of the night[77] he came toward them, walking on the sea, and he wanted to pass by them. 49But seeing him walking on the sea they thought he was a phantom, and they cried out. 50They all saw him and they were terrified.

At once he spoke with them and said,

---

[74] Denarii is a plural of denarius, a silver Roman coin worth about the day's wages of a laborer.

[75] Here the word is specifically "men" rather than people, from the Greek ἀνήρ (aner), ἀνδρός (andros). Another word for "man" is ἄνθρωπος (anthropos), which may mean "man" or also "a genderless person." It is possible, though unlikely, that the multitude consisted entirely or largely of men. Probably the text followed the habit in most languages of men meaning "people" (male and female).

[76] Bethseda from the Greek Βηθσαϊδά (Bethsaida), from the Hebrew בֵּית צַיְדָא (beit tzaida), which is a place north of the Sea of Galilee.

[77] About three in the morning.

Take courage. It is I. Don't be afraid.

51Then he climbed into the boat and the wind fell, and deep in themselves they were astonished. 52They had not understood about the loaves and their hearts hardened.

The sick on stretchers at Gennesaret

53When they crossed over to the land, they came to Gennesaret[78] and anchored. 54They got out of the ship, and people immediately recognized him 55and rushed about over the countryside and began to bring the sick on litters to wherever they heard he was. 56Wherever he went, into villages or cities or into the farmland and in the marketplaces, they laid out the sick and begged that they might touch even the fringe of his garment. And those who touched him were healed.

 CHAPTER 7

On ways of washing

The Prushim and some scholars who had come from Yerushalayim gathered around him. 2They saw that some of his students were eating bread with impure, that is, unwashed, hands. 3The Prushim and all the Jews will not eat unless they wash, hand against fist, so keeping the tradition of the elders, 4and eat nothing from the markets unless they wash. And they keep many other traditions about washing cups and pots and copper cauldrons. 5The Prushim and the scholars questioned him, "Why do your students not walk according to the tradition of our elders, but eat bread with impure hands?"

6Yeshua said to them,

Yeshayah prophesied rightly about you hypocrites,
as it is written:
"This people honors me with their lips
but their hearts are far away from me.
7They worship me in vain,
teaching teachings that are commands of men."[79]
8You abandon God's commands, you hold to human ways.

---

[78] Village on the north side of the Sea of Galilee.

[79] Isa. 29.13. Isaiah says that "these are rules taught by men," suggesting that the commandments do not come from God.

9And he said to them,

> You have a fine way of setting aside the commandment
> of God
> so your tradition can stand.
> 10Mosheh said, "Honor your father and your mother"
> and "Whoever reviles[80] a father or mother must die."
> 11Yet you say if a person tells his father or mother,
> "What you might have got from me is Korban[81]
> (meaning a gift), 12then you are free to do nothing
> for your father and mother,"
> 13and you erase God's word by the way you interpret
> tradition.
> You do many things like that!

Parable of food and defilement

14Then he called the crowd again, and said to them,

> Hear me all of you and understand.
> 15There is nothing outside a person
> which by going in can defile,
> but what comes out,
> these are the things that defile a person.

17When he entered a house from the crowd, the students asked him about the parable. 18He said to them,

> Are you that mindless? Don't you understand,
> anything that goes into a person from the outside
> cannot defile
> 19since it doesn't enter the heart but the stomach
> and goes into the sewer, purging all foods.

20He said,

> What goes out of a person defiles
> 21since evil thoughts come out of the heart—
> copulations, thefts, murders, 22adulteries,

---

80 From the Greek κακολογέω (kakologeo), "to speak poorly" or "evilly" or "reviling." Literally, it is "badspeaking," which is close in spirit to "bad mouthing."

81 Corban is from the Greek κορβᾶν (corban), from the Hebrew קָרְבַּן (korban), meaning "an offering to God," as in Leviticus 1.2 and Numbers 7.13. Mark uses "corban" in a convoluted way to suggest that one can declare an offering to God and so avoid supporting one's parents. The notion appears to have no earlier meaning as Mark defines it, and the later Mishnah states that one can break vows of payment to the synagogue if one is without means of supporting one's parents.

greeds, wickednesses, deceit, lasciviousness,

evil eye, blasphemy, pride, and folly.

23All these wicked things of the earth

come out from within and defile.

Greek girl with a demon

24Arising from there he went off to the region of Tzor. He entered into a house and wanted no one to know, but he could not remain hidden.

25But a woman, whose little daughter had an unclean spirit, immediately heard about him. She came and fell down at his feet. 26The woman was a Greek, by birth a Phoenician from Syria, and she asked him to expel the demon from her daughter.

27He said to her,

Let the children first be fed,

for it is not good to take the bread of the children

and throw it to the dogs.

28But she answered and said to him, "Sir, even the dogs under the table eat the children's crumbs."

Then he told her,

29Because of this word, go.

The demon has left your daughter.

30She left and went into her house, found the child lying on her bed, and the demon was gone.

Fingers and spittle for a deaf mute

31Once again on leaving the region of Tzor, he came through Tzidon to the Sea of the Galil and into the middle of the region of Dekopolis. 32They brought him a deaf mumbler who could barely speak, and they begged him to lay his hand on him. 33He took him away from the crowd where they were alone, put his fingers into the man's ears, spat, and touched his tongue. 34Then after looking up into the sky, he groaned and said to him, *Effatha!*,[82] which means "Be opened!"

35The man's ears were opened, the bond of his tongue loosened, and he spoke plainly.

36Then Yeshua ordered them to tell no one, but the more he ordered, the more they spoke of it everywhere. 37People were overcome with wonder, saying, "He has done everything good, he makes the deaf hear and the dumb speak."

---

[82] From the Greek ἐφφαθά (effatha), which is derived from the Aramaic.

CHAPTER 8

Bread for the four thousand in the desert

In those days again there was a great crowd who had nothing to eat, and calling his students together he said to them,

2I have pity for the crowd,

for they have already been with me three days

and have nothing to eat.

3If I send them hungry to their homes,

they will collapse on the road

and some have come from far away.

4His students answered him, "Where will anyone find bread to feed them here in the desert?"

He asked them,

5How many loaves do you have?

"Seven," they said.

6Then he ordered the crowd to lie back on the ground. He took the seven loaves, and after giving thanks he broke them and gave them to his students to serve.

They served the crowd.

7They had a few small fish. After giving thanks for them he gave them to the students and ordered these to be served also.

8They ate and were filled. And there were seven basketfuls of leftover pieces. 9There were about four thousand people and he sent them off.

10At once he got into his ship with his students and came into the region of Dalmanutha.[83]

A sign from the sky

11Then the Prushim came out and began to argue with him, asking him for a sign from the sky. They were testing him.

12Groaning in his soul, he said to them,

Why does this generation ask for a sign?

Amen I say to you.

No sign will be given to this generation.

---

[83] Matthew says he went to Gennesaret (Matt. 15.39). They may be different names for the same place or two places near each other. Variant readings are Magadan, Magedan, and Magdala, the latter suggesting it may be Magdala, as in Miryam of Magdala.

Understanding bread

₁₃He left them, and got into his ship again and left for the other side.

₁₄They forgot to take bread, and except for one loaf they had nothing for themselves on the boat.

₁₅Yeshua gave orders, saying,

> Look, and watch out for the Prushim's leaven
>
> and the leaven of Herod.

₁₆They argued with one another about not having bread.

₁₇Knowing, he said to them,

> Why do you argue about not having bread?
>
> Do you still not see or understand?
>
> Has your heart hardened?
>
> ₁₈You have eyes, do you not see?
>
> You have ears, do you not hear?
>
> and don't you remember ₁₉when I broke the five loaves
>
> for the five thousand,
>
> how many baskets filled with scraps you picked up?

They said to him, "Twelve."

> ₂₀When it was seven for the four thousand,
>
> how many baskets filled with scraps did you pick up?

They said to him, "Seven."

₂₁And he said to them,

> Do you still not understand?

Saliva on a blindman's eyes

₂₂They came to Beit Tzaida. Some people brought him a blindman and they begged him to touch him.

₂₃He took the blindman's hand and took him outside the village and spat on his eyes, lay his hands on him, and asked him,

> Can you see?

₂₄He looked up and said, "I see people but they look like trees walking."

₂₅Then Yeshua again put his hands on the blindman's eyes.

The man looked hard, his eyes were restored, and saw all things clearly.

₂₆Then he sent him to his house, saying,

> Don't go into the village.

Who do people say I am?

₂₇Then Yeshua and his students went out to the villages of Caesarea Filippi.[84] On the way he questioned his students, saying to them,

---

[84] Caesarea Philippi.

Who do people say I am?

28They answered, saying, "Yohanan the Dipper, and others say, Yeshayah, but others one of the prophets."

29He asked them,

But who do you say I am?

Kefa[85] said to him, "You are the mashiah."

30He warned them not to tell anyone about him.

I will die and be arisen

31He began to teach them that the earthly son[86] must suffer many things and be rejected by the elders and the high priests and the scholars, and be killed and after three days rise. 32And he said the word openly.[87]

Kefa took him aside and began to warn him.

33But Yeshua turned and looked at his students and reproved Kefa, and said,

Go behind me, Satan!

Because you are thinking not the things of God

but of earthly beings.

Follow me

34Then calling the crowd together with his students, he said to them,

If some of you would follow me,

deny yourself and take up your cross

and follow me.

Losing life to find the soul

35Whoever of you would save your life

will lose it.

Whoever of you loses your life for me

and for the good news

will save it.

36How does it help a person to gain the whole world

and forfeit the soul?

37What can a person give in exchange for the soul?

Whoever is ashamed of me

38Whoever of you is ashamed of me and my words

---

[85] Peter.

[86] Son of Man.

[87] Others translate "said the thing" or "said all this," and so forth, but "said the word" is literal, mysterious, yet less vague.

in this adulterous and wrongful generation,
the earthly son will be ashamed of you
    when he comes
in the glory of your father with the holy angels.

❖ CHAPTER 9

Tasting death

And he said to them,
    Amen I say to you,
    there are some of you standing here
    who will not taste death
    until you see that the kingdom of God has come
    with power.

Transfigured, his clothing gleaming white

2After six days Yeshua took Kefa and Yaakov and Yohanan and led them up a high mountain, alone, by themselves. And he was transfigured[88] before them, 3and his clothing became a white so gleaming that no bleach on the earth could so whiten them. 4And there appeared to them Eliyah with Mosheh talking to Yeshua.

5Then Kefa said to Yeshua, "Rabbi, it is good for us to be here, and let us make three shelters,[89] one for you and one for Mosheh and one for Eliyah."

6He didn't know what to say, they were so terrified.

7Then a cloud came and cast a shadow over them, and a voice came out of the cloud:

    This is my beloved son. Hear him.

8And suddenly as they looked around, they no longer saw anyone but Yeshua, alone with them.

---

88 Verses 2–8 are commonly called the Transfiguration. Following the tradition of Jewish apocalypticism, Yeshua is supernaturally transformed into a dazzling white vision of the mashiah in heaven.

89 Tabernacle from the Greek σκηνή (skene), "tent," from the Hebrew סֻכָּה (sukkah), "shelter," or "tent." The three tents are associated with the Jewish Sukkah, also called Sukkoth, or the Festival of the Tabernacles or Booths, חַג הַסֻּכָּה (hag hasukkah), an eight-day celebration for the autumnal harvest, beginning on the eve of the 15th of Tishri. The sukkah is a small lean-to-like tent in the fields. One dwells in the sukkah in commemoration of God's protection of Israel when it was wandering in the desert (the wilderness) after their escape from Egypt.

Eliyah has come

₉As they came down the mountain, he ordered them to tell no one what they had seen until the earthly son has risen from the dead.

₁₀And they kept that word to themselves, discussing what is "to rise from the dead." ₁₁They asked him, saying, "Why do the scholars say that first Eliyah must come?"

₁₂He said to them,

> Eliyah will come first and restore everything.
>
> How has Yeshayah written about the earthly son
>
> that he must suffer much and be rejected?[90]
>
> ₁₃But I tell you that Eliyah has come
>
> and, as written,
>
> they did with him whatever they pleased.

A mute child foaming and grinding his teeth

₁₄When their party came to the students, they saw a great crowd around them and the scholars arguing with them. ₁₅The whole crowd when they saw him were at once amazed and ran up to him and greeted him.

₁₆He asked them,

> What are you arguing about with them?

₁₇Someone from the crowd answered him, "Rabbi, I brought my son to you. He has a speechless spirit. ₁₈When it seizes him, it throws him down, he foams and grinds his teeth and becomes stiff.[91] I asked your students to drive it out, but they could not."

₁₉Yeshua responded to them, saying,

> You faithless generation, how long will I be with you?
>
> Bring him to me.

₂₀And they brought him to him. When the spirit saw Yeshua, at once it convulsed the boy, who fell on the ground and rolled about, foaming.

₂₁Then Yeshua asked his father,

> How long has this been happening to him?

"Since childhood," he said, ₂₂"and often it threw him into the fire and into the water to destroy him. But if you can do anything, have pity on us."

---

[90] Isa. 52.13–53.12, the suffering servant passage. In Isaiah we read of the messianic figure who "grew up before God like a tender shoot" (Isa. 53.2); who was despised and rejected (53.3), who was pierced for our transgressions, whose pain brought us peace and by whose wounds we are healed (53.5); he was led like a lamb to the slaughter (53.7); and after his suffering he will see the light (53.11); he bore the sins of many, and for his suffering will gain God's place with the great (53.12). These passages are standardly interpreted in Christian reading of the Hebrew Bible as prophecy of the suffering, crucifixion, and resurrection of the Christ.

[91] The boy has the symptoms of epilepsy.

₂₃Yeshua said to him,

If you are able, all things are possible for the one believing.

₂₄At once the child's father cried out, saying, "I believe! Help my unbelief!"

₂₅Yeshua, seeing that the crowd was growing around him, warned the unclean spirit, saying to it,

Speechless and deaf spirit, I command you,
come out of him, and enter him no more.

₂₆After screaming and convulsing the boy greatly, it came out and the child became like one dead, and many said he had died.

₂₇But Yeshua holding his hand lifted him and he stood up.

₂₈When he went into a house his students asked him privately, "Why were we unable to cast it out?"

₂₉And he said to them,

This kind will come out only through prayer.

I will die and be arisen

₃₀After leaving there they went through the Galil, and he didn't wish anyone to know. ₃₁He was teaching his students and said to them,

The earthly son will be handed over into human hands
and they will kill him,
and three days after being killed he will arise.

₃₂But they didn't understand his word and they were afraid to ask him.

The first will be last but who receives the child receives me

₃₃Then they came into Kfar Nahum⁹² and once in the house he questioned them,

On the road what were you arguing about?

₃₄They were silent, for they argued on the road about who was the greatest.

₃₅He sat down and called the twelve and said to them,

Who would be first will be last
and a slave to all.

₃₆Then he took a child and placed him in their midst and taking him into his arms he said to them,

₃₇Whoever welcomes a child like one of these
in my name
welcomes me.
And whoever welcomes me, not only welcomes me
but the one who sent me.

---

⁹² Capernaum.

Demons and a cup of water

38Yohanan said to him, "Rabbi, we saw someone casting out demons in your name, and we stopped him because he was not one who followed us."

39But Yeshua said,

Don't stop him,
for no one can perform a power[93] in my name
and speak poorly about me.
40Whoever is not against us is for us.
41Whoever gives you a cup of water to drink in my name
because you are of the mashiah,
I say to you that he won't lose his reward.

A millstone around the neck

42Whoever makes one of these little ones who believes
    stumble,
it would be better for him to hang a millstone[94]
    around his neck
and be thrown into the sea.

43And if your hand makes you stumble, cut it off.
It is better for you to enter life maimed
than to have two hands and go into Gei Hinnom,[95]
into unquenchable fire.
45And if your foot makes you stumble, cut it off.
It is better for you to enter life maimed
than to have two feet and go into Gei Hinnom.
47And if your eye makes you stumble, tear it out.
It is better for you to enter one-eyed into the kingdom
    of God
than to have two eyes and be flung into Gei Hinnom
    48where the worm does not die
    and the fire is unextinguished.[96]

---

[93] Elsewhere translated as "a deed of power" or "a miracle."

[94] Literally, "donkey stone," meaning that a mule turned a great millstone. Verses 42–48 are the first warnings of hell and its pains.

[95] Gehenna from the Greek γέεννα (Geenna), from the Hebrew גֵּיא הִנֹּם (gei hinnom), meaning the "valley of Hinnom." Gei Hinnom is a special pit of darkness of the Hebrew Bible. Gei Hinnom and Sheol are normally translated into English as "hell."

[96] Isa. 66.24.

Salted with fire

49Everyone will be salted with fire.

50Salt is good, but if salt loses the taste of salt,

what will you season it with?

Keep the salt in yourselves and be at peace

with one another.

CHAPTER 10

What God joined together let no one separate

Rising from there he came into the region of Yehuda and beyond the Yarden, and again crowds gathered around him, and again as was his custom he taught them. 2The Prushim came near and asked him if it was allowable for a man to divorce his wife. They were testing him.

3He answered and said to them,

What did Mosheh command you?

4They said, "Mosheh allowed a man to write a notice of separation[97] and to divorce his wife."

5Then Yeshua said to them,

Because of your hardheartedness he wrote this commandment

for you.

6But from the beginning of creation:

he made them male and female.[98]

7Because of that a person will leave the father and mother

8and the two will be one flesh.[99]

So they are no longer two but one flesh.

9Therefore what God joined together let no one separate.[100]

10The students in the house again questioned him about that.

11And he said to them,

---

97 The separation stated in the Greek ἀποστάσιον (apostasion) has its root meaning in "standing apart from." In contemporary translation, there is a temptation to use contemporary legal terms. It may be interpreted as "a divorce," "a legal transfer of property," or "the act of releasing or dismissing."

98 Gen. 1.27. "He" is God.

99 Gen. 2.24.

100 The injunction against separation (divorce) is Yeshua's addition to the Hebrew verses in Genesis and remains the source for the Christian sanctity of marriage.

Whoever divorces his wife and marries another
commits adultery with her.
12And if she divorces her husband and marries another,
she commits adultery.

Let the children come to me

13Then they brought him children for him to touch them, but the students scolded them. 14Seeing this, Yeshua became angry and said,

Let the children come to me.
Do not stop them. For the kingdom of God
belongs to them.
15I tell you,
whoever does not receive the kingdom of God
like a child
will never enter therein.

16And he took them in his arms and blessed them and placed his hands on them.

Dilemmas of a rich man

17As he went out on the road, a man ran up and kneeling before him asked him, "Good rabbi, what must I do to inherit eternal life?"
18Yeshua said to him,

Why do you call me good?
No one is good but God alone.
19The commandments you know:
"Do not murder.
Do not commit adultery.
Do not steal.
Do not bear false witness.
Do not defraud.
Honor your father and mother."[101]

20He said to him, "Rabbi, all those things I have kept since my youth."
21Then Yeshua looked at him and loved him, and said,

One thing you lack. Go, and sell all you own
and give to the poor
and you will have a treasure in heaven.
Then come follow me.

---

[101] Exod. 20.12–16; Deut. 5.16–20.

₂₂But he was downcast by the word and went away grieving. He had many possessions.

Heaven through the eye of a needle
₂₃Then Yeshua looked around him and said to his students,

>How hard it will be for those who have money
>
>to enter the kingdom of God!

₂₄His students were astonished by his words.

But Yeshua said to them again,

>Children, how hard it is to enter the kingdom of God.
>
>₂₅It is easier for a camel to go through the eye
>
>of a needle
>
>than for a rich person to enter the kingdom of God.[102]

₂₆They were even more astonished and said to each other, "Then who can be saved?"

₂₇Looking at them, Yeshua said,

>For humans it is impossible, but not for God.
>
>All things are possible for God.

The last will be first
₂₈Kefa began to say to him, "Look, we left everything and have followed you."
₂₉Yeshua said,

>Amen, amen, I say to you,
>
>There is no one who gave up home or brothers or sisters
>
>or mother or father or children or farms
>
>for my sake and for the good news,
>
>₃₀who will not receive a hundredfold,
>
>now in this age—houses and brothers

---

[102] This famous passage has often been commented on for its hyperbole of a camel passing through the eye of a needle. Because such an event is utterly impossible, it is removed from ordinary reality to an allegorical or surreal level, which permits it to be accepted. The reader is informed not to reject the comparison for reasons of exaggeration, but to accept it "symbolically." So this wonderful literary trope works. In all probability we have a happy accident of conversion from the Aramaic or the Hebrew source. The root consonants for "camel" and "coarse thread" are the same in the Semitic original (vowels distinguishing meaning and pronunciation were written under the letters only much later in the Masoretic texts). Were we to have an accurate translation of the probable meaning of the aphorism, "It is easier for a coarse thread to pass through the eye of a needle than for a rich person to enter the kingdom of God," we would have a bland and forgettable bit of wisdom verse. Although it is always astonishing to read Yeshua conversing in Greek with Jewish peasants rather than in Aramaic and quoting Hebrew to them, in this instance, in comparison with the extant Greek translation, the passage probably suffers in the original.

and sisters and mothers
and children and farms with persecutions—
and in the age to come life everlasting.
31But many who are first will be last
and the last will be first.

I will die and be arisen[103]

32They were on the road going up to Yerushalayim, and Yeshua was leading them. They were astounded, and those following them were afraid. He
took the twelve aside again and began to tell them what was going to happen
to him,

33Look. We are going up to Yerushalayim
and the earthly son will be handed over to the high priests
    and the scholars,
and they will condemn him to death
and hand him over to the gentiles[104]
34and they will ridicule him and spit on him and flog him
    and kill him,
and after three days he will rise again.

Seated in glory

35Yaakov and Yohanan—the sons of Zavdai[105]—came up to him, saying,
"Rabbi, we want you to do for us whatever we ask you to."
36He said to them,

What do you want me to do for you?

37And they said to him, "Let one of us sit on your right and one on your left
in your glory."
38Yeshua said to them,

You do not know what you are asking.
Can you drink the cup I am drinking
or be dipped in the waters I am dipped in?[106]

39They said to him, "We can."
Then Yeshua said to them,

The cup I will drink you will drink
and the waters I am dipped in
you will be dipped in.

---

[103] This is the third time Yeshua foresees his death and resurrection.
[104] Foreigners or non-Jews.
[105] The sons of Zebedee (Zavdai) are the Boargenes (Benei Regesh), known for their fiery zeal.
[106] Presumably "the waters of the spirit."

₄₀Yet to sit on my right or my left is not mine to give.
It is for those for whom it was prepared.

To be first, be a slave

₄₁When the other ten heard about this, they began to be angry with Yaakov and Yohanan, ₄₂and Yeshua called them and said to them,

Among the gentiles, those who are called the rulers
lord over the people and their great ones wield power.
You know that. ₄₃But it's not so with you.
Whoever would be great among you must become
your servant.
₄₄Whoever would be first must be the slave of all.
₄₅The earthly son did not come to be served
but to serve
and give his life as ransom for the many.

A blind beggar in Yeriho

₄₆They came to Yeriho.[107] As he and his students and a large crowd were leaving Yeriho, Bar Timai, son of Timai,[108] a blind beggar, was sitting by the road. ₄₇When he heard that Yeshua the Natzrati was coming, he began to cry out and to say, "Son of David, have pity on me!"

₄₈Many warned him to be quiet.

₄₉But Yeshua stopped and said,

Call him.

And they called the blindman, saying to him, "Be happy. Stand up. He's calling you."

₅₀Then throwing off his cloak, he sprang up and came to Yeshua.

₅₁And answering him Yeshua said,

What do you want me to do?

The blindman said to him, "Rabboni,[109] let me see again."

₅₂And Yeshua said to him,

Go, your faith has cured you.

At once he saw again and followed him on the road.

---

[107] Jericho from the Greek Ἰεριχώ (Ieriho), from the Hebrew יְרִיחוֹ (yeriho).

[108] Bartimeus from the Greek Βαρτιμαῖος (Bartimaios), from the Aramaic בַּר טְמַי (bar timai). *Timai* is a Greek word in Aramaic and Hebrew, probably τιμή (time), meaning "value" or "honor," or a shortened form of Τιμόθεος (Timotheos), Timothy, meaning "valued by God."

[109] *Rabboni,* meaning "my great rabbi."

CHAPTER 11

Entering Yerushalayim on a colt

And as they neared Yerushalayim, at Beit Pagey[110] and Beit Aniyah[111] toward the Mountain of Olives, he sent two of his students 2and said to them,

> Go into the village before you
>
> and once you are inside you will find a tethered colt
>
> on which no one has sat.
>
> Untie it and bring it.
>
> 3If someone tells you, "Why are you doing this?" say,
>
> "His master needs it and he will send it back at once."

4They went away and found a colt tethered to a door out on the street and they untied it.

5Some of those standing there said to them, "What are you doing untying the colt?"

6They told them just what Yeshua had said to them.

And they let them alone.

7Then they brought the colt to Yeshua and piled their clothing on the colt, and he sat on it. 8Many people spread their clothing on the road, and others strewed leafy branches they had cut in the fields. 9The ones leading and the ones following cried,

> Hosanna!
>
> Blessed is the one who comes in the name
>
> > of the lord.
>
> 10Blessed is the coming kingdom of our father
>
> > David.
>
> Hosanna in the highest.[112]

11Then he entered Yerushalayim, into the Temple, and looking around at everything, since the hour now was late, he went out to Beit Aniyah with the twelve.

---

110 Bethphrage from the Greek Βηθφαγή (Bethfrage), from the Hebrew בֵּית פַּגֵּא (beit pagey). Bethphrage is thought to be a village east of Jerusalem on the Mountain of Olives.

111 Bethany from the Greek Βηθανία (Bethania), from the Hebrew בֵּית אֲנָיָה (beit aniyah). Beit Aniyah is also east of Jerusalem, near Beit Pagey.

112 Ps. 118.25–26.

Cursing the fig tree

12On the next day as they left from Beit Aniyah, he was hungry. 13And seeing a fig tree in leaf in the distance, he came to see if he might find something on it. When he came to it he found nothing but leaves. It was not the season for figs. 14He spoke out, saying to it,

Let no one ever eat your fruit again.

His students heard him.

Driving the traders and dove sellers from the Temple

15Then they came to Yerushalayim. And Yeshua entered the Temple and began to drive out those who sold and bought in the Temple. He overturned the tables of the money changers and the chairs of those selling doves. 16He did not allow anyone to carry goods through the Temple.[113] 17He taught and said to them,

Is it not written in Yeshayah and Yirmiyah:[114]

"My house will be called a house of prayer
for the nations?"[115]

But you have made it into "a cave of robbers"?[116]

18The high priests and scholars heard and looked for a way to destroy him. They feared him, for the crowd was amazed by his teaching.

19When it was late they went out of the city.

The fig tree dried up

20In the morning as they passed by, they saw the fig tree dried up from the roots.

21Then Kefa remembered and said to him, "Rabbi, look! The fig tree you cursed has dried up."[117]

---

[113] Market merchants would have been outside the restricted Temple, in the adjacent courtyards where the sacrificial animals were taken to be sold in specific areas reserved for commerce and where non-Jews were permitted to buy and sell. Since commerce was restricted to courtyards, it casts doubt on the location of Yeshua's house cleaning as within the Temple itself.

[114] Jeremiah from the Greek Ἰερεμίας (Ieremias), from the Hebrew יִרְמְיָה (yirmiyah).

[115] Isa. 56.7.

[116] Jer. 7.11.

[117] Destructive miracles are uncommon in the New Covenant, though not infrequent in noncanonical scripture. Here the conventional theological explanation is that Yeshua's curse on the fig tree is a metaphor for the future punishment of the faithless Jews for failing to be fruitful in recognizing Yeshua as the mashiah and is a prophecy of "the destruction of the temple that similarly failed to bear proper religious fruit" (*HarperCollins Bible Dictionary*, 1993, 338).

Moving mountains

22Yeshua answered, saying to them,

> Have faith in God. 23Amen I say to you,
> if you tell this mountain, "Rise and leap into the sea,"
> and have no doubt in your heart
> but believe what is said will happen,
> it will be yours.
> 24So I say to you,
> all you pray for and ask, believe you have received it
> and it will be yours.
> 25When you stand praying, if you hold something
> against someone, forgive
> so your father will also forgive your wrong steps.[118]

Back in Yerushalayim, outwitting priests and scholars

27They came again to Yerushalayim. As he was walking about in the Temple, the high priests and scholars and elders came to him 28and said, "By what authority do you do these things?" or "Who gave you this authority to do these things?"

29Yeshua said to them,

> I will ask you one word, and answer me
> and I will tell you by what authority
> I do these things.
> 30Did Yohanan's immersion come from heaven
> or from people? Tell me.

31They discussed this among themselves, saying, "If we say 'From heaven,' he will say, 'Why don't you believe him?' 32But if we say, 'From human beings.'" . . . They were afraid of the crowd, for everyone held Yohanan to be truly a prophet.

33They answered Yeshua, saying, "We do not know."

And Yeshua said to them,

> Then neither will I tell you by what authority
> I do these things.

---

[118] From the Greek παράπτωμα (paraptoma), meaning "wrong or false step," "transgression," or "sin." The usually translated "trespasses" or "transgressions" are Latin words that also have the original image in them of stepping elsewhere, but that through usage have lost their primary image and metaphor and convey a conceptual meaning of "fault" or "sin." Unless the primary image remains, the metaphor is lost, and the two cognitive levels of image and concept do not intensify each. "Wrong steps" restores the strong image in the Greek of *ptomata,* "steps," and *para,* "gone astray."

CHAPTER 12

The unbridled tenants

And he began to speak to them in parables,

> A man planted a vineyard and put a fence
> around it, dug a wine vat, and built a tower.[119]
> He rented it to farmers and left the country.
> 2At the harvest he sent a slave to the farmers
> to take back some fruits from the vineyard.
> 3But they seized him, lashed him, and sent him away
> empty. 4Again he sent another slave to them
> and him they struck on the head and insulted.
> 5He sent another and that one they killed,
> and many more, lashing some, killing others.
> 6He still had one beloved son. He sent him
> finally to them, saying, "They will respect
> my son." 7But those farmers said to one another,
> "This is the heir. Come, let us kill him
> and the inheritance is ours." 8They seized him
> and killed him and threw him outside the vineyard.
> 9What will the owner of the vineyard do?
> He will come and destroy the farmers and give
> the vineyard to others. 10Have you not read
> in the Psalms: "A stone that the builders rejected
> became the cornerstone. 11From the lord
> it came to be and is wonderful in our eyes."[120]

12The priests and scholars were seeking a way of arresting him, but feared the crowd that knew he told the parable against them. So they let him go away.

Paying coins to Caesar

13Then they sent some Prushim and Herodians to him to trap him in a word. 14They came and said to him, "Rabbi, we know that you are truthful, and favor no one. You do not look at a person's face but rather you teach the way of

---

[119] Tower from the Greek πύργος (purgos). *Purgos* is the common word for "tower" and often is translated as "watchtower," as in Jehovah Witnesses' Watchtower.

[120] Ps. 118.22–23.

God in accordance with truth. Is it right to pay the tax to Caesar or not? Should we give or not give?"[121]

15But he saw their hypocrisy and said to them,

Why are you testing me?

Bring me a denarius to look at it.

16They brought one.

And he said to them,

Whose image is this and whose name?

They said to him, "Caesar's."

17Yeshua said to them,

The things of Caesar give to Caesar

and the things of God give to God.

And they were amazed at him.

Who is one's wife in heaven?

18Then Tzadokim[122] came to him, who say there is no resurrection, and they questioned him, saying, 19"Rabbi, Mosheh wrote for us that if 'a man's brother dies and leaves a wife and no child, the brother should take the wife and raise the seed for his brother.' 20There were seven brothers and the first took a wife and when he died he left no seed. 21The second took her and he died without leaving seed. And the third likewise. 22The seven did not leave seed. Last of all the woman died. 23In the resurrection, whose wife will she be? Seven had her as a wife."

24Yeshua told them,

Are you not wrong in not knowing the scriptures

or the power of God?

---

[121] Historically, this period (preceding all-out rebellion against Roman rule, culminating in 70 C.E. with the destruction of the Temple) was a touchy time of contention between Jew and Roman over religious matters—such as Caligula's attempt in 44–45 C.E. to set up a statue of himself in the Temple. In the gospels, however, the Romans are not perceived as occupiers of a suppressed Israel. Since the scriptural position sees Roman authority as good and Jewish authority as bad (as represented by the Pharisees, who historically strongly opposed both Hellenization and Roman occupation), it is imperative to prove that tribute to Rome in the form of payment to Caesar does not interfere with tribute to God. So this passage of the coin showing Caesar's head establishes three principles: Yeshua's recognition of the authority of the emperor for things of the emperor, the hypocrisy of Jewish authorities who cast doubt on the authority of the emperor, and that payment to the emperor does not imperil the things that are God's. Reflecting loyalties in the gospels, while deeming it proper to pay coins to Rome, Yeshua disdains the yearly upkeep tax for local Temple tax in Capernaum (Kfar Nahum). To avoid scandal, he orders Peter to pay it with a coin he will find in the mouth of a fish he will hook in the sea (Matt. 17.24–27).

[122] Sadducee from the Greek Σαδώκ, from the Hebrew צדוק (tzadok). Sadducees (pl.) is Tzadokim. Tzadok (Tsadok) means "high priest" and "the just."

25When they rise from the dead they do not marry

nor are they given away in marriage.

They are like angels in the skies.

26As for raising the dead, in the Book of Mosheh

have you not read how at the thornbush

God spoke to Mosheh saying,

"I am the God of Avraham and the God of Yitzhak

and the God of Yaakov"?[123]

27He is not the God of the dead but of the living.

You are deeply wrong.

Hear O Yisrael[124]

28One of the scholars came near, heard them debating, and seeing that he had answered them well, asked him, "What is the first commandment of all?" 29Yeshua answered,

The first is:

"Hear O Yisrael, the lord our God, the lord is one.

30And you shall love the lord your God with all your heart

and all your soul and all your mind and all your strength."[125]

31The second is:

"You shall love your neighbor like yourself."

There is no commandment greater than these.

32The scholar said to him, "Well said, rabbi, you are right in saying that he is one and there is no other but he. 33To love him with all your heart and with all your understanding and with all your strength, and to love your neighbor like yourself is greater than all burnt offerings and sacrifices."

34Yeshua seeing that he answered wisely said to him,

You are not far from the kingdom of God.

Nobody dared question him further.

Watch out for scholars

35While he was teaching in the Temple, he said,

How can the scholars say the mashiah is David's son?

36Through the holy spirit David himself declared,

"The lord said to my lord,

---

[123] Exod. 3.6, 15.

[124] Israel from the Greek Ἰσαήλ, from the Hebrew יִשְׂרָאֵל (yisrael).

[125] Deut. 6.4–5.

'Sit at my right
until I put your enemies under your feet.'"[126]
37David calls him lord so how can he be his son?
The great crowd heard him with delight.
38And in his teaching he said,

Beware of the scholars, the ones in long robes
who love to stroll about, be greeted in the marketplaces,
39and claim the best seats in the synagogues
and the foremost couches at dinners,
40who eat up the widows' houses
and solely for show say long prayers.
They will receive the greater condemnation.[127]

The widow's copper coins

41Then he sat down opposite the treasury and observed how the crowd threw copper coins into the treasury. Many rich tossed in many coins. 42A poor widow came and threw in two lepta, worth a penny. 43He called his students and said to them,

Amen, amen, I say to you,
That poor widow threw in more than all who cast money
into the treasury.
44All have thrown in from their abundance.
She has thrown in from her poverty,
She gave all that she had for living on.

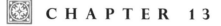 **CHAPTER 13**

The great buildings will be thrown down

As he was leaving the Temple, one of his students said to him, "Rabbi, look, what enormous stones, what enormous buildings!"
2Yeshua said to him,

Do you see these great buildings?

---

[126] Ps. 110.1.

[127] The scholars of Torah were dependent on patrons for their salary. Here they are condemned for their vanity and exploitation of vulnerable widows.

No stone on stone will be left that will not
> be thrown down.[128]

3When he was sitting on the Mountain of Olives opposite the Temple, Kefa and Yaakov and Yohanan and Andreas[129] asked him privately, 4"Tell us when these things will be and what will be the sign when they will be fulfilled."

5Yeshua began to say to them,

Beware that no one leads you astray.

6Many will come in my name saying, "I am,"[130]

and they will lead many astray.

7But when you hear of wars and rumors of wars

do not be frightened. These things must occur.

But the end is not yet.

8Nation will rise against nation, kingdom against kingdom,

there will be earthquakes in the lands

and there will be famines.

These things are the beginnings of the last agonies.[131]

Lashed in the synagogues

9Look out for yourselves. They will hand you over

to the Sanhedrin[132] and lash you in the synagogues

---

128 This famous prophecy of the destruction of the Temple in 70 C.E. suggests a dating of Mark after the year 70 or, if as early as 66 as some venture, a later scribal interpolation. Mark's prophecy is in the tradition of the oracle writing of the Sibyls. The Sibyls were women who proclaimed future events in a state of ecstasy. Usually, their prophecies were placed in a period earlier than that of their authors', so that the catastrophes foretold had already occurred, thereby guaranteeing the Sibyl's accuracy. For a discussion of the Greek, Jewish, Christian-Jewish, and Christian sibyllines, see Barnstone "The Sibylline Oracles," 501–505, and "Christian Sibyllines," 554–566, in *The Other Bible* (San Francisco: HarperSan Francisco, 1984).

129 Peter and James and John and Andrew.

130 From the Greek ἐγώ εἰμι (ego eimi), "I am." *Ego eimi* suggests "I am he," meaning "the messiah," or colloquially "it's me," as the response to "Who is it?" or "Who's here?" However, the strong literal meaning in Greek of *Ego eimi*, "I am," also conveys an oracular tone of stating his existence, as in the Hebrew Bible "I am that I am," which any of these common English translations loses.

131 The gospels were written following the destruction of the Temple and the consequent diaspora of both Jews and contending Christian Jews, and the memory and implications of that catastrophe permeate the scriptures. In the Sermon on the Mount, the prediction of rebellion of nation against nation, kingdom against kingdom, and, specifically, Israel against Rome, tells the price paid for revolution: the dispersal of both Jews and Christian Jews from Israel; the destruction of Israel as a religious power base for Jews as well as Peter's and James's messianic Jews in Jerusalem; and, as a result of the diaspora, an increasing distinction in identity between Jews and Christian Jews, leading in foreign lands to the creation of two interdependent but separate religions, in larger domains outside of Israel, greatly increasing the proselytizing of others to both Judaism and emerging Christianity. The destruction of Israel "is not the end," not the apocalypse, for, as the following lines show, after much suffering, humiliation, and death, "the good news [of the messiah] will be proclaimed to all nations."

132 Councils.

and you will stand before governors and kings
because of me and testify to them. And first
10the good news must be preached to all peoples.
11When they turn you over and bring you to trial,
don't worry beforehand about what you will say.
Whatever is given to you in that hour, say it,
for it is not you who speaks but the holy spirit.
12Then brother will hand over brother to death
and father his child, and children will rise up
against parents and put them to death.
13And you will be hated by everyone
because of my name. But whoever survives
to the end, that person will be saved.

Desolation

14When you see the "abomination of desolation"[133]
standing where it should not—let the reader
understand—then let those in Yehuda flee
to the mountains, 15and someone on the rooftop
not come down or go into the house
to take things away, 16and a man in the fields
not go back to pick up clothing left behind.
17Grief to women with a child in the womb
and to women nursing babies in those days!
18Pray that it may not happen in the winter.
19In those days there will be an affliction
which has not happened since the beginning
of creation, which God created, until now,
and will in no way again take place.
20And if the Lord had not shortened the days,
no flesh would be saved. But for the one
whom he chose, he did shorten the days.

The earthly son comes in the clouds

21And then, if someone says to you, "Look,
here is the mashiah, look, he is there,

---

[133] The phrase is from Daniel 9.27, and alludes to the Hellenistic ruler's attempt in the second century B.C.E. to convert the Temple into a shrine for Zeus. In Daniel we have, "And on a wing of the temple he will set up an abomination that causes desolation." This example from the past is also interpreted as a prelude to the apocalyptic destruction by Titus of the Temple and of Israel three and a half decades after Yeshua's death.

do not believe. 22False mashiahs and false prophets
will rise up and perform signs and wonders
to mislead the chosen, if they can.
23But beware! I have forewarned all to you.
24But in those days after that affliction,
> the sun will be darkened
>> and the moon not give its light
> 25and the stars will fall out of the sky[134]
>> and the powers in the skies will quake.
26Then you will see the earthly son coming
on clouds with great power and glory.
27Then he will send out angels and gather in
the chosen from the four winds from the end
of the earth to the end of the sky.

Stay awake for the coming
28From the fig tree learn the parable.
When its branch is tender again and shoots out leaves,
you know that summer is near.
29So when you see these things happening
you know that the earthly son is near the doors.
30Amen, amen I say to you,
This generation will not pass away before
all these things have come about.
31The sky and the earth will pass away
but my words will not pass away.
32But of that day or the hour no one knows,
neither the angels in heaven nor the son.
Only the father. 33Be watchful, stay awake.
You do not know when the time will come.
34It is like when a person goes on a journey
and puts slaves in charge, to each his task,
and commands the doorkeeper to be watchful.
35Be watchful then, you never know when the lord
of the house comes, in the evening or midnight
or at cockcrow or dawn, 36or coming suddenly
he may find you asleep.
37What I say to you I say to everyone. Beware.

---

[134] Isa.13.10 and 34.4.

CHAPTER 14

Plotting

After two days it would be Pesach,[135] the Supper of the Matzot Bread,[136] and the high priests[137] and the scholars were looking for a way to arrest him by treachery and to kill him. 2"Not at the festival," they were saying, "for there would be an outcry from the people."

Anointed in the house of the leper

3While he was in Beit Aniyah in the house of Shimon the leper, reclining, a woman came with an alabaster jar of myrrh, a pure and costly spikenard ointment. Breaking the alabaster jar she poured it on his head. 4Now some grumbled to each other, "Why was there this waste of myrrh?" 5This ointment could have been sold for more than three hundred denarii and the money given to the poor. And they scolded her.

6But Yeshua said,

Let her be. Why do you bother her?
She has done a good thing for me.
7You always have the poor with you
and whenever you want you can do good for them.
But me you do not always have.
8She did what she could.
She prepared ahead of time to anoint my body
    for the burial.
9I say to you,
wherever in the whole world the good news
    is preached, also what
this woman did will speak her memory.

---

135 On the first two evenings of Passover is the Seder, the supper of the Matzot (unleavened bread). Pesach is Passover from the Greek πάσχα (pasha), from the Hebrew פֶּסַח (pesah), "to pass over," referring to the escape from bondage in Egypt. Pesach is celebrated at the Seder by eating the paschal lamb. See Exodus 12.1–13.16.

136 The Greek word ἄζυμος (azymos) means "unleavened bread," which is a translation from the Hebrew מַצּוֹת (matzot), meaning "unleavened bread." The matzot bread is sometimes called a loaf, which suggests round and oblong. It was more likely flat like East Indian bread or a tortilla. It is not indicated in the Torah or Mishnah that, like modern Matzos, it was dry, heavily salted, and brittle.

137 High priests are the *cohanim*. A high priest is a *cohen* or *kohen*. In Torah (Pentateuch), the priesthood is limited to the Levites, the family of Levi, son of Jacob. Matthew, to whom the Gospel of Matthew is traditionally attributed, is said to be a second-generation Christian Jew whose name, in Matthew, is Levi.

Yehuda and the promise of silver

10Yehuda, man of Keriot,[138] one of the twelve, went to the high priests to betray him to them.[139]

11Hearing of this they were happy and promised to give him silver.

He was looking for an easy way of betraying him.

Planning the Seder in an upper room

12On the first day of the Feast of the Matzot, when the Pesach lamb was sacrificed, his students said to him, "Where do you want us to go to arrange for you to eat the Pesach lamb?"

13And he sent two of his students and said to them,

Go into the city and you will meet

a man carrying a clay pot of water.

Follow him 14and wherever he enters tell

the owner of the house, "The rabbi[140] asks,

'Where is my guest room where I may eat

the Pesach supper with my students?'"

15And he will show you a large upper room

furnished and ready. There prepare for us.

16And the students left and came into the city and found things just as they were told and they prepared the Pesach meal.

One of you will betray me

17 When it was evening, he came with the twelve. 18As they were reclining at the table and eating, Yeshua said to them,

Amen, amen, I say to you,

One of you will betray me,

one who is eating with me.

19They became forlorn and said to him, one by one, "Surely not me?"

20He said to them,

One of the twelve who is dipping matzot in the bowl.[141]

21The earthly son will go just as Yeshayah wrote of him.[142]

---

138 Judas Iscariot.

139 See Afterword for Midrashic origin of the betrayal tale and the choice of the name Yehuda, signifying "Jew," in the betrayal of Yeshua.

140 In his instructions, where he wishes to assert his authority for a Jewish ceremonial feast, it is unlikely that Yeshua would not have used the normal epithet "rabbi" rather than *didaskalos* (διδάσκαλος) or *epistates* (ἐπιστάτης) for "teacher."

141 Presumably dipping "bread" in the bowl.

142 The Greek says "just as it is written," meaning, for the informed reader, Isaiah 1–12, in which Isaiah describes the birth, life, and sacrificial death of the coming mashiah. The "earthly son" translates the probable meaning of a human as opposed to a heavenly being, but here, more clearly than elsewhere, Yeshua

But a plague on him who betrayed the earthly son!
It would be good for him had he never been born!

This is my body, this is my blood

22While they were eating he took the matzot, and blessing it he broke it and
gave it to them and said,

Take it. This is my body.

23And he took a cup and after giving thanks,[143] he gave it to them, and they
all drank from it. 24And he said to them,

This is my blood of the covenant[144]

which is poured out for many.

25Amen, amen, I say to you,

I will no longer drink the fruit of the wine

until that day when I drink it new in the kingdom

of God.

Before the cock crows twice

26After singing the psalm they left for the Mountain of Olives.

27Then Yeshua said to them,

You will all stumble and fail me as Zeharyah wrote:[145]

"I will strike down the shepherd

and the sheep will be scattered."

28But after I am raised up I will lead the way

for you into the Galil.

---

explains his self-given epithet as being the mashiah, making "mashiah" a reasonable translation of *ho huios tou anthropou*, (ὁ υἱὸς τοῦ ἀνθρώπου) but such would be explanation, not translation.

[143] The word "Eucharist" is derived from the Greek εὐχαριστία (euharistía), "thanksgiving," which appears in this passage of the Pesach supper (14.23).

[144] From the Greek διαθήκη (diatheke), "the covenant," and in Hellenistic Greek, "testament" or "will." In the King James Version, the word "new" is added and so it reads, "This is my blood of the new testament." "New" (καινη) is not in the Greek text. In Greek and East European orthodoxy, the title for the scriptures is "New Covenant." New Testament came into Latin and modern West European languages through Jerome's mistranslation of *diatheke* as *testamentum*, "testament" rather than "covenant." "Covenant" derives from the Hebrew בְּרִית (berit). "New Covenant" in the Greek is Καινὴ Διαθήκη (Kaine Diatheke), and in Torah בְּרִית חֲדָשָׁה (berit hadashah), found in Jeremiah 31.30.

The "blood of the covenant" derives from the covenant between God and Moses at Sinai: "Moses then took the blood, sprinkled it on the people and said, 'This is the blood of the covenant that the Lord has made with you in accordance with all these words'" (Exod. 24.6–8). Moses has set up "twelve stone pillars representing the twelve tribes of Israel." The sacred symbolism of the twelve, representing all the tribes of Israel, is repeated in having Yeshua choose to be followed by twelve students. The major covenants in the Hebrew Bible between God and Israel and the patriarchs are through Noah (Gen. 9.9), Abraham (15.18), Moses (Exod. 19.5, 24.7), and David (2 Sam. 7.14). In the New Covenant there are covenants in Matt. 26.28; Mark 14.24; 1 Cor. 11.25; and Heb. 7.22, 8.8–13, 9.15, and 12.24.

[145] Zechariah or Zacharias from the Greek Ζαχαρίας (Zaharias), from the Hebrew זְכַרְיָה (zeharyah).

29But Kefa said to him, "Even if everyone stumbles and fails, I will not."

30And Yeshua said to him, "Amen, I say to you,"

> Today on this same night before the cock crows twice
>
> you will deny me three times.

31But he said forcefully, "If I must die for you, I will not deny you."
And all of them said the same.

Terror and prayer at Gat Shmanim

32And they came to a place whose name was Gat Shmanim[146] and he said to his students,

> Sit here while I pray.

33And he took Kefa and Yaakov and Yohanan with him and he began to feel terror and anguish 34and he said to them,

> My soul is in sorrow to the point of death.
>
> Stay here and keep awake.

35And going a little farther he threw himself on the ground and prayed that, if it were possible, the hour might pass from him. 36And he said,

> Abba,[147] my father, for you all things are possible.
>
> Take this cup from me. Yet not what I will
>
> but what you will.

37And he came and found them sleeping, and said to Kefa,

> Shimon,[148] are you sleeping? Did you not have
>
> the strength to keep awake for an hour?
>
> 38Stay awake and pray that you are not tested.
>
> Oh, the spirit is ready but the flesh is weak.

39He went away again and prayed, saying the same words.

40And he came again and found them sleeping. Their eyes were very heavy, and they did not know what to say to him.

41And he came a third time and said to them,

> Sleep what is left of the night and rest.
>
> Enough! The hour has come.
>
> Look, the earthly son is betrayed
>
> into the hands of those who do wrong.
>
> 42Get up and let us go.
>
> Look, my betrayer is drawing near.

---

146 Gethsemane from the Greek Γεθσημανὶ (Gethsemani), from the Hebrew גַּת שְׁמָנִים (gat shmanim), meaning "olive press." It was the name of an olive orchard on the Mountain of Olives.

147 Abba from the Greek Αββα ὁ πατήρ (abba o pater). Abba from Aramaic אַבָּא (abba, father).

148 "Shimon Kefa" is Simon Peter.

The rabbi is kissed and arrested

43Immediately, while he was still speaking, Yehuda,[149] one of the twelve, arrived, and with him a crowd with swords and clubs from the high priests and the scholars and the elders. 44His betrayer gave them the signal, saying, "The one I kiss is the one. Hold him and take him away under guard."

45When he came, at once he went up to Yeshua and said, "Rabbi," and kissed him.

46They got their hands on him and held him.

47But someone standing near him drew his sword and struck the slave of the high priest and cut off his ear.

48Then Yeshua spoke out to them,

> As against a thief have you come with swords
>
> and clubs to arrest me?
>
> 49I was with you every day in the Temple, teaching,
>
> and you did not seize me,
>
> but only now
>
> so that the scriptures may be fulfilled.

50And all left him and fled.

51And one young man followed him, dressed in linen cloth around his naked body, and they seized him. 52But he left the linen cloth behind and fled.

False testimony in the Sanhedrin

53They led Yeshua to the high priest. All the high priests and the elders and the scholars were assembled.[150]

54Kefa followed him from a distance until he was inside the high priest's courtyard and he sat together with the servants, warming himself near the light of the fire.

55The high priest and the whole Sanhedrin were looking for evidence against him to put him to death, but they didn't find any. 56Many gave false testimony against him, and their testimonies did not agree. 57Some stood up and gave false testimony against him, saying, 58"We heard him say, 'I will tear down this Temple that was made with hands and after three days I will build another not made with hands.'" 59But on this point too their testimony did not agree.

---

[149] Judas the Iscariot. Judas from the Greek Ἰούδας (Ioudas), from the Hebrew יְהוּדָה (yehuda). The name for the messenger (apostle) Judas in Hebrew, *Yehuda*, was surely invented because it suggests the Hebrew word for "Jew," which is יְהוּדִי (yehudi); thereby the betrayer of Yeshua among his followers was a Jew, as opposed to the others who escape that identity.

[150] The night session at the Sanhedrin is problematic, raising many questions. Trials during Passover as well as night trials were forbidden by Jewish law. By Roman law, Jews could not pass death sentences. There is no document or testimony outside the gospels or testimony in the gospels as to how such conversations were recorded and obtained about false testimony.

₆₀Then the high priest stood up in their midst and questioned Yeshua, saying, "Won't you answer anything that they have testified against you?"

₆₁But he was silent and gave no answer to anything.

Again the high priest questioned him and said to him, "Are you the mashiah, the son of the blessed one?"

₆₂Yeshua said,

> I am.
>> "And you will see the earthly son
>>> seated on the right of the power"
>> and "coming with the clouds of heaven."[151]

₆₃The high priest tore his own tunic, saying, "What further need do we have of witnesses? ₆₄You heard this blasphemy. How does it seem to you?"

They all judged him as deserving death.

₆₅And some began to spit on him and to cover his face and beat him. They said to him, "Prophesy!" And the servants took hold of him and pummeled him.

Kefa and the crowing cock

₆₆While Kefa was below in the courtyard, one of the serving maids of the high priest came ₆₇and when she saw Kefa warming himself she stared at him and said, "You were also with the Natzrati,[152] with Yeshua."

₆₈But he denied it, saying, "I don't know or understand what you are saying." Then he went outside into the forecourt. [And the cock crowed.][153]

₆₉And the maid seeing him began again to say to those standing by, "This is one of them."

₇₀Again he denied it.

After a short while those standing by said to Kefa, "Surely you must be one of them, since you are a Galilean."

₇₁He began to curse and to swear, "I don't know this man you're talking about."

At once the cock crowed a second time.

₇₂And Kefa remembered the words Yeshua said to him,

> Before the cock crows twice
>> you will deny me three times.

And he broke down and wept.

---

[151] Lines 1 and 3 of Hebrew scripture cited are from Daniel 7.13, and line 2 from Psalms 110.1.

[152] Nazarene.

[153] "And the cock crowed" is omitted in other texts and bracketed in the Nestle-Aland, which is used here.

CHAPTER 15

Pilatus[154] *asks, Are you the king of the Jews?*

As soon as it was morning, the high priests with the elders and scholars held a meeting. And they bound Yeshua, led him away and handed him over to Pilatus.

₂Pilatus asked him, "Are you the King of the Jews?"

Answering him, he said,

   You say it.

₃The high priests brought many charges against him.

₄Pilatus again questioned him, saying, "Have you no answer? Look how much you are accused of."

₅But Yeshua still said nothing.

Pilatus was amazed.

Crucify him!

₆Now at that festival he used to release one prisoner to the people, whichever one they asked for. ₇There was a man called Bar Abba[155] who was bound along with other revolutionaries, who in the uprising had committed murder.

₈So the crowd came and began to ask Pilatus for what he did for them.

₉But Pilatus answered them, saying, "Do you want me to release the King of the Jews?" ₁₀He knew that the high priests had handed him over to him out of envy.

₁₁But the high priests incited the crowd to release Bar Abba instead to them.

₁₂Pilatus again answered, saying to them, "What do you want me to do with the King of the Jews?"

₁₃"Crucify him!"[156]

---

[154] Pilate from the Latin, *Pilatus.*

[155] Barabbas from the Greek Βαραββᾶς, from the Aramaic בַּר אַבָּא (bar abba), meaning "son of Abba" (father). Nothing is known of Barabbas, but from his revolutionary activities it is assumed that he was a Zealot, a member of a Jewish sect that was rebelling against Roman occupation. Insurrectionists were treated by the Romans as seditionists and hence crucified. It is only from the gospels that we have the notion that the Romans had the custom of releasing one prisoner during the Passover. In Matthew, his name is given as Yeshua Barrabas. Barrabas means "son of the father," or "son of God." See Matthew 27.17.

[156] This pivotal but unlikely scene that has the crowd shout "Crucify him," which is to say "crucify a dissident rabbi," suggests not the voice of a Jewish mob in the street but the voice of Rome enunciated in highly redacted texts attributed to the evangelist. The voice of Rome comes through more emphatically in Matthew's elaboration of the same scene, in which Pilate declares both his own innocence and Yeshua's innocence, and blames the crowd: "When Pilatus saw that he could do nothing and that an uproar was starting, he took water and washed his hands before the crowd, saying, 'I am

₁₄Pilatus said to them, "What wrong did he do?"

But they cried out louder, "Crucify him!"

₁₅So Pilatus, wanting to satisfy the crowd, released Bar Abba to them, and had Yeshua flogged and handed him over to be crucified.

Soldiers clothe him in purple and a crown of thorns and club him

₁₆The soldiers led him away into the courtyard, which is the praetorium,[157] and assembled the whole cohort. ₁₇And they clothed him in purple and twisted some thorns into a wreath, and placed it on his head. ₁₈Then they began to salute him, "Hail, King of the Jews." ₁₉They beat him on the head with a reed club and spat on him, and going down on their knees they worshiped him. ₂₀And after mocking him, they stripped off the purple and put his own clothes on him. Then they led him out to be crucified.

Gulgulta, the Place of the Skull

₂₁And a certain Shimon of Cyrene,[158] the father of Alexandros and Rufus, was passing by from the countryside, and they forced him to carry his cross. ₂₂They brought him to the place Gulgulta,[159] which translated is the Place of the Skull. ₂₃And they gave him wine mixed with myrrh,[160] but he didn't take it.

₂₄And they crucified him.

The soldiers divided his clothes, casting lots to see who would take them.[161]

Crucifying him

₂₅It was the third hour, nine in the morning, when they crucified him. ₂₆The inscription of the charge against him was written above:

THE KING OF THE JEWS.

---

innocent of the blood of this man. You see to it'" (Matt. 27.24). In Mark, to clear himself and, by extension, Rome, of responsibility for the crucifixion, Pilate asks the crowd, "What wrong did he do?" By revealing to the crowd—and to the reader—his conviction that Yeshua did no wrong, he places himself squarely on Yeshua's side at the very moment that he orders the rabbi to be flogged and crucified. Mark paints Pilate as the helpless tool of a murderous mob whom he feels obliged to please. The Eastern Orthodox Church will later elevate the same Roman governor to sainthood. The historical view of Pilate depicts the procurator of Judea, Idumea, and Samaria, 26–36 C.E., as an unusually brutal ruler of peoples under Roman occupation. He was recalled to Rome for the massacre of the Samaritans in 36 C.E. It should also be noted that crucifixion was a Roman means of execution, one neither practiced by Jews nor conceivably ordered by Jews against a Jew. Unless Yeshua were a common thief, such punishment would have been for an opponent of Roman occupation, and it may be assumed that Yeshua was an opponent of Roman rule, which earned him his death.

[157] The governor's residence.

[158] Cyrene. Modern Lybia.

[159] Golgotha from the Greek Γολγοθᾶ (Golgotha), from the Aramaic גָּלְגָּלְתָּא (gulgulta).

[160] In the Talmud, incense is mixed with wine to deaden pain.

[161] Ps. 22.18. These passages contain many citations from Psalms.

27With him they crucified two thieves, one on the right and one on the left of him.

29And those passing by blasphemed him, shaking their heads, and saying, "Ha! You who would destroy the Temple and rebuild it in three days, 30save yourself by coming down from the cross." 31Likewise the high priests mocked him among themselves and with the scholars said, "He saved others but he can't save himself. 32The King of Yisrael, let him now come down from the cross so we can see and believe." And those who were crucified with him taunted him.

Darkness at noon

33At when it was the sixth hour, at noon, the whole earth became dark until three in the afternoon. 34At three o'clock, Yeshua called out words from the Psalms in a loud voice,

Eloi Eloi, lama sabachtani?

which translated is,

My God, my God, why do you abandon me?[162]

35Some of those standing near heard him and said, "See, he calls to Eliyah."[163] 36And someone ran up with a sponge soaked in vinegar,[164] placed it on a reed stick, and gave it to him to drink, saying, "Let him alone. Let us see if Yeshayah comes to take him down."

37But Yeshua let out a great cry and breathed his last breath.

38And the curtain of the Temple tore in two from top to bottom.

39The centurion who was near saw him breathe his last and said, "Truly this man was the son of God."[165]

His women look on

40There were also women looking on from a distance, among whom were both Miryam of Magdala[166] and Miryam mother of Yaakov the younger and of

---

[162] Ps. 22.1. Yeshua's words are in Aramaic.

[163] The bystanders mistakenly heard "Eliyah" for "Eloi," "my God."

[164] From the Greek *oxous,* meaning "vinegar" or "sour wine."

[165] A centurion was a commander of 100 Roman soldiers. In the story of the crucifixion, after Yeshua has been mocked by Jewish bystanders, the high priests and those crucified with him, and the curtain in the Temple has sympathetically torn in two, foretelling the Temple's imminent doom, the first to recognize that Yeshua was the son of God is the commander of the execution squad. This exoneration of Roman leadership, who now are not only guiltless in Yeshua's execution but the first in Jerusalem to state his divinity, follows the pattern of preparing the move of the authority of Yeshua's messiahship to Rome. See footnote 34, p. 52.

In Hebrews 9.8–10, 12; and 10.19–20, Paul tells us that the tearing of the curtain means that Yeshua has entered heaven for us so that we too now may enter God's presence.

[166] Mary Magdalene from the city of Magdala.

Joses,[167] and Shlomit,[168] 41who were in the Galil following him and serving him, and there were many other women who had gone up with him to Yerushalayim.

The body in linen entombed in rock

42Evening had already come, and since it was Friday (day of Preparations), the Day-Before-Shabbat,[169] 43Yosef of Arimathaia,[170] a prominent member of the council, who was also looking for the kingdom of God, boldly went to Pilatus and asked for the body of Yeshua.

44Pilatus wondered if he was already dead and called the centurion, and asked him if he was already dead. 45Informed by the centurion, he gave the corpse to Yosef.

46Then Yosef bought a linen cloth, took him down, and wrapped him in the linen cloth and placed him in a tomb which had been cut out of the rock, and he rolled a stone against the entrance to the tomb.

47Miryam of Magdala and Miryam of Joses saw where he was laid.

CHAPTER 16

The women in the empty tomb

When Shabbat was over, Miryam of Magdala and Miryam of Yaakov and Shlomit bought aromatic spices so they might go and anoint him. 2And very early on the first day of the week, they came to the tomb as the sun was rising.

---

[167] It is not known who Miryam mother of Yaakov the younger and of Joses is. She may be Yeshua's mother, though there is not a consensus in favor of this view. Since she is called the mother of Yaakov rather than of Yeshua, it is is unlikely that Mark intended to identify her as Miryam mother of Yeshua. Elsewhere Yeshua's brothers are identified as James, Joses (Joseph), Judas, and Simon, that is, Yaakov, Yosef, Yehuda, and Shimon. In Mark, Yeshua's mother is not portrayed sympathetically, but by Luke, the last synoptic gospel, Miryam is glorified. The virgin birth is stated in the birth stories of Matthew and Luke, and the nativity in Luke fixes her later image. Please see note 52, p. 56.

[168] Salome from the Greek Σαλώμη (Salome), from the Hebrew שְׁלֹמִית (shlomit or shelomit). Salome may be the wife of Zebedee and so the mother of James and John.

[169] The Greek word for "preparation," παρασκευη (paraskevi), has come to mean "Friday" in the Greek. Here, it means both Friday and preparation for the Pesach. Another word for Friday is Prosabbaton (προάββατον), meaning "the day before Shabbat (the Sabbath)."

[170] Yosef of Arimathea was presumably a member of the Sanhedrin, the council that, according to the gospels, asked for Yeshua's death. This apparent contradiction of role may be softened by the description of his piety and vision of the kingdom of God. Arimathea is from the Greek Ἀριμαθαία (Arimathaia,) and is identified with either Ramathaim or Rentis, fifteen or twenty miles east of Jaffa.

₃They said to each other, "Who will roll away the stone for us from the entrance to the tomb?" ₄They looked up and saw that the stone had been rolled away. And it was huge. ₅Then on going into the tomb they saw a young man sitting on the right, dressed in a white robe, and they were utterly astonished.[171]

₆He said to them, "Don't be alarmed. You are looking for Yeshua of Natzeret, the one who was crucified. He was raised. He is not here. See the place where they laid him. ₇But go tell his students and Kefa, 'He is going ahead of you to the Galil. There you will see him, just as he told you.'"

₈So they went out and fled from the tomb, seized by trembling and ecstasy. And they said nothing to anyone. They were afraid.[172]

---

[171] Matthew identifies the young man as an angel (28.2).

[172] The earliest manuscripts end with the dramatic fear of the women in *ekstasis*, here rendered "ecstasy," which conveys the literal meaning of "being outside themselves" as well as "ecstasy" with its multiple meanings of "amazement" in "being elsewhere" and "beside themselves" with fear.

There are two "orphan" supplements, now generally held to be added later, which are said to smooth out the "abrupt" ending. They are now considered to be later additions to make Mark conform to the appearances of the resurrected messiah as revealed in the other gospels.

TWO SUPPLEMENTS TO MARK

THE ENDING OF MARK HAS BEEN CALLED ABRUPT, ALTHOUGH NOT IN THIS TRANSLATOR'S OPINION OR IN THAT OF MANY SCHOLARS. The ending is mysterious and dramatic, reflecting the uncertain movement during a period of turmoil. The notion of "abruptness" or "incompletion" has probably been suggested to consider or justify the inclusion of two orphan supplements, the shorter and the longer, that do not appear in the Codex Vaticanus or the Codex Sinaiticus, the two earliest manuscripts of the New Covenant. The dating and authorship are unknown. While dating and authorship for all books of the New Covenant and the Hebrew Bible are in question (with the exception of seven of Paul's letters), these orphans, as they are called, cannot be considered part of original Mark. Therefore, without manuscript evidence for inclusion, these supplements are not found in Lattimore and recent translations. When included in others, they are bracketed to indicate that they are pseudepigraphical.

The shorter supplement is a few lines, the longer about a page, continuing chapter 17 from 9–19. The purpose of the "Shorter Ending" is to mend fences with Peter and Peter's faction in Jerusalem. Peter fares poorly in the last chapters, having been rebuked by Yeshua for his irresolution. There is the briefest suggestion of resurrection in that Yeshua is sending through the Peter circle the message of eternal salvation. It is a dull, bureaucratic anticlimax. The "Longer Ending" is more substantive and may be a second-century addition to make Mark conform to the appearances of the resurrected messiah as revealed in the other gospels. Belief in Yeshua's resurrection was crucial to second-century emerging Christianity. The earliest gospel is Mark (it is not known when the theory of order was "first" generally accepted), and to let Mark, either the foundation of the Synoptics or at the very least a core member, not end with a resurrection scene is a serious inconsistency that could cast doubt on the historical reliability of the other gospel documents. Hence, the compiler or compilers assumed their tasks and composed these suitable didactic summaries, these new orphan endings that abruptly change the tensely fearful tone and dramatic climax to Mark.

THE SHORTER ENDING OF MARK

All that had been commanded they reported briefly to those around Kefa. After that, Yeshua himself, from east to west, sent through them the holy and deathless proclamation of eternal salvation. Amen.[173]

THE LONGER ENDING OF MARK

9Now after he rose early on the first day of the week, he appeared first to Miryam,[174] from whom he had cast out seven demons. 10She left and informed those who had been with him, who were mourning and crying. 11But those who had heard that he was alive and was seen by her did not believe her.

12After this he appeared in another form to two of them as they were walking into the countryside. 13And they returned and reported it to the rest, but they did not believe them.

14But later, as the eleven were reclining at the table, he appeared and rebuked them for their disbelief and hardheartedness, for they did not believe those who had seen him risen. 15And he said to them,

Go into all the world and proclaim the good news
    to all creation.
16Who believes and is immersed will be saved,
and who is unbelieving will be condemned.

---

[173] Some ancient authorities give, what is clearly a later addition, inserted between 16.14 and 16.15 of the Longer Ending of Mark: "And they excused themselves, saying 'This age of lawlessness and unbelief is under the sway of Satan, who does not allow the truth and power of God to prevail over the unclean things of the spirits. Therefore reveal your justice now.' In such way they spoke to Christ. And Christ replied to them, 'Satan's term of years has been fulfilled, but other terrible things are coming. Because of those who sinned I was delivered to death so that they may return to the truth and no more sin all in order that they may inherit the spiritual and imperishable glory of justice that lies in heaven.'"

[174] Miryam of Magdala.

17And signs will accompany them.

In my name they will cast out demons,

18and speak in new tongues.

They will pick up serpents with their hands,[175]

and if they drink poison, it will not harm them.

19They will lay their hands on the sick

who will be well again.

20After speaking to them, lord Yeshua was taken up into the sky, and he sat down at the right hand of God. And they went out and preached everywhere. The lord was working with them and confirmed the word through accompanying signs.

---

[175] "With their hands" appears bracketed as doubtful in this UBS 4th Corrected Edition of the Greek texts.

MATTAI[1]
(MATTHEW)

---

[1] Matthew's name in English comes from the Greek Μαθθαῖοσ (Maththaios), from the Hebrew מַתִּתְיָהוּ (Mattityahu) or מַתִּתְיָה (Mattityah), meaning "gift of Yahweh." Another candidate for Matthew's name is the Hebrew Mattai or the Aramaic Matai. These shorter forms are more likely to have been heard in first-century Hebrew speech. Here I have chosen Mattai which preserves Matt from Matan (מַתָּן), meaning "gift," and *ai* the root *yh*, from *yah* (יה), which is short for Yahweh or YHWH (יהוה), the ineffable word for "God."

MATTAI (MATTHEW)

T HE AUTHORSHIP AND PLACE AND DATE OF COMPOSITION OF THE
GOSPEL OF MATTHEW ARE MATTERS OF SPECULATION. IN THE GOS-
pel itself, the writer is identified as Levi the tax collector. "Matthew" is apparently the apostolic name of Levi, given to him by churchmen in the second
century. Biblical scholarship describes Matthew as steeped in rabbinical reference and learning and as a Greek-speaking Christian Jew of the second generation. Though there is no scholarly consensus about the dating of the gospels,
Matthew was probably composed at least a decade after 70 C.E., the year of the
destruction of the Temple by Titus, which is alluded to in Matthew and in the
other gospels. The allusion to this specific historical event of 70 C.E. is sufficient
evidence to place the composition of all the gospels at least after that year.

Traditionally, Matthew is placed first in the order of the gospels, but this placement is not chronological, for Matthew derives from Mark and probably from
a lost sayings gospel, the so-called Q source. The gnostic Gospel of Thomas
found at Nag Hammadi, Egypt, in 1945 is a sayings gospel and may have been
one of those sayings books of Yeshua's aphorisms and parables that fed into the
sources from which Matthew derives. Matthew begins with a genealogy (most
certainly appended at a later date) and with the birth of Yeshua. Since Luke
also begins with a genealogy and is followed by the famous nativity scene of
Yeshua's birth in Bethlehem in a feeding trough, the manger, and in terms of the
story of Yeshua's life, there is as much reason for beginning the New Covenant
with Luke as with Matthew, though it appears in terms of dating and influence that Matthew precedes Luke. That Mark is the earliest of the gospels and
a direct source for Matthew and Luke is widely accepted, and in recent years the
traditional presentation of the gospels has been changed, placing Mark at the
beginning of the New Covenant, as in the Richmond Lattimore and the Jesus
Seminar translations.

There are more allusions to the Hebrew Bible in this gospel than in the
others. Matthew wrote to persuade Jews that Yeshua was the foretold messiah
so they might become Christian Jews. Biblical scholarship suggests that passages
of extreme anti-Semitism, such as "Let his blood be upon us and upon our children!" (27.25), in which the Jews in the street shout a curse upon themselves

now and on their progeny forever, are later interpolations, thereby creating a polemic external to Matthew and his days.

Matthew may be said to be the most aphoristic and poetic of the gospels and closest to a sayings book. This teaching book does not have the same austere plainness and drama of Mark, which is more uniformly narrative and ends abruptly at a moment of fear and ecstasy in the cave where Yeshua's body has disappeared. But Matthew also has a deep pathos and conveys a sense of Yeshua as a leader of the poor, of the disenfranchised, in an epic of hunger and hope. Matthew covers many aspects of Yeshua's life and mission, including his discourse dealing with death, resurrection, and immortality (24.1–25.46). Many of the critical moments in the New Covenant are fully elaborated in Matthew, including the coming of the Magi, the birth of Yeshua, the baptizing mission of John the Baptist, John's arrest and execution, and the passion week scene of Yeshua's arrest, crucifixion, and the risen Yeshua. Matthew's most extraordinary literary and philosophical contribution is the Sermon on the Mount (5.1–7.29), including the Beatitudes (5.3–12) and the Lord's Prayer (6.9–13). Much of the material in the Sermon on the Mount also appears dispersed through the other synoptic gospels (Matthew, Mark, and Luke, but not John), and the Lord's Prayer, in a shorter form, also appears in Luke 11.2–4. Apart from Apocalypse (Revelation), which, as I have stated, is the epic poem of the New Covenant, the poetry in Matthew takes its place among the great bodies of world poetry.

CHAPTER 1

Yeshua's genealogy[2]

The book of the generation[3] of Yeshua the Mashiah[4] son of David son of Avraham.[5] 2Avraham fathered Yitzhak,[6] and Yitzhak fathered Yaakov,[7] and Yaakov fathered Yehuda[8] and his brothers, 3and Yehuda fathered Peretz[9] and Zerah whose mother was Tamar,[10] Peretz fathered Hetzron,[11] and Hetzron fathered Ram,[12] 4and Ram fathered Amminadav,[13] Amminadav fathered Nahshon, and Nahshon fathered Salmon, 5and Salmon fathered Boaz, whose mother

---

[2] The genealogy in Matthew importantly establishes Yeshua's Davidic descent. While Luke's genealogy (3.23–31) traces Yeshua's lineage all the way back to Adam, the son of God, Matthew's begins with Avraham, the father of the Jewish people. It goes forward, ending with "and Yaakov engendered Yosef, the husband of Miryam, from whom was born Yeshua who is called the mashiah." Matthew states that Yeshua was born of Miryam. Since the genealogy is patrilineal, it traces Yeshua's origin not through Miryam's ancestors but Yosef's lines, which go back to Avraham. If it is to be understood that Yeshua was born of the virgin Miryam (seeded by the Holy Ghost) and that Yosef was *not* his biological father, then Matthew's patrilineal genealogy fails to establish Yeshua's blood descent from Avraham, David, and the listed ancestors, and pertains to Yeshua only in affirming who was his mother. To explain this genealogical dilemma, scholars have said that Matthew traces the *legal* descent of Yeshua, since Yosef was Yeshua's legal father, if not his blood relative.

The genealogy (Matt. 1.1–7) is prefatory to the gospel and its author uncertain. It may have been added in a later period.

[3] Generation may also be translated as "birth," "beginning," "history," or "genealogy." The two first words of Matthew are βίβλος γενέσεως (biblos geneseos), "the book of the generation." The beginning parallels Genesis 1.1, "In the beginning"; Genesis 2.4, "These are the generations of the heavens and the earth when they were created"; and exactly Genesis 5.1, "This is the book of the descendants" (זֶה סֵפֶר תּוֹלְדֹת, ze sefer toldot). In *An Introduction to the New Testament* (New York: Doubleday, 1997), Raymond E. Brown notes the competitive meaning of Matthew 1.1: "A polyvalent sense of *genesis* is a possibility: The phrase prefaces the ancestral origin, birth, and beginnings of Jesus; but it also encompasses a view of the whole story of Jesus as a new creation, even greater than the old" (174).

[4] Jesus from the Greek Ἰησοῦς (Iesous), from the Hebrew יֵשׁוּעַ (yeshua), from the Hebrew יְהוֹשֻׁעַ (yehoshua), and Christ from the Greek Χριστός (Hristos) translated from the Hebrew מָשִׁיחַ (mashiah). The Greek translation of Yeshua the Mashiah is Jesus the Christ. Mashiah is a free transliteration of Hebrew Mashiah. After the initial presentation of Yeshúa, the accent is dropped. See Mark, note 2.

[5] Abraham.

[6] Isaac.

[7] Jacob.

[8] Judas.

[9] Perez.

[10] Tamar, Thamar.

[11] Hezron or Esrom.

[12] Aram.

[13] Amminadab.

was Rahav,[14] and Boaz fathered Obev,[15] whose mother was Rut,[16] and Obev fathered Jesse, 6and Jesse fathered David the King.

And David fathered Shlomo,[17] whose mother had been Uriyah's wife, 7and Shlomo fathered Rehavam,[18] and Rehavam fathered Aviyah,[19] and Aviyah fathered Asa,[20] 8and Asa fathered Yehoshafat,[21] and Yeshoshafat fathered Yoram,[22] and Yoram fathered Uziyah,[23] 9and Uziyah fathered Yotam,[24] and Yotam fathered Ahaz, and Ahaz fathered Hizikiah,[25] 10and Hizikiah fathered Menasheh,[26] and Menasheh fathered Amon, and Amon fathered Yoshiyah,[27] 11and Yoshiyah fathered Yehoniah[28] and his brothers at the time of the exile to Babylon.

12After the exile to Babylon, Yehoniah fathered Shaltiel,[29] and Shaltiel fathered Zerubavel,[30] 13and Zerubavel fathered Avihud,[31] and Avihud fathered Elyakim,[32] and Elyakim fathered Azur,[33] 14and Azur fathered Tzadok,[34] and Tzadok fathered Yahin,[35] and Yahin fathered Elihud,[36] 15and Elihud fathered Elazar,[37] and Elazar fathered Mattan,[38] and Mattan fathered Yaakov, 16and Yaakov fathered Yosef, the husband of Miryam,[39] from whom was born Yeshua (Yehoshua) who is called the mashiah.

17So all the generations from Avraham to David are fourteen, and from David until the exile in Babylon fourteen generations, and from the exile in Babylon until the mashiah fourteen generations.

---

[14] Rahab.
[15] Obeb.
[16] Ruth.
[17] Solomon.
[18] Rehoboam.
[19] Abijah.
[20] Asaph. (Matthew gives Asaph, confusing King Asa, son ot the Judean king Aviyah, with a minor figure named Asaph.)
[21] Jehosphaphat.
[22] Joram.
[23] Uzziah.
[24] Jotham.
[25] Hezekiah.
[26] Manasseh.
[27] Josiah, Josias.
[28] Jechoniah.
[29] Salatiel.
[30] Zerubbabel.
[31] Abiud.
[32] Eliakim.
[33] Azor.
[34] Zadok.
[35] Achim.
[36] Eliud.
[37] Eleazar.
[38] Matthan.
[39] Mary.

An angel in Yosef's dream tells of Miryam with child

₁₈The birth of Yeshua the Mashiah happened in this way. Miryam[40] his mother was engaged to Yosef,[41] yet before they came together she discovered a child in her womb, placed there by the holy spirit. ₁₉Yosef her husband, a just man and loath to expose her, resolved to divorce her secretly. ₂₀But as he was making plans, look, an angel of the Lord[42] appeared to him in a dream and said,

> Yosef, son of David, do not fear to take Miryam as your wife.
>
> The child engendered in her came from the holy spirit,
>
> ₂₁and she will give birth, and you will name him Yeshua,
>
> for he will save[43] his people from their wrongdoings.

₂₂All this was done to fulfill the word of God uttered through his prophet Yeshayah,[44] saying,

> ₂₃"Listen. A young woman will have a child
>
> in her womb
>
> and give birth to a son, and his name will be Immanuel."[45]

₂₄When Yosef rose from a dream, he did what the angel of the Lord told him, and he accepted her as his wife, ₂₅yet he did not know her until after she gave birth, and he called the child the name Yeshua.

---

[40] Mary from the Greek Μαρία (Maria), from the Hebrew מִרְיָם (miryam).

[41] Joseph from the Greek Ἰωσήφ (Iosef), from the Hebrew יוֹסֵף (yosef).

[42] Angel of the Lord from the Greek ἄγγελος κυρίου (angelos kyriou), from the Hebrew מַלְאָךְ יהוה (malakh yahweh), as in Genesis 48.16. A literal rendering would be *Yahweh's malakh* or "messenger." *Malakh* (מַלְאָךְ) is the Hebrew word for "angel." "Angel" is a Greek word meaning merely "a messenger," associated with Hermes, without the divine powers of Yahweh's *malakh*. In biblical Greek, however, "angel" has taken on meanings of divinity and connotes "great beauty" and "fear."

[43] The naming of the infant messiah as Jesus, *Iesous* in the Greek, is followed by the reason for naming him Jesus, explaining that the name means "he will save." But Jesus in the Greek, *Iesous* (Ἰησοῦς), has no meaning in the Greek other than being a transliteration of the Hebrew Yeshua, from *Yehoshua*, which does mean "Yahweh saves." This passage suggests either an earlier text in the Hebrew or the Aramaic or that the author of the Greek Matthew was a Greek- and Hebrew-speaking Jew who had in mind the Hebrew or Aramaic name Yeshua or Yehoshua for the salvific lord and expected the readers or listeners to understand the name of the salvific lord in Hebrew embedded in the name Yeshua or Yehoshua. There seems to be no other explanation for attributing "for he will save" to a Greek name which itself is meaningless.

[44] Isaiah from the Greek Ἠσαίας (Esaias), from the Hebrew יְשַׁעְיָה (yeshayah). Isaiah is not mentioned in the text, but the passage quoted is by the prophet Isaiah (7.15). Since an ancient reader or listener presumably knew, or was expected to know, which prophet was being cited—and the modern reader would normally not have such knowledge—the name of the prophet here, and in each instance where the text attributes a passage to a prophet or to a book in the Hebrew Bible, is included in the text itself rather than in the margin or in bottom-of-page annotation.

[45] Immanuel means "God is with us."

CHAPTER 2

A star in the east

Now when Yeshua was born in Beit Lehem[46] in Yehuda[47] in the days of King Herod, look, some Magi, astrologer priests from the east, came to Yerushalayim[48] 2and said,

> Where is he who was born King of the Jews?
>
> We saw his star in the east
>
> and we came to worship him.

3Hearing this, King Herod was troubled and all Yerushalayim with him, 4and calling together all the high priests and the scholars of the people, he asked them where the mashiah was born.

5And they said to him, "In Beit Lehem in Yehuda, for so it is written by the prophet Malaci":

> 6And you, Beit Lehem, in the land of Yehuda,
>
> you are in no way least among the leaders of Yehuda,
>
> for out of you will come a leader
>
> who will be a shepherd of my people Yisrael.[49]

7Then Herod secretly called in the Magi astrologers and learned from them the exact time of the star's appearance, 8and he sent them to Bethlehem, saying, "Go and inquire precisely about the child. When you find him, bring me word so that I too may go to worship him."

9After hearing the king they set out, and look, the star, which they had seen in the east, went before them until it stood above the place where the child lay. 10When they saw the star, they were marvelously glad. 11And they went into the house and saw the child with Miryam his mother, and fell to the ground and worshiped him. Opening their treasure boxes, they offered him gifts of gold and frankincense and myrrh. 12Then having been warned in a dream not to go back to Herod, they returned by another road to their own country.

---

[46] Bethlehem from the Greek Βηθγέεμ (Bethleem), from the Hebrew בֵּית לֶחֶם (beit lehem), meaning "house of bread."

[47] Judea from the Greek Ἰουδαία (Ioudaia), from the Hebrew יְהוּדָה (yehuda). Also is the name Yehuda.

[48] Jerusalem from the Greek Ἰερουσαλήμ (Yerousalem), from the Hebrew יְרוּשָׁלַיִם (yerushalayim).

[49] Israel from the Greek Ισραήλ, from the Hebrew יִשְׂרָאֵל (yisrael).

An angel warns and a family flees to Egypt

13When they had gone, an angel appeared to Yosef in a dream, saying, "Arise, take this child and his mother, and fly into Egypt, and remain there until I tell you. Herod is looking for the child to destroy him."

14Then he arose and took the child and his mother through the dark of night and went to Egypt, 15and he stayed there until the death of Herod, thereby fulfilling the word uttered through Hoshea[50] his prophet, saying,

Out of Egypt I have called my son.

Herod enraged and killing

16When Herod saw that he had been outfoxed by the three astrologers, he was in a great rage and sent his men to kill all the male children in Beit Lehem[51] and in all the coastal region, who were two years and under, according to the exact time of the star, ascertained from the Magi. 17Thereby was fulfilled the word spoken through the prophet Yirmiyah,[52] saying,

18A voice was heard in Ramah,

weeping and grave lamentation,

Rahel[53] weeping for her children,

and she would not be comforted,

because her children are gone.

Back into the land of Yisrael

19Now when Herod died,[54] look, an angel flew down, appearing in a dream to Yosef in Egypt, 20saying,

Arise, take the child and his mother

and go to the land of Yisrael.

Those who sought the child's life are dead.

21Yosef arose, took the child and the mother, and went to the land of Yisrael. 22But when he heard that Archelaos was now King in Yehuda, replacing his father Herod, he was afraid to go there. And being warned in a dream, he with-

---

50 Hosea from the Hebrew הוֹשֵׁעַ (hoshea).

51 Bethlehem.

52 Jeremiah from the Greek Ἰερεμίας (Ieremias), from the Hebrew יִרְמְיָה (yirmiyah).

53 Rachel from the Greek Ῥαχήλ (Rahel), from the Hebrew רָחֵל (rahel).

54 The story of Herod's massacre of the sons at the birth of Yeshua as it is written echoes pharaoh's massacre of the sons at the birth of Moses (Exod. 1.12–22), thereby making a parallel between Moses and Yeshua and Yeshua as leader of their Israel, each having been called by God "out of Egypt."

drew to a place in the Galil,[55] where he went 23 and lived in a city called Natzeret.[56] So the prophets' word was fulfilled:

And he will be called a Natzrati.[57]

CHAPTER 3

Yohanan the Dipper in the desert

In those days came Yohanan the Dipper[58] preaching in the desert of Yehuda, 2 saying,

Repent, for the kingdom of the skies is near.

3 He was the one mentioned by the prophet Yeshayah,[59] saying,

A voice of one crying in the desert:

Prepare the way of the Lord and make his road straight.

4 Now Yohanan wore clothing made of camel's hair and a belt of hide around his waist, and his food was locusts and wild honey. 5 At that time the people of Yerushalayim came to him and also all of Yehuda and the whole countryside about the Yarden.[60] 6 He immersed them in the river Yarden, and they confessed their sins. 7 But when he saw many of the Prushim and Tzadokim[61] coming to the dipping, he said to them,

You offspring of vipers, who warned you to flee from

the coming wrath? 8 Prepare fruit worthy of your repentance.

9 And do not plan to say among yourselves,

"We have Avraham as our father."

For I say to you that out of these stones

God is able to raise up children to Avraham.

---

55 Galilee from the Greek Γαλιλαία (Galilaia), from the Hebrew גָּלִיל (galil). Galil is a "circle," "district," or "province." It is often used in the phrase גְּלִיל הַגּוֹיִם (galil hagoyim), meaning "province of the goyim (gentiles)."

56 Nazareth from Greek Ναζαρέτ (Natzaret), from unknown villiage in Galilee probably spelled Natzeret.

57 Nazarene from the Greek Ναζαρηνός (Nazarenos), from the Natzeret, that is, a Natzrati.

58 John the Baptist. John is from the Greek Ιωάννης (Ioannes), from the Hebrew יוֹחָנָן (yohanan). The Dipper is from the Greek ὁ βαπτίζων (ho baptizon), meaning "one who dips, washes, or immerses," as in Jewish ritual washings.

59 Isaiah.

60 Jordan from the Greek Ιορδάνς (Iordanes), from the Hebrew יַרְדֵּן (Yarden).

61 Pharisees from the Greek Φαρισαῖος (Farisaisos), from the Hebrew פְּרוּשִׁים (prushim). Pharisee (s.) is Parush. Sadducee from the Greek Σαδώκ, from the Hebrew צָדוֹק (tzadok). Sadducees (pl.) is Tzadokim.

10 Even now the axe lies set against the root of the trees,
and so every tree that fails to yield good fruit
is cut down and cast into the fire.

11 I immerse you in water for repentance,
but after me will come one stronger than I,
and I am not fit to carry his sandals.
He will dip you in the holy spirit and fire.
12 His winnowing fork is in his hand,
and he will clear his threshing floor and put his grain
in the storehouse
but he will burn the chaff in unquenchable fire.

Yeshua immersed

13 Then came Yeshua from the Galil to the Yarden and to Yohanan to be immersed by him. 14 Yohanan tried to stop him, saying, "I need to be immersed by you, yet you come to me?" 15 But Yeshua answered, saying to him,

Leave things as they are.
It is right for us in this way to fulfill
all that is just.
Then Yohanan consented.
16 And when Yeshua was immersed, at once he came out of the water and look, the skies opened, and he saw the spirit of God coming down like a dove, coming down upon him. 17 And look, a voice from the skies said,

This is my son whom I love,
in whom I am well pleased.

CHAPTER 4

Temptation in the desert

Then Yeshua was led by the spirit up into the desert to be tempted by the devil. 2 And he fasted forty days and forty nights, and afterward he hungered. 3 And coming up to him, the tempter said,

If you are the son of God, speak
and make these stones loaves of bread.
4 But Yeshua answered, saying,
It is written in Deuteronomy:

One lives not on bread alone

but on every word coming through the mouth of God.[62]

5Then the devil took him to the holy city, and set him on the parapet of the Temple 6and said to him,

If you are the son of God, cast yourself down,

for in the Psalms it is written:

He will command his angels to care for you,

and with their hands they will hold you up

so you will not smash your foot against a stone.[63]

7Yeshua said to him,

Again in Deuteronomy it is written:

You must not tempt the lord, your God.[64]

8Once more the devil led him to a very high mountain and showed him all the kingdoms of the world and their glory, 9and said to him,

All this I will give you

if you fall down before me and worship me.

10Then Yeshua said to him,

Go away, Satan, for it is also written:

You will worship God and you will serve him alone.[65]

11Then the devil left him, and look, angels came down and cared for him.

Preaching in the Galil

12Now when he heard that Yohanan had been arrested, Yeshua withdrew to the Galil, 13and leaving Nazareth he came to and settled in Kfar Nahum[66] by the great lake, in the districts of Zvulun and Naftali. 14He came to fulfill the words spoken through the prophet Yeshayah:

15Land of Zvulun and land of Naftali,

the way to the sea beyond the Yarden,

the Galil of the foreigners,

16the people who were sitting in darkness

saw a great light,

and for those sitting in the land and shadow of death

the light sprang into dawn.[67]

---

[62] Deut. 8.3.

[63] Ps. 91.11–12.

[64] Deut. 6.16.

[65] Deut. 6.13.

[66] Capernaum. Latin *Capernaum* from the Greek Καφαρναούμ (Kafarnaom) from Hebrew כְּפַר נָחוּם (kfar nahum), meaning "village of Nahum."

[67] Isa. 9.1–2.

17From that instant Yeshua began to preach his word and said,

Repent, for the kingdom of the skies is near.

Gathering the fishermen

18And as he was walking by the Sea of the Galil, he saw two brothers, one called Kefa,[68] and his brother Andreas,[69] casting their net into the sea, for they were fishermen. 19He said to them,

Come, and I will make you fishers of people.

20And they immediately dropped their nets and followed him.

21Going on from there he saw two more brothers, Yaakov[70] the son of Zavdai[71] and Yohanan his brother, in the boat with Zavdai their father, mending their nets. He called out to them. 22And they left their boat and their father, and followed him.

Healing the possessed

23Yeshua went all over the Galil, teaching in the synagogues, preaching the good message of the kingdom, and healing every sickness and infirmity among the people. 24His fame spread into all of Syria. And they brought him all who suffered diverse diseases and were seized by pain and those who were possessed by demons, epilepsy, and paralysis, and he healed them. 25And huge crowds followed him around from the Galil and Dekapolis and Yerushalayim, Yehuda, and from beyond the Yarden.

CHAPTER 5

Teaching from the mountain[72]

And seeing the crowds, he went up the mountain. When he was seated, his students came to him. 2And he opened his mouth and from the mountain gave them his teachings:

---

[68] Peter from the Greek Πέτρος (Petros), translated from the Aramaic כֵּיפָא (kefa), meaning "rock" or "stone."

[69] Andrew.

[70] James (Jacob) from the Greek Ἰάκωβος (Iakobos), from the Hebrew יַעֲקֹב (yaakov).

[71] Zebedee from the Greek Ζεβεδαῖος (Zebedaios), from the Hebrew זַבְדִּי (zavdai).

[72] Chapters 5–7, 10, 13, 18, 24–25 are commonly known as the Sermon on the Mount, a phrase that does not appear in the New Covenant. The Sermon is a compilation of wisdom sayings of Yeshua and contains the Beatitudes ("blessings") (5.3–12). Parts of the Sermon are found dispersed in the other gospels and have a counterpart in Luke's Sermon on the Plain (Luke 6.20–49).

3 Blessed are the poor in spirit
for theirs is the kingdom of the skies.
4 Blessed are they who mourn the dead
for they will be comforted.
5 Blessed are the gentle
for they will inherit the earth.
6 Blessed are the hungry and thirsty for justice
for they will be heartily fed.
7 Blessed are the merciful
for they will obtain mercy.
8 Blessed are the clean in heart
for they will see God.
9 Blessed are the peacemakers
for they will be called the children of God.
10 Blessed are they who are persecuted for the sake
   of their justice
for theirs is the kingdom of the skies.
11 Blessed are you when they revile, persecute, and speak
   every cunning evil[73] against you, lying,
   because of me.
12 Rejoice and be glad, for your reward in the heavens is huge,
and in this way did they persecute the prophets before you.

Salt and light
13 You are the salt of the earth.
But if the salt has lost its taste, how will it recover its salt?
Its powers are for nothing except to be thrown away
   and trampled underfoot by others.

14 You are the light of the world.
A city cannot be hidden when it is set on a mountain.
15 Nor do they light a lamp and place it under a basket,
   but on a stand,
and it glows on everyone in the house.

---

[73] The adjective *poneros* (πονηρός) in classical Greek often has a positive meaning, as in "nimble-witted" or "cunning" Odysseus, and has retained that specific earthly meaning into modern Greek. Some sense of the shade of cunning or earthiness is desired in the New Covenant usage, where it is usually rendered "evil" or "wicked."

16So let your light glow before people so they may see
    your good works and glorify your father
    of the skies.

Law and prophets

17Do not think that I have come to destroy the law or the prophets.
I have not come to destroy but to fulfill.
18 And yes I say to you, until the sky and the earth are gone,
not one tiny iota or serif will disappear from the law
    until all has been done.
19Whoever breaks even the lightest of the commandments
    and teaches others to do the same
will be esteemed least in the kingdom of the skies,
but whoever performs and teaches them
will be called great in the kingdom of the skies.
20I say to you, if you don't exceed the justice
of the scholars and the Prushim,
you will never enter the kingdom of the skies.

Anger and the fire of Gei Hinnom

21You have heard our people in ancient times commanded in Exodus,
    You must not murder.
    and whoever murders will be liable to judgment.
22I say to you, whoever is angry with a companion will be judged
    in court,
and whoever calls a companion a fool will go before the Sanhedrin,
    the highest court,
and whoever calls a companion a scoundrel will taste the fire of
    Gei Hinnom.⁷⁴
23If then you bring your gift to the altar,
and there you remember your companion holds something
    against you,
24leave your gift before the altar,
and go first to be reconciled with your companion
and then come back and present your offering.

---

74 Gehenna from the Greek γέεννα (Geenna), from the Hebrew גֵּיא הִנֹּם (gei hinnom), meaning the
    "Valley of Hinnom." Gei Hinnom and Sheol are normally translated as "hell."

25When you see your adversary walking in the street on the way
    to the court,
quickly, be of good will toward him and reconcile
26or your accuser will hand you over to the judge,
    the judge to the bailiff,
and you will be thrown into prison.
I tell you, there will be no way out
until you have paid back the last penny.

Adultery in the heart

27And you have heard in Exodus the words,
"Do not commit adultery."
28Yet I say, if a man looks at a woman with lust
he has already slept with her in his heart.
29So if your right eye takes you to scandalous sin,
tear it out and cast it away.
It is better to lose a part of your body
than for your whole body to be cast into Gei Hinnom.
30And if your right hand takes you to scandalous sin,
cut it off and cast it away.
It is better to lose a part of your body
than for your whole body to be cast into Gei Hinnom.

Sending a wife away

31And you have heard in Deuteronomy, if a man sends
    his wife away,[75]
give her a proper bill of divorce,
32but I also tell you that any man divorcing and sending
    his wife away,
except for dirty harlotry,
makes her the victim of adultery;
and any man who marries a woman divorced and sent away
is himself an adulterer.

Do not swear

33You have heard said in ancient times in Exodus,
You must not swear false oaths,

---

[75] Deut. 4.1.

but make good your oaths before God.

34 But I tell you not to swear at all:

not by heaven, for heaven is God's throne,

35 nor by earth, for earth is God's footstool,

nor by Yerushalayim, for Yerushalayim is the city of the great king.

36 Do not swear by your own head,

since you cannot make one hair white or black.

37 If your word is yes, say yes.

If your word is no, say no.

To say more is to indulge in evil.

Turn your cheek

38 And you have heard in Exodus,

"An eye for an eye and a tooth for a tooth."

39 But I tell you not to resist the wicked person,

and if someone strikes you on the right cheek,

turn your other cheek as well.

40 If someone wants to sue you for your shirt,

give him your cloak as well.

41 If someone forces you to go a mile with him,

go a second mile with him.

42 Give to who asks you. And do not turn away one

who wants to borrow from you.

Love your enemies

43 You have heard it said in Leviticus,

"You will love your neighbor and hate your enemy."[76]

44 I say to you to love your enemies

and pray for those who persecute you

45 so you may become the children of your father of the skies,

for he makes the sun rise over the evil and the good,

and he brings the rains to the just and the unjust

among us.

46 If you love those who love you, what reward have you?

Do not even the tax collectors do the same?

47 If you greet only those who are your friends,

---

[76] Lev. 19.18.

how have you done more than others?
48 Have you done more than the gentiles?
Be perfect as your father the heavenly one is perfect.

 # CHAPTER 6

Actors in the synagogue

Take care not to perform your good deeds before other people
    so as to be seen by them,
for you will have no reward from your father of the skies.
2 When you give alms, don't sound a trumpet before you
like the actors[77] in the synagogues and in the streets,
who seek the praise of the onlookers.
I say to you, they have their reward.
3 Yet when you give alms, do not let the left hand know
    what the right hand is doing
4 so the alms may be given in secret,
and your father seeing you in secret will repay you.

5 And when you pray, do not do so like the actors.
They love to stand in our synagogues and on the corners
of the open squares, praying
so they will be seen by others.
I say to you, they have their rewards.

A secret prayer

6 When you pray, go into your inner room and close the door
and pray to your father who is in secret,
and your father who sees you in secret will repay you.
7 Yet when you pray, do not babble empty words like the gentiles,
for the gentiles think by uttering a glut of words
they will be heard.

---

[77] Actor from the Greek ὑποκριτής (hypokrates). An "actor" or "player" is the ancient meaning. In New Covenant Greek, an actor is a pretender or hypocrite. In this instance of ostentatious acting in the synagogue, for the metaphor for hypocrisy to work it is essential that the primary meaning of "actor," rather than the moral abstraction of "hypocrite," come through first.

8 Do not be like them,
for your father knows what you need before you ask him.

Prayer to the father in the firmament
9 And pray like this:
Our father in the heavens,
let your name be holy
10 and your kingdom come
and your will be done
on earth as in heaven.
11 Our daily bread give us today,
12 and release us from our debts
as we have released our debtors.
13 Do not lead us into temptation,
but rescue us from the cunning one.[78]
[For yours is the kingdom,
and the power and the glory
forever and ever. Amen.][79]

Forgiving
14 If you forgive those who have stumbled and gone astray,
then your heavenly father will forgive you,
15 but if you will not forgive others,
your father will not forgive your missteps.

Oil on your head when fasting
16 When you fast, do not scowl darkly like actors.
They distort their faces to show others they are fasting.
Yes, they have their reward.
17 But when you fast, anoint your head with oil
to make it smooth and wash your face
18 so your fasting will be unknown to people
and known only to your father who is not visible.
Your father who sees you in secret will repay you.

---

[78] The figure referred to is probably the devil.
[79] This famous ending of the Lord's Prayer is in brackets, since it does not appear in the earliest Greek texts. It does appear in the later Majority Greek text, in Tyndale, and in the Authorized translations. See Introduction for further discussion.

Treasures in heaven

19 Do not hoard your treasures on earth
where moth and earthworms consume them,
where thieves dig through walls and steal them,
20 but store your treasures up in heaven
where neither moth nor earthworms consumes
and where thieves do not dig through the walls and steal,
21 since your treasure
is there where your heart will also be.

Lamp of the body

22 The lamp of the body is the eye.
If your eye is clear, your whole body is filled with light,
23 but if your eye is clouded, your whole body will inhabit
darkness.
And if the light in your whole body is darkness,
how dark it is!

Dilemma of two masters

24 No one can serve two masters.
You will either hate one and love the other
or cling to one and despise the other.
You cannot serve God and the mammon of riches.

Life more than food

25 So I tell you, do not worry about your life
or say, "What am I to eat? What am I to drink?"[80]
and about the body, "What am I to wear?"
Isn't life more than its food, and your body more than
its clothing?

Birds of the sky and lilies of the field

26 Consider the birds of the sky.
They do not sow or reap or collect for their granaries,
yet your heavenly father feeds them.
Are you not more valuable than they?

---

[80] "What am I to drink?" is missing in many texts.

Who among you by brooding can add one more hour
    to your life?

27 And why care about clothing?

28 Consider the lilies of the field, how they grow.
They do not labor or spin
29 but I tell you not even Shlomoh[81] in all his splendor
was clothed like one of these lilies.
30 And if the grass of the field is there today
and tomorrow is cast into the oven
and in these ways God has dressed the earth,
will he not clothe you in a more stunning raiment,
you who suffer from poor faith?

Brooding about tomorrow
    31 Do not brood, mumbling, "What is there to eat or drink?"
Or "What shall we wear?"
32 All those things the gentiles set their hearts on.
Your heavenly father knows you need all these things.
33 But seek first his kingdom and his justice,
and all things will be given to you.
34 Do not worry about tomorrow,
for tomorrow will worry about itself.
Each day has enough troubles of its own.

CHAPTER 7

Splinter in the eye
    Do not judge so you may not be judged,
2 for by your judgment you will be judged
and by your measure you will be measured.
3 Why do you gaze at the splinter in your brother's eye

---

81 Solomon from the Greek Σογομών (Solomon), from the Hebrew שְׁלֹמֹה (shlomoh).

yet not recognize the log in your own eye?
4Or why say to your brother,
"Let me take the splinter out of your eye"
when your own eye carries a log of wood?
5You hypocrite, first remove the wood from your own vision,
and you will see clearly enough
to pluck the sliver from your brother's eye.

Pearls and pigs
6Do not give the holy to the dogs
or cast your pearls before the pigs.
They will probably trample them underfoot
and turn and tear you to pieces.

Knock and the door will be opened
7Ask and it will be given to you.
Seek and you will find.
Knock and the door will be opened for you.
8Everyone who asks receives
and the seeker finds,
and the door will be opened to one who knocks.
9And who among you if your son asks for bread
will give him stone?
10Or if he asks for fish
will give him snake?
11If you, who are cunning, know how to give good gifts
    to your children,
how much more will your father of the skies
give good gifts to those who ask him?

Doing for others
12Whatever you wish others to do for you,
so do for them.
Such is the meaning of the law and the prophets.

Narrow gate
13Go in through the narrow gate,
since wide is the gate and spacious the road

that leads to destruction,

and there are many who go in through it.

14 But how narrow is the gate and cramped is the road

that leads to life,

and there are few who find it.

Wolves in sheep's clothing

15 Beware of the false prophets,

who come to you in sheep's clothing,

but who inwardly are wolves.

Tree and fruit

16 From their fruit you will know them.

Can you gather grapes from thorns or pick figs from thistles?

17 Every good tree bears delicious fruit,

but the diseased tree bears rotting fruit.

18 A good tree cannot yield rotting fruit,

nor a diseased tree delicious fruits.

19 Every tree incapable of delicious fruit is cut down

and tossed in the fire.

20 So from their fruit you will know them.

Who enters heaven

21 Not everyone who says to me, "Adonai, Adonai," [82]

will come into the kingdom of the skies,

but only one who follows the will of my father,

who is in the heavens.

22 On that day of judgment many will say to me,

"Adonai, Adonai, didn't we prophesy in your name

and in your name cast out demons

and in your name take on great powers?"

23 And then I will say my word clearly to them:

"I never knew you. Go from me,

you who are working against the law."

---

[82] Kyrie, kyrie (κύριε κύριε) lord. When the scriptures give *theos*, "God," it is uncertain which of the multiple words for God would have been used by Yeshua in the Hebrew or the Aramaic. However, when *kyrie* is used to mean "Lord as God," it may be as in *Adonai*, "my Lord," from the Hebrew אָדוֹן (adon) "Lord," or from *Yahweh* יהוה, another word for "God" or "Lord." Kyrie can also mean simply "sir," "lord," or "master."

Wind battering houses

₂₄Everyone who hears my words and follows them
will be like the prudent man who built his house upon the rock.
₂₅The rain fell and the rivers formed
and the winds blew and battered that house
and it did not fall down
because it was founded upon the rock.
₂₆But everyone who hears my words and doesn't follow them
will be like the young fool who built his house upon the sand.
₂₇The rain fell and the rivers formed
and the winds blew and battered that house
and it fell down and it was a great fall.

₂₈And it happened that when Yeshua ended these words, the crowds were amazed at his teaching, ₂₉for he taught them as one who has authority and not like one of their scholars.

 **CHAPTER 8**

With a leper

When he came down from the mountain, many multitudes followed him. ₂And look, a leper [83] came near and bent low before him, saying,
Sir, if you want to, you can make me clean.
₃Stretching out his hand, Yeshua touched him and said,
Yes, I want to. Be clean.
And at once his leprosy was cleansed away.
₄And Yeshua said to him,
Be sure to say nothing, but go to the priest
and offer the gift that Mosheh commanded.
Offer it to them as proof of your cure.

₅When he came into Kfar Nahum, a centurion, a Roman officer, came near, ₆beseeching him. "Sir, my servant boy is lying paralyzed in my house, and in terrible pain."

---

[83] The word "leper" can refer to several skin diseases.

7 And he said to the centurion,

I will come to heal him.

8 The centurion answered, "Sir, I don't deserve to have you under my roof. Only say a word and my son will be healed. 9 I am also a man under orders, with soldiers under me, and I say to this man, 'Go,' and he goes, and to another, 'Come,' and he comes, and to my slave, 'Do this,' and he does it."

10 Hearing him, Yeshua was amazed and said to his followers,

Yes, I tell you, in all of Yisrael

I have found no one with such deep faith,[84]

11 and I tell you, many from the east and west

will come and lie down beside the table

to eat with Avraham and Yitzhak and Yaakov

in the kingdom of the skies.

12 And other sons of the kingdom will be thrown out

into the far outer darkness.

There will be weeping and gnashing of teeth.

13 Yeshua said to the centurion,

Go back to your home. Since you have had faith,

let the event take place for you.

And his son was healed in that hour.

Healing at the house of Kefa

14 Then Yeshua went into the house of Kefa, whose mother-in-law he saw lying in bed with a fever, 15 and he touched her hand and the fever left her. She got up and served him.

16 That same evening they brought him many who were afflicted with demons. With a word he cast out the spirits and he healed all their sicknesses. 17 He was fulfilling the words of the prophet Yeshayah:

He attended our sicknesses

and removed our diseases.[85]

---

84 Matthew portrays the centurion as humble toward Yeshua, but of a faith greater than anyone in Israel. This astonishing portrait of an officer of the Roman army is repeated when the centurion who commands the execution squad is the first to recognize and announce Yeshua's divinity immediately upon Yeshua's death on the cross (27.54). This benign view of members of an army hostilely occupying Israel, which executed Yeshua and other Jews and, subsequently, great numbers of Christians, is consistent with the exoneration of Rome in the gospels by an early Christian church whose seat was in Rome and in the new Roman empire in Constantinople. See Afterword. The portrait ends with Matthew's familiar warning that earlier Hebrew Bible patriarchs, Avraham, Yitzhak, and Yaakov (Abraham, Isaac, and Jacob), as well as those from east and west (gentiles), will dine in heaven but those other sons of the kingdom (Jews who do not accept Yeshua as the messiah) will be thrown into the darkness and torment of Gei Hinnom.

85 Isa. 53.4.

I will follow you

18Now when Yeshua saw the great crowds all about him, he ordered them to cross over the water to the other side. 19A scholar came up to him and said, "Rabbi, I will follow you wherever you go."

20And Yeshua answered,

Foxes have holes in the earth and birds of the sky
    have nests,
but the earthly son[86] has no place to rest his head.

21Another student said to him, "Sir, first let me go and bury my father."

22But Yeshua told him,

Follow me
and let the dead bury their own dead.

Dead calm

23When he got into the ship, his students followed him. 24And suddenly a great storm sprang up on the sea, so powerful that the ship was hidden under the waves, but he was sleeping. 25And they came and woke him and said,

Sir, save us, we are perishing!

And he said to them,

26Why are you frightened, you of little faith?

Then he got up and admonished the winds and the sea, and there was a dead calm.

27And the people marveled, and said,

What kind of a man is he?
Even the winds and the sea obey him.

Demoniacs and pigs

28When he crossed over into the country of the Gadarenes, two men possessed by demons, coming out of the tombs, accosted him on the road. They were wild and fierce and no one could get through. 29Suddenly they screamed, "What do you want with us, son of God? Are you here before your time simply to torment us?"

30Far off there was a herd of many pigs, feeding.

31And the demons pleaded, "If you cast us out, send us into the herd of pigs!"

32And he said to them,

Go!

---

86 See note 30 on Mark 2.10 for "earthly son."

So they came out and entered the pigs and look, the whole herd raced down the slope into the sea and died in the waters. ₃₃Those tending the pigs ran off, and when they came to their city they told the story of those who had been possessed by demons.

₃₄And look, the whole city came out to meet Yeshua. But when they saw him they begged him to leave their region.

CHAPTER 9

Stand up and walk

Then he stepped back into a ship, crossed over the sea, and came to his own city. ₂And look, the people brought him to a paralytic lying on a bed. When he saw their faith, he said to the paralytic,

Be happy, my child, your wrongs are forgiven.

₃And look, some of the scholars said among themselves, "This man is blaspheming."

₄When Yeshua noticed what they were thinking, he said,

Why do you harbor bad thoughts in your hearts?
₅Which is easier: to say, "Your wrongs are forgiven"
or to say, "Stand up and walk"?
₆So that you will know that the earthly son
has the power to forgive sins,
stand up, take your bed with you, and go home.

₇And the paralytic stood up and went off to his house.

₈When the crowds saw this, they were afraid and glorified God, who gave such powers to people.

Dining with a tax collector

₉As Yeshua walked along, he saw a man seated in the toll house. His name was Mattai,[87] and he said to him,

Follow me.

And Mattai stood up and followed him.

₁₀And it happened that while he was eating in Mattai's house, look, many other tax collectors and sinners came to recline at the table to dine with Yeshua

---

[87] Matthew. Also called Levi, Λευί (לֵוִי), by Mark 2.13 and Luke 5.20. See note 31 in Mark.

and his students. 11When the Prushim saw this, they were saying to the students, "Why does your rabbi eat with tax collectors and sinners?"

12Yeshua heard them and responded,

> The strong and healthy do not need a doctor
> but the sick do. Go and learn the meaning of
> 13"I wish mercy and not sacrifice." [88]
> I came not to call on the upright but the sinners.

Fasting and the bridegroom

14Then Yohanan's students came and asked him,

> Why do we and the Prushim often fast,
> but your students do not fast?

15Yeshua answered,

> Surely the members of the wedding party cannot mourn
> while the bridegroom is with them?
> But the days will come when the groom is taken away
>   from them,
> and then they will be fasting.

Unshrunk cloth and new wine

> 16No one sews a patch of unshrunk cloth on an old coat,
> since the patch pulls away the form of the coat
> and makes the tear worse.
> 17Nor do they pour new wine into old wineskins.
> If they do, the skins burst, the wine gushes out,
> and the wineskins are ruined.
> No, they pour new wine into fresh wineskins
> and both are preserved.

Dead girl and a bleeding mother

18While he was saying these things, a leader of the synagogue[89] came near, bowed low before him, and said,

> My daughter has just died.
> But come and put your hand on her
> and she will live.

---

[88] Hos. 6.6.
[89] The Greek lacks "of the synagogue."

19Yeshua rose and he and his students followed the official. 20And look, a woman, who had been bleeding for twelve years, came from behind him and touched the fringe of his cloak. 21She was saying to herself,

> If only I might touch his garment I will be healed.

22Yeshua turned and saw her and said,

> Be happy, daughter. Your faith has healed you.

And in that instant the woman was healed.

23When Yeshua entered the official's house and saw the flute players and the noisy crowd, 24he said,

> Go away. The girl has not died. She is asleep.

They laughed at him.

25But when the crowd was put outside, he went in and took her hand, and the girl woke.

26And the news of this spread throughout the land.

With the blind

27As Yeshua was leaving, two blind men followed him, weeping and saying, "Pity us, son of David."

28When he had gone indoors, the blind men came to him, and he asked them,

> Do you believe that I can do this?

They said to him, "Yes, lord."

29Then he touched their eyes and said,

> As you have faith, let your eyes be healed.

30And their eyes were opened.

Then Yeshua warned them sternly,

> See that no one knows of this.

31But they left and spread the news throughout the land.

With a mute

32And just as they were going out, look, they brought him a mute and he was possessed by a demon. 33When he cast the demon out, the mute spoke. The crowd stood in wonder and exclaimed,

> Never have these things happened in Yisrael!

34However, the Prushim said,

> He drives out demons through the prince of demons.

Sheep and a shepherd

35Then Yeshua went through all the cities and villages, teaching in their synagogues, and preaching the good news of the kingdom, and healing every disease and sickness. ₃₆When he saw the crowds, he felt pity for them, because they were harassed and helpless like sheep without a shepherd. ₃₇Then he said to his students,

The harvest is abundant but the field workers are few.

₃₈ Ask the harvest owner to send his workers into the fields.

 CHAPTER 10

Missions for the twelve on the road

Then he called his twelve students together, and gave them authority over unclean spirits to cast them out, and to heal every disease and sickness. ₂The names of the twelve messengers⁹⁰ are: first, Shimon,⁹¹ who is also called Kefa, and his brother Andreas, and Yaakov the son of Zavdai, and his brother Yohanan, ₃Filippos and Bartalmai, Toma,⁹² and Mattai the tax collector, Yaakov the son of Halfi,⁹³ and Taddai,⁹⁴ ₄Shimon the Zealot, and Yehuda of Keriot,⁹⁵ the one who betrayed him.

₅These twelve Yeshua sent out with instructions, saying,

Don't go on the road where there are gentiles

and don't enter the city of the Shomronims.⁹⁶

₆Go rather to the lost sheep of the house of Yisrael.

₇And as you go, preach

and say that the kingdom of the skies is coming near.

₈Heal the sick, raise the dead, cleanse the lepers,

and cast out the demons.

Freely you have received, freely give.

₉Don't take gold and silver and copper in your belts,

⁹⁰ Apostles. See note 41 on Mark 3.14.

⁹¹ Simon from the Greek Σίμων, from the Hebrew שִׁמְעוֹן (shimon).

⁹² Thomas.

⁹³ Alphaeus from the Greek Ἀλφαῖος (Halfaios), from the Hebrew חַלְפִּי (halfi).

⁹⁴ Thaddeus from the Greek Θαδδαῖος (Thaddaois), from the Hebrew תַּדַּי (taddai).

⁹⁵ Judas the Iscariot. Judas from the Greek Ἰούδας (Ioudas), from the Hebrew יְהוּדָה (yehuda). The name for the messenger (apostle) Judas in Hebrew, *Yehuda,* was surely invented because it suggests the word in Hebrew for "Jew," which is יְהוּדִי (yehudi), thereby the betrayer of Yeshua among his followers was a Jew, as opposed to the others who escape that identity.

⁹⁶ Samaritans. Samaritans are from Samaria, from the Greek Σαμαρία (Samaria), from the Hebrew שֹׁמְרוֹן (shomron). A Samaritan is a Shomronim.

10or a bag for the journey
or two tunics or sandals or a staff,
for the laborer earns his food.

Shake the dust from your feet

11In whatever city or village you enter,
find out who in it is worthy
and stay there until you leave.
12As you go into a house, greet it,
13and if the house is worthy
let your peace be upon it.
But if the house is not worthy,
let your peace return to you.
14If someone doesn't welcome you
or listen to your words,
as you go out of that house or city
shake the dust from your feet.
15Amen, I say to you,
Sedom and Amorah[97] will be more tolerable
on the day of judgment
than the fate of that city.

Be crafty as snakes, innocent as doves

16Look, I send you out as sheep among wolves,
so be crafty as snakes and innocent as doves.
17Be careful of people who will hand you over to the councils
and flog you in their synagogues.
18You will be dragged before governors and kings,
because of me, to bear witness before them
and before the gentiles.
19But when they hand you over,
do not worry about how and what you are to say.
In that hour what you say will be given to you,
20for you will not be speaking.
The spirit of your father will be speaking through you.

21Brother will turn in brother over to death,
and a father will turn in his child,

---

97 Sodom from the Hebrew סְדֹם (sedom) and Gomorrah from the Hebrew עֲמֹרָה (amorah).

and children will rise against their parents
and have them put to death.
22 You will be hated by all because of my name,
but the one who endures to the end will be saved.
23 And when they persecute you in one city,
escape to another.
Amen I say to you,
you will not have gone through the cities of Yisrael
before the coming of the earthly son.

Student to teacher, slave to master

24 A student is not above the teacher,
nor a slave above the master.
25 It is enough for the student to be like the teacher
and the slave like the master.
If they call the master of the house Baal Zevul,[98]
lord of the flies,
how much worse will they call the members of
the household!

Uncovering darkness

26 So do not fear them.
There is nothing concealed that will not be revealed
and nothing hidden that will not be known.
27 What I say to you in darkness, speak in the light,
and what you hear whispered in your ear,
proclaim from the housetops.
28 And have no fear of those who kill the body
but are unable to kill the soul.
Fear rather the one who destroys both soul and body
    in Gei Hinnom.

Two sparrows and a penny

29 Are two sparrows not sold for a penny?
Yet not one of them will fall to the earth
without your father,
30 Even the hairs of your head are each one of them
    counted,

---

[98] Beelzebub.

31So have no fear.

You are worth more than many sparrows.

Heralding or denying

32 Anyone who heralds me before others,

I will herald before my father of the skies,

33and whoever denies me before others,

I will deny before my father in the skies.

Not peace but a sword

34Do not think I have come to bring peace on the earth.

I have not come to bring peace but a sword.

Micah said,

35I came to set a man against his father

and a daughter against her mother,

and a bride against her mother-in-law

36and one's enemies will be in one's household.[99]

Finding soul

37If you love your father or mother more than me,

you are not worthy of me,

if you love your son or daughter more than me,

you are not worthy of me,

38and if you do not take up the cross and come along

behind me,

you are not worthy of me.

39Whoever finds the soul will lose it,

whoever loses the soul, because of me, will find it.

Even a cup of cold water

40Whoever accepts me, accepts the one who sent me.

41Whoever accepts a prophet in the name of the prophet

will have the reward of a prophet,

and whoever receives a just person in the name

of a just person

will have the reward of the just.

42And whoever gives even a cup of cold water

---

[99] Mic. 7.6.

to one of these children in the name of a student,
I tell you none will go unrewarded.

CHAPTER 11

Teaching in the cities

And when Yeshua had finished instructing his twelve students, he left the region to teach and preach in their cities.

Word from Yohanan in jail

₂When Yohanan heard in prison what the mashiah was doing, he sent his own students ₃to ask him, "Are you the one who is to come[100] or shall we look for another?"

₄And Yeshua answered, saying to them,
Go and tell Yohanan what you see and hear.
In the words of our prophet Yeshayah:
> ₅The blind will see again and the lame walk,
> the lepers are made clean and the deaf hear,
> the dead are raised and the poor hear the good news.[101]
> ₆Blessed is the one I have not caused to fall.

Yohanan, who is Eliyah preparing the way

₇As Yohanan's students were leaving, Yeshua began to speak to the crowd about Yohanan,
> What did you go into the desert to see?
> A reed shaken by the wind?
> ₈But what did you go out to see?
> A man dressed in soft robes?
> Look, those who wear soft clothing are in the houses of the kings.
> ₉What did you go out to see?
> A prophet? Yes, I tell you, and he is more than a prophet.
> ₁₀He is the one of whom the prophet Malachi wrote:
>> See, I send my angel messenger before your face,
>> who will prepare the way before you.[102]

---

[100] "who is to come" refers to "the mashiah (Christ)."
[101] Isa. 35.5–6. See also Isa. 26.19; 29.18; 42.7, 18; 61.1.
[102] Mal. 3.1.

₁₁I say to you, no one risen among us born of women
is greater than Yohanan the Dipper.
Yet who is least in the kingdom of the skies
    is greater than he is.
₁₂From the days of Yohanan the Dipper until now
the kingdom of the skies has been violated
and violent men seize it.
₁₃The prophets and even the law prophesied all
that was to lead to Yohanan's coming,
₁₄and, if you are willing to accept it,
Yohanan is the Eliyah who is about to come.
₁₅Whoever has ears to hear, hear.

Like children sitting in the market place
₁₆But to what shall I compare our generation?
We are like children sitting in the market places,
calling out to one another, ₁₇saying,
"We played the flute for you and you didn't dance.
We sang a dirge and you didn't mourn."
₁₈When Yohanan came he was not eating or drinking,
and they say, "He has a demon."
₁₉The earthly son came eating and drinking,
and they say, "Look at that glutton and drunk,
a friend of tax collectors and sinners,"
yet wisdom is justified by her deeds.

Punishment of cities
₂₀Then he began to blame the cities in which his greatest powers[103] were revealed, because they had not changed their ways,
    ₂₁A plague on you, Horazim[104] and Beit Tzaida![105]
If these powers had been revealed in Tzor[106] and Tzidon[107]

---

[103] Powers from the Greek δύναμις (dynamis), meaning "power." *Dynamis* is traditionally translated as "miracle," though not in most new versions, where it is rendered as "power" or "deed of power," its classical as well as koine meaning in the Greek.

[104] Chorazin from the Greek Χοραζίν (Horazin). The Hebrew "Horazim" is uncertain.

[105] Bethseda from the Greek Βηθσαϊδά (Bethsaida), from the Hebrew בֵּית צַיְדָא (beit tzaida), which is a place north of Lake Gennesaret.

[106] Tyre from the Greek Τύρος (Turos), from the Hebrew צוֹר (tzor), צֹר (tzor), or טוּר (tur), meaning "hard quartz" or "a flint knife," from the Aramaic טוּר (tur), meaning "a rock."

[107] Sidon from the Greek Σιδών (Sidon), from the Hebrew צדון (tzidon).

that were revealed among you,
long ago they would have repented in sackcloth and ashes.
22But I tell you, it will be more tolerable for Tzor and Tzidon
on the day of judgment than for you.
23 And you, Kfar Nahum,
    Will you be raised into the skies?
    No, you will descend into the pits of hell.[108]
If these powers had been revealed in Sedom
that were revealed among you,
Sedom would be here today.
24Yet I tell you, it will be more tolerable for the land
of Sedom on the day of judgment than for you.

Revealed to little children

25 At that time Yeshua said,
    I praise you, lord of the sky and of the earth,
    because you have hidden these things from the wise
        and the learned,
    and revealed them to little children.

Father and son

26Yes, father, in this way it was pleasing to you.
27 All things were given to me by my father,
and no one knows the son except the father,
and no one knows the father except the son
and any to whom the son wishes to reveal it.

Rest for your souls

28Come to me, all who labor and are sorely burdened,
and I will give you rest.
29Take my yoke upon you and learn from me
because I am gentle and humble in heart,
and you will find rest for your souls[109]
30 for my yoke is easy and my burden is light.

---

[108] Isa. 14.13, 15.
[109] Ps. 34.18.

◉ CHAPTER 12

Shabbat[110] in the grain fields

At that time Yeshua walked on the Shabbat through the sown fields. His students were hungry and they began to pick the ears of grain and eat them. ₂But the Prushim saw it and said to him, "Look, your students are doing what is forbidden to do on Shabbat."

₃But he said to them,

Have you not read what David did
when he and his companions were hungry?
₄How he went into the house of God
and ate the bread for presentation,[111]
which he was not permitted to eat,
as were not those who were with him,
for that bread was for the priests alone?
₅Haven't you read in the law that priests in the Temple
break the Shabbat by their labors,
yet they must be held innocent?
₆I tell you here is something greater than the Temple,
₇and if you knew what our prophet Hoshea
meant by "I wish mercy and not sacrifice,"[112]
you would not condemn the innocent.
₈The lord of the Shabbat is the earthly son.

A sheep in a pit, a withered hand

₉And leaving that spot he went inside the synagogue ₁₀and suddenly he saw a man with a withered hand. They asked him, "Is it lawful to heal on Shabbat?" They questioned him, hoping to trap and accuse him. ₁₁But he said to them,

If you who had only a single sheep
and it fell on Shabbat into a pit,
wouldn't you grab it and pull it out?
₁₂A person is worth more than a sheep,
so on the Shabbat one can do good.

---

[110] Sabbath from the Greek σάββατον (sabbaton), from the Hebrew שַׁבָּת (shabbat).

[111] Twelve consecrated loaves of bread, changed weekly, set out in the synagogue as a symbol of communion with God. Also called "the bread of presence."

[112] Hos. 6.6.

13Then he said to the man,

>Hold out your hand.

And it was restored, sound like the other one.

14But the Prushim went out and plotted against him to destroy him.

Yeshayah and hope for foreigners

15Aware of this, Yeshua departed. And many followed him and he healed them all. 16But he warned them not to reveal who he was 17in order that he might fulfill the prophecy of Yeshayah, saying,

>18Look, here is the servant I have chosen,
>
>my love in whom my soul delights.
>
>I will insert my spirit into him
>
>and he will announce judgment for the foreigners.[113]
>
>19He will not quarrel or shout;
>
>No one will hear his voice in the main streets.
>
>20He will not break a bruised reed
>
>or quench a smoking wick of flax
>
>until he brings in the victory of judgment.
>
>21In his name the foreigners will hope.[114]

With a blind and deaf demoniac

22Then they brought him a blind and deaf demoniac and he healed him, so that the mute was able to speak and to see. 23The crowds were amazed and were saying, "Is he not the son of David?"

Yeshua and demons

24But the Prushim heard this and said, "This man doesn't drive out demons except through Baal Zevul,[115] the prince of the demons."

25Yeshua knew their thoughts and said to them,

>Every kingdom divided against itself turns into a desert,
>
>and every city or house divided against itself will not stand.
>
>26And if Satan casts out Satan, he is divided against himself.
>
>How then will his kingdom stand?

---

[113] Foreigner or gentile.

[114] Isa. 42.1–3.

[115] Baal Zevul is Beelzebul, Satan, and orginally a Philistine deity worshiped at Ekron, twenty-two miles west of Yerushalayim (2 Kings 1.2–18). Beelzebul is from the Greek Βεελζεβούλ (Beelzeboul), from the Hebrew בַּעַל זְבוּל (Baal Zevul). Elsewhere we find Baal Zevuv, who is Beelzebub from Greek Βεελζεβούβ (Beelzeboub), from Hebrew בַּעַל זְבוּב (Baal Zevuv). Baal Zevul may mean "Lord of Dung," and Baal Zevuv may mean "Lord of the Flies." In John Milton's *Paradise Lost* Beelezebub is the prince of evil spirits and Satan's chief lieutenant.

27If through Baal Zevul I cast out the demons,
through whom do your sons cast them out?
Therefore they will be your judges.
28But if through the spirit of God I cast out the demons,
the kingdom of God has come to you.

Plundering a strong man's house.

29Or how can one enter the house of a strong man
and carry off his possessions
without first tying up the strong man?
Then his house can be plundered.

Standing firm

30Who is not with me is against me
and who will not assemble with me scatters my gatherings.
31So I tell you, every sin and blasphemy
by people will be forgiven,
32and whoever speaks against the earthly son will be forgiven,
but whoever speaks against the holy spirit
will not be forgiven,
either in this age or in the age to come.

Fruit, vipers, and words

33Either make the tree good and its fruit good
or make the tree bad and its fruit bad,
because from the fruit the tree is known.
34Offspring of vipers, how can you speak of the good
    when you are evil?
The mouth speaks from an abundance in the heart.
35The good person from a good storehouse draws good,
the evil one from an evil storehouse draws evil.
36But I tell you, that each idle word you utter
you will account for on the day of judgment,
37for by your words you will be justified
and by your words you will be condemned.

The sign of Yonah

38Then some of the scholars and Prushim answered him, saying, "Rabbi, we
wish to see a sign from you."
39He answered and said to them,

A corrupt and adulterous generation asks for a sign
but no sign will be given to it
except for the sign of Yonah [116] the prophet.
40 For as Yonah was in the belly of the sea monster
three days and three nights,
so three days and three nights
the earthly son will be in the heart of the earth.
41 The men of Ninevah will stand up on the day of judgment
of this generation,
and they will condemn it,
because they repented with the preaching of Yonah,
and look, there is more than Yonah here.
42 The Queen of the South [117] will rise on the day of judgment
of this generation,
and they will condemn it,
because she came from the ends of the earth to listen
to the wisdom of Shlomoh,
and look, there is more than Shlomoh here.

Unclean spirit

43 When the unclean goes out of a person, it wanders
through waterless places,
seeking a place to rest and finds none.
44 Then it says, "I will return to the house I came from,"
and finds it empty and swept and put in order.
45 Then it goes and picks up seven other spirits,
each worse than itself.
And they go into the house and live there,
and the end for that man is worse than the beginning.
Such it will also be with this evil generation.

Yeshua rejects Miryam and his brothers

46 While he was still talking to the crowds, look, his mother Miryam and his brothers were standing outside, wanting to speak with him. 47 And someone said to him, "See, your mother and your brothers are standing outside, wanting to speak with you." [118]

---

[116] Jonah from the Greek Ἰωνᾶς (Ιωνασ), from the Hebrew יוֹנָה (yonah).
[117] The Queen of Sheba (1 Kings 10.1–13; 2 Chron. 9.1–12).
[118] Verse 47 is omitted in some texts.

48 And Yeshua answered him,

    Who is my mother and who are my brothers?

49 And pointing to his students, he said,

    Look at my mother and my brothers.

    50 Whoever does the will of my father of the skies

    is my brother and my sister and my mother.

CHAPTER 13

Parables by the sea

On that day Yeshua went out of his house and sat by the sea. 2 And a great multitude gathered before him, so that he got into a boat and sat there, and all the crowd stood on the shore. 3 And he told them many things in parables.

The sower

    He said,

        Look, a sower went out to sow

        4 and as he was scattering the seed,

        some of the grain fell on the path

        and some birds came and ate it.

        5 Other seed fell on stony ground

        where there was not much soil

        and the grain sprang up quickly,

        for the soil had no depth.

        6 But when the sun came up

        the seedlings were parched

        and, having no roots, withered.

        7 Some fell among the thorns

        and the thorns grew and choked them.

        8 But some fell on good earth and bore fruit.

        A hundredfold and sixty and thirty.

        9 Whoever has ears to hear, hear.

Why parables?

10 Then the students came near him and asked, "Why do you talk to them in parables?"

11 He answered them and said,

You are given a knowledge of the secrets
of the kingdom of the skies,
but that knowledge is not given to them.
12When one has, more is granted; when one has not,
that little is taken away.
13So I talk to them in parables,
for while they see, they do not see,
and while they hear, they do not hear or understand.

14And so the prophecy of Yeshayah is fulfilled, saying,
You hear, yet in hearing, you do not understand
and you see, yet in seeing, you do not see.
15For the heart of this people has become calloused
and with their ears they hear poorly and their eyes are closed,
otherwise they might see with their eyes, and hear
with their ears
and with their heart understand and turn
and I would heal them.[119]

16But blessed are your eyes because they see and your ears
because they hear.
17I say to you that many prophets and good people
have longed to see what you see and did not see it.
And to hear what you hear and did not hear it.

Sower parable given light
18Now listen to the parable of the sower.
19When someone hears the word of the kingdom
and does not understand it,
the evil one comes and seizes what was sown in the heart.
That is what was scattered on the path.
20The seed dropped into the stony ground is the one
who hears the word and at once accepts it with joy.
21But that sower has no roots within himself,
all is brief and transitory,
and when affliction or persecution comes because of the word,
that sower weakens and falls away.
22Now the seed dropped among the thorns is the one

---

[119] Isa. 6.9–10.

who hears the word, but the worries of the age
and the lure of riches choke the word and it gives no fruit.
23 But the seed sown in the good earth is the one
who hears the word and understands,
and who bears fruit a hundredfold and sixty and thirty.

Weeds sown among the wheat
24 He set another parable before them, saying,
The kingdom of the skies is like someone
who sowed good seed in his field
25 and while the people were asleep
his enemy came and sowed weeds among the wheat
and went away.
26 When the plants grew and bore fruit
then the weeds also appeared.
27 The slaves came to the master of the house,
    and said to him,
"Sir, did you not sow good seed in the field?
Where do the weeds come from?"
28 The master told them, "My enemy did this."
"Do you want us to go and pull them out?"
    said the slaves.
29 "No, in pulling the weeds you would uproot the wheat.
30 Let both grow together until the harvest.
Then at the harvest I'll tell the reapers,
'First pull the weeds and tie them in bundles to burn,
but store the wheat in my granary.'"

Mustard seed and the birds
31 He set another parable before them, saying,
The kingdom of the skies is like a mustard seed
that someone took and planted in the field,
32 which is the smallest among all the seeds
but when it grows it is the greatest of the green shrubs
and becomes a tree
so the birds of the sky come and nest in its branches.

Yeast and heaven
33 He set another parable before them, saying,
The kingdom of the skies is like yeast

a woman hid in three measures of flour
so that the dough was leavened and rose.

Parables opening the hidden

34All this Yeshua told the crowd in parables, and he talked solely in parables 35so as to fulfill the words spoken by the prophet in the Psalms, saying,

I open my mouth in parables,
I will pour out what has been hidden since the creation.[120]

Weed parable given light

36Then he left the crowds and went into the house and his students came up to him and said, "Clarify the parable of the weeds in the field for us."

37And he answered,

The one who sows the good seed is the earthly son
38and the field is the cosmos,
the good seeds are the children of the kingdom,
but the weeds are the children of the evil one,
39and the enemy who sowed them is the devil.
The harvest is the end of an age,
and the reapers are angels.
40Then as the weeds are pulled up and burned in the fire
so it will be at the end of the age.
41The earthly son will send out his angels
and he will gather from his kingdom
all scandalous things and those practicing lawlessness
42and cast them into the furnace of fire
where there will be weeping and gnashing of teeth.
43Then the just will shine like the sun in the kingdom
   of the father.
Whoever has ears to hear, hear.

Three parables:

Of treasure

44The kingdom of the skies is like treasure
   hidden in a field,
which someone found and concealed,
   and out of his joy

---

120 Ps. 78.2.

he goes away and sells everything he ever bought
    and buys that field.

Of a pearl

45 Again, the kingdom of the skies is like a merchant
    seeking fine pearls.
46 After finding one valuable pearl he sold everything
    he had,
and bought that pearl.

Of a net

47 Again, the kingdom of the skies is like a net cast into
    the sea
and catching every kind of fish.
48 When it was full and they dragged it up on the shore,
they sat down and put the good fish in baskets,
but the rotted ones they threw out.
49 So it will be at the end of the age.
The angels will come and separate the evil from the just
50 and will cast them into the furnace of fire,
where there will be weeping and gnashing of teeth.

51 All these things, did you understand them?
52 "Yes," they said to him.
And he said to them,
    Every scholar who is learned about the kingdom
        of the skies
    is like one who is master of a household,
    who takes the new and the old
    from the storeroom of the treasures.

Prophets without honor

53 And it happened that when Yeshua finished the parables, he left the region 54 and came to his home country and taught them in their synagogue. They were astonished and they said, "Where has this man found his wisdom and powers? 55 Isn't he the carpenter's son? Isn't his mother called Miryam, and his brothers Yaakov and Yosef and Shimon and Yehuda? 56 And aren't all his sisters with us too? Where did this man get all these powers?" 57 And they were offended by him.

But Yeshua said to them,

A prophet is not dishonored
except in his own country and house.

₅₈And due to their lack of faith, he performed few deeds of power there.

 **CHAPTER 14**

Herod and Yohanan's head

At this time Herod the tetrarch[121] heard the reports about Yeshua, ₂and he said to his servants, "This is Yohanan the Dipper. He has risen from the dead, which is why these powers are at work in him."

₃Herod had seized Yohanan and bound him and put him in prison, because of Herodias, the wife of Filippos his brother. ₄Yohanan had said to him, "It is not lawful for you to have her." ₅Herod wanted to kill Yohanan, but he feared the crowd, because they held him to be a prophet.

₆Now on Herod's birthday celebration, it happened that the daughter of Herodias danced before them and she captivated Herod, ₇and he took an oath and agreed to give her anything she asked for. ₈The daughter, guided by her mother, said, "Bring me, here on this platter, the head of Yohanan the Dipper."

₉The king was distressed, but because of his oath and his dinner guests he ordered that it be given her, ₁₀and sent word and had Yohanan beheaded in prison. ₁₁The head was brought in and given to the girl, and she took it to her mother.

₁₂Yohanan's students came and took the body away and buried it. Then they left and reported it to Yeshua.

Bread for five thousand on the grass

₁₃When Yeshua heard what had happened, he withdrew quietly from there by boat to a desolate place. But when the crowds found out, they followed him on foot from the villages. ₁₄When he came ashore, he saw a great crowd and pitied them and healed the sick among them.

₁₅When it was evening, his students came to him and said, "This is a deserted place and it is already late. Send the crowds away so they can return to the villages and buy food."

₁₆But Yeshua said to them,

---

121 Tetrarch. Greek for "ruler." Also referred to as "king."

They need not go away.

You give them something to eat.

17"We have only two loaves of bread and two fish," they answered.

18But he said,

Bring them here to me.

19Then he ordered the crowd to sit down on the grass, and took the five loaves and two fishes, gazed into the sky, and gave a blessing, broke the bread and gave the loaves to his students. The students gave them to the crowds. 20And everyone ate and was satisfied. They picked up the broken pieces of the leftovers in twelve baskets full. 21And those who ate were about five thousand men apart from the women and children.

Yeshua walking on the sea at daybreak

22Then he made the students board the ship, and go on ahead of him to the other side while he dispersed the multitude. 23And when the crowds had vanished, he went up on the mountain, by himself, and prayed. When evening came, he was alone there.

24By this time the ship was a great distance from the land and battered by the waves, for the wind was against them. 25In the fourth watch of the night, near dawn, he came toward them, walking on the sea. 26When the students saw him walking on the sea, they were terrified. "It's a phantom!" they said, and cried out in fear.

27Yeshua quickly spoke to them,

Take heart, it is I. Do not be afraid.

28"Sir, if it is you, command me to come to you on the waters," answered Kefa.

29And he said,

Come.

Kefa climbed down from the boat and walked on the waters and he went toward Yeshua. 30But when he saw the storm he was frightened, and began to sink, and cried out, "Lord, save me!"

31At once Yeshua stretched out his hand, caught him, and said,

You of poor faith, why did you doubt?

32As they climbed into the ship, the wind ceased. 33Those who were on the ship worshiped him and said, "Truly you are the son of God."

Touching the sick in Gennesaret

34Then they crossed over and went to the land of Gennesaret. 35The men in that area recognized him and sent word all over the surrounding country and brought him all who were afflicted with sicknesses, ₃₆and they begged him just to let them touch the fringe of his cloak. And those who touched it were cured.

CHAPTER 15

You hypocrites!

At this time, Prushim and scholars came to Yeshua from Yerushalayim, saying, ₂"Why do your students break the tradition of the elders? They don't wash their hands before eating bread."

₃But he answered them,

Why do you also break the commandment of God
because of our tradition? ₄God said,
Honor your father and your mother,[122]
and whoever curses his mother or father must die.
₅You claim whoever tells their mother or father,
"Whatever help you might have had from me
is a gift to God," need not honor the father.
₆So you have made empty the word of God,
because of our tradition. ₇You hypocrites!
Our Yeshayah was right when he prophesied
about you, saying,
₈This people honors me with their lips,
    but their heart is remote from me.
₉They worship me in a hollow way.
    Their teachings are the rules of men.

Parable of food and defilement

₁₀Then calling the crowd together, Yeshua said to them,

Hear and understand,
    ₁₁Not what goes into the mouth defiles
    but what comes out of the mouth.

₁₂Thereupon his students came near him. "Do you know that the Prushim were offended when they heard your words?" they asked.

₁₃He answered, saying,

Every plant that my heavenly father has not planted
will be uprooted.

---

[122] Exod. 20.12.

14 Leave them. They are blind guides of the blind.

When the blind lead the blind,

they both fall into a pit.

15 But Kefa said to him, "Explain this parable to us."

And he said,

16 Kefa, don't you understand yet? Don't you know

17 that everything that goes into the mouth

goes into the stomach and into the sewer?

18 But what comes out of the mouth comes from the heart,

and that makes a person unclean,

19 for from the heart come vile thoughts, murders, adulteries,

fornications, thefts, false testimonies, and blasphemies.

20 These are what make a person unclean.

But eating with unwashed hands does not defile.

Not only the lost sheep of Yisrael

21 Then Yeshua left that place and withdrew to the districts of Tzor[123] and Tzidon.[124] 22 And look, a Canaanite woman from that region came out crying and saying, "Pity me, lord, son of David. My daughter is tormented by a demon."

23 But he didn't say a word to her.

His students came near, and urged him, saying, "Send her away, for she is following us, and keeps crying out."

24 He answered her,

I was sent here solely for the lost sheep

of the house of Yisrael.

25 But she came and bowed before him, saying, "Lord, help me."

26 He answered her,

It is not good to take the children's bread

and throw it to the dogs.

27 But she said,

Yes, sir, but even dogs eat the crumbs

fallen from the tables of their masters.

28 Then he responded, saying to her,

Woman, great is your faith.

Let your wish be carried out.

And her daughter in that hour was healed.

---

123 Tyre.
124 Sidon.

To his mountain came the lame

29Then Yeshua left that place and came to the shores of the Sea of the Galil. He went up the mountain 30and sat there. Great crowds of people came to him, bringing with them the lame, blind, crippled, deaf, and dumb, and many others, and they flung themselves at his feet. And he healed them. 31The crowd was amazed to see mutes talking, cripples healthy, the lame walking around, and the blind seeing.

And they glorified the God of Yisrael.

Bread for four thousand on the shore

32Yeshua summoned his students and told them,

> I pity the crowd. They have stayed with me
> for three days and have nothing to eat.
> I don't wish to send them away hungry
> for fear they will collapse on their way.

33His students asked him, "Here in the desert, where can we find enough loaves to feed such a crowd?"
34He asked them,

> How many loaves of bread do you have?

"Seven loaves and a few fish," they said.
35He told the crowd to sit down on the ground. 36He took the seven loaves and the fish, gave thanks, and he broke them and gave them to his students, and the students to the crowds. 37And everyone ate and was satisfied. And the broken pieces of the leftovers were seven baskets full. 38And those who ate were four thousand men, apart from the women and children.

39Then he sent the people away and got into his ship and came to the region of Magadan.

CHAPTER 16

A sign from the sky

Then Prushim and Tzadokim came to him, and tested him, asking him to show them a sign in the sky.
2He told them,

> Evening comes and you say it will be good weather,
> for the sky is fire red.

3Dawn comes and today will be stormy weather,
for the sky is fire red and very dark.
Do you know how to judge the face of the sky
and not make out the signs of the times?
4A corrupt and adulterous generation asks for a sign
but no sign will be given to it
except for the sign of Yonah the prophet.
Then he left them and went away.

Understanding bread

5When the students crossed to the other side they forgot to take the bread.
Yeshua said to them,

6Be alert and beware of the yeast of the Prushim
and Tzadokim.

7But they were talking it over among themselves, saying, "We didn't bring
the bread."

8Yeshua knew their thoughts. He asked them,

Why are you talking it over among yourselves?
You of poor faith, talking about having no bread.
9Don't you see, don't you remember the five loaves
for the five thousand and all the full baskets
you took away? 10Or the seven loaves for the four thousand
and how many baskets you took away?
11Couldn't you see that I wasn't talking about bread?
But guard against the yeast of the Prushim and Tzadokim.

12Then they understood. He did not say to guard against the yeast of the
bread but against the teachings of the Prushim and the Tzadokim.

Keys of the kingdom

13When Yeshua came into the region of Caesarea Filippi,[125] he questioned
his students,

Who do the people say is the earthly son?

14They said to him, "Some say Yohanan the Dipper, some Eliyah,[126] and
others say Yirmiyah[127] or one of the prophets."

---

[125] Caesarea Philippi.
[126] Elijah.
[127] Jeremiah from the Greek Ἰερεμίας (Ieremias), from the Hebrew יִרְמְיָה (yirmiyah).

He said to them.

15But you, who do you say I am?

16Kefa, called Shimon Kefa, "You are the mashiah, the anointed, the son of the living God."

17Yeshua answered him, saying,

> You are blessed, Shimon bar Yonah.[128]
>
> It was not the flesh and blood that revealed to you this vision,
>
> but my father who is in the skies.
>
> 18And I tell you that you are Kefa the stone
>
> and upon this stone I will build my church,[129]
>
> and the gates of Gei Hinnom will not overpower it.
>
> 19I will give you the keys of the kingdom of the skies,
>
> and whatever you close upon the earth
>
> will be closed in the heavens,
>
> and whatever you open on the earth
>
> will be open in the heavens.

20Then he warned his students not to tell anyone that he was the mashiah.

I will die and be arisen

21From that time on Yeshua began to explain to his students that he must go to Yerushalayim, and to suffer much from the elders and the high priests and the scholars, and be killed and on the third day after his death be raised.

22But Kefa took him aside, and began to rebuke him, saying, "God forbid it! Sir, this must never happen!"

23Yeshua turned to Kefa and said,

> Go behind me, Satan!
>
> To me you are an obstacle,
>
> for you are thinking not the thoughts of God
>
> but of earthly beings.

---

[128] Barjonah, son of Jonah from the Greek Βαριωνᾶ (Bariona), from the Hebrew בַּר יוֹנָה (bar yonah). Some have suggested a secondary derivation from the Hebrew בַּר יוֹחָנָן (bar yohanan).

[129] The Greek words ἐκκλησία (ekklesia) and συναγωγή (synagogi) mean an "assembly," "gathering," or "congregation," and both words can refer to "synagogue." However, ekklesia (except in the Septuagint Greek version of the Hebrew Bible) is normally translated as "church" and is the common Greek word designating the later Christian church, while synagogos is the common word for "synagogue." Here, in Yeshua's prophecy, the intentional futurity of "I will build my church" is contrasted with the old Jewish tradition represented by Gei Hinnom, the Hebrew word for "hell." Yeshua's dramatic message is that he will build on a rock the *new church* that will overcome the *old synagogue*, and that *Christian heaven* will overcome *Jewish hell*. In his lifetime there was no Christian church, and Yeshua preached in the synagogues. For this observant Jew to say that he would "build a church" is an anachronism, revealing not his voice but that of churchmen many decades later when a Christian church as a building and institution did exist. The superimposition of later terminology, theology, and history on the figures of Yeshua and his followers remains the essential dilemma of the New Covenant.

Losing life to find the soul

24 Then Yeshua said to his students,
    If anyone wishes to be my follower,
    deny yourself and take up the cross
    and follow me.

25 If anyone wishes to save the soul
    you will lose it.

    But if you lose your soul
    because of me,
    you will find it.

26 What good will it do you
    to gain the whole world
    but you forfeit your soul?

    And what will you give
    in exchange for your soul?

27 The earthly son will come,
    with his angels in the glory of his father,
    and reward you by your deeds.

28 Some of you who stand here
    will not even taste death

    until you see the earthly son
    coming in his kingdom.

CHAPTER 17

Transfigured, his face like the sun

After six days, Yeshua took Kefa and Yaakov and Yohanan his brother, and led them up a high mountain and they were alone. 2 And he was transfigured before them and his face shone like the sun, 3 and his clothing became white as light. And look, Mosheh and Eliyah were talking with him.

₄Kefa said to Yeshua, "Lord, it is good for us to be here. If you wish I will set up three shelters,[130] one for you and one for Mosheh and one for Eliyah."

₅While he was speaking, look, a shining cloud covered them in shadow and a voice from the cloud was speaking,

> This is my son
> whom I love,
> in whom I am happy.
> Listen to him.

₆When his students heard this, they fell on their faces and were greatly afraid. ₇But Yeshua came and touched them and said,

> Arise and do not be afraid.

₈When they raised their eyes, they saw no one but Yeshua alone.

₉And as they were coming down the mountain, Yeshua instructed them, saying,

> Speak to no one of the vision
> until the earthly son is raised from the dead.

Who is coming first?

₁₀Thereupon his students asked him, "Why do the scholars say Eliyah must come first?"

He replied,

> ₁₁Eliyah is coming and will set all things right.
> ₁₂But I tell you Eliyah has already come
> and they didn't know him and did with him as they cared to.
> So also the earthly son is to suffer at their hands.

₁₃Then his students understood that he was talking about Yohanan the Dipper.

A boy who falls into fire and water

₁₄As they neared the crowd, a man came who kneeled before him and said, ₁₅"Sir, take pity on my son. He is epileptic and suffers deeply. He often falls into the fire and falls into the water. ₁₆I took him to your students and they were not able to heal him."

₁₇Yeshua answered, saying,

> You faithless and depraved generation!
> How much longer must I be with you?

---

[130] Sukkah or Tabernacle, for the Festival of the Tabernacles or Booths. See Mark 9.5, note 89.

How much longer must I endure you?

Bring him to me here.

18 Yeshua scolded him and the demon went out of him, and from that hour on the child was cured.

19 His students came to Yeshua privately, and asked, "Why could we not cast it out?"

20 He said to them,

You failed because of your poor faith.

I say to you, even if your faith is no bigger

than a mustard seed,

when you say to the mountain to move

it will be moved

and nothing will be impossible for you.[131]

The earthly son will die and be arisen

22 And when they came back together in the Galil, Yeshua said to them,

The earthly son is about to be handed over

to human hands

and they will kill him

23 and on the third day he will be raised.

And they felt bitter sorrow.

A coin for the Temple

24 When they all reached Kfar Nahum, those who collect the half-shekel Temple tax came up to them.[132] "Doesn't your rabbi pay the Temple tax?" they asked Kefa.

"Yes," he answered.

25 And Kefa went into the house. Yeshua anticipated his student's thoughts, and told him,

Kefa, what are you thinking?

From whom do the kings of the earth collect duty

and taxes?

From their children or from strangers?"

26 "From strangers," Kefa said.

---

131 The earliest manuscripts do not contain line 21 found in later ancient manuscripts: "But this kind does not come out except by prayer and fasting."

132 Half-shekel. Greek has *didrachma*, a two-drachma coin. The half-shekel tax was paid each March for the upkeep of the Temple.

₂₇Yeshua responded,

> Then the children are free of them.
> But so as not to offend them, go to the sea and cast
> a fishhook into the waters
> and take the first fish coming up, open its mouth.
> You'll find a coin. Take it,
> and give it to them, for me and you.¹³³

 **CHAPTER 18**

Becoming like children

In that hour the students came to Yeshua and asked, "Who is the greatest in the kingdom of the skies?"

₂He called a little child to him and had her stand among them and told them,

> ₃I tell you, unless you change and become like children,
> you will never enter the kingdom of the skies.
> ₄But whoever becomes little like this child
> will be greatest in the kingdom of the skies,
> ₅and whoever in my name accepts a child
> like this one also accepts me,
> ₆but whoever leads one of these children astray
> who believes in me, for him it would be better
> to hang a donkey's millstone around his neck
> and be drowned in the depth of the sea.

Better to enter life one-eyed

> ₇A plague on the world because of troubles that are caused.
> These troubles must occur
> but a plague on one through whom these troubles come.
>
> ₈And if your hand or foot causes you to stumble,
> cut it off and throw it away from you.
> It is better for you to enter life maimed or lame

---

¹³³ See note 121 on coins, Mark 12.13–17.

than to have two hands or two feet
and be hurled into eternal fire.

9 And if your eye causes you to stumble,
rip it out and throw it away.
It is better for you to enter life one-eyed
than to have two eyes
and be hurled into the Gei Hinnom of fire.

Parable of a little sheep lost

10 Take care. Do not despise one of these little ones.
I tell you that the angels in the air constantly gaze
at the face of my father
who is in the heavens.[134]
12 What seems right? If a person has a hundred sheep
and one of them wanders away,
won't she leave the ninety-nine on the mountain
and go and look for the one who has wandered off?
13 And if she happens to find him,
I tell you she is happier than over the ninety-nine
who never went astray.
14 So it is the wish of your father in the heavens
that none of these little ones be lost.

A brother hurting you

15 If your brother hurts you, go alone and show him
your hurt. If you are heard, you have won the brother.
16 But if you are unheard take one or two witnesses
so two or three may confirm each word from your mouth.
17 But if you are still unheard, take it to the synagogue
and if he will not even hear the synagogue
let that one be to you like a gentile or a tax collector.

On earth and in heaven

18 I tell you, whatever you close on earth
will be closed in heaven

---

134 Other ancient authorities add verse 11: "For the earthly son came to save the lost."

and whatever you free on earth
will be free in heaven.
19 Again I say, if two agree about everything on earth they ask for,
it will be done for them by my father of the skies.
20 Where two or three come together in my name,
there I am among them.

How many forgivenesses?
21 Then Kefa came to him and said, "Sir, how many times shall I forgive my
brother? As many as seven times?"
22 Yeshua said to him,
I do not say to you as many as seven
but as many as seventy times seven.[135]

Parable of a king and an unforgiving slave
23 So the kingdom of the skies is like a king
who wished to settle accounts with his slaves.
24 As he was counting, a debtor of ten thousand talents
was brought in 25 who could not pay,
and his master ordered him to be sold,
and also his wife, children, and all they possessed
in order that his owner be repayed.
26 Then the slave fell on his knees before him
and said to him, "Delay your anger with me
and I will pay you back everything."
27 The lord had compassion for his slave
and he pardoned him and forgave the debt.
28 The slave went out and met a fellow slave,
who owed him one hundred denarii,
and he seized him and choked him.
"Pay me back what you owe me," he said.
29 His fellow slave fell to the ground and begged him,
"Delay your anger, and I will repay you,"
30 but the freed slave was unwilling
and he left and threw him into prison
until his fellow slave could pay the debt.
31 When the other slaves saw this they grieved immensely
and went and reported these things to their master.

---

[135] Others render the number seventy-seven.

32The master called the wicked slave to him
and said, "I forgave you because you begged me.
33Should you not have pity on your fellow slave
as I had compassion for you?"
34 And his master was angry and handed him
    over to the torturers in the prison
until he payed back everything he owed.
35 In this way my father in the skies will handle
each one of you unless you forgive
your brother or sister from your heart.

 # CHAPTER 19

What God joined together let no one separate

Now it happened that when Yeshua finished speaking these words, he left
the Galil and came into the regions of Yehuda beyond the Yarden, 2and huge
crowds followed him and there he healed them.

3Then Pharisees came near him and to trap him they asked, "Is it lawful for
a man to divorce his wife for any reason?"

4He answered,

Have you not read in Genesis that "in the beginning"
the creator "made them male and female"?[136]
5And it is said, "because of this a man will leave his father
    and his mother,
and he will be joined to his wife
and the two will be one flesh."[137]
6So they are no longer two but one flesh
and what God joined together let no one divide.

7Then they asked him, "Why did Mosheh decree that one might give a cer-
tificate of divorce and divorce her?"

He replied to them,

8It is solely because of your hard hearts
that Mosheh let you divorce your wives.
Yet it was not so from the beginning.

---

136 Gen. 1.27 and 5.2.
137 Gen. 2.24.

9 I say that he who divorces his wife,
except in the instance of harlotry,
and marries another is an adulterer.

Eunuchs and the gift of celibacy

10 His students asked him,
If this is so between husband and wife,
is it not better not to marry?
11 Yeshua replied,
Not everyone can understand this word.
Only those to whom it is given.[138]
12 There are eunuchs who from their mother's womb
were born to be sterile.
And there are eunuchs who were made into eunuchs by others,
and there are eunuchs who made eunuchs of themselves
for the sake of the kingdom of the skies.
Let anyone who can accept, accept.

Let the little children come to me

13 Then children were brought to him that he might lay his hands on them
and pray for them. But his students scolded those who brought them in.
14 Yeshua said,
Let the children be and do not stop them
from coming to me,
for of such is the kingdom of the skies.
15 And he laid his hands on them, and went on his way.

Dilemmas of a young rich man

16 And look, someone came to him and said,
Rabbi, what good deed must I do to have eternal life?
17 He replied,
Why do you ask me about the good?
There is only one who is good. But if you wish
to enter into life,
keep the commandments.
And he said, "Which ones?"
18 And Yeshua said,
You must not murder or commit adultery or steal

---

[138] Probably the gift of celibacy, which being a eunuch ensures.

or bear false witness. ₁₉You must honor your father
>and mother,
and love your neighbor as yourself.
₂₀The young man replied,
>All these commandments I have observed.
>What am I missing?
₂₁Yeshua said to him,
>If you wish to be perfect, go and sell
>what belongs to you
>and give it to the poor,
>and you will have a treasure in heaven.
>Then come and follow me.
₂₂The young man was downcast when he heard these words, and went away grieving since he had many possessions.

Heaven through the eye of a needle

₂₃And Yeshua said to his students, ₂₄"Amen, I say to you,"
>It will be hard for a rich man
>to enter the kingdom of the skies.
>I say it is easier for a camel to go through the eye of a needle
>than for a rich man to enter the kingdom of God.[139]
₂₅When the students heard this, they were greatly amazed and asked, "Who then can be saved?"
₂₆Yeshua looked at them and said,
>For people this is impossible
>but for God all things are possible.

Life everlasting

₂₇Kefa answered him, saying, "Look, we have given up everything and followed you. What will there be for us?"
₂₈He responded to them, "Amen, I say to you,"
>In the next life when the earthly son is seated on his throne
>>of glory,
>you who have followed me
>will also be seated on the twelve thrones
>and judge the twelve tribes of Yisrael.
₂₉And anyone who has given up houses or brothers
>or sisters or father or mother

---

[139] See note 102 on Mark 10.25.

or children or fields in honor of my name,
will have them back a hundred times over
and inherit life everlasting.

30 Many who are first will be last, and the last will be first.

 CHAPTER 20

Parable of the laborers in the vineyard
The kingdom of the skies is like a man,
the master of a house, who went out at daybreak
to hire laborers for his vineyard.
2 After agreeing on a silver denarius a day,
he sent the laborers into the vineyard.
3 About the third hour after dawn he went out
and saw others standing idle in the marketplace,
4 and said to them, "Go into the vineyard
and I will give you what is right."
5 And they went to the vines.
Again about the sixth and the ninth hour
he went out and did the same.
6 And about the eleventh hour after dawn
he saw others standing idle
and he asked them, "Why have you been standing
    here all day, idle?"
7 They told him, "Because no one hired us."
He said to them, "Go into the vineyard."
8 When evening came the owner of the vineyard
    told his foreman,
"Call the laborers and give them their wages,
beginning with the last who came
and then going on to the first."
9 And those who had come at the eleventh hour
each took away a silver coin.

10 And those who had come first thought their pay
    would be greater

but each took away a silver coin.

11When they took it they grumbled against the master,

12saying, "The last ones worked an hour

and you made them equal to us

who bore the weight of the day and the heat."

13But he told them, "Friend, I am not cheating you.

Didn't you agree with me on one silver coin?

14Take what is yours and go.

But I wish to give to the last as I gave to you.

15Can't I do what I want with what is mine

or is your eye envious that I am kind?"

16So the last will be first and the first will be last.

I will die and be arisen

17Then as Yeshua went up to Yerushalayim, he took the twelve with him aside, and on the road said to them,

18Look, we are going up to Yerushalayim

and the earthly son will be given into the hands

of the high priests and scholars

and they will condemn him to death.

19And they will give him into the hands of the gentiles [140]

to mock and flog and crucify,

and on the third day he will be raised.

Seats for my sons

20Then the mother of the sons of Zavdai [141] came to him, along with her sons, and bowed before him. She had a request.

21He said to her,

What do you want?

She said to him, "Tell me that my two sons will sit on your right hand and on your left in your kingdom."

22And Yeshua answered,

You don't know what you are asking for.

Can you drink the cup I'm about to drink?

The brothers said to him, "Yes, we can."

23He told them,

---

140 Here "gentiles" would be the Roman soldiers.

141 Yeshua's students Yaakov and Yohanan (James and John).

You will drink from my cup,
yet to be seated on my right and my left is not for me
    to grant.
These places belong to those who have been chosen
    by my father.

24Hearing this, the other ten were indignant about the two brothers.

25But Yeshua called them together and said,

You know that the rulers of the gentiles
lord it over their people
and the high officials tyrannize them.
26It will not be so for you,
for whoever among you wishes to be great
will be your servant,
27and whoever among you wishes to be first
will be your slave.
28So the earthly son did not come to be served
but to serve
and to give his own life for the redemption
of the many.

Touching blind eyes in Yeriho

29As they were leaving Yeriho, a great crowd followed him. 30And look, two blind men were sitting beside the road. When they heard that Yeshua was passing by they cried out, saying, "Have pity on us, lord, son of David."

31The crowd scolded them and told them to keep quiet, but again they cried out, saying, "Have pity on us, lord, son of David."

32Yeshua stopped and called to them, saying,

What do you want me to do for you?

They said, 33"Lord, let our eyes be opened."

Yeshua pitied them and touched their eyes and at once they saw and followed him.

C H A P T E R   2 1

Entering Yerushalayim on a colt

Then as they came near Yerushalayim and reached Beit Pagey[142] at the Mountain of Olives, Yeshua sent two students ahead, 2 saying to them,

> Go on into the village ahead of you
> and soon you will find a donkey tethered
> and her foal beside her.
> 3Untie them and bring them to me.
> And if anyone should say anything to you,
> say that their master needs them.
> And he will send them at once.

4This was done to fulfill the word spoken
by our prophets Zeharyah[143] and Yeshayah, saying,

> 5Tell the daughter of Zion,
> Look, your king is coming to you,
>   modest and riding on a donkey,
>   and with a colt, the son of the donkey.[144]

6His students went and did as Yeshua instructed them. 7They brought the donkey and the colt and placed their cloaks upon them, and he sat on them. 8 And the enormous crowd spread their cloaks on the road. Others cut branches from the trees and spread them on the road. 9 And the crowds who went ahead and those who followed were shouting,

> Hosanna to the son of David!
> Blessed is he who comes in the name of the lord!
> Hosanna in the highest realm!

10When he entered Yerushalayim, the whole city trembled, saying, "Who is this?"

11 And the crowds were saying, "This is the prophet Yeshua of Natzeret in the Galil."

---

[142] Bethphage from the Greek Βηθφαγή (Bethfage), from the Hebrew בֵּית פַּגֵּא (beit pagey).
[143] Zechariah or Zacharias from the Greek Ζαχαρίας (Zaharias), from the Hebrew זְכַרְיָה (zeharyah).
[144] Isa. 62.11; Zech. 9.9.

Driving the traders and dove sellers from the Temple

12Then Yeshua entered the Temple and drove out all who bought and sold in the Temple, and he overturned the tables of the coin changers and the chairs of those who sold doves. 13He said to them,

> As it is written in Yeshayah and Yirmiyah,[145]
> "My house will be called a house of prayer,"
> but you have made it a den of robbers.

Healing in the Temple and consternation of priests

14And the blind and the lame came to him in the Temple, and he healed them.

15But when the high priests and the scholars saw the wonders[146] he performed and the children crying out in the Temple, "Hosanna to the son of David," they were indignant, 16and said to him, "Do you hear what they are saying?"

And Yeshua answered,

> Yes. Have you never read in the Psalms:
> "From the mouths of children and infants
> you have composed praise for yourself"?[147]

17And he left them and went out of the city to Beit Aniyah[148] where he spent the night.

Cursing and drying up the fig tree

18Early in the morning he came back to the city, and he was hungry. 19And seeing a single fig tree by the road, he went up to it and found nothing on it but leaves, and said to it,

> Let you bear no fruit forevermore.

And at once the fig tree dried up.[149]

20His students seeing it were astonished, and asked, "How did the fig tree suddenly dry up?"

21Yeshua answered them, saying,

> Amen I say to you.
> If you have faith and do not doubt,

---

[145] Isa. 56.7; Jer. 7.11.

[146] From the Greek τὰ θαυμάσια (ta thaumasia), meaning "wonders" or "wonderous things." "Wonder" from the Greek θαυμαστός (thaumastos) and "power" from the Greek δύναμις (dynamis) are the words in the gospels for "miracle."

[147] Ps. 8.2 (Septuagint).

[148] Bethany from the Greek Βηθανία (Bethania), from the Hebrew בֵּית אָנִיָּה (beit aniyah).

[149] Here the incident in Mark is developed to say that, had the fruit tree had faith, its fruit would not have dried up, but with faith one can move mountains. For more on the metaphor, see note 117 on the withering of the fig tree, Mark 11.20–21.

not only what happened to the fig tree
will be in your domain,
but you can say to the mountain,
"Rise up and hurl yourself into the sea,"
and it will be done.
₂₂ All things you ask for in prayer with faith
you will receive.

By what authority?

₂₃Now when he had gone into the Temple and was teaching there, the high priests and the elders of the people came to him, saying, "By what authority do you do these things?"

₂₄And Yeshua replied to them,

I too will ask you one thing, and if you tell me
I will tell you by what authority I do these things.
Where did Yohanan's baptism come from?
Was it from heaven or from people on earth?

₂₅They discussed it among themselves, and said, "If we say 'from heaven,' he will tell us, 'Then why did you not believe him?' ₂₆But if we tell him 'from people on earth,' we will fear the crowds, for everyone holds Yohanan to be a prophet."

₂₇So they told Yeshua, "We do not know."

He said to them,

Then neither will I tell you by what authority
I am doing these things.

Parable of the two sons

₂₈What do you think?
A man had two children.
To the first he said, "Son, go out today and work in the
vineyard."
₂₉But the son said, "I don't want to."
Later, he changed his mind and went.
₃₀To the second he asked the same.
He said, "I will go, sir," but didn't go.
₃₁Which of the two did the father's will?
They said, "The first."
Yeshua responded, telling them, "Amen, I tell you,"
The tax collectors and the prostitutes
will go before you into the kingdom of God.

32Yohanan came to you on the path of justice
and you did not believe him,
but the tax collectors and the prostitutes
believed in him,
and even after you saw, you did not later repent
and believe him.

Parable of the wicked tenants
33Listen to another parable.
There was a man who was a landowner
who planted a vineyard and put a fence around it,
and dug a wine press in it,
and built a tower and leased it all to farmers
and left the country.

34 And when the time of the vintage was near,
he sent his slaves to the farmers to take the vintage.
35But the farmers seized the slaves
and one they beat, one they killed, one they stoned.
36 Again he sent slaves, more than the first group,
and they dealt with them the same.

37 After this he sent his son, saying,
"They will respect my son."
38 But once the farmers saw his son,
they said among themselves, "He is the heir.
Come, let us kill him and take his inheritance."
39 And they seized him, threw him out of the vineyard,
and they killed him.

40Now, when the lord of the vineyard came,
what will he do to those farmers?
41They said to him, "Those wicked ones he will destroy and he will lease the
vineyard to other farmers who will give him his share of the grape at vintage
time."
And Yeshua replied,
42Have you never read in the Psalms:
"The stone that the builders rejected,
it has become the cornerstone.

It was made by the lord
>and is a wonder to our eyes"?[150]

43For this reason I tell you,
the kingdom of God will be taken away from you
and given to a people producing its harvest.
[44And the one falling on the stone will be broken
and it will crush anyone on whom it falls.][151]

45And when the high priests and the Prushim heard his parables, they knew that he spoke of them. They were looking for a way to seize him, but they feared the crowds, since they held him to be a prophet.

◉ CHAPTER 22

Parable of the wedding guest without a wedding garment
Once more Yeshua spoke to them in parables, saying,
2The kingdom of the skies is like a king
who held a wedding banquet for his son.
3And he sent out his slaves to call on those invited
>to the feast
but they did not wish to come.
4He sent out more slaves, telling the guests,
"Look, I have prepared a dinner. The oxen and fatted calves
>are slaughtered,
and all is ready. Come to the wedding."
5But they were unconcerned and went their way,
one going to lands, one to business,
6while others seized the slaves and outraged them
and killed them.

7So the king was angry and sent out his armies
and destroyed those murderers and burned their city.
8He said to his slaves, "The wedding feast is ready,
but our invited guests were unworthy.
9So go out to the open crossroads and invite everyone
>to the wedding."

---

150 Ps. 118.22–23.
151 Other early texts lack verse 44.

10 And those slaves went out to the roads
and gathered everyone they found, good and bad,
and filled the wedding hall with guests.

11 But when the king went in to observe them at dinner,
he saw a man not wearing a wedding garment.
12 He said to him, "Friend, how did you come in
without a wedding garment?"
The man was speechless.
13 Then the king said to his servants,
"Bind his hands and legs and cast him into the outer darkness
where there will be weeping and gnashing of teeth."
14 Many are called, few are chosen.

Paying coins to Caesar

15 Then the Prushim went and conferred on how to trap Yeshua through his words. 16 They sent their students, along with supporters of Herod, saying, "Rabbi, we know that you are truthful and you teach the way of God in the truth and show no favor to anyone, for you do not judge people by their face. 17 So tell us what seems right. Is it right to pay taxes to Caesar, or not?"

18 But aware of their craftiness, Yeshua said,

Why do you test me, hypocrites?
19 Show me the tax coin.

And they brought him a denarius.
20 And he said to them,

Whose image is this and whose name?
21 "Caesar's," they said to him.

He told them,

Then give the things of Caesar to Caesar
and the things of God to God.[152]

22 When they heard this, they were left in wonder, and they turned and went away.

A wife in heaven

23 On that same day the Tzadokim, who say there is no resurrection, came to him and questioned him, saying, 24 "Rabbi, Mosheh told us that if someone dies without children, his brother must marry the widow and raise offspring for his

---

[152] This episode presents the prevailing view in the gospels to cooperate with Roman rule. For more information, see note 121 on Mark 12.14.

brother. ₂₅Now there were seven brothers among us. The first one married, and not having children he left his wife to his brother. ₂₆The second did the same, also the third and all the way until all seven had married her. ₂₇Last of all, the woman died. ₂₈So in the resurrection, whose wife will she be? For they all had her as wife."

₂₉Yeshua responded,

> You are wrong not to know the Torah[153] or the power of God.
> ₃₀In the resurrection they do not marry or given in marriage
> but are like angels in the air.
> ₃₁As to the resurrection of the dead,
> haven't you read God's word in Exodus speaking to you:
> ₃₂"I am the God of Avraham and the God of Yitzhak
>   and the God of Yaakov"?
> God is not God of the dead but of the living.

₃₃And hearing this, the crowds were struck with wonder by his teaching.

Loving God and neighbors

₃₄When the Prushim learned how he had silenced the Tzadokim, they assembled together, ₃₅and one of them, an expert in the law, questioned him in order to test him. ₃₆"Rabbi, which is the great commandment in the Torah?"

₃₇And Yeshua said to them,

> "You shall love the lord your God with all your heart
> and with all your soul and with all your mind."
> ₃₈This is the great and first commandment.
> ₃₉And the second is like it:
> "Love your neighbor like yourself." ₄₀All the law
> and the prophets hang on these two commandments.

Son and lord of David

₄₁When the Prushim were gathered together, Yeshua questioned them, saying,

> ₄₂What do you think is right concerning the mashiah?
> Whose son is he?

"The son of David," they told him.

He said,

> ₄₃How then did David, moved by the spirit,
> call him lord? For it says in the Psalms,
>   ₄₄"The lord says to my lord,

---

[153] Torah is specifically the five books of Moses but is normally a synecdoche for the Hebrew Bible.

'Sit at my right hand until I make your enemies
a footstool under your feet.'"[154]

45 If then David calls him lord, how can he be his son?

46 And no one could say a word in reply, and from that day on no one dared
to ask him any more questions.

CHAPTER 23

They speak and do nothing

Then Yeshua spoke to the crowds and to his students, 2saying,
On the seat of Mosheh[155] sit the scholars and Prushim.[156]
3Do and observe all that they tell you,

---

[154] Ps. 110.1.

[155] Moses represents the covenant of Sinai that is transcended by the New Covenant. The Pharisees sit
on Moses' seat, identifying these wicked scholars with the Jewish Bible and its old law and commandments now superceded by Matthew's sermons and good news, although elsewhere the Torah is
cited as the authenticating source of Yeshua as the promised messiah, who is dignified by his Davidic
sonship as in Matthew 1.1. See note 2 on Matthew 1.1 and Raymond E. Brown's analysis of "the
story of Jesus as a new creation, even greater than the old."

[156] Matthew 23 "is a litany of angry fulminations against (some of) the Pharisees" (*The New Oxford Annotated Bible*, 417). And literarily it is a compendium of great poetic curses. It represents the views of
an already competitive early Christian polemic against the Pharisees, though we have no idea when
these denunciations may have been composed or added to a changing text, constantly recopied and
freely redacted. Some contemporary scholars conjecture that Yeshua was a Pharisee rabbi, which is
why, in the early assembling of a New Covenant text, it became necessary to distance Yeshua furi-
ously from his Jewish source, a view elaborated by Burton Mack and Hyam Maccoby among others.
(See Afterword for more on Pharisees.) If Yeshua was not a Pharisee, he was at the very least closer to
them than to the Essenes, with whom he is often compared, in that the Pharisees took up and emphasized ideas that are essential to New Covenant eschatology: a belief in the messiah and his resurrection and in the immortality of the soul, which had been a dominantly Greek Platonic rather than
a Jewish notion. The Pharisees also represented an oral Jewish tradition that was constantly changing.
Of the some seventeen sects of Jews at the time of Yeshua (as identified by James H. Charlesworth),
the Pharisees as a prominent sect distinguished themselves from the Sadducees, who did not believe
in the immortality of the soul, resurrection, or angels, but who, in contrast to the Pharisees, did support the Hasmonean priest-kings, who represented Hellenization and who during Yeshua's life were
surrogates for Roman rule. The prevailing politics of the gospels is an exoneration of Pilate, depicted
as innocent, and of Rome and the Roman occupation of Israel. Since the Sadducees were the natural
allies of the Hasmonean-Roman power base, in the gospels they do not receive the sustained
polemic reserved for the Pharisees. By contrast, the hated Pharisees, by sharing Yeshua's views, made
their rejection imperative if Christianity were to distinguish itself from its early reality as a Jewish
sect of Christian (messianist) Jews. Yeshua was, like the Pharisees (as opposed to the cooperative Sadducees) troublesome, and probably deemed a revolutionary figure. The Romans saw fit to crucify
him as they did thousands of Jewish opponents in the first century. "Innocent" Pilate had a dominantly bloody role in the massacres.

but do not do as they do. They speak and do nothing.
4They tie up heavy bundles
and lay them on the shoulders of other men,
but will not lift a finger to move them.
5All they do is for show.
They spread their tephillin[157] and lengthen their tassels
6and love the foremost couch at the dinners,
the front seats in the synagogues,
7to be greeted in the market places
and to be called rabbi by the people.

8But you must not be called rabbi,
for you have one teacher and are all students.
9On earth call no one father. You have one father
    in heaven
10and do not call yourselves instructors.
You have one instructor, the mashiah.
11The greatest among you will be your servant.

12Whoever raises himself high will be brought low
and whoever is brought low will be raised high.

A plague on you!

13A plague on you, scholars and Prushim, hypocrites!
You lock people out of the kingdom of the skies.
You do not enter, nor let others go in.[158]
15A plague on you, scholars and Prushim, hypocrites!
You sweep the sea and the dry land
to enroll a single convert,
and make your convert into a child of Gei Hinnom
and twice as much of hell as you.

16A plague on you, blind leaders who say, "If you swear
    by the Temple, it means nothing,
but if you swear by the gold of the Temple, it is binding."

---

[157] Phylacteries.

[158] Verse 14, not found in the most ancient texts, is omitted in the UBS 4th edition used here, but appears in other ancient texts and translations as "A plague on you, scholars and Pharisees, hypocrites! You devour widows' houses and for appearance make long prayers. So you will receive the greater condemnation."

17Fools and blindmen, which is greater,
the gold or the Temple that hallows the gold?
18 And if you swear by the altar, it means nothing,
but if you swear by the gift on the altar, is it binding?
19Blindmen, which is greater, the gift or the altar that hallows
    the gift?

20So one who swears by the altar swears by it and by everything
    on it.
21 And one who swears by the Temple swears by it and by the one
    who dwells in it.
22 And the one who swears by heaven swears by the throne
    of God
and by the one sitting upon it.

23 A plague on you scholars and Prushim, hypocrites,
because you pay a tenth on the mint and the anise and the cumin
and pass over what is grave in the law: justice and mercy
    and faith.
You should have done the last and not passed over the first.
24Blind leaders, you strain the gnat but swallow the camel.

25 A plague on you scholars and Prushim, hypocrites,
because you clean the outside of the cup and the dish
but the inside is filled with greed and dissipation.
26Blind Parush, first scour the inside of the cup
so the outside will also be clean.

27 A plague on you scholars and Prushim, hypocrites,
because you are like graves that are whitewashed,
which on the outside seem beautiful
but the inside are filled with the bones of the dead
    and all uncleanness.
28So you too on the outside seem to the people to be just
but on the inside you are filled with hypocrisy and lawlessness.

29 A plague on you scholars and Prushim, hypocrites,
because you build the tombs of the prophets
and decorate the monuments of the just
30and say, "Had we lived in the days of our fathers,

we would not have been guilty of spilling the blood
   of the prophets."
31So your witnesses against yourselves are the children
of those who murdered the prophets
32and you are the full measure of your fathers.
33Snakes, offspring of vipers, how can you escape
from the judgment of Gei Hinnom?[159]

34Therefore, look, I am sending you prophets and sages and scholars,
some of them you will kill and crucify,
and some of them you will flog in the synagogues
and chase from city to city
35so that all the righteous blood spilled on the earth
will descend upon you,
from the blood of Hevel[160] the just to the blood
of Zeharyah[161] son of Berekyah[162]
whom you murdered between the Temple and the altar.
36Amen, I say to you,
all this will descend on this generation.[163]

Yerushalayim, Yerushalayim

37Yerushalayim, Yerushalayim, who kills the prophets
and stones those who were sent to her,
how many times I wished to gather in your children
as a hen draws her brood under her wings,
but you would not let me.
38Look, your house has been left desolate.
39I say to you that you will not see me until you say,
"Blessed is the one who comes in the name of the lord." [164]

---

[159] In 31–32, Yeshua accuses the Jews, as represented by Moses and the Pharisees, of being the children of the "murderers" of the prophets and tells them that as offspring of vipers they will be sent to hell. So the guilt of the fathers is transferred to the children, always with the implicit charge of killing the messiah. The legend of killing the prophets and the charge of killing the foretold Righteous One is repeated in Acts 7.52–53: "Which of the prophets did your ancestors not persecute? They killed those who foretold the coming of the Righteous One, and now you have become his betrayers and murderers."

[160] Abel from the Greek Ἄβελ (Abel), from the Hebrew הֶבֶל (hevel).

[161] Zechariah.

[162] Barachiah from the Greek Βαραχίας (Barahais), from the Hebrew בֶּרֶכְיָה (berekyah).

[163] The preceding attacks on the scholars and Pharisees are called the seven woes (plagues) or seven denunciations.

[164] Ps. 118.26.

CHAPTER 24

Prophecy of the Temple stones thrown down

And Yeshua left the Temple and was on his way when his students came to him to show him the buildings of the Temple. 2But he said to them,

> Do you not see all this? Amen, I tell you,
> nothing here will escape destruction. No stone
> upon a stone will not be thrown down.

Earthquakes, famines, signs of the end and the coming[165]

3While he was sitting on the Mountain of Olives, his students came to him privately. "Tell us," they said, "when will this happen and what will be the sign of your coming and the end of the world?"

4And Yeshua answered them,

> See to it that no one leads you astray,
> 5because many will come in my name, saying,
> "I am the mashiah,"
> and they will lead many astray.
> 6You will hear of wars and rumors of wars.
> See to it that you are not alarmed.
> For this must happen, but it is not yet the end.
> 7Nation will rise up against nation
> and kingdom against kingdom
> and there will be famines and earthquakes
> in place after place.
> 8All these are the beginning of birthing pains.
>
> 9Then they will hand you over to be tortured
> and they will kill you and you will be hated
> by all the nations because of my name.
> 10And many will fall into sin
> and they will betray and hate one another
> 11and many false prophets will rise and lead many astray.
> 12And through the abundance of lawlessness,
> the love of many will grow cold.
> 13But the one who endures to the end will be saved

---

165 Parousia. "The coming." The parousia is the "coming of the messiah."

14and the good message of the kingdom will be preached
throughout the world as a testimony,
and then the end will come.

15So when you see the abomination of desolation
standing in the holy place,
foretold through Daniel the prophet
(let the reader understand),
16then let those who are in Yehuda flee to the mountains.
17Let no one on the roof come down
to carry away anything from the house.
18Let no one in the field go back to pick up his cloak.

19 A plague on you pregnant women and mothers nursing
babies.
20Pray that your flight not come in the winter or on Shabbat,
21 for then there will be great affliction
unequaled from the beginning of the world till now
and never equaled again.
22And if those days had not been cut short,
there would be no living flesh saved,
but for the sake of the chosen ones those days will be cut short.

23 If anyone tells you, "Look, here is the mashiah,
he's here," don't believe it. 24 False mashiahs will arise
and false prophets and they will give great signs
and portents to lead astray, if possible, even the chosen.
25Look, I have warned you.
26 If they tell you, "Look, he is in the desert,"
don't go out to it, or "Look, he's in the inner rooms,"
don't believe it.
27For as lightning comes out of the east and flashes
as far as the west,
so will be the coming of the earthly son.
28Wherever the corpse may be, the vultures will gather.

Coming of the earthly son
29 And suddenly after the suffering of those days,
the sun will be darkened
and the moon not give its light

and the stars fall out of the skies
   and the powers of the heavens be shaken.[166]
30Then the sign of the earthly son will shine in the sky,
and all the tribes of the earth will beat themselves mourning
and they will see
   the earthly son coming on the clouds
      in the high air
   with power and multiple glory,[167]
31and he will send out his angels with a great ram horn blast
and the chosen will gather from the four winds,
from one peak of the skies to the other peak.

Lesson of the fig tree
32From the fig tree learn the parable,
   When its branch is already tender and issues leaves
   you know that summer is near.
   33So when you too see all these things,
   you know that he is near, at your doors.

34Amen, I say to you,
   This generation will not fade before all these things
      are done.
   35The sky and earth will disappear
   but my words will not pass away.

36As to that day and hour, no one knows.
Not angels in the air [nor the son].[168]
None but the father alone.
37For as the days of Noah came,
so will be the coming of the earthly son.
38For as in those days before the flood,
they were eating and drinking, marrying husbands and wives
until the day Noah went into the ark,
39and they knew nothing until the flood came
and carried everything away,
so will be the coming of the earthly son.

---

[166] Isa. 13.10, 13 and 34.4. The language echoes Isaiah as well as other prophets.
[167] Dan. 7.13–14.
[168] Lacks Greek in some earlier texts.

40Then two men will be in the field:
one is taken away and one is left.
41Two women will be grinding flour at the mill:
one is taken away and one is left.
42So be watchful, since you don't know on what day
your lord is coming.
43But you know that if the master of the house
had known at what hour of the night the thief was coming,
he would have kept awake
and not allowed his house to be broken into.
44Therefore, you also must keep awake,
for in an hour unknown to you comes the earthly son.

Master and slaves

45Who then is the faithful and wise slave
whom the master sets over the household
to give out the food at the proper time?
46Blessed is that slave found working away
when the master barges into the room.
47I tell you, the master will choose only him
to be in charge of all his possessions.
48But if that other wicked slave says in his heart,
"My master is delayed and will not come soon,"
49and he begins to flog his fellow slaves
and he eats and drinks with the drunkards,
50the master will come on a day of surprise
and at an hour when he is not expected,
51and he will cleave him into small pieces
and deliver the parts to the hypocrites,
and there will be weeping and gnashing of teeth.

 CHAPTER 25

Ten virgins and their oil lamps

Then the kingdom of the skies can be compared
to ten young virgins who picked up their lamps
and went out to meet the bridegroom.

₂Five of them were foolish and five were wise.
₃The fools took their lamps but not the oil.
₄The clever ones took flasks of oil with their lamps,
₅but when the bridegroom was delayed,
the virgins all grew drowsy and fell asleep.

₆In the middle of the night there was a shout.
Look, it is the bridegroom. Go out to meet him.
₇Then the women woke and trimmed their lamps,
₈but the fools said to the wise, "Give us some
of your oil, because our lamps are going out."
₉But the wise ones answered, saying, "No,
there would never be enough for us and you.
Better go out to the merchants and buy some for yourselves."

₁₀And while they were gone to buy the oil,
the groom came and the virgins ready with light
went with the groom into the wedding,
and the door was shut. ₁₁Soon the others came crying,
"Lord, lord, open the door to us!"
₁₂But the master answered them in turn,
"I tell you, I don't know you." ₁₃Be watchful,
for you do not know the day or the hour.

Landlord and slaves

₁₄Again, it is like a man going on a journey
who called his slaves together and handed his possessions
over to them.
₁₅And to one he gave five talents, meaning many pounds
of silver coins,
to another slave two sacks of coins,
and to another one talent, each according to his skills,
and he went off at once on his journey.

₁₆The one who received five talents left at once,
put his money to work, and gained another five.
₁₇Likewise the one with two gained another two.
₁₈But the one who received one talent went out
and dug a hole in the ground and hid the money
that his master had given him.

19 After a long time the master of those slaves came back
and settled accounts with them.
20 The slave who got five talents came forward
and showed the other five to him, saying,
"Master, you gave me five talents. See, I have made five
    talents more."
21 His master said, "Well done, good and faithful slave.
You were faithful in small things. I will put you in charge
    of much. Enter into your master's joy."
22 And the slave who got two talents came forward
and showed the other two to him, saying,
"Master, you gave me two talents. See, I have made two
    talents more."
23 His master said, "Well done, good and faithful slave.
You who were faithful over a few things
now I will put you in charge of many things
so you can share the joy of your master."
24 And the slave with one talent came forward, saying,
"Master, I knew you were a harsh man,
harvesting where you didn't sow and gathering
where you didn't scatter seed.
25 And so I was frightened and went away
and hid my one sack of silver coins in the ground.
Here, I return to you what is yours."
26 The master of the mansion answered him,
"Wicked and timid slave, so you knew that I harvest
where I don't sow, that I gather where I don't scatter seed?
27 You should have placed your money with the bankers
and I would have received my part with interest.
28 So take away the sack of coins from him
and give it to him who has ten talents."
29 To all who have will be given, even in excess,
and from those who have nothing,
even what they do have will be taken from them.
30 And cast this worthless slave into outer darkness.
There will be weeping and gnashing of teeth.

Judgment day for the kingdom
31 When the earthly son comes in his glory
and all the angels with him,

then he will sit upon the throne of his glory.
32 And all the nations will be assembled before him
and he will separate them one from the other
as the shepherd separates the sheep from the goats.
33 And he will place the sheep at his right hand
but the goats he will place at his left.

34Then the king will say to those at his right,
"Come, you who are the blessed by my father,
and inherit the kingdom prepared for you
since the creation of the world.
35For I was hungry and you gave me to eat,
I was thirsty and you gave me to drink,
I was a stranger and you took me in,
36 I was naked and you gave me clothing,
I was sick and you took care of me,
I was in prison and you came to me."

37Then the just will answer the king, saying,
"Lord, when did we see you hungry and feed you,
or thirsty and give you to drink?
38 And when did we see you a stranger and take you in,
or naked and give you clothing?
39 And when did we see you sick or in prison
and come to you?"
40 And the king will answer them, saying,
"I tell you that all those things you have done
for one who was least in my family,
you have also done for me."

41 And he will say to those at his left,
"Go from me, cursed, into the everlasting fire
prepared for the devil and his angels.
42For I was hungry and you didn't feed me,
I was thirsty and you gave me nothing to drink,
43I was a stranger and you didn't take me in,
naked and you didn't give me clothing,
sick and in prison and you didn't come to me."

44Then they will also answer him, saying,
"Sir, when did we see you in hunger or thirst
or as a stranger or naked or sick or in prison
and we did not help you?"

45And the king will answer them,
"Amen, I say to you, since you did nothing for one
who was least of my family, you did nothing for me."
46And these will go into everlasting punishment,
but the just will enter life everlasting.

CHAPTER 26

Plotting

And it happened that when Yeshua finished saying all these words, he told his students,

2You know that in two days the Pesach comes,[169]
and the earthly son will be given over to be crucified.

3Then the high priests and the elders gathered in the courtyard of the high priest, whose name was Kayfa,[170] 4and they made plans to capture Yeshua by treachery and kill him. 5But they said, "Not during the feast days, or there might be a noisy riot among the people."

Anointed in the house of the leper

6Now while Yeshua was in Beit Aniyah[171] in the house of Shimon the leper, 7a woman came to him with an alabaster flask of precious myrrh and poured it on his head, anointing him, while he was reclining at the dinner table. 8When his students saw this, they were indignant and said, "Why this waste? 9This ointment could have been sold for a great price and the money given to the poor."

10Yeshua heard them and said,

Why are you troubling this woman
who has done a good thing for me?

---

169 Passover, the Feast of Unleavened Bread.
170 Caiaphas from the Greek Καϊάφας (Kaiafas), from the Hebrew כֵּיפָא (kayfa).
171 Bethany.

11The poor you always have with you,
but me you will not always have.
12When she poured myrrh on my body,
she prepared me for my burial.
13Amen, I say to you, where in all the world
the good news is proclaimed,
what she has done will be told
in memory of this woman.

Yehuda and the silver

14Then one of the twelve, who was called Yehuda of Keriot, went to the high priests and 15said, "What are you willing to give me if I hand him over to you?"

And they weighed out thirty pieces of silver for him.

16And from that moment, Yehuda looked for a chance to betray him.

Planning the Seder in an upper room

17On the first day of the Feast of the Matzot Bread, the students came to Yeshua, saying, "Where do you wish us to make preparations to eat the Pesach[172] supper?"

18And he said,

Go into the city to a certain man and tell him,
"The teacher says: My time is near. With you
I will celebrate the Pesach with my students."

19And the students did as Yeshua instructed and they prepared the Seder.

One of you will betray me

20When evening came, he took his place reclining at the table with the twelve. 21And as they were eating, he said,

I tell you that one of you will betray me.

22Bitterly sorrowful, they began to say to each other, "Surely not I, lord?"

23He answered, saying,

The one who has dipped his hand
in the bowl with me will betray me.

24Yes, the earthly son departs
as the prophets wrote of him,

---

[172]The Pesach supper is the Seder. The Feast of the Matzot is the Festival of Unleavened Bread. The Greek word ἄζυμος (azymos) means "unleavened bread," which is a translation from the Hebrew מַצּוֹת (matzot), "unleavened bread." See Mark, note 136. Pesach is Passover from the Greek πάσχα (pasha), from the Hebrew פֶּסַח (pesah), "to pass over," referring to escape from bondage in Egypt, celebrated at the Seder by eating the paschal lamb. See Exodus 12.1–13.16.

but agony is prepared for him

who betrayed the earthly son.

Better had he not been born!

25 Then Yehuda, the one betraying him, said,

Surely not I, Rabbi?

Yeshua replied,

You have said it.

This is my body, this is my blood

26 As they were eating, Yeshua took the matzot, and after giving thanks he broke it, gave it to his students, and said,

Take it and eat.

This is my body.

27 Then he took the cup and after giving thanks, he gave it to them, saying,

Drink from it, all of you,

28 for this is my blood of the covenant,[173]

poured out for the many for forgiveness of sins.

29 I tell you, I will no longer drink this fruit of the vine

until that day I drink it new with you

in the kingdom of my father.

30 And they sang a psalm and went out to the Mountain of Olives.

Before the cock crows twice

31 Then Yeshua said to them,

You will all desert me this night,

for it is written in Zeharyah:

I will strike down the shepherd

and the sheep of his flock will be scattered.[174]

32 But after I am raised up,

I will go ahead of you to the Galil.

33 "Though all the others fail you, I will never fail you," Kefa protested.

34 Yeshua said to him,

---

173 From the Greek διαθήκη (diatheke), "the covenant," and in Hellenistic Greek "testament or will." In the King James Version, the word "new" is added and so it reads, "This is my blood of the new testament." "New" (καινη) is not in the Greek text. In Greek and East European orthodoxy the title for the scriptures is "New Covenant." New Testament came into Latin and modern West European languages through Jerome's mistranslation, or repetition of an earlier mistranslation, of *diatheke* as *testamentum*, "testament" rather than as "covenant." "Covenant" derives from Hebrew בְּרִית (berit). New Covenant in Greek is Καινὴ Διαθήκη (Kaine Diatheke), and in Torah בְּרִית חֲדָשָׁה (berit hadashah), found in Jeremiah 31.31.

174 Zech. 13.7.

Amen, I say to you.

During this night before the cock crows,

you will deny me three times.

35"Even if I must die with you, I will not deny you," Kefa answered.
And all the students said the same.

Terror and prayer at Gat Shmanim

36Then Yeshua went with them to a place called Gat Shmanim and he told
his students,

Sit down here while I go over there to pray.

37He took with him Kefa and the two sons of Zavdai and then he fell into
pain and sorrow. He told them,

38My soul is in anguish to the point of death.

Stay here and keep awake with me.

39And going a little farther, he threw himself down on his face and prayed,

My father, if it is possible,

let this cup pass from me,

but not as I wish, but as you wish.

40Then he went back to the students and found them sleeping, and said to
Kefa,

Were you not strong enough to stay awake

with me for one hour? 41Stay awake and pray

that you are not brought to the test.

The spirit is eager but the flesh is weak.

42Again he went off and prayed, saying,

My father, if this cup cannot pass from me

without my drinking it,

let your will be done.

43And returning once more, he found them sleeping, for their eyes were heavy.
44He went off a third time and prayed and said the same words as before. 45Then
he came back to his students and told them,

Are you still asleep and resting?

Look, the hour is near,

and the earthly son

will be betrayed into the hands of sinners.

46Wake up, let us go.

Look, the one betraying me is near.

The rabbi is kissed and arrested

47While he was speaking, look, Yehuda, one of the twelve, came, and with him a great crowd with swords and clubs from the high priests and the elders of the people. 48And the betrayer told them the signal, which was, "The one I kiss is the man. Seize him."

49And at once he came up to Yeshua and said, "Hello, Rabbi."

And he kissed him.

50And Yeshua said,

> Friend, do what you are here to do.

Then they came and laid their hands on Yeshua and seized him.

51And look, one of those with Yeshua put out his hand, drew his sword, and struck the high priest's slave, cutting off his ear. 52But Yeshua said to him,

> Put your sword back into its place,
> for all who draw the sword will die by the sword.
> 53Do you suppose I don't have the power to call on my father
> to send me at once twelve legions of angels?
> 54How else would the scriptures be fulfilled
> that say in this way these things must happen?[175]

55At that moment Yeshua said to the crowds,

> Have you come to arrest me with swords and clubs
>   as if I were a robber?
> Day after day I sat in the Temple, teaching,
> and you did not take hold of me.
> 56But all this happened so the scriptures of the prophets
>   might be fulfilled.

Then all his students deserted him and fled.

False testimony in the Sanhedrin

57But those who had seized Yeshua led him to Kayfa the high priest, where the scholars and the elders had gathered.[176] 58And Kefa followed him at a distance, as far as the courtyard of the high priest, and went inside and sat down with the servants to see the outcome. 59The high priests and the entire San-

---

[175] 2 Kings 6.15–17; Ps. 24.8–10; Rev. 19.14.

[176] The night session at the Sanhedrin is problematic, raising many questions. Trials during Passover as well as night trials were forbidden by Jewish law. By Roman law, Jews normally could not pass death sentences, but by the first century "the Roman authorities voluntarily authorized the Sanhedrin and the High Priest to try capital cases," M. Stern writes in "The History of Judea Under Roman Rule," in H. H. Ben-Sasson, ed., *A History of the Jewish People* (Cambridge, MA: Harvard University Press, 1976), 250. However, this authority would not have extended to the instance of Yeshua whom, it is generally agreed, was tried as a seditionist, as the "King of the Jews."

hedrin were looking for false witnesses against Yeshua so they could put him to death. 60But they found none, though many false witnesses came forward.

Later, two came forward 61and declared, "This man said, 'I can tear down the Temple of God and rebuild it within three days.'"

62The high priest stood up and said to the captive, "Do you answer nothing? What is this testimony these men bring against you?"

63But Yeshua was silent.

And the high priest said to him, "I charge you under oath by the living God to tell us if you are the mashiah, the son of God."

Yeshua told him,

64You said it. But I say to you,

from now on you will see the earthly son

seated at the right hand of the power

and coming upon the clouds of the sky.[177]

65Then the high priest tore his clothing and said, "He has blasphemed! Why do we still need witnesses? Look, now you have heard the blasphemy. 66What do you think?"

They responded, "He deserves death."

67Then they spat in his face and struck him with their fists. And slapped him, 68and said, "Tell us your prophesy, mashiah. Who hit you?"

Kefa and the crowing cock

69Now Kefa was sitting outside in the courtyard, and a servant girl came to him and said, "You were with Yeshua of the Galil."

70But he denied it before everyone, saying, "I do not know what you are saying."

71When he went to the gate, another girl saw him and said to the people there, "He was with Yeshua of Natzeret."

72And again he denied it, with an oath, saying, "I do not know the man."

73A little later, those who were standing there came up to Kefa and said, "Certainly you are one of them. Your Galilean accent betrays you."

74Then he began to curse, and he swore an oath, "I do not know the man!"

At that moment a cock crowed.

75Kefa remembered what Yeshua had said,

Before the cock crows you will deny me.

And he went outside and wept bitterly.

---

[177] Daniel 7.13, which he cites, reads, "I saw one like a person / coming upon the clouds of the sky."

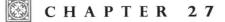

CHAPTER 27

Yeshua before Pilatus

When early morning came, all the high priests and the elders of people held a meeting against Yeshua to have him put to death. ₂They bound him and led him away and handed him over to Pilatus the governor.

Yehuda with silver and rope

₃When Yehuda, who betrayed him, saw that Yeshua was condemned to die, he was seized with remorse, and returned the thirty silver coins to the high priests and the elders.

₄"I have sinned in betraying innocent blood," he told them.

But they said, "What is that to us? You live with it."

₅He flung the silver coins into the Temple and left. Then he withdrew and hanged himself.

₆After the high priests picked up the silver coins, they said, "It's not permitted to put this into the treasury, since it is blood money."

₇Then they took counsel again, and used the money to buy the potter's field to bury foreigners in. ₈To this day that field has been called the Field of Blood.

₉With this, the word spoken through Yirmiyah the prophet was fulfilled, saying,

> And they took the thirty silver coins,
>
> the price fixed on him by the children of Yisrael,
>
> ₁₀and used them to buy the potter's field
>
> as the lord commanded me.[178]

Pilatus asks, Are you the king of the Jews?

₁₁Later, Yeshua stood before the governor, and the governor asked him, "Are you the king of the Jews?"

And Yeshua said,

> You say so.

₁₂When the high priests and the elders accused him, he answered nothing.

---

[178] The passage is not from Jeremiah, though Jeremiah mentions buying land and visiting a potter. The passage is loosely derived from Zechariah 11.12–13.

13Then Pilatus said to him, "Do you not hear all the charges against you?"

14But he gave no reply to a single charge, and the governor was greatly amazed.

Crucify him!

15For the holidays of Pesach, the governor had the custom of releasing a prisoner to the crowd, whichever one they wished. 16At that time they had a learned prisoner,[179] who was called [Yeshua] Bar Abba.[180] 17So after they assembled, Pilatus said to them, "Which one do want me to release to you, Yeshua Bar Abba[181] or Yeshua who is called the mashiah?" 18He knew that out of jealousy the latter had been handed over to him.

19While Pilatus was sitting on the judgment seat, his wife sent word to him, saying, "Have nothing to do with that just man, for I have suffered much today because of a dream about him."

20But the high priests and the elders persuaded the crowds to ask for Bar Abba and to destroy Yeshua.

21The governor again said to them, "Which of the two do you want me to release to you?"

"Bar Abba!" they cried.

22"Then what should I do with Yeshua, who is called the mashiah?" he asked.

"Let him be crucified," [182] they all said.

23"What harm has he done?" he told them.

But they screamed all the more, "Crucify him!"

24When Pilatus saw that he could do nothing and that an uproar was starting, he took water and washed his hands before the crowd, saying, "I am innocent of the blood of this man.[183] You see to it."

25Then all the people answered, "Let his blood be upon us and upon our children!"[184]

---

179 The prisoner's epithet is from the Greek ἐπίσημον (epistemon), which means "learned," "sagacious," "prudent," or "wise." In virtually all translations Barrabas is "notorious," with the exception of the KJV, which is neutral to positive, where he is called "a notable prisoner."

180 Barabbas from the Greek Βαραββᾶς, from the Aramaic בַּר אַבָּא (bar abba), meaning "son of Abba" (father).

181 Jesus Barabbas. Barabbas means "son of the father" or "son of God." It is assumed that Jesus Barabbas was a revolutionary of the Zealots, a Jewish sect which opposed payment of taxes to the Roman emperor, use of the Greek language, and Roman occupation of Israel. Their rebellion, referred to in the "uprising" in Mark 15.7, ended with the Roman assault on the fortress at Massada and their mass suicide in the fortress after which the sect disappeared.

182 See note 156 on Mark 15.13 for questions arising from this scene.

183 For more on Pilate's "innocence" and his subsequent sainthood in the Eastern Orthodox Church, see note 156 on Mark 15.13.

184 This line, "Let his blood be upon us and upon our children!," has given rise to much dispute and skepticism. The Jews in the street are shouting, "Let the guilt of his murder be upon us, the Jews, forever."

₂₆So Pilatus released Bar Abba to them.

He had Yeshua flogged and sent him off to be crucified.

Soldiers clothe him in scarlet and a crown of thorns and club him

₂₇Then the soldiers of the governor took Yeshua to the governor's residence[185] and drew up the whole battalion around him. ₂₈And they stripped him and wrapped a scarlet robe around him, ₂₉and twisted thorns in a wreath and put it on his head and placed a reed staff in his right hand. Then they knelt before him and mocked him, saying, "Hail, king of the Jews!" ₃₀And they spat at him and took his reed staff and struck him on the head with it. ₃₁After mocking him, they took off his scarlet robe and dressed him in his own garments and led him away to be crucified.

Gulgulta, the Place of the Skull

₃₂As they came out they found a man from Cyrene by the name of Shimon. They forced him to carry the cross. ₃₃And they came to a place called Gulgulta, which is called the Place of the Skull.[186] ₃₄They gave him wine mixed with gall to drink. When he tasted it, he didn't wish to drink it.

Crucifying him

₃₅Then they crucified him, divided up his clothing by casting lots, ₃₆and sat there and kept watch over him. ₃₇Above his head they put the charge against him, which read,

THIS IS YESHUA THE KING OF THE JEWS.

₃₈They crucified two thieves with him, one on his right and one on his left. ₃₉And those who passed by cursed him, shaking their heads, ₄₀and said, "You who can tear down the Temple and rebuild it in three days, save yourself if you are the son of God, and come down from the cross." ₄₁So too the high priests along with the scholars and the elders mocked him, saying, ₄₂"He saved others, but cannot save himself. He is the king of Yisrael. Let him come down now from the cross and we will believe in him. ₄₃He trusted in God. Let God rescue him now if he wants him, for he said, 'I am the son of God.'"

₄₄And similarly the thieves who were crucified with Yeshua taunted him.

On Passover evenings the Jews would be in their houses, celebrating the Passover meal. They would not be in the street asking the Romans to crucify a rabbi, and, had they been, they would not be shouting for crucifixion and at once declaring their guilt forever for shouting for crucifixion.

[185] The praetorium.

[186] Golgotha from the Greek Γολγοθᾶ (Golgotha), from the Aramaic גֻּלְגָּלְתָּא (gulgulta), meaning "skull."

Darkness at noon

45From noon on, darkness came over all the land until three in the afternoon.[187] 46And about three o'clock, Yeshua cried out in a great voice,

Eli, Eli, lama sabachthani?

meaning,

My God, my God, why have you forsaken me?

47Some of those standing there heard and said, "This man is calling for Eliyah."

48All at once one of them ran and took a sponge, filled it with poor wine,[188] put it on a stick, and gave it to him to drink. 49But the others said, "Leave him alone. Let's see if Eliyah comes to save him."

50And Yeshua again let out a great cry and breathed his last breath.

51And look, the curtain of the Temple tore in two from top to bottom, and the earth shook and the rocks were split, 52and the tombs opened and many bodies of the saints[189] who had fallen asleep were raised. 53And after his resurrection they came out of their tombs and went into the holy city and they appeared to many people there. 54When the centurion and those with him guarding Yeshua saw the earthquake and all that took place, they were terrified, and said, "Surely he was the son of God!"[190]

---

[187] In Greek, noon is the sixth hour, and three in the afternoon is the ninth hour.

[188] A popular wine of the poor, also translated "vinegar" or "vinegared wine," from the Greek ὄξος (oxos), which was supposed to be more effective than water in eliminating thirst. The classical Greek definition of *oxos* gives "poor wine," that is, a wine poor in quality and for the poorer classes. The King James Version gives "vinegar" and most modern translations "soured wine." The standard annotation explains that the motive of the sponge soaked with sour wine was not to comfort Yeshua but to revive him and prolong his agony, and is taken as a symbol of Jewish malice to their enemy, fulfilling scripture, as in Psalm 69.20–21: "I looked for pity, but there was none, and for comforters, but I found none. They gave me poison (gall) for my food (meat) and vinegar to drink." Line 27.48 in Matthew states only that after Yeshua's plea to God, a bystander who heard got a sponge soaked with poor wine and ran forward and put it to Yeshua's lips to drink. Whether this was the act of a brave sympathizer or a taunting foe cannot be known, since no motive is indicated in verse 27.48, nor is it clarified by turning to verses in Psalm 69 of David, which begins with a Jew saying, "Save me, O God, for the waters have come up to my neck. I sink in deep mud where there is no foothold." However, the next verse does seem to depict the offerer as a comforter rather than a villain since he is derided by another bystander who says, "Leave him alone. Let's see if Eliyah comes to save him" (27.49).

[189] Saints or, literally, the "holy ones." The Greek word (*agios*, saint), normally refers to a Christian saint, and in this instance is probably an anachronism since there were not yet Christian saints to fall out of their tombs. If they were meant to be pre-Christian Jewish saints, this meaning does not come through.

[190] Centurion is a Roman commander of a century, that is, one hundred soldiers. Here the centurion is the head of the execution squad that mocks and crucifies Yeshua, and he and his soldiers are also the first to state that Yeshua is the son of God.

His women look on

₅₅And there were many women watching from a distance. They had followed Yeshua from the Galil and had provided for him. ₅₆Among them were Miryam of Magdala,[191] and Miryam the mother of Yaakov and Yosef, and the mother of the sons of Zavdai.[192]

The body in linen entombed in rock

₅₇When evening came, a rich man from Arimathaia[193] named Yosef appeared. He was also a student of Yeshua. ₅₈He went to Pilatus and asked for the body of Yeshua. Then Pilatus ordered it to be given to him. ₅₉Yosef took the body, wrapped it in clean linen, ₆₀and laid it in his own new tomb, which he had cut out of the rock. He then rolled a great stone to the door of the tomb and went away.

₆₁Miryam of Magdala and the other Miryam were there, sitting opposite the tomb.

Guard at the tomb

₆₂On Shabbat, the next day after Preparation Day,[194] the high priests and the Prushim gathered before Pilatus ₆₃and said, "Sir, we remember what the imposter said while he was alive, 'After three days I will rise again.' ₆₄Therefore, command that the tomb be guarded until the third day so his students will not come and steal his body and say to the people, 'He has been raised from the dead.' And that will be the ultimate deception, worse than the first."

₆₅Pilatus said to them, "You have a guard of soldiers. Go, and make it as secure as you know how."

₆₆And they went to police the tomb and they secured the stone with the guard.

---

[191] Mary Magdalene from the Galilean town of Magdala.

[192] Mother of the sons of Zebedee. Her sons were Yaakov and Yohanan. Of the three Miryams at the crucifixion, Miryam, mother of Yeshua, is notably absent in Mark, Matthew, and Luke. However, in John, Miryam, mother of Yeshua, is there, and there is a moving recognition: "Woman, here is your son." Then Yeshua says to the student he loved, "Here is your mother." The unknown student then takes Miryam to his own home (John 19.2–27). In the gospels, it is Miryam of Magdala who goes to the tomb and speaks to the risen Yeshua in the garden.

[193] Arimathea from the Greek Ἀριμαθαία (Arimathaia) and identified with either Ramathaim or Rentis, fifteen or twenty miles east of Jaffa.

[194] Friday.

❖ CHAPTER 28

The women at the empty tomb

After Shabbat, at the first dawnlight of Sunday, Miryam of Magdala and the other Miryam came to look at the tomb. ₂And look, there was a great earthquake. An angel of Yahweh came down from the sky and approached the tomb, rolled away the stone, and was sitting on it. ₃And his appearance was like lightning and his clothing white as snow. ₄And those who were on guard shook with fear, and became like dead men.

₅But the angel said to the women,

Don't be afraid. I know you are looking for Yeshua
who was crucified.
₆He is not here. He has risen just as he said.
Come see the place where he lay.
₇Then go quickly and tell his students,
"He has risen from the dead, and look,
he goes before you into the Galil.
There you will see him." Look, I have told you.

Risen

₈The women left the tomb with fear and great joy, and ran to tell the news to the students. ₉And look, Yeshua met them and said,

Hello!
And they came near him and grabbed his feet and worshiped him.
₁₀Yeshua said to them,

Do not fear. Go and tell my brothers and sisters
to go to the Galil and there they will see me.

Report of the guards

₁₁And while the women were on their way, look, some of the guards went into the city to report to the high priests all that had happened. ₁₂And they met with the elders and took enough silver coins to give to the soldiers ₁₃and told them, "Say that during the night the students came and stole his body while we were sleeping. ₁₄And if the governor hears of this, we will confer with him and keep you out of trouble."

₁₅The soldiers took the money and did as they were instructed. And this story is known among the Jews to this day.

Yeshua in the Galil with his students

₁₆Now the eleven students went to the Galil, to the mountain where Yeshua had commanded them to go. ₁₇And look, when they saw him they worshiped him, but some doubted. ₁₈And Yeshua came up to them and spoke to them, saying,

> To me was given all authority in heaven and on earth.
>
> ₁₉Go and make students of all nations,
>
> washing them in the name of the father and the son
>
>   and the holy spirit,
>
> ₂₀teaching them to hold to all I have commanded you.
>
> And know I am with you
>
> all the days until the end of the age.[195]

---

[195] "Age" in Greek is αἰών (aion). The King James and Lattimore versions have chosen to translate the completion of the aeon as "the end of the world," which is more dramatic and beautiful. The Greek wording also has a mysterious note conveying "until the end of eternity."

LOUKAS
(LUKE)

LOUKAS (LUKE)

THERE IS GENERAL AGREEMENT AMONG SCHOLARS THAT LITTLE IS CERTAIN ABOUT AUTHORSHIP, PLACE, AND DATE WITH REGARD TO Luke. While this uncertainty exists for all the gospels, Luke remains a special case. Older scholarship has given us the authorial name Luke and the places of his gospel composition as Rome or cities in the East such as Achaia, Ephesus, or Caesarea in Israel. The name Luke appears to come from bishop Irenaeus (late second century), who claimed that Luke was Paul's "inseparable collaborator" in Antioch. But the depiction of Paul in the Acts, which is also ascribed to Luke, has little to do with the self-portrait of Paul that emerges in the apostle's own letters. There are also traditions, of no more certainty, that speak of Luke as "the beloved physician," as a "convert" to the Christian Jews, and as the evangelist who wrote for gentile converts. There is no substantial evidence for any of this. It is clear that Luke the author never read or even knew of Paul's letters, and hence all attempts to identify who the author of Luke was, who were his associates, for whom he wrote, and what city or country he wrote in, fall apart. Luke was almost certainly not the companion of Paul. Regardless of unproved speculations about the person of Luke, the Gospel of Luke is a splendid achievement.

Luke is the longest of the gospels, and, according to most commentators, the most skillfully constructed one, composed in an elegant Greek at times approaching classical Hellenistic Greek of the first century. The main example cited by scholars to demonstrate Luke's classical Greek is the brief prologue (1.1–4). This text resembles the prologue to Acts and has been used as proof that Luke is the common author of the Gospel of Luke and the Acts of the Apostles. While it is true that the prologue is a good example of the Hellenistic complexity of rhetoric, its convoluted discourse is polite and also heavy. The prologue, in fact and in spirit, is not by the same author who wrote the rest of the Gospel of Luke. And whether or not the same author wrote Luke and the Acts should not be proven by the similarities of the prologues, which in Acts, again, does not share the spirit of the scripture it prefaces. Once we go beyond the prologue, the Greek of Luke is different, is more inflected, but not decisively removed from Mark and Matthew.

The Gospel of Luke reads as a fluent late text, greatly enlarging the scope of the New Covenant. Its immediate sources in the synoptic chain are the unknown Q source, which is presumed to be a sayings gospel, and both Mark and Matthew. Luke expands on Mark and Matthew, and we cannot explain the sources for this additional material. Perhaps the most original and beautiful passages in Luke (for which there are no counterparts in the other gospels) are the annunciation (1.26–38), Mary's visit to Elizabeth (1.39–56), the nativity scene of the birth of Yeshua in the manger (2.1–7), the parable of the Good Samaritan (10.29–37), and the parable of the Prodigal Son (15.11–32). Only the rich treasure of Luke gives us the birth of John the Baptist (1.5–25, 57–80), the angelic announcement and the visit of the shepherds (2.8–20), as well as the prayers of Simeon and Anna (2.25–38). Among the poetic masterpieces in the New Covenant is Mary's song, the "Magnificat" (1.39–55), beginning "My soul magnifies the lord."

Much has been written about Luke as the great narrator, which is true, and Luke's means are often contrasted with Mark's more modest style. The comparison is mistaken. Both Mark and Luke are master narrators of the New Covenant, and Luke is closer to Mark than is normally acknowledged. The clichés of Mark as a rude populist and Luke as an elegant Henry James are unfounded. In their best moments, especially in the rush and drama of the passion week, the two authors are cut from the same cloth. Although Mark has no resurrection scene and Luke does, the ending of Luke resembles the narrative genius of Mark. Luke speaks of Yeshua, who has come back to life and is walking the roads of Israel, startling his disciples and friends, and engaging in the most profound and compelling conversations of the gospels.

PROLOGUE[1]

So you may know the truth, excellent Theofilos

Since many have set their hand to composing a narrative of those things which have been fulfilled among us 2as they were handed on to us from the beginning by eyewitnesses and servants of the word, 3it seemed also good for me, since I was the first to follow everything closely, to write them down in good order for you, excellent Theofilos, 4that you may know the truth concerning these words about which you have been instructed.

CHAPTER 1

Angel with good news for barren Elisheva

5In the days of Herod, king of Yehuda,[2] there was a certain priest named Zeharyah,[3] from the priestly order of Aviyah,[4] and his wife came from the daughters of Aharon[5] and her name was Elisheva.[6] 6They were both upright before God, walking blamelessly in all the commandments and regulations of God. 7But they had no child, because Elisheva was barren, and both of them were advanced in their days.

8Now it happened that in his priestly duty when it was the turn of his division to be before God, 9Zeharyah was chosen by lot, according to the custom of the priesthood, to go into the Temple of the lord and burn incense. 10And a huge gathering of people was praying outside at the hour of the

---

1 In Paul's Letter to Philemon 1.24, Luke is Paul's "fellow worker," and in Colossians 4.14 he is "the beloved physician." Acts begins: "In the first book, Theophilos, I wrote about everything that Yeshua did and taught. . . ." This reference to "the first book" has been taken as an allusion to the Gospel of Luke and remains at the center of the Luke-Acts' controversy over authorship. While these late brief prefaces do not prove common authorship for Luke and Acts, their almost identical voice, each addressed to the honorific patron Theofilos, may mean their own single authorship, or one author imitating another. The heart of Luke is composed in graceful popular Greek, and the notion of the elevated classical style is rumor.

2 Judea (and Judas, Juda, Judah, Jude, and feminine of Jew) from the Greek Ἰουδαία (Ioudaia), from the Hebrew יְהוּדָה (yehuda).

3 Zechariah from the Greek Ζαχαρίας (Zaharias), from the Hebrew זְכַרְיָה (zeharyah).

4 Abijah from the Greek Ἀβιά (Abia), from the Hebrew אֲבִיָּה (aviyah).

5 Aaron from the Greek Ἀαρών (Aaron), from the Hebrew אַהֲרוֹן (aharon).

6 Elizabeth from the Greek Ἐλισάβετ (Elisabet), from the Hebrew אֱלִישֶׁבַע (elisheva).

incense offering. 11Then an angel of the Lord appeared to him, standing to the right side of the incense altar. 12He was terrified at what he saw and fear fell upon him.

13But the angel said to him:[7]

Do not be afraid, Zeharyah, your prayer
was heard and your wife Elisheva will bear
you a son and you will name him Yohanan[8]
14and he will be your joy and exultation,
and many will rejoice at his birth,
15for he will be great before the eye of the lord
and he will never swallow wine or strong drink
and he will be filled with the holy spirit
while still in his mother's womb, and will turn
16many sons of Yisrael[9] toward the lord their God.
17And he will advance with Eliyah's spirit and power
to turn the hearts of fathers toward their children
and the disobedient to the wisdom of the just,
and to prepare a people ready for the lord.

18And Zeharyah said to the angel,

How will I know this? I am an old man
and my wife is weak in the years of her life.

19The angel answered, saying to him,

I am Gavriel.[10] I stand in the presence of God
and was sent to speak to you and to announce
these things to you. 20And look, you will be silent,
unable to speak till the day these things happen
because you did not believe my words,
which will be fulfilled in their own time.[11]

21Now the people were waiting for Zeharyah and they wondered at the time he spent in Temple. 22But when he came out he could not speak to them, and they knew he had seen a vision in the Temple. He kept nodding to them and

---

7 The poem that follows is in the manner of the Hebrew Bible as Luke understood it through the Septuagint (the Greek translation of the Hebrew Bible for the Jews of Alexandria, 250–100 B.C.E.), and such phrases as "It happened that" (1.5), the first words of the narrative after the prologue, are in conscious imitation of the Septuagint phrasing, with words taken from Num. 6.1–4; Jud. 13.4; Jer. 1.5; Mal. 4.5–6; and Gen. 17.17.

8 John from the Greek Ιωάννης (Ioannes), from the Hebrew יוֹחָנָן (yohanan).

9 Israel from the Greek Ἰσραήλ, from the Hebrew יִשְׂרָאֵל (yisrael).

10 Gabriel.

11 She would become pregnant, and her child would become known as John the Baptist.

remained speechless. ₂₃And it happened that when the days of his liturgies[12] were completed, he went to his house.

₂₄After those days his wife Elisheva conceived, and she hid away for five months, saying,

₂₅This is what the lord has done for me

in the days he looked on me with favor

and took away my disgrace among people.[13]

Angel with troubling news for Miryam[14]

₂₆In the sixth month the angel Gavriel was sent by God to a city in the Galil[15] called Natzeret,[16] ₂₇to a virgin engaged to a man whose name was Yosef,[17] from the house of David, and the name of the virgin was Miryam.[18] ₂₈And he came near her and said,

Hello, favored one, the lord is with you.

₂₉But Miryam was deeply troubled by his words and pondered what kind of greeting this might be.

₃₀The angel said to her,

Do not fear, Miryam, for you have found favor with God.

₃₁Look, you will conceive in your womb and bear a son

and you will name him Yeshua.

₃₂He will be great and be called son of the highest,

and the lord God will give him the throne of his father David,

₃₃and he will rule over the house of Yaakov through the ages,

and of his kingdom there will be no end.

₃₄But Miryam said to the angel,

How will this be since I do not know a man?[19]

---

12 From the Greek λειτουργία (leitourgia), "liturgy." Usually translated as "ministries" (King James) or "service(s)" in modern versions, but liturgy also means, as in English, a liturgy, "a ceremonial chant in service of attending a parishioner." The root meaning of the word is "work for people." Since both the musical notion of ceremonial liturgy and work are suggested in the Greek, it is important to convey this in English.

13 Elizabeth's disgrace was for having been infertile.

14 In the *Harper NRS Study Bible*, the subtitle is *The Birth of Jesus Foretold;* in the Jerusalem Bible it is *The Annunciation.*

15 Galilee from the Greek Γαλιλαία (Galilaía), from the Hebrew גָּלִיל (galil). Galil is a "circle," "district," or "province" and is usually written in the Hebrew as גְּלִיל הַגּוֹיִם (galil hagoyim), meaning "province of the goyim (gentiles)."

16 Nazareth from the Greek Ναζαρέτ (Natzaret), from unknown village in Galilee probably spelled Natzeret.

17 Joseph from the Greek Ιωσήφ (Iosef), from the Hebrew יוֹסֵף (yosef).

18 Mary from the Greek Μαρία, from the Hebrew מִרְיָם (miryam).

19 The old versions in English, Tyndale, and the Rheims in the sixteenth century and James in the seventeenth century, accord the English version of this phrase the accurate dignity of the Greek ἄνδρα

35The angel answered her,

> The holy spirit will come to you
> and the power of the highest will overshadow you.
> So the one being born will be called the holy son of God.
> 36And look, Elisheva your kinswoman
> has also conceived a son in her old age
> and this is her sixth month, she who had been called barren.
> 37With God nothing is impossible.[20]

38Miryam said,

> Look, here I am, the slave of the lord.
> May it happen to me according to your word.

The angel left her.

Miryam visits Elisheva

39And Miryam rose up in these days and went into the hill country to a city in Yehuda.[21] 40She entered the house of Zeharyah and greeted Elisheva.[22]

Elisheva sings

41It happened that when Elisheva heard Miryam's greeting, the child leapt in her womb. And Elisheva was filled with the holy spirit. 42She spoke out, with a great cry,

> You are blessed among women
> and blessed is the fruit of your womb.

> 43How has it happened to me that the mother
> of my lord comes to me?

> 44Look, as soon as the sound of your greeting came
> to my ears, a child in my womb leapt for joy!

> 45Blessed is she believing in the fulfillment
> of what was told her by the lord.

οὐ γινώσκω (andra ou ginosko?). Tyndale: "I know not a man?" Rheims: "I know not man?" James: "I know not a man?" However, modern versions commit the heresy of explanation. NIV: "I am a virgin?" NRSV: "I am a virgin?" New American Standard: "I am a virgin?" Oxford Inclusive Version: "I am a virgin?" Going further into explanation, the New American Bible reads: "I have no relations with a man?" The Annotated Scholars reads: "I've not had sex with any man." As usual, Lattimore breaks the modern mold and returns to the Greek: "I know no man?" His interpretation differs slightly in that here the negative is connected with the verb, and Lattimore negates the object noun.

[20] The texts vary on line 1.37, some putting it in doubt.

[21] Judea. See note 2, p. 203, on Judea.

[22] Harper NRSV has *Mary Visits Elizabeth*; the Jerusalem *The Visitation*.

Miryam sings

46And Miryam sang,[23]

47My soul magnifies the lord
and my spirit is joyful in God my savior,

48for he has looked upon his young slave
in her low station.

Hereafter all generations will call me blessed,
49for through his powers the great one did wondrous

things for me. His name is holy.
50His mercy goes from generation to generation

to those who fear him.
51He has shown the strength of his arm,

and scattered those who were proud
in the mind of their heart.

52He has toppled monarchs from their thrones
and raised the poor to their feet.

53He filled the hungry with good foods
and sent the rich away empty.

54He has helped Yisrael his servant and child
through the memory of his mercy,

55just as he spoke to our fathers,
to Avraham and to his everlasting seed.

56Miryam stayed with Elisheva about three months and went back to her own house.

Yohanan born

57Now for Elisheva the time was completed for her to give birth, and she bore a son. 58Her neighbors and relatives heard that the lord had made great his mercy to her and they rejoiced with her.

---

[23] Miryam's song, popularly known through the Latin title the Magnificat, resembles Hannah's song over Samuel's birth (1 Sam. 2.1–10) and the immediately preceding Elisheva's song.

Yohanan circumcised and named

59And it happened on the eighth day they came to circumcise the child and they were calling him by the name of his father Zeharyah.

60His mother said, "No, but he will be called Yohanan."

61They told her, "There is no one among your relatives who is called by that name."

62And they made signs to his father to learn what he wanted to call him.

63He asked for a tablet and wrote, "Yohanan is his name."

And all were amazed.

64His mouth was open and his tongue immediately set free, and he spoke praising God.

65Then fear took hold of all those living near them, and in all the hill country of Yehuda those sayings were on everyone's lips. 66All who heard them placed them in their heart, saying, "What will this child be?"

The hand of the lord was with him.

Zeharyah's prophecy

67His father Zeharyah was filled with the holy spirit and he prophesied, saying,
68Blessed be the lord God of Yisrael.
He visited his people and shaped their deliverance
69and raised a horn of salvation for us
in the house of his servant David 70as he spoke
through the mouth of the ancient holy prophets:
71We will be delivered from our enemies
and from the hand of those who hate us.
72He will show mercy to our fathers
and remember his holy covenant
73in which he swore to Avraham our father:
74to grant us deliverance without fear
from the hand of our enemies
and that we serve him 75in holiness and justice,
and be before him all of our days.
76You, child, will be called the highest prophet.
You will go before the lord to make ready his ways,
77to give knowledge of salvation to his people
through the forgiveness of their sins.
78Through the tender mercies of our God
the dawn sun will visit us from its heights
79to illuminate those of us who are sitting

in darkness and the shadow of death,
and to guide our feet along the way of peace.

Yohanan in the deserts

80And the child grew and became strong in spirit, and he was in the deserts[24] until the day of his appearance before Yisrael.

CHAPTER 2

Yeshua born in a stable

It happened in those days that a decree was sent out from Caesar Augustus to enroll the whole world.[25] 2This was the first census, when Quirinius was governor of Syria. 3And all went to their own cities to be registered.

4Now Yosef also went up from the Galil, from the city of Natzeret,[26] to Yehuda, to the city of David which is called Beit Lehem,[27] because he was of the house and family of David. 5He went to be enrolled with Miryam, who was engaged[28] to him and who was pregnant.[29] 6And it happened that while they were there, the days were completed for her to give birth, 7and she bore a son, her first-born, and she wrapped him in strips of cloth and laid him in a feeding trough[30] of a stable because there was no room for them in the inn.

8And there were shepherds in the region, camping in the fields at night and keeping guard over their flock. 9An angel of the lord stood before them and the glory of the lord shone about them, and they were terrified.

---

[24] "In the deserts" from the Greek ’εν ταις ἐρήμοις (en tais eremois) is often translated as "in the wilderness."

[25] A census presumably in the whole Roman world that could be used for purposes of taxation and military service.

[26] Nazareth.

[27] Bethlehem from the Greek Βηθλέεμ (Bethleem), from the Hebrew בֵּית לָחֶם (beit lehem), meaning "house of bread."

[28] To make plausible Miryam's virginity, Yosef was engaged, not married, to Miryam. There is no reference in the gospels to a later marriage between Yosef and Miryam, though Yeshua will later have four brothers, who are named, and probably two sisters, who are unnamed.

[29] It was important to establish Yeshua's lineage through Joseph, who was of the family of David, as indicated in Luke's genealogy, 3.23–37, but with the reservation "so it was thought." The virgin birth would, it would seem, deprive Yeshua of the biological paternal link back to David, but through Mary there was a blood line.

[30] From the Greek φάτνη (fatne), "feeding trough." "Manger" is a feeding trough for animals. Though a beautiful and evocative word, "manger" has come, incorrectly, to signify the stable itself rather than the feeding box, which conveys a more extraordinary incident.

10The angel said to them,

> Don't be afraid. Look, I tell you good news,
> a great joy for all people.
> 11Because on this day was born to you in the city of David
> a savior who is the mashiah the lord.
> 12Here is your sign. You will find a child wrapped in cloths
> and lying in a feeding trough of a stable.

13And suddenly with the angel there was a multitude of the heavenly army praising God and saying,

> 14Glory to God in the highest sky
> and on earth peace among people of good will.[31]

15And it happened that after the angels had gone from them into the sky, the shepherds said to one another, "Let us go to Beit Lehem and see what has taken place, which the lord has made known to us."

16And they left, hurrying, and found Miryam and Yosef, and the baby boy lying in the feeding trough. 17When they saw them, they made known what had been said to them about the child. 18And all who heard were amazed at what the shepherds told them.

19But Miryam took all these words in and pondered them in her heart.

20The shepherds returned, glorifying and praising God for all they had heard and seen, as it had been told them.

Yeshua circumcised and named

21Now after eight days had passed it was time for his circumcision, and he was called by the name Yeshua, the name called by the angel before he was conceived in the womb.

22When the days for their purification[32] had passed, according to the law of Mosheh,[33] they brought him up to Yerushalayim[34] to present him before the lord, 23as it is written in Exodus[35] in the law of the lord:

> Every male child who opens the womb
> will be called holy to the lord.[36]

---

[31] From the Greek εὐδοκία (eudokia), "of goodwill" or "good pleasure," or variously translated as "whom he favors."

[32] Forty days after the birth of a male child.

[33] Moses from the Greek Μωϋσῆς (Moyses), from the Hebrew משֶׁה (mosheh).

[34] Jerusalem from the Greek Ἰερουσαλήμ (Yerousalem), from the Hebrew יְרוּשָׁלַיִם (yerushalayim).

[35] Exod. 13.2.

[36] This famous passage of the nativity scene, based on Exodus 13.2, is translated accurately from Luke's Greek, without interpretation, in the KJV and in Lattimore. Luke has made a loose reference to Exodus 13.2. Perhaps to complete Luke's free reference to Exodus 13.2, most standard contemporary translations, including NRSV, NIV, Jerusalem, and Oxford Inclusive, have added and subtracted words in their versions of Luke. NRSV has "Every firstborn shall be designated as holy to the Lord."

24And a sacrifice was offered according to what is said in the law of the lord,

A pair of turtledoves or two young pigeons.

Song of Shimon

25And look, there was a man in Yerushalayim whose name was Shimon,[37] and he was just and circumspect and he looked forward to the consolation of Yisrael,[38] and the holy spirit was upon him. 26It had been revealed to him by the holy spirit that he would not see death until he saw the mashiah of the lord. 27And through the spirit he came into the Temple. When the parents brought in the child Yeshua, to do for him what was the custom under the law, 28Shimon took him in his arms and praised God and said,

29Rabbi, in accordance with your word,

now you release your slave in peace,

30for my eyes have seen your salvation,[39]

31which you prepared before the face of all the people,[40]

32a light of revelation to the gentiles[41]

and a glory to your people Yisrael.

33And his father[42] and mother were in wonder at the things said about their child.

34Then Shimon blessed them and said to Miryam his mother,

See, the child is appointed for the fall and rise

of many in Yisrael,

NRSV's own version of Luke's source (probably by way of the Septuagint) in Exodus 13.2 reads "Consecrate to me all the firstborn; whatever is the first to open the womb among the Israelites." Luke does not say "firstborn," which most modern translations add. But Luke does repeat the very strong Hebrew metaphor, "open the womb," here in the Greek διανοίγον μήτραν (dianoigon metran), which modern translations omit.

[37] Simon from the Greek Σίμων (Simon), from the Hebrew שִׁמְעוֹן (shimon).

[38] The consolation that the coming of the messiah would bring to Israel.

[39] Isa. 52.10 and 46.13.

[40] Isa. 42.6 and 49.6; John 8.12b.

[41] Gentiles from the Greek ἔθνος (ethnos), "a nation" or "people." "Gentile" is from the Latin gens, gentis, "a nation," equivalent to the Greek ethnos, and the Hebrew goy. The gentiles (ethnoi) were the "ethnics" or non-Jews. In unfriendly reference, the ethnos is translated as "pagan," and when wholly foreign or wicked and infidel as "heathen." When friendly or Christian, ethnos is "gentile." The gentile and Jewish communities co-existed in politics and trade, and many were proselytes, becoming the Christian Jews who followed Yeshua. In Christian Jewish communities of the diaspora, after 70 C.E., the gentile converts to messianism dominated and gentile came to mean "a Christian." Here, since Luke, the nominal author of Luke, was traditionally called the non-Jew among the four evangelists, the appearance of "the gentiles" in the Song of Simeon is said by commentators to reflect Luke's careful emphasis on affirming that salvation is offered to gentile as well as Jew.

[42] The reference to Joseph as πατὴρ (pater), "father" rather than "stepfather," reveals the difficulty of speaking of Yeshua's parents without raising the question of his lineage.

and destined to be a sign that will be opposed,
35and through your own soul a sword will pierce
so that secrets from many hearts may be revealed.

Hannah, Temple prophet

36And there was Hannah,[43] a prophet, daughter of Fanuel, of the tribe of Asher. She was well advanced in her days, having lived with her husband seven years after her virginity,[44] 37and she was a widow until she was eighty-four years. She did not leave the Temple, serving there with fasting and prayers night and day. 38At that hour she came in, standing near, and praised God and spoke of the child to all who looked forward to the deliverance of Yerushalayim.

Yeshua's childhood in Natzeret

39When they completed everything according to the law of the lord, they went back to the Galil to the city of Natzeret. 40And the child grew and became strong, filled with wisdom, and the grace of God was upon him.

After Pesach in Yerushalayim, twelve-year-old Yeshua stays on alone to talk with the rabbis in the Temple

41Now his parents journeyed every year to Yerushalayim for the Seder of the Pesach.[45] 42And when he was twelve years old, they went up as was their custom for the Seder. 43When the feast days were over and they returned, the boy Yeshua remained in Yerushalayim, but his parents did not know it. 44Thinking he was with a caravan of travelers, they went a day on the road, looking for him among their relatives and acquaintances. 25When they didn't find him, they went back to Yerushalayim and searched for him.

46And it happened that after three days they found him in the Temple, sitting among the rabbis, listening to them and asking them questions. 47And all who listened to him were amazed at his intelligence and his answers.

---

[43] Anna from the Greek Ἄννα, from the Hebrew חַנָּה (hannah). Phanuel from Greek Φανουήλ (Fanouel), from Hebrew פְּנוּאֵל (fenuel). Hannah's words and Shimon's song are seen as prophecies.

[44] Virginity from the Greek παρθενία (parthenia), "virginity," "purity," or "maidenhood." Here the word means from her *marriage* as indicated by the time since maidenhood was lost. It is important not to lose in translation the physical immediacy of the Greek word for "virginity," which may suggest marriage but does not say it, by giving its less rich equivalent or an explanation. As with many expressions, the Greek works from a metaphorical image, which the reader understands at both ends of the metaphor. In his 1525 New Testament, William Tyndale and the 1611 KJV translate "parthenia" as "virginity."

[45] Passover feast or Seder, a ceremonial meal on the first or first two evenings of Pesach, a festival commemorating the escape of the Jews from captivity in Egypt.

48And when his parents saw him they were astonished, and his mother said to him, "Son, why did you do this to us? Look, your father and I were in sorrow, searching for you."

49And he said to them,

> Why were you looking for me?
> Didn't you know I must be in my father's things?[46]

50And they didn't understand the words he spoke to them.

Yeshua in Natzeret grows into manhood

51Then he went down with them and they came to Natzeret, and he was under their authority.[47] And his mother kept all his sayings in her heart.

52Yeshua increased in wisdom and in stature and in the favor of God and people.

 # CHAPTER 3

Yohanan the Dipper in the desert

In the fifteenth year of the reign of Tiberius Caesar,[48] while Pontius Pilatus[49] was governor of Yehuda, and Herod was tetrarch of the Galil, and his brother Filippos[50] was tetrarch of the region of Ituraea and Trachonitis, and Lysanias was tetrarch of Abilene, 2during the priesthood of Hannan[51] and Kayfa,[52] the word of God came to Yohanan son of Zeharyah in the desert. 3And he went into all the surrounding region of the Yarden,[53] preaching ritual washing of repentance for the forgiveness of sins, 4as it is written in the book of words of the prophet Yeshayah,

> I am the voice of one crying out in the desert:
> "Prepare the way of Adonai, make his paths straight!
> 5Every ravine will be filled
> and every mountain and hill will be leveled low,

---

46 Other translations have rendered "my father's things" as "my Father's house," which is not stated in the Greek, and while it may be implied, the range of meanings of "things" thereby becomes limited by specific interpretation.

47 A polite way of saying he was obedient to them.

48 Literally, "hegemony." The reign of Tiberius Caesar (14–37 C.E.).

49 Pontius Pilate.

50 Philip from the Greek Φίλιππος (Filippos).

51 Annas. Hannan, or Anan, means "high priest" in the Hebrew, from the Greek ῎Αννας (Annas), from the Hebrew חָנָן (hannan), "priest" or "gracious one."

52 Caiaphas. From the Greek Καϊάφας (Kaiafas), from the Hebrew כַּיְפָא (kayfa), meaning "a depression." The high priests were under Rome and subject to appointment. Kayfa was appointed by Valerius Gratus, governor of Judea.

53 Jordan from the Greek Ἰορδάνης (Iordanes), from the Hebrew יַרְדֵּן (yarden).

and the crooked will be straight

and the rough roads smooth

₆and all flesh will look upon the salvation of God."⁵⁴

Yohanan forewarns the offspring of vipers

₇Yohanan said to the crowds that came out to be dipped by him,

Offspring of vipers!,

who warned you to flee from the coming anger?⁵⁵

₈Bear fruits that are worthy of repentance,

and do not begin to say among yourselves,

"We have Avraham for our father."⁵⁶

For I say to you that out of these rocks

God can raise up children for Avraham.

₉Even now the ax is set against the root of trees

so every tree that does not bear good fruit

is cut down and cast into the fire.

₁₀And the crowds questioned him, saying, "What should we do then?"

₁₁Yohanan answered them, saying,

One who has two coats should share them

with one who has none.

One who has meat⁵⁷ should share it

in the same way.

₁₂Then came tax collectors to be dipped, and they said to him, "Rabbi, what should we do?"

₁₃He said to them,

Collect no more than you are ordered to.

₁₄Then soldiers in service also questioned him, saying, "What should we do?"

And he said to them,

---

⁵⁴ The prayer, which appears in other gospels, comes from Isaiah 40.5.

⁵⁵ The furious curse and anger by Yohanan at his entrance are taken as a warning of forthcoming punishment to the people who do not recognize the messiah, which is the coming destruction of the Temple in 70 c.e., which has occurred by the time of the gospel's composition. The familiar anger against Jews is historically anachronistic, since Yohanan belonged to the same tribe as the "offspring of vipers." The Annotated Scholars edition translates the phrase "offspring of vipers" (Matt.23.33) as "You spawn of Satan," so interpreting "vipers" to be both "the snake as Satan in the garden" and "the snake as Jew." This early segment of warning and condemnation in Luke, given in Yohanan's voice, duplicates the word and sentiment found in the other gospels, however, at later moments in the narrative. Here the curse is introduced early in Yohanan's voice. Another such example of a curse by a Jew on Jews is the implausible passage in Matthew in which the Jews are out in the street, shouting their own future and eternal punishment, "Let his [Yeshua's] blood be upon us and upon our children!" (Matt. 27.25).

⁵⁶ 2 Chron. 20.7.

⁵⁷ Also translated as "food."

Do not slanderously blackmail, do not extort,

and be satisfied with your wages.

Who is the mashiah?

15And as the people had great expectations and wondered in their hearts about Yohanan, whether he might be the mashiah, 16Yohanan answered them all, saying,

I wash you with water,

but one is coming who is stronger than I,

and I am not worthy to untie the strap of his sandals.

He will immerse you in holy spirit and fire.

17His winnowing fork is in hand to clean out the threshing floor

and to gather the grain into his storehouse,

but the chaff he will burn up in quenchless fire.

18And with many other words of exhortation, Yohanan proclaimed the good news to the people.

Yohanan imprisoned

19But Herod the tetrarch, whom Yohanan had rebuked about Herodias his brother's wife and about all the misdeeds that Herod had done, 20added one more to them all: he locked Yohanan up in prison.[58]

Yeshua baptized

21Now it happened that in washing all the people and also Yeshua while he was praying, the sky opened 22and the holy spirit descended on him in the bodily form of a dove. A voice came out of the sky, saying,

You are my son whom I love.

In you I am pleased.[59]

His ancestry

23And Yeshua was about thirty years old when he began his work, being the son (as it was thought) of Yosef, son of Eli,[60] 24son of Mattat,[61] son of Levi, son of Malki,[62] son of Yannai,[63] son of Yosef, 25son of Mattatias, son of Amos,[64] son of Nahum, son of Hesli,[65] son of Naggai, 26son of Mahat,[66] son of Mattathi-

---

[58] According to Josephus, Yohanan was imprisoned in Machaerus, Herod Antipas's fortress palace overlooking the Dead Sea, later in Yeshua's life (*Antiquities* 18.5.2).

[59] Other manuscript readings give, "Today I have begotten you."

[60] Heli.

[61] Matthat.

[62] Melchi.

[63] Jannai.

[64] Amos, as in the prophet, is not to be confused with Amoz, the father of Isaiah.

[65] Esli.

[66] Maath.

yah, son of Shimi,[67] son of Yoseh,[68] son of Yodah,[69] 27son of Yohanan,[70] son of Reisha,[71] son of Zerubavel,[72] son of Shaltiel,[73] son of Neri, 28son of Malki, son of Addi, son of Kosam,[74] son of Elmadan,[75] son of Er, 29son of Yeshua, son of Eliezer, son of Yoram,[76] son of Mattat, son of Levi, 30son of Shimon, son of Yehuda, son of Yosef, son of Yonam, son of Elyakim,[77] 31son of Malah,[78] son of Manah,[79] son of Mattatah,[80] son of Natan,[81] son of David, 32son of Yishai,[82] son of Obev,[83] son of Boaz, son of Salmon, son of Nahshon, 33son of Amminadav,[84] son of Admin, son of Arni, son of Hetzron,[85] son of Peretz,[86] son of Yehuda, 34son of Yaakov, son of Yitzhak, son of Avraham, son of Terah, son of Nahor, 35son of Serug, son of Reu, son of Peleg, son of Ever,[87] son of Shelah, 36son of Keinan,[88] son of Arpahshad,[89] son of Shem, son of Noah, son of Lemeh,[90] 37son of Metushelah,[91] son of Hanoh,[92] son of Yered,[93] son of Mahalalel,[94] son of Keinan, 38son of Enosh,[95] son of Shet,[96] son of Adam, son of God.

---

[67] Semein.

[68] Josech.

[69] Joda.

[70] Joanan, John. The Hebrew name passing through the Greek comes out as Joanan, when referring to a Hebrew Bible figure, and John, when a New Covenant figure, taking it from the Greek Ἰωάννης (Ioannes), from the Hebrew יוֹחָנָן (yohanan). John in English is further removed from its Semitic source than is Yohanan.

[71] Rhesa.

[72] Zerubbabel.

[73] Shealtiel.

[74] Cosam.

[75] Elmadan.

[76] Jorim.

[77] Eliakim.

[78] Melea.

[79] Menna.

[80] Mattatha.

[81] Nathan.

[82] Jesse.

[83] Obed.

[84] Amminadab.

[85] Hezron.

[86] Perez.

[87] Eber.

[88] Cainan.

[89] Arphaxad.

[90] Lemech.

[91] Methuselah.

[92] Enoch.

[93] Jared.

[94] Mahalaleel.

[95] Enos.

[96] Seth.

CHAPTER 4

Temptation in the desert

Filled with the holy spirit, Yeshua returned from the Yarden[97] and was led by the spirit into the desert 2for forty days, being tested by the devil. And he ate nothing in those days and when they were ended, he hungered.

3The devil said to him,

If you are the son of God,

tell this stone to become bread.

4And Yeshua responded to him,

As it is written in the Torah:

"One does not live by bread alone."[98]

5Then the devil led him very high and showed him all the kingdoms of the world in a flash of time, 6and said to him,

I will give you authority over all these places

along with the glory of these things,

since this has been handed over to me,

and I give it to whomever I please.

7If you worship me it will all be yours.

8And Yeshua answered, saying to him,

It is written in the Torah:

"You will worship the lord our God

and will serve him alone."[99]

Temptation from the Temple rooftop

9The devil led him to Yerushalayim and placed him on the pinnacle of the Temple and said to him,

If you are the son of God, leap down from here,

10for it is written in Psalms:

He will command his angels to protect you,

11and on their hands they will hold you up

so you won't smash your foot against a stone.[100]

12Yeshua answered, saying to him,

---

[97] Jordan.

[98] Deut. 8.43. The Torah is specifically the five books of Moses but is normally used as a synecdoche for the entire Hebrew Bible.

[99] Deut. 6.3.

[100] Ps. 91.11–12.

You will not test the lord your God.[101]

13When the devil had completed every test, he left him for a better time.

Teaching in synagogues in the Galil

14And Yeshua returned in the power of the spirit to the Galil. And rumor went out about him in the surrounding countryside. 15He taught in their synagogues, honored by all.[102]

Saying Yeshayah's prophecy in synagogue in Natzeret

16He came to Natzeret where he had been raised, and on Shabbat[103] he entered the synagogue as was the custom, and stood up to read. 17He was given the book of the prophet Yeshayah. And he unrolled the scroll[104] and found the place where it was written,

18The spirit of the lord is upon me,
> through which he anointed me
>> to bring good news to the poor.

He sent me to preach release of captives
> and vision to the blind,
>> to let the downtrodden go free,
19to proclaim the year of the lord's favor.[105]

20He rolled up the book, gave it back to the servant, and sat down. And the eyes of all in the synagogue were fixed on him. 21He began to speak to them,

Today the Torah is fulfilled in your ears.

Prophet unwelcome in one's country

22And all spoke well of him and marveled at the grace in the words that came from his mouth, and said, "Isn't this Yosef's son?"

23He said to them,

---

[101] From the Greek πειρασμός (peirasmos), "test." Also translated as "temptation," which lightly heightens specific "test" to conceptual religious "temptation."

[102] From the Greek ἐν ταῖς συναγωγαῖς αὐτῶν (en tais synagogais auton), "in their synagogues." *Auton,* meaning "of them" or "their," is a crucial distancing pronoun, since, decades before the fact; it implies a distinction of identity between Yeshua and the Jews of the synagogue. If Yeshua, a Galilean, is to be fully identified as a Jew, it should be "in *the* synagogues" or "in *his* synagogues," since he was in his homeland of Galilee. One would not say that Augustine taught "in their churches." Augustine would be teaching "in the churches," for he and the congregation were identified as one, whether it was Galilee or Rome.

[103] Sabbath from the Greek σάββατον (sabbaton), from the Hebrew שַׁבָּה (shabbat).

[104] The Greek uses βιβλίον (biblion), "book." Here a "book" is a "scroll."

[105] The basic tenets of Yeshua's ministry and his later title appear in this passage from Isaiah 61.1–2 and 58.6: the spirit of the lord in him; anointment by God; bringing the good news (the evangels); setting free captives; vision to the blind (in physical and metaphorical sense); freeing the poor; a year of the lord's favor (coming of the time of deliverance).

Surely you will tell me the parable,

"Doctor, heal yourself," and you will say,

"All that we heard that happened in Kfar Nahum,[106]

accomplish here in my own country."

24But he said, "Amen, I tell you,"

No prophet is welcome in his own country.[107]

25But truly there were many widows in Yisrael in the days of Eliyah[108]

when the sky was closed for three years and six months

and so there was great famine over all the land

26and Eliyah was sent to no one except to a widow

at Tzarfat[109] in Tzidon.[110]

27And many lepers were in Yisrael in days of the prophet Elisha,

and none of them was made clean except Naaman the Syrian.

28Then all those in the synagogue were filled with anger when they heard these things 29and rose up and drove him out of the city. They led him up to the edge of the hill, on which the city was built, to fling him over. 30But he passed through their midst and went on his way.

With a demoniac

31And he went down to Kfar Nahum, a city in the Galil, and he taught them on days of Shabbat, 32and they were astonished at his teaching because of the authority of his word.

33And in the synagogue there was a man who had the spirit of an unclean demon[111] and he cried out in a great voice, 34"Ha! What are you to us, Yeshua of Natzeret?[112] Did you come to destroy us? I know who you are, the holy one of God!"

35Yeshua reproved him, saying,

Be silent and come out of him.

The demon threw the man down in the middle of them and he came out of him without harming him.

---

[106] Capernaum.

[107] See note 56 on Mark 3.35.

[108] Elijah from the Greek Ἠλίας (Elias), from the Hebrew אֵלִיָּה (eliyah).

[109] Zarephath from the Greek Σάρεπτα (Sarepta), from the Hebrew צָרְפַת (tzarfat).

[110] Sidon from the Greek Σιδών (Sidon), from the Hebrew צדון (tzidon).

[111] Reflecting the pattern of inserting or elevating a religious significance to the lexicon, "demon," from the Greek δαίμων (daimon), is translated as "devil" in Tyndale, James, and other early versions. After the Revised, "demon" is translated as "demon." In classical Greek, as in Homer's theogony, *daimon* is a "divinity" or "god."

[112] Nazareth from the Greek Ναζαρέτ (Nazaret). Since the town is not mentioned by name in the Hebrew Bible or the Talmud, the Hebrew form of the word is uncertain. It could be from Netzeret, meaning "sentinel" or Natzoret, meaning "watchtower."

₃₆Then wonder came over everyone and they talked to one another, saying, "What is this word that in its authority and power he commands unclean spirits and they come out?"

₃₇And rumor went out about him into every place of the surrounding region.

Shimon's feverish mother-in-law

₃₈Then he rose up from the synagogue and entered the house of Shimon.[113] Shimon's mother-in-law was suffering from a great fever and they asked him about her.

₃₉He stood over her and reproved the fever and it left her.

At once she got up and served them.

Demons cry, "You are God's son"

₄₀As the sun was setting, all who had people sick with various diseases brought them to him, and he laid his hands on each of them and healed them. ₄₁Demons came out of many of them, shouting, "You are the son of God."

But he rebuked them, forbidding them to speak, because they knew he was the mashiah.

From a deserted place Yeshua goes on to preach in Yehuda

₄₂When day came he left and went into a deserted place and the crowds were looking for him and came up to him and held him back so that he could not go away from them. ₄₃But he said to them,

I must preach the good news of the kingdom of God
in other cities,
since for this I was sent.

₄₄And he preached in the synagogues of Yehuda.[114]

CHAPTER 5

Calling his first students, who are fishermen

Now it happened that while the crowd pressed in around him to hear the word of God, Yeshua was standing beside the lake of Gennesaret. ₂He saw two ships there beside the lake. But the fishermen had got out of them and were

---

[113] In this brief episode, Shimon or Simeon will be Shimon Kefa (Simon Peter). See note 44 on Mark 3.16 for the derivation of Simon Peter.

[114] Other early texts, which the King James used, say Galilee rather than Judea. The Nestle-Aland gives Judea.

washing their nets. ₃He climbed into one of the ships, one that was Shimon's, and asked him to take him out a little away from the shore. Then he sat down and from the boat he taught the crowds.

₄When he stopped speaking, he said to Shimon,

Go out into the deep waters
and drop your nets and fish.

₅Shimon answered and said, "Rabbi, all through the night we worked hard and caught nothing. But on your word I will lower the nets."

₆And when they did this, they caught such an abundance of fish that their nets were breaking. ₇They signaled their partners in the other ship to come help them. They came and they filled both ships so much it was sinking them.

₈Shimon Kefa fell down at Yeshua's knees and said, "Go away from me, lord. I am a sinful man."[115]

₉He and all who were with him were amazed at the haul of fish they took in. ₁₀And so were Yaakov and Yohanan, sons of Zavdai,[116] who were partners with Shimon.

Yeshua said to Shimon,

Do not be afraid. From now on
you will be catching people.

₁₁And they beached their boats and left everything and followed him.

With lepers

₁₂It happened that while he was in one of the cities, look, there was a man full of leprosy. On seeing Yeshua, he fell on his face and implored him, saying, "Sir, if you want to, you can make me clean."

₁₃Then stretching out his hand, Yeshua touched him, saying,

I want to. Now be clean.

And at once the leprosy left him.

₁₄He ordered him,

Tell no one but go,
and then show yourself to the priest
and, as Mosheh commanded, make an offering
for your cleansing,
and do this as a testimony to them.

₁₅But the word about him spread even more, and great crowds came together to hear him and be healed of their sicknesses.

₁₆Yeshua withdrew into the desert and was praying.

---

[115] "Sinful" from the Greek ἁμαρτωλός (hamartolos) is the usual New Covenant translation. In ancient Greek, the word means one who "misses the mark," who "fails" or "goes astray."
[116] Zebedee from the Greek Ζεβεδαῖος (Zebedaios), from the Hebrew זַבְדִּי (zavdai).

A paralytic

17It happened that on one of those days while he was teaching, seated there were Prushim[117] and rabbis of the law, who had come from every village of the Galil and Yehuda and from Yerushalayim. The power of the lord was in him to heal. 18And look, men, carrying a man on a stretcher, who was paralyzed, and they tried to carry him in and place him before Yeshua. 19And finding no way to bring him in because of the crowd, they went up on the roof and lowered him on the stretcher through the tiles into the middle, in front of Yeshua. 20When he saw their faith he said,

> Friend, your sins are forgiven.

21Then the scholars and the Prushim began to reason, saying, "Who is this who speaks blasphemies? Who can forgive sins but God alone?"

22Yeshua perceived their reasoning, and answered, saying to them,

> Why do you reason in your hearts?
> 23Which is easier: to say, "Your sins are forgiven,"
> or to say, "Stand up and walk"?

Then to the paralytic, he said,

> 24But for you to know that the earthly son
> has authority on earth to forgive sins,
> I tell you, "Stand up and take up your bed
> and go to your house."

25And at once he stood up before them all, and took up what he was lying on, and he left for his house, glorifying God.

26And ecstasy overcame everyone, and they glorified God and they were filled with fear, saying, "Today we saw the extraordinary."

With Levi the tax collector

27After these things he went outside and saw a tax collector named Levi,[118] sitting in the tax booth. And he said to him,

> Follow me.

28Leaving everything behind, he got up and followed him.

29And Levi arranged a great feast for him in his house, and there was a throng of tax collectors and others who were with him reclining at the table.

30The Prushim and their scholars were grumbling to Yeshua's students, saying, "Why do you eat and drink with sinners?"

31And Yeshua answered and said to them,

---

[117] Pharisees from the Greek Φαρισαῖος (Farisaisos) from the Hebrew פְּרוּשִׁים (prushim). Pharisee (s.) is Parush.

[118] Levi from the Greek Λευί (Levi), from the Hebrew לֵוִי (levi), is identified with the evangelist Matthew.

The healthy do not need a physician
but the sick do.
32I did not come to call the just to repent
but the sinners.

33But they said to him, "The students of Yohanan often fast and say prayers, and so too the students of the Prushim, but your students eat and drink."

34Then Yeshua said to them,

Can you ask the members of the wedding party to fast
while the bridegroom is still with them?[119]
35The day will come when the bridegroom
will be taken away from them,
and in those days they will fast.

New wine in old wineskins

36He told them a parable,

No one tears a patch of cloth from a new coat
to sew on an old coat
for the new one will tear
and the piece from the new will not match the old.
37No one pours new wine into old wineskins,
since the new wine will split the skins
and the wine be spilled and the skins destroyed.
38But new wine must be put in new skins.

And he added,

39Yet no one drinking old wine wants the new.
The old is good.

CHAPTER 6

Shabbat in the grain fields

It happened on Shabbat[120] that he passed through grain fields, and his students picked and ate the ears of grain, rubbing them in their hands.

2And some of the Prushim said, "Why are you doing what is not permitted on Shabbat?"

---

119 Members of the wedding from the Greek υἱοὺς τοῦ νυμφῶνος (uious tou numfonos), meaning "sons" or "children of the bridal chamber" and may also be understood as "attendants of the bridegroom."

120 Sabbath.

₃Yeshua answered and said to them,

> Have you not read what David did when he
> was hungry and those with him were hungry,
> ₄how he went into the house of God
> and took the show bread and ate it
> and gave bread to those who were with him,
> which can only be eaten by the priests?

₅And he said to them,

> The earthly son is the lord of Shabbat.[121]

Man with a shriveled hand

₆And it happened that on another Shabbat he went into the synagogue and taught. There was a man there and his right hand was crippled. ₇The scholars and the Prushim were watching Yeshua to see whether he healed on Shabbat so they might accuse him. ₈But he knew their thoughts, and said to the man with the crippled hand,

> Rise and stand before everyone.

And he rose and stood there.

₉Yeshua said to them,

> I ask you if it is lawful to do good or do evil
>> on Shabbat,
> to save or to destroy?

₁₀And after looking around at all of them, he said to him,

> Stretch out your arm.

And he did so and his arm was restored.

₁₁But they were filled with fury and talked with each other about what they could do to Yeshua.

Choosing his twelve messengers

₁₂And it happened in those days that he went out to the mountains to pray, and he spent the whole night in prayer to God. ₁₃And when it was day he summoned his students and chose twelve of them, whom he named messengers.[122] ₁₄Shimon whom he named Kefa,[123] and Andreas[124] his brother, and Yaakov,[125] and

---

[121] There exists in English the beautiful phrase "Lord of the Sabbath," which comes from Luke 6.5. The Internet search engine Google lists 165,000 entries of "Lord of the Sabbath," carrying us from Tyndale to Dylan Thomas.

[122] Apostles. See note 41 on Mark 3.13.

[123] Paul called him "Cephas" (Greek transliteration of Kefa), meaning "stone" or "rock" in Aramaic.

[124] Andrew from the Greek Ἀνδρέας (Andreas). Andreas, like Markos and Loukas, are Greek names used by Jews in Israel.

[125] James (Jacob) from the Greek Ἰάκωβος (Iakobos), from the Hebrew יַעֲקֹב (yaakov).

Yohanan and Filippos and Bartalmai,[126] 15and Mattai[127] and Toma[128] and Yaakov son of Halfi,[129] and Shimon who was called the Zealot, 16and Yehuda[130] son of Yaakov, and Yehuda, man of Keriot,[131] who became a traitor.

Sermon on the Plain[132]

17He went down with them and stood on the plain,[133] and there was a huge crowd of students and a great multitude of people from all Yehuda and Yerushalayim and the coastal region of Tzor[134] and Tzidon.[135]

18Those who came to hear him and be healed of their diseases, and those troubled with unclean spirits were cured. 19And all in the crowd tried to touch him.

Blessings

20He raised his eyes to the students and said,[136]

Blessed are the poor
for yours is the kingdom of God.

21Blessed are you who are hungry now
for you will be fed.

Blessed are you who weep now
for you will laugh.

22Blessed are you when people hate you,
when they ostracize you and blame you

and cast your name about as evil because of the earthly son.
23Be happy on that day and spring and leap,

---

126 Bartholomew from the Greek Βαρθολομαῖος (Bartholmaios), from the Hebrew בַּר תַּלְמַי (bar talmai).

127 Matthew from the Greek Μαθθαιοσ (Maththaios), from the Hebrew מַתִּתְיָה (mattityah) or from the Aramaic (mattai).

128 Thomas from the Greek Θωμᾶς (Thomas), from the Aramaic תְּאוֹמָא (toma).

129 Alphaeus from the Greek Ἀλφαῖος (Halfaios), from the Hebrew חַלְפִּי (halfi).

130 Judas from the Greek Ἰούδας (Ioudas), from the Hebrew יְהוּדָה (yehuda).

131 Iscariot from the Greek Ἰσκαριώθ (Iskarioth), from the Hebrew אִישׁ קְרִיּוֹת (ish keriot), meaning "man of Keriot." In English, "Keriot" is also written "Kerioth."

132 The Sermon on the Plain (the title does not appear in the New Covenant), 6.20–49, is often compared to the larger Sermon on the Mount in Matthew in chapters 5–7, 10, 13, 18, 24–25.

133 Literally, a level place.

134 Tyre from the Greek Τύρος (Tyros), from the Aramaic טור (tur), from the Hebrew צֹר (tzor), meaning "hard quartz" or "a flint knife."

135 Sidon.

136 20–23. These four passages are commonly called the "Beatitudes" or "blessings," as in Matthew's eight Beatitudes, 5.3–10.

for look, your reward is great in the sky.
For in the same way their fathers treated the prophets.

Plagues

24But a plague on you the rich,[137]
for you have received your consolation.

25A plague on you who are filled now,
for you will hunger.

A plague on you who laugh now,
for you will mourn and weep.

26A plague on you when all people speak well of you,
for so did their fathers treat the false prophets.

27But I say to you who listen,
love your enemies, do good to those who hate you,
28and praise those who curse you.

Sayings of love and enemies

Praise those who curse you.
Pray for those who abuse you.

29When one slaps you on the cheek,
offer the other cheek as well.

From one who takes your coat,
do not withhold your shirt.

30To all who ask you,
give what you have.

From one who takes what is yours,
ask nothing back.

---

[137] 24–26. These are commonly called the "woes" or "curses." The word "woe" is archaic in English. The
cliché "a plague on" comes closer to the Greek "woe" than does "woe" or "curse."

31As you wish people to do for you,
do for them.

32If you love those who love you, what grace is yours?
Even sinners love those who love them.

33And if you do good to those who do good,
what grace is yours? Sinners do the same.

34If you lend to those from whom you hope return,
    what grace is yours?
Even sinners lend to sinners for a like return.

35But love your enemies and do good,
and when you loan, ask nothing in return.

Your reward will be great.
You will be the children of the highest.

He is kind to the ungrateful as he is to the cunning.[138]
36Be compassionate as your father is compassionate.

Sayings of judgment

37Do not judge and you will not be judged.
Do not condemn and you will not be condemned.

Forgive and you will be forgiven.
38Give and you will be given.

A good measure of wheat[139] shaken, packed down
and overflowing will be placed in your lap,

since the measure of your measure
will be the measure of your return.

---

[138] Also has the New Covenant meaning of "wicked."

[139] "Wheat" is not in the Greek. The implication is probably that a measure of wheat will be pressed into the fold of the garment and overflow.

Sayings and parables

39Then he told a parable,
Surely the blind cannot guide the blind?
Will they not both fall into a pit?

40A student is not above the teacher,
but fully trained, everyone is like the teacher.

41Why do you see the splinter in the eye of your brother
when the log in your own eye you cannot perceive?

42How can you say to your brother, "Let me take out
the splinter in your eye"
when the log in your eye you do not see?

Hypocrite! First take the log out of your eye
and then you will see clearly to take the splinter
out of the eye of your brother.

Tree and its fruit

43No good tree bears rotten fruit,
and so no rotten tree bears good fruit.
44Each tree is known by its own fruit.

Not from thorns are figs gathered
nor from brambles are grapes picked.

45The good person from the good treasure house of the heart
brings forth good,
and the cunning person out of cunning brings forth cunning.

Out of the fullness of the heart, the mouth speaks.

Parable of house and foundation

46Why do you call me "lord, lord,"[140] and do not do
what I say?

---

[140] Lord from the Greek κύριος (kyrios) is always ambivalent, since it means "Lord," "lord," "master,"
and "Mr." and "Sir." Here it appears to mean primarily "Adonai," that is, "Lord," which in the Aramaic and Hebrew of Yeshua's day would be אָדוֹן (adon) "lord," or "Adonai, my lord." Lord could also
have been YHVH, from the Hebrew יַהְוֶה, the Hebrew Tetragrammaton representing the name of
God. Adonai, my lord, is one of the alternate ways of expressing the presumably unsayable YHWH

₄₇When anyone comes to me and hears my words
 and does them,
I will show you who that person is like.
₄₈That person is like the man building a house
who dug and went down deep and laid a foundation
 on rock.
The flood came and the river burst against that house
and it was not strong enough to shake it,
because the house was well built.
₄₉But one who hears and does not do
is like the man who built a house on the earth
 without any foundation,
against which the river burst
and at once the house collapsed under the river
and the ruin of that house was great.

CHAPTER 7

With a Roman officer's slave boy

After he had completed all his sayings for the people to hear, he entered Kfar Nahum. ₂A centurion[141] had a certain slave, whom he highly prized, who was sick and near death. ₃Hearing about Yeshua, the Roman sent some Jewish elders to go to Yeshua, asking him to cure his slave. ₄When they came to him, they pleaded with him urgently, saying, "He is worthy of your doing this, ₅for he loves our people and he built our synagogue."[142]

₆And Yeshua went with them.

(or YHVH), made up of the letters *yodh he vav he.* However, the vowels under the letters do make YHWH pronounceable as Yahweh or Yahveh. See glossary for Yahweh and YHWH.

[141] A Roman officer usually commanding one hundred men.

[142] The role of Roman officers is presented as benevolent. In these years of common Roman crucifixion, Rome is portrayed in the gospels as benign, and her destruction of the Temple in 70 C.E. is prophesied as a fit punishment of the Jews, both for their wickedness in opposing Rome and their failure to recognize Yeshua as messiah. The centurion commanding the execution squad and the squad itself are the first to affirm the crucified Yeshua as God's son. In the above passage, implausibly, the Jewish elders claim that the Roman officer loves the nation and has built their synagogue. And in Luke 7.9, Yeshua tells us that the Roman officer's faith goes beyond that of anyone in Israel, and so beyond that of his own followers and students. Passages such as Yeshua's heaping praise on the officer's faith reflect layers of scribal emendation that make the gospels an apology for Rome and the later Christian church in Constantinople and Rome. As such, the gospels stand in contrast to Apocalypse, which is

But when he was not far from the house, the centurion sent friends to tell him, "Sir, do not trouble yourself, for I am not fit to have you come under my roof. 7Therefore I didn't think myself worthy to come to you. But say the word, and let my boy be healed. 8I am also a man placed under orders, with soldiers under me. I say to this one, 'Go,' and he goes, and to another, 'Come,' and he comes, and to my slave, 'Do this,' and he does it."

9Yeshua hearing this was amazed by him, and he turned to the crowd following him and said,

I tell you,

I have not found such faith in Yisrael.

10When those who had been sent returned to the house they found the slave in good health.

Touching a coffin in Naïn

11And it happened on the next day that he went to a city called Naïn,[143] and his students and a large crowd went along with him. 12As he came near the gate of the city, look, there was a dead man being carried out, the only son of his mother, and she was a widow. A sizable crowd from the city was with her.

13When he saw her, the lord pitied her and said to her,

Don't weep.

14And coming near he touched the coffin, and those carrying it stopped, and he said,

Young man, I tell you, stand up.

15And the dead man sat up and began to speak, and Yeshua gave him to his mother.

16Fear seized all of them and they glorified God saying,

A great prophet has risen among us!

God has looked on his people!

17The word about him went out through Yehuda and in all the surrounding countryside.

Who is mashiah? Who is prophet?

18Yohanan's students brought him news of all these things. And Yohanan summoned two of his students 19and sent them to Yeshua to say,

Are you one who is to come

or should we look for another?

---

violently anti-Roman, revealing the plight of early Christian Jews and Christian gentiles, who, as in Cappadocia, built churches in underground caves and lived in terror of Roman purpose and acts.
[143] Nain. Probably Naim in the Hebrew.

₂₀And when the men came to him they said, "Yohanan the Dipper sent us to ask you, 'Are you the one who is to come or should we look for another?'"

₂₁In that time he healed many with diseases and afflictions and evil spirits and many blind he graced with sight. ₂₂He answered, saying to them,

Go and tell Yohanan what you have seen and heard.

"The blind see again, the lame walk, lepers are cleansed,

the deaf hear, the dead arise,

the poor are told good news."

₂₃And blessed is one who does not stumble

and fall into wrong because of me.

Yeshua commending Yohanan

₂₄When the messengers of Yohanan left, Yeshua began to talk about Yohanan to the crowds,

What did you come into the desert to see?

A reed shaken by the wind?

₂₅But what did you come out to look at?

A man dressed in soft clothing?

Look, those who are in splendid clothing

and luxury are in the palaces of the kings.

₂₆But what did you go out to see? A prophet?

Yes, I tell you. And more than a prophet.

₂₇This is he about whom Malachi writes:[144]

"Look, I send my messenger before your face

who will prepare the way before you."

₂₈I tell you, among those born of women

there is no one greater than Yohanan.

But there is one who is the very least,

yet in the kingdom of God greater than he.

₂₉And all the people who heard this, including the tax collectors, found justice in God, since they had been cleansed with Yohanan's immersion. ₃₀But the Prushim and the lawyers rejected God's will, since they had not been immersed by him.

They call me a glutton and a drunk

Yeshua said,

₃₁What are the people of this generation like

---

144 Mal. 3.1. The words are directly from Malachi, but they also appear earlier in Exodus 23.20. Malachi comes from the Hebrew מַלְאָכִי (malachi), meaning "messenger" or "angel."

and to whom shall I compare them?
32They are like children in the marketplace,
sitting and calling out to each other, who say,

We played the flute for you
and you did not dance.
We sang a dirge
but you did not weep.

33Yohanan the Dipper came and ate no bread
and drank no wine, and you say, "He has a demon."
34The earthly son comes and eats and drinks
and you say, "Look, this man is a glutton and a drunk,
a friend of tax collectors and sinners."
35But wisdom is proved right by all her children.

A woman washes Yeshua's feet with her tears and dries them with her hair

36One of the Prushim asked Yeshua to eat with him, and he went into the house of the Parush and reclined at the table. 37And look, there was a woman of the city who was a sinner.[145] When she learned that he was reclining in the house of the Parush, she brought in an alabaster jar of myrrh. 38Standing behind his feet and weeping, she began to wash his feet with her tears. She dried them with her hair and kissed his feet and anointed them with myrrh.

39When the Parush who had invited him saw this, he said to himself, "If this one were a prophet, he would have known who and what kind of woman is touching him, since she is a sinner."

40Yeshua answered and said to him,

Shimon, I have something to say to you.

"Rabbi," he said, "Speak."

41A money lender had two people in his debt.
One owed five hundred denarii, another fifty.
42When they couldn't pay, he forgave them both.
Now which of them will love him more?

43Shimon answered, saying, "I suppose the one whom he forgave more." He said to Shimon,

You judged right.

44And turning to the woman, he said to Shimon,

Do you see this woman?
I came into your house.

---

[145] A prostitute.

You did not give me water for my feet,

but she washed my feet with her tears.

45You gave me no kiss,

but from the time I came in

she has not stopped kissing my feet.

46You did not anoint my head with olive oil,

but she anointed my feet with myrrh.

47Therefore, I tell you, her many sins

are forgiven, for she loved much.

But one who is forgiven little, loves little.

48And he said to her,

Your sins are forgiven.

49And those who were reclining at the table began to say to each other, "Who is this who even forgives sins?"

50And he said to the woman,

Your faith has saved you. Go in peace.[146]

CHAPTER 8

Women with Yeshua

And it happened after this that he went through every city and village preaching and bringing good news of the kingdom of God, and the twelve were with him. 2And some women were cured of crafty spirits and sicknesses: Miryam who was called Miryam of Magdala[147] from whom seven demons had gone out, 3Yohannah[148] wife of Herod's steward Kuza,[149] and Shoshannah,[150] and many others.

These women provided for Yeshua and the twelve from their own possessions.

Parable of the sower

4When a large crowd assembled and people from every city made their way to him, he said through a parable,

---

146 "Go in peace" in the Hebrew is שָׁלוֹם (shalom).

147 Mary Magdalene from the Galilean town of Magdala.

148 Joanna from the Greek Ἰωάννα or Ἰωάνα (Ioanna or Ioana), probably a feminine form of John from the Greek Ἰωάννης (Ioannes), from the Hebrew יוֹחָנָן (yohanan), from which Yohannah is derived.

149 Chuza.

150 Susanna from the Greek Σουσάννα (Sousanna), from the Hebrew שׁוּשָׁן (shushan), "lily," from which the name Shoshannah, שׁוֹשַׁנָּה (shoshannah) is derived.

5The sower went out to sow his seed
and as he sowed some seed fell by the road
and it was trampled down and birds of the sky ate it.
6And some fell on the rock
and after growing it dried up because it had no moisture.
7And some fell in the midst of thorns,
and when the thorns grew they choked it.
8And some fell into good earth
and after growing it made a hundredfold of fruit.
As he said these things, he called out,
Whoever has ears to hear, hear.
9Then his students asked him what the parable meant.
10And he said,
You are given knowledge of the mysteries of the kingdom
of God
but to others I speak in parables
so that, as Yeshayah says,
Looking they may not see,
and hearing they may not understand.[151]

Telling the mysteries
11Now this is the parable:
The seed is the word of God.
12The ones on the side of the road are those who heard.
Then comes the devil, who takes away the word
from their heart
so they will not believe and be saved.
13Those on the rock are those who when hearing
the word receive it joyfully. But they have
no root. They believe for a while and in time
of trial fall away. 14As for what fell among
the thorns, they are the ones who hear
but are choked with worries and riches
and pleasures, and nothing they do bears fruit.
15What is in the good soil are those who hear
the word with a good and generous heart
and hold to it and bear fruit with patience.

---

[151] Isa. 6.9.

Lamp and light

16No one lights a lamp and puts it in a jar
   or under the bed.
One puts it on a lampstand
so that those who come in may see the light.
17For nothing is hidden that will not become visible,
and nothing is obscure[152] that will not be known
and come into the light.

Who has and has not

18See how you listen, for to anyone who has,
more will be given,
and whoever has not, even what one thinks one has
will be taken away.

Yeshua rejects his mother and brothers

19Then his mother and his brothers came to him, but could not reach him because of the crowd. 20Word came to him, "Your mother and brothers are standing outside, and wish to see you."
21But he answered, saying to them,
   My mother and my brothers are those
   who hear the word of God and do it.[153]

Calming the storm and the sea

22Now it happened on one of those days, he got into a ship, he and his students, and he said to them,
   Let us cross to the other side of the lake.
   And they set out.
23While they sailed he fell asleep, and a wind storm fell down on the lake and they were filling with water and were in danger.
24They went to him and woke him and said, "Rabbi, rabbi, we are lost!"

---

152 Obscure from the Greek ἀπόκρυφον (apokrefon) here translated as "obscure" but may also be rendered "secret" or "hidden." This lamp parable appears again, with variations, in 11.33–36.

153 This instance of Yeshua's rejection of his mother Miryam and his brothers (and sisters) for their apparent lack of faith in his messiahship occurs in the other gospels in various forms. Here, as in Mark 3.21 and 31–32 and in John 7.5, Yeshua states that his true mother and brothers are those in the fields listening to him. When Yeshua avoids his mother and brothers who unsuccessfully seek him out in the fields, the poignancy of familiar conflict is heightened. The scene corresponds to his earlier complaint: "No prophet is welcome in his own country" (Luke 4.24).

But he woke and rebuked the wind and the rough water and they stopped and it was calm. ₂₅And he said to them,

Where is your faith?

And they were afraid and wondered, saying to one another, "Who is this who commands even the winds and the water and they obey him?"

Demoniac and the pigs

₂₆Then they sailed down to the country of the Gerasenes, which is across from the Galil. ₂₇And as he came upon the land, a man from the city met him, a man who had demons[154] and for some time had worn no clothing and did not live in a house but in the tombs. ₂₈When he saw Yeshua, he cried out and fell down before him and in a great voice said, "What am I to you, Yeshua son of the highest God? I beg you, don't torment me."

₂₉For Yeshua had ordered the unclean spirit to come out of the man.

Often it had seized him and he had been bound with chains and shackles and was guarded, but he would break his bonds and go, driven by the demon into the desert.

₃₀But Yeshua asked him,

What is your name?

"Legion," he said, because many demons had entered him.

₃₁Now the demons implored him not to command them to drop back into the abyss.

₃₂There was a herd of pigs feeding on the mountain. The demons begged him to let them enter them.

And he let them.

₃₃When the demons came out of the man, they entered the pigs, and the herd rushed down the slope into the lake and drowned.

₃₄When those feeding them saw what happened, they fled and reported it in the city and in the farmlands. ₃₅Then people came out to see what happened and came to Yeshua and they also found the man, from whom the demons left, seated at the feet of Yeshua, clothed and in his right mind. And they were afraid. ₃₆Those who had seen it told them how the demon-possessed was saved.

---

[154] Demons from the Greek δαιμόνια (daimonia), "demons." In Tyndale, "demon" (δαίμων) is translated as "devil" or "fiend." In KJV and even the Jerusalem Catholic version, the Greek δαίμων is also "devil." In the Revised and most contemporary versions δαίμων is translated as "demon." The older translation practice of making "demons" into "devils" is a *devilizing* (not *demonizing*) of the many demon-possessed figures in the gospels. Contrary to common perception, here Luke's treatment of the episode gives us a richer and more psychologically complex picture of the wild man. He has not fully demonized him. The wild man is initially described as being possessed by "unclean spirits," not "demons." Once cured, however, he is referred to as "the man who had been demonized."

37The whole population of the region asked him to leave them, because they were seized by great fear. So he got into his ship and returned.

38The man from whom the demons had gone out pleaded to go with him, but he sent him away, saying,

39Return to your house and declare how much

God did for you.

And he went away, proclaiming throughout the city how much Yeshua did for him.

Girl near death and a woman bleeding

40When Yeshua returned, the crowd welcomed him, for they were all expecting him. 41And look, a man came to him whose name was Yair,[155] who was a leader in the synagogue, and he fell at Yeshua's feet. He pleaded with him to enter his house 42because his only daughter, who was twelve, was dying.

42As he went the people were crowding around him. 43There was a woman who had been bleeding for twelve years, and [though she had spent all she had on physicians,] no one could heal her.[156] 44Coming from behind she touched the hem of his cloak and immediately her flow of blood stopped.

45Then Yeshua said,

Who touched me?

When everyone denied it, Kefa said, "Rabbi, the crowds are pressing in and squeezing you."

46But Yeshua said,

Someone touched me. I felt the power go out

from me.

47When the woman saw that she had not gone unnoticed, she came trembling and fell down before him. And in the presence of all the people, she declared why she had touched him and how she had been healed at once.

48He said to her,

Daughter, your faith has saved you.

Go in peace.

49While he was speaking, someone came from the house of the leader of the synagogue, saying to him, "Your daughter is dead. Do not trouble the rabbi any longer."

50But Yeshua heard and answered him,

Do not be afraid. Only believe and she

will be saved.

---

[155] Jairus from the Greek Ἰάϊρος (Iairos), from the Hebrew יָאִיר (yair).
[156] Other editions lack the passage enclosed in brackets.

51And he went into the house and did not let anyone enter with him except Kefa and Yohanan and Yaakov and the father of the child and the mother. 52All were weeping and mourning her, but he said,

> Do not weep. She did not die
>
> but is sleeping.

53And they laughed at him, knowing that she was dead. 54He took her hand, and called out, saying,

> Child, get up!

55The spirit came back to her and at once she stood up and he ordered them to give her something to eat.

56Her parents were amazed, but he instructed them to tell no one what happened.

 CHAPTER 9

Missions for the twelve on the road

And he called together the twelve and gave them power and authority over all demons and to heal sicknesses. 2He sent them out to preach the kingdom of God and to heal. 3And he said to them,

> Take nothing for the road,
>
> no staff, no bag, no bread, no silver,
>
> not even two tunics.
>
> 4Whatever house you go into, stay there,
>
> and leave from there.
>
> 5And whoever does not receive you,
>
> as you go out of that city shake the dust
>
> from your feet
>
> in testimony against them.

6And they went out going around through each village, preaching the good news and healing everywhere.

Herod and Yohanan's head

7Now Herod the tetrarch heard about these things happening everywhere, and he was perplexed because it was said by some that Yohanan had been raised from the dead, 8by some that Eliyah had appeared, but by others that one of the ancient prophets had arisen. 9And Herod said, "Yohanan I beheaded, but who is this about whom I hear such things?" And he sought to see him.

The twelve withdraw with Yeshua to Beit Tzaida

₁₀The messengers returned and told him what they had done. And taking them with him, he withdrew privately to a city called Beit Tzaida.[157] ₁₁When the crowds learned of it, they followed him. After welcoming them, he spoke to them about the kingdom of God, and those in need of treatment he healed.

Bread for five thousand on the grass

₁₂The day began to fade, and the twelve came to him, and said to him, "Send the crowd away so that they may go into the surrounding villages and farms to find places to sleep and food to eat. Here we are in a desolate place."

₁₃And he said to them,

  You give them something to eat.

But they said, "We have only five loaves and two fish unless we go to buy food for all these people."

₁₄There were about five thousand men.

He said to his students,

  Have them sit down in groups of fifty.

₁₅And they did so and they made everyone sit down.

₁₆Then he took the five loaves and the two fish and looked up to the sky, and blessed them and broke them and gave them to the students to set before the crowd.

₁₇And they ate and all were fed. What was left over by them was picked up and filled twelve baskets with broken pieces.

Who do you say I am?

₁₈Once when Yeshua was praying alone, the students were with him, and he asked them, saying,

  Who do the crowds say I am?

₁₉They answered, saying,

  Yohanan the Dipper, but others say Eliyah,

  and some say an ancient prophet has risen.

₂₀And he said to them,

  You, who do you say I am?

Kefa answered,

  The mashiah of God.

₂₁He warned them and ordered them to tell no one of this.

---

[157] Bethseda from the Greek Βηθσαϊδά (Bethsaida), from the Hebrew בֵּית צַיְדָא (beit tzaida), which is a place north of the Sea of Galilee.

I will die and be arisen
   22And he said,
      The earthly son must suffer much
      and be rejected by the elders and high priests and scholars
      and be killed
      and on the third day be raised up.

Deny and follow me
   23Then he said to everyone,
      Whoever wants to come after me,
      deny yourself
      and raise your cross each day
      and follow me.

Losing life to find the soul
      24Whoever wants to save the soul
      will lose it,
      but whoever loses the soul because of me
      will save it.

      25What benefit is there to gain the whole world
      and lose or punish yourself?

Earthly son in his kingdom
      26Those who are ashamed of me and my words
      will be ashamed of the earthly son
      when he comes in his glory
      and the glory of his father and the holy angels.
      27But I tell you truth:
      There are some standing here who will not taste death
      until they see the kingdom of God.

Transfigured, his clothing lightning white
   28And it happened about eight days after these sayings, Yeshua took Kefa and Yohanan and Yaakov with him and they went up to the mountain to pray. 29While he was praying, the appearance of his face changed and his clothing was lightning white. 30And look, two men were talking with him, Mosheh and Eliyah, 31who shone in glory, spoke about his departure, which he was to fulfill in Yerushalayim.
   32Kefa and those with him were heavy with sleep. But they woke and saw his glory and the two men who were standing with him. 33And it happened that as

they left him, Kefa said to Yeshua, "Rabbi, it is good for us to be here. Let us make three shelters,[158] one for you and one for Mosheh and one for Eliyah." He didn't know what he was saying.

34While he spoke, a cloud came and overshadowed them. They were frightened as they went into the cloud. 35And a voice came out of the cloud saying,

This is my son, the chosen,[159] hear him!

36And as the voice vanished, Yeshua was found alone. They were silent and no one in those days reported anything they had seen.

Down the mountain to a boy foaming at the mouth

37On the next day when they came down from the mountain a large crowd met him. 38And look, a man from the crowd cried out, saying, "Rabbi, I beg you to look at my son, for he is my only son. 39And look, a spirit takes hold of him and suddenly he screams and it convulses him and he foams at the mouth, it bruises him, and barely leaves him.[160] 40I begged your students to cast it out, and they could not."

41And Yeshua answered, saying,

O unbelieving and crooked generation,
how long will I be with you and endure you?
Bring your son to me.

42While he came near him, the demon threw the boy to the ground and convulsed him, but Yeshua rebuked the unclean spirit and healed the child and returned him to his father.

43And all were astounded at the greatness of God.[161]

I will die

And while all were in wonder at all he was doing, he said to his students,

44Store these words in your ears,
for the earthly son is to be turned over
into human hands.

---

158 Tabernacle from the Greek σκηνή (skene), "tent," from the Hebrew סֻכָּה (sukkah), "shelter" or "tent." The three shelters are associated with the Jewish Sukkoth, the Festival of the Tabernacles or Booths, חַג הַסֻּכָּה (hag hasukkah), an eight-day celebration for autumnal harvest, beginning on the eve of the 15th of Tishri. The sukkah is a small lean-to-like shelter in the fields. One dwells in the sukkah in commemoration of God's protection of Israel when the people were wandering in the desert after their escape from Egypt.

159 Other ancient Greek texts have "my beloved."

160 Symptoms of epilepsy.

161 Only in Luke is there a frequent equation of Yeshua and God before the resurrection. As the latest of the synoptic gospels, there is a formalization of ideas in which the notion of a messiah, born of humans, "the earthly son," and divine God are one.

45But they did not understand this saying. It was hidden from them so they might not perceive it, and they were afraid to ask him about it.

Greatness and the child

46Then there arose a dispute among them as to who might be the greatest of them.

47Yeshua, seeing the thought in their heart, took a child standing near him, 48and he said to them,

> Whoever receives this child in my name
> receives me,
> and whoever receives me receives the one
> who sent me.
> For whoever is smallest among you all,
> that one is great.

Of one not our follower

49And Yohanan said, "Rabbi, we saw someone in your name casting out demons and we tried to stop him, because he is not one of our followers."

50But Yeshua said,

> Do not stop him.
> Whoever is not against you is for you.

Shall we burn the Shomronim village with heaven's fire?

51And it happened that as the day of his ascension came near, he set his face to go to Yerushalayim. 52And he sent messengers ahead of him. They went into a village of Shomronims[162] to make things ready for him, 53but they did not receive him because his face was set for going to Yerushalayim. 54When his students Yaakov and Yohanan saw this, they said,

> Lord, do you want us to summon fire
> down from heaven to consume them?

55But Yeshua turned and reproved them.[163] 56And they went to another village.

Rest nowhere

57As they went along the road, someone said to him, "I will follow you wherever you go."

---

[162] Samaritans. Samaritans are from Samaria, from the Greek Σαμαρία (Samaria), from the Hebrew שמרון (shomron). A Samaritan is a Shomronim.

[163] Having just been given powers of healing and over demons, the messengers (apostles) test Yeshua, asking whether they should use holocaust fire to consume the village and the lives of these inhospitable Samaritans, but Yeshua quickly scolds them and they go on to the next village.

58And Yeshua said to him,
> Foxes have holes and birds of the sky have nests,
> but the earthly son has no place to lay his head.

Let the dead bury the dead

59And he said to another,
> Follow me.

But the man said, "Let me go first to bury my father."
60But Yeshua said to him,
> Let the dead bury their own dead,
> and as for you,
> go and proclaim the kingdom of God.

Do not look back

61And another said, "I will follow you, lord, but first let me say goodbye to my people in my house."
62But Yeshua said,
> No one who puts a hand on the plow
> and looks back
> is fit for the kingdom of God.

CHAPTER 10

Seventy lambs on the road

After these things, the lord appointed seventy[164] others and sent them two by two ahead of him into every city and place where he was going to go. 2And he said to them,
> The harvest is abundant, but the workers few.
> So ask the master of the harvest
> to send out workers into his harvest.
> 3Go forth. Look, I send you as lambs
> into the midst of wolves.
> 4Carry no purse or a bag or sandals,
> and greet no one along the road.

---

[164] Other texts have seventy-two.

Shake the dust from your feet

5Whatever house you enter, first say, "Peace to this house."
6And if a child of peace is there,
your peace will stay with that one.
And if not, it will return to you.
7Remain in the same house, eating and drinking with them,
for the worker deserves his wages.
Don't wander from house to house.
8And when you go into any city and they receive you,
eat what they set before you
9and heal those who are sick and say to them,
"The kingdom of God is near."

10But when you go into any city
where they do not receive you,
go out into its open places and say,
11"Even the dust from this city clinging to our feet
we wipe off against you.
But know this. The kingdom of God is near."
12I tell you on that day it will be more bearable
for Sedom[165] than for that city.

What awaits unrepentant cities

13A plague on you, Horazim,[166] a plague on you, Beit Tzaida.
If the miraculous powers[167] shown among you
had been shown in Tzor and Tzidon,
they would have repented long ago,
and sat in sackcloth and ashes.
14But for Tzor and Tzidon at the day of judgment
it will be more tolerable than it will be for you.
15And you Kfar Nahum, as said in Yeshayah:

---

[165] Sodom from the Greek Χόδομα (Sodoma), from the Hebrew סְדֹם (sedom or sdom).

[166] See note on Matt. 11.21.

[167] Powers from the Greek δύναμις (dynamis), "power." The translation of *dynamis* splits between the RSV and Lattimore that render "powers," which is the immediate classical meaning, and "miracles" in NIV and older versions, which is certainly the intended meaning. If the reader knows that "powers" has taken on the meaning of a "miracle," then to give the vital "powers" would be preferable. However, most readers do not know the ambiguity of the word. Therefore, here, "miracles" seems the appropriate choice, since Luke is, in its majority, a book of miracles. The reader is asked, however, to sense the original meaning of "powers" operating behind the event, which is interpreted as the miracle.

"Will you be exalted to the sky?
No. You will be thrown into Sheol."[168]

16Whoever hears you hears me
and whoever rejects you rejects me
and whoever rejects me rejects the one who sent me.

Return of the seventy

17And the seventy returned with joy, saying, "Sir, even the demons submit to us in your name."

He said to them,

18I saw Satan falling from the sky like a flash of lightning.
19Look, I have given you authority to walk on snakes
    and scorpions,
and over all the power[169] of the enemy,
and nothing will ever harm you.
20But do not rejoice that the spirits submit to you.
Rejoice that your names are written in the skies.

Revealing only to the children

21In that same hour Yeshua rejoiced in the holy spirit, and said,
I thank you, holy father, lord of sky and earth,
for you have hidden these things from the wise and the learned
and revealed them to little children.
Yes, father, for so it pleased you.
22All was given to me by my father,
and no one knows who the son is except the father
and who the father is except the son
and anyone whom the son wishes to reveal it to.

---

168 Sheol from the Greek ᾅδης (Hades), from the Hebrew שְׁאוֹל (sheol). These two lines of exaltation and damnation are a translation from Isaiah 14.13–15, taken directly from the Septuagint version of the Torah. In the Hebrew text of Isaiah 14.15, Sheol means "pit" or "underworld of the dead," which may be thought of as a relatively benign Greek Hades as opposed to fiery Gei Hinnom (Gehenna), which, as a *fiery* pit outside Jerusalem, suggests the more fierce notion of Old Norse hell. Both the Septuagint Greek Bible and the Greek gospels erroneously translate Isaiah's Sheol into English as "Hades." In doing so they follow the New Covenant pattern of Hellenizing the Hebrew Bible, here taking an essential Jewish figure and replacing it with a figure from Greek myth and religion. "Sheol," an accurate transliteration of the Hebrew, is a strong word to represent "the underground place of the dead" and to return its geography from Greece to Israel.

169 The same tradition that makes Yeshua's "powers" be rendered as "miracles" can also make the powers of the enemies understood to be "miracles."

What his students have seen

23And turning to his students privately, he said,

Blessed are the eyes that see what you have seen.

24I tell you that many prophets and kings

wanted to see what you see and have not seen,

and to hear what you hear and have not heard.

How to find eternal life?

25And look, a lawyer stood up to test him, saying, "Rabbi, what must I do to inherit eternal life?"

26And he said to him,

What is written in the law of the Torah?[170]

How do you read it?

27The man answered and said,

"You will love the lord your God with all your heart,

with all your soul, with all your strength

and with all your mind,

and you will love your neighbor as yourself."

28And Yeshua said to him,

You answered right. Do this and you will live.

Parable of the Good Shomronim[171]

29But wishing to justify himself he said to Yeshua,

And who is my neighbor?

30Yeshua answered and said,

A man was going down from Yerushalayim

to Yeriho[172] and fell into the hands

of robbers. They stripped him and beat him

and went away leaving him half dead.

31By chance a priest went down the same road

and when he saw him he passed by on the other side.

32And a Levite also came by and saw him

and passed by on the other side.

33But a Shomronim on his journey came near

and when he saw him he pitied him.

34He went to him and bound his wounds

and poured olive oil and wine over him,

---

170 Here these basic commandments come from Deuteronomy 6.5 and Leviticus 19.18.

171 Samaritan. See note 54 on John 4.9.

172 Jericho from the Greek Ἰεριχώ (Iericho), from the Hebrew יְרִיחוֹ (yeriho).

and set him on his own beast, and took him
to an inn where he cared for him.
₃₅And on the next day he took out and gave
two denarii to the innkeeper and said,
"Take care of him and what costs you still may have,
I will repay when I return."
₃₆Which of the three seems to you the neighbor
of the man who fell before the robbers?
₃₇And the lawyer said,
The one who treated him with mercy.
Yeshua told him,
Go and you too do the same.

With Marta and Miryam

₃₈And on their journey he went into a certain village. A woman named
Marta[173] took him in. ₃₉And she had a sister named Miryam, who sat at the feet
of the lord and listened to his word. ₄₀But Marta was distracted by her many
house duties and stood near him and said, "Sir, do you not care that my sister
has left me to serve by myself? Tell her to help me."
₄₁And he answered, saying to her,
Marta, Marta, you worry and fret
about many things, ₄₂yet few are needed.
Miryam chose the good portion,
and it will not be taken from her.

 **CHAPTER 11**

How to pray

And it happened that while he was praying in a certain place, when he
stopped, one of his students said to him, "Sir, teach us to pray, as Yohanan
taught his students."
₂And he said to them that when you pray, say,
Father, may your name be holy
may your kingdom come.
₃Give us each day our morning bread

---

[173] Martha from the Greek Μάρθα (Martha), from the Hebrew מָרְתָא (marta).

₄and forgive us when we do wrong
since we shall forgive all in debt to us,
and do not bring us to temptation.[174]

Midnight friend and bread
  ₅And he said to them,
    Who among you has a friend and will go
    to him at midnight and say to him,
    "Friend, lend me three loaves, ₆because my friend
    has come in from the road to my house
    and I have nothing to set before him."
    ₇And the one inside answers and says,
    "Don't bring me troubles. I've already locked
    the door and my children are in bed.
    I cannot get up to give you anything."
    ₈I tell you, even if he will not get up
    and give it to him because he is a friend,
    yet he will wake up and give him
    what he needs because of his persistence.

Knock and the door opens
    ₉I tell you, ask and it will be given you,
    seek and you will find,
    knock and the door will be opened for you.
    ₁₀For all who ask receive
    and the seeker finds,
    and for who knocks the door will be opened.

Son asking for a fish
    ₁₁Who among you has a son who would ask his father
      for a fish
    and instead of a fish he will give him a snake?
    ₁₂Or even if he asked for an egg,
    will he give him a scorpion?
    ₁₃If then you who are cunning know how to give
      good gifts to your children,

---

[174] The King James Version uses other texts that add "And deliver us from evil (cunning)," but modern texts do not include this sentence, which does appear in Matthew's Lord's Prayer.

by how much more will the father from the sky
give holy spirit to those who ask him?

Division and desolation

14He was casting out a deaf man's demons. And it happened that as the demons came out, the deaf man spoke and the crowds marveled.

15Yet some of them said, "It is through Baal Zevul[175] ruler of the demons that he cast out the demons." 16Others tested him, asking him to bring a sign down from the sky. 17But he knew their thoughts, and said to them,

Every kingdom divided against itself becomes desolate
and a house against its own house falls.

18And if Satan is also divided against himself,
how will his kingdom stand?

How I cast out demons

You say I cast out demons through Baal Zevul.
19But if through Baal Zevul I cast out demons,
by whom do your sons cast them out?
So they will be your judges.
20Yet if through the finger of God I cast out demons,
then the kingdom of God has come to you.

Strong man and peace

21When a strong man, fully armed, guards his own castle,
his possessions are in peace.
22But when one stronger than he attacks and overpowers him,
he takes off his armor in which he trusted
and gives away his plunder.

Who is not with me

23One who is not with me is against me
and who does not gather with me scatters.

---

175 Baal Zevul is Beelzebul, Satan, and originally a Philistine deity worshiped at Ekron, twenty-two miles west of Yerushalayim (2 Kings 1.2–18). Beelzebul is from the Greek Βεελζεβούλ (Beelzeboul), from the Hebrew בַּעַל זְבוּל (Baal Zevul). Elsewhere we find Baal Zevuv, who is Beelzebub from Greek Βεελζεβούβ (Beelzeboub), from Hebrew בַּעַל זְבוּב (Baal Zevuv). Baal Zevul may mean "Lord of Dung," and Baal Zevuv may mean "Lord of the Flies." In John Milton's *Paradise Lost* Beelezebub is the prince of evil spirits and Satan's chief lieutenant.

Wanderings of unclean spirit

24When an unclean spirit goes out of a person,
it goes through waterless places seeking a place to rest,
and finding none, it says,
"I shall return to my house from which I came out of."
25And when an unclean spirit goes back,
it finds the house swept and in order.
26Then it goes and picks up other spirits slyer than itself,
seven of them who all go in and live there,
and the last condition for that person
is even worse than the beginning.

The blessed

27And while he was saying this, a woman in the crowd raised her voice and said
to him, "Blessed is the womb that carried you and the breasts that you suckled."
28But he said,
Blessed rather are those who hear the word
of God and obey it.

Sign of Yonah

29As the crowds increased he began to say,
This generation is a malicious generation.
It seeks a sign and it will be given no sign
except for the sign of Yonah.[176]
30Just as Yonah became a sign to the people of Nineveh,
so is the earthly son for this generation.
31The Queen of the South[177] will rise up
on the day of judgment with the men of this generation
and she will condemn them, for she came
from the ends of the earth[178] to hear the wisdom of Shlomoh,[179]
and look, one greater than Shlomoh is here.
32The men of Nineveh will rise up
on the day of judgment with this generation
and condemn it because they repented

---

[176] Jonah from the Greek Ἰωνᾶς (Ιωνασ), from the Hebrew יוֹנָה (yonah). Jonah was three days in the huge fish as Yeshua was buried for three days before his resurrection.
[177] The Queen of Sheba.
[178] Ethiopia.
[179] Solomon from the Greek Σολομών (Solomon), from the Hebrew שְׁלֹמֹה (shlomoh).

on hearing the preaching of Yonah,
and look, one greater than Yonah is here.

Lamp on a stand

33No one lights a lamp and puts it in a hidden place,
    but on the lampstand[180]
so that those who come in may see the light.
34The lamp of the body is your eye.
When your eye is clear, then your whole body
    is filled with light.
35But when it is clouded, then your body is darkness.
36So if your whole body is filled with light,
    with no part dark,
you will be all light as when the lamp illumines you
    with its beams.

Insulting Prushim

37While he was speaking, a Parush asked him to dine with him. So he went inside and reclined at the table. 38The Parush saw this and was astonished that he did not first wash before the meal.

39But the lord said to him,

You Prushim clean the outside of the cup
and dish, but inside you, you are full of greed
and cunning. 40You fools! Did not the one
who made the outside make the inside too?
41But give away what is inside as charity,
and look, everything will be clean for you.
42But a plague on you Prushim![181]
Though you tithe mint and rue and every herb
you neglect justice and the love of God.
You should have practiced tithing
without neglecting to do the others.
43A plague on you Prushim! Because
you love the place of honor in the temples
and the greetings in the marketplaces.
44A plague on you! You are like invisible graves;
people walk over you and don't know it.

---

180 Other texts add "nor under a measuring bucket."
181 These are the six tribulations.

Insulting lawyers

45One of the lawyers answered, saying to him, "Rabbi, in saying these things
you insult us too."

46But Yeshua said,

> And a plague on you too, lawyers!
> You burden people with loads hard to carry,
> yet you don't touch the loads with one
> of your fingers. 47A plague on you
> because you build the tombs of the prophets,
> but your fathers killed them. 48And you are witnesses
> and you approve of the deeds of your fathers,
> since they killed them and you build their tombs.
> 49That is why the wisdom of God has said,
> "I will send them prophets and messengers,
> some of whom they will kill and persecute."
> 50So this generation will be charged
> with the blood spilled of all the prophets
> from the creation of the world, 51from the blood
> of Abel to the blood of Zeharyah,
> who was killed between the altar and the Temple.
> Yes, I tell you, this generation will be charged.[182]
> 52A plague on you lawyers, because

---

[182] Through the voice of Yeshua, Luke reminds the reader that the Jews are murderers of their own
prophets, and that this generation approves the killing deeds of their fathers and hence is guilty of all
the blood spilt from the blood of Abel to the blood of Zechariah, and hence charged "from the creation of the world to this generation." The figures of Abel and Zechariah are cited as examples of
prophets whom the Jews killed, Abel by his brother Cain (Gen. 4.8–10), and Zechariah a priest
murdered in the Temple (2 Chron. 24.20–22). In the Hebrew Bible they are not identified as
prophets. The role of the prophet was firmly established in the pre-exilic monarchic society of Israel,
and there are no references in Hebrew scripture to killing prophets. This particularly strong vitriol
against the Jews of the Hebrew Bible reflects the imagination of later churchmen rather than the utterance of a first-century itinerant rabbi.

At the time of the composition of the gospels, the early Christian Jews and gentile converts had
only the Hebrew Bible (Tanak) as scripture, which was seen with disturbed ambivalence as their own
book but also as the book of Jews from whom they urgently wished to distinguish themselves. While
the Hebrew Bible is quoted abundantly and in a positive light on virtually every page of the gospels,
it is also fiercely condemned as the *Old* Covenant, as opposed to the *New* Covenant. Troubling to resolve was that the people of the Hebrew Bible—the patriarch Abraham, king Solomon, and the
prophet Isaiah—were Jews as were Yeshua and all his lifetime followers. The problem of identity was
imperfectly resolved by having Yeshua condemn his contemporary Jews as inheritors of the guilt of
being murderers of their Jewish prophets, while he, his followers, and his family are presented less
distinctly as Jews and exempt from the wicked inheritance of the Jews and the consequent punishments. In this instance, now even the vaguely unscathed "Israelites," who inhabit the translations of
the Hebrew Bible, have become Jews and are associated with Jews of the New Covenant, who bear
the guilt of their ancestors for having killed their prophets.

you took away the key of knowledge.

You did not go in yourselves, and blocked

the way of those who tried to go in.

53When he went outside, the scholars and the Prushim were fiercely hostile to him and questioned him closely about many things, 54plotting to trap him on something out of his mouth.[183]

CHAPTER 12

Be on guard against the Prushim

Meanwhile, as a crowd of thousands gathered and trampled one another, he began to speak first to his students,

Be on guard against the yeast of the Prushim,

which is their hypocrisy.

Hidden into light

2There is nothing hidden that will not be revealed,

and nothing secret that will not be known.

3What you have said in darkness will be heard in the light,

and what you said to the ear in inner rooms

will be proclaimed on the housetops.

Fear and killing the body

4I tell you my friends, do not be fearful of those who kill

the body

but after that can do nothing more.

5I will show you one to fear.

Fear the one who after killing you has the power

to throw you into Gei Hinnom.[184]

Yes, I tell you, that one you should fear.

---

[183] Out of his mouth from the Greek ἐκ τοῦ στόματος αὐτοῦ (ek tou stomatos autou). Contemporary translations do not render the powerful, literal metaphor "out of his mouth," but the Tyndale and the King James versions follow the Greek to the word. The Revised and later versions explain the metaphor as "something he might say" or "something he might let fall" (Lattimore) or "with his own words" (Annotated Scholars).

[184] Gei Hinnom from the Greek γέεννα (Geenna), "hell," from the Hebrew גיא הנם (gei hinnom), meaning the "Valley of Hinnom." Gei Hinnom is a "special pit of darkness" of the Hebrew Bible. Gei Hinnom and Sheol are normally translated into English as "hell."

God's memory of sparrows and pennies

₆Are five sparrows not sold for two pennies?[185]
And not one of them is forgotten before God.
₇But even the hairs of your head are all counted.
Do not fear.
You are worth more than many sparrows.

Accepted or denied by angels of God

₈I tell you, whoever accepts me before people,
the earthly son will accept before the angels of God.
₉But whoever denies me before people
will be denied before the angels of God.
₁₀And whoever speaks a word against the earthly son
will be forgiven,
but one who blasphemes against the holy spirit
will not be forgiven.
₁₁And when they bring you before the synagogues
and its rulers and authorities,
do not worry how or what you should speak in your defense
or what you should say.
₁₂For in that very hour the holy spirit will teach you
what you must say.

Rich man and death

₁₃Someone in the crowd said to him, "Rabbi, tell my brother to share his inheritance with me."
₁₄But he said to him,
Sir, who appointed me to be the judge
or arbiter between both of you?
₁₅He said to them,
Look and guard against every kind of greed.
Life is not in the possessions one piles up.
₁₆Then he told them a parable, saying,
The farm of a rich man bore excellent crops
₁₇yet he asked himself, "What should I do

---

[185] Pennies or assars from the Greek ἀσσάριον (assarion), a Roman copper coin, worth about one-sixteenth of a denarius. Three words are used for Roman coins: denarius or denar (δηνάριον) or denarion, assarion (diminutive of Latin *as*), and kodrantes (κοδράντης), a loan word from the Latin *quadrans*, and worth about a quarter of a cent. The assarion is translated as "penny," "nickel," "copper," or "farthing."

since I have no place to store my crops?"
18And said, "I'll tear down my barns and build bigger ones.
I'll gather all my grain and goods there
19and say to my soul, 'You have many goods
stored away for many years. Rest, eat, drink, and be happy.'"
20But God said to him, "You fool. This night they demand
your soul.
To whom will go all you have prepared?"
21So it goes for one who stores up treasures
for himself but is not rich before God.

Consider the ravens of the sky

22And Yeshua said to the students,
So I tell you this. Do not worry about your life,
what you eat, about your body, or how you clothe yourself.
23The soul is more than food and the body more
   than clothing.
24Consider the ravens who do not sow or reap,
who have no storehouse or barn,
and God feeds them.
How much more are you worth than the birds!
25Who among you by brooding can add one more hour
   to your life?
26If you cannot do a little thing, why worry about the rest?

Consider the lilies

27Consider the lilies, how they grow.
They do not labor or spin,
but I tell you, not even Shlomoh in all his glory
was clothed like one of these lilies.
28But if God so dresses the grass of the field
which is here today
and tomorrow is cast into the oven,
how much better he will clothe you,
O you of little faith!

Setting hearts on the kingdom

29And look not for what you can eat and drink,
and do not worry.
30All the nations of the world seek them,

but your father knows you are in need.
31Seek only his kingdom
and these things will be added for you.
32Little flock, do not fear, for your father
is happy to give you the kingdom.

Give and no moth or thief destroys

33Sell your possessions and give charities.
Make yourselves purses that never wear out,
be an inexhaustible treasure in the skies
where no thief comes near or moth destroys.
34Where your treasure is,
there also will be your heart.

Master may come at any hour

35Let your loins be girded about and the lamps burning
36and be like people waiting for their master
when he comes back from the wedding,
so that when he comes and knocks
they will open for him at once.
37Blessed are the slaves whom the lord
on his return finds wide awake.
Amen, I tell you, he will gird himself up
and have them recline to eat and he will come near
and he will serve them.
38And if he comes in the second watch[186] or third watch[187]
and finds them alert,
they will be blessed.
39But know this. If the master of the house
knew what time the thief was coming,
he would not have let his house be broken into.
40Be ready, for the earthly son comes
in the hour when you least expect him.

Lashes and death for slaves unprepared for the master's return

41And Kefa said, "Lord, is your parable for us or do you speak to everyone?"
42And the lord said,

---

[186] Midnight.
[187] Three in the morning.

Who is the faithful steward, the prudent one,
whom his master will set over his servants
to give them their measure of bread
at the right time? 43Blessed is that slave
whom the lord when he comes will find
at work. 44I tell you truth, he will put him
in charge of all the possessions.
45But if that slave says in his heart, "My master
is long in coming," and he begins to beat
the men servants and women servants,
and to eat and to drink and to get drunk,
46the lord of that slave will come on a day
when he does not expect him and in an hour
which he does not know, and cut him to pieces
and cast him out with the unfaithful.[188]
47That slave who knows the master's will
but who is not prepared or flaunts his own will
will be flogged with many blows.
48But the one who knows nothing and does
what merits a whipping will be flogged lightly.
Everyone to whom much is given will have
much to return. To whom much was entrusted,
even more they will ask from him.

I came with fire
49I came to cast fire over the earth
and how I wish it were already ablaze!

His need to be washed
50There is a dipping I must undergo,
and how I am afflicted until it is done!

I do not bring peace but division
51Do you think I came to bring peace on earth?
No, I tell you, I came to bring division.
52From now on there will be five in one house
dissenting against two and two against three:[189]

---

[188] The fate of the unfaithful, of not accepting the messiah, is death and everlasting punishment.
[189] This passage here and in Matthew 10.34 have traditionally been interpreted to mean that there will
be conflict between the competing religious sects. The contemporary NIV Study Bible, alluding to

53Father will be divided against son
    and son against father,
mother against daughter
    and daughter against mother,
mother-in-law against daughter-in-law
    and daughter-in-law against mother-in-law.

Reading rain clouds and paying debts

54And he said to the crowds,
When you see a cloud rising in the west,
at once you say a rain storm is coming.
55And so it comes. When a south wind blows
you say it will be hot. 56You hypocrites!
The face of the earth and the sky you know
how to read. Why don't you know how to read
these times? 57Why don't you judge on your own
what is right? 58As you go with your opponent
to the magistrate, try on the way there
to reconcile with him, or you may be dragged
before the judge, and the judge will hand you
over to the bailiff and the bailiff throw you
in jail. 59I tell you, you will never get out
of there until you pay back the last penny.

John 8.44 where the Jews are declared the children of the devil ("You are from your father the devil") interprets: "Yet the inevitable result of Christ's coming is conflict—between Christ and the antichrist, between light and darkness, between Christ's children and the devil's children." *The Study Bible, New Revised Standard Version* (New York: HarperCollins, 1993), comments mildly, "The promise of peace . . . becomes a threat of *division* if the messiah is rejected." The passage is a threat of division and fire on the day of judgment. One can also read the passage as a commentary on an already divisive Israel, within families, including Yeshua's family, between sects, which may coincide with meaning of the affirming passage then quoted from Micah 7.6, which reads: "For the son dishonoureth the father, the daughter riseth up against her mother, the daughter in law against her mother in law; a man's enemies *are* the men of his own house" (KJV).

CHAPTER 13

Repent or perish

At that time some who were there told him about the Galileans whose blood Pilatus had mingled with their sacrifices.[190] 2And he answered and said to them,

> Do you think these Galileans, because
> they suffered in this way, were the worst sinners
> of all the Galileans? 3No, I tell you,
> but unless you repent you will all perish
> like them, 4or like those eighteen when the tower
> of Shiloach fell on them and killed them.[191]
> Do you think they were more guilty
> than the people living in Yerushalayim?
> 5No, I tell you, but unless you repent
> you will perish too just as they all did.

Parable of the barren fig tree

> 6Then Yeshua told this parable,
> A man had a fig tree planted in his vineyard
> and he went looking for fruit on it
> and found none. 7He said to the gardener,[192]
> "Look, for three years I have come looking
> for fruit on this tree and have found none.
> Cut it down. Why should it be wasting the soil?"
> 8But he answered and said to him, "Sir, let it go
> for another year while I dig around it
> and throw manure on it. 9Then it may bear fruit
> in the future. And if not, cut it down."

---

[190] This is the only information we have about a slaughter of Galileans in the midst of religious ceremonies. It seems to say that Pilate's soldiers killed some Galilean Jews in the act of their sacrifices and mixed their blood with their offerings. Pilate's brutal reprisals and disdain of religious practice are elaborated in Josephus's *Antiquities* 18.85–89. Other commentators conjecture that Pilate may have been concerned with an insurrection of the Jews (which came much later). Yeshua's anger against Pilate's killing of Galileans conflicts with the benign picture of Pilate, who washes his hands in a symbol of his innocence in ordering the crucifixion of Yeshua.

[191] Siloam. The tower of Shiloach was built inside the southeast section of Jerusalem's walls.

[192] Literally, "vinekeeper" or "vinedresser."

Working good on Shabbat

10He was teaching in one of the synagogues on Shabbat. 11And look, a woman who had a spirit of sickness for eighteen years and she was bent over and unable to stand up straight at all. 12When he saw her, Yeshua called her over and said to her,

> Woman, you are released from your weakness.

13And he placed his hands on her and at once she stood straightened out and was glorifying God.

14But the leader of the synagogue, angered because Yeshua had healed on Shabbat, said to the crowd, "There are six days on which one must work. So come and be healed on these days and not on the day of Shabbat."

15The lord answered him and said,

> Hypocrites![193] Each of you on the Shabbat,
> do you not untie your ox or your donkey
> from the feeding trough and lead it away
> to give it water? 16And this daughter of Avraham
> whom Satan, look, bound for eighteen years,
> should she not be loosened from this bondage
> even if it is the day of the Shabbat?

17And when he said this, all who opposed him were put to shame, and the entire congregation rejoiced over all the glorious things that came through him.

Mustard seed and kingdom of God

18Then he said,

> What is the kingdom of God like
> and to what shall I compare it?
> 19It is like a mustard seed that a man threw
> into his garden and it grew into a tree,
> and the birds of the sky nested in its branches.

---

[193] After the first statement, the debate concerning the meaning of the Sabbath (Shabbat) turns to severe insult. The inflammatory language by Yeshua was also found commonly in the Hebrew Bible, voiced by prophets and Yahweh himself. There it was perceived as conflict and condemnation within the tribe. In the New Covenant, although the conflict of ideas is still between Jews (Christianity did not exist), it is presented and, more significant, has been virtually universally perceived anachronistically, as a conflict between Christian and Jew, and hence this pattern of vilification has been a primary source of traditional anti-Semitism. It is not known when the invective found its place in scripture, whether it was in the original assemblage or added to it in the course of scribal copying. If the hate word "hypocrites!" did not initiate Yeshua's response, the argument would be perfectly ordinary, and the hearts of the congregation, who are won over to Yeshua's humane interpretation of the Sabbath, would have been no less likely to be won over joyfully. But being there, the invective entirely alters the tone, level, and consequence of the discourse.

Yeast and kingdom of God

20And again he said,

> What is the kingdom of God like?
> 21It is like yeast that a woman took and concealed
> in three measures of wheat
> until it was all leavened.

Narrow gate[194]

22And he walked through cities and villages, teaching and making his way to Yerushalayim. 23Someone said to him, "Sir, will only a few be saved?"

And he said to them,

> 24Struggle to go in through the narrow door,
> because many, I tell you, will try to get in
> and will not succeed, 25for once the master
> of the house wakens and shuts the door,
> you will begin to stand outside and knock,
> saying, "Lord, open for us." And he will answer,
> saying to you, "I do not know you or where
> you come from." 26Then you will begin to say,
> "We ate and drank with you, and you taught
> in our broad streets." 27Then he will tell you,
> "I do not know where you come from.
> Go away from me, all you workers of iniquity!"
> 28There will be the weeping and gnashing of teeth
> when you see Avraham and Yitzhak and Yaakov
> and all the prophets in the kingdom of God,
> but you will be cast alone outside.
> 29And they will come from east and west
> and from north and south and they will recline
> at a table in the kingdom of God. 30And look,
> the last will be first and the first will be last.

A prophet must die in Yerushalayim

31In the same hour some Prushim came near him and said, "Go and make your way out of here, because Herod wants to kill you."

32And he said to them,

> Go and tell that fox, look, I cast out demons

---

194 In Matthew 7.13–14 the narrow gate leads to life; here the narrow gate leads to salvation.

and I perform cures today and tomorrow
and on the third day I am done. 33Yet today
and tomorrow and the next day I must go
on my way, for it is not possible for a prophet
to die outside Yerushalayim. 34Yerushalayim,
Yerushalayim, who kills the prophets
and stones those who are sent to her! How often
I wanted to gather your children together
just as a bird her brood under her wings
and you were unwilling! 35Look, your house
abandons you. But I tell you, you will not
see me until the time you can say: "Blessed
is one who comes in the name of the lord."[195]

CHAPTER 14

Healing a man with dropsy on Shabbat

It happened that when he went into the house of a leading Parush on Shabbat and ate bread, they were watching him closely. 2And look, there was a man before him suffering from dropsy. 3And Yeshua spoke to the lawyers and Prushim, saying,

Is it lawful or not to heal on Shabbat?
4But they were silent.
5And he said to them,

Who among you who has a son or an ox
fallen into a well
will not lift it out immediately
on the day of Shabbat?
6And they were unable to answer.

Choosing a place at the table

7And observing how places of honor at a meal are selected, he told them a parable,

8When you are invited by someone to
a wedding, do not recline at the table

---

[195] Ps. 118.26.

in the place of honor, for possibly one
with more honors than you has been invited
by him. 9Then he who invited you will say
to you, "Give up your place," and you will slip
with shame into the very last place.
10But when you are invited, go and take
the lowest place, so when your host comes
he will say to you, "Friend, move up higher."
Then glory will come to you before all
who are reclining at the table with you,
11because all who exalt themselves high
will be humbled low, and those who choose
to humble themselves will be exalted.

Choosing guests

12He also said to the one who was his host,
When you prepare a lunch or supper,
do not invite your friends or your brothers
or your relations or rich neighbors,
for possibly they will invite you in return
and it will be a repayment to you.
13When you prepare a banquet invite
the poor, the crippled, the lame, the blind.
14Then you will be blessed, for they have no means
to repay you, but you will be repaid
at the resurrection of the good.

Fate of guests who do not come

15Hearing this, one of the guests at the table said to him, "Blessed is one
who eats bread in the kingdom of God."
16Yeshua said to him,
There was a man preparing a great banquet
and he invited many, 17and at the dinner hour
he sent his slave to say to those who were
invited, "Come, because now it is ready."
18Then one and all asked to be excused.
The first said to him, "I bought a field
and I must go out and look at it. I ask
you to excuse me." 19Another said, "I bought
five yokes of oxen and I'm going out

to try them out. I ask you to excuse me."
20Another said, "I took a wife and so
I cannot come." 21When the slave returned
and reported these things to his lord,
then the master of the house got angry
and told his slave, "Go quickly into the squares
and alleys of the city and bring in the poor
and the crippled and the blind and the lame."
22The slave said, "Master, what you ordered
has been done and there is still room." 23The master
said to the slave, "Go out to roads and hedge roads
and compel the people to come in to fill
my house. 24I tell you not one of those men
who were invited will taste my dinner."

Hate your father and mother, renounce everything and follow me

25And there was a large crowd accompanying him and he turned and said
to them,

26If someone comes to me and does not hate
his father and mother and wife and children
and brothers and sisters and even life itself,
he cannot be my student. 27Whoever does not
carry the cross and follow me cannot be
my student. 28Who among you who wants to build
a tower will not first sit down and calculate
the cost to see if you have enough to finish it?
29For if you have put the foundation in place
and cannot finish it, everyone who sees it
will begin to make fun of you 30and say,
"This one began to build and was not able
to complete it." 31Or what king going to war
with another king would not first consider
if with ten thousand he is strong enough
to combat one who comes against him
with twenty thousand? 32If he lacks the force,
while the enemy is still far away, he sends
an envoy to ask for terms of peace.
33So those of you who do not surrender
all possessions cannot be my students.

Taste of salt

34Salt is good. But if salt has lost its taste
how can it be seasoned?
35It is not fit for the land or a dunghill.
They throw it out.
Whoever has ears to hear, hear.

◈ CHAPTER 15

Three parables

Now all the tax collectors and wrongdoers were coming near him to listen
to him. 2And the Prushim and the scholars were grumbling and saying, "This
man welcomes wrongdoers and eats with them."

3But Yeshua told them this parable:

Parable of the lost sheep

4Who among you who has a hundred sheep
and has lost one of them will not leave
the ninety-nine in the wilderness
and go after the one lost until it is found?
5Once he finds it he sets it on his shoulders
and is happy. 6And when he comes home
he calls his friends and neighbors together
and tells them, "Celebrate with me,
for I have found my sheep that was lost."
7I say to you there will be more joy
in heaven over one sinner who repents
than over ninety-nine of the just
who have no need of repentance.

Parable of the lost drachma

8Or what woman who has ten drachmas[196]
if she loses one will not light a lamp
and sweep the house and search carefully

---

[196] The drachma was a Greek silver coin. A drachma was worth about a day's wage.

until she finds it? 9And finding it, she calls
together friends and neighbors, saying,
"Celebrate with me, for I have found the coin
I lost." 10So I tell you, there is joy
among the angels over one sinner who repents.

Parable of the lost son[197]
11And he said,

There was a man who had two sons.
12The younger said to his father, "Father,
give me the share of the property
that will belong to me." So he divided
his resources between them. 13And not
many days later the younger son
got all his things together and went off
to a far country and there he squandered
his substance by riotous living.
14When he had spent everything he had,
there came a severe famine throughout
that country, and he began to be in need.
15And he went and hired out to a citizen
of that land, who sent him to his fields
to feed the pigs. 16He longed to be fed
on the pods the pigs were eating, but no one
gave him anything. 17He came to himself[198]
and said, "How many of the day laborers
of my father have bread left over and here
I'm starving and dying. 18I will rise up
and go to my father and I will say to him,
'Father, I have sinned against heaven
and before you. 19I am no longer worthy
to be called your son. Make me
like one of your hired hands.'" 20And he rose up
and went to his father. While he was still
far off, his father saw him and was filled
with compassion and tears fell on his neck
and he kissed him. 21And the son said to him,

---

[197] Commonly called "The Prodigal Son."
[198] Meaning "he came to his senses."

"Father, I have sinned against heaven
and before you. I am no longer worthy
to be called your son." 22But his father said
to his slaves, "Quick, bring out the finest robe
and put it on him, and give him a ring
for his hand and sandals for his feet.
23And bring the fatted calf, slaughter it,
and let us eat and celebrate, 24for my son
was dead and he came back to life,
he was lost and he has been found."
And they began to celebrate.

25Now the older son was in the fields
and as he drew near the house he heard
music and dancing. 26And he called over
one of his slaves and asked what was going on.
27He told him, "Your brother is here,
and your father has slaughtered the fatted calf
because he took him back in good health."
28He was angry and did not want to go in,
but his father came out and pleaded with him.
29Yet he answered and said to his father,
"Look, so many years I have served you
and never disobeyed an order of yours,
and for me you never gave a young goat
so I could celebrate with my friends.
30But when this son of yours came, who ate up
your property with prostitutes, for him
you slaughtered the fatted calf." 31And he said
to him, "Child, you are always with me,
and everything that is mine is yours,
32but we must be happy and celebrate.
Your brother was a dead man and he lived
and he was lost and has been found."

CHAPTER 16

Crafty steward

Then Yeshua said to his students,

There was a rich man who had a steward[199]
and this steward was accused of squandering
his possessions. 2So he summoned him
and said, "What is this I hear about you?
Give me a statement of your stewardship,
since you can no longer be my steward."
3Then the steward said to himself,
"What will I do now that my master
has taken my stewardship from me?
I am not strong enough to dig. I am
ashamed to beg. 4Now I know what to do
when I am removed from my stewardship
so people will welcome me in their houses."
5And he summoned all the debtors
of his master, one by one. He told the first,
"How much do you owe my master?"
He said, "A hundred measures of olive oil."
6"Take your bills, sit down, and quickly write in
fifty." 7Then to another he said, "How much
do you owe?" "A hundred bushels of wheat,"
he said to him. "Take your bills and write in
eighty." 8And his master praised the steward
for his dishonesty since he had acted shrewdly.
The people of this age are wiser than
the children of light of their generation.
9I say to you: Make friends for yourselves
by way of the mammon of dishonesty,
so when that wealth is gone, you will
be welcomed into the eternal tents.

---

199 Also translated as "manager."

Faithful in money

10One who is faithful in the little thing
is faithful in the bigger, and one who is
dishonest in the little is also dishonest
in the bigger. 11So then if you have not
been faithful with dishonest wealth,
who will believe in you for true riches?
12And if you have not been faithful
with what belongs to another,
who will give you what is your own?

Dilemma of two masters

13No house slave can serve two masters.
Either he will hate one and love the other
or be devoted to one and despise the other.
You cannot serve God and mammon.[200]

Against Prushim who love silver

14When the Prushim, who loved silver,[201] heard all these things, they derided him.

15Yeshua said to them,
You are the ones who justify yourselves
in the eyes of the people, but God knows
your hearts. For what among people is exalted
is in the eyes of God an abomination.

Law and prophets, then the kingdom

16Until Yohanan came it was the law
and the prophets. Since then the kingdom of God
is preached, and all try to force their way in.
17But it is easier for the sky and the earth
to disappear than for one hook of the letter
of the law in the Torah to fall away.

Divorce and adultery

18Anyone who divorces his wife and marries another
commits adultery.

---

[200] Riches or money.
[201] Also means by extension "fond of money."

Anyone who marries a woman divorced from her husband
   commits adultery.

Rich man in burning Sheol, begging help from Avraham in heaven
   19There was a rich man dressed in purple
   and fine linen, and he feasted every day
   in splendor. 20And at the gate lay a poor man
   named Elazar,202 covered with sores,
   21and longing to be fed with the crumbs
   that fell from the rich man's table.
   Even the dogs came to lick his sores.
   22And it happened that the poor man died
   and was carried away by angels to Avraham's side.
   The rich man also died and was buried.
   23And in Sheol203 where he was in torment,
   he raised his eyes and saw Avraham far away
   and Elazar lying on his chest. 24And he called
   and said, "Father Avraham, have mercy on me
   and send Elazar to dip his fingertip into water
   and cool my tongue, for I am in agony
   in this flame." 25But Avraham said, "Child,
   remember that you received the good things
   in your life, and Elazar got the bad.
   But now he is comforted here and you suffer.
   26And more than that, between us and you
   a great chasm has been fixed so that those
   who want to cross over from here to you
   cannot, nor can they cross from there to us."
   27And he said, "Then I ask you, father, to send
   him to my father's house. 28I have five brothers.
   He may warn them so they will not also come
   to this place of torment." 29But Avraham said,
   "They have Mosheh and the prophets. Let them
   listen to them." 30Yet he said, "No, father Avraham,
   if someone goes to them from the dead
   they will repent." 31But Avraham said to him,
   "If they do not listen to Mosheh and the prophets,

---

202 Lazarus from the Greek Λάζαρος (Lazaros), from the Hebrew אֶלְעָזָר (elazar).
203 The underworld.

nothing will persuade them to repent
even if someone rises from the dead."

CHAPTER 17

Millstone to drown one who leads others astray
Yeshua said to his students,
> It is impossible that traps will not be set
> for stumbling into, but a plague on
> anyone who falls in! 2It would be better
> if a millstone were hung around his neck
> and he were cast into the sea
> than to cause these little ones to go astray.

When your brother does wrong
> 3Watch yourselves. If your brother does wrong
> and repents, forgive him. 4And if he does wrong
> seven times a day against you and seven times
> turns around to say, "I repent," forgive him.

Faith uprooting a black mulberry tree
5The messengers said to the lord, "Give us more faith."
6But the lord said,
> If you have faith like a grain of mustard seed
> you could say to this black mulberry tree,
> "Pluck yourself up by the roots and plant yourself
> in the sea," and it would still obey you.

Duty of a slave plowing
> 7But who among you with a slave plowing
> or tending sheep, who comes in from the fields,
> will say to him, "Come here at once and eat
> with me at the table"? 8Will he not say,
> "Prepare something for supper, wrap an apron
> around you, serve me while I eat and drink,
> and after all this, you may eat and drink"?
> 9Does he thank the slave for doing as he
> was commanded? 10So when you too do all
> you were told to do, say, "We're worthless slaves
> and what we did was our duty to do."

With ten lepers

₁₁And it happened on his journey to Yerushalayim, Yeshua passed through the middle of Shomron[204] and the Galil. ₁₂As he went into a certain village ten men who were lepers met him, keeping their distance, ₁₃and raised their voices, saying, "Yeshua, master, have mercy on us!"

₁₄When he saw them, he said to them,

Go and show yourselves to the priests.

And it came about that as they went away they were made clean.

₁₅And one of them, seeing that he was healed, turned, glorifying God in a great voice. ₁₆He fell on his face at his feet, thanking him. And this man was a Shomronim.[205]

₁₇Yeshua answered him and said,

Were not ten made clean? Where now are the nine?

₁₈Has no one come back to glorify God

except this stranger?

₁₉And he said to him,

Rise and go. Your faith has saved you.

Coming of the kingdom of God mysteriously inside

₂₀When he was asked by the Prushim when the kingdom of God was to come, he answered them and said,

The kingdom of God is not coming

in an observable way,

₂₁nor will people say, "Look, it is here!"

or, "It is there!"

For look, the kingdom of God is inside you.

Coming of the earthly son

₂₂Then he said to the students,

The days are coming when you will long to see

one of the days of the earthly son,

and you will not see it.

₂₃And they will say to you, "Look, there!" or "Look, here!"

Do not go after them! Do not follow them!

₂₄For as lightning burns at one end of the sky

and then at the other end of the sky glistens,

so will be the coming of the earthly son.

---

[204] Samaria.
[205] Samaritan.

₂₅But first he must suffer multiple wrongs
and be rejected by this generation.
₂₆And as it happened in the days of Noah,
so it will be in the days of the earthly son.
₂₇The people were eating, drinking, marrying,
and given away in marriage until the day
Noah went into the ark and the flood came
and destroyed all of them.²⁰⁶ ₂₈It was the same
as in the days of Lot. They were eating,
drinking, buying, selling, planting, building.
₂₉But on the day Lot went out of Sedom²⁰⁷
it rained fire and sulfur from the sky
and destroyed everything. ₃₀So it will be
on the day the earthly son is revealed.
₃₁On that day if a man is on the roof and his goods
are in the house, let him not come down
to carry them away. And one in the field
likewise let him not turn back for anything
left behind. ₃₂Remember the wife of Lot.
₃₃Whoever tries to preserve her life will lose it,
but whoever loses it will bring it to life.
₃₄I tell you, on that night there will be two men
in one bed. One will be taken, the other left.
₃₅There will be two women grinding meal
at the same place. One will be taken, the other left.²⁰⁸

₃₇And they asked him, "Where, lord?"
He said to them,
Where the body is, the vultures will assemble.²⁰⁹

---

²⁰⁶ This passage contains a warning of impending apocalypse when Yeshua is revealed. There is established a vital parallel between the suffering of Yeshua and his rejection by "this generation" in Israel,
and an equivalent rejection by the world's population of God's word in the days of the Hebrew
Bible. For this impiety comes a flood, an absolute holocaust, which destroys all living people on
earth except for the single family of Noah. The parallel of apocalyptic judgment is then extended to
the iniquitous inhabitants of Sodom and the lone-surviving family of Lot.

²⁰⁷ Sodom.

²⁰⁸ Other ancient authorities have added verse 36: "Two will be in the field; one will be taken and the
other left."

²⁰⁹ This aphorism may be reworded as "where the corpse is the vultures or eagles will assemble."

CHAPTER 18

Parable of the unjust judge and widow

Then he told them a parable about the need always to pray and not weaken, saying,

2In a certain city there was a judge
who did not fear God or respect people.
3And in that city there was a widow
who was coming to him and saying,
"Grant me justice against my adversary."
4And for a time he would not, but later
he said to himself, "Though I do not fear God
or respect people, 5since this woman gives
me trouble, I will grant her justice for fear
she will keep coming and at last wear me down."
6And the lord said,
Listen to what the unjust judge says.
7Will God not do justice to his chosen ones
who cry out to him day and night?
Will he set them at a distance from him?
8I tell you he will quickly give them justice.
But when the earthly son comes,
will he then find faith on the earth?

Parable of the Parush and tax collector

9And to some who confidently saw themselves as just and looked upon others with contempt, he told this parable,

10Two men went up to the Temple to pray,
one a Parush and the other a tax collector.
11The Parush stood alone and prayed
in this way, "God, I thank you that I am
not like the other people—grasping, unjust,
adulterous—or even like this tax collector.
12I fast twice a week, I give a tithe on all
I have." 13Now the tax collector stood far off
and did not wish to raise his eyes to the sky
and he beat his chest, saying, "God, have mercy
on me a sinner." 14I tell you this man went back

to his house justified while the other,

because he exalted himself, will be humbled,

and he who humbles himself will be exalted.[210]

Let the children come to me

₁₅They even brought him babies for him to touch, and seeing this the students scolded them. ₁₆But Yeshua called for them and said,

Let the children come to me

and do not stop them, for the kingdom of God

belongs to them.

₁₇Amen, I tell you,

whoever does not receive the kingdom of God

    like a child

will never enter therein.

Rich ruler

₁₈And a certain official asked him, "Good rabbi, what do I do to inherit eternal life?"

₁₉And Yeshua said to him,

Why do you call me good? No one is good

except God alone. ₂₀The commandments you know.

Do not commit adultery, do not murder,

---

[210] Officials of the Roman occupation of Palestine (in which Judea, its Roman name, was a Roman province ruled by Roman governors) are seen positively by the evangelists, while the Pharisees, who by their opposition to Roman occupation, during Yeshua's life and during the failed rebellion, by their emphasis on the oral (*Halakhah*) rather than the written word (the domain of the Sadducees), by their belief that the soul survives death, would all seem to place them in Yeshua's camp. While the Sadducees represented the rich and the ruling class, the Pharisees in the first century were typically the liberal theologians, who spoke for the poor and reflected the larger people of Israel, who saw Judaism as a living and changing religion, which was the *Halakic* oral tradition of discourse exemplified in Yeshua's speech of using and at the same time altering the written law. In the gospels, however, the Pharisee is the sinister scapegoat Jew. Although there is disagreement with regard to Pharisee opposition to Herodean (Hasmonean) and Roman authority, Josephus was disturbed by the Pharisees as a dissident group opposing Rome, and Paul, an ultimate dissident who was executed by Rome, who wrote and died before the gospels were composed, was proud of his dissident Pharisee background (Phil. 3.5). The early Christian polemic against the Pharisees as hypocrites and legalistic conspirators is largely discredited as self-justifying rant. But in the gospels the division between supporters of state authority by way of Pilate, centurions, and even a lowly tax collector (Matthew's profession) and opponents by way of the Pharisees is constant, and hence it is natural that in this parable the Pharisee is depicted as a self-exalting hypocrite and the tax collector as a modest repentant who will find salvation. The gospels, through Yeshua's voice, have made Yeshua, who many scholars assert was a Pharisee (as Paul claimed to be), militantly opposed to the Pharisees and an apologist for Rome and some of those in its employ. In this parable, the gospel's prophecy is that Israel will be humbled, Rome exalted, which is the Rome that will crucify Yeshua. In contrast to the gospels, Acts and Revelation narrate Rome's massacre and martyrdom of early Christians, and there is no love affair with Rome.

do not steal, do not bear false witness,
honor your father and your mother.
21And he said, "All those I kept since my youth."
22Hearing this Yeshua said to him,
    You still have one thing missing.
    Sell all you own and give it to the poor
    and you will have a treasure in heaven,
    and then come and follow me.
23But when he heard this, he grieved, for he was rich.
24Yeshua looked at him and said,
    How hard it is for the wealthy to enter the kingdom
        of God!
    25It is easier for a camel to enter through the eye
        of a needle
    than for a rich man to enter the kingdom of God.[211]

Who can be saved?

26Those hearing him said, "And who can be saved?"
27He said,
    What is impossible for people
    is possible for God.

Rewards for abandoning family for the kingdom

28Then Kefa said, "See, we have given up what we had and followed you."
29And Yeshua said to them,
    Amen, amen, I say to you.
    There is no one who has left house or wife
    or parents or children for the kingdom of God
    30who will not receive back many times more
        in this age,
    and in the age to come life everlasting.

I will die and be risen

31Then taking the twelve aside, he said to them,
    Look, we are going up to Yerushalayim
    and all that has been written by the prophets
    about the earthly son will be fulfilled.

---

[211] See note 102 on Mark 10.25.

32He will be handed over to the foreigners,[212]

and they will mock and insult and spit on him,

33and after scourging him they will kill him

and on the third day he will rise again.

34But they understood nothing of this, and this word was concealed from them and they did not know what was being said.

Blind beggar in Yeriho

35And it happened as he drew near Yeriho there was a blind man sitting by the road, begging. 36And when he heard the crowd going by, he asked what was going on. 37They informed him that Yeshua the Natzrati[213] was going by. 38And he cried out, saying, "Yeshua, son of David, have pity on me!"

39Those who were in front of him rebuked him and told him to be quiet, but he cried out much louder, "Son of David, have pity on me!"

40Yeshua stood still and ordered him to be brought to him. Drawing near him, he questioned him,

41What do you want me to do?

And he said, "Lord, let me see again."

42Then Yeshua said to him,

See again. Your faith has healed you.

43And at once he saw again and followed him and glorified God. And all the people, seeing this, gave praise to God.

CHAPTER 19

Zakai, rich tax collector who will be saved

And he entered Yeriho and was passing through it. 2And look, a man named Zakai[214] was a chief tax collector, and he was rich. 3He was trying to see who Yeshua was, but was unable to because of the crowd, since he was short. 4So he ran ahead to the front and climbed a sycamore tree to see him. He was about to pass by. 5As Yeshua came to the place, he looked up and said to him,

Zakai, hurry and come down,

for today I must stay at your house.

---

212 See note 41 on Luke 2.32: gentiles, foreigners, pagans, heathen.

213 Nazarene.

214 Zacchaeus from the Greek Ζακχαῖος (Zakhaios), from the Hebrew זַכַּי (zakai). The Hebrew name in Luke is given in Greek form and is ordinarily Romanized in English. See note 201 on Roman tax collectors, Luke 18.14. Zakai is found in Ezra 2.9 and Nehemiah 7.14.

₆And he quickly climbed down and welcomed him with joy.

₇When they saw this, everyone muttered, saying, "He has gone in to stay with a sinful man." ₈Zakai stood there and said, "Lord, I am giving half my possessions to the poor, and if I have cheated anyone I am paying it back four times over."

₉And Yeshua said to him,

Salvation has come to this house today,

because he too is a son of Avraham.[215]

₁₀The earthly son came to seek out and save the lost.

Parable of the king and his slaves

₁₁As they were listening to this, he went on to tell a parable, because he was near Yerushalayim and they supposed the kingdom of God would appear immediately. ₁₂Then he said,

A man of high birth journeyed to a far land

to acquire a kingdom for himself and then

return. ₁₃He summoned ten of his slaves

and gave them ten minas[216] and told them,

"Carry on the business with this silver

until I return." ₁₄But his citizens hated him

and they sent a delegation after him, saying,

"We do not want this man to rule

over us." ₁₅Now it happened on his return,

after he obtained his appointment as king,

he summoned his slaves to whom he had given silver

so he could find out what profit they made.

₁₆The first one came and said, "Master, your mina

has made you ten minas." ₁₇And he said to him,

"Well done, good slave. Since in every detail

you were faithful, take charge of ten cities."

₁₈And the second came saying, "Master, your mina

made five minas." ₁₉And he also said to him,

"Rule over five cities." ₂₀And the other came

saying, "Master, see the mina you gave me,

which I hid away in a napkin. ₂₁I was afraid

because you are a severe man. You take

what you did not lay down, and you harvest

what you did not sow." ₂₂He said to him,

---

[215] Son of Abraham meant a true Jew and not one to be excluded from society because, as a tax collector, he was working for the Roman occupiers.

[216] One talent is 60 minas, and a mina is 100 drachmas. A drachma is about a day's wage.

"Out of your own mouth I judge you, crafty slave!
Didn't you know I am a severe man
and take what I did not lay down and harvest
what I did not sow? 23Why did you not put
my money into the bank? Then when I came
I could have taken it out with interest."
24And to those who were standing near he said,
"Take this mina from him and give it to the one
with ten minas." 25And they said to him,
26"Master, he has ten minas." "I tell you, everyone
who has will be given. But from one with nothing,
even that nothing will be taken away. As for
27my enemies who have not wanted me to rule,
bring them here and slaughter them before me."[217]

Entering Yerushalayim on a colt

28And after Yeshua said this, he went on ahead, going up to Yerushalayim. 29And it happened as he came near Beit Pagey[218] and Beit Aniyah,[219] near the place called Mountain of Olives, he sent two of his students ahead, 30saying to them:

Go into the village just ahead
and as you enter you will find a tethered colt
on which no one has ever sat.
Untie it and bring it here.
If someone asks you, "Why are you untying it?"
31you will say, "His master needs it."

32So those whom he had sent left and found what he told them. 33While untying the colt, its owners said to them, "Why are you untying the colt?"

34They said, "His master needs it."

35And they led it to Yeshua.

Then after spreading their clothing on the colt, they mounted Yeshua on it. 36And as he rode on they strewed their clothing on the road.

37As he came near the descent from the Mountain of Olives, the whole multitude of his students began joyfully to praise God in a great voice for all the miracles they had seen, 38and said from the Psalms,

---

217 Virtue in this parable is to reward good financial performance and to punish caution and timidity. In the last lines, the slaughter of those who oppose and lack faith in their master as king is ominous. Common interpretation has the overlord's departure to be appointed king an allegory for Yeshua's own departure and exaltation.

218 Bethphage from the Greek Βηθφαγή (Bethfage), from the Hebrew בֵּית פַּגֵּא (beit pagey).

219 Bethany from the Greek Βηθανία (Bethania), from the Hebrew בֵּית אַנְיָה (beit aniyah).

Blessed is the king
who comes in the name of the lord!
Peace in heaven
and glory in the highest.[220]

If his students are silent the stones will cry out

39Some of the Prushim in the crowd said to him, "Rabbi, reprove your students."

40And he answered them and said,

I tell you, if these are silent,
the stones will cry out.

Weeping for Yerushalayim, which will be punished, its children crushed

41As he came near and saw the city, he wept over it, 42saying,

If you only knew on this day those things
creating peace! Yet now they are hidden
from your eyes. 43But days will come upon you
and your enemies will set up ramparts
against you and encircle you and hem you in
from all sides. 44They will crush you and your children
and not leave a stone on a stone intact in you[221]
since you did not know the time of your visitation.

Driving the vendors from the Temple

45And he went into the Temple and began to throw out the vendors, 46saying to them as written in Yeshayah and Yirmiyah,

My house shall be a house of prayer
but you have made it into a cave of robbers.[222]

Teaching in the Temple

47And he was teaching every day in the Temple. The high priests and the scholars sought to kill him, and also did the leaders of the people, 48but they could not find what to do, for the people were all hanging on his words.

---

[220] Ps. 118.26.

[221] In this passage Yeshua foresees the destruction of Jerusalem in 70 C.E. by the Roman general Titus, son of the emperor and future emperor himself. The city will fall because of her disobedience to Rome and her impiety toward Yeshua. For more information, please see Afterword.

[222] Isaiah 56.7 writes: "My house shall be a house of prayer." Jeremiah 7.11 writes: "Has this house, which bears my Name, become a den of robbers to you?"

CHAPTER 20

Sparring with authorities in the Temple[223]

And it happened on one day when he was teaching in the Temple[224] and preaching the gospel, the high priests and the scholars came by, and also the elders, 2and they said to him, "Tell us by what authority you do these things? Who gave you this authority?"

3He answered and said to them,

I too will ask you a word and you tell me.
4Was the immersion of Yohanan come from heaven
or from humans?

5They discussed this among themselves, saying, "If we say from heaven, he will say, 'Why do you not believe him?' 6But if we say from humans, all the people will stone us, for they are convinced that Yohanan is a prophet." 7So they answered that they didn't know where he came from.

8And Yeshua said to them,

Neither will I tell you by what authority
I do these things.

Parable of wicked tenants

9He began to tell the people this parable,

A man planted a vineyard and leased it
to farmers and left the country for some time.
10And when the time came he sent a slave

---

223 The subtitles given in modern translations to conspiracy passages reveal positions of the translator editors. Such unconfirmed private conversations in the New Covenant are, for a historian, true, speculative, or fictional, depending on witness accounts of which there are none outside the gospels. Given the uncertainty and crucial importance of conspiracy passages in the religious politics of the scriptures, the translators may choose neutral or inflammatory speech in their own additions to the texts, which are the subtitles. Reflecting four Bible versions, the 1993 *Harper Study Bible*'s subtitle has "The Authority of Jesus Questioned," the 1986 Zondervan NIV Study Bible also has "The Authority of Jesus Questioned" (normally subtitles in these major translations differ), and the 1995 Oxford *New Testament and Psalms* has "Jesus' Authority is Questioned." However, the 1990 revised edition of the *New Jerusalem Bible* has "The Jews question the authority of Jesus." Here the Jerusalem subtitle is inflammatory, pitting Jews against Yeshua, giving credence to an underlying notion that Yeshua is not of the Jews. "Jew" in their subtitle enforces "Jew" as a loaded hate word, based on the New Covenant fiction that Yeshua and the ordinary inhabitants of Jerusalem and Israel who were Yeshua's followers ceased to be Jews insofar as they became his followers. The anti-Semitism whose voice begins in the Jewish scripture of the New Covenant is intensified in the *New Jerusalem Bible* by its invention of a subtitle that logically makes Yeshua seen as the non-Jew.

224 Yeshua was probably teaching in the Temple courts.

to the farmers so they would give him
some of the fruit of the vineyard.
But the farmers beat him and he came back
empty-handed. 11Then he sent another slave,
but they also beat him and humiliated him
and sent him back with nothing. 12And he sent
a third. They wounded him and threw him out.
13The owner of the vineyard said, "What can I do?
I'll send my beloved son. This one maybe
they will respect." 14But when the farmers saw him,
they talked it over and said, "He is the heir.
Let us kill him so the inheritance
will become ours." 15And they drove him out of
the vineyard and killed him. What will
the owner of the vineyard do to them now?
16He will come and destroy these farmers
and give the vineyards over to others.
And when they heard it they said, "May it never happen!"
17But he looked at them and said,
  What is the meaning of this phrase in Psalms:
    "This stone which was rejected by the builders
      has become the cornerstone"?[225]
  18Anyone who falls on that stone will be broken to pieces
  and anyone it falls on will be crushed.[226]

19The scholars and the high priests were looking for a way to lay their hands on him at that very time but they were afraid of the people, for they knew he had spoken that parable against them. 20And they watched for an opportunity and sent spies who pretended to be just so they might trap him through his word and turn him over to the rulers and authority of the governor.

Paying coins to Caesar

21And they questioned him, saying, "Rabbi, we know that you speak and teach straight, and do not favor any person but truthfully teach the way of God. 22Is it right for us to pay the tax to Caesar?"

---

[225] Ps. 118.22.

[226] The stone is "the new rock of Christianity." Whoever rejects Yeshua will be crushed. When this brief parabolic phrase from the Psalms was added and explained in the New Covenant cannot be known. It is routine in the gospels to draw from the Hebrew Bible to prove the truth of Yeshua as the foretold messiah.

23But he knew their craftiness and said to them,

24Show me a denarius silver coin.

Whose image and name are on it?

"Caesar's," they said.

25And he said to them,

Then give the things of Caesar to Caesar

and the things of God to God.[227]

26And they were not able to catch him on his saying before the people, and they were confounded at his answer and were silent.

A wife in heaven

27Some of the Tzadokim[228] came near him, those who say there is no resurrection. 28They questioned him: "Rabbi, Mosheh wrote for us that if one's brother dies, and he is childless, then his brother should marry the widow and raise children for his brother. 29Now there were seven brothers. And the first who married the widow died childless, 30and the second took her and the third, 31and in the same way all seven died childless. 32Finally, the woman died too. 33In the resurrection whose woman will she be? For all seven had her as wife."

34Yeshua said to them,

The sons in this age marry, are given in marriage,

35but those who are thought worthy

in this age to attain life in the resurrection

from the dead do not marry or are given

in marriage. 36But they can no longer die

for they are like angels, they are children

of God, being children of the resurrection.

37That the dead are raised Mosheh revealed

in the burning bush,[229] where he calls the lord

the God of Avraham and Yitzhak and Yaakov.

38But God is not of the dead but of the living,

because to him everyone is alive.

39Some of the scholars answered and said, "Rabbi, you have spoken well." 40They no longer dared to question him on anything.

---

227 This episode of the coin presents the synoptic gospels' view of cooperation with Roman officials. For more information, see note 121 on Mark 12.14.

228 Sadducee from the Greek Σαδώκ, from the Hebrew צדוק (tzadok). Sadducees (pl.) is Tzadokim. Tzadok (Tsadok) means "high priest" and "the just."

229 Exod. 3.2.

The mashiah is son and lord of David

41And Yeshua said to the people,

How can they say that the mashiah is the descendant
  of David?
42For David himself says in the book of Psalms:
  "The lord said to my lord,
    'Sit at my right side
      43while I make your enemies your footstool.' " 230
44Since David calls him lord, how can he be his son?

Condemning scholars

45And in the hearing of all the people, he said to his students,
  46Beware of the scholars, who like to walk around
  in long robes, who love to be greeted
  in market places, in their high seats in the synagogues
  and at the places of honor at the dinners,
  47who eat up the houses of the widows,
  and, for mere appearance, say lengthy prayers.
  They will receive the harshest judgment.

⊞ CHAPTER 21

The widow's copper coin

Then he looked up and saw the rich casting their gifts into the treasury.
2And he saw a poor widow casting in two copper leptas.231 3And he said, "Truly
I tell you,"

  This widow who is poor
  has cast in more than anyone else.
  4All of them put in gifts from their abundance
  while she in her poverty cast in
  all the pennies she had to live on.

---

230 Ps. 110.1.
231 A small copper coin of which 100 make a drachma.

Destruction of the Temple foretold

₅And when some were saying that the Temple was adorned with beautiful stones and sacred gifts, Yeshua said,

> ₆As for what you see,
> the days will come
> when there will be
> not one stone on a stone
> not thrown down.[232]

False mashiahs and terrifying signs

₇And they questioned him, saying, "Rabbi, when will this be and what sign when it will take place?"

₈And he said,

> Beware that you are not fooled.
> Many will come in my name, saying, "I am he."
> The time is near. Do not follow them.
> ₉When you hear about wars and uprisings,
> do not be alarmed, for these must happen first,
> but the end will not come soon.

₁₀Then he said to them,

> Nation will rise up against nation
> and kingdom against kingdom.
> ₁₁There will be great earthquakes,
> and in many places there will be famines and plagues,
>   and horrors,
> and there will be great signs from the sky.

Betrayal and persecutions because of my name

> ₁₂But before all these things, they will lay their hands on you
>   and persecute you
> and turn you over to the synagogues and jails,
> and you will be brought before kings and governors,
> because of my name.
> ₁₃This will be your time to testify.
> ₁₄So keep in your hearts that you must not prepare
> to defend yourselves,
> ₁₅for I will give you such a tongue and wisdom

---

[232] The reference is again to the Romans' taking of Jerusalem and the burning of the Temple.

that all those opposed to you
will not resist or stand against you.

Though parents and friends betray and kill you,
you gain your souls
     16You will be betrayed even by parents
     and brothers and relatives and friends,[233]
     and they will put some of you to death,[234]
     17and you will be hated by all because of my name.
     18Yet not a hair of your head will perish.
     19In your endurance you will gain your souls.

Desolation of the siege of Yerushalayim
     20When you see Yerushalayim encircled
     by armies, then know that its devastation is near.
     21Then those in Yehuda must flee to the mountains
     and those in the city must escape
     and those in the fields not go into her,
     22for these are days of vengeance to fulfill
     all that has been written by the prophets:
     23A plague on those women who have a child
     in their womb and women who are nursing
     in those days. There will be great distress
     on the earth and anger against the people.
     24And they will fall to the edge of the sword
     and they will be taken away as captives
     into all nations, and Yerushalayim
     will be trampled by foreigners until the time
     of the foreigners has run its course.[235]

---

[233] The betrayal by parents and brothers reflects Yeshua's by-now frequent indignation not only in the broader sense against those who are not followers but also against his own family and the failure of his mother and brothers and sister to have faith in him as the messiah. See Luke 4.24 and 8.19.

[234] Reference of this prophecy is to Stephen in Acts 7.54–60 and James in Acts 12.2. Yeshua's prophecies, here and throughout the scriptures, indicate that the author of Luke created these words for Yeshua since Stephen's death took place after his crucifixion. All knowledge by Yeshua, including the destruction of Jerusalem elaborated in Luke 19.41–44 and 21.20–24, suggests either that Yeshua had knowledge of the future or that in the future the assemblers of the scriptures put knowledge of the future into Yeshua's speech.

[235] These prophecies of disaster are from Isaiah 63.4–5, and 63.18, and Daniel 8.13 and 9.24–27.

Cosmic disasters and coming of the earthly son

₂₅There will be signs in sun and moon and stars,
and on the earth the dismay of foreign nations
in bewilderment at the sound of the sea
and surf. ₂₆People will faint from fear
and foreboding of what is coming upon the world,
for the powers of the skies will be shaken.
₂₇And then they will see the earthly son coming
on a cloud with power and enormous glory.[236]
₂₈When these things happen, stand up straight
and raise your heads, for your redemption is near.

Parable of the budding fig tree

₂₉And he told them a parable,
Look at the fig tree and all the trees.
₃₀When they sprout leaves, you look at them
and know that summer is already near.
₃₁So too when you see these things happening
you know the kingdom of God is near.
₃₂I tell you truth. This generation will not
pass by until all these things take place.
₃₃The sky[237] and the earth will pass away
but my words will not pass away.

Don't burn up before the day rushing
in on all of us on the face of the earth

₃₄Be careful that you don't weigh down your hearts
with dissipation and drunkenness and worries of life
lest that day suddenly come upon you ₃₅as a trap,
for it will rush in on all
who are sitting on the face of the whole earth.

---

[236] Dan. 7.13–14.

[237] Sky from the Greek οὐρανὸς (ouranos), translated as "sky" or "heaven." In Greek, as in many languages, the word for heaven and earth is the same. Normally, translations raise the possible religious or moral meaning of words, and hence *ouranos* is regularly translated as "heaven" regardless of context, as it is in this instance by NRSV and NIV, with the notable exception of Richmond Lattimore and the Annotated Scholars' translation. In this version, the intention is not to blur the distinction between heaven and the physical sky above the earth, for then the image of paradise, God's abode and the abode of the saved, would also be blurred. So either "heaven" or "sky" is used to translate *ouranos*, depending on its usage, and in very many cases the choice is difficult, because either or both meanings are possible.

36Be alert and pray at all times for strength
to escape the many things that are to happen,
and to stand before the earthly son.

Days in the Temple, nights on the Mountain of Olives

37Now during those days he was in the Temple, teaching, and in the nights he went out and stayed on the mountain, the one called "Of the Olives."[238] 38And all the people rose at dawn to go to the Temple to hear him.

 **CHAPTER 22**

Plotting before Pesach

The Feast of the Matzot Bread[239] was approaching, which is called Pesach.[240] 2The high priests and the scholars were looking for ways to destroy him, because they were afraid of the people. 3Then Satan entered Yehuda, who is called the one from Keriot, who was one of the number twelve.[241] 4And he went to speak with the high priests and generals[242] about a way to hand him over to them. 5They were very happy and agreed to pay him money. 6And he consented and looked for an opportunity to betray him when the crowd was not there.

Preparation for the Seder

7The day of the Matzot Bread came when it was necessary to sacrifice the Pesach lamb. 8And he sent Kefa and Yohanan, saying,

Go and prepare the Pesach meal for us
so we can eat.

238The Mountain of Olives.

239 Matzot Bread from the Greek ἄζυμος (azymos), "unleavened bread," from the Hebrew מַצּוֹת (matzoh).

240 Festival of the Matzot Bread is the Festival of Unleavened Bread. Pesach is Passover from the Greek πάσχα (pasha), from the Hebrew פֶּסַח (pesah), "to pass over," referring to escape from bondage in Egypt, celebrated at the Seder by eating the paschal lamb. See Exodus 12.1–13.16. In other instances I have transliterated the Hebrew heth, ח as "h," so it is Yohanan, not Yochanan, which would also be acceptable and emphasize the guttural "ch." However, "ch" may also be understood in English as "ch" in "child." Hence ח is always "h" except in Pesach (chosen rather than Pesah), since Pesach is already a Hebrew word used in English and found in English dictionaries.

241 The demonization of the Jew is epitomized by introducing an earlier Midrashic story of the betrayer into the gospels and giving the Midrashic figure the name Judas (Yehuda), meaning "the Jew." Please see Afterword, page 490, for more discussion.

242 Temple officers.

₉And they said to him, "Where do you want us to prepare it?"
₁₀And he said to them,

> Look, as you go into the city,
> a man carrying a jar of water will meet you.
> Follow him into the house he enters
> ₁₁and say to the owner of the house,
> "The rabbi says to you, 'Where is the guest room
> where I am to eat the Pesach meal
> with my students?' " ₁₂And he will show you
> a large upstairs room, already furnished.
> Prepare it there.

₁₃So they left and found things just as he had told them and they prepared the Pesach supper.

The Seder

₁₄When the hour came, he reclined at the table, and the messengers with him. ₁₅And he said to them,

> I greatly desired to eat this Pesach with you
> before I suffer.
> ₁₆I tell you truth,
> I will not eat it again until it is fulfilled
> in the kingdom of God.

₁₇And taking the cup he gave thanks and said,

> Take this cup from me and share it among you.
> ₁₈I say to you,
> as of now I will not drink of the fruit
> of the vine
> until the kingdom of God comes.

₁₉And taking the matzot he gave thanks, broke it, and gave it to them, saying,

> This is my body [which is given for you.
> Do this as a memory of me.[243]

₂₀And he did the same with the cup, after supper, saying,

> This cup is the new covenant[244] in my blood,
> which is poured out for your sake.]

---

[243] The ceremony of the thanksgiving, known as the Eucharist, from the Greek εὐχαριστία (eucharistia), "giving thanks (to God)."

[244] From this Greek phrase, καιὴ διαθήκη (kaine diatheke), we have "New Covenant," the Greek name for the Christian scriptures.

Foretelling the hand of the betrayer
> 21But look, the hand of the betrayer is with me
> on the table.
> 22Because the earthly son is going away
> as has been determined,
> but a plague on that man who betrayed him.

23And they began to ask each other who of them would do this.

Who is the greatest?

24Then a quarrel took place among them as to who was thought to be the greatest.

> 25And he said to them,
> The kings of nations lord it over them
> and those in power are called benefactors,
> 26but with you it is not so.
> Let the greatest among you be the youngest
> and the leader the one who serves.
> 27Who is greater?
> The one who reclines at the table
> or the one serving?
> I am among you as one who serves.

You will eat and drink at my table in my kingdom
> 28You are the ones who have stood by me
> in my trials. 29And just as my father
> has conferred a kingdom on me, I confer on you
> 30that you may eat and drink at my table
> in my kingdom, and you will sit on thrones
> and judge the twelve tribes of Yisrael.

Shimon Kefa, you will deny me
> 31Shimon, Shimon, look, Satan asked for you
> to sift you like wheat,
> 32but I have prayed that your faith not fail you,
> and you, when you return,
> strengthen your brothers.

33And he said to him, "Lord, with you I am ready to go to prison and to death."
34He said to him,
> I tell you, Kefa, the cock will not crow today
> until you have three times denied knowing me.

Now go out with a purse, bag, and sandals
and buy a sword

35And Yeshua said to them,

> When I sent you without a purse and bag
> and sandals, were you in need of anything?

They answered, "Nothing."

36And he said to them,

> But now let the one who has a purse
> let him take it, and also the bag,
> and the one who has no sword,
> let him sell his coat and buy one.
> 37For I tell you, what Yeshayah wrote
> must be fulfilled in me.[245]
> "Even he was counted among the lawless."
> And what is said about me
> will find its resolution.

38And they said to him, "Lord, look, here are two swords."

He said to them,

> It is enough.

An angel comes to him while he is praying
on the Mountain of Olives

39He came outside, and then, as was his custom, he went to the Mountain of Olives. And the students followed him. 40When he came to the place he said to them,

> Pray that you do not come
> to the time of trial.

41And he withdrew from them about a stone's throw, went to his knees, and prayed, saying,

> 42Father, if you choose, take this cup from me,
> and let not my will but yours be done.

43[Then an angel from the sky appeared, giving him strength. 44And being in agony he prayed more intensely. His sweat became drops of blood falling on the ground.][246]

---

245 Isa. 5.12.
246 22.43–44 appear in some texts and not in others.

Why are you sleeping?

45He stood up from prayer and went to his students and found them sleeping after their grief. 46And he said to them,

> Why are you sleeping? Get up and pray
> that you may not enter the time of trial.

The rabbi is kissed and arrested

47Yet while he was speaking, look, a crowd came, and the one called Yehuda, one of the twelve, was leading them, and he came up to Yeshua to kiss him.

48And Yeshua said to him,

> Yehuda, are you betraying the earthly son
> with a kiss?

49When his companions saw what was to happen, they said, "Sir, shall we strike with a sword?"

50And one of them struck a slave of the high priest and cut off his right ear. 51But Yeshua answered and said,

> No more of this!

And he took hold of the man's ear and he healed him.

52Yeshua said to the ones coming against him, high priests and generals of the Temple and elders,

> Did you come out with swords and clubs
> as if I were a robber?
> 53Each day I was with you in the Temple,
> you did not lay your hands on me.
> But this is your hour and the power of darkness.

Kefa and the crowing cock

54They seized him and led him away and took him to the house of the high priest. Kefa was following at a distance. 55And when they lit a fire in the middle of the courtyard and sat down together, Kefa was among them. 56When a serving girl saw him sitting near the light, she stared at him and said, "This man was also with him."

57But he denied it, saying, "Woman, I do not know him."

58And after a short while someone else saw him and said, "You are also one of them."

But Kefa said, "Sir, I am not."

59And after an hour passed, another insisted, saying, "Truthfully, this man also was with him. He is even a Galilean."

60But Kefa said, "Sir, I do not know what you are saying."

And suddenly while he was speaking the cock crowed.

61The Lord turned and looked at Kefa, and Kefa remembered the words of the Lord, how he had told him,

> "Before the cock crows today
> you will deny me three times."

62And he went outside and wept bitterly.

Men holding Yeshua mock and beat him

63And the men who had hold of Yeshua ridiculed him, beat him, 64and blindfolding him questioned him, saying, "Prophesy! Who is it who hit you?"

65And they uttered many other blasphemies against him.

Before the Sanhedrin

66And when it was dawn, the elders of the people assembled, high priests and scholars, and they led him away to the Sanhedrin.[247] They said, 67"If you are the mashiah, tell us."

But he said to them,

> If I tell you, you will not believe me,
> 68and if I question you, you will not answer.
> 69But from now on the earthly son
> will be sitting on the right of the power of God.[248]

70And they all said, "Then you are the son of God?"

But he said to them,

> You say that I am.

71Then they said, "Why do we still need a witness? For we ourselves have heard it from his mouth."

◈ CHAPTER 23

Yeshua before Pilatus

Then the whole assembly rose as a multitude and led him before Pilatus.[249] 2And they began to accuse him, saying, "We found him misleading our nation,

---

247 The council.
248 Ps. 110.1.
249 Pilate.

forbidding taxes to be paid to Caesar[250] and saying that he is the mashiah and king."

3Pilatus questioned him, "Are you the king of the Jews?"

He answered him and said,

> You say it.

4And Pilatus said to the high priests and the crowds, "I find no guilt in this man."[251]

5But they insisted, saying, "He inflames the people with his teaching throughout all Yehuda, from the Galil where he began and up to here."

6When Pilatus heard this, he asked whether the man was a Galilean, 7and learning that he was under the authority of Herod, who in these days was also in Yerushalayim, he sent him off to Herod.

Yeshua before Herod

8Herod was exceedingly pleased to see Yeshua, for he had heard about him and hoped to see him perform a miracle.[252] 9And he questioned him at some length, but Yeshua gave him no answer.

10The high priests and scholars stood there, vehemently accusing him. 11Herod and his soldiers despised and mocked him, putting shining clothing on him, and sent him back to Pilatus. 12Herod and Pilatus became friends on that same day, though earlier they had been enemies.

Yeshua again before Pilatus

13Pilatus assembled the high priests and the leaders and the people 14and said to them, "You brought this man before me as one who was inciting the people to rebellion, and look, I have judged him in your presence and found him not guilty of any charges you bring against him. 15Nor did Herod, for he sent him back to us. And look, he has done nothing to deserve death. 16So I will have him flogged and release him."[253]

18But they all screamed together, "Take him away and release Bar Abba to us!"[254]

19Because of some uprising in the city, and a murder, he was there in prison.

20And again Pilatus spoke to them, wanting to let Yeshua go.

---

[250] For more information on this passage, please see Afterword.

[251] In this passage begins Pilate's exoneration.

[252] In this context, the Greek σημεῖον (semeion), "sign," may be translated as "miracle."

[253] Other ancient authorities add verse 17: "Now he was obliged to release someone for them for the festival."

[254] Barabbas from the Greek Βαραββᾶς, from the Aramaic בַּר אַבָּא (bar abba), meaning "son of abba" (father).

21But they cried out saying, "Crucify! Crucify him!"

22A third time, he said to them, "What harm has this man done? I found nothing in him to deserve death. I will have him flogged[255] and let him go."

23But in loud voices they insistently demanded that he be crucified.

24And Pilatus decided to grant their demand. 25And he released the one they asked for, who had been thrown into prison for insurrection and murder. But Yeshua he delivered to their will.

Shimon a Cyrenian forced to carry the cross

26As they led him away, they seized a man named Shimon, a Cyrenian,[256] who was on his way in from the country, and they loaded the cross on him to carry it behind Yeshua. 27A huge crowd of people followed him and women who mourned and lamented him.

28And Yeshua turned to them and said,

Daughters of Yerushalayim,[257] don't cry for me,
but cry for yourselves and for your children,
29for look, the days are coming when they'll say,

Blessed are the barren and the wombs
that do not bear and breasts that do not nurse.

30Then they will say to the mountains,
"Fall upon us,"
and say to the hills,
"Cover us."[258]
31If they do this when a tree is wet and green
what may happen when it is dry?[259]

Crucifying him

32Two other men, both criminals, were led away to be executed. 33When they came upon a place called Skull,[260] there they crucified him and the criminals, one on the right, one on the left. 34[And Yeshua said,

---

255 Flogged from the Greek παιδεύω (paideuo), meaning "to discipline as in whipping, flogging, or scourging."

256 From Cyrene, a city in Libya, where there was a large Jewish community.

257 The epithet "Daughters of Yerushalayim" from the Greek θυγατέρες ʼ Ιερουσαλήμ (thigateres Ierousalem), from the Hebrew בְּנוֹת יְרוּשָׁלַיִם (benot yerushalayim) is from the Song of Songs.

258 Hos. 10.14. Can be read, by extension, as "bury us."

259 Ezek. 20.47. In his last speech prior to his resignation, as always Yeshua speaks in aphoristic verse, citing the prophets, here enigmatically, probably to suggest that if the messiah is here now to help them, what will happen when he is gone.

260 In the other gospels, the Place of the Skull is identified as Golgoltha. Golgotha is from the Greek Γολγοθᾶ (Golgotha), from the Aramaic גָּלְגָּלְתָּא (gulgulta).

Father, forgive them.

They do not know what they are doing.][261]

The soldiers divided up his clothing and cast lots for it. 35The people stood around watching.

But the leaders ridiculed him, saying, "He saved others, let him save himself if he is God's mashiah, the chosen one."

36The soldiers also came up to him, ridiculed him, offering him sour wine,[262] and they said, 37"If you are king of the Jews, save yourself!"

38And there was a sign over him:

This One the King of the Jews.

With me in paradise

39One of the criminals hanging there insulted him and said, "Are you not the mashiah? Save yourself and us!"

40But the other one reproved the first criminal and said, "Do you not fear God, since you shared the same sentence? 41And we were justly punished, and are getting what we deserve, but he did nothing wrong." 42Then he said, "Yeshua, remember me [when you enter your kingdom]."

43And Yeshua replied,

Amen, I say to you, today you will be with me
in paradise.

Darkness at noon

44And it was noon and darkness came over the whole land until three in the afternoon,[263] 45the sun was eclipsed, and the curtain of the Temple was torn down the middle.

46Yeshua cried out in a great voice,

Father, into your hands I commend my spirit.[264]

As he said this he breathed his last.

---

[261] The passage in brackets is not included in many ancient texts and is often omitted or placed in notes.

[262] Also translated as "poor wine" or "vinegar." See note 188 on Matthew 27.48 where a sympathetic bystander, not a soldier, offers the wine.

[263] The Greek has the sixth hour (noon) and the ninth hour (three in the afternoon). Yeshua had been on the cross since the third hour, about nine in the morning.

[264] In Luke we have a Yeshua who is without protest and with confidence in paradise that very day, for himself and his companion on the cross. His last words bespeak faith in the father to whom he is returning: "Father, into your hands I commend my spirit." In Mark and Matthew, however, Yeshua's last words leave us in doubt and with open interpretation. The human immediacy of those last words "Lord, why have you abandoned me?" makes Yeshua into a supremely solitary soul bespeaking human desperation and reproof at his abandonment by the father who, it appears, has not intervened to alter his pain and momentary death.

47When the centurion, commander of the company of soldiers, saw what had happened, he glorified God, saying, "Surely this was a just man."265

48And when all the crowds gathered for this spectacle saw what had happened, they beat their chests and went away. 49But those who were known to him and also the women who had followed him from the Galil stood at a distance, watching all this.

The body in linen entombed in rock

50And look, there was a man by the name of Yosef, and though a member of the Sanhedrin,266 he was a good and a just man 51and had not agreed with the council and their action. He was from Arimathaia,267 a city of the Jews, and he was waiting for the kingdom of God. 52He came to Pilatus and asked for the body of Yeshua. 53Then he took it down, wrapped it in linen cloth, and placed it in a tomb cut in the rock where no one had yet been laid. 54It was the day of Preparation and Shabbat was dawning.268

55The women who had come from Galil with him followed Yosef and saw the tomb and how his body was laid in it. 56Then they returned and prepared spices and myrrh. And on Shabbat they rested according to the commandment.

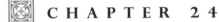

CHAPTER 24

The women at the empty tomb

On the first day of the week at early dawn the women came to the tomb, bringing the spices which they had prepared. 2And they found that the stone had been rolled away from the tomb, 3and when they went inside they did not find the body [of the lord Yeshua].269

---

265 Innocent from the Greek δίκαιος (dikaios), translated literally as "just" or "righteous," may be read by implication as "innocent." That the military commander of the Roman death squad, who presumably oversaw executions on a routine basis, should at the instant of killing his victim glorify the Jewish God Yahweh and declare Yeshua a righteous or innocent man suggests a miracle of conversion or an invention by author or copyist. This specific apology for Rome, making the executioner pious, jolts human credulity. For more information on the centurion, see note 142 on Luke 7.2 and note 165 on Mark 15.39.

266 The council or Sanhedrin, which was said to have voted to have Yeshua killed.

267 Arimathea from the Greek Ἀριμαθαία (Arimathaia). Among places the city may be is ancient Ramathaim, also called Ramah, the birthplace of Samuel. It is identified uncertainly with present-day Ramallah, fifteen or twenty miles east of Jaffa.

268 Shabbat (the Sabbath) begins at sunset on Friday evening. The dawning of Shabbat leaves unsaid the time between Friday sunset and Saturday dawn.

269 The words in brackets are omitted in some manuscripts.

₄And it happened that while they were at a loss about this, look, two men stood near them in clothing that gleamed like lightning.

₅The women were terrified and bowed their faces to the earth but the men said to them,

> Why do you look for the living among the dead?
> ₆He is not here, but has risen.
> Remember how he spoke to you when you were in the Galil,
> ₇"The earthly son must be delivered into the hands
>   of the wrongdoers
> and be crucified
> and on the third day he shall rise again."

₈And they remembered his words.

Women inform messengers

₉When they returned from the tomb they reported all this to the eleven and to the others. ₁₀The women were Miryam of Magdala and Yohanna and Miryam of Yaakov and the other women with them. They told the messengers these things, ₁₁and to them their words seemed madness. They did not believe them.

₁₂[But Kefa got up and ran to the tomb and bending over saw only the linen cloth, and he left, wondering what had happened.]²⁷⁰

On the road to Emmaous

₁₃And look, on the same day, two of them were traveling to a village about seven miles from Yerushalayim, whose name was Emmaous,²⁷¹ ₁₄and they were speaking to each other about all that took place. ₁₅And it happened that during their talk and discussion Yeshua came near and went with them. ₁₆But their eyes were kept from recognizing him.

₁₇He said to them,

> What are these words you are exchanging
> with each other as you walk along?

And they stood still, downcast. ₁₈One of them whose name was Kleopas answered and said to him, "Are you the only one visiting Yerushalayim who does not know what happened there in these days?"

₁₉He said to them,

> What things?

---

²⁷⁰ The words in brackets are omitted in some manuscripts.

²⁷¹ Emmaous from the Greek Ἐμμαοῦς (Emmaous). The location of the village cannot be stated with certainty.

And they said to him, "The things about Yeshua the Natzrati,[272] who was a prophet powerful in act and word, before God and all the people, 20and how our high priests and leaders[273] handed him over to the judgment of death and they crucified him. 21We had hoped that he was going to redeem Yisrael. But now it is already the third day since these things occurred. 22And more, some women among us amazed us. They went at dawn to the tomb, 23and did not find the body and came back saying they saw a vision of angels who say that he is alive. 24Then some of us went back to the tomb and found it as the women said, but did not see him.

25And he said to them,

O what fools and slow of heart you are to believe

all that the prophets spoke!

26Did not the mashiah have to suffer this

and enter into his glory?

27And starting with Mosheh and through all the prophets he explained to them all the things in the Torah concerning himself.

28And as they approached the village they were traveling to, he pretended to be going on further. 29They entreated him, "Stay with us. It is almost evening and the day has fallen."

So he went in to stay with them.[274]

30And it happened that as he reclined at the table with them, he took the bread and blessed it and broke it and gave it to them.

31Then their eyes opened and they recognized him. But he vanished from them.[275]

---

272 Nazarene. Also translated as "Yeshua of Natzeret."

273 "Our" from the Greek ἡμῶν (hemon) "our," the gen. pl. Here, in the resurrection, in contrast to earlier ethnic and religious detachment from identity with Jewish priests and authorities, the speakers at last say "our," mending their estrangement from Jewish identity. Prior to this moment, the evil ones, meaning those without faith in Yeshua as the messiah, have been "they" or "the Jews," implying that "they" the accusers were not themselves Jews. These shifts in pronouns for purposes of religious politics reflect later scribal redaction. At the end of Luke, the "their" has become "our" high priests and authorities, and the Jewish sects are seen under one emblem, while the "they" that follows is reserved for the Roman crucifiers. These pronominal changes are of significance, since this recounting of Yeshua's life and death and resurrection is a didactic interruption in the dramatic narration of Yeshua's companionship with his followers on the road to Emmaous.

274 Verse 27 is another interruption in the drama. After Yeshua's taunting of his followers as fools for their less than total faith in him as the messiah, which he has confirmed through his suffering and death for them, there appear two contrasting messages: one, the routinely didactic lines from the imagination of later churchmen reporting the Hebrew Bible, from Moses on, as an unbroken prophesy concerning the coming of Yeshua; and two, the climactic passage of Yeshua walking through the village with his students, who entreat him to stay with them. His students feel, yet do not know, who he is until the instant that he vanishes from them when they recognize him by his presence and speech and because their hearts have been on fire.

275 Or "he became unseen to them."

₃₂They said to each other, "Were our hearts not burning inside us when he talked to us on the road as he revealed the Torah to us?"

Yeshua with the eleven messengers in Yerushalayim

₃₃And they rose up in that very hour and returned to Yerushalayim, and found the eleven and those with them.

₃₄They said, "The lord has truly risen and he appeared to Shimon."

₃₅Then they described the things on the road and how they recognized him in the breaking of the bread.

₃₆While they were saying these things, he stood in their midst [and said to them:

Peace be with you.]²⁷⁶

₃₇They were startled and full of fear and thought they were looking at a ghost.

₃₈And he said to them,

Why are you shaken and why do doubts rise
in your hearts?
₃₉Look at my hands and my feet
and see I am myself.
Touch me and see,
because a ghost does not have flesh and bones
which as you see I have.

₄₀[And when he said this, he showed them his hands and feet.]²⁷⁷

₄₁And when in their joy they still could not believe him and wondered, he said to them,

Do you have something to eat?

₄₂They gave him a piece of broiled fish.

₄₃And he took it and in their presence he ate it.

₄₄Then he said to them,

These are my words which I spoke to you
while I was still with you:
all that was written about me in the law of Mosheh
and the prophets and Psalms must be fulfilled.²⁷⁸

₄₅Then he opened their minds to an understanding of the Torah, ₄₆and he said to them,

---

₂₇₆ The words in brackets are omitted in some texts.

₂₇₇ Other authorities lack verse 40.

₂₇₈ In these words the author of Luke has Yeshua declare his Hebrew Bible inheritance as the foretold messiah.

It is written that the mashiah is to suffer and to rise
from the dead on the third day,
47and in his name you will preach repentance
and forgiveness of sins to all nations,
beginning with Yerushalayim.
48You are the witnesses.
49And look, I am sending the promise of my father
    to you.
So stay in the city
until you are clothed with power from on high.[279]

In Beit Aniyah Yeshua raises his hands and blesses
and is carried into the sky

50And he led them out as far as Beit Aniyah, and raised his hands and blessed them. 51And it happened that while he blessed them, he departed from them [and was carried up into the sky].[280]

52And they [worshiped him and][281] returned to Yerushalayim with great joy, 53and they were constantly in Temple blessing God.

---

[279] Mark ends abruptly, powerfully, and mysteriously; Matthew and John dramatically and with great pathos. Here the drama is also intense until these last ecclesiastical instructions to prepare witnesses for the missionary duties of the church. The instructions "to stay in the city / until you are clothed with power from on high" serve as a perfect afterword to the road and house scenes, and this last formal message contains hope and a promise of power to be delivered from the father on high to the faithful, who will go out from the city to preach the good news. The dramatic narration of the post-crucifixion gospel ends by verse 44, however, preceding the send off, with the immensely poignant gloom of the followers at the earthly loss of the messiah, their joy at the recognition on the road and at the breaking of the bread, the plain reality and immediacy of his instructions to look at his mutilations of hand and feet—"Touch me and see"—and his last human act, which is to ask for food and then, in the presence of the intimates, to eat the cooked fish.

[280] The words in brackets are omitted in some texts.

[281] The words in brackets are omitted in some texts.

YOHANAN[1]

(JOHN)

---

[1] John from the Greek Ἰωάννης (Ioannes), from the Hebrew יוֹחָנָן (yohanan). It can also be written as Yochanan.

YOHANAN (JOHN)

THE PROLOGUE OF THE GOSPEL OF JOHN, "IN THE BEGINNING WAS THE WORD," IMITATES THE FIRST WORDS OF THE CREATION IN Genesis, "In the beginning God created the heavens and the earth." The word in Greek is *logos,* and logos was a familiar philosophical term, already in Greek currency through its usage by the pre-Socratic philosopher Heraclitus and by the Stoics. John uses logos to convey a specific message. The word is the divine savior, who comes into the world to bring hope and eternal life. The "word become flesh" is Yeshua, God's emissary incarnated in the world. In contrast to the synoptic gospels (Mark, Matthew, and Luke), where Yeshua's divinity is always elusive—there and not there—John suggests that Yeshua is the messiah, that the messiah is divine, and he is the son of God.

In the prologue there is also an emphasis on light and darkness, on truth and lies, which seems to be in harmony with dichotomies found in the Dead Sea Scrolls of the Essene community. And finally, in the richest and most eloquent passages of spiritual inquiry, which characterize John, there must be observed a strong gnostic element. In short, John is a mirror to a time of diverse beliefs and philosophies. Key terms and concepts, from the Neoplatonist Jew Philo of Alexandria to the scrolls of the Essenes and the gnostics, flash in and out of his text with unusual intensity.

The authorship of John is a complex puzzle for which there is no solution. Traditionally, the author is John, son of Zebedee, one of Yeshua's disciples and apostles. For many reasons, including the probable dating of the work, this view is not generally accepted today. We do not know the name of the author. Some scholars suggest that the author of the prologue may not be the author of the rest of the gospel or that it may even be the work of a Johannine community (those who followed John's ideas).

John is distinct from the synoptic gospels in many ways. There is no Sermon on the Mount. Yeshua tells no parables (except of the good shepherd), heals no lepers. Demons are not exorcised, there is no Lord's Prayer or Last Supper, and the notion of religious instruction and moral teachings found in the synoptics is transformed into metaphysical discourse. As in the other gospels, the Book of John does use miracles as "signs" to prove the powers of the messiah and God. However, by contrast, Yeshua is a more abstracted figure; and the presentation of his crucifixion, in contrast to that of the other gospels, is not of an especially suffering man, tortured and dying for human sin, but of a controlled, even aloof, figure, following his own divine purpose without fear. There are similarities to the language of Apocalypse, which is ascribed to John. In both texts Yeshua is the Word and the Lamb of God. But it should be emphasized that the apocalyptic nature of Revelation—the epic vision of heaven and hell, the phantasmagoric images—is wholly apart from anything found in the Gospel of John and alone discredits the traditional notion of common authorship.

There is a special problem with regard to the Jews, who did not accept Christ as the promised messiah. Like Matthew, John is a deeply Jewish gospel, steeped in Old Covenant thought and allusion. But more than Matthew, the reference to Jews as the opponents is fierce and constant, while at the same time the gospel presents Yeshua as a Jew and rabbi. One explanation for John's presentation of this intramural struggle between Jews lies in the politics of his own later time. If, as many scholars believe, John dates from early in the second century, anywhere from 100 to near 150 A.D., then it is probable that he is addressing the increasingly tense struggle in many parts of the diaspora world, especially in Asia Minor, between Christian Jews and non-Christian Jews for their place in the synagogues.

Above all, John is a literary document of the Bible. The prologue is magic for believers or nonbelievers, surely one of the summit moments in world literature. As Mark is the most poignant and dramatic, Matthew perhaps the most poetic, Luke the most literarily accomplished in its telling of the nativity and the parables, John is the most spiritual, philosophical, and independent of the gospels.

C H A P T E R   1

In the beginning was the word
>In the beginning was the word[2]
>and the word was with God,
>and God was the word.
>2The word was in the beginning with God.
>3Through it[3] everything came about
>and without it not a thing came about.
>What came to be 4in the word was life
>and the life was the light of people
>5and the light in the darkness shines
>and the darkness could not apprehend it.

Yohanan came to proclaim light[4]
>6There was a man sent from God.
>His name was Yohanan.[5]
>7He came as a witness in testimony of the light
>so that all might believe through him.
>8He was not the light,

---

2   John informs us in "In the beginning was the word," Ἐν ἀρχῇ ἦν ὁ λόγος (En arhe en ho logos)
   (John 1.1). God created through the word, ὁ λόγος. With that utterance God translates divine sound
   into matter and being, thereby bringing the cosmos, the earth, and the earth's inhabitants, great and
   small, into temporal existence. The creation through the word in John parallels the creation in Genesis 1.1 of the Hebrew Bible: "In the beginning when God created the heavens and the earth": הָאָרֶץ
   בְּרֵאשִׁית בָּרָא אֱלֹהִים אֵת הַשָּׁמַיִם וְאֵת (bereshit bara elohim et hashamayim veet ha-aretz). God in Genesis uses "the word" to speak the world into being through his order, "Let there be light," יְהִי אוֹר (yehi
   or), while in John "the word" of creation may be spoken or written, but it also is the initial cause of
   creation. And as in the Hebrew Bible, that word is immediately commingled with light. It has been
   observed that in John's prologue, the use of the logos offers a link between the divine mind and the
   human mind, which is rational and apprehends the word through reason, reason being another meaning of "logos." This beginning is often presumed to be a separate poem added or adapted to the gospel.
      John is considered the most gnostic of the gospels, and especially in its prologue. The logical se-
   quence of this poem also suggests the syllogistic reasoning of the Sophists as well as the Cynics to
   whom leading theologians sometimes compare Yeshua. See John Dominic Crossan in *The Birth of
   Christianity* (San Francisco: HarperSan Francisco, 1998), and Burton L. Mack in *Who Wrote the New
   Testament?* (San Francisco: HarperSan Francisco, 1995). More broadly, "logos" may be given multiple meanings: the word of God, knowledge, science, the Greek principle of reason ordering the universe, and a Kabbalist principle of the primacy of creating words and, before words, an alphabet of
   letters, so that God has the means of speaking the universe into being.
3   "Through it" is also translated as "Through him."
4   Yohanan the Dipper (John the Baptist).
5   John from the Greek Ἰωάννης (Ioannes) from the Hebrew יוֹחָנָן (yohanan).

but came to testify about the light.[6]
9The light was the true light
which illuminates every person
who comes into the world.

Light was in the world

10He was in the world
and through him the world was born,
and the world did not know him.[7]
11He went to his own
and his own did not receive him.[8]
12To all who received him
he gave power to become the children of God,
to those who believed in his name,
13who were born not from blood
or from the will of the flesh
or from the will of a man,
but were born of God.

Word became flesh

14And the word became flesh
and lived among us.[9]
And we gazed on his glory,
the glory of the only son born of the father,
who is filled with grace and truth.

Yohanan cries out about him who will come after and who was before

15Yohanan testifies about him and cries out, saying,
He is the one of whom I said,

---

[6] Yohanan was not the light, meaning not Yeshua the Mashiah, but the lamp carrying the light, defining the testimony of Yohanan the Dipper (John the Baptist) as prophetic but in a secondary role to Yeshua, who is the messiah, and also suggesting rivalry between early followers of the messiah, some favoring Yohanan, who electrified Judaism with his arrival in ways foretold in Isaiah (Isa. 9.2, 42.6–7, 60.1–3). The majority favor Yeshua, but there is considerable evidence that by the second century of the common era the number of those favoring Yohanan over Yeshua as the messiah was increasing alarmingly.

[7] Yeshua the Mashiah.

[8] The Jews in Isaiah and other prophets spoke of one messiah, whom the majority of Jews did not accept when he came. Those Jews, who did recognize Yeshua, the early messianics, who late in the first century broke off from mainstream Jewry, were the Christian Jews (meaning "messianics," followers of the messiah). They shared with traditional Jews the Torah as their sole holy scripture, since the New Covenant was not to be firmly set and canonized until centuries later.

[9] God's word became human flesh in the person of Yeshua.

"One who will come after me was before me,

because before me he was."

16From his bounty we have all received grace upon grace,

17and as the law was given through Mosheh,[10]

grace and truth have come through Yeshua the Galilean.

18No one has ever seen God.

Only the one born of God,[11]

who is in the heart of his father,

he has made him known.

In the desert Yohanan the Dipper denies being the mashiah

19And this is the testimony of Yohanan the Dipper when the Jews[12] sent priests and Levites from Yerushalayim[13] to ask him, "Who are you?"

20And he confessed and made no denial, but confessed, "I am not the mashiah."

21They asked him, "What then? Are you Eliyah?"[14]

He said, "I am not."

"Are you the prophet?"

He answered, "No."

22"Who are you? Give us an answer for those who sent us here. What do you say about yourself?"

23He said,

I am the voice of one crying out in the desert:

"Make straight the way of Adonai,"

as the prophet Yeshayah said.[15]

24Now they had been sent by the Prushim. 25They questioned him and said to him, "Why do you dip if you are not the mashiah or Eliyah or the prophet?"

---

[10] Moses from the Greek Μωϋσῆς (Moyses), from the Hebrew משֶׁה (mosheh).

[11] Other texts have "only begotten son."

[12] The Jews. All the people in these scenes are Jews. The appellation "Jew" here and in most places in John has two functions: to distinguish Jews who do not believe Yeshua to be the son of God from those who do; and to cast hatred on and condemn the unbelievers to immediate and eternal punishment at the day of judgment. Such usage of "Jew" cannot reflect initial texts of John but is an anachronism of later interpolators. The followers of Yeshua were initially few in number among the many sects that made up the Jewish population. All thought themselves Jews—Jews and Christian Jews. Therefore, naming the Jews as a hated community existing alongside Yeshua and his follower Jews is linguistically unlikely. Such usage reflects the later competitive period of nascent Christianity when the Jews had expelled Christian Jews from the synagogues and when the traditional Jews, in turn, became the vilified enemy.

[13] Jerusalem from the Greek Ἰερουσαλήμ (Yerousalem), from the Hebrew יְרוּשָׁלַיִם (yerushalayim).

[14] Elijah from the Greek Ἠλίας (Elias), from the Hebrew אֵלִיָּה (eliyah).

[15] Isa. 40.3. Isaiah from the Greek Ἡσαΐας (Esaias), from the Hebrew יְשַׁעְיָה (yeshayah). Pharisees from the Greek Φαρισαῖος (Farisaisos), from the Hebrew פְּרוּשִׁים (prushim). Pharisee is Parush.

₂₆He answered them,

    I dip in water.

    Among you stands one you do not know,

    ₂₇one who will come after me,

    whose sandal strap I am unworthy to loosen.

₂₈All this happened in Beit Aniyah,[16] across the Yarden,[17] where Yohanan was dipping.

The lamb of God

₂₉The next day Yohanan saw Yeshua coming toward him and said,

    Look, the lamb of God who takes away the wrong of the world.

    He is the one of whom I have said,

    ₃₀"A man is coming after me who was before me,

    because before me he was."

    ₃₁And I did not know him,

    but so that he might be known in Yisrael[18]

    is why I came dipping in water.

Spirit descending like a dove

₃₂And Yohanan testified, saying,

    I saw the spirit descending like a dove from the sky

    and it rested on him ₃₃and I did not know him,

    but the one who sent me to dip in water said,

    "The one on whom you see the spirit descend and rest,

    he is the one dipping in holy spirit."

₃₄And I have seen and I have testified that he is the son of God.

We have found the mashiah, meaning "the anointed"

₃₅The next day Yohanan again was standing with two of his students. ₃₆When he saw Yeshua walking by, he said,

    Look, the lamb of God.

₃₇His two students heard him speaking and they followed Yeshua.

₃₈And Yeshua turned and saw them following him and said,

    What are you looking for?

"Rabbi," which translated means teacher,[19] "where are you staying?"

---

[16] Bethany from the Greek Βηθανία (Bethania), from the Hebrew בֵּית אֲנִיָּה (beit aniyah).

[17] Jordan from the Greek Ἰορδάνης (Iordanes), from the Hebrew יַרְדֵּן (yarden).

[18] Israel from the Greek Ἰσραήλ (Israel), from the Hebrew יִשְׂרָאֵל (yisrael).

[19] After Yeshua is addressed as Rabbi, the next phrase, ῥαββί, ὃ λέγεται μεθερμηνευόμενον διδάσκαλε (rhabbi, o legetai methermeneuomenon didaskale), which translated means "teacher," is a scribal aside that appears to be a later interpolation, whose purpose is to persuade the reader that

39"He told them,

> Come and see.

So they came and saw where he was staying, and stayed with him that day. It was about four in the afternoon.

40One of the two who heard Yohanan and followed him was Andreas,[20] brother of Shimon[21] Kefa.[22] 41First he found his own brother Shimon and told him, "We have found the mashiah" (meaning "the anointed").[23]

42He led Shimon to Yeshua.

Looking at him, Yeshua said,

> You are Shimon, the son of Yohanan.
>
> You will be called Kefa,

(which is translated Petros).[24]

Rabbi, you are the son of God

43The next day Yeshua wished to go out to the Galil.[25] He found Filippos[26] and said to him,

> Follow me.

44Now Filippos was from Beit Tzaida,[27] the city of Andreas and Kefa. 45Filippos found Natanel[28] and said to him, "The one whom Mosheh wrote about

---

"rabbi" meant a "teacher" or "scholar" rather than a rabbi of the Jews, whose profession was to lead a congregation and interpret Jewish law. Rabbi is a Greek word, reproducing in the Hebrew רַבִּי (rabbi), meaning "rabbi," "master," "great one," or "teacher."

20 Andrew from the Greek Ἀνδρέας (Andreas).

21 Simon from the Greek Σίμων, from the Hebrew שִׁמְעוֹן (shimon).

22 Shimon Kefa is Simon Peter. Peter from the Greek Πέτρος (Petros), translated from the Aramaic כֵּיפָא (kefa), meaning "rock" or "stone." In 1 Corinthians 1.12 and elsewhere, Paul Hellenizes כֵּיפָא (kefa), calling Peter Κηφᾶς (Kefas), traditionally Latinized in English as "Cephas." In Greek, as in French (but not in English), the name and the word for "stone" are related as in "Pierre" (the name) and "pierre" (stone).

23 Anointed is the Christ. Christ is from the Greek Χριστός (Hristos), "the anointed," an attribute of the messiah; in the New Covenant Greek, Χριστός is used almost synonymously with Μεσσίας (Messiah), a Hellenized transliteration of the Hebrew מָשִׁיחַ (mashiah). The parenthetical scribal aside, "meaning 'the anointed,' " suggests an earlier text in Aramaic or Hebrew.

24 By calling Peter "Kefa," meaning "stone," Yeshua is here suggesting that Peter will be the rock of the church. There is an irony in this prediction, since elsewhere in the gospels Yeshua chooses Peter to ridicule among his students, predicts that Peter will deny him three times, and, after the crucifixion, Peter is beaten by Yeshua's unnamed but "most beloved" student in their race to find Yeshua in the empty tomb. Here the parenthetical scribal aside, "which is translated into Greek as Petros," suggests an earlier text in the Aramaic.

25 Galilee from the Greek Γαλιλαία (Galilaia), from the Hebrew גָּלִיל (galil). Galil is a "circle," "district," or "province." It is often used in the phrase גְּלִיל הַגּוֹיִם (galil hagoyim), meaning "province of the goyim (gentiles)."

26 Philip from the Greek Φίλιππος (Filippos). Accent is on the first i.

27 Bethseda from the Greek Βηθσαϊδά (Bethsaida), from the Hebrew בֵּית צַיְדָא (beit tzaida), which is a place north of Lake Gennesaret.

28 Nathanael from the Greek Ναθαναήλ (Nathanael), from the Hebrew נְתַנְאֵל (natanel).

in the Torah[29] and whom the prophets describe, we have found, Yeshua, son of Yosef,[30] from Natzeret."[31]

46And Natanel said to him, "Can anything good come out of Natzeret?"

"Come and see!" Filippos replied.

47Yeshua saw Natanel coming to him and said of him,

Look, a true Jew,[32] one in whom there is no cunning.

48"How do you know me?" Natanel said.

Yeshua answered,

Before Filippos called you,

you were under the fig tree and I saw you.

49Natanel answered, "Rabbi, you are the son of God! You are the king of Yisrael!"

50Yeshua responded, saying,

Because I told you I saw you under the fig tree,

do you believe?

51You will see even greater things.

And he said to him,

Amen, amen, I say to you,

You will see the sky open

and angels of God ascending and descending

upon the earthly son.[33]

---

29 "The Law" in Hebrew is "Torah." Torah most commonly means the Five Books of Moses as well as the entire Hebrew Bible.

30 Joseph from the Greek Ἰωσήφ (Iosef), from the Hebrew/Aramaic יוֹסֵף (yosef).

31 Nazareth from the Greek Ναζαρέτ (Natzaret), unknown villiage in Galilee probably spelled Natzeret.

32 The Greek reads Ἰσραηλίτης (Israelites), from the Hebrew (yisraeli), corresponding to "Israeli." Because translations from the Hebrew Bible translate יִשְׂרְאֵלִי as Israelite (rather than Israeli, which is accurate), and the Greek New Convenant uses the word "Jews" exclusively for the bad Jews and avoids labeling Yesuha or his followers as Jews, here, where the obvious word in Greek should, in first-century Aramaic and Hebrew, be "Jew," the Greek text resurrects "Israelite" Ἰσραηλίτης) in shocking consistency with its pattern of depicting good Jews as vaguely non-Jews, like John the Baptist and Mary, and non-followers as Jews. In the odd instance of Natanel, there is no recourse but to reach back to the Hebrew Bible and, ignoring time, safely call him an untainted, true *Israelite*. Had any earlier translation gone directly to the Hebrew for *Israelite*, rather than to its Greek version, it would have found Hebrew יִשְׂרָאֵלִי, that is, Israeli, not Israelite, and it would be clear to today's reader that a biblical Israeli and Jew are one and the same. Israelite is from the Greek nominative case version of Israeli.

33 See note 30 on Mark 2.10 for "earthly son."

CHAPTER 2

Wine and water at a wedding in Kana

On the third day there was a wedding in Kana[34] in the Galil, and Yeshua's mother was there. ₂Yeshua and his students had also been invited to the wedding. ₃And when the wine gave out, Yeshua's mother said to him, "They have no wine."

₄Yeshua said to her,

> What is that to me and you, woman?[35]
>
> My hour has not yet come.

₅His mother said to the servants, "Do what he tells you."

₆Now there were six waterpots of stone standing there for the Jewish custom of washing,[36] each holding two or three measures.[37]

₇Yeshua said to them,

> Fill the pots with water.

They filled them to the brim.

₈And he said to them,

> Now pour some of the water out
>
> and take it to the master of the feast.

They took it.

₉When the master of the feast tasted the water become wine, not knowing where it came from—though the servants knew, those who had drawn the water—he called the bridegroom ₁₀and said to him, "Everybody serves the good wine first, and when the guests are drunk brings out the inferior kind. You have been saving the good wine till now."

₁₁Yeshua did this, the first of his miraculous signs in Kana in the Galil, and he revealed his glory, and his students believed in him.

Days in Kfar Nahum with family and students

₁₂After this he went down to Kfar Nahum[38] with his mother and brothers and students. They stayed there for a few days.

---

[34] Cana. A village, probably Khirbert Qana, some miles north of Nazareth.

[35] The gruff use of γύναι (gynai), "woman," rather than κυρία (kyria), "lady," is softened in many translations to "Dear woman" (NIV), and "Madame" (Lattimore). However, in KJV and NRSV it remains "woman."

[36] Washing hands in rite of purification.

[37] Twenty or thirty gallons.

[38] Capernaum. Latin *Capernaum* from the Greek Καφαρναούμ (Kafarnaoum), from the Hebrew נחום

Pesach in Yerushalayim and driving
vendors from the Temple

13It was almost the Pesach[39] of the Jews and Yeshua went up to Yerusha-layim. 14In the Temple he found the people selling oxen and sheep and doves, and the coin changers sitting there. 15He made a whip out of ropes and drove out all the animals, the sheep and the oxen. He also scattered the coins of the changers and knocked over their tables. 16To the dove sellers he said,

> Get these things out of here!
> Do not make the house of my father
> a house of business![40]

17His students remembered how the Psalms say:

> Zeal for your house will consume me.[41]

18Then the Jews said to him, "What sign can you show us for doing this?"
19Yeshua answered,

> Destroy this Temple
> and in three days I shall raise it up.

20Then the Jews said, "This Temple was built over forty-six years, and you will raise it up in three days?"

21But he was speaking about the Temple of his body. 22After he was raised from the dead, his students remembered what he said and they believed the scripture and the word which Yeshua said.

Yeshua's wondrous signs in Yerushalayim and his knowledge of people

23When he was in Yerushalayim during the Pesach suppers, many people believed in his name, seeing the wondrous signs he was doing. 24But Yeshua would not entrust himself to them, because he knew all people 25and because he had no need to have anyone testify about a person and he knew what was in a person.

כְּפַר (kfar nahum), meaning "village of Nahum." A prosperous town or city near the north end of the Sea of Galilee that Yeshua made a center for his work.

[39] Passover from the Greek πάσχα (pasha), from the Hebrew פֶּסַח (pesah). Festival of the Matzot Bread is the Festival of Unleavened Bread. Pesach, meaning "to pass over," refers to the escape from bondage in Egypt, celebrated at the Seder by eating the paschal lamb. See Exodus 12.1–13.16.

[40] For location of vendors see note 113 on Mark 11.16.

[41] Ps. 69.9.

CHAPTER 3

With Nakdeimon, speaking of spirit and light

Now there was a Parush named Nakdeimon,[42] a leader of the Jews. ₂He came to Yeshua at night and said, "Rabbi, we know that you came as a teacher from God since no one can perform these wondrous signs if God were not with him."

₃Yeshua answered, "Amen, amen, I say to you,"

Unless you are born from above

you cannot see the kingdom of God.

₄"How can one be born when one is old?" he asked. "One cannot enter a mother's womb a second time and be born."

₅Yeshua answered, "Amen, amen, I say to you,"

Unless you are born from water and the wind of God[43]

you cannot enter the kingdom of God.

₆What is born from the flesh is flesh,

what is born from the wind is wind.

Do not wonder that I told you

₇you must be born again from above.

₈The wind blows where it wants to and you hear its sound

but you cannot know where it comes from and where it goes.

So it is for everyone born from the wind of God.

₉"How can these things happen?" Nakdeimon asked.

₁₀Yeshua said to him,

You are the teacher of Yisrael and do you not know this?

₁₁Amen, amen, I say to you,

We speak of what we know and we testify to what we have seen,

yet you do not receive our testimony.

₁₂If I tell you of earthly things and you do not believe,

how if I tell you of heavenly things will you believe?

₁₃And no one has gone up into the sky

---

42 Nicodemus from the Greek Νικόδημος (Nikodemos). Originally a Greek word, Nikodemos was Hebraized to נַקְדִּימוֹן (nakdeimon). A Parush is a Pharisee.

43 In John 3.5, from the Greek πνεύματος (pneumatos), "of the wind." The Greek τό πνεῦμα (to penuma) is "the wind," and in the New Covenant, by metaphorical abstraction, may also mean "the spirit." Verse 3.8 begins "The wind [τό πνεῦμα] blows," where πνεῦμα clearly retains its classical, particular meaning of "wind."

except the one who came down from the sky, the earthly son.
14And as Mosheh raised up the snake in the desert,
the earthly son must be raised up
15so that all who believe in him will have eternal life.

16God loved the world so much he gave his only son
so that all who believe in him might not be destroyed but have eternal life.
17For God did not send his son into the world to judge the world
but so through him the world might be saved.
18One who believes in him is not judged
but one who does not believe is judged already
for not believing in the name of God's only son.
19And this is the judgment:
Light came into the world
and people loved the darkness rather than the light,
for their works were cunning.
20For all who do shoddy things[44] hate the light
and do not come toward the light
so that their works will not be exposed.
21But those who do the truth come toward the light
so their works may shine as accomplished through God.[45]

Yeshua dipping in Yehuda

22After this Yeshua and his students came into the land of Yehuda.[46] He stayed there with them and dipped.

Yohanan dipping and speaking of the mashiah

23Yohanan also was dipping in Einayim[47] near Shalem,[48] since there were many waters there, and the people came and were immersed. 24Yohanan had not yet been thrown into prison.

25There was a dispute between Yohanan's students and a Jew[49] about cere-

---

[44] From the Greek φαῦλα (faula), "slight," "trivial," "rough," or "paltry" rather than normal "evil" or "wicked." "Shoddy" suggests "sloppy work" with a darker implication.

[45] Yeshua's distinctions between darkness and light and his emphasis on light as spiritual knowledge and salvation imbue this entire passage with gnostic tenets.

[46] Judea from the Greek Ἰουδαία (Ioudaia), from the Hebrew יְהוּדָה (yehuda). Also is the name Yehuda.

[47] Ainon, Aenon from the Greek Αἰνών (Ainon), from the Hebrew עֵינַיִם (einayim), meaning "springs."

[48] Salim from the Greek Σαλίμ (Salim), from the Hebrew שָׁלֵם (shalem).

[49] In this context the Greek μετὰ᾽Ιουδαίου (meta Ioudaiou), "with a Jew," has been explained as a man from Judea (Yehuda) as opposed to another region of Israel. More likely it is simply to distinguish Yohanan from the Jews, which is how it comes through in Greek and English. Verse 22 already indicates that Yohanan is in Judea.

monial washing. 26They came toward Yohanan and said, "Rabbi, the one who was with you across the Yarden, to whom you testified, look, he is dipping all who come to him."

27Yohanan answered,

No one can receive anything unless it comes from heaven.

28"You are my witnesses. I said,

"I am not the mashiah but I am sent before him."

29He who has the bride is the groom.

The groom's friend who stands near and hears him

is filled with joy at the groom's voice.

So my happiness is completed.

30He must increase and I be diminished.

31The one who comes from above is above all.

The one who is of the earth is of the earth

and speaks from the earth.

The one who comes from the sky is above all.

32To what he has seen and heard he testifies,

yet his testimony no one receives.

33Who receives his testimony proves that God is true.

34Whom God sent speaks the words of God,

for the wind of spirit he gives out is beyond measure.

35The father loves the son and has given all things into his hand.

36Who believes in the son has eternal life,

but one who disbelieves the son will not see life.

The wrath of God remains upon him.

CHAPTER 4

With a Shomronim woman needing water

Now when Yeshua realized that the Pharisees had heard that Yeshua was converting and immersing more students than Yohanan (2though it was not Yeshua himself who dipped them but his students), 3he left Yehuda and went again into the Galil. 4But it was necessary to pass through Shomron.[50] 5He

---

[50] Samaria from the Greek Σαμαρία (Samaria), from the Hebrew שֹׁמְרוֹן (shomron). A Samaritan is a Shomronim.

315

came to a town in Shomron called Shehem[51] near the piece of land that Yaakov[52] gave his son Yosef. 6There was a well of Yaakov there. Yeshua was tired from the trip and sat down by the well. It was near noon.[53]

7A Shomronim woman came to draw water.

Yeshua said to her, "Give me a drink." 8His students had gone off to the town to buy food.

9The Shomronim woman said to him, "How can you a Jew ask to be given a drink by me, a Shomronim? Jews do not mingle with Shomronims."[54]

10Yeshua answered, saying to her,

If you knew the gift of God and who is saying to you

"Give me a drink,"

you would have asked and he would have given you living water.

11She said to him, "Sir, you have no bucket and the well is deep. Where do you have this living water? You are not greater than our father Yaakov 12who gave us the well and who himself drank and whose sons and cattle drank."

13Yeshua answered her, saying,

Everyone who drinks this water will be thirsty again.

14But whoever drinks the water I give them

will not be thirsty again.

The water I give them will become in them

a fountain of water springing into eternal life.

---

[51] Sychar. Sychar is the Aramaic. The Greek Σψηὰρ (Syhar) is probably a corruption of Συχέμ (Syhem), from the Hebrew שְׁכֶם (shehem). Sychar, written Shechem in the King James Version, can also be written Shekhem or Shehem. It is identified with nearby Jacob's Well (Bir Yaakov), and modernly with the city of Nablus.

[52] James (Jacob) from the Greek Ἰάκωβος (Iakobos), from the Hebrew יַעֲקֹב (yaakov).

[53] Literally, "the sixth hour."

[54] "Jews do not mingle with Samaritans" in other editions is put in brackets, parentheses, or a bottom-of-page note, which in effect acknowledges a later scribal commentary. It could be either way, and here it may be better not to set the phrase off as spurious. This notable identification of Yeshua as a Jew by an "outsider" Samaritan contradicts the prevalent dejudaizing of Yeshua and his circle and the normal use of Jew as Yeshua's deadly opponent. Revealed once again is the disturbed and confused nature of the scriptures, as we have it from multiple hands, which in contingent passages esteems and scourges the Jew. To speak of the Samaritan as not a Jew is problematic, since the Samaritans, from Samaria, were Jews among the main sects of Jews, which included Hasids, Essenes, Sadducees, and Pharisees, among whom, as suggested here with regard to Jerusalem Jews and Samaritan Jews, there was much intense rivalry. Individual branches often claimed to be the true Jews. The later rivalry after Yeshua's death between "traditional" and Christian Jews as to the messiah, laws, and rites was to lead to the main schism in Judaism. As to differences between Samaritans and other Jews, the sacred Samaritan capital was at Shechem, not Jerusalem, and its Temple, then in ruin, on Mount Gerizim. The Samaritans had their own version of the Torah (only the first five books were accepted by them), which was slightly different, and they claimed to be the true Israel, following Mosaic law, and opposing Jews from Jerusalem and its Temple. Here the Samaritan woman speaks of their common ancestor Jacob and common father, meaning "God."

₁₅The woman said to him, "Sir, give me this water so I won't be thirsty or have to come here to draw it up."

₁₆He said to her,

Go and call your husband and come back here.

₁₇She answered and said to him, "I have no husband."

Yeshua said to her,

You are right to say, "I have no husband."

₁₈You had five husbands and the one

you have now

is not your husband.

What you spoke is the truth.

₁₉The woman said to him, "Sir, I see that you are a prophet. ₂₀Our parents[55] worshiped on this mountain and you say Yerushalayim is the place where we must worship."

₂₁Yeshua said to her,

Believe me, woman, the hour is coming

when not on this mountain

nor in Yerushalayim will you worship the father.

₂₂You worship what you do not know.

We worship what we know

since salvation is from the Jews.

₂₃But the hour is coming and it is now

when the true worshipers will worship the father

in spirit and truth,

for the father seeks such people to worship him.

₂₄God is spirit

and those worshiping must worship him

in spirit and truth.

₂₅The woman said to him, "I know a mashiah is coming who is called the anointed. When he comes he will declare all things to us."

₂₆Yeshua said to her,

I am he, talking to you.

---

55 Our parents from the Greek οἱ πατέρες ἡμῶν (hoi pateres hemon) "our fathers." As in Greek, in contemporary European languages "our fathers" (as in the Spanish *nuestros padres* or the French *nos pères*) is the common word for "parents" and, by extension, "ancestors" or "forefathers."

Students and Shomronims are amazed by Yeshua

27At this his students came and were amazed that he was talking with a woman,[56] but no one said, "What are you looking for?" or "Why are you talking with her?"

28Then the woman left her waterpot and went back into the town and said to the people, 29"Come see a man who told me everything I ever did. Can he be the mashiah?"

30They went out of the town and came toward him.

31Meanwhile the students were saying, "Rabbi, eat."

32But he said to them,

I have a meat[57] to eat which you do not know.

33Then the students said to each other, "Could someone have brought him something to eat?"

34Yeshua said to them,

My meat is to do the will of him
who sent me and to complete his work.

Grain for eternal life

35Do you not say,
"Four more months and then comes the harvest?"
Look, I say to you, lift up your eyes
and you will see the fields are white for harvest.
36Already the reaper is taking his wages
and gathering the grain for the eternal life
so sower and reaper alike may be happy.
37The words of the proverb are true:
"One sows and another reaps."
38I sent you to reap what you did not labor.
Others worked and you entered their work.

Shomronims believe

39And many Shomronims from the city believed in him, because of what the woman said when she testified, "He told me everything I ever did." 40So when they came near him, the Shomronims asked him to stay with them.

He stayed there two days.

---

[56] It remains unclear whether the students' amazement is due to Yeshua's talking to a woman, a Samaritan woman, or perhaps to both notions.

[57] Meat from the Greek βρφσις (brosis), also means "food."

41And many more believed because of his word, 42and they said to the woman, "It is no longer because of your talk that we believe. We ourselves have heard and we know that he is truly the savior of the world."

Yeshua is received in the Galil

43After two days he went from there to the Galil, 44for Yeshua himself had testified that a prophet has no honor in his own country.[58] 45But when he came to the Galil, the Galileans welcomed him, for they had seen all the things he did in Yerushalayim during the festival days, since they too had gone to the festival.

In Kana, treating a sick prince

46Then he came again to Kana in the Galil, where he had made the water wine. There was a certain prince whose son was sick in Kfar Nahum.[59] 47When he heard that Yeshua had come from Yehuda into the Galil, he went to him and asked him to come down and heal his son, for he was near death.

48Yeshua said to him,

Unless you see signs and wonders

you will not believe.

49The prince said to him, "Sir, come down before my child dies."

50Yeshua said to him,

Go, your son lives.

The man believed the word Yeshua told him and left. 51And as he was going down, his slaves met him and told him that his son was alive.

52So he asked them at what hour[60] he had gotten better.

They told him, "Yesterday at the seventh hour[61] the fever left him."

53Then he realized it was the same hour that Yeshua told him, "Your son lives,"and he believed and along with all his household.

54And Yeshua had performed a second sign[62] after coming from Yehuda to the Galil.

---

[58] "Honor in his own country." See texts and/or notes on Mark 3.35, 6.4; Matt. 13.57; and Luke 4.24, 8.21.

[59] Capernaum.

[60] "At what time" or "at what hour." The answer "one in the afternoon" is "the seventh hour."

[61] At one in the afternoon.

[62] Miracle from the Greek σημεῖον (semeion) "sign." "Sign" in this context should be understood as "miracle."

CHAPTER 5

In Yerushalayim at sheep pool called Beit Zaita,
Yeshua treats a sick man

After this it was the Pesach of the Jews and Yeshua went up to Yerushalayim. ₂In Yerushalayim by the Sheep Gate, there is a pool, whose name in Hebrew is Beit Zaita.[63] It has five porches. ₃By the porches lay a crowd of the sick, blind, lame, and paralyzed [₄waiting for the water to move, for an angel of the lord came down into the pool, and whoever was first to go into the water after it was stirred was healed of affliction].[64]

₅There was one man there who had been sick for thirty-eight years.

₆Seeing him lying there and knowing how long he had been there, Yeshua said to him,

Do you want to get well?

₇The sick man answered, "Sir, I have no one to put me down into the pool when the water is stirred up. And while I am going there, someone else gets there ahead of me."

₈Yeshua said to him,

Stand,

take up your bed[65]

and walk.

₉And immediately the man was healthy and he took up his bed and walked around.

Healing on Shabbat

And that day was Shabbat.[66] ₁₀The Jews said to the healed man, ₁₀"It is Shabbat and it is unlawful for you to carry your bed."

₁₁But the man answered them, "The one who made me healthy told me to take up my bed and walk."

---

[63] Bethzatha from the Greek Βηθζαθὰ (Bethzatha) is thought to be from the Hebrew בֵּית זֵיתָא (beit zaita), "house of olives." The more common form is Bethesda from the Greek Βηθεσδὰ (Bethesda), from the Aramaic בֵּית חֶסְדָּא (beit hesdda), meaning "house of mercy." Hence Bethesda's use as a name for hospitals. The meaning and source of Bethesda is debated. It is thought that Bethesda is the pool by Sheep Gate and Bethzatha the location.

[64] Verse 4, in many manuscripts, is omitted or bracketed in most translations. It is probably an explanatory gloss inserted by a later copyist to show the pool's miraculous healing powers.

[65] Bed from the Greek κράβαττόν (krávatton). Can also be understood as a "mat" or "pallet."

[66] Sabbath from the Greek σάββατον (sabbaton), from the Hebrew שַׁבָּת (shabbat).

12"Which man told you to take up your bed and walk?" they asked him.

13The healed man didn't know who he was, for Yeshua had disappeared into the crowd that was there.

14Afterward Yeshua found him in the Temple and said to him,

Look, you have become healthy.

Sin no more

or something worse may happen to you.

15The man went off and told the Jews it was Yeshua who cured him. 16And for this the Jews began to persecute Yeshua, because he healed on Shabbat.

17But Yeshua responded to them,

My father is still doing his work

and I am doing mine.

18For this the Jews sought all the more to find him and kill him, since he was not only breaking Shabbat but he even called God his own father, making himself equal to God.

19Yeshua answered and said to them, "Amen, I say to you,"

The son can do nothing by himself unless he sees

the father doing the same,

for what he does the son does likewise.

20The father loves the son and shows him everything

that he is doing,

and he will show him greater works than these

so you will marvel.

21Just as the father wakes the dead and gives them life,

so the son gives life to whom he will.

22The father judges no one,

for he has given all judgment to his son

23so all will honor the son as they honor the father.

One who does not honor the son

does not honor the father who sent him.

24Amen, amen, I say to you,

One who hears my word and believes him

who sent me

has eternal life and does not come to judgment,

but passes out of death to life.

25Amen, amen, I say to you,

A time is coming and it is now

when the dead will hear the voice of the son of God
and those who hear will live.
26Just as the father has life in himself,
so he has given the son life to have in himself.
27And he has given him authority to judge
because he is the earthly son.
28Do not wonder at this,
for the hour is coming when all who are in their graves
will hear his voice
29and will come out:
those who have done good will go to a resurrection of life,
but those who have done evil will go to a resurrection
    of judgment.
30I can do nothing from myself.
As I hear I judge,
and my judgment is just,
since I do not seek my will but the will of him
who sent me.

Yeshua's testimony and Mosheh's words in the Tanak

31If I testify about myself, my testimony is not true.
32There is another who testifies about me.
33You have sent to Yohanan[67] and he has testified
    to the truth.
34But from no living man do I take my testimony
and I say this so you may be saved,
35yet that man was a lamp that burns and shines
and you wished to exult for an hour in his light.

36Yet I have a testimony greater than Yohanan's,
for the works that my father gave me to fulfill,
these my own works, testify that the father has sent me.
37And the father who has sent me has testified for me.
His voice you have never heard, and his shape
    you have never seen,
38and his word does not live inside you
since you do not believe the one whom he sent you.

---

[67] John the Baptist.

39You search the writings of the Tanak[68]

because you think in them is eternal life

and it is they that testify about me

40but you do not want to come to me

so that you may have life.

41I do not accept glory from living people,

42but I know you and that you do not have the love

 of God in you.

43I have come in the name of my father

and you do not accept me.

If someone else comes in his own name,

that one you will accept.

44How can you believe when you take glory from each other

and do not seek the glory from the only God?

45Do not suppose I will accuse you before the father.

Your accuser is Mosheh in whom you have hoped.

46But if you believed in Mosheh you would believe in me,

for he wrote about me.

47But if you do not believe his writings in the Tanak,

how will you believe my words?

◼ CHAPTER 6

Bread for five thousand on the grass

After this Yeshua left for the other side of the Sea of the Galil, also called Lake Tiberius.

2And a big crowd followed him, because they saw the miraculous signs he performed on the sick.

3Yeshua went up the mountain and there he sat down with his students. 4Pesach was near, the holiday of the Jews. 5Yeshua raised his eyes and seeing a big crowd coming toward him, said to Filippos,

 Where can we buy some bread so they can eat?

6But he said this to test him, for he already knew what he would do.

---

[68] The Hebrew Bible. Also written "Tanakh" or "Tanach."

7Filippos answered him, "Two hundred denarii worth of bread are not enough for everyone to have a bite."

8One of his students, Andreas, the brother of Shimon Kefa, said to him, 9"There is a young boy here who has five barley loaves and two fish. But what is that for all these people?"

10Yeshua said,

Have the people sit down.

Now there was a lot of grass in this place. So the men lay back on the ground, five thousand of them.[69]

11Then Yeshua took the loaves, and gave thanks and passed out the bread to the people who were reclining there. So also the fishes, as much as they wanted. 12And when they were filled, Yeshua said to his students,

Pick up the leftover pieces so nothing is lost.

13So they picked up and filled twelve baskets with pieces from the five barley loaves that were left over by those who had eaten.

14And when the people saw the miraculous signs he did, they said, "Certainly he is the prophet, the one who is coming into the world."

Yeshua alone on the mountain

15Yeshua, knowing they were about to come and seize him to make him king, went off again to the mountain to be alone.

Walking on the sea

16When evening came the students went down to the sea, 17and got into a boat to cross over the sea to Kfar Nahum. By now it was dark and Yeshua had not come to them. 18Since there was a strong wind the sea was rough. 19When they had rowed three or four miles, they saw Yeshua walking on the sea and coming close to the boat, and they were afraid.

20But he said to them,

It is I.

Do not be afraid.

21Then they wanted to take him up into the boat, and at once the boat reached the land where they were going.

---

[69] It is unlikely that such a crowd would consist only of men, and, though some translations say "they" or "people," the Greek says "men."

Looking for Rabbi Yeshua who preaches to them
in the synagogue at Kfar Nahum

22Next day the crowd that had stayed on the other side of the sea saw that there had been only one boat there. They also saw that Yeshua had not gone aboard the ship with his students, but the students had set out alone. 23Then some boats from Lake Tiberius came near the place where they had eaten the bread.[70] 24When the crowd saw that neither Yeshua nor his students was there, they got into the boats and went to Kfar Nahum, looking for Yeshua.

25When they found him on the other side of the sea, they said to him, "Rabbi, when did you come here?"

26Yeshua answered them, saying, "Amen, amen, I say to you,"

You look for me not because you saw signs

but because you ate the loaves and were filled.

27Do not work for the food that spoils

but for the food that lasts for eternal life,

which the earthly son will give you,

since on him God who is father set the seal.

28Then they said to him, "What can we do to do the work of God?"

29Yeshua answered and said to them,

The work of God is to believe the one he sent.

30So they said to him, "Why don't you do a sign so we may see and believe in you and in what you do? 31Our parents ate manna in the desert, and as Mosheh wrote in Exodus, 'He gave them bread from the sky to eat.'"

32Then Yeshua said to them, "Amen, amen, I say to you,"

It was not Mosheh who gave you bread from the sky,

but my father gives you bread from the sky,

the true bread,

33for the bread of God comes out of the sky

and gives life to the world.

34Then they said to him,

Sir, always give us this bread.

35Yeshua said to them,

I am the bread of life.

Who comes to me will not be hungry,

and who believes in me will not be thirsty again.

36Yet I said to you,

you have seen me and do not believe.

---

70 Some manuscripts continue the sentence, "after the Lord gave thanks." The phrase referring to Yeshua as "Lord" is probably a scribal addition and is omitted in recent translations.

37All that my father gives me will come to me
and anyone who comes to me I will not turn away,
38since I have come down from the sky
not to do my own will but the will of him who sent me.

39And this is the will of him who sent me,
that I should lose nothing of all he gave me
but raise it up on the last day.
40This is the will of my father,
that all who see the son and believe in him
may have eternal life,
and I will raise them up on the last day.

The Jews murmur about Yeshua, who responds to his coreligionists

41Then the Jews murmured about him because he said, "I am the bread that came down from the sky." 42Isn't he Yeshua, Yosef's son, whose father and mother we know? How can he now say he has come down from the sky?"
43Yeshua said to them,

Do not murmur gossip among yourselves.
44No one can come to me
unless drawn in by the father who sent me,
and I will raise that person up on the last day.
45It was written by the prophet Yeshayah,[71]
"They will all be taught by God."
Everyone who has heard from the father and learned
comes to me.
46Not that anyone has seen the father
except one who is from God.
This one has seen the father.

47Amen, amen, I say to you,
One who believes has eternal life.
48I am the bread of life.
49Your parents[72] ate the manna in the desert and died.
50This is the bread that comes from the heavenly sky,
so anyone may eat it and not die.

---

[71] Isaiah 54.13. See also Jeremiah 31.34.
[72] Can also be translated as "ancestors." See note 55, p. 317.

51I am the living bread
who came down from the sky.
Whoever eats this bread will live forever,
and the bread is my flesh,
which I will give for the life of the world.

The Jews argue with each other and Yeshua
speaks to them in the synagogue

52The Jews were arguing with each other, saying, "How can this man give us
his own flesh to eat?"

53So Yeshua said, "Amen, amen, I tell you,"
Unless you eat the flesh of the earthly son
and drink his blood,
you have no life within you.
54The one who eats my flesh and drinks my blood
has eternal life
and I will raise that person up on the last day,
55for my flesh is the true meat and my blood is
the true drink.

56The one who eats my flesh and drinks my blood
lives in me and I in them.[73]
57As the living father sent me and I live
because of the father,
so the one who eats me will live because of me.
58This is the bread that came down from the sky,
not like what our parents ate and died.
Who eats this bread will live forever.

59These things Yeshua said in a synagogue while teaching in Kfar Nahum.

Yeshua's students also murmur about him, revealing disbelief

60Many of his students heard these things, and said, "His teaching is abra-
sive. Who can bear to hear it?"

61But Yeshua knew inside himself that his students were complaining about
his words, and he said to them,

Does this shock you?
62What if you see the earthly son ascend to where he was before?

---

73 "Them" is literally "him."

63The breath[74] keeps us alive.
The flesh is of no help.
The words I spoke to you are the breath of spirit
and are life.
64But some among you do not believe.

Yeshua knew from the beginning who among them didn't believe and who would betray him. 65And he said,

I have told you that no one can come to me
unless it be granted by the father.

66Because of this many of his students withdrew to their own place and would no longer walk about with him.

67Then Yeshua said to the twelve,

You too, do you not want to leave?

68Shimon Kefa answered,

Lord, whom can we go to? You have the words
of eternal life,
69and we have believed and known that you are
the holy one of God.

70Yeshua responded,

Did I not choose you the twelve?
Yet one of you is a devil.

71He was speaking of Yehuda son of Shimon of Keriot,[75] for he, among the twelve, was about to betray him.

✦ CHAPTER 7

Yeshua in danger

And after that Yeshua went about in the Galil. He did not want to go about in Yehuda because the Jews were trying to kill him.

---

[74] Breath from the Greek πνεῦμα (pneuma) means "breath" and by extension "spirit."
[75] Iscariot from the Greek Ἰσκαριώθ (Iskarioth), from the Hebrew אִישׁ קְרִיּוֹת (ish keriot), meaning "man of Keriot." In English, "Keriot" is also written "Kerioth."

Yeshua's brothers, who do not believe in him, urge him to go
into Yehuda and up to the Sukkoth festival in Yerushalayim

₂Now the Jewish harvest feast of Sukkoth[76] was near, ₃and his brothers[77] said to him, "Leave here and go into Yehuda so your students will see the works you do. ₄No one acts in secret who wants to be widely known. Since you do these things, show them to the world."

₅Even his own brothers did not believe in him.

₆Then Yeshua said to them,

My time has not come, but your time is always here.

₇The world cannot hate you, but it hates me,

for I testify concerning it that its works are evil.

₈You go up to the festival [I will not go],

because my time has not yet been completed.

₉And saying these things, he stayed in the Galil.

Yeshua goes to Yerushalayim, teaches in the Temple,
and debates with the people

₁₀When his brothers went up to the festival, he also went up, not openly but in secret. ₁₁So then the Jews were looking for him in the festival and saying, "Where is that man?" ₁₂And the crowds were murmuring about him, some saying, "He is a good man," yet others saying, "No, he is fooling the crowd." ₁₃But no one spoke openly about him for fear of the Jews.[78]

₁₄About the middle of the festival, Yeshua went up into the Temple and taught.

₁₅The Jews were astonished and said, "How can this man have learning when he has not instructed?"

Yeshua answered them,

₁₆My teaching is not mine but is his who sent me.

---

[76] Tabernacle from the Greek σκηνή (skene), "tent," from the Hebrew סֻכָּה (sukkah), "shelter," "tent." The three tents are associated with the Jewish Sukkoth, the Festival of the Tabernacles or Booths, חַג הַ־סֻכָּה (hag hasukkah), an eight-day celebration for autumnal harvest, beginning on the eve of the 15th of Tishri. The sukkah is a small lean-to-like tent in the fields. The Festival, lasting eight days, commemorates the forty years that Moses and the Jews spent in the desert after escaping from Egypt and before entering Canaan.

[77] Yeshua had four brothers, James, Joseph, Judas, and Simon (Yaakov, Yosef, Yehuda, and Shimon), mentioned in Mark 6.3 and Matthew 13.54–56. His sisters are also mentioned in these passages, but not by name.

[78] In these passages the word "Jew" cannot mean "Jew" with respect to the people of Jerusalem, since the people in the crowd are Jews, including Yeshua. But here "Jew" refers to any presumed opponent of Yeshua, thereby demarking enemies as Jews, and rabbi Yeshua who is there to teach in the Temple as some undefined other.

17Whoever wants to do the will of God

will know whether the teaching is from God

or whether I speak on my own.

18The person who speaks only from inside

seeks a personal glory,

but the person who seeks the glory of God who sent us

is true and has nothing false inside.

19Did Mosheh not give you the law?

Yet none of you keeps the law.

Why are you trying to kill me?

20The crowd responded, "You have a demon inside you. Who is trying to kill you?"

21Yeshua answered,

I performed one work and you are amazed.

22So Mosheh gave you circumcision—

not that it comes from Mosheh but from the patriarchs—

and on Shabbat you circumcise a man.

23If a man receives circumcision on Shabbat

in order not to break the law of Mosheh,

are you angry with me for making

a man's whole body healthy on Shabbat?

24Do not judge by appearance

but with the judgment of justice.

Gossip in Yerushalayim about Yeshua as mashiah

25Now some were saying in Yerushalayim, "Isn't this the man they are trying to kill? 26And look, here he is, speaking openly, and they say nothing to him. Perhaps the rulers know that this man is the mashiah. 27But we know where this man comes from. When the mashiah comes, no one will know where he comes from."

Yeshua preaches in the Temple

28Then Yeshua cried out in the Temple while teaching, and said,

You know me and know where I am from,

and I have not come on my own,

but he is true, the one who sent me,

and you do not know him.

29I know him because from him I am

and he sent me.

30Then they sought to seize[79] him and no one had laid a hand on him, because his hour had not yet come. 31Many in the crowd believed in him, however, and said, "When the mashiah comes, will he do more signs than this man did?"

Look for me, but I am going where you cannot come

32The Prushim heard the crowd murmuring these things about him, and the high priests and Prushim sent servants[80] to seize him.

33And Yeshua said,

> For a little more time I am still with you
> and then I go away to the one who sent me.
> 34You will search me out and not find me,
> and where I am you will not be able to come.

35Then the Jews said to each other, "Where is this man about to go where we cannot find him? Is he about to go to the diaspora among the Greeks and teach them?[81] 36What is the meaning of the words he said,

> You will search me out and not find me,
> and where I am you will not be able to come?"

Last day of Sukkoth Yeshua cries out in the Temple
to the crowd of the promise of living water

37On the last and greatest day of Sukkoth, Yeshua stood up and cried out,

> Let anyone who is thirsty come to me and drink!
> 38For one who believes in me, as it says in the scriptures,
> "Rivers out of his belly will flow with living water."[82]

39He said this about the spirit, which the believers in him were to receive. But the spirit was not yet because Yeshua was not yet glorified.

---

[79] From the Greek πιάσαι (piasai), "to seize" or "to grab." Often the verb is translated as "arrest," but while the notion of "arrest" may be implied as a later consequence of seizing, here it means only "to seize." "Arrest" initially meant "to stop" or "to seize."

[80] Servants from the Greek ὑπηρέτας (hyperetas) means "servants" and also has been translated as "officers" or "policemen."

[81] In 7:35, "Is he [Yeshua] about to go to the diaspora among the Greeks" seems like a prophecy of Yeshua's students who indeed later went to preach in the synagogues of the Greek Jews in Greek lands to announce the good news of Yeshua as the messiah. Although the "diaspora" is a common word for the dispersion of the Jews abroad, this phrase has puzzlingly been interpreted to mean ethnic Greeks, not Greek-speaking Jews in Greek lands. The largest center of diaspora Jews was probably in Alexandria, for whom the Septuagint Bible was translated from Hebrew into Greek (second century B.C.E.). At this time, the Jews were dispersed in great numbers from Alexandria and Antioch to Thessaloniki and Rome; most were Greek-speaking, in contrast to the figures in the New Covenant who spoke Aramaic, with Hebrew the language of the synagogue.

[82] The scripture intended is uncertain. It may be Isaiah 44.2–3 or Zechariah 14.8. Zechariah is read at Sukkot.

More crowd discussion of Yeshua as mashiah

40Some of the crowd hearing these words said, "This man is truly the prophet."

41Others were saying, "He is the mashiah."

But some were saying, "Surely, the mashiah cannot come from the Galil? 42Didn't Micah say in scripture that the mashiah will come from the sperm of David and from the village of Beit Lehem[83] where David lived?"

43So there was a split in the crowd over him, 44some wanting to seize him, but no one laid a hand on him.

Nakdeimon, a Parush, defends Yeshua before the council

45Then the servants went back to the high priests and Prushim, who said to them, "Why didn't you bring him?"

46"No one ever spoke like this man," the servants answered.

47The Prushim retorted, "Have you too been taken in? 48Surely none of the rulers believed in him. 49But the crowd[84] that does not know the law is cursed."

50Nakdeimon,[85] who had gone to Yeshua before, and was one of the council, said to them, 51"Surely our law doesn't judge a person unless it first hears and knows what that person is doing?"

52They replied, saying to him, "You are not also from the Galil, are you? Search and you will find no prophet is to rise from the Galil."

53[Then each went to his own home, but Yeshua went to the Mountain of Olives.[86]

---

83 Bethlehem from the Greek Βηθλέεμ (Bethleem), from the Hebrew בֵּית לֶחֶם (beit lehem), meaning "house of bread."

84 The crowd, from the Greek ὄχλος (ohlos). Until this moment, *ohlos* has been translated as "crowd," carrying no pejorative undertones. In this context, where the crowd has been cursed for not knowing the law, the translation remains accurately "crowd" in the NRSV. However, in others versions, it is rendered as "mob" or "rabble," thereby effectively heightening anger against Jewish authorities and Pharisees for having used the unfriendly term "mob" or "rabble" with respect to a crowd in the Temple favorable to Yeshua as the messiah. So the word for "crowd" astonishingly becomes "mob" in the NIV and "rabble" in the Jerusalem, Lattimore, Funk, and Hoover (Jesus Seminar), and other earlier versions. The King James Version, however, moves in another direction. It renders ὄχλος with precise and wondrous majesty, "But this people who knoweth not the law are cursed." However, turning "this crowd" into "this people" cannot but have the ominous and familiar tone of a curse not only on the crowd but also on the people.

85 Nakdeimon. Nicodemus.

86 Normally the last half of verse 7.53 is printed as 8.1, after the chapter break. It makes more sense to leave 7.53 as a last complete sentence in chapter 7. Adding to the confusion, scholars agree that the movingly adroit story of the adulterous woman was not originally part of the gospel but an emendation based on oral tradition. Lines 7.53 through 8.11 are bracketed.

CHAPTER 8

Woman taken in adultery

₂At dawn he went into the Temple and all the people came to him and he sat down and taught them. ₃The scholars and Prushim led a woman in who had been caught in adultery, and they stood her before them ₄and said to him, "Rabbi, this woman was caught in the act of adultery. ₅In the law, Mosheh charged us to stone such women. Now, what do you say?"

₆They said this to test him so they could have a charge against him. But Yeshua stooped down and with his finger wrote on the ground. ₇When they kept questioning him, he stood up and said to them,

> The one among you without sin[87]
>
> let him first cast a stone at her.

₈And again he stooped down, writing on the ground, ₉and those who heard him went away, one by one, beginning with the older ones. And he was left alone with the woman standing before him.

₁₀Yeshua stood up and said to her,

> Woman, where are they?
>
> Has no one condemned you?

₁₁And she said, "No one, sir."

And Yeshua said,

> Neither do I condemn you.
>
> Go, and from now on sin no more.][88]

Yeshua, light of the world

₁₂Then Yeshua spoke to them again,

> I am the light of the world.
>
> Whoever follows me will not walk in darkness
>
> but will have the light of life.

---

[87] The Greek is sparse and needs no fleshing out, saying word for word, "The blameless you [gen.] first at her throw stone." The Greek ἀναμάρτητος (anamartetos) means "one without fault, failing, or wrong" or "one who misses the mark," which in biblical Greek came to mean primarily "sin."

[88] 7.53–8.11 is not in early manuscripts and is thought to be an addition. Although an interruption in the flow of Yeshua's debate in the Temple and whether authentic or spurious, it still adds to the narrative complexity.

Telling the Prushim who is his father

13Then the Prushim said to him, "You are testifying about yourself. Your testimony isn't true."

14Yeshua answered and said to them,

Even if I testify about my self, my testimony is true.

I know where I came from and where I am going.

And you do not know where I came from

or where I am going.

15You judge according to the flesh.

I judge no one.

16And if I do judge, my judgment is true

because I am not alone,

but I and the father who sent me.

17And in your law[89] it is written in Deuteronomy

that the testimony of two people is true.

18I am he who testifies about myself,

and testifying about me is the one who sent me,

my father.

19They said to him, "Where is your father?"

Yeshua answered,

You know neither me nor my father.

If you knew me,

you would also know my father.

20These words he spoke in the treasury while teaching in the Temple. And no one seized him, because his hour had not yet come.

Yeshua not of this world

21Then he said to them again,

I am going and you will look for me

and you will die in your sins.[90]

Where I am going you cannot come.

---

[89] Deut. 17.6, 19.5. The Greek reads *"your* law," thus separating Yeshua from his adversaries. While Yeshua was questioning the law, it was still his law, as is clear from the immediately preceding passages citing Mosaic law. Insofar as the story is set in a historical period, "your" rings like a later redaction when the Hebrew Bible was diminished in authority, and was the "old" rather than the "new" covenant.

[90] Sins. In the classical Greek, ἁμαρτία (hamartia) means "missing the mark," "failure," "wrong," and sometimes "sin." In biblical Koine it has been translated as "sin," though some object. In *Three Gospels* (New York: Scribners, 1996), Reynolds Price translates ἁμαρτία as "wrong" or "error," explaining that the word "appears to have fewer connotations of the fleshpot than the English word *sin,* so long ago hijacked by the puritan and hypocrite" (18). I have translated ἁμαρτία as "sin" when the intention is harsh, and "wrong" or "error" when the intention is more sympathetic to the wrongdoer.

₂₂Then the Jews said to one another, "He won't kill himself, will he, when he says, 'Where I am going you cannot come'?"

₂₃And he said to them,

> You are of things below.
>
> I am of things above.
>
> You are of this world,
>
> I am not of this world.
>
> ₂₄So I have told you
>
> you will die in your sins.
>
> If you do not believe that I am,[91]
>
> you will die in your sins.

₂₅Then they were saying to him, "Who are you?"

Yeshua said to them,

> I am what from the beginning I told you.
>
> ₂₆I have much to say about you and much to judge,
>
> but the one who sent me is true
>
> and what I heard from him I speak in the world.

₂₇They did not know he was speaking to them about the father.

₂₈Then Yeshua said,

> When you raise up the earthly son,
>
> then you will know that I am[92]
>
> and from myself I do nothing,
>
> but I speak as my father taught me.
>
> ₂₉And the one who sent me is with me.
>
> He did not leave me alone,
>
> for what I do pleases him always.

₃₀When he was saying this, many believed in him.

The truth will set you free

₃₁Then Yeshua said to the Jews who believed in him,

> If you remain with my word,
>
> then you are truly my students,
>
> ₃₂and you will know the truth
>
> and the truth will set you free.[93]

---

[91] This phrase is normally translated "I am he," but the Greek says ἐγώ εἰμι (ego eimi), "I am." "I am he" may be implied, or "I am myself," or the solitary mystery of "I am." It is richer to give only what the Greek gives, "I am," and then, not bound by interpretation in translation, read the verse creatively. As for Yeshua's take on the phrase, in the next line he is asked the essential enigma, "Who are you?" His answer is a riddle, which should be respected.

[92] See note 91 above.

[93] The passages "You are of things below. / I am of things above," "I am the light of the world," and "the

Children of Avraham

₃₃They answered him, "We are of the sperm of Avraham[94] and have never been enslaved. How can you say that we will be set free?"

₃₄Yeshua said, "Amen, amen, I say to you,"

Everyone who sins is a slave to sin

₃₅but the slave does not stay in the house forever.

The son remains forever.

₃₆If the son frees you, then you will be really free.

₃₇I know you are the sperm of Avraham

but you are trying to kill me

because my word has no place in you.

₃₈I tell what I have seen with the father.

So, what you have heard from the father, do.

₃₉They responded and said to him, "Our father is Avraham."

Yeshua said to them,

If you are the children of Avraham,

then do what Avraham did,

₄₀yet now you are seeking to kill me,

a man who has told you the truth

which I heard from God.

That is not what Avraham did.

₄₁You are doing your father's work.[95]

They told him, "We were not born of prostitution.[96] We have one father, God."

Jews, the children of the devil

₄₂Yeshua said to them,

If God were your father you would love me,

for I came out from God and I am here.

I have not come from myself but from the one

who sent me.

₄₃Why do you not know my voice?

---

truth will set you free" reflect the distancing from the world on earth in favor of a spiritual world of light elsewhere. In gnosticism the soul is trapped in darkness on earth and yearns for return to the light principle. As such, these cited passages display the essence of gnostic beliefs and are used to support a common contention of the essential gnostic nature of John with regard to the spirit as light.

[94] Abraham from the Greek Ἀβραάμ (Abraam), from the Hebrew אַבְרָהָם (avraham).

[95] The "your father" makes no sense until the next verses when Yeshua declares that the Jews' purported father of the Hebrew Bible is not God, but another father, the devil, as immediately seen in v. 44.

[96] Of prostitution. From the Greek ἐκ πορνείας (ek porneias). Also translated as "filth," "prostitution," and more freely as "illegitimate" (NRSV).

Because you cannot hear my word.

44You are from your father the devil[97]

and you want to do the desires of your father.

From the beginning he was a murderer

and he does not stand in the truth,

because there is no truth in him.

When he lies he speaks from himself,

since he is a liar and the father of lies.

45And because I speak the truth you do not believe me.

46Who among you proves me in sin?

If I tell the truth, why do you not believe me?

47Whoever is from God hears the words of God.

But you do not hear, for you are not from God.

Yeshua glorified by his father

48The Jews answered him, "Are we not right to say that you are a Shomronim and have a demon?"

49Yeshua answered,

I have no demon, but I honor my father

and you dishonor me.

50And I do not seek my glory.

There is one who seeks it and he is the judge.

51Amen, amen, I say to you,

---

[97] "You are from your father the devil / and you want to do the desires of your father. / From the beginning he was a murderer." In this angry demonization of the Jews as children of the devil, who is their murderous father, Yeshua appears to speak not as a contemporary Jew to a Jew but through the voice of a later writer whose hatred for the Jew is undisguised. However, it is wrong to soften the attack in the gospels by disguising the target of the attack in translating Jews as "the people," "opponents," or "rulers," which is done with good intent in the *New Testament and Psalms* (New York: Oxford University Press, 1995) and in other versions. Here the Jews are portrayed both as unrelated to their Jewish Bible God, yet also related to Abraham, whom Yeshua states that he preceded. This violent attack on his coreligionists also reaches Abrahamic Judaism and the inferiority of the Hebrew Bible compared to the New Covenant, though here the polemic is not as specific as elsewhere in the gospels, where the Jews are the murderers of their own prophets as they will be the murderers of their foreseen messiah, Yeshua. However, in these passages the Jews of the New Covenant are irrevocably separated from the Jews of the Hebrew Bible, who are called "the Israelites" (Greek for "Israelis"), which safely eases the passage into fiction to readers unfamiliar with the sundry names for Jews.

Before the chapter's last delimiting of Abrahamic Judaism and self-proclamation, "Before Avraham was born I am," Yeshua states that Abraham himself would have seen and exulted at Yeshua's coming. It is not likely that this pride, unpleasant anger, and retribution have much to do with a historic Yeshua and his messianic center in the formation of later Christianity. Rather, we are reading late, redacted documents in Greek, a foreign language to the participants, reflecting a nascent church and its torrid rejection of the parent creed and its member Jews, excluding rabbi Yeshua and followers, who escape all retribution for their birth and observed religion.

Whoever honors my word
will not look on eternal death.

52The Jews said to him, "Now we know that you have a demon. Avraham died, as did the prophets, and you say, 'Whoever honors my word will not look on eternal death.' 53Can you be greater than our father Avraham who died? And the prophets who died? Who do you think you are?"

54Yeshua answered,

If I glorify myself my glory is nothing.
My father glorifies me,
of whom you say, "He is our God,"
55though you do not know him.
But I know him.
And if I say that I do not know him
I will be like you, a liar,
but I know him and I keep his word.
56Your father Avraham was glad that he could see
my day.
He saw it and exulted.

57Then the Jews said to him, "You are not yet fifty and you have seen Avraham?"

58Yeshua said,

Amen, amen, I say to you,
Before Avraham was born I am.

59Then they took up stones to throw at him, but Yeshua hid and went out of the Temple.

 **CHAPTER 9**

Rabbi Yeshua and a blindman

Going on he saw a man blind from birth.

2His students asked him, saying, "Rabbi, who sinned, this man or his parents that he was born blind?"

3Yeshua answered,

Neither he nor his parents did wrong.
He was born blind so the work of God
might be revealed in him.
4We must do the work of him who sent us
while it is day.

Night is coming when no one can work.

5While I am in the world,

I am the light of the world.

6After saying that, he spat on the ground and made mud with the spit and smeared mud on the man's eyes, 7and said to him,

Go wash in the pool of Shiloah.[98]

Then he went and washed and came back seeing.

8The neighbors and those who had seen him as a beggar said, "Isn't he the one who sat and begged?"

9Some said, "That's him."

Others said, "No, but it looks like him."

The man said, "It's me."

10So they kept asking him, "How were your eyes opened?"

11He answered, "The man called Yeshua made mud and smeared[99] it on my eyes and said to me, 'Go wash in the pool of Shiloah.' So I went and after washing I saw."

12And they asked him, "Where is he?"

"I don't know," he said.

Prushim question and revile the former blindman

13They took the former blindman to the Prushim. 14Now it was a Shabbat day when Yeshua made the mud and opened his eyes. 15Then the Prushim in turn asked him how he regained his sight.

And he told them, "He put mud on my eyes and I washed and now I see."

16Some of the Prushim said, "This man is not from God, for he doesn't observe the Shabbat." But others said, "How can a man be a sinner who does such signs?" And there was division among them.

17They said to the blindman again, "What do you have to say about him because he opened your eyes?"

"He is a prophet," he said.

18The Jews did not believe he was blind and then regained his sight until they called on the parents of the one who saw again. 19And they said to them,

---

98 Siloam from the Greek Σιλωάμ (Siloam), from Hebrew שלח (shiloah). Siloam is followed by an interpolation: "which translated means the one who has been sent." Shiloah is found also in Isaiah 8.6.

99 Smear from the Greek ἐπέχρισεν (epehrisen) here also means "the anointed," from the same root as the noun "anointed," χριστός (hristos), as in Yeshua the Anointed, but here the verb means simply "smear" or "spread." The KJV, shifting to third person and upgrading the verb to convey the power of the messiah (the anointed), translates this phrase freely and beautifully, "And he anointed the eyes of the blind man."

"This is your son whom you say was born blind? How is it that he can see now?"

20His parents answered, saying, "We know that this man is our son and that he was born blind. 21But we don't know how it is that now he sees, nor know who opened his eyes. Ask him, he is of age. He will speak for himself."

22His parents said these things because they were afraid of the Jews, for the Jews had already agreed that anyone who confessed that Yeshua was the mashiah would be barred from the synagogue. 23That is why his parents said, "Ask him, he is of age."

24So for a second time they called the man who was blind and said to him, "Glory to God. We know that this man is a sinner."

25This man answered, "If he is a sinner I do not know. One thing I do know. I was blind and now I see."

26"What did he do to you? How did he open your eyes?" they said to him.

27"I told you already and you don't listen," he said to them. "Why do you want to hear it again? Could it be that you too want to be his students?"

28And they reviled him and said, "You are his student, but we are Mosheh's students.[100] 29We know that God spoke to Mosheh, but we don't know where this man is from."

30The man answered, saying, "Here is what is astonishing, that you don't know where he is from, yet he opened my eyes. 31We know that God does not listen to sinners, but if one is devout and does his will, he hears. 32From the beginning of time we have not heard of one who opened the eyes of a blindman. 33If this man were not from God, he could not have done anything."

34They answered and said to him, "You were born wholly in sins, and you are teaching us?"

And they threw him out.

Yeshua gives a blindman light

35Yeshua heard that they threw the blindman out and he found him and said,

> Do you believe in the earthly son?

36The man replied to him, "And who is he, sir, that I may believe in him?"

37Yeshua said to him,

> You have seen him
> and he is the one talking with you.

---

[100] A reference to the superiority of Yeshua's teaching over that of Moses and, by extension, of the New Covenant over the Jewish Bible.

₃₈And he said, "I believe, lord."

And he worshiped him.

₃₉And Yeshua said,

>I came into this world for judgment
>
>so those who cannot see may see
>
>and those who see may go blind.

Yeshua and the sighted Prushim

₄₀Some of the Prushim who were near him heard this and said to him, "Surely, we are not blind?"

₄₁Yeshua said to them,

>If you were blind you would have no sin.
>
>Since you say, "We see," your sin remains.

 # CHAPTER 10

Good shepherd at the gate, who lays down his life for the sheep

Again Yeshua said, "Amen, amen, I tell you,"

>I am the gate of the sheepfold
>
>Whoever enters the sheepfold not through the gate
>
>but climbs up and goes in another way,
>
>>is a thief and a robber,
>
>₂but whoever enters through the gate,
>
>>is the shepherd of the sheep.
>
>₃The gatekeeper opens to him
>
>and the sheep hear his voice
>
>and he calls his own sheep by name
>
>and he leads them out.
>
>₄When he has put all his own outside,
>
>he goes in ahead of them and the sheep follow
>
>because they know his voice.
>
>₅They will not follow a stranger, but flee from him.
>
>They do not know the voice of strangers.

₆Yeshua told them this parable, but they failed to understand what he was saying to them.

₇So again Yeshua said, "Amen, amen, I say to you,"

I am the gate of the sheepfold.
8All who came before me are thieves and robbers.
The sheep did not listen to them.
9I am the gate.
Whoever enters through me will be saved
and will go in and go out and find pasture.
10The thief comes only to steal and kill and destroy.
I came that they may have life, and have abundance.

11I am the good shepherd.
The good shepherd lays down his life[101] for the sheep.
12The hired man who is not a shepherd
and is not the owner of the sheep
sees the wolf coming and leaves the sheep and runs,
and the wolf ravages and scatters them
13since he is a hired man
and cares nothing about the sheep.

14I am the good shepherd
and I know my own and my own know me
15as the father knows me and I know the father.
And I lay down my life for the sheep.
16And I have other sheep which are not from this fold.
And I must also bring them in
and they will hear my voice
and there will be one flock and one shepherd.

17Therefore my father loves me
because I lay down my life to receive it again.
18No one takes it from me.
But I lay it down of my own accord.
I have the right to lay it down
and I have the power to receive it again.
This command I have received from my father.
    19At these words there was again division among the Jews. 20Many were say-
ing, "He has a demon and he's mad. Why listen to him?" 21Others said, "These
words are not the words of one with a demon. Can a demon open the eyes of
the blind?"

---

[101] Literally "spirit" but figuratively "life."

Hanukkah in Yerushalayim, Yeshua announces he is the son of God

22Then came Hanukkah in Yerushalayim, the Festival of Lights. It was winter, 23and Yeshua was walking around in the Temple, on the colonnade of Shlomoh.[102] 24The Jews surrounded him and said to him, "How long will you hold our soul suspended? If you are the mashiah tell us plainly."

25Yeshua answered them,

> I told you and you do not believe.
> The works I do in my father name
> are my witness. They speak for me,
> 26but you do not believe because you are not of my sheep.
> 27My sheep hear my voice
> and I know them and they follow me.
> 28I give them eternal life
> and they will not perish forever
> and no one will pluck them out of my hand.
> 29What my father gave me is greater than all,
> and no one can pluck it out of the father's hand.
> 30I and the father are one.

31Then the Jews picked up stones again to stone him.

32Yeshua answered them,

> I have shown you many good works from the father.
> For which of these works will you stone me?"

33The Jews answered him, "For good work we do not stone you, but for blasphemy, and because you are a man and make yourself God."

34Yeshua replied to them,

> Is it not written in your[103] law,
> "I have said that you are gods"?[104]
> 35If God called gods those to whom the word of God came,
> and scripture cannot be set aside,
> 36can you say that I whom the father sanctified
> and sent into the world am blaspheming
> because I said, "I am the son of God"?

---

102 Shlomoh from the Greek Σολομών (Solomon), from the Hebrew שְׁלֹמֹה (shlomoh).

103 Again a question of distancing through the choice of possessive pronouns. "your" in "your law" appears to be implausible, since Yeshua is a Jew and the law is also *his* law, which means the Bible (Torah). Only "the law" or "our law" is sensible if Yeshua is speaking in his own time. To prove his argument, in the following phrase Yeshua cites the law in Psalms 82.6, "you are gods." Then, confirming their mutual possession of biblical law, he adds "and scripture cannot be set aside." Yeshua argues as if he were not a Jew and the law were not *his* law; yet, as a Jew, he uses their common law to prove his point.

104 Ps. 82.6.

343

₃₇If I do not do the works of my father,

do not believe me.

₃₈But if I do them, even if you do not believe me,

believe the works

so you may know and see that the father is in me

and I am in the father.

₃₉They tried to seize him again, and he slipped out of their hands.

Yeshua withdraws to other side of Yarden

₄₀And he went away again across the Yarden to the place where Yohanan was earlier dipping and he stayed there.[105] ₄₁Many came to him and said that Yohanan had not performed a wondrous sign, but everything that Yohanan said about Yeshua was true. ₄₂And many believed in him there.

 CHAPTER 11

With Elazar who is dead

There was a man who was sick, Elazar[106] from Beit Aniyah,[107] from the village of Miryam[108] and Marta,[109] her sister. ₂It was Miryam who anointed the rabbi with oil of myrrh and wiped his feet with her hair. Her brother Elazar was sick. ₃So the sisters sent word to him, saying, "Rabbi, look, one whom you care for is sick."

₄When Yeshua heard this, he said,

This sickness is not close to death

but to the glory of God that through it

the son of God may be glorified.

₅Now Yeshua loved Marta and her sister and Elazar. ₆Therefore when he heard that he was sick, he remained in the place he was for two days. ₇After this he said to his students,

Let us go to Yehuda again.

---

105 Bethany, where John the Baptist dipped his followers, lies beyond the Jordan, and its location is unknown. In some manuscripts it is written Bethabara. This appears not to be the Bethany on the slope of the Mountain of Olives some two miles east of Jerusalem, where Yeshua visited his friends Mary and Martha and where tradition says Lazarus is buried.

106 Lazarus from the Greek Λάζαρος (Lazaros), from the Hebrew אֶלְעָזָר (elazar).

107 Bethany.

108 Mary from the Greek Μαρία (María), from the Hebrew מִרְיָם (miryam).

109 Martha from the Greek Μάρθα (Martha), from the Hebrew מָרְתָא (marta).

8His students said to him, "Rabbi, the Jews were just now trying to stone you[110] and are you going there again?"

9Yeshua replied,

> Are there not twelve hours in the day?
> Whoever walks around in the day doesn't stumble
> since one sees the light of this world.
> 10Whoever walks around in the night stumbles
> since the light is not in that person.

11These things he said, and then he told them,

> Our friend Elazar has fallen asleep,
> but I am going there to awaken him.

12So the students said, "Sir, if he has fallen asleep, he will be cured."[111]

13Yeshua had spoken about his death, but they thought he was talking about restful sleep.

14Then Yeshua told them plainly,

> Elazar died, 15and I am happy for you
> that I was not there so that you may believe.
> But now let us go to him.

16Toma,[112] who was called the Twin, said to his fellow students, "Let us also go so that we may die with him."

I am the resurrection

17When Yeshua arrived, he found that Elazar had already been four days in the tomb. 18Now Beit Aniyah was near Yerushalayim, about two miles away, 19and many of the Jews had come to console Marta and Miryam for their brother. 20When Marta heard that Yeshua was coming, she went out to meet him, but Miryam sat in her house. 21Then Marta said to Yeshua, "Sir, if you had been here, my brother would not have died. 22Even now I know that whatever you ask God, God gives you."

23Yeshua said to her,

---

110 "Rabbi, the Jews were just now trying to stone you." The conjunction of "rabbi" and "the Jews" is an anomaly, whose contradiction in identity befuddles the purpose of making the Jews appear abhorrent. In like passages in Matthew and Luke, "rabbi" has been changed to "master," "teacher," or "Lord," and so the anomaly is less apparent.

111 From the Greek σωθήσεται (sothesetai) means primarily "he will save or preserve" and by extension "he will cure." So both cure and salvation are implicit. The students have not understood "falling asleep" as a euphemism for death and understand *sothesetai* to mean "he will cure the (sleeping) body." But Yeshua, skillfully using the verb for his purpose, means "he will save the soul" of the dead man, and in this instance save it for his body, which he will bring back to life.

112 Thomas from the Greek Θωμᾶς (Thomas), from the Aramaic תאומָא (toma). Because תאומָא means "twin," Thomas has frequently been identified as Yeshua's twin brother, but his name is not one of the four names listed in the gospels as Yeshua's brothers.

Your brother will rise again.

24Marta said to him, "I know he will rise in the resurrection on the last day."

25Yeshua said to her,

I am the resurrection [and the life].

Those who believe in me even if they die

will live.

26And everyone who lives and believes in me

will not die into eternity.

He asked her, "Do you believe this?"

27She said to him, "Yes, lord. I believe that you are the mashiah, the son of God, who is coming into this world."

Raising Elazar

28After she said this, she left and called her sister Miryam, telling her secretly, "The teacher is here and calls for you."

29When that woman heard she got up quickly and came to him.

30Now Yeshua had not yet come into the village, and he was still at the place where Marta had met him.

31The Jews who were with her in the house, consoling her, saw Miryam quickly get up and go out, and they followed her, thinking that she was going to the tomb to weep there.

32Miryam came to where Yeshua was, and seeing him she fell at his feet, saying to him, "Sir, if you had been here my brother would not have died."

33When Yeshua saw her weeping and the Jews who had come with her were weeping, he raged at his own spirit, harrowed himself, 34and said,

Where have you laid him?

They said to him, "Sir, come and see."

35Yeshua wept.

36Then the Jews were saying, "See how he loved him."

37But some of them said, "Couldn't he who opened the eyes of the blindman have done something so this man wouldn't die?"

38Yeshua again raged inwardly and went to the tomb.

It was a cave, and a stone was lying against it.

39Yeshua said,

Lift the stone.

The sister of the one who died, Marta, said to Yeshua, "Sir, he already stinks.[113] It's the fourth day."

---

[113] Stinks from the Greek ὄζει (oksei), meaning "strong." Many translations tone it down, but the KJV renders it "he stinketh."

₄₀Yeshua said to her,

> Did I not tell you that if you believed
> you would see the glory of God?

₄₁So they lifted the stone.

Yesha lifted his eyes up and said,

> Father, I thank you for hearing me,
> ₄₂and I know that you hear me always
> but because of the crowd standing here
> I spoke so they would believe you sent me.

₄₃After saying this, in a great voice he cried out,

> Elazar, come out!

₄₄The one who had died came out, bound feet and hands in graveclothes and his face wrapped around in a cloth.

Yeshua said to them,

> Unbind him and let him go.

The Jews plotting to kill Yeshua

₄₅Then many of the Jews who had come to Miryam and seen what he did believed in him. ₄₆But some of them went away to the Prushim and told them what Yeshua had done.

₄₇So the high priests and the Prushim called a meeting of the Sanhedrin,[114] ₄₈and said, "What can we do about this man who is performing so many miraculous signs? If we leave him like this, everyone will believe in him, and the Romans will come and take away our holy place and nation."

₄₉But one of them, Kayfa,[115] who was high priest for that year, said to them, "You know nothing. ₅₀You haven't understood that it is better for one man to die for the sake of the people and not have the whole nation perish."

₅₁This he did not say on his own, but as high priest for that year he prophesied that Yeshua would die for the sake of the nation, ₅₂and not only for the nation but so that he might bring together the scattered children of God.

₅₃From that day on they planned to kill him.[116]

₅₄So Yeshua no longer walked openly among the Jews but went away from

---

114 Council.

115 Caiaphas from the Greek Καϊάφας (Kaiafas), from the Hebrew כָּיְפָא (kayfa).

116 The conversations and substance of a conspiracy plot to kill Yeshua, like all conversations and events in the New Testament, have no recorded or otherwise historical evidence to corroborate their authenticity outside the gospels themselves. It is reasonable and probable to assume that such material was conceived and shaped by the authors of the gospels, based on unconfirmed story, testimony, or their own emendation.

there to the country near the desert, to a city called Efrayim,[117] and he stayed there with the students.

As Pesach draws near, will Yeshua return to Yerushalayim?

₅₅Now the Pesach of the Jews was near, and many went up from the country to Yerushalayim before Pesach to purify themselves. ₅₆They were looking for Yeshua and said to one another as they stood in the Temple, "What do you think? That he won't come to the festival?"

₅₇But the high priests and the Prushim had given orders that if anyone knew where he was, he should report it so they might seize him.

CHAPTER 12

Miryam anointing Yeshua's feet and wiping them with her hair

Six days before Pesach, Yeshua came to Beit Aniyah where Elazar was, whom he had raised from the dead. ₂So they prepared a supper for him, and Martha served, and Elazar was one of those reclining at the table with him. ₃Then Miryam took a pound of spikenard ointment, pure and precious, anointed the feet of Yeshua, and wiped his feet with her hair. And the house was full of the fragrance of the unguent.

₄Yehuda of Keriot,[118] one of his students, who was about to betray him, said, ₅"Why was this ointment not sold for three hundred denarii[119] and given to the poor?" ₆But he said this not because he cared about the poor, but because he was a thief and he was the keeper of the money box and was removing what was dropped into it.

₇So Yeshua said,

Let her be, so she may keep it for the day
of my burial.
₈The poor you always have with you,
but me you do not always have.[120]

---

[117] Ephraim from the Greek Ἐφραίμ (Efraim), from the Hebrew אֶפְרַיִם (efrayim).

[118] Judas Iscariot. Judas the Iscariot. Judas from the Greek Ἰούδας (Ioudas), from the Hebrew יְהוּדָה (yehuda). The name for the messenger (apostle) Judas in Hebrew, *Yehuda*, was surely invented because it suggests the Hebrew word for "Jew," which is יְהוּדִי (yehudi), thereby the betrayer of Yeshua among his followers was a Jew, as opposed to the others who escape that identity.

[119] Three hundred denarii could be a year's wages.

[120] Similar stories about anointing Yeshua's body appear in Mark and Luke. In Mark, the earliest of the gospels and main source of the synoptic gospels Matthew and Luke as well as John, it is the house of

The high priests plot to kill Elazar

9Then a great crowd of Jews learned that he was there, and they came, not only because of Yeshua but to see Elazar, whom he had raised from the dead. 10But the high priests planned also to kill Elazar 11since because of him many of the Jews were going away and believing in Yeshua.

Yeshua, king of Yisrael, enters Yerushalayim

12On the next day the great crowd that came to the festival heard that Yeshua was coming to Yerushalayim. 13They took palm branches and went out to meet him and, as in Psalms, they cried,

> Hosanna!
> Blessed is he who comes in the name of the lord,
> the king of Yisrael.[121]

14And Yeshua found a young donkey and was seated on it just as it is written in Zeharyah:[122]

> 15Do not fear, daughter of Zion.
> Look, your king is coming,
> sitting on a foal of a donkey.[123]

16His students did not understand these things at first, but when Yeshua was glorified, then they remembered that these things had been written about him and these things had been done for him.

17The crowd that was with him when he raised Elazar from the tomb bore witness to it all. 18That was why the crowd went to meet him, for they heard that he had performed the miraculous sign.

19So the Prushim said to one another, "You see, you can do nothing. Look, the world has gone over to him."

Yeshua foretells death and glorification

20Now there were some Greek Jews[124] among those who went up to worship at the festival. 21They came to Filippos from Beit Tzaida of the Galil and asked him, saying, "Sir, we wish to see Yeshua."

Shimon the Leper, not Elazar (Lazarus). The grumbling about the money wasted on anointing Yeshua that might have gone to the poor is voiced by unnamed diners, not Yehuda (Judas), who was surely added to the supper table in order to further darken his portrait. In Luke, the scene is more erotic; there is also a Shimon, the speech about the poor is almost the same, and Yehuda is not mentioned.

121 Ps. 118.25–26.

122 Zechariah or Zacharias from Greek Ζαχαρίας (Zaharias), from the Hebrew זְכַרְיָה (zeharyah).

123 Zech. 9.9.

124 Ethnic Greeks who had converted to Judaism.

22Filippos came and told Andreas. Andreas and Filippos came and told Yeshua.

23And Yeshua answered them, saying,

> The hour has come when the earthly son is glorified.[125]

24"Amen, amen, I say to you,"

> Unless a grain of wheat falling into the earth dies,
> it remains alone.
> But if it dies it brings forth a great harvest.[126]

25Whoever loves life will lose it,
and whoever hates life in this world
will keep it for life everlasting.

26Let anyone who serves me, follow me,
and where I am, there also will be my servant.
Whoever serves me, the father will honor.

Yeshua speaks of his death and tells others
to be children of light

> 27Now my soul is shaken
> and what shall I say?
> Father, save me from this hour?
> But I came for this hour.
> 28Father, glorify your name.

A voice came out of the sky,

> I have glorified it, and I shall glorify it again.

29Then the crowd standing there heard it. They said,

> It has thundered.

Others said,

> An angel has spoken to him.

30Yeshua answered and said,

> Not because of me has this voice come
> but because of you.
> 31Now is the judgment of the world,
> now the ruler of this world will be cast out.
> 32And if I am raised above the earth
> I shall draw all people to me.

---

[125] Glorification is the hour of his death, resurrection, and ascension.

[126] Fruit from the Greek καρπός (karpos). καρπός is often translated as "harvest" or "crop," since here it refers specifically to the fruit of a wheat grain, which would be a harvest or crop.

33This he said, signifying what kind of death he was to die.

34The crowd answered him, "We heard from the law that the mashiah remains forever. How can you say the earthly son must be raised? Who is this earthly son?"

35Yeshua said to them,

> For a little time longer the light is with you.
> Walk about while you still have the light
> so that the darkness may not overtake you.
> And someone walking in the darkness
> does not know where she is going.
> 36While you have light, believe in the light
> so you may be the children of light.

Of the unbelievers

Yeshua said this and went away and went into hiding from them. 37Though he had performed so many miraculous signs before them, they did not believe in him 38so that the word spoken by the prophet Yeshayah[127] will be fulfilled,

> Lord, who has believed in our message?
> and to whom was the arm of the lord revealed?[128]

39This is why they could not believe, because since Yeshayah said elsewhere,

> 40He has blinded their eyes and hardened their heart
> so that they might not see with their eyes
> and understand with their hearts and turn their ways around
> so that I might heal them.[129]

41Yeshayah said these things because he saw his glory and he spoke about him. 42Still even among the rulers many believed in him, but because of the Prushim they did not admit it so that they would not be put out of the synagogue. 43They loved human glory more than the glory of God.

44But Yeshua cried out and said,

> Who believes in me does not believe in me
> but in the one who sent me.
> 45Who looks at me also looks at him who sent me.
> 46As light into the world I have come
> so that who believes in me will not reside in darkness.
> 47And who hears my words and does not keep them
> I do not judge

---

[127] Isaiah.
[128] Isa. 53.1. See also Rom. 10.16.
[129] Isa. 6.10. See also Matt. 13.15; Mark 4.12.

for I have not come to judge the world
but to save the world.

48Who rejects me and will not receive my words
has a judge waiting.
The word I spoke will judge him on the last day.
49Because I did not speak from myself but the one
who sent me,
the father has given me his commandment,
what I should say and how I should speak.
50And I know his commandment is life everlasting.
So what I say, as the father told me, I say it.

 CHAPTER 13

Washing his students' feet

Before the feast of the Pesach, Yeshua knew that his hour had come to pass from this world to the father. In this world he had loved his own people and he loved them to the end. 2And when supper was served, the devil had already put in the heart of Yehuda,[130] son of Shimon of Keriot, that he should betray him. 3Yeshua, knowing that the father had placed everything in his hands and that he had come from God and was going to God, 4rose from the supper table, took off his garment, took a towel and girded his waist. 5And he poured water into the basin and began to wash the feet of his students and to wipe them with the towel he had tied around himself. 6Then he went to Shimon Kefa.[131]

Kefa said to him, "Lord, are you washing my feet?"
7Yeshua said to him,

What I do for you, you do not know now,
but these things later you will understand.
8Kefa told him, "You will not wash my feet forever."
Yeshua answered him,

Unless I wash you, you have no part of me.
9Shimon Kefa said to him, "Lord, not just my feet but also my hands and head."
10Yeshua told him,

130Judas from the Greek Ἰούδας (Ioudas), from the Hebrew יְהוּדָה (yehuda).
131 Simon Peter.

One who has bathed need wash nothing
except his feet
and he is wholly clean, and you are clean
but not all of you.
11He knew his betrayer. That is why he said,
Not all of you are clean.
12So when he washed their feet and put his garments back on and took his
place again reclining at the supper table, he said,
Do you know what I have done for you?
13You call me the rabbi and lord,[132]
and what you say is right, for so I am.
14So if I your lord and rabbi washed your feet,
you also ought to wash each other's feet.
15For I have given you an example
for you to do as I have done to you.

16"Amen, amen, I say to you,"
A slave is not greater than his master,
nor is the sent one greater than he
who sent her.
17If you know these things
you are blessed if you do them.
18I am not speaking of all of you—
I know whom I chose—
but to fulfill the scripture:
The one who ate my bread[133]
lifted his heel against me.
19I tell you now before it happens
so that when it happens
you will believe that I am I.
20Amen, amen, I say to you,
The one who accepts one I send
also accepts me,
and whoever accepts me
accepts him who sent me.

---

[132] Lord or Adonai from the Greek κύριος (kyrios). When referring to the divine lord, the Greek
κύριος (kyrios) may be translated "lord" or "Adonai" (אֲדֹנִי) as here in the Hebrew text cited from
Isaiah; when referring to Jesus, *kyrios* may be translated as "sir," "master," "teacher," or "rabbi," when
the implicit Hebrew source is רַבִּי (rabbi).
[133] Ps. 41.9.

₂₁After he said this, Yeshua was troubled in his soul, and bore witness, and said,

> Amen, amen, I say to you,
> One of you will betray me.

₂₂The students looked at each other, wondering whom he was speaking about. ₂₃One of the students was leaning back on Yeshua's chest, one whom Yeshua loved.¹³⁴

₂₄So Shimon Kefa nodded to him to ask who it was he was talking about. ₂₅The man who was leaning on Yeshua's chest said to him, "Sir, who is it?"

₂₆Yeshua answered,

> It is the one for whom I will dip the matzot
> and give it to him.

So he took the matzot and gave it to Yehuda, man of Keriot.

₂₇And after he received the matzot, Satan entered into him.

So Yeshua said to him,

> Do what you will do quickly.

₂₈But no one of those lying back at the table knew why he said this to him. ₂₉Some thought that since Yehuda had the money box, Yeshua was telling him,

> Buy what we need for the supper
> or something to give to the poor.

₃₀But he took the crust of bread and went out at once. Now it was night.

In a short while goodbye. Now love.

₃₁When Yehuda left, Yeshua said,

> Now the earthly son has been glorified
> and God has been glorified in him.
> ₃₂If God has been glorified in him
> God will glorify him in himself
> and will glorify him at once.

> ₃₃Children, I am with you a short while.
> You will look for me,
> and I tell you now as I said to the Jews,
> "Where I go you cannot also come."
> ₃₄I give you a new commandment
>   to love each other.

---

134 "The beloved student." The mysterious, unnamed student whom Yeshua loves will appear in the last lines of John as the one Yeshua loves most, who outruns Kefa to his empty tomb, and who will not die until Yeshua comes again.

As I loved you, you also must love each other.

35By this everyone will know

you are my students

if you love each other.

Yeshua tells Kefa what he will do

36Shimon Kefa said to him, "Lord, where are you going?"

Yeshua answered him,

Where I go

you cannot follow me now,

but you will follow later.

37Kefa said to him, "Lord, why can I not follow you now? I will lay down my life for you."

38Yeshua answered him,

You will lay down your life for me?

Amen, amen, I say to you

that the cock will not crow

before you have disowned me three times.

CHAPTER 14

I am the way

Do not let your hearts be shaken.

Believe in God and believe in me.

2In my father's house there are many rooms.

If there were not, would I have said to you

that I go to prepare a place for you?

3And if I go to prepare a place for you,

I will come again and take you to me

so that where I am you may also be.

4And where I go you know the way.

5Toma said to him, "Lord, we do not know where you are going. How can we know the way?"

6Yeshua said to him,

I am the way and the truth and the life.

No one comes to the father but through me.

7If you had known me, you would have also known
    my father,
and now you know him and have seen him.
8Filippos said to him, "Lord, show us the father, and that is enough for us."
9Yeshua said to him,
    All this time I have been with you
    and do you not know me, Filippos?
    Who has seen me has seen the father.
    How can you say, "Show us the father"?
    10Do you not believe that I am in the father
    and the father in me?
    The words I speak to you I do not speak
        from myself,
    but the father who lives in me does his works.
    11Do you not believe that I am in the father
    and the father in me?
    And if not, believe because of his works.

12"Amen, amen, I say to you,"
    Who believes in me will also do the works I do
    and you will do ones greater than these,
    because I am going to the father.
    13And whatever you ask in my name I will do
    so that the father may be glorified in the son.
    14If you ask for anything in my name,
    that I will do.

    15If you love me, keep my commandments,
    16and I will ask the father for another comforter[135]
    to be with you forever,
    17the spirit of truth that the world cannot accept
    because it cannot see or know it.
    You know it because it dwells with you
    and in you will be.
    18I will not leave you orphans.
    I am coming to you.

---

[135] The Paraclete has been identified with the Advocate, who will work on behalf of the "sinning believer," and, in John 7.39, an editorial comment inserted in the text identifies the Paraclete with the
Holy Spirit.

19A little time and the world will not see me,
but you will see me.
Because I live, you also live.
20On that day you will know I am in my father,
and you are in me and I am in you.
21Who has my commands and keeps them
loves me.
You who love me will be loved by my father,
and I will love you
and reveal myself to you.

I leave you peace

22Yehuda said to him (not the man of Keriot), "Sir, what has happened that you are to show yourself to us and not to the world?"
23Yeshua answered him and said,

Anyone who loves me will keep my word,
and my father will love you
and we will come to you and make our home with you.
24Anyone who does not love me
does not keep the word that you hear,
and what I say is not mine
but from the father who sent me.

25This I have told you while I remain with you
26but the comforter, the holy spirit,
whom the father will send in my name,
will teach you all things and recall all things
that I have said to you.

27I leave you peace. My peace I give to you.
Not as the world gives, I give to you.
Do not be shaken in your heart or frightened.
28You heard what I told you.
"I am going away and I am coming to you."
If you loved me you would be happy
that I am going to the father
since the father is greater than I.

29And now I have told you before it occurs
so when it happens you may believe.

30I will no longer talk much with you,
for the ruler of the world is coming,
and he owns no part in me.
31But so the world knows I love the father,
what the father has commanded me I do.

Rise up. Let us go from here.

 **CHAPTER 15**

I am the true vine and my father is the gardener
I am the true vine and my father is the gardener.
2Each branch in me bearing no fruit he cuts off,
and each branch bearing fruit he also prunes clean
that it may bear even more fruit.
3You are already clean because of the word
I have spoken to you.

4Abide in me as I in you.
As the branch cannot bear fruit by itself
unless it stays on the vine,
you too cannot unless you dwell in me.
5I am the vine, you the branches.
You who dwell in me as I in you
bear much fruit,
but without me you can do nothing.

6Anyone who does not remain in me
is cast away like a branch and dries up,
and these are gathered and thrown into the fire and burned.
7If you dwell in me and my words dwell in you,
ask whatever you wish and it will be given you.

8So my father is glorified that you may bear much fruit
and be my students.
9As the father has loved me I have loved you.
Dwell in my love.

10If you keep my commandments
you will stay in my love,
just as I have kept the father's commandments
and dwell in his love.
11These things I have told you so my joy may be in you
and your joy be full.

Love each other as I have loved you
12This is my command,
That you love each other as I have loved you.
13No one has greater love than this,
than to lay down one's life for one's friends.
14You are my friends if you do what I command you.
15No longer will I call you slaves
because the slave does not know what the master does.
But you I have called friends
because all things I heard from my father
I have made known to you.

16You did not choose me
but I chose you and appointed you to go and bear fruit
and your fruit will last
and so whatever you ask for in my name
he may give you.
17These things I command you
so you may love one another.

A world hating us without cause
18If the world hates you,
know that before you it hated me.
19If you were from the world
the world would love you as its own.
But I have chosen you out of this world
and because you are not of this world
the world hates you.

20Remember the word I said to you:
No slave is greater than his lord.
If they persecuted me, they will persecute you also.
If they kept my word, they will also keep yours.

21But all this they will do to you
because of my name,
because they do not know the one who sent me.

22If I had not come and spoken to them,
they would have no sin,
but now they have no cloak[136] to wrap around their sin.[137]
23Who hates me also hates my father.
24If I had not done among them things
that no one else has done,
they would have no sin.
But now they have seen and hated both me and my father.
25And to fulfill the word written in the law,[138]
"They hated me openly and without cause."[139]

When the comforter comes
26When the comforter comes,
whom I will send you from my father,
the breath of truth who comes from the father,
he will testify about me.
27You also will be my witness
since from the beginning you are with me.

CHAPTER 16

I will go away so the comforter will come
This I have told you so you will not go astray.
2They will expel you from the synagogue
and the hour is coming when those who kill you
will suppose they are serving God.
3And they will do this because they know
neither the father nor me.
4But this I have told you so when the hour comes

---

[136] Cloak, in that there is no possible concealment and therefore no excuse.
[137] Or "guilt."
[138] "Law" as Torah (Hebrew Bible), which in this case is the Psalms.
[139] Pss. 35.19 and 69.4.

you will recall that I told you.
I did not tell you at the beginning, since I was with you.
5But now I am going to the one who sent me,
and not one of you asks me, "Where are you going?"
6But because I have said these things to you,
sorrow has filled your heart.

7I tell you the truth: It is better for you that I go away.
If I do not go, the comforter will not come to you.
But if I go away, I will send him to you.
8And when he comes he will expose the world
concerning wrongdoing and justice and judgment:
9wrongdoing, since they do not believe in me;
10justice because I am going to the father
and you will no more see me.
11Judgment because the ruler of this world has been judged.
12I still have many things to tell you
but you cannot bear to hear them now.
13When the spirit[140] of truth comes
he will be your guide to the whole truth.
For he will not speak from himself but what he hears
and will report to you what is to come.
14He will glorify me
since he will take what is mine and report it to you.
15All that the father has is mine,
so I said he will take what is mine and report it to you.
16In a little while you will no longer see me
and again in a little while you will see me.

I will go, but when I return grief will turn into joy

17Now some of his students said to each other, "What does he mean by 'In a little while you will no longer see me and again in a little while you will see me,' and 'because I am going to the father'? 18What is this 'in a little while'? We don't know what he is saying."

19Yeshua knew they wanted to question him and said to them,

Are you asking each other what I meant by,

"In a little while you will no longer see me

---

[140] Or "breath." The words in both the Hebrew and the Greek mean "wind" and by extension "spirit." There is usually a crossover in meaning which no one word in English has.

and again in a little while you will see me"?
20Amen, amen, I say to you,
You will weep and mourn but the world will be joyful.
You will be grieved but your grief will turn to joy.
21When a woman gives birth she grieves
because her hour has come,
but when she has borne her child she no longer remembers
    her pain
because of the joy that a child was born into the world.
22So now you are in sorrow, but I will see you again
and your heart will be happy
and your gladness no one will take from you.
23And on that day you will ask me nothing.

Amen, amen, I say to you,
Whatever you ask the father in my name,
he will give you.
24Till now you ask nothing in my name.
Ask and you will receive so your joy may be complete.

25These things I have told you in riddles,
but the hour is coming when no longer in riddles
will I speak to you, but plainly I will declare
concerning the father.
26On that day you will ask in my name.
And I do not say to you I will ask the father on your behalf.
27The father loves you because you have loved me
and believed that I have come from God.
28I came from the father and have come into the world.
I leave the world again and go to the father.

Through me, have peace. I have conquered the world
29His students said, "See, now you are speaking plainly and no longer in riddles. 30Now we know that you know all things and we have no need to question you. By this we know that you came from God." 31Yeshua answered them,
    Now do you believe?
    32Look, the hour is coming and it has come
    when you will be scattered each on his own

and you will leave me alone.
But I am not alone, because the father is with me.

33These things I have said to you
so through me you may have peace.
In the world you have pain. Courage.
I have conquered the world.

❖ CHAPTER 17

Yeshua raises his eyes, converses with the father,
and prays for his students

Yeshua said this, then raised his eyes to the sky and said,
Father, the hour has come.
Glorify your son so that your son may glorify you
2as you gave him authority over all flesh[141]
so he may give life everlasting to all you have given him.

3And this is the life everlasting
so that they may know you, the only true God,
and he whom you sent, Yeshua the Anointed.[142]
4I glorified you on earth
by completing the work you gave me to do.
5And now glorify me, father, with yourself,
with the glory I had with you before the world was.

6I made your name known to the people
whom you gave me from the world.
They were yours and you gave them to me
and they have kept your word.
7Now they know that all you gave me comes from you.
8Because the words you gave me I gave them.
And they accepted them,
and they knew the truth that I came from you
and believed that you sent me.

---

[141] All flesh from the Greek πάσης σαρκός (pases sarkos), which in a larger sense means "all people."
[142] The Greek ᾽Ιησοῦς ὁ χριστὸς (Iesous o hristos) can be translated as "Yeshua the Anointed" or "Yeshua the Mashiah."

₉I ask for their sake.
I am not asking for the sake of the world
but for the ones whom you gave me
because they are yours.
₁₀And all that is mine is yours and yours is mine
and I am glorified in them.

I am not in this world

₁₁And I am no longer in the world
but they are in the world,
and I am coming to you.
Holy father, [keep them in your name,
which you gave me,]¹⁴³
so they may be one as we are one.
₁₂When I was with them,
through your name I kept those whom you gave me.
I guarded them and not one of them was lost
except the son of perdition
so that the scripture be fulfilled.

I am coming to you

₁₃Now I am coming to you
and these things I say in the world
so my elation be fulfilled in them.
₁₄I gave them your word and the world hated them
since they are not of the world
as I am not of the world.

Sanctify them in the truth

₁₅I do not ask you to take them from the world
but to keep them from the cunning one.¹⁴⁴
₁₆They are not of this world as I am not of this world.
₁₇Sanctify them in the truth.
Your word is truth.
₁₈As you sent me into the world so I sent them
into the world.

---

¹⁴³ This phrase is included in this text but not in other ancient texts.

¹⁴⁴ "From the cunning one." From the Greek ἐκ τοῦ πονηροῦ (ek tou ponerou) can be translated as "from the evil one" or "from the devil."

₁₉And for them I sanctify myself
so they may also be sanctified in truth.

I ask for all believers
₂₀I do not ask for them alone,
but for those believing in me through their word
₂₁that we may all be one
as you, father, are in me and I in you;
that the world may believe that you sent me.
₂₂The glory you gave me I gave them
so they may be one as we are one.
₂₃I in them and you in me
so they may be made perfect as one,
so the world may know that you sent me
and loved them just as you loved me.

₂₄Father, wherever I am I want the ones you gave me
also to be with me and see my glory,
which you gave me since you loved me
before the foundation of the world.
₂₅Just father, the world did not know who you were,
but I knew you
and these ones knew that you had sent me.
₂₆I made your name known to them
and I shall make it known
so the love you have had for me
may be in them and I in them.

CHAPTER 18

Yehuda brings soldiers to arrest Yeshua

After saying these words, Yeshua went out with his students across the ravine[145] where there was a garden which he and his students entered.

---

[145] Cedron from the Greek Κεδρών (Kedron), from the Hebrew קִדְרוֹן (kidron). The valley (or ravine) lies east of Jerusalem, on the way to the Mountain of Olives.

₂Now Yehuda, who betrayed him, also knew the place, since Yeshua often met there with his students. ₃Then Yehuda got a band of soldiers and serving men of the high priests and Pharisees, and went there with lamps and torches and weapons.

₄Yeshua, who knew everything that was to happen to him, went out and said to them,

>Who are you looking for?

₅They answered him, "Yeshua the Natzrati."[146]

₆He said to them,

>I am he.

And they stepped backward and fell to the ground.

₇So he asked them again,

>Who are you looking for?

And they said, "Yeshua the Natzrati."

₈Yeshua replied,

>I told you that I am he.

>If you are looking for me, let these men go.

₉All this happened to fulfill the word he said,

>"I have not lost one of those you gave me."

Kefa cuts off the slave's ear

₁₀Then Shimon Kefa had a knife and took it out and struck the slave of the high priest and cut off his right ear. The slave's name was Maleh.[147]

₁₁But Yeshua said to Kefa,

>Put your knife back in its sheath.

>Shall I not drink the cup the father gave me?

Yeshua bound and taken to Hannan[148] and Kayfa[149]

₁₂Then the guard and the commander and servants of the Jews took Yeshua and bound him. ₁₃And first they led him to Hannan, who was the father-in-law of Kayfa, the high priest for that year. ₁₄Now it was Kayfa who advised the Jews that it is better for one man to die for the people.

---

[146] Nazarene from the Greek Ναζαρηνός (Nazarenos), from Natzeret, that is, a Natzrati.

[147] Malchus from the Greek Μάλχος (Malhos), probably from the Hebrew מֶלֶךְ (meleh), meaning "king."

[148] Annas. Hannan, or Anan, means "high priest" in Hebrew, from the Greek Ἅννας (Annas), from the Hebrew חָנָן (hannan), "priest" or "gracious one."

[149] Caiaphas.

Kefa disowns Yeshua in the high priest's court

₁₅Shimon Kefa and another student followed Yeshua. And that student, who was known to the high priest, went with Yeshua into the high priest's court. ₁₆But Kefa stayed outside the door. So the other student, an acquaintance of the high priest, spoke to the doorkeeper and brought Kefa inside.

₁₇Then the girl who was at the door said to Kefa, "Aren't you one of that man's students?"

He said, "I am not."

Yeshua answers the high priest, and a servant beats him

₁₈Now the slaves and assistants stood around a charcoal fire they had made, since it was cold and they were warming themselves. Kefa also was standing there with them, keeping warm.

₁₉Then the high priest questioned Yeshua about his students and about his teaching.

₂₀Yeshua replied to him,

I have spoken openly to the world.
I always taught in a synagogue and in the Temple
where all the Jews gather. And in secret
I spoke nothing. ₂₁Why question me?
Ask those who heard what I said to them.
Look, they know what I said.

₂₂When he said this, one of the serving men slapped Yeshua, "Is that how you answer the high priest?"

₂₃Yeshua answered him,

If I spoke wrong, testify to the wrong.
But if I spoke right, why do you beat me?

₂₄Then Hannan sent him bound to Kayfa the high priest.

Kefa disowns Yeshua a second and third time

₂₅Shimon Kefa was standing and warming himself. So they said to him, "Aren't you also one of his students?"

He denied it and said, "I am not."

₂₆One of the high priest's slaves, a relative of the one whose ear Kefa cut off, said, "Didn't I see you in the garden with him?"

₂₇Again Kefa denied it and at once the cock crowed.

Yeshua before Pilatus. Pilatus asks, Are you the king of the Jews?

₂₈They led Yeshua from Kayfa to the praetorium.[150] It was early morning. They didn't enter the praetorium, so as to avoid defilement that might prevent them from eating the Pesach meals. ₂₉So Pilatus emerged and said to them, "What charge do you bring against this man?"

₃₀They answered him and said, "Unless he was doing wrong, we would not have turned him over to you."

₃₁Pilatus said to them, "Take him and judge him according to your law."

Then the Jews said to him, "It is not lawful for us to put anyone to death."

₃₂This happened to fulfill Yeshua's word when he foretold what kind of death he was to die.[151]

₃₃Then Pilatus again went into the praetorium and called Yeshua and said to him, "Are you the king of the Jews?"

₃₄Yeshua answered,

> Are you speaking for yourself
> or did others tell you about me?

₃₅"Am I a Jew?" Pilatus answered. "Your people and the high priest handed you over to me. What did you do?"[152]

₃₆Yeshua responded,

> My kingdom is not of this world.
> If my kingdom were of this world
> my servants would have fought to keep me
> from being delivered to the Jews.[153]
> But now my kingdom is not here.

₃₇Then Pilatus said to him, "Then you are a king?"

Yeshua answered,

> You say I am a king.

---

[150] Governor's house.

[151] Verse 32, a commentary and interpretation interrupting the narration, may be a scribal interpolation and is usually placed in parentheses or brackets.

[152] Pilate's essential question, "What did you do?" would suggest that Pilate is unaware of wrongdoing. Among historians there is a consensus that Rome executed Yeshua as a seditionist, as one opposed to Roman occupation. Pilate's question to Yeshua, however, as preserved in scripture, means that Yeshua had committed no grievance against Rome, but Pilate would carry out a punishment for the Jews, to crucify a rabbi, because of disagreement with coreligionists on vital issues. Without historical evidence, Pilate's question is not plausible. Its consequence is to accuse coreligionists of initiating Yeshua's execution and to emphasize Rome's unwilling and marginal involvement in it.

[153] Here the "we and them" reference to Jews signifies that the speaker and his supporters are not to be identified as Jews. A Jew has not been crucified, although Yeshua's teaching in the Temple has been to persuade Jews that he represents true Judaism. Near death, the rabbi might disagree with other Jews but not himself deny that he is a Jew, that he symbolically is king of the Jews. The placement of the denial is odd, since it follows immediately upon Pilate's own identification of Yeshua as a Jew in his statements "Are you the king of the Jews?" and "your people."

For this I was born
and for this I came into the world
that I might testify to the truth.
Everyone born of truth hears my voice.

₃₈Pilatus said to him, "What is truth?"

Pilatus before the Jews, who shout for Bar Abba

And after he said this, again he went out to the Jews and told them, "I find no fault in him. ₃₉But you have this custom that I should release someone to you at Pesach. So do you want me to release the king of the Jews?"

₄₀They shouted back saying, "Not this man but Bar Abba!"

Now Bar Abba[154] was a robber.

◈ CHAPTER 19

Crucify!

Then Pilatus took Yeshua and flogged him. ₂And the soldiers wove a wreath out of thorns and put it on his head and threw a purple robe around him. ₃And they went up to him and said, "Hello, king of the Jews!"

And they struck him in the face.

₄And Pilatus again went outside and said to them, "Look, I am bringing him out to you so you may know I find no fault in him."

₅Then Yeshua came out, wearing the wreath of thorns and the purple robe. And Pilatus said to them, "Look at the man."

₆When the high priests and the serving men saw him, they shouted,
    Crucify, crucify!

Pilatus said to them, "You take him and crucify him. I find no fault in him."

₇The Jews answered him, "We have a law and according to that law he should die, because he made himself son of God."

Pilatus, afraid, yields to the Jews and orders crucifixion

₈When Pilatus heard this word, he was more frightened. ₉Again he went back into the praetorium and said to Yeshua, "Where are you from?"

But Yeshua didn't answer him.

---

[154] Barabbas from the Greek Βαραββᾶς, from the Aramaic בַּר אַבָּא (bar abba), meaning "son of abba" (father).

₁₀Then Pilatus told him, "You don't speak to me? Don't you know that I have the authority to free you and I have the authority to crucify you?"

₁₁Yeshua answered him,

> You would have no authority over me at all
>
> were it not given to you from above.
>
> Therefore the one who handed me over to you
>
> has the greater sin.[155]

₁₂Thereupon Pilatus sought to release him, but the Jews cried out, saying, "If you free this man, you are not a friend of Caesar! Everyone who makes himself a king defies Caesar."

₁₃When Pilatus heard these words, he led Yeshua outside and sat on the judgment seat called Stone Pavement, but in Hebrew Gabta.[156]

₁₄Now it was Friday, the Preparation Day for the Pesach, the sixth hour which is noon. He said to the Jews, "Look, here is your king."

₁₅Then they shouted, "Take him away, take him away and crucify him!" Pilatus said to them, "Shall I crucify your king?"

The high priest answered, "We have no king but Caesar."

₁₆So he gave him to them to be crucified.[157]

---

[155] Yeshua fully exonerates Pilate, who is acting not through his authority or free will but by the authority given to him from the father. The Jews, however, have acted freely and therefore their sin is greater.

[156] Gabbatha from the Greek Γαββαθα̂ (Gabbatha), from an unknown Aramaic word that would be transliterated as *gabta*.

[157] "So he gave him to them to be crucified." With reference to the "them" in 19.16, the commentary in the Jesus Seminar translation in *The Five Gospels* reads: "The resulting implication that all the Jews/Judeans, or perhaps only some Jewish officials, crucified Jesus—as Pilate had suggested—is wholly inaccurate. In historical fact, whatever Pilate's view of Jesus' guilt, it was certainly he who saw to the execution; crucifixion was never practiced by Jews. The monstrous unreality of this half-verse, if it reads as intended, must be entirely a function of theological or political polemic" (Robert W. Funk and Ray W. Hoover, eds., New York : Macmillan, 1993).

In the introduction to John in Robert J. Miller's *The Complete Gospels: Annotated Scholars Version* (Sonoma, CA : Polebridge Press, 1992–1994), under "A Jewish Christian gospel," there is a full discussion of references to "the Jews." "The ideological milieu of this gospel is thoroughly Jewish: even the abstract and dualistic symbolism (such as light/darkness) comes from a world that has very little to do with Gentile culture. Nevertheless, this document is ardently anti-Jewish. Only here are the Jewish people spoken of monolithically and from the outside; in the other gospels Pilate alone uses the phrase 'the Jews.' The explanation appears to be that this group of Christian Jews has recently been expelled from the synagogue (9.22, 34; 12.42; 16.2) and therefore has a highly ambivalent, and frequently hostile, attitude to *Ioudaioi*. . . . This gospel has given rise, still more than Matthew, to savage Christian anti-Semitism down the subsequent centuries."

Carrying his cross to the Place of the Skull,
Gulgulta, where they crucify him

They took Yeshua. 17Carrying the cross himself, he went to what was called
the Place of the Skull, which in Hebrew is Gulgulta,[158] 18where they crucified
him, and with him two others, one on either side with Yeshua in the middle.

19Pilatus wrote a placard and put it on the cross. It read,

YESHUA THE NATZRATI THE KING OF THE JEWS.

20Many Jews read the placard because the place where Yeshua was crucified
was near the city. And it was written in Hebrew, Latin, and Greek. 21So the
high priests of the Jews said to Pilatus, "Do not write, 'The King of the Jews,'
but write what he said: 'I am king of the Jews.'"

22Pilatus answered, "What I've written I've written."

The soldiers cast lots for Yeshua's clothes

23When the soldiers crucified Yeshua, they took his clothes and divided
them in four parts, one part for each soldier. And they took his tunic too. Now
his tunic shirt was seamless, woven in one piece from the top straight down.
24So they said to each other, "Let's not tear it, but casts lots for it to see whose
it will be. This was to fulfill the words written in the Psalms saying,

They divided my clothes among them
and for my clothes they cast lots.[159]

That is what the soldiers did.

Woman, here is your son

25But near the cross of Yeshua stood his mother and his mother's sister
Miryam of Klofa[160] and Miryam of Magdala.[161]

26Then Yeshua, seeing his mother and the student he loved standing near,
said to his mother,

Woman, here is your son.[162]

---

[158] Golgotha from the Greek Γολγοθᾶ (Golgotha), from the Aramaic גָּלְגָּלְתָּא (gulgulta), meaning "skull."

[159] Ps. 22.18.

[160] Clopas from the Greek Κλωπᾶς (Klopas), from the Aramaic קְלוֹפָא (klofa). The name cannot be explained with certainty, but it is said to refer to a person who is the husband of the Mary near the cross, or is the father of James, and others identify him with Cleopas to whom the risen Yeshua appeared on the road to Emmaus (Luke 24.18). Cleopas is a Greek name from Κλεοπᾶς (Kleopas). See note 167 on Mark 15.40.

[161] Magdalene from the Greek Μαγδαληνή (Magdalene), meaning "from Magdala," from the Greek Μαγαδάν (Magadan), from the Aramaic Magdala. A village of uncertain location near Lake Gennesaret.

[162] Literally, "Woman, look, your son," which is followed by "Look, your mother." In the synoptic gospels, Miryam, Yeshua's mother, does not appear. Here she appears briefly, but her name goes unmentioned. The other Miryams (Marys) appear by name.

27Then he said to the student,

>Here is your mother.

And from that hour the student took her into his home.[163]

I am thirsty. It is ended.

28After this Yeshua, knowing that all had been done to fulfill the words of the Psalms, said,

>I am thirsty.

29A jar filled with cheap wine[164] was lying there. So they put a sponge soaked with the vinegar on a branch of hyssop and held it to his mouth. 30Then when Yeshua had taken the wine, he said,

>It is ended.

And bowing his head he gave up his spirit.[165]

A spear in Yeshua's side

31Since it was Friday the Preparation Day, the Jews asked Pilatus that their legs be broken and they be taken away so that the bodies would not remain on the cross on Shabbat. 32The soldiers came and broke the bones of the first man and then of the other one crucified with him. 33But when they came to Yeshua and saw that he was already dead, they did not break his legs. 34But one of the soldiers stabbed his side with his spear, and at once blood and water came out.

35And the one who saw this has testified to it, and the testimony is true, and he knows he is speaking the truth so that you may also believe.[166]

36These things happened to fulfill the scripture: "No bone of his will be broken."[167] 37And in Zeharyah it says, "They will look at him whom they stabbed."[168]

---

163 Although "home" or "care" may be the implied translation, it says no more than "He took her into his own," probably meaning "her own place."

164 Vinegar from the Greek ὄξος (oksos), "cheap wine," "sour wine," or "vinegar."

165 Breath or spirit from the Greek πνεῦμα (peneuma), meaning "spirit" or "wind/breath." Here again the word πνευμα, with its double meaning of particular "breath" and more general "spirit," retains in the Greek its double message, that is, he stopped breathing and surrendered his spirit. The phrase παρέδωκεν τὸ πνεῦμα (paredoken to pneuma) in KJV is rendered movingly as "gave up the ghost."

166 Much of the New Covenant centers around questions of belief, particularly in Yeshua's miracles and divinity. Belief is a moral signal of good or evil. In this unusual insertion into the narration, the narrator notes the specific event of blood and water issuing from Yeshua's side and concludes that the event has been witnessed, the testimony is true, and "you may believe." What is apparently miraculous is that water as well as blood has issued from the wound. Raymond E. Brown renders a standard interpretation: "The scene of the piercing of the dead Jesus' side is peculiarly Johannine, fulfilling both 7.37–39 that from Jesus would flow living water symbolic of the Spirit, and (since the bones of the paschal lamb were not to be broken) 1.29 that he was the Lamb of God" (An Introduction to the New Testament, 358).

167 Ps. 34.20; Exodus 12.36; Num. 9.12.

168 Zech. 12.10.

₃₈After these things Yosef of Arimathaia,[169] being a student of Yeshua, but a secret one for fear of the Jews,[170] asked Pilatus if he could take away Yeshua's body.

Pilatus allowed it.

Then he came and took the body.

₃₉Nakdeimon came too, the one who first came to him during the night, and he brought a mixture of myrrh and aloes, about a hundred pounds. ₄₀So they took the body of Yeshua and wrapped it in aromatic spices in linen cloths, as is the burial custom of the Jews.[171]

₄₁Now in the region where he was crucified there was a garden, and in the garden a new tomb in which no one had been placed. ₄₂So because it was Friday, the Preparation Day of the Jews, and the tomb was near, in it they placed Yeshua.

 CHAPTER 20

Miryam of Magdala discovers the empty tomb

On Sunday the first day of the week, Miryam of Magdala came to the tomb early while it was still dark and saw that the stone had been removed from the tomb. ₂So she ran and came to Shimon Kefa and to the other student whom Yeshua loved and said to them, "They took the lord from the tomb and we don't know where they put him."

₃Then Kefa and the other student came out and went to the tomb. ₄The two ran together, but the student ran faster than Kefa and reached the tomb first. ₅And he stooped down and saw the linen cloths lying there, but didn't go in. ₆Then Shimon Kefa came, following him, and he went into the tomb, and saw the linen cloths lying there, ₇but the kerchief which had been on his head was not lying next to the cloths but apart and folded up in its own place. ₈And then the other student, who had come first to the tomb, saw and believed. ₉They didn't yet know the scripture[172] that he must rise from the dead.

---

[169] Arimathea from the Greek Αριμαθαία (Arimathaia), and identified with either Ramathaim or Rentis, fifteen to twenty miles east of Jaffa.

[170] "For fear of the Jews." Though a Pharisee and member of the Sanhedrin, by being presented as one in fear of the Jews, Yosef of Arimathaia is at once delivered from his religious identity and wears no stain of Jewish villainy.

[171] As is the Jewish custom. Please see commentary to this passage in the Afterword.

[172] There is a resurrection of the dead in Isaiah 26.19 and Daniel 12.2. The notion of resurrection of the dead and immortality of the soul is derived from Jewish apocalyptic literature and probably the influence of Plato, Neoplatonism, and contemporary pagan notions.

Miryam of Magdala cries Rabboni!

10Then the students went off to their own places.

11But Miryam stood by the tomb, weeping. Then as she was weeping, she stooped and looked into the tomb 12and saw two angels in white sitting there, one at the head and one at the feet where the body of Yeshua had lain.

13And they said to her,

> Woman, why are you weeping?

She said to them, "They have taken my lord away and I don't know where they put him."

14Saying this she turned around and saw Yeshua standing there and didn't know it was Yeshua.

15Yeshua said to her,

> Woman, why are you weeping?
>
> Whom are you looking for?

Thinking he was the gardener, she said to him, "Sir, if you took him away, tell me where you put him and I will take him."

16Yeshua said to her,

> Miryam!

She turned and said to him in Hebrew, "Rabboni!" (which means teacher).[173]

17Yeshua said to her,

> Do not hold on to me,
>
> since I have not yet gone up to the father.
>
> But go to my brothers and tell them:
>
> "I am ascending to my father and your father
>
> and my God and your God."

18Miryam of Magdala went and announced to the students, "I have seen the lord." And she told them that he had said these things to her.

Yeshua appears in the locked house of the students

19So when it was early evening of that first day of the week and the doors of the house where the students met were locked for fear of the Jews, Yeshua came and stood in their midst and said to them,

> Peace to you.

20And saying this he showed his hands and his side to them.

The students were overjoyed when they saw the lord.

21So Yeshua said to them again,

---

[173] Miryam would have been speaking Aramaic, and in "She turned and said to him in Hebrew, 'Rabboni!'" *rabboni* is Aramaic, not Hebrew. The scribal intrusion, "which means teacher," fails to silence the idea that to Miryam, in her moment of dramatic recognition, Yeshua is truly a rabbi.

Peace to you.

As the father sent me

so I send you.

22And saying this he breathed over them and said to them,

Receive the holy spirit.

23For any whose sins you forgive,

their sins are forgiven.

For any whose sins you do not release,

they are not released.

Yeshua tells doubting Toma to touch his wounded side

24But Toma, who was one of the twelve, called the Twin, was not with them when Yeshua came.

25So the other students were saying to him, "We have seen the lord."

But he said to them, "Unless I see the mark of the nails in his hands and I put my finger into the place of the nails and I put my hand into his side, I shall not believe."

26After eight days the students were again in the house and Toma with them. Though the doors were shut, Yeshua stood in their midst and said,

Peace to you.

27Then he said to Toma,

Bring your fingers here and see my hands,

and bring your hand and put it in my side,

and do not be without faith but of faith.

28Toma answered saying to him, "My lord and my God."

29Yeshua said to him,

Do you believe because you have seen me?

Blessed are they who have not seen and believe.

30Yeshua performed many other signs before his students, which have not been written in this book. But these things were written that you may believe that Yeshua is the mashiah, the son of God, and that in believing you may have life in his name.

✪ CHAPTER 21
(A SUPPLEMENT)[174]

Yeshua causes fish in Lake Tiberius to be
plentiful near the students' boat

After this, Yeshua again showed himself to the students at Lake Tiberius. And this is how he showed himself. ₂Gathered together were Shimon Kefa and Toma called the Twin and Natanel from Kana in the Galil and the sons of Zavdai[175] and two other students.

₃Shimon Kefa said, "I'm going fishing."

They told him, "We're coming with you."

They went out and got into the boat, and all that night caught nothing.

₄At daybreak Yeshua was standing on the beach. But the students didn't realize that it was Yeshua.

₅Yeshua said to them,

Children, have you any fish?

"No," they answered him.

₆And he said to them,

Cast the net in the waters to the right side
of the ship and you will find some.

So they cast, and they weren't strong enough to haul it back in because of the swarm of fish.

Yeshua attends a breakfast fishbake

₇Then that student[176] whom Yeshua loved said to Kefa, "It is the lord."

When Shimon Kefa heard it was the lord, he put on his outer garment, for he had stripped naked and thrown himself into the sea.

₈But the other students came in a small boat—they were not far from the land, about a hundred yards away—dragging the net full of fish.

₉When they came out on the shore, they saw a charcoal fire and a small fish placed on it, and bread.

---

174 Or "orphan ending."

175 Zebedee from the Greek Ζεβεδαῖος (Zebedaios), from the Hebrew זַבְדִּי (zavdai).

176 Apparently the unknown student, who ran faster to the empty tomb than Peter, believed what he saw (20.5, 8). When fishing, the beloved student, not Peter, recognized Yeshua on the shore (21.4, 7). In the same supplement, however, Peter appears to be elevated to leadership (21.18) by virtue of his foretold crucifixion in service of the church. In the missions of the Jerusalem church, Peter, as the "rock" on which the church was founded, was conventionally entrusted with the circumcised and Paul with the uncircumcised (Gal. 2.7).

10Yeshua said to them,

> Now bring some of the fish you caught.

11So Shimon Kefa went on board and dragged the net onto the land, filled with big fish, a hundred fifty-three of them, yet with so many the net didn't tear.

12Yeshua said to them,

> Come have breakfast.

None of the students dared ask, "Who are you?" They knew that it was the lord.

13Yeshua came and took the bread and gave it to them, and also the fish.

14This was already the third time that Yeshua appeared to the students after he was raised from the dead.

Yeshua questions Shimon Kefa's love

15So when they had breakfasted, Yeshua said to Shimon Kefa,

> Shimon son of Yohanan, do you love me
> more than they do?

Shimon said to him, "Yes, lord, you know that I love you."

Yeshua said to him,

> Feed my lambs.

16He asked Shimon a second time,

> Shimon son of Yohanan, do you love me?

Shimon said, "Yes, lord, you know that I love you."

17He said to Shimon son of Yohanan for the third time,

> Do you love me?

Kefa was hurt that he had asked him for the third time, "Do you love me?" And he said to him, "Lord, you know all things, you know that I love you."[177]

Yeshua replies,

> Graze my sheep.

Yeshua foretells Shimon Kefa's death

And he said to him, 18"Amen, amen, I say to you,"

> When you were younger,
> you fastened your own belt
> and walked about where you wished.
> But when you grow old
> you will stretch out your hands

---

[177] Peter's threefold profession of love parallels his earlier threefold denial.

and another will fasten your belt

and take you where you do not wish to go.[178]

19This he said, signifying by what death he would glorify God.

After he said this, he told him,

Follow me.

The unknown, most-loved student who is writing this passage

20Kefa turned and saw the student whom Yeshua loved following them, the one who also lay next to his chest at the supper and who had said, "Who is betraying you?"

21When Kefa saw him, he said to Yeshua, "Lord, what about him?"

22Yeshua said to Kefa,

If I want him to stay until I come,

what is that to you?

Follow me.[179]

23So word went out to the brothers that the student would not die. But Yeshua did not tell Kefa that the student would not die, but rather, "If I want him to stay until I come, what is that to you?"

24This is the student who testifies to these things and who has written these things, and we know that his testimony is true.

The world not big enough to hold books describing Yeshua's doings

25And there are many other things that Yeshua did. If they were written down one by one, I think the world itself would not have room to hold the books that would be written.

---

178 "Stretch out your hands." This passage suggests Peter's later crucifixion, which is uncertain.

179 This testy exchange, in which Yeshua tells Peter to follow him and not to question him further about the unnamed other student whom Yeshua loves most, is mystifying. The student will be there when Yeshua comes again, will not die, and declares himself to be the one testifying to and writing the final lines in colophan 21.24–25.

APOCALYPSE
(REVELATION)

APOCALYPSE (REVELATION)

A POCALYPSE IS THE ALTERNATE TITLE OF REVELATION, AND IN 1.1
APPEARS THE WORD "APOCALYPSE" FROM THE GREEK Ἀποκάλυψις
(apokalypsis), meaning "revelation," "disclosure," and literally an "uncovering."[1]
The title conveys the visionary and apocalyptic nature of the book.

Visionary writing is a habit of the Hebrew Bible, found in Isaiah, Ezekiel,
and Jeremiah, and in the Book of Daniel, which contains four formal apocalypses. The apocalyptic form is found in virtually all religions of the world, be
it as murals in a Tibetan monastery or in the Egyptian Book of the Dead.
These allegorical works, usually prompted by some historical conflict, have
enormous spatial dimensions. In Apocalypse, characters float between earth,
heaven, and hell, and, with Christ's help, the good, on defeating the wicked,
enter the fulfillment of a New Age. God declares himself the Alpha and the
Omega, and he appears with the mystery of the seven stars in his hand. The four
Horsemen of the Apocalypse ride by. A woman gives birth in midair. The
angel Michael fights the dragons. Christ and his army throw the beasts of evil
into a lake of fire, whereupon a heavenly Jerusalem descends to replace the
earthly city, and the millennium arrives.

In the second century Bishop Irenaeus ascribed the Book of Apocalypse to
the evangelist John son of Zebedee, one of the twelve apostles, who is also
credited with writing the Gospel of John and the three Letters of John. Modern scholars, however, find the style, language, thought, and historic circumstance of Apocalypse so different from the Gospel of John as to obviate the
notion of single authorship. John does identify himself as "John" in 1.9, "I
Yohanan your brother," and there is good reason to suppose that the author
was a Christian Jew named Yohanan, which is anglicized as John. On the basis
of the Greek style, which has elements of Hebrew syntax and vision, it is speculated that the author was a native of Israel who emigrated to Asia Minor, perhaps in the diaspora after the Jewish revolt against Rome (66–70 C.E.) when
many had to flee from Jerusalem. One may wonder why one should have
falsely ascribed Apocalypse to the evangelist John. It should be remembered
that books of the Hebrew Bible and of the New Covenant as well as scripture

---

[1] Revelatory writing, as in Isaiah and Daniel, is conveyed in the Hebrew גָּלָה (galah), "to reveal" or "un-
cover."

of the Intercovenant period were regularly ascribed to great figures so that such scripture might be taken into the canon. So we have works attributed to Enoch and Moses well into the first and second centuries C.E. in order to give those religious texts major significance. Six of the thirteen letters ascribed to Paul are thought not to be by Paul. Similarly, the attachment of the evangelist's name John to Apocalypse gave great authority to the book and surely helped it find its way into the canon.

There is a crypt in a monastery on Patmos, the Greek island to which John was exiled for two years, and in a small cave at the edge of this crypt John is said to have composed Apocalypse. Since the speaker in the book says that the risen Christ appeared to him on the island of Patmos, then part of a Roman province, and ordered him to write the book, there is good reason to suppose that Apocalypse might have been written there. Efesos is given as an alternative place of composition. The date is uncertain. Because of the scarcely disguised anger against the Romans who were persecuting Jews and Christians, some suggest that the book was composed during the rule of the Roman emperor Nero (54–68 C.E.), who massacred both Christian Jews and Christian gentiles, or during the rule of Domitian (81–96 C.E.).

During the Intercovenant period when Revelation was written, the apocalypse form was a common, indeed a popular, form, and there are significant extant examples, such as the Book of Enoch (Jewish), the Apocalypse of Peter (Christian), and the Apocalypse of Thomas (Christian). To the apocalyptic mind, a visionary experience yields a revelation of the future, of a holy city of redemption, or a terrible hell of punishment. Apocalypse is peopled by angels, monsters, four-headed beasts, who may represent Satan or a Roman emperor, a woman clothed with the sun, representing the faithful people of God, or the great whore of Babylon, representing nefarious Rome. God in his glorious city of gold and precious stones remains the blessing in wait for the pious reader. Though bestial and chaotic creatures of evil battle against heavenly forces, the heavens will triumph through the intervention of Christ as the Christian message will triumph over the hostility of Rome.

Clearly, between the writing of the gospels and their papal canonization in 405 C.E., many hands shaped the words and theology. Apocalypse, which was probably composed in early draft at the end of the first century and the first decades of the second, was one of many apocalypses and, obscure and uncertain in doctrine as it is, barely made it into the final canon, which is perhaps why it may have been less tampered with. This visionary book of the future and of heaven and hell is not only anti-Roman, but the Roman soldiers are symbolized as demon monsters of hell, Rome is Babylon, and the beast, whose code name is 666 (13.18), is probably not the Babylonian Captivity of Israel in the sixth century B.C.E. but primarily the wicked Nero. Under Nero and Domitian, Christians and Jews were slaughtered, and there was every reason to feel unfriendly toward Rome the oppressor. When Rome became the seat of Christianity, the politics in the Bible's texts was reshaped and reinterpreted, but little of that apparently in Revelation.

As a genre of revelatory and visionary works, Apocalypse is narrated by a prophet in the first person and contains great disasters and heavenly salvation. The main source is Daniel. The beasts and surreal dream atmosphere of this late mythical book historically reflect two periods of oppression: the Babylonian Captivity of the Jews, and its mirror, the Roman occupation and oppression that color John's Apocalypse. As a single poem, Apocalypse is the great epic work of the New Covenant, with epic length, high conflict, and elevated speech. It was not the custom to lineate either the Hebrew Bible or the New Covenant Greek in verse. After the nineteenth-century Revised Edition, large sections of the Hebrew Bible—the Psalms, Proverbs, Song of Songs, Job, and long passages in Isaiah and the other prophets—were uniformly rendered in verse. But not until the mid-twentieth century French *La Bible de Jérusalem* were even Hebrew Bible verse passages quoted in the New Covenant rendered into verse. Apocalypse, like the Book of Job, is an extended poem, as densely poetic as Blake's *Jerusalem,* Whitman's *Leaves of Grass,* or Gerard Manley Hopkins's *The Wreck of the Deutschland.* Here it is rendered in loose blank verse. The language is richly symbolic, obscure, allusive; the work is highly structured, yet, like the Song of Songs, it is a collage of recapitulations. Apocalypse is a prophecy of doom and salvation, ending with a description of the walls and streets burning in the bejeweled city of heaven.

As an epic poem, Apocalypse takes its place with *Gilgamesh* (Babylonian ca. 2000 B.C.), *Beowulf* (eighth century), and John Milton's *Paradise Lost* (1667) as one of the world's critical visionary poems. As a single, unified work,

Apocalypse may be seen as the literary masterpiece of the New Covenant. The symbolism is complex and obscure, a vision blindingly fearful and beautiful. Although an intensely luminous book, it suggests more mysteries than it discloses. For that reason, the book is unfinished, as great books are, and its open ending permits the reader endless meditation. There is a circular phenomenon in the fact that the Apocalypse, composed probably on a pagan Greek island, stands as the last work in the Asian New Covenant, which returns, as no other volume in Christian scriptures, to the speech, vision, and hopes of salvation of the Jewish Bible visionaries.

CHAPTER 1

Prologue

The Apocalypse[2] of Yeshua the Mashiah,[3] which God gave him to show his slaves what must soon happen. And he signified it by sending it through his angel to his slave Yohanan,[4] 2who bore witness to the word of God and the testimony of Yeshua the Mashiah of everything he saw. 3Blessed is the one who reads and blessed are they who hear the words of this prophecy and who keep what is written in it. For the time is near.

Alpha and Omega

4Yohanan said to the seven churches in Asia,
　　Grace be with you and peace from one who is,
　　and one who was, and one who is to come,
　　and from the seven spirits before his throne,
　　5and from Yeshua the Mashiah, faithful
　　witness who is the firstborn of the dead
　　and is the ruler of the kings of the earth.
　　To him who loves us and freed us from our sins
　　by his own blood, 6and who made us a kingdom,
　　and made priests labor for the God and father,
　　to him glory and dominion forevermore.
　　　　　　　　　　　　　　　Amen.
　　7Look, he is coming with the clouds, and every eye
　　　　will see him,
　　and even they who stabbed him,
　　and all the tribes of the earth will mourn him.[5]
　　　　　　　　　　　　　　　Amen.

---

2 Apocalypse from the Greek ἀποκάλυψις (apokalypsis), "revelation" or "disclosure of secrets" (literal meaning) or "a vision of heaven, hell, and the end of the world" (in the referential sense).

3 Jesus Christ. Jesus is from the Greek Ἰησοῦς (Iesous), from the Hebrew יֵשׁוּעַ (yeshua), traditionally translated Joshua, a later form of Yehoshua (יְהוֹשֻׁעַ). Christ is from the Greek Χριστός (Hristos), "the anointed," an attribute of the messiah. In the New Covenant Greek, Χριστός is used almost synonymously with Μεσσίας (messiah), a Hellenized transliteration of the Hebrew מָשִׁיחַ (mashiah).

4 John from the Greek Ἰωάννης (Ioannes), from the Hebrew יוֹחָנָן (yohanan).

5 Dan. 12.10; Zech. 12.10, 14.

8"I am the Alpha and the Omega," says the lord,
"who is and who was and who is coming,
and who is the ruler of all, the pantokrator."[6]

Yohanan's vision

9I Yohanan your brother, who through Yeshua
share with you suffering and kingdom and endurance,
was on the island called Patmos for the word
of God and testimony of Yeshua.
10I was fixed in the spirit on the lord's day
and I heard behind me a great voice like a ram's horn[7]
11saying: "What you have seen, write in a book
and send it off to the seven churches,
to Efesos,[8] Smyrna, Pergamos,[9] and Thyatira,
to Sardis and Philadelphia and Laodikeia."[10]

Yeshua amid seven gold lamps

12And I turned to see the voice speaking to me,
and when I turned I saw seven gold lamps,
13and in the midst of the lamps was one like
the earthly son[11] clothed in a robe down to his feet,
and girt around his breasts[12] with a gold belt.
14His head and his hair were white like white wool
like snow and his eyes like a flame of fire,

---

6 Pantokrator from the Greek παντοκράτωρ (pantokrator), from the Hebrew צְבָאוֹת (tzvaot), meaning "the Almighty," "all powerful," or "ruler of all," "of hosts." In the Greek Orthodox church "pantokrator," meaning "all powerful," from pan ("all") and kratos ("strong"), is regularly used in the Greek liturgy to signify "Almighty." Here it is chosen to reflect the Greek usage. However, since these first two verses come from Isaiah 6.3, "Almighty" better reflects the tradition of translation from the Hebrew Bible. In Isaiah 6.5, we find the origin of "pantokrator" (or "pantocrator" Romanized) in the set phrase יְהוָה צְבָאוֹת הַמֶּלֶךְ (hamelech yahweh tzvaot), "the king," "lord all powerful" (all powerful, almighty of hosts, etc.).

7 The trumpet (meaning "horn") in Apocalypse is not the modern brass instrument but the shofar, a "ram's horn," sounded as a battle signal.

8 Ephesus from the Greek Ἔφεσος (Efesos).

9 Pergamun from the Greek Πέργαμος (Pergamos).

10 Laodicea from the Greek Λαοδίκεια (Laodikeia).

11 "Son of Man" or "son of man" is the usual translation from the Greek ὁ υἱὸς τοῦ ἀνθρώπου (ho huios tou anthropou), which literally means "son of a person" or "son of people." The Greek ἀνθρώπου is not "man" but without gender, like "person." In the Hebrew Bible, "son of people" was an idiomatic way of saying "human being." In the gospels it may also suggest "the son on earth" as opposed to "the son in heaven," the "earthly son" rather than the "heavenly son." Hence, "earthly son," rather than "son of man," "son of people," or "human being," may work better poetically and theologically.

12 Although the Greek mastois means "breasts," it is commonly translated as "chest" or "waist" or sometimes the singular form "breast."

₁₅his feet like fine bronze as if fired in a furnace
and his voice like the sound of many waters.
₁₆And in his right hand he held seven stars
and from his mouth came a sharp two-edged sword
and his face was like the sun shining in its power.
₁₇When I saw him I fell at his feet like a dead man
and he placed his right hand on me and said,
"Don't be afraid. ₁₈I am the first and last
and the living one, and I have been dead,
and look, I am alive forevermore
and I have the keys to death and of hell.
₁₉So write what you have seen and what you see
and after this what is about to happen.
₂₀The mystery of the seven stars you saw
in my right hand, and seven golden lamps.
Seven stars are angels for the seven churches
and seven golden lamps are the seven churches."

 CHAPTER 2

*Efesos*¹³

"To the angel of the church in Efesos write:
'So speaks one holding seven stars in his right hand,
one walking amid the seven gold lamps:
₂"I know your work and labor and endurance
and that you cannot tolerate bad men.
You have tried those who say they are apostles
and yet are not, and you have found them false.
₃You have patience and for the sake of my name
you have persevered and not grown weary.
₄But I blame you for abandoning your first love.
₅Remember the height from which you have fallen
and repent and return to your first works.
If not, I'll come to you and take your lamp

---

¹³ Efesos (Ephesus), an important early Christian center and the largest city of the Roman province of
Asia. These next parts, commonly called "letters," are messages or edicts to the seven churches
of Asia.

from its place unless you repent. ₆But you
have this in your favor: You hate the deeds
of the church of Nikolaos,[14] which I also hate.
₇Who has an ear, hear the spirit speaking to
the churches. To the victor I will give food
to eat which comes from the tree of life
and which stands in the paradise of God.'

Smyrna[15]

₈"To the angel of the church in Smyrna write:
'So speaks he who is the first and the last,
who was dead and came back into life:
₉"I know your suffering and your poverty,
but you are rich, and I know the blasphemy
of those who say they are Jews and are not
but come out of a synagogue of Satan.[16]
₁₀Do not fear what you are about to suffer.
Look, the devil will throw some of you in prison
to test you and you will suffer for ten days,
and I will give to you the crown of life.
₁₁Who has ears, hear the spirit speaking to
the churches. And the victor won't be harmed
by the second death.'

Pergamos[17]

₁₂"To the angel of the church in Pergamos write:
'So speaks one who has the sharp two-edged sword:
₁₃"I know where you live, where Satan's throne is,
and you keep my name, even in the days of Antipas[18]
my witness, my faithful one, who was killed
among you in the place where Satan lives.

---

[14] The heretical Nicolaitians were antimonian sects associated with Efesos and Pergamos, accused of compromising with pagan idolatry and of being libertine gnostics. Most scholars now doubt these specific references, and think Nikolaos, from the Greek Νικόλαος (conqueror of people), is a wordplay parallel to Balaam (Rev. 2.14–15), from the Hebrew בִּלְעָם (bilam), meaning "he destroyed people."

[15] A harbor city north of Efesos.

[16] Satan from the Greek σατάν (satan) or σατανᾶς (satanas), from the Hebrew שָׂטָן (satan). The demonization of the Jews in the gospels persists in Apocalypse.

[17] An important Roman city with an imperial cult and major Hellenistic culture.

[18] Antipas was, according to tradition, roasted to death in a bronze kettle by those worshiping the Roman emperor at the Asian capital city of Pergamos ("Pergamum" in Latin). Pergamos, meaning "citadel," also held one of the great libraries of antiquity, before Alexandria, and our word "parchment" derives from the Greek pergamenos. Parchment was first achieved in Pergamos.

14But I have a few things I hold against you,
for there you keep the teachings of Bilam[19]
who taught Balak[20] to snare the sons of Yisrael,
to eat food sacrificed to idols and go with whores."[21]
15So you also hold to the teachings of Nikolaos.
16Repent then or soon I will come to you
and battle them with the sword of my mouth.
17Who has ears, hear the spirit speaking to
the churches. To the victor I'll give hidden manna
and I will give a white stone, and on the stone
will be written a new name no one knows
except for the one who will receive it.'

Thyatira

18"To the angel of the church in Thyatira[22] write:
'These are the words of the son of God
whose eyes are like the flame of fire
and whose feet are like burnished bronze.
19"I know your works—your love, faith, your service
and endurance—last longer than the first.
20But I blame you that you forgive Izevel,[23]
who calls herself prophet and teaches and tricks
my slaves to go with whores and consume food
sacrificed to idols. 21And I gave her time
in which to repent, but she would not repent
her harlotry. 22See, I will cast her on a bed
and will hurl those who copulate with her
into great suffering if they don't repent
of going with her. 23And I'll kill her children
with death. And all the churches will know

---

[19] Balaam from the Greek Βαλαάμ (Balaam), from the Hebrew בִּלְעָם (bilam).

[20] Balak, from the Greek Βαλάκ (Balak), from the Hebrew בָּלָק (balak), was king of Moab. Fearful after the Jews defeated the Amorites, Balak summoned Balaam to curse them (Num. 22–24). Balaam, in turn, urged Balak to persuade Israel to idolatry with the help of the women of Moab (Num. 25.1–3).

[21] "To go with whores" from the Greek πορνεύω (proneuo), "to practice prostitution." The colorful "commit fornication" used in earlier translations does not refer specifically to prostitutes.

[22] Inland, between Pergamos and Efesos.

[23] Jezebel from the Greek Ἰεζάβελ (Iezabel), from the Hebrew אִיזֶבֶל (izevel). The Canaanite queen of King Ahab of Israel (1 Kings 18–19; 2 Kings 9) who induced Ahab to worship Canaanite deities. John gave this name to a Christian sect, probably the Nicolaitians, who were leading Christians astray.

that I am the one who searches their minds
and hearts. And I will give to each of you
according to your works. ₂₄To the rest of you
in Thyatira who do not hold this teaching,
who have not known the depths of Satan,
I will not lay another weight on you.
₂₅But hold to what you have until I come.
₂₆To one who conquers and keeps my works
until the end, and as it says in the Psalms,²⁴

> I will extend power over the nations
> ₂₇and will shepherd them with a staff of iron
> as pottery is broken.

₂₈And as I have received from my father
I will give away the morning star. ₂₉Who has an ear,
hear the spirit speaking to the churches.'

⊞ CHAPTER 3

*Sardis*²⁵

"To the angel of the church in Sardis write:
'These words are from one holding seven spirits
of God and seven stars: "'I know your works,
in name you are alive yet you are dead.
₂Come and awake and strengthen what is left
and which is soon to die, for I have found
your works were not enacted before God.
₃Remember then the things you have received
and heard, and hold on to it and repent.
If you don't wake I'll come in as a thief
and you won't know what hour I'll come to you.
₄But you have the names of a few in Sardis
and they have not defiled their garments.
They will walk with me in white because
they're worthy. ₅The victorious like them

---

²⁴ Ps. 2.8–9.
²⁵ Ancient capital of Lydia, then a Seleucid kingdom. It had a temple to Artemis and, along with
  Laodikeia, received harsh criticism in Apocalypse for its spiritual "soiled clothes."

will be clothed in white clothing. I will never
obliterate your name from the book of life,
and I will confess your name before my father
and before his angels. ₆Who has an ear,
hear what the spirit is saying to the churches.'

Philadelphia

₇"To the angel of the church in Philadelphia²⁶ write:
'These are the words of the saint, the true one,
and as Yeshayah²⁷ says,

 Who holds the key of David,
  who opens and none will close,
  who closes and none will open.²⁸

₈"'I know your works, look, I have set before you
an open door and no one can shut it,
since you have little strength and kept my word
and you did not deny my name. ₉Look, I give you
those who are from the synagogue of Satan,
who say they are Jews and are not. They lie.
Look, I will make them come and worship
before your feet and know I gave you my love.
₁₀Since you have kept my word of my patience,
I too will keep you from the hour of trial
about to come upon the entire world
to test the inhabitants of the earth.
₁₁I'm coming soon. Hold fast to what you have
so none can take your crown away from you.
₁₂If you conquer I'll make you a pillar in the temple
of my God and you will never leave it,
and on you I will write the name of my God
and the name of the city of my God,
the new Yerushalayim descending from
the sky, and will record my own new name.
₁₃Who has an ear, hear what the spirit
is saying to the churches.'

---

²⁶ Near Sardis, Philadelphia appears in Apocalypse as a place of rivalry between Christianity and the
 Jewish community (Rev. 3.9).
²⁷ Isaiah from the Greek Ἡσαΐας (Esaias), from the Hebrew יְשַׁעְיָה (yeshayah).
²⁸ Isa. 22.22.

Laodikeia[29]

₁₄"To the angel of the church in Laodikeia write:
'These are the words of the Amen,[30] the faithful
and true witness, the origin of God's creation:
₁₅"'I know your works, that you are neither cold
nor hot, ₁₆and since you are lukewarm, not hot
nor cold, I will spit you out of my mouth.
₁₇Because you say I am rich and prospered
and need nothing, and you do not know
that you are the wretched and the pitiful
and the poor and the blind and the naked,
₁₈I counsel you to buy from me a gold
made pure in fire so that you may be rich,
and have white clothes to wear on your body
so the shame of your nakedness not appear,
and salve to rub on your eyes so you can see.
₁₉And those I love I rebuke and discipline.
So strive relentlessly and then repent.
₂₀Look, I'm standing at the door, and knock.
If you can hear my voice, open the door,
and I'll come in to you and eat with you
and you with me. ₂₁The victor I will ask
to sit with me on my throne as I too
was victorious and sat with my father
on his throne. ₂₂Who has an ear, hear
what the spirit is saying to the churches.'"

 CHAPTER 4

An emerald rainbow around a throne in heaven
After this I looked, and there a door opened
in the sky, and the voice of the first I heard

---

29 A commercial center one hundred miles east of Efesos. During Paul's Ephesian ministry, its church
was led by a woman named Nympha (Col. 4.15).
30 Not "Amen" of liturgical response, but a transliteration from the Hebrew of "master workman," here
signifying Yeshua. The term is also found in Proverbs 8.30, "then I was beside him like a master
worker."

was a ram's horn speaking with me saying,
"Come up here and I will show you what
must happen after this." ₂At once I was enveloped
in the spirit and saw a throne standing in the sky
and one seated on the throne. ₃The one seated
looked like stone of jasper and carnelian,
and around the throne was a rainbow like an emerald.
₄And around the throne were twenty-four thrones
and seated on the thrones were twenty-four elders
clothed in white garments, and on their heads
were gold crowns. ₅From the throne poured out
lightning flashes and voices and booming thunder,
and before the throne were seven lamps of fire
burning, which are the seven spirits of God,
₆and before the throne a sea of glass like crystal.

And in the middle and around the throne
were four live animals teeming with eyes
in front and in back.³¹ ₇The first was like a lion
and the second animal was like a calf³²
and the third animal had a human face,
₈the fourth creature was like a flying eagle.
And each of the live animals had six wings
and were full of eyes around them and inside,
and day and night they never ceased saying,
    Holy, holy, holy,
      lord God the pantokrator,
      the one who was and is
      and is to come.³³
₉And when the animals gave glory and honor
and thanks to the one seated on the throne
and to the one who lives forevermore,
₁₀the twenty-four elders cast their crowns
before the throne, and said,
    Our lord and God,

---

³¹ The description of the four animals or "living creatures" is derived from Ezekiel 1.5–10. Since Irenaeus, these four animals were used as symbols iconographically for the four evangelists.
³² "Calf" in earlier translations rendered as "ox."
³³ Isa. 6.2–3.

you are worthy to receive this glory, honor,
     and power,
   for you made all things,
and by your will they were and were created.

◇ CHAPTER 5

The scroll and the lamb
   And I saw in the right hand of him sitting
   on the throne a scroll written on the inside
   and on the back, and sealed with seven seals.
   2And I saw a strong angel who cried out
   in a great voice, "Who is worthy to open
   the book scroll and break its seven seals?"
   3And no one in the sky or on the earth
   or under the earth could open the book
   or look at it, 4and I wept much since no one
   was found worthy to open the book
   or look at it. 5And one of the elders said to me,
   "Don't weep, see, the lion from the tribe
   of Yehuda, the scion of David, has conquered
   and will open the book and its seven seals."

   6I saw, between the throne and the four animals
   and elders, a lamb standing as if slaughtered,
   with seven horns and seven eyes which are
   the seven spirits of God sent all over the earth.
   7And he came and took it from the right hand
   of the one seated on the throne. 8And when he took
   the book the four animals and twenty-four elders
   fell before the lamb, each holding a harp and gold bowls
   filled with incense, which are the prayers of saints.
   9And they sang a new song, saying,[34]
       You are worthy to take up the book scroll
           and to open the seals upon it

---

[34] "A new song." From Psalms. 33.3 and 96.1 and Isaiah 42.10, "Sing to the Lord a new song."

since you were slaughtered and by your blood
  you bought [35] people for God
from every tribe and language and nation,
  10and for our God
you made them be a kingdom and priests
  and they will reign over the earth.

11I looked and heard the voices of many angels
around the throne and animals and the elders,
and they numbered myriads of myriads
and thousands and thousands, 12saying in a great voice,
  Worthy is the lamb who was slaughtered
    to receive the power and riches
  and wisdom and strength and honor
    and glory and blessing.
And every creature which is in the sky,
on the earth and under the earth and on the sea,
and everything in these, 13I heard them saying,
  To the one seated on the throne
    and to the lamb,
  blessings and honor and glory and dominion
    forevermore.
14And the four animals said, "Amen,"
and the elders fell down and worshiped.

CHAPTER 6

Seven seals

And I saw the lamb open one of the seals
and I heard one of the four animals saying
in a voice that seemed like thunder, "Come!"
2and I saw, and look, a white horse
and its rider had a bow and was given a crown
and he went out conquering and to conquer.

---

[35] Bought from the Greek ἀγοράζω (agorazo), to "buy." "Buy" is the immediate common meaning of *agorazo*, which may in context take on a religious level of "redemption" (also a financial word) but remains an explanation of a metaphor, not the financial metaphor itself.

₃And when the lamb opened the second seal,
I heard the second animal saying, "Come!"
₄Another horse of fire red came out.
Its rider was ordered to take peace away
from earth so men might kill each other,
and he was given an enormous sword.

₅And when the lamb opened the third seal,
I heard the third animal saying, "Come!"
And I saw, and look, a black horse,
and its rider held a pair of scales in his hand.
₆And I heard what seemed to be a voice
in the midst of the four animals, saying,
"A measure of wheat for a single denar
and three measures of barley for a single denar,
and do not damage the olive oil with wine."

₇And when the lamb opened the fourth seal,
I heard the voice of the fourth animal saying,
"Come!" ₈and I saw, and look, a pale green horse,
and the name of his rider was Death, and Hell
was following him. Power was given them
over a quarter of the globe to kill
by sword and by hunger and by death
and by the wild beasts of the earth.

₉And when the lamb opened the fifth seal,
I saw under the altar the souls of those
who were slaughtered for the word of God
and the testimony which they held.
₁₀And they cried out in a great voice saying,
"How long, O absolute ruler, holy and true,
will you wait to judge and avenge our blood
from those who live upon the earth?"
₁₁They were each given a white robe and told
to rest a little time until the number was reached
of their fellow slaves, brothers and sisters
who are to be killed as they were killed.

₁₂When the lamb opened the sixth seal I looked
and there took place a great earthquake
and the sun became black like sackcloth of hair
and the full moon became like blood,
₁₃and the stars of the sky fell to the earth
as the fig tree drops its unripe fruit
shaken by a great wind. ₁₄And the sky
vanished like a scroll rolling up
and every mountain and island of the earth
was torn up from its place and moved.
₁₅And the kings of the earth and the great men
and commanders of thousands and every slave
and the free hid in caves and mountain rocks,
₁₆and said to the mountains and rocks, "Fall on us
and hide us from the face of him who is sitting
on the throne and from the anger of the lamb
₁₇because the great day of his anger has come,
and before him who has the force to stand?"

 CHAPTER 7

144,000 sealed from the tribes of Yisrael
After that I saw four angels standing on
the four farthest corners of the earth,
holding back the four winds of the earth
so that no wind might blow upon the earth
or upon the sea or upon any tree.
₂And I saw another angel going up
the sky from the rising place of the sun,
carrying the seal of the living God,
and he cried in a great voice to the angels
granted power to harm the earth and sea,
₃"Do not harm the earth or the sea or the trees
until we have marked the slaves of our God
with a seal on their foreheads."
₄And I heard

the number of those who were marked, a hundred
forty-four thousand were marked from every tribe
    of the children of Yisrael:[36]
5From the tribe of Yehuda twelve thousand sealed,
from the tribe of Reuven[37] twelve thousand,
from the tribe of Gad twelve thousand,
6from the tribe of Asher twelve thousand,
from the tribe of Naftali[38] twelve thousand,
from the tribe of Menasheh[39] twelve thousand,
7from the tribe of Shimon twelve thousand,
from the tribe of Levi twelve thousand,
from the tribe of Yisahar[40] twelve thousand,
8from the tribe of Zvulun[41]twelve thousand,
from the tribe of Yosef twelve thousand,
from the tribe of Binyamin[42] twelve thousand
    marked with the seal.

9After that I looked, and suddenly a multitude
whose number no one could count, from every
nation and tribe and people and tongue,
standing before the throne and before the lamb,
wearing white robes, holding palms in their hands.
10And they cried out in a great voice, 12saying,[43]
    Salvation to our God who is sitting
    on the throne and to the lamb.
11And all the angels stood around the throne
and around the elders and the four animals,
who fell down before the throne on their faces
and they worshiped God, 12with these words:
    Amen, blessing and glory and wisdom
    and thanksgiving and honor and power
    and strength to our God forevermore.
                         Amen.

---

[36] Israel.

[37] Reuben from the Greek Ῥουβήν (Rouben), from the Hebrew רְאוּבֵן (reuven).

[38] Naphtali from the Greek Νεφθαλίμ (Nefthalim), from the Hebrew נַפְתָּלִי (naftali).

[39] Manasses from the Greek Μανασσῆς (Manassis), from the Hebrew מְנַשֶׁה (menasheh).

[40] Issachar from the Greek Ἰσσαχάρ (Issahar), from the Hebrew יִשָּׂכָר (yisahar).

[41] Zebulun from the Greek Ζαβομλών (Zaboulon), from the Hebrew זְבֻלוּן (zvulun).

[42] Benjamin from the Greek Βενιαμίν (Beniamin), from the Hebrew בִּנְיָמִין (binyamin).

[43] Ps. 8.3.

₁₃Then one of the elders asked me, saying,
"These people who are clothed in robes of white,
do you know who they are, where they are from?"
₁₄And I replied to him, "My lord, you know."
And he said to me, "These people came from
great suffering and they have washed their robes
and whitened them in the blood of the lamb.
₁₅So they stand before the throne of God,
and serve him day and night in his temple.
Seated on his throne he'll spread his tent over them.⁴⁴
₁₆They'll not be hungry or thirsty any more,
no sun will fall on them and scorch their skin,⁴⁵
₁₇because the lamb in the middle of the throne
will shepherd them and lead them to the springs
of the waters of life,⁴⁶ and from their faces
God will wipe away every tear from their eyes."

 # CHAPTER 8

Angel and censer of fire
And when the lamb opened the seventh seal,
there was a half hour of silence in the sky.
₂I saw the seven angels standing before God
and they were given seven ram's horns.
₃And another angel came and stood by the altar,
with a gold censer, and was given much incense
to offer with the prayers of all the saints
on the gold altar which was before the throne.
And coming with the prayers of the saints,
₄then the smoke of varied incense arose
out of the hand of the angel before God.

---

⁴⁴ See Lev. 26.11 and Ezek. 37.27.
⁴⁵ An allusion to the idyllic conditions described in Isaiah 49.10. See also Revelation 21.4.
⁴⁶ For the shepherd metaphor for king (and Yeshua), see 2 Samuel 7.7; Isaiah 44.28; and Jeremiah 3.15. For living springs, see Isaiah 49.10.

5And the angel took the censer and filled it
with fire from the altar and threw it down to earth,
and there came thunders and voices and lightning
flashes and earthquake. 6The seven angels
holding the ram's horns prepared to blow them.

7The first angel blew the ram's horn. There came hail
and fire mingled with blood and it was thrown
to the earth, and a third of the earth burned up,
and a third of the trees burned up, and all green grass
    caught fire.

8And the second angel blew the ram's horn
and something like a great mountain on fire
was cast into the sea. A third of the sea was blood
9and a third of the creatures in the sea died,
who had been alive. A third of the ships sank.

10And the third angel blew the ram's horn.
From the sky a great star fell, a blazing torch,
and the star fell on a third of the rivers
and across the springs of the waters,
11and the name of the star is called Wormwood,
and a third of the waters became wormwood
and many people died from the waters
because they were made bitter.

12And the fourth angel blew the ram's horn
and a third of the sun was struck by it,
and a third of the moon, a third of the stars,
and a third of their light was darkened,
and the day lost a third of its brilliance
and likewise the night.

13And I looked and I heard an eagle flying
in mid-sky, crying out in a great voice,
"Despair despair despair to the inhabitants
of the earth at the blasts of more ram's horns
that the three angels are about to blow."

CHAPTER 9

A star fell from the sky

And the fifth angel blew his ram's horn
and I saw a star fall out of the sky
and down to the earth, and the angel was given
the key to the shaft of the bottomless pit.
2He opened the shaft of the bottomless pit
and smoke rose from the shaft like fumes
from a great furnace. And the sun was darkened
and the air was darkened from the smoke
of the shaft. 3And out of the smoke came locusts
upon the earth, and they were given powers
like the powers of scorpions of the earth.
4They were told not to damage the earth's grass,
or any green thing, or any tree, but only people
who don't wear the seal of God on their foreheads.
5They were told not to kill them but to torture them
for five months, and their torture should equal
the scorpion's torture when it strikes a person.
6And in such days the people will seek death,
but not find it, and they will desire to die
but death will escape from them.

7The locusts looked like horses prepared for war.
On their heads it was like the crowns of gold
and their faces were like the faces of people,
8and they had hair like the hair of women,
and the teeth in their jaws resembled lions.
9Their breastplates seemed to be made of iron,
and the noise of their wings was like the noise
of many horse chariots galloping into battle.
10And they have tails like scorpions and stings,
and in their tails the power to harm people.
11They have a king over them who is the angel
of the abyss, whose name in Hebrew is Abaddon

and in Greek he has the name of Apollyon.[47]
12The first despair is over. After the first,
look, there are still two more despairs to come.

13And the sixth angel blew his ram's horn,
and I heard a voice coming from the four horns
of the gold altar standing before God,
14telling the sixth angel who held the ram's horn,
"Release the four angels who are bound
at the great river Euphrates." 15The four angels
were freed, prepared for the hour and day
and month and year to kill a third of the people.
16And the number of cavalry of their armies
is two hundred million. I heard their number.
17And so I saw the horses in the vision
and the riders on them were wearing breastplates
of fire red and hyacinth blue and yellow sulfur
and the heads of horses were like heads of lions
and fire, smoke and sulfur[48] came from their mouths.
18From these three plagues a third of humankind
was killed by the fire and smoke and sulfur
spewing from their mouths. 19The power of the horses
resides in their mouths and in their tails
because the tails are like serpents with heads
and with them they do harm.

20The rest of the people who had not been killed
in the plagues did not repent of the work
of their hands so they might go on worshiping
the demons and the idols of gold and silver
and bronze and stone and wood, which cannot
see or hear or walk. 21And they did not repent
of their murders or their poison sorceries
or their dirty copulations or their thefts.

---

[47] Abbadon is the realm of the dead, and Apollyon means "destroyer," an attribute of Apollo.
[48] Sulfur from the Greek θεῖον (theion) is also translated as "brimstone."

CHAPTER 10

An angel clothed in cloud

I saw another strong angel coming down from
the sky, clothed in cloud, and the rainbow
was on his head, and his face was the sun,
and his feet like pillars of fire. 2In his hand
he held a little book open. He planted his right foot
on the sea and his left foot on the land
3and cried out in a great voice like a roaring lion.
When he cried out, the seven thunders spoke
in their own voices. 4When the seven thunders spoke,
I was about to write, but heard a voice in the sky,
saying, "Seal what the seven thunders have spoken
and do not write them down." 5Then the angel,
whom I saw standing on the sea and on the earth,
lifted his right hand to the sky 6and he swore
by him who is alive forevermore,
who created the sky and what lives in it,
and the sea and what lives in it, and he said
that the time will be no more. 7But in the days
of the sounding of the seventh angel, when he
is about to blow his ram's horn, right then
the mystery of God will be fulfilled
as he informed his slaves who were the prophets.

8And the voice I heard from the sky again
spoke to me, saying, "Go take the open scroll
in the hand of the angel standing on the sea
and on the earth." 9And I went to the angel,
telling him to give me the little book.
And he said to me, "Take it and eat it
and it will make your stomach bitter,
but in your mouth it will be like sweet honey."
10And I took the book from the angel's hand
and ate it and in my mouth it was as sweet
as honey but it made my stomach bitter.
11Then they said to me, "You must prophesy

again about many peoples and their tongues,
and about many nations and their kings."

 CHAPTER 11

Two witnesses in sackcloth

The angel gave me a reed like a staff. He said,
"Stand up and measure the temple of God
and the altar and those who worship there.
2But omit the courtyard outside the temple
and do not measure it, since it has been given
to the gentiles. They will trample the holy city
for forty-two months. 3I will give power to
two of my witnesses and they will prophesy
for a thousand two hundred days, wearing sackcloth."
4These are the two olive trees and the two lamps
that stand before the lord of the earth.
5And if anyone wants to harm them, then fire
comes out of their mouths and eats their enemies;
and if anyone wants to harm them,
in this way that person must be killed.
6These have the power to close the sky
so no rain will drench their days of prophecy,
and they have a power over the waters
to turn them into blood and strike the earth
with every plague as often as they want.

7And when they finish their testimony,
the beast rising from the bottomless pit
will make war with them and conquer them
and kill them. 8Their dead bodies will lie
in the square of the great city,[49] which is called
spiritually Sedom, and Egypt where their lord
was also crucified. 9For three days and a half,

---

[49] The great city in Apocalypse is normally Babylon, but is also identified as Rome, Jerusalem, Egypt, and Sodom, all condemned for crimes against prophets, God's messengers, and Yeshua.

members of the tribes and tongues and nations
will stare at their corpses and not let them be placed
in graves. ₁₀And those who dwell on the earth
will be happy over them and be cheerful
and send each other gifts, since these two prophets
tormented those who dwell upon the earth.

₁₁But after three days and a half, the breath
of life from God went into them, and they
stood on their feet, and great fear fell upon
those who saw them. ₁₂They heard a great voice out
of the sky, saying to them, "Come up here."
And they went up into the sky in a cloud.
Their enemies saw them. ₁₃And in that hour
there was a great earthquake and a tenth of
the city fell. And in the earthquake were killed
seven thousand of the inhabitants,
and the rest were terrified and gave glory
to the God of the sky. ₁₄The second despair
is over. Look, the third despair comes soon.

The seventh ram's horn

₁₅And the seventh angel blew his ram's horn
and there were great voices in the sky, saying,

> The kingdom of the world is now the kingdom
> > of our lord and his mashiah,
> > and he will reign forevermore.[50]

₁₆And the twenty-four elders, sitting on their thrones
before God, fell on their faces and worshiped God,
₁₇saying,

> We thank you, lord God the pantokrator,
> > the one who is and was,
> because you have taken your great power
> > and become king.
> ₁₈The gentile nations raged[51]
> > and your anger came

---

[50] Ps. 2.22, 29.
[51] Ps. 2.1.

and also the time for judging the dead
and giving wages to your slaves, the prophets
and your saints, and to all who fear your name,
    the small and the great,
and to destroy the destroyers of the earth.

19Then the temple of God in the sky was opened
and the ark of his covenant[52] was seen in his temple
and there came lightning flashes and voices
and thunders and an earthquake and great hail.

 ## CHAPTER 12

Woman, child, and the dragon

Then there was a great portent in the sky,
a woman clothed in the sun, and the moon
under her feet, and on her head a crown
of seven stars. 2In her womb she had a child
and screamed in labor pains, aching to give birth.
3And another portent was seen in the sky,
look, a great fire-red dragon with seven heads
and ten horns, and on his heads seven diadems.
4His tail dragged a third of the stars of heaven
and hurled them to the earth. The dragon stood
before the woman about to give birth
so when she bore her child he might devour it.
5She bore a son, a male, who will shepherd
all nations with a rod of iron,
and her child was snatched away to God
and to his throne. 6And the woman fled
into the desert where she has a place
made ready by God that they might nourish
her one thousand two hundred sixty days.

---

52 "The ark of his covenant" was an acacia wood chest (Deut. 10.1–2), symbolizing the presence of God
among his people, kept in the Temple in Jerusalem probably until the Temple's destruction in the
early sixth century B.C.E. by the Babylonian king Nebuchadnezzar.

7And in the sky were Mihael[53] and his angels
battling with the dragon. 8The dragon and his angels
fought back, but they were not strong enough.
No longer was there place for them in the sky.
9The great dragon, the ancient snake, who is called
Devil and Satan, the deceiver of the whole
inhabited world, was flung down to earth
and his angels were flung down with him.
10And I heard a great voice in the sky, saying,
"Now has come the salvation and the power
and the kingdom of our God and the authority
of his mashiah, for the accuser of our brothers
and sisters has been cast down, and the accuser
abused them day and night before our God.
11They defeated him through the blood of the lamb
and by the word to which they testified
and did not cling to life while facing death.
12Be happy, skies, and those who set their tents
on you. Earth and sky, you will know grief,
because the devil has come down to you
in great rage, knowing he has little time."

13When the dragon saw that he had been cast
down on the earth, he pursued the woman
who had borne the male child. 14And she was given
two wings of the great eagle that she might fly
into the desert to her place where she is nourished
for a time, and times, and half a time away
from the face of the snake. 15But from his mouth
the snake cast water, a flood behind the woman,
so he might sweep her away on the river.
16But the earth helped the woman, and the earth
opened its mouth and swallowed the river
which the dragon had cast out of his mouth.
17The dragon was enraged at the woman and left
to battle against her remaining seed,

---

53 Michael from the Greek Μιχαήλ (Mihael), from the Hebrew מִיכָאֵל (mihael) in Daniel 12.1, "the great prince, the protector of your people, shall arise." From Michael as the special protector of Israel came the covenant meaning of "the protecting archangel."

those who keep the commandments of God
and keep the testimony of Yeshua.

18Then the dragon stood on the sand of the sea.[54]

CHAPTER 13

Beast from the sea

Then I saw a beast coming up from the sea,[55]
with ten horns and seven heads and on his horns
ten diadems, and on his heads were the names
of blasphemy. 2The beast I saw was like a leopard,
his feet like a bear and his mouth like the mouth
of a lion. And the dragon gave him his power
and his throne and fierce power of dominion.
3One of his heads seemed to be stricken to death
but the wound causing his death was healed
and the whole world marveled after the beast.
4They worshiped the dragon since he had given
dominion to the beast, and they worshiped the beast,
saying, "Who is like the beast and can battle him?"
5He was given a mouth to speak great things
and blasphemies. And he was given dominion
to act for forty-two months. 6Then he opened
his mouth to utter blasphemies against God,
blaspheming his name and his tenting place,
and those who have set their tent in the sky.
7He was given powers to battle the saints
and to overcome them, and was given powers
over every tribe and people and tongue and nation.
8All who dwell on the earth will worship him,
each one whose name has not been written since
the foundation of the world in the book of life
of the slaughtered lamb. 9Who has an ear, hear
Yirmiyah:[56]

---

[54] Other ancient texts have this line at the beginning of Chapter 13.
[55] Rome and its emperors are represented as the sea monster Leviathan (Ezek. 29.3; 2 Esd. 6.47–52).
[56] Jeremiah from the Greek Ἰερεμίας (Ieremias), from the Hebrew יִרְמְיָה (yirmiyah).

10He who leads into captivity goes into captivity.
He who kills with the sword will be killed
     by the sword.[57]
Such is the endurance and faith of the saints.

Beast from the earth

11Then I saw another beast rising from the earth
and he had two horns like a lamb and he spoke
like a dragon. 12He exercises all the dominion
of the first beast before him, and makes the earth
and its inhabitants worship the first beast,
whose wound of death was healed. 13He does great portents,
even making a fire plunge from the sky
down to the earth in the sight of the people.
14He fools the inhabitants on the earth
by means of the portents he contrives to make
on behalf of the beast, creating an image
to show the beast as wounded by the sword
yet coming out alive. 15And he had the power
to give breath[58] to the image of the beast
and the image of the beast could even speak
and cause all who would not worship the beast
to be killed. 16He causes all, the small and great,
the rich and poor, the free and the slaves,
to be marked on the hand and the forehead
17so that no one can buy or sell without the mark,
the name of the beast or number of his name.
18Here is wisdom. Who has a mind, calculate
the number of the beast, which is the number
for a human. And the number is 666.[59]

---

[57] Jer. 15.2, 14.11.

[58] Breath from the Greek πνεῦμα (pneuma) is "breath" and by extension "spirit," and sometimes, as in
the prologue of John, it means both.

[59] The number of the beast corresponds in Hebrew to a code, which may be the name of Nero Caesar.

CHAPTER 14

Lamb on Mount Zion

    Then I saw, and look, the lamb standing on
Mount Zion and with him one hundred forty-four
thousand who had his name and the name of
his father written on their foreheads. ₂And
I heard a voice out of the sky like the voice
of many waters, like the voice of great thunder,
and the voice I heard was like the voice of harpists
playing on their harps. ₃They sing a new song
before the throne and before the four animals
and the elders, and no one could learn the song
except the hundred and forty-four thousand
who have been bought⁶⁰ from the earth. ₄These are
the men who were not defiled by women,
since they are virgins. They follow the lamb
wherever he goes. These were bought from men
as a first fruit for God and the lamb. ₅And in
their mouths no lie was found. They are blameless.

    ₆Then I saw another angel flying in midair
with an eternal gospel to proclaim
to those inhabiting the earth and each nation,
and tribe and tongue and people, ₇saying
in a great voice,

        Fear God and give him glory.

        The hour of his judgment is come,

   and worship him who made the sky and earth,

        the sea and the springs of water.

  ₈Another angel, a second, followed, saying,

        Great Babylon is fallen, is fallen.⁶¹

    She made all nations drink her wine of passion

        and her filthy copulations.

---

⁶⁰ See note 35, page 394, on "bought" and "redeemed."
⁶¹ Isa. 21.9. Babylon may be a code name for Rome.

₉Another angel, a third, followed them, saying
in a great voice, "All those who worship the beast
and his image and receive a mark on the forehead
or on the hand, ₁₀even those humans will drink
the wine of the wrath of God, which his poured
undiluted into the cup of the anger
of their God, and they will be tormented
in fire and in sulfur before the holy angels
and before the lamb. ₁₁The smoke of their torment
will rise forevermore, and there's no rest
day and night for any who worship the beast
and his image or wears the mark of his name."
₁₂Such is the endurance of the saints, who keep
the commandments of God and faith in Yeshua.

₁₃And I heard a voice out of the sky, saying,
"Write. Blessed are the dead who from now on
die in the lord." "Yes," the spirit says, "so they
may rest from their labors. Their works
will follow after them."

Earthly son on a white cloud and angels with harvest sickles
   ₁₄Then I looked and there was a white cloud,
and seated on the cloud was one who seemed
to be the earthly son, wearing a gold crown
on his head, and he was carrying in his hand
a sharp sickle. ₁₅Another angel came out
of the temple, crying in a great voice
to the one sitting on the cloud, "Take out
your sickle and reap, for the hour to reap
has come, because the harvest of the earth
is ripe." ₁₆And the one sitting on the cloud
swung his sickle on the earth, and reaped the earth.
₁₇Another angel came out of his temple
in the sky, and he carried a sharp sickle.
₁₈Another angel came out of the altar,
who is in charge of fire, and he called
in a great voice to him with the sharp sickle,
"Thrust in your sharp sickle and gather up
the clusters of the vine upon the earth,

because her grapes are ripe." ₁₉And the angel
thrust his sickle into the ground and gathered
the vintage from the earth and threw it into
the great winepress of the anger of God.
₂₀And the winepress was trodden outside the city
and blood came from the press up to the bridles
of horses for a distance of four hundred furlongs.⁶²

 CHAPTER 15

Sea of glass mingled with fire
> And I saw another great portent in the sky,
> great and wonderful, seven angels with seven plagues,
> the last ones, since the anger of God is fulfilled
> in them. ₂I saw what seemed a sea of glass
> mingled with fire, and victors over the beast
> and his image and the number of his name,
> standing on the sea of glass, holding harps of God.
> ₃They sang the song of Mosheh the slave of God
> and the song of the lamb:
>> Great and wonderful are your works,
>>> lord God the pantokrator.
>> Just and true are your ways,
>>> O king of nations!
>> ₄Who will not fear you, lord,
>>> and glorify your name?
>> Because you alone are holy,
>>> because all nations come
>>> and worship before you,
>> because your judgments are revealed.⁶³

---

⁶² Furlong from the Greek στάδιον (stadion). The Greek says 1,600 stadia. A stade is 606 feet, and 1,600 stadia is about 200 miles. "Stade" is commonly translated as "furlong," 220 feet; hence 400 furlongs.
⁶³ The song of Moses, from Deuteronomy 32.1–47 and Exodus 15.1–18, was sung on Sabbath evenings in the synagogues to celebrate Israel's deliverance from Egypt.

Seven gold bowls with the anger of God
    5After this I looked. The temple of the tent[64]
of testimony was opened in the sky,
6and the seven angels with the seven plagues
came out of the temple. They were robed in linen
clean and bright, and gold belts girding their breasts.
7One of the four animals gave the seven angels
seven gold bowls filled with the anger of God
who lives forevermore. 8The temple was filled
with smoke from the glory of God and from
his power, and none could enter the temple until
the seven plagues of the seven angels were done.

CHAPTER 16

Angels emptying bowls of God's wrath on the earth
    Then I heard a great voice out of the temple,
saying to the seven angels, "Go and pour out
the seven bowls of the anger of God
onto the earth." 2So the first went, and poured
the bowl out onto the earth, and a sore
and painful wound came on those with the mark
of the beast and those worshiping his image.

    3Then the second poured his bowl on the sea
and it turned into blood like a dead man's,
and every living soul died in the sea.
4And the third poured his bowl on the rivers
and springs of waters, and it turned into blood.
5I heard the angel of the waters saying,

    You are just, the one who was,
       the holy one,
    for you have judged these things.
    6Because they shed the blood of saints
       and prophets,

---

[64] Tent from the Greek σκηνή (skene), "tent," from the Hebrew סֻכָּה (sukkah), "shelter," or "tent."

you gave them blood to drink
    as they deserve.
7And I heard the altar respond,
    Yes, lord God, the pantokrator,
    your judgments are true and right.

8And the fourth poured his bowl onto the sun
and he was able to burn people with great fire.
9And the people were burned in a great blaze
and they blasphemed the name of his God,
who holds dominion over these plagues,
and they failed to repent and give him glory.

10And the fifth poured out his bowl on the throne
of the beast, and his kingdom turned dark,
and they chewed their tongues from pain.
11They blasphemed the God in the sky because
of their pains and their sores and did not repent
from their works.

        12And the sixth poured out his bowl
on the great Euphrates river. Its water dried up
so as to make ready the way for the kings
from the rising sun. 13I saw coming out
of the mouth of the dragon, from the mouth
of the beast, from the mouth of the false prophet
three unclean breaths like frogs. 14For these are breaths
of demons performing portents that go out
to the kings of the whole inhabited world,
to poise them for the battle of the great day
of God the pantokrator. 15("Look, I'm coming
like a thief! Blessed is the one who watches
and cares for his clothes so he doesn't walk
about naked and his shame become seen.")[65]

---

[65] This unforeseen parenthetical voice, "I'm coming like a thief!" gives the common metaphor for the unexpected arrival of Yeshua, as in Matthew 24.42–44 and Luke 12.39–40.

₁₆And they brought them together in a place
which is called in Hebrew Har Megiddo.⁶⁶

₁₇The seventh poured out his bowl upon the air,
and a great voice came out of the temple
from the throne, saying, "It happened!" ₁₈There were
the lightning flashes, voices and the thunders.
There was an earthquake greater than any since
people inhabited the earth, it was so violent.
₁₉The city was sundered into three parts
and the cities of the nations fell. Then Babylon
the great was remembered before God,
who gave her the wine cup of the fury of his wrath.
₂₀Every island fled and mountains were not found.
₂₁Huge hail, heavy as talents, fell from the sky
upon the people, and they blasphemed God
for bringing a plague with this enormous hail,
because the plague was exceedingly great.

 **CHAPTER 17**

The great whore on a scarlet beast
    Then came one of the seven angels who held
    the seven bowls and he spoke with me, saying,
    "Come, I'll show you the judgment on the great whore
    sitting on the many waters, ₂with whom the kings
    of the earth have copulated, and with the wine
    of her copulations the dwellers of the earth
    have got drunk." ₃He took me off to a desert
    in the spirit. I saw a woman sitting
    on a scarlet beast who was filled with the names
    of blasphemy, with seven heads and ten horns.
    ₄The woman was wearing purple and scarlet

---

⁶⁶ Armageddon or Har Magedon from the Greek Ἁρμαγεδών (Armagedon), from the Hebrew מְגִדּוֹ
הַר (har megiddo), meaning, "Mountain or Hill of Megiddo," an ancient archaeological site and city
in central Israel of decisive battles, by Megiddo, a major Canaanite city in Manasseh. The site has
taken on a mystical quality about which there is much fuss and uncertainty.

and was adorned with gold and precious stones
and pearls. She held a gold cup in her hand,
full of the abominations of filth
of her harlotry. 5On her forehead a name
was written:

MYSTERY

BABYLON THE GREAT

THE MOTHER OF THE WHORES

AND THE ABOMINATIONS OF THE EARTH[67]

6And I saw the woman drunk on the blood of saints
and from the blood of the witnesses of Yeshua.
I was amazed, looking at her with wonder.
7The angel said to me, "Why do you marvel?
I will tell you the mystery of the woman
and the beast with seven heads and ten horns
who carries her. 8The beast you saw was
and is not and is about to come up out of
the bottomless abyss and go to his perdition.
And the inhabitants of earth will be stunned,
whose names have not been written in the book
of life from the foundation of the world,
when they see the beast that is and is not
and is to come. 9Here is the mind with wisdom:
the seven heads are seven mountains where
the woman sits on them. They are seven kings.
10Five have fallen, one is, the other has not
yet come, and when he comes, short is the time
he must stay. 11The beast who was and is not,
he too is the eighth and comes from the seven
and goes to his perdition. 12The ten horns
you saw are ten kings who did not yet take
a kingdom, but they will have their kingdom
as kings for one hour along with the beast.
13These are of one mind and render the power
and dominion to the claws of the beast.
14They will make war with the lamb and the lamb
will conquer them, because he is the lord

---

[67] The great whore is often a metaphor for "a godless city" as in Isaiah 1.21 and 23.16–17.

of lords and king of kings. Those on his side
are the called and the chosen and the faithful."

₁₅Then the angel said to me, "The waters you saw
where the whore sits, there are peoples and crowds
and nations and tongues. ₁₆The ten horns you saw
and the beast, they will all hate the whore
and will make her desolate and naked,
and eat her flesh and will burn her up with fire.
₁₇For God put in their hearts to do his will
and act with one mind to give their kingship
until the words of God will be fulfilled.
₁₈And the woman you saw is the great city[68]
with dominion over the kings of the earth."

 ## CHAPTER 18

All nations have drunk the wine of copulation with fallen Babylon
After this I saw another angel coming down
out of the sky and with great authority
and the earth was lighted with his glory.
₂And he cried out in a powerful voice, saying,
    Fallen fallen is Babylon the great.[69]
    She has become a home for demons
    and a prison of every foul spirit
    and a prison of every foul bird
    and a prison of every foul and
    detested beast, ₃since all the nations

---

[68] The great city is Babylon but may signify Rome, or hell, or all three.

[69] Again a reference to Isaiah 21.9 and Jeremiah 51.8, foreseeing Rome's fall. These many references to Rome as the terrible enemy reflect how Apocalypse remained outside the redaction process that fashioned the gospels so as to favor Rome (despite its crucifixion of Yeshua), to justify her destruction of "sinful" Jerusalem of the Jews, and, by implication, to speak for Rome's later church. Although the gospels are replete with references to the Hebrew Bible, each page of Apocalypse draws deeply from the Jewish scriptures. Written while the division between Jews and Christian Jews was still a blur of rivalry and not a schism, it is, after Daniel, the other great apocalypse of which we have several Jewish and Christian Jewish texts from the Intertestamental period. See James H. Charlesworth, ed., *The Old Testament Pseudepigrapha* (Garden City, NY: Doubleday, 1983–1985, two vols.), and Willis Barnstone, *The Other Bible* (San Francisco: HarperSan Francisco, 1984).

have drunk the wine of passion
of her copulation, and the kings
of the earth have copulated with her,
and the merchants of the earth
have grown rich on her lechery.[70]

Of merchants, captains, and seafarers who mourn and now cry out
   ₄Then I heard another voice out of the sky, saying,
     Come out of her, my people,
     so you will not join in her sins,
     so you won't take on her plagues,
     ₅because her sins are piled up
       and reach the sky.
     God has remembered her iniquities.
     ₆Render to her as she has rendered,
       mix her a double portion
       in the cup she has mixed.
     ₇As she gloried in the luxury of the flesh,
     give her equal torment and sorrow.
       In her heart she says,
         "I sit, a queen.
         I am not a widow
           and will never know grief."
     ₈But soon the plagues will come to her,
     death and sorrow and famine,
       and in fire she will burn,
     for powerful is the lord God who has
       judged her.

   ₉The kings of the earth, who have copulated
with her and lived in lechery, will weep
and beat themselves over her when they see
the smoke of her burning. ₁₀Standing far off
because they fear the torment, they say,
     Despair despair is the great city
       Babylon, the strong city,
     for in an hour your judgment came.
   ₁₁The merchants of the earth cry out and mourn

---

[70] Lechery or sensuality from the Greek στρῆνος (strenos), which may also be translated as "luxury."

over her, since no one buys their cargo now,
12cargo of gold and silver and precious stones
and pearls and fine linen and purple cloth
and silk and scarlet and every cedar wood
and every ivory vessel and every vessel
of precious wood and bronze and iron and marble
13and cinnamon and spice and incense and myrrh
and frankincense and wine and olive oil
and fine flour and wheat and cattle and sheep,
and horses and chariots and bodies and souls.

> 14And the autumn fruit your soul longed for
> > has gone from you,
> and all the luxurious and the brilliant
> > are lost to you
> > and never will be found.

15The merchants of these things, who became rich
from her, will stand far off because they fear
her torment, her weeping and her mourning,
16which say,

> Despair despair is the great city
> who was clothed in fine linen
> and purple cloth and scarlet
> and decorated with gold
> and precious stone and pearl.
> > 17In an hour that wealth was desert.

And all captains and seafarers on the ship
and sailors and all those who work the sea
stood far off 18and cried out as they saw
the smoke of her conflagration, saying,

> What city was like this great city?

19And they threw dust upon their heads
and they cried out with tears and groans,

> Despair despair is the city,
> where all who owned ships on the sea
> grew rich from her prosperity.
> In an hour came only desolation.

20Heaven and saints, celebrate her downfall,
and apostles and prophets, for God has judged
against her for you. 21Then one strong angel

picked up a boulder like a great millstone
and hurled it down into the sea, saying,
> With such violence Babylon will be cast down
> > and will be found no more.
22And the voices of harp players and singers,
> > the pipers and ram-horn blowers
> > will be heard no more in you,
> > and the artisan of any trade
> > will be found no more in you,
> > and the sound of the mill
> > will be heard no more in you,
23and the light of a lamp
> > will shine no more in you,
> > the voice of the groom and bride
> > will be heard no more in you.
Your merchants were the great men of the earth
and all nations were fooled by your sorcery.
24In her was the blood of prophets and saints
and all those who were slaughtered on the earth.

 # CHAPTER 19

A great voice in the heaven crying Halleluyah![71]
> After this I heard a great voice in the sky,
> like a huge crowd shouting,
> > > Halleluyah!
> Salvation and glory and honor and power
> > > to our God,
> 2True and just are his judgments,
> He judged the great whore
> who has corrupted the earth with her harlotry.
> He avenged the blood of his own slaves
> > > against her hand.

---

[71] Halleluyah from the Greek ἀλληλουϊά (hallelouia), from the Hebrew הַלְלוּיָהּ (halleluyah), meaning "praise Yahweh."

₃A second time they said,
> Halleluyah!
And her smoke ascends forever and ever.
₄Then the twenty-four elders and four animals
fell down and worshiped God, who was seated
on the throne, and said,
> Amen Halleluyah!
₅And a voice came from the throne, saying,
> Praise our God
and all his slaves and those who fear him,
> the small and the great.

₆And I heard the voice of a huge crowd
like the voice of many waters and thunders,
saying,
> Halleluyah!
Because the lord God and pantokrator reigns.
₇Let us be happy and exult and give him glory,
for the wedding of the lamb has come,
> and his bride got ready
₈and she had to clothe herself in fine linen
> bright and clean,
a linen of the good acts of the saints.
₉The angel said to me, "Write. Blessed are
those called to the supper of the wedding
of the lamb." And the angel said, "These words
are the true words of God." ₁₀I fell before
his feet to worship him. He said to me,
"You must not do that! I am your fellow slave
and of your brothers and sisters who keep
the testimony of Yeshua. Worship God.
To witness Yeshua is the spirit of prophecy."

Rider on a white horse
₁₁I saw the sky open, and look, a white horse
and the rider on him called Faithful and True,
and in the right he judges and makes war.
₁₂His eyes are flames of fire, and on his head
many diadems, with names written known
alone by him. ₁₃And he wore a mantle

dipped in blood and his name is called the word
of God. 14The armies in the sky followed him
on white horses, clothed in fine linen white
and clean. 15And from his mouth goes a sharp sword
to smite the nations. He will shepherd them
with a rod of iron. He will trample the wine press
of the fury of the anger of God, the pantokrator.
16He wears on his mantle and on his thigh
a name written:

KING OF KINGS AND LORD OF LORDS

Into the lake of fire
17I saw an angel standing in the sun
and he cried out in a great voice, saying,
"To all the birds flying in the middle air,
come, gather for the great supper of God
18to eat the flesh of kings and flesh of captains
and flesh of strongmen and flesh of horses
and of their riders and flesh of both the free
and slaves and small and great." 19I saw the beast
and kings of the earth and their armies poised
to make war against the rider on his horse
and against his armies. 20Then the beast
was captured and with him the false prophet
who had worked miracles on the beast's behalf
and so deceived those who received the mark
of the beast and those who worshiped the image
of the monster. The two of them were cast alive
into the lake of fire burning with sulfur.
21The rest were killed by the sword of the rider
on the horse, the sword that came from his mouth;
and all the flying birds gorged on their flesh.

CHAPTER 20

Angel with a great chain in his hand
I saw an angel coming down from the sky.
He was holding a great chain on his hand

and the key of the bottomless pit. 2He seized
the dragon, and ancient snake, who is the devil
and Satan; he bound him for a thousand years
3and cast him into the bottomless pit
and closed it tight and sealed it over him
so he couldn't fool the nations any more
until the thousand years should be fulfilled.
After that he must be released a short time.
4Then I saw thrones, and those who sat on them
were given the power to judge. I saw
the souls of those beheaded for their testimony
to Yeshua and for the word of God
and those who had not worshiped the beast
nor the image of him and did not take
his mark on their forehead and on their hand,
and they came to life and reigned with Yeshua
for a thousand years. 5The rest of the dead
did not come to life until the thousand years
were over. This is the first resurrection.

Devil in sulfur and fire forever

6Blessed and holy are they who take part in
the first resurrection: on these the second death
has no power. They will become priests of God
and of Yeshua and with him they will reign
a thousand years. 7And when the thousand years
should be fulfilled, Satan will be released
from his prison 8and will come out to fool
the nations in the four corners of the earth,
Gog and Magog,[72] to lead them into battle,
whose number is like the sand of the sea.
9Then they climbed up and over the width
of the earth and encircled the encampment
of the saints and their beloved city,
but fire came down from the sky and consumed

---

[72] Ezek. 38–39. Gog and the king of Magog, two names that represent those nations in league who will march against Jerusalem. They seem to appear after the first thousand-year reign of the messiah. In Apocalypse, their defeat, meaning that of Satan and of his forces, will herald the triumph of the Lamb in the New Jerusalem. The war of Gog and Magog is commented on in the Babylonian Talmud.

the attackers. ₁₀The devil, who had fooled them,
was cast into the lake of fire and sulfur
where both the beast and the false prophet are
and will be tormented forevermore.

Of the dead written in the book
    ₁₁I saw a throne great and white, and sitting
on it was he from whose face fled the earth
and the sky, and no place was found for them.
₁₂I saw the dead, the great and small. They stood
before the throne and there the books were opened.
Another book was opened, which is the book
of life. The dead were judged according to
their works as they were written in the books.
₁₃The sea gave up the dead in it, and hell
gave up the dead in it, and they were judged,
each one according to their works. ₁₄And Death
and Hell were cast into the lake of fire.
This is the second death, the lake of fire.
₁₅And anyone not written in the book
of life was cast into the lake of fire.

 CHAPTER 21

A new Yerushalayim descends from heaven
    And I saw a new sky and a new earth,
for the first sky and the first earth were gone
and the sea was no more. ₂I saw the holy
city, the new Yerushalayim, coming down
out of the sky from God who prepared her
like a bride adorned for her groom. ₃And then
I heard a great voice from the throne, saying,
"Look, now the tent of God is with them. They'll be
his people, and he God will be with them,
₄and he will wipe away each tear from their eyes
and death will be no more. And grief and crying
and pain will be no more. The past has perished."

I am the Alpha and the Omega

5And he who sat upon the throne said, "Look,
I made all new." And he said, "Write, because
these words are true and faithful." 6And he said
to me, "It's done. I am the Alpha and the Omega,
the beginning and the end. And to the thirsty
I will give a gift from the spring of the water
of life. 7The victor will inherit these things
and I will be his God and he will be
a son. 8But to the cowards and unbelieving
and abominable and murderers and copulators
and sorcerers and all who are false, their fate
will be the lake burning with fire and sulfur,
which is the second death."

The city clear gold like clear glass

9One of the angels came with the seven bowls
full of the seven last plagues, and he spoke
with me, saying, "Come, I will show you the bride,
the wife of the lamb." 10And he took me away
in spirit onto a mountain great and high,
and showed me the city of holy Yerushalayim
coming down out of the sky from God,
11wearing the glory of God, and her radiance
like a precious stone, like a jasper stone
and crystal clear. 12She has a great and high wall
with twelve gates and at the gates twelve angels,
their names inscribed on them: the twelve tribes
who are the sons and daughters of Yisrael.
13On the east three gates and on the west three gates,
on the south three gates and on the west three gates.
14The walls of the city have twelve foundations,
and on them twelve names, the twelve apostles of
     the lamb.
15The angel speaking to me had a gold
measuring rod to gage the city and her gates
and walls. 16The city lies foursquare, its length
and width the same. He gaged the city with

the reed, twelve thousand furlongs in length,[73]
her length and width and height the same. 17He gaged
her wall a hundred forty-four cubits,[74]
by human measurement like the angel's.

18The wall is built of jasper and the city
clear gold like clear glass. 19The foundations of
the city are adorned with precious stones,
the first foundation jasper, the second sapphire,
third of agate, fourth of emerald, 20fifth of onyx,
the sixth carnelian, seventh of chrysolite,
the eighth beryl, ninth of topaz, tenth of chrysoprase,
eleventh jacinth and the twelfth amethyst.
21The twelve gates are twelves pearls, each gate
a single pearl, and the great square in the city
is clear gold like diaphanous glass.

City without need of sun or moon
22I saw no temple in her, for the temple
is lord God the pantokrator and the lamb.
23The city has no need of sun or moon
to shine on her, for the glory of God
illumined her and her lamp is the lamb.
24The gentile nations will walk around
through her light, and the kings of the earth
bring glory into her. 25Her gates will never
be shut by day, and night will not be there.
26Her people will bring the glory and honor
of nations into her. 27But no common thing[75]
will enter her, or anyone who stoops
to abominations and lies, but only those
written in the book of life of the lamb.

---

[73] About 1,500 miles.
[74] Almost 200 feet.
[75] Common from the Greek κοινός (koinos), meaning "common," "of little value," or "communal" (in the sense of being shared). Here this word, as with many ordinary words in New Covenant lexicons, is given a religious boost by translating it as "profane," which suggests "in contrast to the sacred." But its sense of "common" or "plain" contrasts in a lovely way with the luminous magnificence of the city in the sky, which is lost when "common" has an ecclesiastical ring.

CHAPTER 22

River of the water of life

The angel showed me a river of the water
of life shining like crystal and issuing
from the throne of God and of the lamb.
2Between the great plaza and the river
and on either side stands the tree of life
with her twelve fruits, yielding a special fruit
for every month, and the leaves of the tree
are for healing the nations. 3All curses
will cease to exist. The throne of God
and of the lamb will be in the city.
His slaves will serve him; 4they will see his face. His name
will be on their foreheads. 5And night will not
be there and they'll need no light of a lamp
or light of sun, for the lord God will glow
on them, and they will reign forevermore.

I'm coming quickly!

6Then he said to me, "These words are faithful
and true, and the lord God of the spirits of
the prophets sent his angel to show his slaves
those things which soon must take place. 7Look,
I'm coming quickly! Blessed is the one
who keeps the words of this book's prophecy."
8I Yohanan am the one who heard and saw
these things. And when I heard and saw I fell
and worshiped before the feet of the angel
showing me these things. 9And he said to me,
"You must not do that! I am your fellow slave
and of your brothers and prophets and those
who keep the words of this book. Worship God."
10And he tells me, "Do not seal the words
of prophecy of this book. The time is near.
11Let the unjust still be unjust, the filthy
still be filthy, the righteous still do right,
and the holy one be holy still." 12"Look,

I'm coming quickly, and my reward is with me
to give to each according to your work.
13I am the Alpha and the Omega, the first
and the last, the beginning and the end."

To the tree of life

14Blessed are they who are washing their robes
so they will have the right to the tree of life
and can enter the city through the gates.
15Outside will be the dogs and sorcerers
and copulators and murderers and idolators
and everyone who loves to practice lies.

I am the offspring of David the bright morning star

16"I Yeshua sent my angel to you
to testify these things for the churches.
I am the root and the offspring of David,
the bright morning star." 17The spirit and bride
say, "Come." Let you who hear say, "Come."
"Let you who thirst come, and let you who wish
take the water of life, which is a gift."

Come, lord Yeshua!

18I give my testimony to all who hear
these words of the prophecy of this book.
If anyone adds to these, then God will add
to them the plagues recorded in this book.
19If anyone takes away from the words
of this book's prophecy, God will cut off
their share of the tree of life and the holy
city, those things recorded in this book.[76]
20And he who is the one who testifies
to all this says, "Yes, I am coming quickly!"
Amen. Come, lord Yeshua! 21And may
the grace of lord Yeshua be with you all.

---

[76] These last commands and warnings are from Deuteronomy 4.2 and 12.32.

AFTERWORD

Translation History, Anti-Judaism,
Authors and Sources, Yeshua to Jesus,
Passover Death and Rome,
and Yeshua the Voice of Spirit

A BRIEF HISTORY OF
THE TRANSLATOR'S WAY

A HISTORY

JOHN WYCLIF

In the conversion of holy scripture each word faces the risky test of theology, canon, and history. From the fourteenth to the sixteenth centuries in England and France, translators burned. John Wyclif (1320–1384), Master of Balliol College and called the flower of Oxford scholarship, was a dissenter against the rich princes of the church. He engaged in open war with Rome, which reserved the reading of the Bible for its clergy. For Wyclif it was not enough to overhear the priest's Latin language in the church. He held that the emancipation of the individual soul lay in the possibility of reading the Bible in one's native tongue. He was the first translator of the entire Bible into vernacular English, for a public which could not read its Latin translation. He also addressed another language rivalry: the political and class conflict between Norman French and English. With Chaucer writing his masterpieces in English and the Wyclif English Bible reaching large numbers of people orally and in manuscript—this was still the manuscript age—English established itself as the language of England, and Wyclif contributed to its early domination. The Wyclif Bible was immensely popular (some two hundred manuscripts of the Wyclif versions have survived, many times the number of extant copies of Chaucer's *Troilus* or the *Canterbury Tales*), and it was also to serve as source and dictionary for the later Tyndale New Testament in 1525 and Coverdale's Bible in 1535.

There was a price for Wyclif's populist outrages. The official church was not deaf to the sounds of all this theological and related linguistic activity from Oxford lectures and in the churches and streets in England. It would not remain silent. In 1401 Archbishop Arundel denounced Wyclif as heretical. He fumed: "The peal of the Gospel is scattered abroad and trodden underfoot by swine." He further wrote in his report to claimant John XXIII: "This pestilent and wretched John Wyclif, of cursed memory, that son of the old serpent . . . endeavored by every means to attack the very faith and sacred doctrine of Holy

Church, devising—to fill up the measure of his malice—the expedient of a new translation into the mother tongue."

The scholar's death, by natural causes, saved him. Some associates and readers of Wyclif were, however, burned alive for the sins of unauthorized vernacular translation. John Purvey, his follower and author of the second widespread revision of his work, was thrown into prison under the 1401 acts against heresy, *De haeretico comburendo,* and under torture abjured his Lollard principles (the vernacular "mutterings" of poor preachers). Wyclif was by then safely in the earth, or so it seemed. In 1424, forty years after his burial, his bones were dug up, burned, and thrown into the River Swift.

ÉTIENNE DOLET

In France the pre-Renaissance scholar Étienne Dolet (1509–1546), historian, painter, printer, and translator of the Bible, was tried and convicted of heresy by the French church for his secularized translation of Plato—not for his scripture. He was burned at the stake. He became the first martyr in the cause of secular translation.

WILLIAM TYNDALE

Meanwhile, in England, Dolet's near contemporary William Tyndale (ca. 1494–1536) was establishing the Renaissance English language of the Bible. The larger part of the Authorized New Covenant (and that part of the Hebrew Bible that Tyndale lived to translate) is Tyndale's phraseology. His prose is clear, modern, minimally Latinized, and with unmatched narrative powers. Everything is fresh, including the use of very common words, unelevated for religious respectability. So where the Authorized Version has "and the Lord was with Joseph and he was a prosperous man" (Gen. 39.2), Tyndale has "the Lord was with Joseph and he was a luckie felawe." We have been trying and failing for centuries to get back to that speech which is at once dignified and ordinary, which a Bible from common but inspired people should be. Working from original sources, Tyndale made the English of his day the language of the Bible, and his vision of biblical speech imposed itself on all subsequent versions in English, particularly the Geneva, which carried the cadence and ordinary magnificence of his words under its own rubric to the masters of English literature.

Not only did Tyndale translate the Bible into English to make it readable for the literate and hearable for the unlettered church-goer, but he did so with the enthusiastic assertion that English was an excellent language to translate into from Hebrew and Greek, and far better than Latin. English is so flexible that one can translate into it word for word, and not paraphrase as one must in Latin. And Tyndale, working hard to stay close in word and syntax to the original, more than any Renaissance translator, avoided paraphrase, equivalents, and explanation. But he did so with his special gift for finding the grace and sweetness of the English language:

> They will say it cannot be translated into our tongue, it is so rude. It is not so rude as they are false liars. For the Greek tongue agreeth more with the English than with the Latin. And the properties of the Hebrew tongue agreeth a thousand times more with the English than with the Latin. The manner of speaking is both one, so that in a thousand places thou needest not but to translate it into the English word for word when thou must seek a compass in the Latin and yet shall have much work to translate it well-favouredly, so that it have the same grace and sweetness, sense and pure understanding with it in the Latin as it hath in the Hebrew. A thousand parts better may it be translated than into the Latin. ("Obedience of a Christian Man" in Alter and Kermode, 648)[1]

But Tyndale's courageous venture into English did not escape the wrath of those who saw heresy in his vernacular, in his translations which he rendered "for the ploughboy in the fields." The bishop of London called them "persiferous and most pernicious poison." As a sign of those noisy times, Sir Thomas More (who was to lose his head to the axe in 1535) devoted a book, *Dialogue Concerning Tyndale* (1529), to blasting Tyndale the man, reviling the language of his revisionist translation, and even transforming its author into a barking hound: "He barketh against the sacraments much more than Luther" (*Dialogue*, 315). And no one in his day could surpass More in his sonorous alliterations and orchestration of rhythmic denunciations. But he surpassed his own alliterative flair and brutal magnificence in the rhetoric of insult when he called Tyndale "the devilish drunken soul . . . this drowsy drudge hath drunken so deep in the devil's dregs that if he wake and repent himself the sooner he may hap to fall into draff that the hogs of hell shall feed upon."

For his "cunning counterfeit" and a choice of offensive words—"congregation," not "church"; "senior" and "elder," not "priest"; and "love," not "charity,"

---

[1] The lines from Tyndale are taken from Gerald Hammond's essay "English Translations of the Bible" in Robert Alter and Frank Kermode, eds., *The Literary Guide to the Bible* (Cambridge, MA: Harvard University Press, 1967). Hammond's essay and his volume *The Making of the English Bible* (New York: The Philosophical Library, 1983) contain uniformly sensitive and informed remarks on Bible translation.

all lacking ecclesiastical correctness—Tyndale was arrested for heresy in Antwerp, then under the rule of Charles V. By this time he had completed the Pentateuch, Jonah, and the Second Book of Chronicles. In 1535 he was imprisoned near Brussels at Vilvorde, where he continued to translate. Even in prison Tyndale was a hero of translation. We read from a letter to the marquis of Bergen, "And I ask to be allowed to have a lamp in the evening; it is indeed wearisome sitting alone in the dark. But most of all I beg and beseech your clemency to be urgent with the commissary, that he will kindly permit me to have the Hebrew bible, Hebrew grammar, and Hebrew dictionary, that I may pass the time in that study." On October 6, 1536, William Tyndale was taken to the stake, strangled by the hangman, and burned. His last words were, "Lord, open the King of England's eyes."

TRANSLATION REGISTERS

The grace of Tyndale's word lay in his chosen way, which I place midway in translation registers.[2] On one side of the register is a straightforward transfer of information to the reader, student, and scholar in need of a denotative crib to read scripture in Hebrew or Greek. On the other side is free re-creation or imitation, such as John Dominic Crossan's adroit transformations of Yeshua's sayings into minimalist poems. And the middle ground, which is Tyndale's, is autonomous restatement.

Interlinear Greek Bibles (Greek text with English between lines under each word or phrase) provide accurate word-for-word information, without syntax, with which the instructed reader can decipher the Greek scripture. The interlinear page usually contains a parallel column translation, with King James or a standard modern version, to help the reader return to the Greek. It is the Rosetta Stone of translations.

In the mid-range of the spectrum, the translation stands solitary on the page, without the Greek, as an autonomous text to be read in English as scripture. I should say at the outset that the translation should express, not indulge

---

2 In *Poetics of Translation: History, Theory, Practice* (New Haven: Yale University Press, 1993), I suggest a division of three registers: interlinear or Benjamin's word-by-word; Horace's and Cicero's sense-by-sense middle ground; and Dryden's imitation. In a derogatory way, the middle ground is often eliminated, and the work is accused of either unenlightened literalism or infidel license. Actually, the middle ground is very wide, as it should be, and includes both "the chaste, close, responsible version, in which the original author is always visible and the source culture is often allowed to retain an imposing flavor in the target language, and, in opposition, a free transference, in which the translator is most visible, where the work seems to be native and at home in the target language, not a naturalized immigrant, but, as the Spanish mystic Fray Luis de León posited, 'as if born and natural in the language'" (*Poesías*, Vega 15) (*Poetics*, 28).

in, "the heresy of explanation," as Robert Alter states in his introduction to *Genesis* (1996). Insofar as the translation does explain, it lacks autonomy to be read as an expressive text and returns in essential function to the interlinear level, that is, it becomes a useful aid, for student and teacher, to read and study the original Greek text. A self-contained literary version needs no self-explanation. Explanation and interpretation go into commentary wherever that is placed—on the page, at the back, or in another volume—but not within the translation itself. The Jesus Seminar translation of the gospels, worthy but heavy in explanation and conceptualization of image and metaphor, uses key words to clarify rather than to express, and operates, unintentionally, very much like an interlinear version, that is, as a bridge back to study and interpretation of the Greek. The frequent *e basileia ton ouranon* (ἡ βασιλεία τῶν οὐρανῶν), "the kingdom of the skies" (or traditionally "kingdom of heaven") is rendered as "God's imperial rule." The image and metaphor are lost to abstraction and explanation. Neither God, empire, or rule is in the Greek. That is interpretation.

At the other end of the register are those who freely re-create literary texts, as Robert Lowell cunningly and brilliantly did in his imitations. The imitator enters into an artistic partnership with the earlier writer. Much of our best literature is imitation—from hunks of Chaucer, Crashaw, and Racine to Yeats, Pound, and Lowell. Some declare their imitations openly as Racine, Pound, and Lowell did, and Chaucer, Crashaw, and Yeats did not seem to. Lowell entitled his collected translations *Imitations,* but Richard Crashaw's well-known poem on Saint Teresa de Avila, "A Song," with its key line, "I dy even in desire of death," is actually a rewording of Teresa's best-known poem, "Vivo sin vivir en mí." Similarly, William Yeats's "When you are Old" is an imitation of Pierre de Ronsard's most famous sonnet, "Quand vous serez bien vieille."

So here are two extremes that can be satisfied happily: a gloss for the reader who wants help in reading the source text, and imitation for the writer who wants to collaborate with, adapt, or rewrite a precursor's work as Dryden did with Shakespeare's *Anthony and Cleopatra* or Anouilh with Euripides' *Antigone.* As for the free approach, it is perfectly fine if the reader knows what it is. But, like the informational gloss, a free imitation should not pass for a close literary translation. It has another creative purpose. Recent free translations of *Gilgamish* by David Ferry and of Dante by Robert Pinsky are magnificent, and there is no subterfuge of method. There is a sharing of authorship that has resulted in versions superior to predecessors, close or free, and these works will endure.

There is also a middle ground between gloss and imitation, whose purpose is to hear the source author more clearly than the translator author. To say what this way is, I offer a brief visual parable rather than the wearily abstract terminology in translation studies (of which I am an offending user). When Robert Fitzgerald decided to translate the Odyssey, he went to see Ezra Pound at Saint Elizabeth's Hospital where the poet was incarcerated. He asked Pound how he should do it. Pound replied, "Let Homer say everything he wanted to say" (Edwin Honig, *The Poet's Other Voice*, 113). This was not Pound's normal practice. He himself took tremendous freedoms, imitated, and intimately collaborated with or overcame the author in his best translations from Anglo-Saxon and Chinese—and they may be his own best poems. But Pound gave Fitzgerald generously right advice. Fitzgerald followed it and produced—because he was a great poet in the act of translations—the major literary version of his era. Alter, with equal art, did the same in rendering Genesis and David in 1 Kings and 2 Kings.

This is the difficult middle way.

In looking for a right and good voice for the New Covenant, I read and thought but did not experiment. After a certain period it was there, and I was grateful it was clear. I wished to let the Greek talk, not me, and behind the Greek voice a restoration of the Semitic biblical names to temper the lexical anti-Semitism where its source seems to be the eager accretions of later redactors. In short, I believe I have found a plain and close voice—as distinct from gloss, interpretation, or a free authorial collaboration. The great discovery for me was the invisible poet hitherto hidden in unlineated Greek prose.

The closeness, the plainness, and the poetic is just what Fitzgerald and Alter have done in making the literal literary. I quickly add that those who hear "literal" and think "literalist thug" or "academic clunk" are usually right. "Literal" is usually a dismissive word and most often describes the laziest, worst, and least imaginative type of mechanical "correct" translation, with minimal reaches of valence and voice. By "literal," I mean a deep respect for all aspects of the source text; and, to make a distinction in definition, I say "literal," not "literalist," the one being as different from the other as "sentiment" from "sentimental." So the literal should be literary (not the literary's antagonist) and be as literary as any version on the way to pure imitation. To be close to the word and its full connotations need imply no lessening of tonality or song or semantic richness.

Gerald Hammond, in his superb essay on English translations of the Bible, praises the Authorized over more interpretive modern versions, which by their very interpretations not only lose in accuracy and literature but limit ambiguity by making choices for us. He writes, "The Renaissance translators were still close to a Protestant Reformation which stressed the primacy of the Bible's literal sense, as opposed to the various allegorical readings which the Catholic

Church had foisted upon it. Stressing the literal sense very often involves treating the story with as much care as any writer of narrative should do" (in Alter and Kermode's *Literary Guide to the Bible*, 664).

The translator in service of the source author becomes more invisible as the art intensifies, permitting the reader to *see* Homer or Dante or the Bible and, as Pound suggested, to hear them have *their* say. By contrast, in the inevitable collaboration between author and translator, as we move from re-creation to imitation, the earlier author tends to disappear, overcome by the voice of the translating author.

It is hard to hold that middle ground, to be both literal and literary. The literal tends to move one toward information transfer, the literary toward imitation. But these difficulties of balance also liberate. With the imperative to preserve fidelity to both raw content and artistic form, the translator is saved from first-glance easy solutions. To overcome the obstacles, one must leap up or track through the mind to come upon many possibilities until the right, or almost right, one surprisingly appears. Is such translation truly possible? Of course not, in an absolute sense, since *a* is not *b*. But the fact of impossibility makes the translation richer and more desirable, and differences in languages are a plus to all sides. It is good to wrestle with the words, as Jacob wrestled with God until daybreak, for the child of that struggle will come up intact, imperfect, and handsome.

Finally, I restate my enthusiasm for the at-last excellent versions of Genesis and Kings that have recently appeared, and my debt to the beloved Richmond Lattimore of the Greek classics, whose last work was the New Covenant. To fulfill the required words about translation practice, it should be enough to ignore what has been done and affirm one's own ways and wait—while acknowledging the debt to others. I have saved particular praise for the older versions, done in dangerous times when a life could be lost to the axe or stake. The King James and especially the Tyndale conversion remain the joy of the literal become literary. I would wish, just wish, the speech and song here to be so plain and lucid for Tyndale's "ploughboy in the fields."

KING JAMES VERSION

The model for high and good translation of the New Covenant remains the King James Authorized Version of 1611. Strictly speaking, the King James is, as its title states, "a version" rather than a translation, since about eighty percent of its New Covenant comes directly, with minimal change in letter or punctuation, from the William Tyndale translation, which appeared between 1525 and 1536. In rendering about half the Hebrew Bible directly from the

Hebrew and the complete New Covenant from the Greek, Tyndale produced a lucid version, beautiful in its cadences, plain in its lexicon, favoring the Anglo-Saxon over the Latin word. Erasmas saw in Tyndale "the evangelist of the poor." However, the near century that separates Tyndale from the Authorized, a century of rapid change in the language, also distances Tyndale that much more from contemporary spelling. Consequently, without modernization, the Authorized remains the great Bible of the past and present that can still be read with perfect linguistic ease. Principally for reason of access, the King James is the most attractive version in English. It has, as Gerald Hammond sees, "the kind of transparency which makes it possible for the reader to see the original clearly" (in Alter and Kermode's *Literary Guide to the Bible,* 664).

The "forty and seven scholars who devised the Book of the World" knew the art of translation. And it was in their famous preface (omitted, alas, in almost all editions) that Miles Smith said his unforgettable, "Translation it is that openeth the window, to let in the light." The Authorized let in the light with bright focus and minimum distortion. In comparing nineteenth-century and contemporary versions of the New Covenant, I've noted how the King James, with all its recognized magnificence of word, is plainer, less convoluted than any contemporary version, closer to the Greek text, and more accurate (despite the frequent slamming the KJV takes for deficient Greek texts and errors). Its authors were genial in deciphering complexity in the Greek and rendering straightforward English prose. Its strength and emotional impact lie not only in the by-now-sacred majesty of memorable phrasing but in its clear and comprehensible speech. No serious writer in English can afford to ignore its speech, and since its publication few major writers have not been strongly affected by it.

The downside of the King James is heard often enough. It is true that recent translations have earlier and more reliable texts than did the king-appointed translators of the seventeenth-century Bible. However, since the present, "more reliable" texts are at best questionable, the common criticism should be softened. It is also true that the King James abounds in archaisms and holds some problems of uncertain meaning for the modern reader; the New King James Bible, which appeared in 1979, responded to those attested frailties, and it modernized spelling, corrected mistakes as it saw them, and moderated gender bias. I confess that I prefer the unmodernized version, as I would an unmodernized Shakespeare, for the Authorized is close enough to be perfectly readable. If one wants to read a modern-spelling version of a text that is endlessly beautiful but not perfectly readable in the old spelling because of the extensive spelling changes in the late sixteenth century, then the David Daniell edition of William Tyndale is fully satisfying and still "old" enough in spelling and speech to make it of the earlier age. There is not a stilted or churchy phrase in Tyndale's everyday words, no obtrusive inversions. Tyndale's English is as plain and compelling as Mark's ordinary Greek.

Having said all these good things about Tyndale and the original Authorized, why a new translation? First, I should say that praise for the Authorized, as praise for Chapman's Homer, does not lessen the need, since we are dealing with translation, not an original Shakespearean play, whose difficulties and obscurities we gladly accept rather than modernize. The Greek and Roman classics, despite the Chapman, Dryden, Pope, and Shelley versions, have been given life today through the dignity and beauty of modern English in translations by Richmond Lattimore, Robert Fitzgerald, and Robert Fagles. They have given readership to the classics. By comparison, the Bible has fared poorly. I have mentioned the exceptions—Lattimore's *Four Gospels* and Alter's *Genesis*—which I am certain mark the beginning of good things.

My reasons for the translation are literary and philosophical. I want to let the Greek speak, that is, to be close and literal, but make the literal literary. I've also reasoned that the poetry of the New Covenant, principally of Yeshua and Yohanan of Patmos and Efesos, should breathe good light. As noted, I have, when possible, restored proper names to their Hebrew or Aramaic original forms, which will also help clarify the identity of the people. I favor both the rhetoric of the ordinary and the magic of the simple line, whether in straightforward Mark or in the poetry of soaring Apocalypse, the epic poem of the New Covenant.

ANTI-JUDAISM
IN THE NEW COVENANT

NEW LIGHT OF THE GOSPELS

In considering Jews as the people of the New Covenant—those who received and those who did not receive Yeshua as the messiah—George W. E. Nickelsburg in "Jews and Christians in the First Century: The Struggle Over Identity" (in *Neotestamentica* 27[2], 1993), states categorically:

> That the first "Christians" were Jewish followers of Jesus of Nazareth is indisputable. At the very least, Paul attests this in 1 Cor. 15:5–7. Thus, while it may seem tautological, it is worth emphasizing that Christianity begins among *Jews* who are *distinguished from other Jews* by virtue of their belief in the special status or role(s) of Jesus of Nazareth. Thus, from the beginning certain Jews (i.e., Christian Jews) isolated a particular factor as crucial to their self-identity as Jews. (367)

The aim of this translation of the last book of the Bible should provide open reading for Jews, Christians, and all peoples and faiths or nonfaiths, without exclusion, without worry whether one is of the elect or the eternally damned. Jews should be able to read this book of marvels, of their authorship, about themselves, about some Jews who believe they have found the Jewish messiah, whose offspring become known as messianics or Christians. It is imperative to remember that it is not the gentiles (non-Jews) but a body of Jews who nourish and first proclaim Yeshua to be their messiah. Near the end of the first century, these *messianic* Jews are called *Christians*, which is "messianic" in Greek translation. The messianic Jews have a different name for themselves in Greek, *Christians;* hence the popular confusion by way of names of first separating Jew from Christian, of separating Yeshua's family, followers, and ultimately Yeshua himself from his people and his faith. Yeshua was a rabbi of the synagogue, not a priest of the church. This translation—having made Yeshua's Judaism obvious through its restoration of Jewish names and its annotation and afterword—should encourage Jews to read the New Covenant without terror, without fear for their very lives and souls. If that degree of enlightenment is accomplished, apart from literary aspirations, this version will be a happy one.

One cannot alter scripture to eliminate angry slurs, nor erase a resultant history of good-news gospels bringing bad news to Jews. The gospels have been the significant factor during dark centuries of dismal exclusion of the Jew from ordinary society. However, once the gospels are absolutely and clearly understood as a book by Jews arguing among themselves about authority and dominion, we have a new book, with new light, and that light invites us to read one of the essential wonders of spirit and art. In this sense, the Jews should be as deeply concerned readers of the Greek Covenant as they are of the Hebrew Bible, for, however it is presented, it is their history, too, of the last Jewish prophet and of their people—not of Europeans, Australians, or Chinese—and it is a history they share with later Christians and the world. Christians in turn should be able to recognize their origin, to read the New Covenant as a book about a Jewish messiah, to share the book with Jews and the world, and read it *without* the grave weight of Christian shame and guilt for the gospels' condemnations and polemical exclusions.

In regard to the New Covenant as a tract against Jews, Krister Stendahl, a Christian scholar, speaks of Christian complicity in making the New Testament the first instrument of anti-Semitism. He speaks of the burden that Christianity carries for its record of misuse of its developing majority status with regard to the Jewish minority:

> But the Christians burdened by the horrendous history of anti-Semitism have urgent reasons to recognize how the rhetoric of a fledgling and beleaguered minority turned into the aiding and abetting of lethal hatred when endowed with the power of being in the majority. Anti-Semitism could be branded the most persistent heresy of Christian theology and practice. ("Anti-Semitism," 34)[3]

Anti-Semitism begins its decisive and horrendous world history in the New Covenant. Yet had anyone attempted to accuse Yeshua or Paul of not being a Jew, he would have been scandalized.[4] And, by extension, Jeremiah, Isaiah, and Amos were no less harsh in their internal denunciations of Jews; yet theirs is

---

[3] "Anti-Semitism" in *The Oxford Companion to the Bible,* ed. Bruce M. Metzger and Michael D. Coogan (New York: Oxford University Press, 1993).

[4] Through the Letters, Paul speaks of himself as a Jew certain that the Jewish messiah has come. In Galatians 2.14–15, he rebukes Peter—whom he addresses as Cephas, Greek for Kefa—for not acting like a Jew, "I said to Cephas before them all [at Antioch], 'If you, though a Jew, live like a Gentile and not like a Jew, how can you compel the Gentiles to live like Jews? We ourselves are Jews by birth and not Gentile sinners.'"

not received as anti-Judaism but self-criticism for purposes of higher virtue. How does such criticism differ in the New Covenant?

The circumstance that permits a polemic against the Jew in the Covenant is the misrepresentation of the historical period and the identity of the contending parties. Internal squabbles between Jewish sects during the life of Yeshua are presented in the gospels as shivering conflicts between foreign forces, of gentile Christians without Jewish identity against Jews. How did such flagrant distortions enter the gospels? Although the gospels' narrations read as the history of the life and death of Yeshua, they are not historical documents of key days in Jerusalem but late compositions imposing the political interest and theological professions of a later period on an earlier one. They invent actions and conversations. They devise new personages—such as the figure of Judas, meaning the Jew—in a rehashed version of the traditional betrayer tale; and they shape the character of known personages, such as the benevolent Pilate and his soldiers, who unwillingly crucify yet also love and believe in the divinity of their victim. The gospel narration, without annotation to contextualize these compositions, cannot be easy reading for a Jew. Who wishes to see oneself portrayed as deeply evil, demonic, and destined for eternal condemnation?

As noted, we possess no undisputed fact about the historical Yeshua other than his death by Roman crucifixion. But we know that during his lifetime he had proponents, for within a hundred years of his death his descendants developed a new form of messianic Judaism. During Yeshua's lifetime, he was a local rabbi of Galilee and Judea with a following. By anachronistic retelling, the events of his life became a black-and-white conflict between divine and demonic forces.

The horrifying denunciations reflect the fury of a new sect denouncing its parent, inflamed by Rome, textual corruption, and patristic exegesis. The holy books seem to justify the bleak history of Christian oppression and the slaying of Jews for being Jews. So it is perfectly understandable why the gospels, though Jewish books, have become a *noli me tangere*—don't-touch-me—terrain for Jewish readers. As a result, even today, apart from scholars who in the last decades have turned importantly to the New Covenant, Jews at all levels of education instinctively hold the New Covenant at bay as a dread document, not to be read, whose subtext signifies death to the Jews.

The time is long overdue for translations and editions of the New Covenant in English that permit the reader to see beyond the demonization of those outside the later Christian fold. The special attack on Jews must be shown to be implausible, since Yeshua and those he attends are Jews. With that knowledge, his love for the hurt, the hopeless, and those harrowed by poverty of body and thought might prevail. The gospels are unequaled works of art and spirit, extraordinary achievements that should not be rejected because of their sectarian blemishes. The itinerant Yeshua, wise in the tradition of mythical Gautama Siddhartha, Laozi, and all the great oral teachers on the continent of Asia, where Yeshua lived and died, deserves more. Only with joy should the covenant be received, and by everybody. It contains the poetic speech of the last charismatic Jewish prophet. For those who receive him as the messiah, he gave word of life here, of pain here, and of salvation. For those without belief in his messiahship, he remains, like Socrates or the Buddha, an articulate wisdom figure whose word is indispensable to the life of the spirit.

ON THE GOSPELS' AUTHORSHIP,
TEXTS, AND ELUSIVE
SEMITIC SOURCES

THE GOSPELS' UNKNOWN SOURCES

The puzzle of the gospels' unknown sources remains the most disturbing enigma of the Greek scriptures. Much imaginative scholarship has gone into supposing oral or graphic records to fill in the nearly half century between Yeshua's death and the earliest gospels. The lonely absence of any record remains.[5] The question of unknown sources also beset the Hebrew Bible with respect to the canonical Apocrypha. By Old Testament criteria, the gospels are the canonical Apocrypha of the New Covenant. As in the instance of the canonical Apocrypha of the Hebrew Bible, we also lack an original Hebrew or Aramaic text to support them. Is it not a wonder that the Church Fathers were not as concerned with the absence of a source text for the canonical gospels as they were with Hebrew Bible Apocrypha? The decision by Jerome (347–419/420), the great translator of the Hebrew and Greek Bibles into Latin, to give apocryphal status to the Apocrypha (and to name the Apocrypha) was based on the absence of a Hebrew original, a measure he discarded with respect to the gospels. But that secondary status of the Apocrypha was such that the Jews, Catholics, and Greek and Russian Orthodox churches considered them deuterocanonical, and the Reformation Protestants excluded them altogether from the canon. Among those books in the Septuagint[6] accepted as

---

[5] If the Gospel of Thomas indeed predates the canonical gospels, which is unlikely, it would not shed any light on the narrative, since Thomas is wisdom sayings and no story. Q is the main linguistic reconstruction, which is discussed on p. 449.

[6] The Septuagint is commonly dated as a third-century B.C.E. translation, a notion still shared by the editors of the Tanak Bible published in English in 1985 by the Jewish Publication Society, and standard fare in recent Bible dictionaries and the latest *American Heritage Dictionary,* all of which repeat information contained in the Alexandrian *Letter of Aristeas.* Aristeas's *Letter* describes the translation of the Hebrew Bible by seventy-two scholars representing the twelve tribes of Israel, in seventy-two days, for the Jews of Greek-speaking Alexandria who could no longer read Hebrew. The work is the earliest document on the theory and practice of literary translation. In his edition of the *Letter of Aristeas,* 1951, the late Moses Hadas shows that Aristeas's letter as well as the completed Septuagint (which he states took between one hundred and one hundred and fifty years, rather than the legendary seventy-two days, to complete) could itself not have been written earlier than the second century B.C.E. Septuagint, meaning seventy in Latin, refers to the number of scholars, who were legendarily seventy-two. The frequent quotations from the Hebrew Bible in the New

canonical apocryphal writings by the Jews are Tobit, Judith, The Wisdom of Solomon, and Ecclesiasticus; and accepted by the Roman Catholics are First and Second Books of Maccabees, Susanna, and extensive portions of the Book of Esther.

The main difference between the apocryphal status of the gospels and the canonical Apocrypha is that, while we still have no earlier documents to authenticate or trace the tradition of the gospels, since the discovery of the Dead Sea Scrolls[7] we now have fragments in Hebrew and Aramaic for some of the Greek Septuagint Apocrypha. Such original source texts in Hebrew had been the indispensable measure for inclusion in the Bible as fully canonical scripture. Since the translation from the rest of the Hebrew Bible into the Septuagint Bible is remarkably accurate, it is reasonable to believe that the translation from the lost Hebrew scriptures into what we call the Apocrypha may be similarly accurate. The Dead Sea Scroll fragments in Hebrew of the Apocrypha, including Tobit, confirm the closeness of the translation. Indeed, Robert Alter notes in his translation of Genesis (*Genesis: Translation and Commentary*, 1996) that he has looked to the Septuagint for alternate meanings of the Hebrew, for the second-century B.C.E. Septuagint translation is in fact older than the Hebrew Bible texts in the form we know them, as established by the Masoretic scholars centuries later into the Common Era.

As for a similar fidelity in transmitting "the lost gospel," that is, the unknown Semitic sources, written or oral, into the gospels, the parallel breaks down. There are no original fragments in Hebrew or Aramaic and little hope that there will be any found. While as the Essenes came to life through the Dead Sea Scrolls and the Apocrypha found fragmentary Hebrew and Aramaic originals, no Semitic scriptures have been found as a source for the gospels.

Covenant are not direct translations from the Torah but come largely from its Greek Septuagint translation.

[7] The Dead Sea Scrolls or Qumran Literature, containing ten scrolls and thousands of fragments, were found in 1947 in caves near Qumran on the northwest shore of the Dead Sea. The Qumran Scrolls include fragments of the Apocrypha, and we now have resolved the question of a Semitic language origin for Septuagint Apocrypha. There are one Hebrew and four Aramaic manuscripts of the book of Tobit, fragmentary of course. Tobit was officially published in Joseph Fitzmyer, *Discoveries in the Judaean Desert* 19 (Oxford: Clarendon Press, 1995), 1–76. And newer translation is available in the editions of the Scroll translations by Florentino García Martínez, ed., *The Dead Sea Scrolls Translated* (New Orleans: E. J. Brill/Grand Rapids, MI: W. B. Eerdmans, 1996) and Geza Vermes, *The Complete Dead Sea Scrolls in English* (London: Allen Lane/Penguin, 1997), 559–65. Since we now have evidence of a Hebrew original, it may be time to move Tobit from deuterocanonical to canonical status in the churches where it resides among the Apocrypha and to be admitted into the Protestant Bibles. All this is not crucial—Tobit has not even entered Writings (Kethuvim), the appropriate place in the Hebrew Bible. Yet clearly the Dead Sea Scrolls have again raised those ancient questions of canonicity that once occupied religious councils.

Before the Greek scriptures is the void. Since there is not a written phrase or verse or record of an overheard word, the gospels, as they exist in Greek, are what we have to read and work with. It is unknown how they moved from Semitic sources into Greek, from conversations carried on largely in Aramaic, except for the words of Pilate, who was speaking Latin. It is not likely that Pilate ever addressed Yeshua in Latin, and whether or not Yeshua had Latin to respond to him is unknown. It is similarly unlikely that Pilate and Yeshua spoke to each other in Greek. If they spoke, it was through interpreters. And because of language differences, it is also improbable that they exchanged those austere life-and-death questions and retorts heard dramatically in the gospels. What fidelity of phrase was there when the Latin of Pilate and the Aramaic of Yeshua moved into the Greek of the gospels? No scholar has been able to answer these critical questions.

As they stand today, the subject of the Greek scriptures is the history of early first-century Jews. However, the writings send both early Jewish and later Christian signals, reflecting a perception of a century or two after the events. It is inconceivable that these accounts about Yeshua the Messiah were not deeply adjusted or invented in the course of their establishment in Greek by the emerging churches, which were not anxious to own up to Rome's execution of a seditious rabbi.[8] As for specific additions to the gospels, there are the well-known "orphan endings" appended to Mark. The "longer ending to Mark" adds a resurrection scene. Its initial absence in Mark raises questions as to what was the model for the resurrection accounts in the later gospels. The resurrection scene, like the entire gospel narration, leads back to its formation during the gap after Yeshua's death around 30 B.C.E. and the penning of the first gospel by Mark at least four decades after the crucifixion.[9] Once the evangelist Mark—or rather the unknown figure who in the second century was designated as Mark—wrote the earliest gospel, there began the amorphous period of the shaping of the gospels, the redactions, the orphan contributions, and the Christianizing of Jewish events into the narrations that exist today. This writing and shaping of the gospels occurred during the later part of the first century and well into the second. By the third century, despite small variations indicated in brackets in the competing texts of today, the gospels found their final form.

---

[8] Raymond E. Brown, in *An Introduction to the New Testament* (New York: Doubleday, 1997), notes in his foreword: "Most of the main NT figures and possibly all the writers were Jews, and NT affirmations have had a major role (often devastating) in relations between Jews and Christians" (xi).

[9] Paul, who like the evangelists, did not personally know Yeshua, wrote and died during the period before the gospels were formulated, but his work was apparently not known, or if known, not accounted for, in the gospels and so in no way serves as a source or bridge to the gospels.

As for that strangely silent gap of about forty years between the crucifixion and the first gospel, were we to come upon in some cave or burial site the equivalent of the Dead Sea Scrolls of the Essenes or the Nag Hammadi Library of the Gnostics (gifts of the mid-1940s), imagine the monumental news of the discovery of an ur-gospel or letters composed in Hebrew or Aramaic, shortly after Yeshua's death, recording the circumstances of Yeshua's life and death and his messianic movement. Such information would have unimaginable consequences in regard to our understanding of the early formation of Christian Judaism, which by the end of the second century, as accounted in Acts and in the Letters, had evolved into Christianity. Its resemblance to or departure from the extant gospels would test and perhaps reshape existing Christian doctrine and faith.

AUTHORSHIP

The names of the evangelists are, as Robert W. Funk and Roy W. Hoover observe in their introduction to *The Five Gospels* (New York: Macmillan, 1993), "guesses or perhaps the result of pious wishes." About a century after Yeshua's death, the names occur in the writing of the later Church Father Papias (ca. 130 C.E.), as reported by Eusebius (d. 325), who suggested the names Matthew and Mark. Matthew, who introduces himself in Matthew 9.9 as the tax collector, is identified in Mark 2.14 as Levi. As for Luke, Funk and Hoover say, "Like the other attributions, this one, too, is fanciful." And John (ca. 180 C.E.) "was produced by a 'school' of disciples, probably in Syria."[10] They sum up: "All the gospels originally circulated anonymously. Authoritative names were later assigned to them by unknown figures in the early church" (20). They affirm what Emily Dickinson perceived in the uncertainty of the blurry faces behind the books in her lines: "The Bible is an antique Volume—/ Written by Faded Men." The additional cognomens of Matthew the lion, Mark the ox,

---

[10] The formation of the Book of John is the most intriguing and, because of its separate sources from the Synoptics, has given rise among scholars to much speculation. Frank Kermode tells us: "Earlier in the present century there were those who strongly believed John to have been related to a particular form of gnosticism, the Mandean. This belief was abandoned after the discovery of the Dead Sea Scrolls, which were the work of Jewish writers before the time of John, and which anticipated some of his characteristic imagery and habits of thought. John is now seen to derive from a tradition that is fundamentally Jewish, however influenced by Hellenistic ideas. Such considerations and others, such as the accuracy of his Palestinian topography, have induced most scholars to reject the view that John's was a late theological reworking of the material, lacking direct contact with the original tradition. It is now commonly thought that the Fourth has sources as old as, though largely independent of, those available to the Synoptics" (Robert Alter and Frank Kermode, eds., *The Literary Guide to the Bible* [Cambridge, MA: Harvard University Press, 1967], 43).

Luke the man, and John the eagle derive fancifully from the four living creations in Revelation 4.7.

The tradition of false attribution relates to the pseudepigrapha, which includes many intertestamental scriptures or noncanonical apocrypha assembled largely in the centuries between the closing of the Hebrew Bible and the canonization of the New Covenant.[11] Most of the traditional names given the books of the Hebrew Bible—the Psalms of David, Solomon's Song of Songs, the three Isaiahs—also fall into the category of the pseudepigraphical.

The earliest and most reliable texts with regard to both author and the validity of the Greek are Paul's letters, which were written as letters, not scripture, but whose inclusion in the canon made them scripture. By and large they do not have the problems of sources and later tampering by inventive hands—by Church Fathers, scribes, and evangelists—that make the gospels a subject of intense debate. However, Paul's Pastoral letters to Titus and to Timothy are not considered authentic, and the authorship of Ephesians, Colossians, and Thessalonians 1 and 2 is in question. As a historical figure, a Jew born in the Hellenistic city of Tarsus, Paul as a person, name, and author is the least controversial of any figure associated with books of the New Covenant. And his actuality as a person, in the seven letters categorically attributed to him, bestows a historic liveliness to what he wrote. In the conceptual, not the manuscript, sense, he was the great translator. He transposed biblical law into Christian practice; he seems to have transformed the Jewish hope for the messiah into a Christian accomplishment. In the same way that he converted Shaul into Paul, in the diaspora synagogues of the Mediterranean and the Near East, Paul translated Judaism into what after his life became a strong foundation for Christianity.

There are problems, however, with this traditional interpretation of Paul's role in giving us the earliest scripture. First, it must be said that Paul knew Yeshua only "after the flesh," and so wrote from accounts and faith. However, Burton Mack points out in great detail in *Who Wrote the New Testament?: The*

---

[11] The compendium of pseudepigrapha related to the Hebrew Bible (though most of it is in Greek and other languages) is collected in *The Old Testament Pseudepigrapha*, ed. James H. Charlesworth. *The Other Bible*, ed. Willis Barnstone, contains pseudepigrapha as well as noncanonical apocrypha of Torah, New Covenant, gnostic scriptures, The Dead Sea Scrolls, and other intertestamental writings. There is an overlapping in this terminology, pseudepigrapha meaning "works of false attribution and noncanonical apocrypha." I use "intertestamental" when referring to works not necessarily written between the last books of the Hebrew Bible and the conjectured dates of the Greek scriptures, but in the wider sense of the gap of centuries (first B.C.E. to fifth C.E.) between the canonization of the Hebrew Bible and that of the Greek scriptures. During that period many works were written, ascribed to everyone from Moses to the evangelists, hence pseudepigraphical, with aspirations to find their way back into the Hebrew Bible or into the not-yet-canonized New Covenant.

Making of the Christian Myth (San Francisco: HarperSan Francisco, 1995) how the letters do not reflect the scene of those early followers of Yeshua:

> There are two problems with this view [that of Paul's perception of Christianity]. Paul's conception of Christianity is not evident among the many texts from the early Jesus movements. The other is that Paul's gospel was not comprehensible and persuasive for most people of his time, including many other Christians, as we shall see. For historians this means that the traditional picture of Christian origins derived from Paul's letters is suspect and needs to be revised. Instead of reading the material from the Jesus movements through the eyes of Paul, we need to read Paul as a remarkable movement in the history of the Jesus movement. (99)

To whatever extent Paul reflects the actual moment or determines the future Yeshua movement (which is more probable), the existence of his letters, despite early controversy about authenticity, is the most historical frame we have in the writings.

As for the authorship of the gospels, the complexity of the problem and absence of documentary evidence make description of their emergence from the shade difficult. However, we do have factual knowledge of their final emergence, selection, and late canonization. In that final form, the scriptures, consisting of the gospels, letters, apostolic writings and rewritings, represent a small number from a mass of texts that were floating around the ancient world—those rejected pseudepigrapha—including many extant apocalypses, gospels, infancy gospels, psalm books, wisdom poetry, and acts. As mentioned above, by the fourth century the ground was established for the Christian selection and canonization of both the New Covenant and the "Christian" Hebrew Bible (based on the Septuagint). Between 325 and 330 C.E., Constantine ordered Eusebius to make a selection of writings that he copied and included in a Christian book of holy scriptures. These are listed in his *Ecclesiastical History* 3, 25. Jerome's translations of the scriptures into Latin were done in 382 C.E. These translation and editorial events, along with Augustine's arguments for a more inclusive selection from the Hebrew Bible, made way for the Hebrew Bible and Christian scriptures as we have them today in the Latin West.

SELECTION AND CANONIZATION OF SCRIPTURES

With regard to method and purpose, here are some technical thoughts on the gospels, their selection, canonization, and the names of the active cast in them.

In the Western church, the New Covenant was formally canonized in Rome at the beginning of the fifth century. Athanasios[12] was the first to use the word "canon" (from the Greek κανών, kanon, a measuring rod, and, in second-century koine, rule of truth), and his canon, listing the present books of the Greek scriptures, was first proposed in his "Thirty-ninth Easter Letter," written in 369 C.E. It was probably approved at the Synod of Rome in 382, and confirmed by papal declaration in 405. Yeshua's citing of passages from the Torah might have been directly from the Hebrew Bible, not as we have it in the gospels, where the authors and redactors went to the well-known second-century B.C.E. Septuagint translation of the Jewish Bible into Greek.

DETAILS ABOUT THE TEXTS OF THE GOSPELS

The New Covenant, as we have it, is in Greek, containing among its twenty-seven books four gospels, which, in probable order of their composition, are Mark, Matthew, Luke, and John (Markos, Matai, Loukas, and Yohanan). There is an uneven consensus today that Mark precedes Matthew and that Mark used Q, the hypothetical sayings source, whose recent reconstruction by the members of The Jesus Seminar and others was accomplished by collating coincidences of language in Yeshua's sayings. Yet some prominent scholars still give precedence to Matthew and/or question that there was a Q.[13]

Q is from the German word *Quelle*, meaning "source." Our speculations about Q source texts for the New Covenant go back at least one hundred fifty years. In the twentieth century, Rudolf Bultmann[14] and B. H. Streeter[15] each published major studies on the two-source theory, which posits that Matthew

---

[12] Bishop (later saint) Athanasios (ca. 297–373) was a strong opponent of Arianism, Christianity's most powerful heresy, concerning the nature of Yeshua. It was widespread, diverse, among emperors and clergy, and lasted until around 560 when, under Pope Gregory I, it disappeared in Italy.

[13] In his "The Gospel according to the 'Jesus Seminar'" in *The Emergence of the Christian Religion* (Harrisburg, PA: Trinity Press International, 1997), Birger A. Pearson takes on, with meticulous fury, the notions of the Jesus Seminar with respect to their attempts to measure authenticity in the gospels. The Jesus Seminar, a group of hundreds of liberal American theologians, asserts that most of the gospels are spurious and restrict the authentic *historical* (as opposed to the *canonized*) Yeshua to Yeshua's sayings, which they estimate as less than 20 percent of scripture. The notion of voting and ascribing degrees of truth to passages is comparable to searching for historic events in Homer; the allusions to events are there, but the details of those allusions, which contain the great interest, are certainly the least historical. I prefer the approach of Paula Fredriksen in *Jesus of Nazareth, King of the Jews*, who begins with the premise that the single verifiable fact of Yeshua's life is that he was a Jew crucified around 30 C.E. and then speculates.

[14] Rudolf Bultmann, *The History of the Synoptic Tradition*, trans. John Marsh (New York: Harper & Row, 1966). Bultmann sought and ultimately opposed the notion of discovering "a historical Jesus," since it was impossible and theologically illegitimate, and worldly proof took dominion over faith.

[15] Burnett Hillman Streeter, *The Four Gospels: A Study of Origins* (London: Macmillan, 1930).

and Luke derived not only from the Markan account of the life of Yeshua, but also from a hypothetical Q text. With the 1945 discovery of the Coptic-gnostic Gospel of Thomas as one of the documents in the Nag Hammadi Library,[16] found buried near the ancient town of Chenoboskion in Upper Egypt, containing Yeshua's sayings, about 35 percent of which coincide with those sayings of the Synoptics (Mark, Matthew, Luke), there has been a major new impetus to pursue the Q hypothesis. A major book on Q and its actual reconstruction is John Kloppenborg's *The Formation of Q* (Philadelphia: Fortress Press, 1987). Burton L. Mack has carried the reconstruction further in his *The Lost Gospel: The Book of Q & Christian Origins* (San Francisco: HarperSan Francisco, 1993). Following the model of Kloppenborg in his *Q Parallels* (1987), Mack reconstructed an original text in a fresh translation. The Jesus Seminar translation of *The Complete Gospels: Annotated Scholars Version* (1992–1994) provides a two-column reconstruction (based on Luke and Matthew) of Q,which is less easy to read, but which provides helpful annotation. And since the Mack there is finally *The Critical Edition of Q*, under James M. Robinson, a new masterful 600-page work, with a 106-page introduction, including the Coptic for Thomas, and academic translations into English, German, and French.[17]

Since the late eighteenth century, there has been an attempt to apply historical approaches to the oral and script transmission of the gospels and to speculate on order, source, and veracity. These questions will be debated and are not likely be resolved unless there are major finds of earlier versions of the gospels that cast specific light on questions of New Covenant source and composition, or unanticipated related documents. In his introduction to the New Testament in *The Literary Guide to the Bible* (1987), Frank Kermode sums up the problems of order of composition and of Q: "Beginning in the 1830s the view gained ground that priority must be accorded to Mark, and it is probably still the majority opinion that Matthew and Luke used Mark, augmenting him from a collection of sayings (Q) and also from sources peculiar to themselves; there are many variants of this view. Recently, however, inconsistencies and improbabilities in the standard explanation have led to a revival by some of the old assumption that Matthew came first. Other scholars retain the Markan priority but dispense with Q" (377).

Whatever the order, these gospels are the only canonical ones that we acknowledge, and surprisingly we have them in Greek outfit rather than Ara-

---

[16] James M. Robinson, ed., *The Nag Hammadi Library* (San Francisco: Harper & Row, 1977).
[17] James M. Robinson, Paul Hoffman, and John S. Kloppenborg, eds., *The Critical Edition of Q* (Minneapolis: Fortress Press, 2000).

maic or late Hebrew. Traditionally there was more interest in restoring a hypothetical source of information, with little regard for its passage as translation
from its Semitic roots and Jewish thought. In the last decades, however, there
has been a sea change of interest in Yeshua as an Aramaic-speaking observant
Jew, whose words have been presented at one remove in Greek and, for those
in the West, at two removes, going from Aramaic to Greek and then on to the
second language of their translation (and frequently in past at three removes, if
they pass from Aramaic to Greek to Jerome's Latin and then into a West European language). In his *The Changing Faces of Jesus* (New York: Viking Compass, 2000), Geza Vermes attempts to restore "the vague contours of the real
Jesus, the charismatic Hasid" (286), and he comments on the language of
Yeshua and of his Aramaic-speaking followers, on the virtual absence of a
record of their speech, and affirms that the Greek New Covenant is a translation of a Jewish ideology acculturated by an alien pagan Graeco-Roman
world:

> The language of Jesus and his Galilean disciples was Aramaic, a Semitic lan-
> guage akin to Hebrew, then spoken by most Palestinian Jews. It was in Ara-
> maic that Jesus taught and argued with friends and foes. The linguistically
> authentic form of his teaching, with the exception of a dozen or so Aramaic
> words preserved in the Gospels, soon disappeared. If there ever existed a writ-
> ten Aramaic Gospel, it did not survive for long; we certainly no longer have it.
> At the same time, as a consequence of the success of the primitive church in
> the Greek-speaking Gentile (i.e., non-Jewish) world, the whole message
> transmitted by the apostles—the Gospels, the letters, and the rest—was
> recorded in Greek, which is the earliest form of the New Testament that we
> possess. But this Greek New Testament is a "translation" of the genuine
> thoughts and ideas of the Aramaic-thinking and -speaking Jesus and of his
> immediate disciples, a transplantation not just into a totally different language,
> but also a translation of the ideology of the communication and in his familiar
> Semitic tongue. (2–3)

The Greek texts we have are mirrors of lost shadows of Jewish wisdom and
thought, and of Aramaic speech and probably script. Although original Semitic texts are unlikely to materialize, above ground or below, one purpose of
this translation is, through restoration of Semitic names, to reflect more shadows of those disappeared figures and events.

With regard to the preserved Greek gospels and all the books of the covenant, as noted, this bundle of scripture officially entered the canon in Rome in
405 C.E. In Bruce M. Metzger's *The Text of the New Testament: Its Transmission,*

Corruption, and Restoration (New York: Oxford University Press, 3d enlarged edition, 1992), which deals authoritatively on the approximately five thousand manuscripts that contain all or part of the New Testament, there is abundant information about the survival, changes, emendations, and copying tactics, but absolutely no light on the essential mystery by which Yeshua's words and a history of his life and death migrated into this plethora of early Greek texts. In addition to these untraceable canonical gospels, there are seventeen gospels now included in *The Complete Gospels: Annotated Scholars Version,* edited by Robert J. Miller from 1992–1994, including the Gospel of Thomas, which exists in Coptic and fragmentarily in Syriac and Greek (the latter in portions that exist in the *Oxyrhynchus Papyri*). But we also do not know how or from what tongues the Gospel of Thomas was transmitted into Greek, though surely there was an Aramaic or Hebrew source, since only in those languages could one witness and record Yeshua's sayings. So what some scholars claim to be the most authentic of the gospels with regard to Yeshua's wisdom utterances, remains, like all the gospels, a mystery with regard to source.

The Gospel of Thomas, itself a discovery of enormous value—the so-called "Fifth Gospel"—suggests new possibilities as it casts doubt on some older systems of the formation of the gospels. Thomas has passages that parallel the synoptic gospels, and whether indeed it was assembled around 50–55 C.E., as has been asserted (though this early date is unlikely), or whether it simply represents a different line of preservation of Yeshua's sayings, it reveals an ancient, completely distinct Yeshua, who is also free of the problems of the narration of the canonical gospels, since it has none. It is uncertain which is the partial source of the other, the gospels or Thomas, or whether both draw on hypothetical Q. Yeshua in Thomas, like the Buddha and Laoze, lives by his speech rather than the myths that his person and sayings later incited. With only dialogue and no background events, Thomas reveals a Yeshua of metaphysical aphorisms, who breathes the spirit of the formal gnostic scriptures of the Nag Hammadi Library and of their dissident solitude.[18] As a gnostic version of early Christianity, found in Coptic translation from the Greek, these wisdom sayings early went into hiding (they were found buried in Egyptian soil in a leather pouch in Egypt) and did not publicly survive long enough to have gone through the altering of copying, redaction, scribal insertions, and changes which is the history of the canonical gospels. Nor did Thomas have a narration that was exposed to the Christianizing handiwork of later priestly redactors.

---

[18] There are other late sources for a tradition of Yeshua's sayings, especially in Coptic, Syriac, and Arabic, which may be found in Marvin Meyer's *The Unknown Sayings of Jesus* (San Francisco: Harper-San Francisco, 1998).

FAITH AND HISTORY

One may ask: Why is it necessary to verify the gospels by finding an earlier version, a source, an original, and why, without an apparent parentage, do the gospels stand in limbo as documents accepted on faith rather than confirmed by history? Why should the gospels need their lost historical sources? We do not ask for Homer's sources. We do not look askance because the Genesis flood story has almost identical mirrors in much earlier Mesopotamian writings. But Homer is literature and myth, and no longer a religion requiring "truth" and belief. And early Genesis is primeval myth of religion and stands self-sufficiently alone. For most readers, however, the gospels utter a historical statement. They tell the life of an actual wandering Mediterranean rabbi healer and exorcist in the Eastern Roman empire, who irked its local rulers enough to be condemned to suffer Roman political execution, for reasons that remain unclear. Those four biographies, the good news of a messiah, cannot escape into myth and literature. In a word, faith makes the documents self-validating; but history leaves them undocumented beyond themselves.

The events in the evangels concern Jews in the city of Jerusalem and the districts of Judea and Galilee. They are in Greek, a language native to Jews of the diaspora, especially in Alexandrian Egypt, Greece, and the former Greek empire in Asia Minor, but not native to the Jews of Israel, of Judea, Samaria, and Galilee. Consider John the Baptizer. Yeshua's precursor and model was not baptizing in Greek. Not only is the language of the gospels suspect, but the time of their composition raises questions. Since the gospels were composed probably between 70 and 95, none of their reputed evangelists witnessed Yeshua in his lifetime. The gospels did not rise from nothingness. How, then, did their authors come upon their account? As previously mentioned, we have hypotheses of origin and linguistic markers that go back to Hebrew phrases. The existence of the Secret Gospel of Mark, the Secret Book of John, the Gospel of Philip, and the Gospel of Thomas, among other extant noncanonical gospels, offers information on other ways that the speech of Yeshua has reached us. But no original Semitic document in the languages of Yeshua from under the sand or in a cave has come to light.

Scholars are looking—not archeologically but through existent texts or ones they wish to be existent.[19] Burton L. Mack tells a mystery story of a lost gospel

---

[19] The dry sands of Syria, Israel, and Egypt are likely areas for archeological search, since only in virtually waterless areas can papyrus survive, and even later parchment copies, a stronger medium, do not do well in damp climates. Although three major religions (as well as classical Western literature) are based on common interweaving scriptures, there is relatively little exploration. When there are discoveries, enormous political, scholarly, and religious problems materialize to delay or frustrate further exploration. Ancient documents do not carry the economic and political clout of oil and gas.

in *The Lost Gospel* (San Francisco: HarperSan Francisco, 1993), which is based on his composite of Yeshua's sayings from sundry sources. Mack makes the Yeshua community vividly real. He writes: "Jesus was much more like a Cynic-teacher than either a Christ-savior or a messiah with a program for the reformation of second-Temple Jewish society and religion" (245). Yet we scarcely know who the historical teacher was, or what tendencies he shared with the Cynics, the gnostics, the Essenes, the Pharisees, the healing and miracle-making Hasidim (the charismatic holy men), and the messianic tradition of Isaiah. The main documents, the gospels, are examined for clues, as the theogony of Homer is examined to understand Greece, war, and gods of antiquity. And, curiously, the waves of intense yet mutating theory that saturate literature, film, art, history, and anthropological studies are hardly perceptible in biblical studies, which are usually a strange mix of faith, tradition, and academic inquiry. Nevertheless, a common goal among imaginative thinkers is to look for a historical figure called Yeshua and bring him to life.

For reconstructing the life and times of Yeshua, we lack the documentary material of historians, but there is a story of an extraordinary man; there is a new early Jewish sect vying for dominion over other sects. Yeshua's followers were the sect who saw Yeshua as their teacher, leader, and messiah. In all religions, then and now, such conflict between sects is usual. However, one salient aspect of the historical enigma of the gospels is their view of Rome. One may ask how in the New Covenant the military leaders from Rome, Pontius Pilate and his centurion who executed Yeshua, are presented with generously phrased understanding of their difficult assignments. Indeed, they are ultimately seen as ruefully carrying out their role of deicide. The benign view of Yeshua's Roman crucifiers is balanced by the virulently condemnatory view of the Pharisees, who were strong opponents of the Roman occupation and their Hasmonean clerics. Since the gospels reflect a Roman and later church take on the crucifixion of Yeshua, the Romans are spared opprobrium, while opponents of Rome are defamed. Where this leaves Yeshua is the enigma. Since crucifixion was reserved strictly for political insurrection, Yeshua could not have been perceived by his executioners with sympathy, as the scriptures convey. At the same time, why exactly did they crucify him? As Paula Fredriksen points out (*Jesus of Nazareth*, 8–9), the level of insurrection must have been minor, since only Yeshua and none of his followers were killed. Had there been a seriously subversive revolutionary movement, such as the mass rallies in Galilee against Rome that preceded and followed Yeshua's death, there would have been crucifixions galore to accompany "the messiah's" execution.

For many years I have pondered how the gospels could be relentlessly an apology for Rome when its essence, regardless of presumed later tampering in copying and redacting by its editors, was established between the years 70, of Mark's gospel, to the final edition around 150, years of growth but of vast public persecution by Rome, from the catacombs of Rome to the cave chapels and communities in Cappadocia in central Anatolia. Since even despite a few second-century fragments (and these now considered wishfully dated), there is no extant copy in Greek of the gospels before the fourth century, I had to assume, *faute de mieux*, that the most furious Romanizing of the gospel texts occurred between the early decades of the fourth century when Constantine became the first Christian emperor of the Roman Empire, and Athanasios's canon in 367. I asked Professor David Trobisch, the distinguished German manuscript historian, about the anomaly of Christian loyalty to their persecutors. His response: "Think of the perfect parallel in Josephus." Here was the greatest of Jewish historians, I realized, who details the day-to-day marches of Roman armies and the concerns of their commander, Titus, as he heads to Rome. And Josephus takes the same line as the gospels, defending the action of the Roman armies that in 70 were to level the walls, raze the city, destroy the Temple, crucify many of its inhabitants, and exile Jews and Christian Jews alike in the greatest diaspora since the sixth-century B.C.E. Babylonian Captivity, which resulted in the destruction of the first Temple. "Why did Josephus placate the Romans?" His response: "Because he was a Jew, living in Rome in a fine villa, in pleasant captivity, and were he to have taken any other line opposing the emperor it would have been his end, exile or the sword."

To survive and grow under the Roman Empire that demanded loyalty, Josephus and the evangels' editors had no choice if their public churches and their texts were to survive. I thought of the earlier parallel of the Maccabees, who in the second century B.C.E. had fought the invading armies of the Seleucid ruler Antiochus IV, saving Israel and Judaism from extinction, yet their Hasmonean descendents, kings and rulers, including Herod, were by the time of Yeshua both Hellenized and pro-Roman. More, even The Apocalypse, which among the twenty-seven scriptures of the New Covenant remains uniquely and relentlessly anti-Roman, which fully demonizes them to an alert reader, does so only allegorically, going back to the "Whore of Babylonia" and 666, a coded word for a Roman Emperor Nero or more likely Domitian, to show their furious opposition. Even Revelation could not call a Roman a Roman. With these ideas, the riddle of the political orientation in the gospels seemed to find some solution.

While the gospels of the New Covenant may not fit the categories of either historical chronicle or literary fable, they join early Genesis to stand at the summit of the transcendent spirit and of world literature. It also must be stated that uncertainties of origin and sectarian bigotries do not subvert their spiritual and aesthetic impact and the grandeur of their straightforward speech. Even the twentieth-century's indifferent translations, though winning few friends, have not threatened them. Especially in their older English-language incarnations, distinguished by the Tyndale and the King James Versions, the gospels are beautiful, fearful, and dramatic; they dwell in the profound labyrinths of the soul. Their poetry and vision have haunted the world. They persist as creation, parable, conspiracy, mystery, apocryphal testament, and essential holy scripture. For the majority readership of the faithful, the gospels are a manual of salvation.

HOW YESHUA BEN YOSEF
BECAME YESHUA THE MESSIAH
AND JESUS THE CHRIST

HEBREW NAMES IN THE JEWISH BIBLE

In the primordial beginnings of the Torah, until Adam gave names to all cattle and to the birds of the air and to every animal of the field, their existence was unfulfilled. With a name, even the humblest ant or bleak raven had a sound to distinguish it from all other species. Names also distinguish good from bad, pleasant from foul, and are a clue to essence. After God formed Adam, and Adam completed his task of endowing all with names, we find names for deities, people, and beasts whose mere utterance implies good or evil, kindness or cruelty, tribal friend or foreign enemy.

Adam's name, meaning "earth," connects him to the earth, paralleling God's molding of Adam from the earth. In the first creation tale (Gen. 1.26), God makes one he calls not a man but an Adam, that is, "one from the earth." And again in the second creation tale (2.7), God makes Adam (אָדָם, adam) from earth (אֲדָמָה, adamah). Adam is still a man-woman. Only after Genesis 2.18, when God puts Adam to work in the garden and delivers Eve to him, does God distinguish his genderless creations by their sexes. Then Adam jubilantly cries that "from his flesh and bones / this one will be called woman / and this one man" (Gen. 1.23). And God calls Adam man, ish (אִישׁ), and Eve woman, ishah (אִשָּׁה).

Each of these early namings—indeed, most names in the Hebrew Bible—is replete with etymological puns and semantic resonances, from earthly Adam to the pleasant garden of Eden (עֵדֶן, eden), whose name means "delight." By noting the enormous importance of names in the opening passages of Genesis, we have a model for the significance of new names designed for the New Covenant.

GREEK AND ENGLISH NAMES IN THE NEW COVENANT

In choosing names for the cast of the New Covenant, the authors established a semantic code for recognizing Jew, Christian, and gentile. The code, as with all codes, is often muddled, self-contradictory, and inconsistent, but it has worked both in Greek and in translations from Greek to other tongues. Through the naming and renaming of place, people, and movement, the New Covenant has changed identity and position for a new cast of actors who pass distinctly as the messianics (the Christians), and not as another Jewish faction.

How were these linguistic feats accomplished? How was time moved ahead around a hundred years to early in the second century when indeed Christians were beginning to be distinct from Jews? Here, with respect to anachronistic bias, it is important to restate that while the gospels read as contemporary history, Mark, the earliest gospel, was not formulated in Greek until at least forty or fifty years after Yeshua's crucifixion (ca. 30 c.e.) and the others up to seventy years after his lifetime.

The dissociation of the New Covenant as a Jewish book begins with the conversion of Semitic names into Greek names. When referring to members of the messianic movement, the New Covenant uses largely Greek or seemingly Greek names. But the Greek name is usually only a shadow of the original Hebrew name in sound and connotation. James is the name for Yeshua's brother, the son of Miryam, who was later head of the church in Jerusalem. English James scarcely echoes Greek Iakobos ('Ιάκωβος) and Hebrew Yaakov (יַעֲקֹב). So James is removed from his Semitic self in his new British costume. To leap from James back to Yaakov is a stretch, maybe a shocking one to the reader, because of the coded tradition of distinguishing Christian from Jew in days when they were all Jews. But once having understood how far one has been led from the Hebrew name, it should be a pleasure to return and redeem the names that Adam and his descendants dreamed up.

I have earlier noted the problems with the title of the Greek scriptures, namely, that New Testament is a mistranslation of the Greek title New Covenant based on Jerome's intermediate Latin mistranslation, which he rendered as *Novum Testamentum*.[20] The title New Covenant itself derives from

---

[20] For the initial discussion of the origin of the title New Testament, please see note 9, p. 9. Reference to the Vulgata by Jerome should always be tempered by the fact that we do not know if portions of the Vulgata that have come down to us were actually done by Jerome.

In the King James Version (KJV) there is an inconsistency in the translation of *diatheke* (διαθήκη) into English. For the title *diatheke* is "Testament" as it is in 1 Corinthians 11.25. However, in Hebrews 8.8–13, the KJV translates *diatheke* as "covenant" both in citing Jeremiah and in Paul's own speech. Hebrew 8.13 reads: "In that he saith, A new *covenant*, hath made the first old. Now that which decayeth and waxeth old *is* ready to vanish away." In defense of the King James Version's inconsistency, one must applaud the translators of the Authorized (the KJV), who avoided the painful consistencies imposed on the text in many versions, especially in contemporary ones. Absolute consistency of translation suggests that the original word and the context it falls into in the English text always hold the same meaning. That is not how language works. In their preface to the Authorized, the translators say, "We have not tied ourselves to an uniformity of phrasing, or to an identity of words, as some peradventure would wish we had done, because they observe that some learned men somewhere have been as exact as they could that way." Another perhaps more accurate

Luke 22.20, Paul in 1 Corinthians 11:25 and Hebrews 8.8–13.[21] The idea of a "new covenant," we must remember, comes from Paul who takes it directly from Jeremiah 31:31: "I will establish a new covenant with the house of Israel." In Hebrews 8–13, Paul quotes this famous passage in Jeremiah and writes, "In [Jeremiah's] speaking of 'a new covenant,' he has made the first one obsolete. And what is obsolete and growing old will soon disappear."[22] Paul, a Greek-speaking Jew from Tarsos, who knew the Hebrew texts, used *diatheke* to convey its meaning in Hebrew, *berit* (בְּרִית), which is covenant, and also a cut or circumcision, as we shall see when Paul speaks of a "new circumcision of the heart" (Rom. 2.25–29).[23]

FROM YESHUA TO JESUS

The New Covenant's Greek texts were initially addressed largely to Greek-speaking Jews to persuade them that Jesus (*Iesous*—'Ιησοῦς)[24] was not, or not only, a late Jewish prophet, but was their messiah, hence the name Christian for their sect, Christian meaning "messianic."[25] At some point in this process of voyage, the transmission from the probable Aramaic script or oral witness accounts to the Greek, the Hebrew biblical names were Hellenized, that is, they were given to us in a Greek translation or transliteration from late He-

---

translation from Hebrew *berit* into Greek is the word συνθήκη (syntheke), which specifically means "covenant" and "contract." So we would have καινή συνθήκη (kaine syntheke).

[21] Few today would ascribe Hebrews to Paul, though the assumption of Paul's authorship got its place in the canon. In quoting from Hebrews, as in other letters carrying Paul's name but of doubtful ascription, the point is, as in this case, the same, that Paul or another figure of the time asserted this or that.

[22] There has been a raising and lowering of the place of the Old Testament in Christianity. Before the completion of the gospels, the Christian Jews, including gentile converts, had only the Torah as their Bible. Before there was a canonized New Covenant, the second-century gnostic heretic Marcion argued for abolishing the Old Testament. Paul's argument in Hebrews 8–13 that the "new covenant" made the "old covenant" obsolete and that the old one would eventually disappear has been misinterpreted. (Hebrews is one of the letters uncertainly ascribed to Paul.) Paul, or the author of Paul's letter, was not referring to the texts of the Hebrew Bible as obsolete as opposed to the good news of the New Covenant, since in his lifetime no word of the gospels or other books was written other than his own letters that were to be incorporated in the canon of the New Covenant. Paul spoke to the notion of a spiritual versus a physical pact, to a circumcision relating to spirit and the heart rather than to the ritual cutting of the flesh. In the changing status of the Hebrew Bible in Christianity, the effect of the Protestant Reformation was to raise the Old Testament, doing so especially through its translation into vernaculars, along with that of the New Covenant. This was at the heart of bringing "the word of God" directly to the people and not confining it to a Latin translation associated with Rome.

[23] For further discussion on new covenant, see Galatians 3.15ff.

[24] See note 2, p. 47.

[25] Messianic or messianist signifies "one who follows the messiah," which in Greek translation is "Christian." Christian derives from Christ, whose transfer from Hebrew *mashiah* is given above.

brew or Aramaic. So, as we have seen, Yeshua (יֵשׁוּעַ) or, more fully, Yehoshua the Messiah, which comes from יְהוֹשֻׁעַ (yehoshua) and מָשִׁיחַ (mashiah), is rendered into Greek as *Iesous o Hristos* ('Ιησοῦς ὁ Χριστός). *Iesous* is a transliteration of *Yeshua* and *Hristos* (meaning the "anointed"), being a translation of *mashiah*. Greek *Iesous o Hristos* is in turn translated into English as Jesus [the] Christ. Similarly, *Yohanan* (יוֹחָנָן) becomes *Ioannes* ('Ιωάννης) in Greek, *Johannes* in Latin, and *John* in English.[26]

But we are not Greek-speaking Jews and gentiles, the gospels' original audience. We speak English. Why not biblical Yohanan in English rather than Greek John? Why adopt an English transcription of a Hellenized Greek transcription of Hebrew names from the Hebrew Bible? It is roundabout. Since we transcribe biblical names from the Hebrew Bible directly into English with minimum changes (Abraham may be written Avraham since the *b* and *v* in Hebrew, as in Spanish and other languages, are interchangeable), why not transcribe biblical names from the New Covenant directly into English? And without pausing at an intermediary Greek transcription? Hellenizing Yeshua the Messiah, son of God, into Jesus Christ is comparable to Hellenizing Yahweh (YHWH) into Zeus. Then Genesis would begin, "In the beginning Zeus created the heavens and the earth," and the Hebrew Bible would be consonant with the presently Hellenized New Covenant. It is ridiculous and unacceptable, yet the same translators allow the Greek translation of Sheol in Hebrew to carry over into English as Hades, which designates the pagan underworld in Greek religion and mythology.[27]

As for Yeshua's name, his name is key to the Hellenization and Christianization of the last Jewish prophet, who died for some Jews and later Chris-

---

[26] In *The Masks of God: Occidental Mythology* (New York: Viking Penguin, 1964; Penguin Arkana, 1991), Joseph Campbell traces John the Baptist's garb and diet back to Elijah as described in 2 Kings 1.8, but both his baptism practices and his name go back to the water god Ea, "God of the House of Water," from the Sumerian temple city of Eridu. He writes, "In the Hellenistic period, Ea was called *Oannes*, which is in Greek *Ioannes*, Latin *Johannes*, Hebrew *Yohanan*, English *John*." Whether any of these ancient ablutions—and he might have mentioned those of the Essenes—is more than a universal wash is uncertain, but Campbell does trace the journey of the English name John back to Hebrew *Yohanan*. Ea (also known as Enki) goes back to both Sumerian and to Old Akkadian ḥyw, which Hebrew of Eve also goes back to, so that Ea and Eve both have the common Semitic root ḥyh, meaning "living" (as in living water), which is a common phrase both in the gospels and especially in gnostic scriptures that analyze the Gospel of John.

[27] Commonly, a dominant religious faith determines whether a creation or supernatural story is assigned to religious history or mythology; and this determination usually ascribes one's own tales to religious history and the outsider religion to mythology. Hence from our perspective, Hades is part of Greek mythology, although it has slipped into the Christian terminology in the Greek scriptures. Hell is another Germanic/Scandinavian equivalent, but Sheol and Gehenna really deserve a common place in English, and they evoke accurately and spiritually the original meaning of Jewish underworld notions.

tians as the messiah, and who in his life was known by his Jewish name and titles. For the early Christian world the life, death, and resurrection of Yeshua was the fulfillment of Jewish prophetic expectations. Yeshua was the messiah, the Lord's anointed one. George Nickelsburg elaborates:

> Early Christians oriented their world view around the belief that the crucified Jesus was exalted in heaven. There he ruled as Lord and Christ and prepared to return as God's appointed judge, who would vindicate and reward the righteous and punish their oppressors (as if they had such) and the rest of the wicked of this world. They also attached positive value to Jesus' death as a means of dealing with human sin. The categories from which these beliefs were drawn are thoroughly Jewish: the suffering and exalted servant of the Lord; the Lord's Anointed One; the one like a son of man enthroned as the executor of God's reign. Thus these Christians related their self-understanding as heirs of the Israelite tradition to their identification of the crucified and risen Jesus with the aforementioned figures of Jewish expectation. Jesus the crucified, risen, and exalted one was the key to their understanding of their tradition and the polar star by which they oriented themselves. In their view, being a Jew required that one recognize Jesus as the fulfillment of these expectations; to believe in the crucified and exalted Christ was to acknowledge the realization of God's promises to judge all flesh and to extend the divine reign throughout the cosmos. (2.2.6)[28]

The gospels preserve the life and death of the messiah and lord of emerging Christianity, and they preserved him, without excuse or explanation, in Greek scriptures with a Greek name, which may not seem to be at all unreasonable for Greek-reading Jews and gentiles. Yes, why not translate Hebrew names into Greek for Greek readers? Yet the non-Greek reader of these names should not be required to be a textual detective to understand Yeshua's probable Jewish name and ethnicity. In the end it must be clear why and how the title of Yeshua the Messiah[29] becomes in Greek Ἰησοῦς ὁ Χρηστός (Iesous ho Hris-

---

[28] George W. E. Nickelsburg, "Revealed Wisdom as a Criterion for Inclusion and Exclusion: From Jewish Sectarianism to Early Christianity," in Jacob Neusner and Ernest S. Frerichs, eds., *To See Ourselves as Others See Us: Christians, Jews, "Others" in Late Antiquity* (Chico, CA: Scholars Press, 1985).

[29] Coming upon Yeshua the Messiah is not without complication, as we have seen. Christ (from Greek *Hristos*) means "anointed" or "messiah." Jesus (from Greek *Iesous*) can be Yeshua, or *Joshua*, as it is in translations from the Hebrew Bible with the exception of Everett Fox's *The Five Books of Moses,* which restores Joshua to *Yehoshua*. Joshua is simply an older English way of transliterating Yeshua. So we can have *Yeshua the Messiah* or *Joshua the Messiah* or *Yehoshua the Messiah*. We can also return messiah to Hebrew *mashiah,* and then have *Yehoshua Mashiah*. The advantage of saying Joshua the Messiah would be that it reproduces the traditional English spelling used in the Hebrew Bible and makes Joshua the same name in both books. But it seems better to use the closer form in English,

tos). Here, and now in other translations, the movement directly from Hebrew and Aramaic into the target languages is beginning, will persist, and perhaps will prevail.

The name Jesus Christ has no Hebrew resonance or linguistic identity and, as we'll see, has allowed Yeshua to pass as someone other than a Jew, to have been a gentile in his earthly life. At the crucifixion, the Roman soldiers cast lots and offered Yeshua the sour wine and mocked him with the title "the king of the Jews." The soldiers slipped into the truth, and that title, if true in the eyes of the Roman rulers, reinforces the belief that Yeshua was executed by Roman soldiers for sedition, that is, for being a leader and opponent to Roman occupation of Israel. And in the gospels, for the sect of Jews who followed him, Yeshua was certainly the spiritual king of the Jews.

The paramount reason behind the old tradition of *not* using Hebrew biblical names in English in translations of the New Covenant was to distance early Christian Jews and later Christians from Judaism. The immediate effect of bestowing Greek names on the circle of figures around Yeshua created a pantheon of Hellenized venerables who would, by way of a gentleman's agreement, be perceived as Christians rather than Jews and thereby be one step farther removed from their Jewish identity.[30] From the first pages of the Greek gospels, changing names was essential in the process of dejudaizing Yeshua.

---

which is Yeshua, and hope that in future translations of the Hebrew Bible, old Joshua will give way to Yeshua, as Jupiter and Jehovah have importantly given way to Yahweh and YHWH. There is common agreement that Jesus was known in his time as *Yeshua,* the shortened Aramaic and Hebrew version of *Yehoshua,* and I have come, not without other possibilities in mind, to *Yeshua the Mashiah,* which is an understandable shift from *Jesus the Christ. Messiah* translates both meanings of the Hebrew mashiah, of "messiah" and "anointed." The terms Yeshua ben Yosef or Yeshua bar Yosef (fully Aramaic version) are also becoming increasingly common as Yeshua's proper name before he was given the mantle of the messiah.

[30] For an investigation of questions of Jewish and Christian identity in the first century, see two seminal articles by George W. E. Nickelsburg: "Jews and Christians in the First Century: The Struggle Over Identity" in *Neotestamentica* 27(2) (1993): 365–390/1–4.5, and "The First Century: A Time to Rejoice and a Time to Weep" in *Religion and Theology,* Vol. 1/1 (1994): 4–17/1–5. Nickelsburg speaks of the Jewish traditions from which Yeshua comes and the often-noted "parallels between the New Testament and the Qumran documents." Of special importance are his observations on the parallels between the Jewish tradition of "persecution and vindication of the righteous one" with Yeshua's death and his resurrection and exaltation in heaven. Placing Yeshua as the figure of Old Testament prophecy, Nickelsburg writes that Yeshua's sacrificial death makes him the true Son of Man, God's judge in heaven and on earth, and fulfills the multiple tradition of "Second Isaiah's Chosen One, the Servant of the Lord." He also relates Yeshua to the dream vision of the apocalyptic beast who was burned to death and then given glory and everlasting dominion over peoples and nations of the earth, which occurs in Daniel's diaspora novel (Dan. 7.13–15). In short, the main Jewish and Christian-Jewish titles come together in the life and death of Yeshua: "the son of man/chosen One/Anointed One" (Nickelsburg, 2.2.3) and the heavenly figure seated beside God's throne. In these earliest moments of Christianity, Yeshua was a salvific figure who thoroughly fulfilled Isaianic and Danielic scriptural prophecy.

A simple and well-known example of an attempt to free Yeshua in the Greek gospels of the Jewish stain occurs when Andrew and Peter first address Yeshua (John 1.38): "Rabbi—which translated means 'teacher'—where are you staying?" (ῥαββί ὃ λέγεται μεθερμηνευόμενον διδάσκαλε, ποῦ μένεις;[31]). This aside, breaking the narrative flow, seems to be a later scribal interpolation to explain away rabbi as teacher and to blur Yeshua's identity as a rabbi and Jew; and indeed to persuade the reader that rabbi meant an independent teacher or scholar and not a Jewish interpreter of the Bible. Rabbi is a Greek word from Hebrew *rabbi* (רַבִּי), meaning "my master," "great one," or "teacher of the law." That the aside in John 1.38 needs to be "translated" into Greek suggests an earlier version of this passage in late Hebrew or Aramaic. This example of the dejudaizing of Yeshua the Messiah occurs not only in the Greek version, but, as will be shown, in multiple renderings of Greek *rabbi* into English versions of the New Covenant.

In speaking of "the dejudaizing of Jesus," Hugh J. Schonfield writes in *The Original New Testament* (San Francisco: Harper & Row, 1985): "The story of Christian beginnings has commonly been related with little reference to or comprehension of its Jewish aspects . . . it is a deprivation which resulted in a one-sided and very inaccurate viewpoint with horrifying consequences so far as the Jews of Europe were concerned. Jesus was made not only a stranger to his brethren, but their mortal foe seeking their extermination. . . . The dejudaizing of Jesus was appreciably to affect both the Christian Faith, as in the Church Creeds, and the comprehension of the New Testament, since it was responsible for a good deal of mistranslation and misinterpretation of the text" (xix).

Hoping that the practice of dejudaizing Yeshua will cease, in this instance I have followed the now-current practice of translating Greek *rabbi* into English "rabbi." When the Yeshua's title is teacher as in the Greek διδάσκαλος, I follow the definition of *Greek-English Lexicon of the New Testament and Other Early Christian Literature* of διδάσκαλος, giving rabbi or rabboni as the Hebrew word for Yeshua's title: "Used in addressing Jesus (corresp. to the title רַב or רַבִּי, rabbi) Matt 8:19; 12:38; 19:16; 22:16, 24, 36; Mark 4:38; 9:17, 38; 10:17, 20, 35; 12:14, 19, 32; 13:1; Luke 7:40; 9:38 Ῥαββί w. translation John 1:38, also Ῥαββουνί 20:16. W. the art. Mt 9:11; 17:24; 26:18; Mk 5:35; 14:14; Lk 22:11; J 11:28."

In John 1.38, where the scribe comes out of the closet to add an aside in order to exonerate Yeshua of his Jewish identity, the usual religious mutation of rabbi into Greek as teacher, master, sir, or lord has not occurred, but the revelation of rabbi has been explained away. The Romans achieved a similar

---

[31] Greek ";" is English "?".

trompe l'oeil in their Romanization of Greek deities when they created a pantheon of Latin gods by ingloriously making Greek Zeus into Roman Jupiter, Aphrodite into Venus, Artemis into Diana, and Athena into Minerva. As the Jews took the names for God and Beelzebub from earlier Mesopotamian religions, so the Christians appropriated Yeshua as their own, and the Romans appropriated the Greek gods and heroes. Such borrowings and denials are universal and purposeful, and cannot be explained always as linguistic oddities or casualties of translation. It is not easier phonetically to call Yeshua *Jesus* rather than *Yeshua,* or Yaakov *James* rather than *Yaakov* or *Jacob.*

MIGRATION OF YAAKOV TO JAMES

In this translation of the New Covenant, I have in most instances restored the biblical names to their Hebrew equivalents in English. An example is the aforementioned Jacob. It is important to see in some linguistic detail how Yaakov migrated to England as James. Yaakov—in Hebrew יַעֲקֹב—is traditionally transcribed into English as Jacob. The biblical figure Yaakov, son of Yitzhak (Isaac—יִצְחָק), appears in the genealogies of Matthew and Luke as *Iakob,* which is as close as the Greek can transliterate the name. But the same name Yaakov, when applied to Yeshua's brother, is slightly Hellenized; that is, *Iakob* for Jacob is an uninflected foreign borrowing, but when it refers to Yeshua's brother it is given the Greek nominative ending, and we have *Iakobos* in order to distinguish in Greek, if only grammatically, between the Old and New Covenant figures who carry the same Hebrew Bible name. So in Greek the name of Jacob when applied to the Old Testament patriarch remains Jewish, but when applied to a New Testament brother of Yeshua it takes on a Greek form to help him be more comfortable in a Greek epithet. When these Greek names are transcribed into English, *Iakob* becomes Jacob, but *Iakobos* comes out implausibly as James. Now the separation is complete. The original Hebrew name Yaakov, which in its two Greek versions were distinguished only by a declension ending, has generously spawned two entirely distinct names in English, Jacob and James. In having his name taken away from him, Yaakov also loses his cultural and religious identity. As "James" he appears as a fresh New Covenant figure in no danger of being detected as a Jacob or a Yaakov from the Hebrew Bible. In keeping up the pretense of two already distinct religions in Jerusalem, no Old Testament patriarch can have the name James.[32]

---

[32] The word for Yeshua's brother Yaakov in Greek is the declined noun: Ἰάκωβος, οὖ, ὁ (Iakobos, Iakobou, Iakobo). The word for the Jewish patriarch is "indeclinable" Ἰακώβ. In the standard *Greek-English Lexicon of New Testament and Other Early Christian Literature,* there is an explanation. Under

Past translators have been guilty of deceiving the Christian readers. By using non-Jewish names for bibical figures, and worse, by using diffrent Greek and English names for the same Hebrew name to distinguish between people in the Old and New Covenants, translators are putting a linguistic screen between the two books and creating the impression that Christianity did not spring from the messianic tradition in Judaism.

In this version, Iakob and Iakobos, the two Greek translations from the Hebrew, are restored to one Yaakov, and Jacob and James are two memories. The question of what specific traditional biblical name of the time, in late Hebrew or Aramaic, should be restored will always be uncertain. What is certain is that the presently accepted Greek names for Christ and John or the strangely Anglicized names from the Greek such as James and Jude are false names to accept and will in a decade or two give way to names that reflect not Greek but biblical Jewish names. In Homer, for now more than a century Ulysses and Venus have given way to Odysseus and Aphrodite, though the Roman names for the gods still persist in the romance languages, even in translations of Homer. Already in recent standard translations "messiah" is replacing "Christ," when the Greek text refers to the messiah as the savior, as in "the Christ." While the King James gives us "the Christ," most twentieth-century versions give us "the messiah."

In summary, since most of the names in the Greek scriptures are translations or transliterations from the Hebrew, it makes more sense to do in English what the Greeks did: work straight from Hebrew instead of doing a translation of a translation. The Alexandrian Neoplatonic philosopher Plotinus informed his friend and biographer Porphyry that he refused to let a painter paint his picture. His reasoning: "Why paint an illusion of an illusion?"

IN SPAIN THE FATE OF THE SUSPECT ORIGINAL

Curiously, translating a Hebrew name into English through its Greek version begins to make the Hebrew original seem like a suspect illusion, and an attempt to foist that original onto English a radical language act. A "suspect original," or a more general revulsion against the Jewish origins of Christianity, occurs in the drama of the Spanish poet Fray Luis de León (1524–1591), an Augustinian monk and professor of Latin, Greek, and Hebrew at the University of Salamanca, whose student was the mystical poet Saint John of the

---

Ἰακώβ, the entry reads: "indecl. This, the un-Grecized form of the Hebrew Bible, is reserved for formal writing." The dictionary explanation falters, however, since undeclined Ἰακώβ (Iakob) is not "formal writing."

Cross. Luis de León, of convert (*converso*) background, translated Job, Song of Songs, and Psalms directly from the Hebrew, with commentary, in what remain the finest versions of the Bible in the Spanish language. For this, he was four and a half years in the inquisitional prison at Valladolid, accused of judaizing. He had, according to his accusers, translated from "the corrupt original" Hebrew text rather than from the authorized Latin Vulgata. When the esteemed poet was released, his students carried him on their shoulders back in triumph to his university chair at Salamanca.

An aversion and anxiety about drawing from the original texts was not unique to Spain, which in the Middle Ages, because of its large multilingual Jewish population, actually had at least two private translations of the Jewish Bible made directly from Hebrew. They were the Alba Bible, 1422–1433, translated by Rabbi Mossé Arragel de Maqueda, uniquely and restrictively for use in the house of the Duque de Alba, and the Osuna Bible for the house of the Marqués de Santillana. Elsewhere in Europe any translation into a demotic tongue was done at the risk of heresy and punishment. As a result of the domination of Jerome's Vulgate, throughout the Western Middle Ages and in the Renaissance, not only the names in the Bible but the Bible itself contained another layer of Latinizations. The Vulgata was the canonized word of God for the Roman Catholic Church, and, insofar as the Bible went into European tongues, it was rendered exclusively from the approved Latin, not the Greek, which even learned Dante and Petrarcha couldn't read, or the dark original in Hebrew, which only Jews could read. Spain, in the instance of the aristocratic family translations, was the exception. After the 1492 expulsion of Jews from Spain, there soon appeared new versions from the Hebrew Bible into Spanish editions published in Ferrara (with the papal seal of approval), Amsterdam, and Constantinople.

RESTORATION OF ORIGINAL BREATH

After centuries of covering up and condemning the Hebrew language base of the Hebrew Bible and of the Greek scriptures, modern scholarship is moving to correct traditional infelicities. This is an auspicious time for the New Covenant, for the restoration in scholarship and translation of its Semitic names, the religious identity of its main characters as Jews, and above all a spirit of universality which, both in the gospels and their interpretation, has too often been merely divisive. As sectarian differences drop away, a broader bible may come through to include the Hebrew Bible, the Intertestament, and the New Covenant. Easy access to deuterocanonical and non-canonical apocrypha will alone prove the welcome news of diversity. Some may shudder and fume, but such a wider bible will bring in a lot of good news.

As for rethinking old historical assumptions, we may note a biblical prehistory of stories flooding in from Mesopotamia, with many names and many gods, and the spellings of place-names and figures in flux as scholars tinker. Knowledge frees and incites the courage of change. Among obvious changes is the practice of seeking source-language foreign spellings and pronunciations, which is now enjoyably common. Hence Peking has yielded to Beijing (it was always *Beijing,* if one knew how to pronounce the odd Chinese-English code letters that Wade-Giles established). It is not always possible, however, to jar habit, to call Plato *Platon* or Pindar *Pindaros.* So Everett Fox in *The Five Books of Moses* (New York: Schocken Books, 1995) notes that he has retained English Jordan (rather than Hebrew Yarden), while relentlessly returning to a phonetically based English equivalent of most Hebrew names in the Torah. But Everett Fox did something of equal importance to his restoration of Hebrew names: He translated the Torah into verse.

YESHUA BACK HOME

Yeshua's quintessential poetic sayings were of life, light, soul, and death, and of his source in Adonai the Lord. He himself took on, in his followers' eyes, the earthly incarnation of Adonai the Lord, the traditional ever-waited-for messiah of the Jews, who was to appear salvifically on earth. "For to us a son is born. . . . And he shall be called Wonderful, The Counselor, The mighty God, The everlasting Father, The Prince of Peace" (Isa. 9.6, KJV). Through odd concealment of his person, he became universally known as a Greek-speaking figure ostensibly from Galilee (the Galil), but essentially from nowhere. His universality appeared to take away his simple Jewish origin, including his voice, preserved only in Greek or in translations from Greek, and especially into Latin. That same universality, canonized by the Roman State Church, made him so remote from his native language and origin that in his dialogues his own tongue and person were under cover. Imagine if Odysseus spoke only Aramaic and quoted Hebrew verse as he bounced around the Mediterranean, and that he was universally known not as Odysseus but Moses. That reversal of Greek and Hebrew has for two millennia been the destiny of Yeshua ben Yosef, who preached around the hills and villages of the Galil and Yehuda (Galilee and Judea).

This conversion of the New Covenant into English seeks to bring Yeshua back to his Semitic geography and roots. To bring him back home.

HISTORICAL BASES OF YESHUA'S LIFE AND DEATH: JOURNEY FROM EVENT TO GOSPEL

When I was a child growing up in an evangelical part of the Christian Church in the United States, I was convinced that Jesus must have been a Swede or at least an Englishman. Every picture I saw of him, and there were many, portrayed him with fair skin, blonde hair, and blue eyes.

—JOHN SHELBY SPONG, EPISCOPAL BISHOP OF NEWARK
LIBERATING THE GOSPELS

The virgin by the blooming beans is blonde
And her small Jesus is a blond like her
His eyes are blue and pure like the sky or wave
I guess her seeded by the Paraclete.
—GUILLAUME APOLLINAIRE, "THE VIRGIN
BY THE BEAN BLOSSOMS IN COLOGNE"

Carts were dashing though the narrow streets of the city; more going on than usual for this town; everything that evening seemed too satisfied.
Jesus withdrew his hand: It was a movement of childish and feminine pride. "All of you, if you don't see miracles, you don't believe."
—ARTHUR RIMBAUD, "GALILEE," *ILLUMINATIONS*

DISCOVERY OF AN EARLY GOSPEL

Especially since the discovery of the Gospel of Thomas in 1945 in Egypt among the scrolls of the Nag Hammadi Library, the historicity of narrations in the New Covenant has been increasingly studied and questioned. Since the only real source for Yeshua's life had been the gospels, written long after his death, faith rather than historical documents has prevailed to fashion a picture of Yeshua. The Gospel of Thomas has added information. Without narration and relatively free of anti-Jewish bias, it gives what some scholars assert (and others deny) are the earliest words of Yeshua. Through the sayings, it offers some hints about the personality of a historical Yeshua. The dating is significant but ultimately secondary to the greater contribution which is that it represents a profoundly different presentation of Yeshua's words, and is obviously one of the earliest distinct sources we have.

The Gospel of Thomas is found in Coptic translation from the Greek of a text that may have had an Aramaic origin. There are also fragments of Thomas in Syriac. In the gospel, we hear Yeshua in the format of a Platonic dialogue. It is also significant that the "Fifth Gospel" was found together with classical gnostic scriptures, and that Yeshua's appearance in Thomas is itself the centerpiece of early gnosticism. The extraordinary Gospel of Thomas, reflecting a sage's original thought, is focused in 144 concise entries of oral sayings and parables. The tradition of an itinerant sage's oral sayings and parables clearly derives from both the written Bible and extra-biblical literature.

Among the Nag Hammadi scrolls were also the gnostic Gospel of Truth and Gospel of Philip. These documents cast a new light on the Yeshua of gnostic speculation, the special gnosis of light, truth, knowledge, and divinity found inside the person rather than in external scripture. Early Jewish and Jewish-Christian gnosticism, as in the Book of Baruch, linguistically reveals the transition between Judaism and Christianity; but, aside from the closer character and more traditional format, these early gnostic scriptures pose the same enigmas of origin and transmission of information as the canonical gospels, since in this presentation of a Greek and Coptic speaker in gnostic scriptures, the Semitic atmosphere and textual links are missing that should take us back to an Aramaic-speaking Yeshua.[33]

SOURCES AND TRANSMISSION OF TEXTS[34]

The question of historicity pertains to factual information about the people in the New Covenant, their names and identity, what they did and said, the miracle story, events (and especially the Passion narration), and the condition of the texts which offer all this information. As for specific historical references to Yeshua of Nazareth outside the gospels, they are pitifully few and uncertain. There are brief allusions in Tacitus, Suetonius, and Pliny the Younger.

The Jewish historian Josephus (ca. 37–100 C.E.) (Joseph ben Matthias) has a passage of more significance, though its validity is strongly debated. In *The Changing Faces of Jesus* (New York: Viking Compass, 2000), Geza Vermes of-

---

[33] The atmosphere in the Gospel of Thomas will soon change. The fine version of Thomas in English by Marvin Meyer, *The Gospel of Thomas* (San Francisco: HarperSan Francisco, 1992), has a stunning interpretation by Harold Bloom, who places Thomas in its Jewish and gnostic setting. In his forthcoming edition of the Gospel of Thomas for *The Gnostic Bible*, Professor Meyer has, as here, restored all names to their probable Hebrew and Aramaic forms.

[34] For details on authorship, the Q source, and Thomas, see pages 446–452.

fers a balanced view: "In certain circles, Josephus was venerated as the fifth evangelist. Hypercritical scholars consider the entire passage to be spurious, i.e., a Christian gloss inserted into the *Antiquities* to furnish a first-century Jewish proof of the existence of Jesus who was the Messiah. Admittedly, as it stands, the text is unlikely to have originated from the pen of Flavius Josephus. The flat assertions, 'He was the Christ' and that his resurrection on the third day fulfilled the predictions of the prophets are alien to Josephus and must have derived from a later Christian editor of the *Antiquities*" (276–277).

For a spiritual biography of Yeshua we have Paul, who did not know Yeshua in the flesh and who is unconcerned with Yeshua in history. Paul is closer to John of the Fourth Gospel, who wrote three generations after Yeshua's death. Both authors sought and created a messianic and eschatological Yeshua, who corresponded to the emerging ideological development of Jewish Christianity. And then, we have Josephus and Philo to give us specific reporting of the Jews during the life of Yeshua. Of great importance is also the history of Yeshua's time found in the later Talmud (rabbinical writing around 200 C.E., including the Mishnah), which is vital for understanding Yeshua's precursors among the charasmatic Hasidic healers and miracle-makers. However, since the gospels are all we have as a detailed record of the life of Yeshua, they are what we investigate and evaluate and about which we come up with guesses and broad theories. In short, all the historical events of Yeshua's life take place within the frame of unverifiable religious scripture.

In the last decades there have been a number of new "biographies" of Jesus, which, in a novelistic manner, fill in the colorful scenes, describing village life, landscapes, the farmers, carpenters, and fishermen, the crowds as well as main figures of the day, including Herod Antipas and his mass crucifixions of dissidents and enemies, and the stoning to death of Yeshua's younger brother James (Jacob/Yaakov), who was head of the Jerusalem church. An excellent example of such re-creations is Bruce Chilton's *Rabbi Jesus: An Intimate Biography* (New York: Doubleday, 2000). Generally speaking, these biographies reconstruct speech, ideas, and events recorded in the gospels and in Acts. The historical base is scripture (with reservations), Josephus, later rabbinical writings, and factual knowledge of Roman rule. Since these lives of Jesus draw primarily on unverifiable scripture, however skillfully they are handled, there remains the question of what is knowable and what is guided conjecture. In this regard, the outstanding life of Jesus is *The Changing Faces of Jesus* by Geza Vermes. Vermes looks to the gospels for discrete information to shape a picture of Yeshua, and also to the Essenes of the Dead Sea Scrolls (which he edited and translated), and to Yeshua's antecedents and contemporaries among the Hasidic charismatics. Given the multitude of general sources and paucity of specific references to Yeshua outside of the gospels, I think that Vermes may offer us the most persuasive ways of coming to terms with the evasive "historical Jesus."

The gospels concern the late Second Temple period followers of Yeshua (who are sometimes called "the primitive Christians") and, having been written *after* the Roman destruction of the Herodian Temple in 70 C.E., they direly predict the catastrophe and presage the swiftening separation of Jews from Christian Jews that takes place after the diaspora from Jerusalem. It is imperative to remember that these gospels were long to reach their present form, and the editors who copied, emended, and rewrote are all unknown. In speaking about the formation of Mark, John Drury writes, "A welter of oral and fluid tradition about Jesus got fixed into text. Stories which had been the property of Christian preachers, teachers, and prophets were appropriated by a Christian writer. This written gospel is next-door neighbor to thirty or forty years of oral gospeling" (in Alter and Kermode, eds., The *Literary Guide to the Bible*, [Cambridge, MA: Harvard University Press, 1967], 404).

FAITH MOVES MOUNTAINS, AND ITS VEHICLE IS TRANSLATION

As for the four gospels, probably the earliest, the more historical Mark, was not recorded as a written document until around 70 or 80 C.E., generations after Yeshua's death. Mark is closest to the Aramaic-speaking Yeshua, and the few Aramaic words found in the gospels are mainly in Mark: *Rabbuni,* "my rabbi" (10.15), *Abba,* "father" (14.36), and finally, *Eloi, Eloi, lama sabachtani,* "My God, my God, why do you abandon me?" (15.34). In at least this one line from the scripture, the last words Yeshua will utter, we hear the human, Aramaic voice of Yeshua; for the same line in Matthew, Hebrew *Eli, Eli* replaces Aramaic *Eloi, Eloi* (27.46). Each of the gospels reveals a different face of Yeshua.

How did we arrive at the four canonized gospel biographies of Yeshua? Beginning with a changing oral text recorded in now lost sources, the course of translation from original events to the first Greek manuscripts was a very long road. Errors and, more significant, interpretation of those events as they were told and retold (oral copying or oral translation), editorial invention, omission, and alteration on their way to the extant fourth-century codices have all determined the nature of the Christian scriptures. In *A Historical Introduction to the New Testament* (New York: Harper & Row, 1963), Robert M. Grant gives an overview: "The Gospels testify primarily to the faith and the memories of the communities out of which they came, not the historical reliability of their authors. In many respects the Synoptic Gospels (though not John) resemble folk literature more than the creation of individual artists" (108).

The events that happened one day in Jerusalem to a rabbi called Yeshua represent perhaps the major act of literary composition in history. A version of those happenings appeared, and a new religion was born. Christianity arose. For the Romans, this was a day of a routine crucifixion by its army of three Jews in Jerusalem. Descriptive evidence concerning this event, apart from the uncertain sentence of Josephus ("He was the Christ"), lies uniquely in the Greek version of the gospels. Yeshua's teaching was oral, and there is no claim that there were writings by him. Yet scholars continue to debate, arguing as if the true nature of a transcendent God depended in some definitive way on a discovery of further evidence concealed within the translated words in the text. One looks, of course, for the deepest meaning within a text, but always with the awareness that great religious scriptures of the world, in this and apparently all instances, are not tape recordings or photographs, but late transcriptions that have gone through an unknown plethora of transmission activity.

In its journey from event to gospel,[35] the tale was translated from oral reports of Aramaic- and Latin-speaking witnesses, perhaps from written reports in Hebrew including something by a man later designated as Matthew. Finally, decades later, the story reached the pens of Greek-writing Jewish scribes. Grant comments on the bilingual authors of the gospels: "Even though none of the New Testament books was written in Aramaic, the authors of some of them thought in Aramaic, at least at times. And behind the sayings of Yeshua in their Greek versions lies a chain of transmission which began in a Semitic language. Obviously this chain cannot be reproduced in a translation. But it has to be taken into account" (56).

Much talk, memory, imagination, creation, and interpretation went into that story, climaxing with the last of the miracles, the miracle of the resurrection, and its first recording. We know that whether true or false in actuality, the Mark ver-

---

[35] Gospel, meaning "good news," has come also by usage to be used as a specific genre, and many intertestamental works are typed as "gospels," including thirteen other extant gospels, such as the Gospel of Philip, the Gospel of Mary, and the Gospel of Thomas. Some point out anomalies in calling gospel a genre of writing, including David Trobisch who comments, "The term *Gospel* is used to refer to the content of the message as well as to the act of preaching in the New Testament. It is not used to indicate a specific literary genre. And so far no evidence has surfaced in pre-Christian literature, either, that the term can be used to refer to a literary genre" (*The First Edition of the New Testament*, 38). Elsewhere he comments that the books fall into the genre normally called in early Greek βίος (bios), meaning "a life." However, since the publication of the gospels, which Trobisch posits to be around 150, "genre" has persisted as the common term for the life of Yeshua. Prior to the second century, "gospel" had meant something else. For Paul, who died before the gospels were composed or edited, "gospel" refers to the whole Christian message, above all to the eschatological meaning of Yeshua's death, and there could be only one gospel. By the end of the second century, there were many gospels still claiming to be the one true one, but by then, Mark, Matthew, Luke, and John had found their place as the canonical four.

sion of the resurrection is a spurious "orphan" ending (a late appended text), included in the King James Version but omitted from twentieth-century versions such as the widespread New Revised Standard Version. The NRSV is based on the now standard UBS (United Bible Societies) Greek texts edited by Kurt Aland (1979) and a later edition of them in the Eberhard and Nestle *Novum Testamentum Graece* (1993), all of which exclude the orphan. The process of recording the gospels, to use an appropriate metaphor, is an oral and graphic palimpsest with endless layers of changing information. The later translation of the Greek scriptures themselves into Latin and the world's languages brings in further changes, due to error or intention, along with the trauma of textual alterations at the time of the radical conversion of uncial[36] into modern letters. Each new stage of transmission carries with it all the problems of interlingual rewording.

The scriptures are insistent about the truth of their recorded events, about the truth of belief and faith in miracle and the supernatural powers of the divine, and in the punishments awaiting those who fail to believe in these truths. Yet with respect to the authenticity of actual events, dialogue, or miracles, there is no way of corroborating the truth of the events. Discomfort about this absence lurks in the statements of the early Latin Fathers, such as Origen's claim that the Holy Spirit gave each of the evangelists a perfect memory. Even if true with regard to each memory, this solves nothing unless we believe, against widely accepted chronological evidence, that the evangelists were witness to Yeshua's life and death and therefore had a personal recollection of the events which they recorded.

The problems of historicity, of verification of even the most minor facts, remain a barrier to affirming the truth or falsity of gospel events. Despite the documentary vacuum outside the gospels, there is within the gospels, as there would be in any literary document, enormous information that may be examined and conclusions drawn, as I have attempted to do with regard to the straightforward facts of the existing names in the gospels. The danger is to forget, especially during a lifetime of research, that so little is known, and that evidence pertaining to miracles, exorcism, the source of the parables and wisdom sayings, the conspiracy, the crucifixion, and the resurrection can never be ascertained from a literal surface reading of the text. Paula Fredriksen, among so many, states the obvious in her cautionary summary of capturing these oral texts:

---

[36] Uncial letters from the fourth to the eighth centuries were characterized by round capital letters in Greek and Latin manuscripts that provided the model for most modern capital letters.

This is another way of saying that Jesus' audience, like himself, would have been for the most Aramaic-speaking Jews living in Jewish territory, but the language of the evangelists is Greek, their medium written, nor oral. No one knows where the Gospels were composed, nor the identities of their authors— the traditional ascriptions ("Matthew," "Mark," "Luke," and "John") evolved only in the course of the second century: The original texts circulated anonymously. Most scholars assign locations of origin to somewhere in the Greek-speaking cities of the empire. Accordingly, the question of their communities' relations with Gentiles, with Gentile culture, and with imperial government looms much larger for the evangelists than it could have for Jesus himself. (Jesus of Nazareth, 19)

As for transmission by eyewitness testimony, which is the usual way of filling the gap between an event and the late transcription of an event, Fredriksen further states:

But eyewitness testimony is never scientific or objective, first of all because the witness is human. In this particular case their conviction that Jesus has been raised from the dead, or that he was God's special agent working in history for the redemption of Israel and the world, would inevitably have affected the reports that these witnesses gave: Other witnesses, not so convinced, would, and presumably did, speak differently. (20) (cf. Matt. 28.17)

We can only guess at the nature of pre-gospel information. Sometimes, knowledge of the Hebrew or Aramaic source word deflates the magnificence, as in the proverb of it being harder for a rich man to enter heaven than for "a camel to pass through the eye of a needle" (Mark 10.25; Matt. 19.24; Luke 18.25). "Coarse thread" and "camel" turn out to have the same root consonants (vowels are unmarked in Hebrew and Aramaic). Hence the mistake in transmission to the Greek gives us the memorable, beautiful, and surreal image in the maxim. So, apart from external historical and archeological evidence, the main areas of research are in understanding and interpreting material in the gospels themselves and in studying and establishing a history of the great number of surviving complete and fragmentary manuscripts of the gospels.

MANUSCRIPT HISTORY

The earliest fragment of the gospels is a scrap with five verses from John 18, which was recognized by C. H. Roberts in 1934 from shreds of papyri found by Bernard P. Grenfell in 1920 in Egypt. Roberts dated the piece to the first half of the second century, though the date cannot be confirmed. The first substantial manuscripts with portions of the New Covenant are the Bodomer papyrus of John and the Chester Beatty papyrus, which contains ten Pauline letters. These papyri are dated some time in the middle of the third century. The earliest extant uncial parchment manuscript, containing the entire New Covenant, is the Codex Sinaiticus discovered in 1844 at St. Catherine's monastery in the Sinai, dating from the fourth century. These early manuscripts have all the expected erasures, rewriting, emendations, and comments about earlier scribes on them, which is helpful in tracing their history. In the case of the Hebrew Bible, the earliest copies are much later, while the Septuagint Greek translation of the Bible is earlier than any surviving Hebrew text (with the exception now of fragments in the Dead Sea Scrolls). Indeed, almost all the ancient literature that has come down to us from every society consists of copies of copies.

As mentioned, the composition of the gospels took place in the late first and early second centuries. There is no manuscript fragment of the gospels themselves for at least a century after Yeshua's death—and at least two centuries for anything substantial. Because of the information gap after Yeshua's life, we have only guesses to describe the mysterious chemistry that turned a Jewish movement in Jerusalem into Greek Christian scripture.

SPREADING THE WORD OF GOD IN MANY TONGUES

Before looking and studying within the Greek New Covenant, it is important to know how scriptures spread through the world soon after their selection and order were established. Greek scripture moved into new language bodies, and each transformation assumed a distinct means and purpose of translation. As will be clear in later elaboration, the historical content of the scriptures changed not only as events and dialogue reached through silence and mystery to the Greek scripture, but also, and now fully visibly, as they have been moved out of our extant Greek source text into a thousand and another thousand foreign versions.

The first major employment in the West of the translator—of the translating messenger of the Bible—was to spread the word of God. Curiously, in classical Greek and Latin literatures, while there is imitation of Greek in Latin, as when Catullus adapts a poem by Sappho, there is otherwise remarkably little translation per se. Beyond their own literatures, Greeks and Romans had little interest, and decently educated Greeks and Romans read both Greek and Latin. The power of the Greeks and Romans resided in their civilization and the ruling power of the sword. The power of the proselytizing Christians was in the holy word. And Greek was a chosen language for this purpose, since in eastern Europe, much of North Africa, and the Near East, Greek was the lingua franca. But with the growth of Christianity and the necessity for clergy, if not for the largely illiterate laity, to possess canonized scripture, the serious ecclesiastical industry of Bible translation began. Most of the emphasis was on producing vernacular versions of the New Covenant rather than of the Hebrew Bible, for part of the overriding need to propagate Christianity was distinguishing it from its Jewish source. Accordingly, there were soon versions of the Greek scriptures in Syriac, Armenian, Georgian, Ethiopic, Arabic, and even Nubian, Persian, Sogdian, and Caucasian Albanian. In the West, that is, west of the Near East, there was primarily Latin, and then Gothic, Old Church Slavonic, and Anglo-Saxon.[37]

HISTORY OF THE WORD AFTER JEROME'S LATIN DOMINATION

In the early Christian centuries, Latin had the double role of being not only a classical language of Rome but also a true European vernacular, spoken by both clergy and laity in Latin countries before the vulgar Romance tongues predominated. Moreover, like Greek Koine, church Latin in biblical translation and patristic writings had thrown off the artificial elegance of complicated classical Latin syntax. For the common reader it was an easier tongue to read. As the Romance languages gained ground, displacing Latin as the vulgar tongue, the need for a true universal Vulgate arose, which was in large part the handiwork of the Latin scholar Jerome (347–419/420). Saint Jerome, as was his later title, revised earlier versions of the gospels and ultimately settled in Bethlehem and with the help of Jewish friends translated the Hebrew Bible from what he called the "true text." He was lucky to be working from the original Hebrew text for the Old Testament as opposed to the mysterious apocryphal New Covenant gospels, which were one language removed from their Semitic speakers. The New Covenant, like the canonical Apocrypha (until the Dead Sea Scrolls findings), had no Semitic version.[38]

---

[37] For the most thorough description and analysis of early Bible translations, see Bruce M. Metzger's *The Early Versions of the New Testament: Their Origin, Transmission, and Limitations* (Oxford: Clarendon Press, 1977).

[38] For more on the gospels as the New Covenant Apocrypha, see p. 443.

The fifth-century Vulgate dominated the West as the true Bible (the title Vulgate or Vulgata came into being only in the sixteenth century), and by the sixteenth century there was sacred sound but the meaning of the words eluded most of the laity. Latin had remained a learned universal language, but its parish readers were limited. So came the need to bring the biblical story directly to the people and not through a translated version in the priest sermon summary. Hearing the truth of the Bible in a language one could not understand may have been advantageous to clerical authority, but it simply added another layer of the ahistorical to stories already suffering from the absence of verifiable originals. The Protestant Reformation, the break from Rome and Latin, the Roman Catholic language, had at its core the mission of bringing the Bible to the laity in a tongue they could understand.[39]

In returning to the vernacular, the Bible moved back to its original koine (common) purpose, which was to speak to the common people in plain, sharp, uplifting speech. The life-and-death drama of those translation efforts in France, Germany, and England also profoundly affected the language and literatures of each people. In England, the sixteenth-century William Tyndale gave the New Covenant back to the people, to "the plowboy in the field." He followed the aims of Erasmus, who gave us the populist image of the plowboy who could read scripture. In 1529, Tyndale translated *Exhortations for the Diligent Study of Scripture* in which Erasmus asks that the Bible be translated into all tongues, for women and for all peoples and faiths. In Tyndale's lovely words we hear, "I wold to God the plowman wold singe a texte of the scripture at his plow-bene. And that the wever at his lowme with this wold drive away the tediousnes of tyme. I would the wayfaringman with this pastyme wold expelle the weriness of his iorney."

With Tyndale, and in the next century with the spoken grandeur of the King James Version (now raised to a higher rhetorical level beyond the plowboy), the testaments entered the English language popularly as original text, as "the word of the Bible." Such popular confusion about original document and a translation of a translation reveals just how far the lofty beauty of the King James Version can lead one to ascribe absolute authority to its words, though its title modestly calls itself a version. The King James Version is a Protestant translation. The now omitted prefatory "Translation to the Reader" reveals the struggle between Catholic and Protestant, between London and Rome, concerning dominion, doctrine, and moral law. While the leader of the translation

---

[39] Halfway through the twentieth century, the Latin Vulgate gave way to the vernacular, with the exception of a few places such as the Catholic Church in China.

group, Dr. Miles Smith, denounces his rival "Catholicks," whom he defines as "Popish *Romanists*," his introduction ends with a spiritual defense of the art of translation with his plea that translation let in the light.

LOOKING WITHIN THE GOSPELS FOR HISTORICAL AND IMAGINED EVENTS

Unfortunately, as the New Covenant and the Hebrew Bible multiplied in translation throughout Europe, all the tendencies within the Greek scriptures to disenfranchise Yeshua of his religion and ethnicity were not ameliorated but, rather, enhanced. The original history of a Jewish sect recognizing its messiah became more remote from the Galil and the streets of Yerushalayim, and the translation of Greek names into local names increasingly distanced the personages from their Semitic stage. To understand the Greek scriptures in their time, it is helpful to gather information from other writings—some that have remained closer to their linguistic and spiritual sources—including the Dead Sea Scrolls, the Nag Hammadi Library, the intertestamental pseude-pigrapha overlapping with New Testament apocrypha, and, above all, the writings of Philo and Josephus.

The gospels are documents composed as histories of the beginnings of Christianity. Their religious purpose is to prove, to inspire, and to convert. However, the events, the people, the names, the conversations are story, not chronicle or history. In telling its story, every religious document necessarily claims and demands belief in its unique and absolute historical truth. Often the punishment for disbelief or even skepticism has been death, death to "the infidel" or "heretic," meaning one who is unfaithful or dissident to a prevailing orthodoxy. To take the gospels as historical event, which their didactic form prescribes, requires an act of faith. This same reasonable assumption of faith pertains to all religions.

As long as there are sects, there will be polemics over who has the correct faith. But a deeper faith does not need revealed truth in immutable words in our translated scripture. Nor does faith require proof or disapproval by external historic document. Faith survives as a beautiful tautology, since faith requires faith in faith. Scripture, however, which is often the source of faith, is fallible, since it is neither written nor dictated by God but is a human, imperfect endeavor. Those who say that faith carries them beyond the word may have the clearest mind and spirit, for perhaps they understand that words are sounded script, imprecise signs, and sometimes wondrous. And even the word under the word, that pause of silence, will not yield a perfect epiphany. So pitting faith against history or history against faith should be taken as a common human activity of medium importance. In the end, faith and moveable mountains will keep their own terrains. In the instance of my translations and comments, these are another tampering with tradition and perhaps doctrinal faith by seeking to make the words closer to their Greek and Semitic sources. In the cause of progress and frailty, I hope I can add something to the necessary inconstancy of text and their mysterious interpretations.

GOSPEL YESHUA AND HISTORICAL YESHUA

For more than a century, those who look for historical truths in texts sacred and secular have come up with two versions of Yeshua: the gospel Yeshua and the historical Yeshua. The unfriendly dilemma of looking for the historical Yeshua is our expanding awareness of what cannot be known. We do not know even the most fundamental facts of the life of Yeshua—including the nature of his birth, the sect or segment of Jews (Essenes, Galileans, Zealots, Pharisees, Hasidim) whose views reflect his formation, the specific cause of his crucifixion. Lacking resources, we search in the gospels to prove or disprove a gospel event or statement. We look for special elements within the gospel story, and then examine archaeological evidence in Israel, just as in corroborating events in Homer we gaze at the ruins of Troy, its walls, the Labyrinth in Crete, its stone bull, and even Hades as an archaic temple in Southern Epirus. As for patristic documents to confirm the story of Yeshua, the commentary leads not to history but back to the gospels through the Church Fathers' passionate convictions and interpretations. Whatever rigor of dispassionate reason, honesty, and nonpartisan intelligence is applied to this search, there remains the limiting fact that in investigating miracles, events, and intimate conversations that are said to have taken place in houses, in the Sanhedrin,[40] and between Yeshua and his opponents, there is no external evidence to support or reject these matters. As for gospel references to peoples and events in Yeshua's time, we do have historic information: Romans in the Seleucid Near East; Pompey's conquest of Jerusalem in 63 B.C.E.; the Jews in Israel, Alexandria, and in the wider diaspora; the Jewish uprising against the Romans in 66–70 C.E. And this external information helps us to receive the meaning of gospel statements in some historical context.

Because the gospels arrive before us from unknown origin, we have only some "negative" facts. It is certain that the authors (the evangelists or gospel

---

[40] The highest judicial and ecclesiastical council in Jerusalem. Its members were accused of conspiring the death of Yeshua, and secret conversations in the Sanhedrin are reported in the gospels to prove the conspiracy. Reports of overheard conversations behind the walls of the Sanhedrin lack credibility.

writers) are unknown by name or person, that no alleged eyewitness accounts survive, that no intermediary texts exist in Hebrew, Aramaic, Greek, Syriac, Coptic, or Latin—the languages used in areas of early Judaism and Christianity. Where did the evangelists, who were not witness to these events, obtain their information? There is no knowledge about this void. What is known is that a rabbi, whose name was probably Yeshua ben Yosef, was crucified by the Romans for the political crime of conspiring against Rome.

Given this rude circumstance, we do at least have an important option: While we cannot prove the truth of any described event, we can perhaps convincingly assert the untruth or improvability of some events. Such an option may seem meager, but it is not. Demonstrating the improvability of events that are sinister in their implication for the principal participants may in itself be a crucial achievement.

PASSOVER PLOT

The single event in the New Covenant that provides the basis for blaming the Jews for the death of Yeshua is the trial before the council or Sanhedrin where, the gospels say, the high priests and whole council were looking for testimony against Yeshua to put him to death, but they found none. "Many testified falsely against him, and their testimonies were not the same" (Mark 14.55). Similar words occur in Matthew 26.59. How could the evangelists, or anyone outside the Sanhedrin, have known, at least three decades after the words that were supposed to have been exchanged, what deliberations took place behind closed doors in a private residence? How could one know that such a meeting even took place?

Such passages in the gospels were assembled to exonerate the Romans for their crucifixion of Yeshua and to incriminate and place a curse on the Jews for Yeshua's execution. This selective curse incriminating an entire people forever reveals its own folly and senseless cruelty. Why do Yeshua and his family and followers not share the blanket racial and religious guilt laid upon all Jews for all generations? ("Let his blood be upon us and upon our children!" [Matt. 27.25]). And is Yeshua as a Jew not also the devil and a murderer? ("You are from your father the devil / and you want to do the desires of your father. / From the beginning he was a murderer" [John 8.44]). But rabbi Yeshua is exempt from the terrible epithets and curses laid upon his coreligionists.

It should be clear that in the schizoid way in which Yeshua is presented—as rabbi and as denouncer of Jews—there is a deep confusion of conflicting disguises of identity, and diverse voices speaking through his persona. With regard to the curse that Matthew has the Jews call upon themselves and their children, Vermes declares the consequence of demonization: "Matthew laid the foundation of the Christian concept of the universal and permanent Jewish guilt for deicide which, unhesitatingly embraced by the church, was responsible for the shedding of much innocent blood over the ages" (*The Changing Faces of Jesus*, 232). Vermes points out fascinating paradoxes in Matthew, who at one moment has his Yeshua speak as leader of fellow Jews, and the next as a later Church Father: "Matthew's 'schizophrenia' shows itself in many ways. He is more pro-Jewish than Mark, and much more than the Gentile Luke. He portrayed a Jesus who was concerned only with Jews—'I was sent to the lost sheep of the house of Israel' (Matt. 15.24)—and who actually forbade his disciples to take an interest in non-Jews: 'Go nowhere among the Gentiles, and enter no town of the Samaritans, but rather to the lost sheep of the house of Israel' (10.6). However, in a complete volte-face from the chauvinism expressed in the preceding passages, Matthew laid a heavier emphasis than any other evangelist on the Christian mission to all the nations, and on the church being substituted for Israel" (231).

The sundry faces of Yeshua confound, but it must be remembered that an emerging new sect needs to erase its parent. So it was essential to fabricate a Socrates-like trial by villainous Jews in order to free the Romans of their historical execution of Yeshua. Yet there is no historical exoneration of the Romans for Yeshua's execution. The single event in the life and death of Yeshua that all agree is historical is his execution by the Romans. If there were exonerating circumstances that "justified" such execution within the arena of Roman law, such as Yeshua's being an active leader and opponent to Roman rule, a seditionist, a Jewish revolutionary, indeed, the king of the Jews against the Roman governor, that, too, we cannot know. We have no official information on why the Romans ordered the execution but, given that this execution is historical, we cannot go further than to suppose that some form of opposition to Roman rule led to Yeshua's death, since such opposition is the usual cause for the empire's practice of cruel execution for all to see.

Crucifixion was also applied to robbers. However, if there is any truth or significance in the "King of the Jews" placard that the Romans had Yeshua carry, or in the anti-Jewish version, which again made it the politics of the Sanhedrin to convince Rome of Yeshua's disloyalty to Rome, all these hints within the gospels suggest political not civil crime, the latter being normally the responsibility of the occupied people. While nothing is foolproof, it is most unlikely that Yeshua died as a thief.

Despite the negative facts—our absolute ignorance of what led to Yeshua's execution—some excellent scholars, even in books published as late as 1999, perpetuate the myth of ultimate Jewish culpability.

E. P. Sanders states as a firm fact that "Jesus was executed by the Romans as a would-be 'king of the Jews'" (E. P. Sanders, *Jesus and Judaism* [Philadelphia: Fortress Press, 1987], 294).[41] His argument that the Romans killed Yeshua as an insurrectionist is proved by his title "king of the Jews." Since this view puts potential blame on the Romans (whereas the gospels show unwillingness by the Romans to carry out the crucifixion), one can think that here, at last, is a plausible motive that does not reflect the evangelists' pattern of making the Romans mere puppets of wicked Jewish will. But while the "king of the Jews" incident may suggest Roman anger against Yeshua as a rebel leader, Sanders still accepts the gospels' version that the "Jews," through their plot, convinced the Romans of Yeshua's role as seditionist, which throws the guilt again fundamentally back on the Jews for suggesting Yeshua's opposition to Rome.

One implication is that it would be slanderous and sinister for Yeshua to have opposed the Romans. This view is compatible with the gospels' view of diminished Roman responsibility as an agent of justice falsely determined by the plotting Jews. It also suggests that we do have knowledge of what the Jewish leaders said behind closed doors, and we are again back to square one in terms of unverifiable speculation of a Jewish plot to murder Yeshua. Such speculation on the basis of the inherent truth of incidents reported in scripture is common and, until recently, universal. Yet all such speculation founders on its disrespect for the three already noted facts regarding the death of Yeshua: 1) Yeshua died by Roman *crucifixion;* 2) crucifixion was the punishment for *sedition* against Rome, as were some forms of civil crime, but in this instance all parties have ruled out civil crime; 3) outside the gospels we have *no information* on the specific nature of the political crime of sedition—whether it was his actual opposition to Rome or a plot by his Jewish opponents to convince Rome of his opposition—that persuaded the prefect Pilate to make a public example through crucifixion. Scholars who routinely blame the Jews for setting up Yeshua's death founder on fact 3, which is the unverifiable conspiracy scenario.

A regrettable side of the gospels, as they have come down to us, is the apologetic alibi for Roman authorities in their role in the crucifixion (as well as the acceptance of the depravity of opposing Rome for which the fit punishment will be the destruction of the Temple). Evidence in Acts, Apocalypse, and in routine historical documents about the treatment of Christians in the Roman Empire prior to Constantine's conversion shows an unhappy picture that goes beyond the Christian martyr scenes in the Colosseum. All the miseries of the early Christians under the Roman Empire speak out against the

---

[41] Sanders looks for discussion of his ideas among many historians who deal with the trial and execution to A. E. Harvey, *Jesus on Trial* (1976) and Paul Winter, *On the Trial of Jesus* (Berlin/New York: De Gruter, 1974).

revisionary hands that at critical moments cast the gospels' authors as Roman sympathizers during years of terrible persecution when, among the horror of mass crucifixions, in 70 c.e., the earliest Christian Jews, along with the others, were killed or driven by Roman legions from an incinerated Jerusalem.

In the gospels both the Jewish leaders and the Jews in the street are blamed for Yeshua's death. Those scholars who still contend that the Jewish authority put the Romans up to killing Yeshua are in sad concordance with the Second Vatican Council's diplomatic softening of the universal charge of deicide against the Jewish people. After nearly two thousand years, the Roman Catholic Church, in the *Vatican Council II* document *Nostra Aetate,* announced: "Even though the Jewish authorities and those who followed their lead pressed for the death of Christ (cf. John 19.6), neither all Jews indiscriminately at that time, nor all Jews today, can be charged with the crimes committed during his passion." What is the meaning of "neither all Jews indiscriminately at that time, nor all Jews today"? It shifts the blame of "ancient crimes" from all Jews forever to some Jews discriminately in the past and an unspecified number of Jews today. The Vatican offers an improvement that only reinforces the original charge by turning to John 19.6 to validate the ancient, inhuman accusation of deicide. While the Vatican in recent years has officially and courageously acknowledged and apologized for its own crimes over the centuries, here their restatement of Jewish authorities' alleged dominant role in the death of the Galilean is not a happy way of resolving ancient persuasions that have caused so much misery and death.

Graham Stanton comments, "In antiquity crucifixion was the most savage and shameful form of capital punishment. It was so barbarous and inhumane that polite Romans did not talk about it. Crucifixion was carried out by Romans especially on slaves, violent criminals and rebellious subject peoples" (*Gospel Truth?,* 173). With respect to Yeshua's death, Graham Stanton, concurring with E. P. Sanders, states that under Roman law, sedition was a crime for which the crucifixion was a due punishment. But while proposing the accusation of sedition as the active cause of Yeshua's death, like Sanders, Stanton too accepts the plot theory and blames the Jewish Temple authorities for misinformation to the Romans. In both examples, where recent scholars advance a radical and more historical explanation for the crucifixion by seeing more possibilities within the gospel presentation, they assume an impossible premise of knowledge of the intentions and words of the Jewish authorities.

To guess the line of causes of the crucifixion keeps scholars busy speculating about the fate of the historical Yeshua. We do not know the truth of the charge of "king of the Jews." We do not know whether Roman soldiers cast dice for Yeshua's garments, whether he was stabbed with a spear or he was not (the gospels do not concur on the stabbing). We do not know whether the centurion, who was head of the execution squad, had an immediate vision after killing Yeshua. Nor do we know that while he and his troops were gazing in awe at the dead Yeshua, he, the centurion, converted on the spot to later Christian credo and that he declared Yeshua innocent, God, and risen. We cannot know or argue the veracity or falsehood of these scenes other than to say that certain assertions in the gospels seem likely, unlikely, contradictory, or unverifiable. It is unverifiable which of our assertions has dominion.

In fairness to E. P. Sanders, while he does assert the culpability of the Temple authorities, he elaborates the unknowability of these scenes, and observes that not only theologians but historians have their "'history' and 'exegesis' dictated by theology" (*Jesus and Judaism*, 334). He also observes the well-known contradictions and implausibilities about the trial: "It is hard to believe that a formal court actually convened on the first night of Passover, as Matthew and Mark have it. Luke, we should note, states that Yeshua was taken to the Sanhedrin only after daybreak (Luke 22.66). John does not depict a trial before the Sanhedrin at all" (298). Sanders, who speaks of himself as a "secularized Protestant," continues:

> The Gospels are all influenced by the desire to incriminate the Jews and exculpate the Romans. The insistence of the crowd that Jesus be killed, despite Pilate's considering him innocent (Matt. 27.15–26/Mark 15.6–15/ Luke 23. 18–23; cf. John 18.38), shows this clearly enough. The elaborate Jewish trial scenes in the Synoptic Gospels also tend to shift responsibility to Judaism in an official way and help serve the same purpose. (298)

As for why the evangelists should have wanted so much to exculpate the Romans, Sanders says, "This reflects the fact that the early Church had to make its way in the Roman Empire, and did not wish its leader to be thought of as truly guilty in Roman eyes" ("Jesus Christ," in *Eerdmans Dictionary of the Bible*, ed. David Noel Freeman [Grand Rapids, MI/Cambridge, UK: William B. Eerdmans Publishing Company, 2000], 706).

About the actual possibility of the trial and what we can know of it he writes:

> All we need do is to accept the obvious, that we do not have detailed knowledge of what happened when the high priest and possibly others questioned Jesus. We cannot know even that "the Sanhedrin" met. Further, I doubt that the earliest followers of Jesus knew. They were not privy to the membership list; if people hurried into the high priest's house at night there was no one to identify them and tick their names off. . . . I am not proposing that the evangelists have deliberately deceived us. It seems quite clear that they did not

know why Jesus was executed from the point of view of the Jewish leaders. We shall see, in fact, that they were ignorant even about the composition of a Jewish court. New Testament scholars all tell themselves, one another and their students that the Gospels writers were not historians in the modern sense, but we do not apply this fact rigorously enough. (*Jesus and Judaism,* 299)

Sanders observes diverse reasons "that could have led the Romans to think that Yeshua was a threat to public order" as grounds for his execution. And he insists that on that confused night "the trial scene of Matthew and Mark is not historical," "that not only do we not know whether the Sanhedrin convened, but our ignorance of all aspects is also shared by the evangelists." Finally, he states: "That the *internal motives* of the actors were known by those on whom the evangelists drew seems impossible" (300). He also castigates fellow modern historians for making assertions not based on historical evidence, for not being rigorous enough.

With all his annoyance at historical presumptions, Sanders still writes shockingly, "I do not doubt that Jesus was arrested on the orders of the high priest and interrogated" (299). With that declaration Sanders subverts his own detailed and vehement argument that the conspiracy plot, trial, and arrest have no basis in historical reference or probability and that the evangelists wrote to exculpate the Romans. All his argument, historical observations, and his debunking of those who mythologize history and come to facile conclusions disappear. The venom, which entered the gospels and was to persist as a death force directed against Yeshua's coreligionists from early Christendom to the present, is issued once again, implausibly, by an earnest historical interpreter of the gospels.

The story of Jews at the Passover, who kidnap Christian children to perform ritual murder on them to use their blood to prepare the matzoh, a tale that exists in virtually every language in Europe, is not heard today. Yet the source of the satanization of the Jews, leading to such tales, lies in the New Covenant and, as Elaine Pagels has revealed in *The Origin of Satan* (New York: Vintage, 1995), has not faded; and so the venom, of Jew-hating and Jew-killing, has not vanished. The Jew-hating will not disappear for a reader of the New Covenant as long as Yeshua and all his cast continue to have their true identities as observant Jews interacting with Jews obscured. Maybe in a few generations in the Christian West, the dark activity of hatred and killing will vanish. For now, New Covenant scholarship must fully face its responsibility by rejecting as factual history the eternally unforgivable Jewish deeds dramatically presented in the Passion story. Then this Jewish scripture will be read with measured understanding and enlightened pleasure. The demonized Jew will be no more. And Yeshua, who escapes demonization only insofar as he is not perceived as a Jew, will have his dignified religious passion fully and jubilantly restored. For the Christian faithful, the undisguised Jew, Yeshua, can be received as the unblemished incarnation of Jewish messianic aspiration.

RECENT SCHOLARSHIP ON YESHUA, THE JEWISH AUTHORITIES, JUDAS, AND THE CHARGE OF DEICIDE

Today is a good time with respect to questions of the historical Yeshua, immeasurably good compared to yesterday. But today has a memory. It is hard for many scholars, who must draw primarily on the gospels, to move freely from nearly two millennia of theological exegesis to an unprejudiced walk through historical investigation. The holy precincts of Christianity are a powerful tradition and fortress, and judgment contends with almost insuperable temptations of normative belief. To my surprise, however, these approaches, in commentary and translation, have been welcomed with openness and indeed excitement. With respect to translation, the restoration of Semitic names has already been incorporated in other forthcoming translations. There is enthusiasm in the air for change, which is inevitable.

Among those writers who for many years have moved independently and with great scholarly resources are George Nickelsburg, who has given us his excellent study, *Jewish Literature Between the Bible and the Mishnah* (1981), as well as many seminal books and studies on the ties between Judaism and early Christianity. He has dealt meticulously with matters of historicity. Jacob Neusner brings in rabbinic traditions and a knowledge of Mishnaic law. Geza Vermes has pivotal volumes on the historicity of the gospels, including *Jesus the Jew* (1981) and his recent *The Changing Faces of Jesus* (2000). A long important road exists between Albert Schweitzer's *The Quest of the Historical Jesus* back in 1906 and Rudolf Bultmann's *The History of the Synoptic Tradition* (1966), W. G. Kümmel's works on the New Testament, Howard Clark Kee's *Jesus in History* (1977), and recent work by Wayne A. Meeks, Burton L. Mack, Elaine Pagels, Paula Fredriksen, Marcus J. Borg, and Graham Stanton, to mention but a few of the scholars who have been innovative and also reach a wide audience.

In studies pertaining to a historical Yeshua, the sticking point is what is worth discussing as a source of history. The quest for the historical Jesus owes its impetus to eighteenth-century Enlightenment and the orientalist Hermann Samuel Reimarus (1694–1768). Schweitzer begins his work on the historical Jesus with Reimarus as indicated in his title *Von Reimarus zur Wrede*, (1906). Schweitzer elaborates the ethical nature of Yeshua's ministry in first-century Judaism, essentially discounting most information on the historical figure and stressing his idea of a "spiritual kingdom." The Jesus Seminar, which represents a sizable group of contemporary theologians and scholars within the university and clergy, questions the authenticity of Yeshua's words and the events of his life. In their new translations of the New Covenant, the Jesus Seminar scholars rate the historical probability of each chapter and verse (which must be taken, at best, as a symbolic gesture toward correction).

As for the historical origins of anti-Judaism that are to be found in the New Covenant, no one has written more brilliantly and movingly than Elaine Pagels in her *The Origin of Satan*. That disease of anti-Semitism, she informs us, begins with the demonization of the Jews in the Greek scriptures. Pagels finds a historical possibility in the scriptures, however, that leads her to accept, with probability, the story of a Jewish conspiracy, perpetrated by "Jewish leaders" that the New Covenant tells. She writes:

> I agree as a working hypothesis that Jesus' execution was probably imposed by the Romans for activities they considered seditious—possibly for arousing public demonstrations and (so they apparently believed) for claiming to be "King of the Jews." Among his own people, however, Jesus appeared as a radical prophetic figure whose public teaching, although popular with the crowds, angered and alarmed certain Jewish leaders, especially the Temple authorities, who probably facilitated his capture and arrest. (xxii)

Later, in discussing the diverse uses of the term "Jew" in the gospels, she tells us that "John, like the other Gospels, associates the mythological figure of Satan with specific human opposition, first implicating Judas Iscariot, then the Jewish authorities, and finally "the Jews collectively" (105). But, after stating that the gospels associate mythological Satan (presumably unfairly and incorrectly) with both Judas and Jewish authorities in order to blame them for Yeshua's death, she returns to her original premise: "Let us assume, first, that it is historically likely that certain Jewish leaders may have collaborated with Roman authorities in Jesus' arrest and execution" (105). While she absolutely deplores and disdains the accusations of guilt and demonization of the Jews, and colors those accusations as gospel mythology, she, too, believes (at least in these passages) that these accusations are "historically likely" to be true. Like well-intentioned Sanders and Stanton, Pagels provides the demonizers of the Jews with their essential opening for pinning guilt collectively and eternally on the Jews (as Matthew proclaims) for Yeshua's death.

Who can believe that a Jewish mob on the first night of Passover is in the street shouting to a reluctant prefect, "Crucify him!" followed by "Let his blood be upon us and upon our children!"? Would anybody shout a curse upon themselves and their children? The notion is silly but noxious, and has followed the

Jews for two millennia. At the instant before his death, Yeshua cries out to God his despair of abandonment, in Aramaic, his own tongue. At this supreme moment of Yeshua's death as a tortured Jewish man by Roman crucifixion, he may be "King of the Jews" in Roman mockery, but to the evangelists and future followers he is seen as the Christian God, not the Jewish *mashiah*. More, by inventing a scene of mass Jewish guilt that he notably does not share, Yeshua at once ceases to be perceived as a Jew. He is defrocked. He is stripped of his robes of faith and tradition as a messianic Jew preaching redemption.

These hate scenes lack historicity. We know that the church of Rome needed to find the Jews, not the earlier Romans, guilty for Yeshua's death. Pagels explains that those who wrote about Yeshua were "devoted admirers, even as his worshipers" (*The Origin of Satan*, 7), and she writes, further, that the gospels were "wartime literature" (referring to the Jewish-Roman war in 66–70), and composed to persuade other Jews not to agitate against the Romans. These "wartime literature" gospels were, as Pagels interprets them, citing Josephus, Roman-biased documents warning Jews not to resist Rome or else suffer devastation.

In character with recent historical criticism on killing Yeshua the man, William Nicholls, in his book *Christian Anti-Semitism* (Northvale, NY and London: Jason Aronson, 1995), writes:

> Did the Jews kill Christ? We shall discover that the stories in the Gospels that suggest they did are exceedingly improbable. The Jews did not kill Jesus because they had no reason to do so. He was not guilty of any religious offense. It is in the highest degree improbable that such a trial before the Sanhedrin as we read of in the gospels of Mark and Matthew ever took place. What we read in the gospels about the trial of Jesus is the project of later Christian imagination, and it reflects Christian, not Jewish, views of the nature of the Messiah. (17)

Nicholls, Nickelsburg, and Vermes reflect at least a strong component of contemporary historical criticism. While, as noted, other distinguished figures state that there was a Jewish plot to arrest and kill Yeshua the lord, the current mood and scholarship of religious studies in university and seminary generally has, increasingly, little patience for dreadful conspiracy theory.

Elaine Pagels is our most original and eloquent interpreter of the period for Jewish, Christian, and gnostic matters, and a champion of women in her books *The Gnostic Gospels* (New York: Random House, 1979) and *Adam, Eve, and the Serpent* (New York: Vintage, 1988). Yet Pagels, Sanders, Stanton, and a majority of earlier and many contemporary religious historians seem to hold to the premise that Jewish authorities plotted and achieved Yeshua's death through the instrument of the weak, innocent, but acquiescing Roman prefect of Palestine.[42] At the very least they accept an active Jewish involvement in the events leading to Yeshua's crucifixion. They do so without malice, with good conscience, based on their sound historical wisdom and experience in the fields. Yet we cannot know that the Jewish conspiracy is factual. Nor can we know that there was not a conspiracy of Jews against the rabbi Yeshua. And since no truth can be established with regard to the drama of Yeshua's death, we must stop there, and escape from the traditional assumptions so hard to lay to rest. It might be that angry Jews conspired horribly against other Jews and even in worse ways than the theatrical scenes that the New Covenant enacts. The Essenes, the sons of light, certainly declared their intention to wipe out, through war, the Jewish sons of darkness inhabiting Jerusalem. Nothing is surprising in the history of sectarian conflict. Here it is beyond dispute that we have no references to the Jews and the crucifixion outside the frame of the late gospels. The few historical mentions of Yeshua by name say nothing in this regard, including Josephus.

That ultimate condemnation of the Jews will create the terrible history of Jews and Christians. I should also venture that even were there a historical basis for Jewish plot theory, it should no more lead to global and eternal condemnation of selective Jews (since Christian Jews and Yeshua's family have been spared) than the execution of Socrates should lead to an eternal curse on the souls of Greeks.

We can believe through Christian faith in 1) Yeshua's virgin birth, 2) his miracles, and 3) his resurrection. And though the New Covenant is presented not as a tale but a report, many contemporary theologians will shepherd these key notions onto the meadow of faith and demand no historic proof from the gospels. But the alleged conspiracy plot by Jews against Yeshua has nothing to do with Christian faith. We can guess the circumstance of rivalry and self-exoneration that may have induced the early church to fabricate a conspiracy scene. The grave accusation demands historical credibility or dismissal once and for all.

---

[42] Though Marcus Borg in his *Meeting Jesus for the First Time* (San Francisco: HarperSan Francisco, 1994) refutes "the popular image of Jesus" and blames "parts of the New Testament" for constructing a picture of Jews against Yeshua, he too refers to Yeshua's crucifixion and his Jewish "opponents." With the kind intention of exonerating Jews in general from Yeshua's death, he asserts, as fact, the evil of a few enemy Jews. He writes, "But Jesus' opponents did not represent the Jewish people or nation. Rather, the few Jewish persons involved in the events leading to his execution were a small but powerful elite whose power derived from the Romans. Instead of representing the Jews, they might fairly be described as collaborating in the oppression of the Jewish people" (22).

To assume that a powerful elite of Herodian Jews collaborated with Romans, or worse, according to scripture, that unwilling Romans were urged by Jews in the street and from the Sanhedrin to execute Yeshua, returns us to the conspiracy theory of the Greek texts.

After all this, is there anything we can say about the crucifixion scene without falling into the trap of purposeful invention of evidence? Having spoken about what can *not* be said, what specific, historical assumptions *can* we make? There remain pivotal questions that can be reasonably elaborated. We say that there existed a historic Jew named Yeshua of Nazareth, who especially after his death and witnessed resurrection was called the messiah. It is widely doubted that Yeshua himself assumed the title of messiah during his lifetime, but that, too, is speculation. We can also say that the same Yeshua was crucified in the fourth decade of the first century by order of a historical figure, Pontius Pilate, the prefect or governor of Judea. We can say that those sayings attributed to Yeshua in the Gospel of Thomas and repeated and augmented in the gospels, while reflecting a wide oral rabbinic wisdom tradition based on biblical wisdom scripture, may in small or large part be statements originating with Yeshua. Beyond these bare statements, there is historical speculation and faith.

In the search for historicity, we can go a crucial step further than affirming the absence of historical proof. Sometimes there is enough external textual evidence to assert the improbability of certain events, which is a crucial positive step. For example, the figure of Judas lacks historical probability, since this story of the betrayer seems to be lifted intact and anachronistically from Midrashic tale. There is also the convenient parallel in Genesis of the Joseph story, where Judah sells Joseph for twenty pieces of silver. Bishop John Shelby Spong writes eloquently in *Liberating the Gospels* of the Judas story as a Christian invention. The common folklore motif of the betrayer was trumped up, in all its telling details, to use against the Jews as one of the colorful ways of exonerating Rome, and the Christians who inherited Rome, from Yeshua's death.

The motive for the insertion of the Judas story into the gospels is clear. Judas carries the name Judas to make "a Jew" be the betrayer of Yeshua. Judas is from the Greek *Ioudas* ('Ιούδας), from the Hebrew name Yehuda (יְהוּדָה), which signifies the province of Judea as well as "one who pertains to the tribe of Yehudi (יְהוּדִי—yehudi)," that is, a Jew. The Greek word "Judea" is a Latin version of the Greek *Ioudaia* ('Ιουδαία). So in Greek as well as in Hebrew, Judas and Jew are synonymous.

Such is the power of names that *Ioudas* ('Ιούδας) in the King James Version is translated in all other cases as Juda so that Judas will remain uniquely the caricature of the evil Jew of the New Covenant. In modern versions, such as the NRSV, Juda has been given its correct translation of Judas. Gone is the intent of saving Yeshua's own brother Judas from bearing the name of the betrayer. Among the epistles of the New Covenant we still have Jude in the "Letter of Jude" in all translations. The names "Juda," "Judah," and "Jude" are all translation masks to separate Christians Jews from Judas, but in the Greek texts they all have one name, *Ioudas* ('Ιούδας). Judas is a key figure in denigrating the image of the Jew, and his name remains a word in all languages for traitor.

In keeping with making Judas the Jew among the primitive Christians, who are Yeshua and his students, there is a pictorial tradition of making Judas look like the somber thief while the other disciples take on the features of the painter's nation. In the national art museum in Prague in a series of paintings of Yeshua and his disciples, all appear as fair Slavs, except for Judas, who is bent over as the dark, crafty Mediterranean.

THE CHARGE OF DEICIDE

Here we depart radically from the discussion of Rome killing Yeshua as "King of the Jews." Did Rome kill God as well? And, more crucial, can the biblical God be killed? The notion of deicide inevitably takes us to the history of Christological speculation on the human and divine in Yeshua. The early centuries of Christianity saw fearful debates about the nature of Christ, especially in the East. The Docetists (from *dokein*, "to seem"), along with overlapping gnostics, Nestorians, Arians, and Monophysites, were the main contenders for control of doctrines. The Docetists held that the figure on the cross was a simulacrum of Yeshua, since divine Yeshua could not be killed by mortals. By the end of the seventh century, these docetic "heresies" yielded to the prevailing orthodoxy of the Church: the incarnation of the divine word in the flesh as expounded in the prologue of the Gospel of John: "And the word became flesh" (Jn 1.14). In the incarnation, the divine Word (the *Logos*), which precedes the flesh, lives in union with the flesh during Yeshua's life, and after the flesh's death, the Word, which is the divinity of God, survives. Yeshua suffers pain as a human and dies, but the Word residing in him is eternal. The eternal God of the Abrahamic faiths cannot be killed by Jews, Christians, Greeks, Romans, or anyone. Hence, God cannot be the victim of deicide. But the charge of deicide presumes that God dies, and that after the crucifixion he disappears. God's death surely is not acceptable to those who have accused Jews of killing God. Indeed, those who charge deicide do so while firmly believing that God is not only alive but will avenge the deicide. Clearly, deep confusion presides.

While the notion of deicide is self-contradictory, this self-contradiction has persisted for two millennia. The gospels have none of it. The Roman centurion who executes rabbi Yeshua is the first to tell the crowds that Yeshua is God and arisen. He does not announce that his now-recognized God is dead. A man dies, but not God. And paradoxically, three days after his crucifixion, Yeshua returns to earth in human form. At one moment he asks the doubting Thomas to touch his wounds. For the believer, God lives and his everlasting existence has never lapsed. So the notion of deicide is a cruel rhetorical impossibility, and no person or people should be accused of having the desire or the means of committing what is humanly impossible: to kill the biblical God.

As a summary of the three crucial historical questions, *Rome, deicide, and Judas,* I take from Spong's *Liberating the Gospels* two powerful and succinct paragraphs from his chapter on Judas, "Judas Iscariot: A Christian Invention?" After twenty pages of detailing incongruities in the betrayal story, and indicating the source of the spurious betrayal story in Midrashic scripture, Spong concludes:

> I only want to register now that it is a tragedy of enormous dimensions that, by the time the story of Jesus' arrest and execution came to be written, the Christians made the Jews, rather than the Romans, the villains of their story. I suggest that this was achieved primarily by creating the narrative of a Jewish traitor according to the *Midrashic* tradition out of the bits and pieces of the sacred scriptures and by giving that traitor the name Judas, the very name of the nation of the Jews. As a result, from that day to this, the blame for the death of Jesus has been laid on the backs, not just of Judas, the Jewish prototype, but of the entire people of the Jews themselves. "His blood be upon us and upon our children." That was a biblical sentence of death to untold numbers of Jews.
>
> I raise this possibility to consciousness in the hope that as you and I are awakened to the realization of what this story of Judas has done to the Jews of history, we Christians might rise up and deal a death blow to the most virulent Christian prejudice that has for 2,000 years placed on the Jewish people the blame for the death of Jesus. If that result could be achieved, then the darkest clouds that have hung over the Christian Church in our history might finally begin to lift. (276)

CHRISTIAN JEWS OR
JEWISH CHRISTIANS

W e turn now to other aspects of historicity in the gospels, which is the identities of the participants. To understand this first-century setting, it is crucial to look at key Adamic names that describe the contending factions of Jews in the gospels. Traditionally, those who followed Yeshua have been called Christians or, more recently, "Christian Jews" (as there were Essenic Jews or Jews from any of perhaps seventeen sects seeking authority within Second Temple Judaism). Those who did not follow Yeshua are often called "Orthodox Jews," an essentially useless term of identity in a period of contending sects of first-century Jews, including the entourage around Yeshua.

In the touchy and highly charged game of naming people, sects, and places, which is at the heart of religious politics, the epithet "Jewish Christians" became widely popular in the last century, with some daring, as an acceptable title for those Jews who followed Yeshua. There was indeed no singular name for the first-century Jews who accepted Yeshua as the messiah. They were originally widely called Nazoreans, the general name for Aramaic-speaking Christian Jews and specifically for a sect who lived in Borea, which gave us the late second-century Gospel of the Nazoreans. They were also called Ebionites ("the poor") as in the Gospel of the Ebionites,[43] and Sampsaeans ("servants of God"). Since all who first followed Yeshua, who formed the religion that was to be called Christianity, were Jews, some word must account for them. Yet the term "Jewish Christians" is seriously misleading in its emphasis. I prefer "Christian Jews," which is just now coming into usage. "Jewish Christian" suggests that the followers of Yeshua *had* been Jews, and were now apostates who had renounced Judaism and converted to Christianity. This is all wrong, since the early "Christians" certainly thought themselves Jews, and when they addressed Yeshua as rabbi, which happens throughout the gospels, it was not a rabbi of some other religion than Judaism. The followers of the messiah, the

---

[43] For the Gospel of the Ebionites and Gospel of the Hebrews (another Christian Jewish gospel), see Ron Cameron, *The Other Gospels* (Philadelphia: Westminster Press, 1982), 103–106, and Willis Barnstone, *The Other Bible* (San Francisco: HarperSan Francisco, 1984), 333–338.

messianic Jews, were Jews, vying among other sects of Jews for persuasion and dominance.

There are also among the Christian Jews distinctions, and it gets complicated. We will stick to Christian Jews as the main appellation, but it should be understood that in the formation of early Christianity, there were both Jewish and gentile converts to Christian Judaism. Among the Jews who joined the Christian Jews, Paul represented a break from many of the traditional Jewish rites and practices, while the Jerusalem Christian Jews more strictly observed the laws of the Torah. Among the gentile Christian Jews, many welcomed the break from some demanding Jewish rites, while others, as exemplified by those whom Paul addressed in his Letter to the Galatians, were against laxity, and required strict observance of the Torah, including circumcision. Then there is the ambiguous term of "gentile Christians." Initially it means simply those gentiles who converted to the sect of the Christian Jews but later, as Christianity drifts from its center in Judaism—or thinks it does—it will be known simply as the gentiles (the non-Jews), or Christians.

Until the destruction of the Temple in 70 c.e., more than three decades after Yeshua's death, the overwhelming number of the followers of Yeshua remained Jews. Those who were gentile converts were converts not to Christianity but to a first-century Judaism that accepted Yeshua as the biblical messiah. So, insofar as we speak of Jews, Hasmonean Jews, Diaspora Jews, Second Temple Jews, Hasidic Jews, we call the followers of Yeshua the Mashiah "Christian Jews." Since "Christian" means "messianic," a Christian Jew is a messianic Jew who has found the messiah. The Greek word *Hristos* (Χριστός) for Christ, meaning "the messiah" and "the anointed one" from Hebrew *mashiah* (מָשִׁיחַ), would never have been used or understood by those Jewish peasants who looked to Yeshua. For Jews of the day, a central meaning of "messiah" was, as Graham Stanton summarizes, "the hope that an anointed King of David's line would set up a glorious kingdom by removing Israel's enemies" (*Gospel Truth?* 178). Whether there was a more transcendental meaning, which we would presume from Isaiah's reference to a spiritual son or whether he was instead the practical guardian that Stanton suggests he was, there is no question that soon "messiah" became synonymous with Yeshua, in effect his name, and hence his followers eventually took on his name. When the messianic Jews became dominantly Greek-speaking, the sect took on a Greek name and were the Christians. Stanton writes:

> Paul refers to Jesus as "Christ" on every page of his letters—271 times in all in
> his seven undisputed letters. However, with only clear exception and a handful

of marginal cases, "Christ" has become simply a name for Jesus; it no longer refers to the *messiahship* of Jesus. Elsewhere when Paul speaks about the significance of Jesus for Christians, he prefers to use "lord," or "Son"/"Son of God," because these terms made sense to Gentiles. Without explanation, Messiah meant nothing in non-Jewish settings. (*Gospel Truth?* 178)

Unfortunately, even today the word "Christian" has for almost everyone lost its original meaning of "messianic," and consequently Christians rarely understand that "Christian" is not only the name of a religious denomination but is primarily a title of Jewish faith in the messiah. To speak now of "messianics" and "messianic Jews" restores the essence of the meaning of early Christianity (messianism). In the history of Christianity, Yeshua is seen as the messiah and his followers Christian Jews, and this meaning is preferable when referring to intertestamental scripture, which when Jewish with a Christianizing overlay is now almost universally termed "Jewish Christian." To resort to the older term of "primitive Christians" obscures the fact that the followers belonged to a new branch of first-century Judaism, and demeans these followers as "primitive," suggesting that the Christian Jews were the good but uninformed and uninstructed pioneers of a future great faith.

Once having observed that for early Christians Yeshua was the Jewish messiah, he was one of many declared messiahs. The title of messiah is at the heart of Jewish biblical scripture and rabbinic tradition. King David—apart from all his human political accomplishments and swashbuckling passions—assumed for many the anointed role of messiah, and in 1 Samuel 16 he is singled out as the divinely chosen ruler. In Psalm 2.2 he is identified "as God's anointed" whom God addresses as "son." The Jewish messianic hope is one of a promised, ideal future on earth, of a leader from the seed of David (as defined in Ezra 4) who will restore divine rule to Israel and reign in goodness and truth. Christian messianism, primarily fashioned by Paul, was scarcely interested in the teachings of Yeshua who will restore divine rule to Israel and reign in goodness and truth. Messianism for the Christians was less centered on an earthly paradise. Paul, who fashioned the eschatology of Christian messianism, spoke little of the teachings of Yeshua on earth. His Yeshua is the crucified son of God who resurrected brings judged souls into eternal, celestial salvation. His messianism is a vision of ends through which the righteousness of the messiah and his rewards to the believers are revealed. But most of the later gospels are not of the Passion, which inspired Paul, but of Yeshua the wise man of the parables, the healer, and the miracle worker here in this world, and which corresponds to messianic powers of Elisha and Elijah and of the Hasid holy men from Yeshua's Galilee.

Early in Matthew and Luke, the Galilean Yeshua ben Yosef's Davidic seed is established where the evangelists trace his lineage back to King David (Matt. 1.17; Luke 3.23–38). It should be added that these two genealogies are separate in linguistic style and may be later additions to the gospels. Yeshua's contemporary Essenes had their messianic figures as revealed in the Dead Sea Scrolls, but Yeshua appears to come directly out of the strong Hasidic tradition in Galilee, of these holy charismatic men, the healers and miracle workers, who represented not the official religion of the priests in the synagogues, but a popular personal figure, "the man of God" (*ish ha-elohim*). This tradition goes back to the prophets Elisha and Elijah, who were the most revered popular healers and miracle makers in the Hebrew Bible.

As we move to Yeshua's time, in the Apocrypha and the Dead Sea Scrolls, the references to healers and miracles are legion, and especially in northern Israel, which was the site of Yeshua's ministry. The later Mishnah and the Talmud note two major healers: Honi (whom Josephus calls Onias) and his grandson Hanina ben Dosa, a contemporary of Yeshua.[44] Honi, called "the Circle Drawer" in the Mishnah and the Talmud, was a rainmaker. These itinerant charismatics were normally ascetic, caring little for food or personal possessions, which they would share with others. Like Yeshua, Honi was eventually put to death for political reasons, not willing to take sides in disputes between ruling factions (Josephus, *Antiquities* 14.22–24). Hanina ben Dosa from the first century, came from Araba or Gabara, near Yeshua's Nazareth, and was the best known of those who through prayer performed miracles. To follow the road of his many healings, of his changing vinegar into oil (as Yeshua changed water into wine), is to trace the path of Yeshua in his many therapeutic visits to the sick and, when called upon, his miracles of changing few provisions into necessary abundance. Vermes observes the Galilean holy men, whose messianic traits are shared by Yeshua: "Jewish, and perhaps in particular Galilean, popular religiosity tended to develop along the path followed by Honi, Hilkiliah, Hanan, Jesus, and Hanina. Compassionate, caring, and loving, they were all celebrated as deliverers of the Jews from famine, sickness, and the dominion of the forces of darkness, and some of them at least as teachers of religion and morality. . . . The Jesus of the New Testament fits into this picture, which in turn confers on his image validity and credibility; for there is no denying that a figure not dissimilar to the Honis and Haninas of Palestine Judaism lurks beneath the Gospels" (Vermes, *The Changing Faces of Jesus,* 267).

---

[44] For extensive information on healers and miracle workers in Galilee, see "Beneath the Gospels" in Geza Vermes's *The Changing Faces of Jesus,* 246–279.

In late Kabbalah (a body of mystical teachings of rabbinic origin), there are important messianic leaders, especially after the expulsion from Spain when Lurian mysticism established itself in Amsterdam, Safed in Israel, and Constantinople. The most fascinating later messianic is Rabbi Shabbetai Tzevi of Smyrna (1626–1676),[45] who proclaimed himself messiah in 1665. For a century he had thousands of faithful followers among Jews and Muslims, in part because of Nathan of Gaza (ca. 1644–1690), who found a parallel between gnosticism and Kabbalah and explained Tzevi through the Lurian theory of repair, which entailed the descent of the just into the abyss in order to liberate the captive particles of divine light. The chain of "messiahs" continues to our time, where the Hasidim again have a special interest in discovering and proclaiming the revered, anointed leader.[46]

MOVING FROM JEWISH MESSIANISM TO CHRISTIANITY

While the term "Jewish Christian" is widely used today, neither "Jewish Christian" nor "Christian Jewish" is used to describe the gospels. Only writings from non- or extra-canonical scripture, as say those of the Ebionites or the syncretistic Gospel of the Hebrews and Gospel of the Nazoreans, are described as Jewish Christian. How can this be if texts written later than the gospels still carry the epithet "Jewish Christian"?[47] Although the gospels have been traditionally accepted as Christian, they deal with a period before the later followers of Yeshua established a religion now called Christianity. Christian theologians increasingly assert that the gospels are simply Jewish texts. The whole problem of names is crucial here. Historically, a Christian was a Jew who saw Yeshua as the messiah. We are so far from understanding that simple fact, though the word "Christian" (messianic) tells it all, that we must quibble, like parties making peace with each other, who must learn again how to address each other.

---

[45] See Gershom Scholem, *Sabbatai Sevi: The Mystical Messiah, 1626–1676* (Princeton: Princeton University Press, 1973).

[46] Martin Buber (1876–1965) traces the history and tales of Hasidism in *Die Chassidische Botschaft* (Heidelberg: L. Schneider, 1922), which appeared in English as *Tales of the Hasidim* (New York: Schocken Books, 1975), beginning with the revival of Hasidic speculation in the eighteenth century as exemplified by the clairvoyant charismatic Jacob Isaac (d. 1815) of Lublin in Poland.

[47] Among the important noncanonical gospels is the Gospel of the Hebrews, which is preserved in fragments recorded in Cyril of Jerusalem, Jerome, and Clement, and may precede Mark. It contains the second saying in the very early gnostic Gospel of Thomas. In the Gospel of the Hebrews, James (Jacob/Yaakov), brother of Yeshua, is mentioned as the first to see the resurrected appearance of Yeshua. The fragments confirm the authority assigned to James, who was the leading figure of the conservative Jewish church in Jerusalem that followed Yeshua.

The quibbling over names should, one hopes, bring us back to history and to who these followers of Yeshua were. During his lifetime and for at least four decades after his death, the followers of Yeshua were Jews. This means they thought themselves Jews and were also made up largely of Jews in the ethnic sense, and seldom of gentile (ἐθνικῶς) background until after the diaspora of 70 C.E. The historical establishment of an independent Christian Church was not yet the issue during that intra-Jewish struggle for dominance in the recognition of the messiah. Christians did not come to recognize Yeshua when the Jews failed to do so (a falsehood repeated to death as gospel truth). On the contrary, there were originally no outsiders, no gentiles, who recognized Yeshua.[48] Only Jews did, messianic (Christian) Jews. Precisely from those Christian Jews grew a body of followers and also a quartet of Jewish gospels concerning the life of rabbi Yeshua, which became the centerpiece of an independent religion, and which eventually gained the unhyphenated title of Christianity.

By the end of the first decades of the second century of the Common Era, the Jewishness of the two covenants, the wrangling over biblical imperatives, and the religion and ethnicity of the principal figures in this first-century Israel drama were denied and forgotten. It was necessary for the early Christians to make this final divorce. Forgotten was the Jewish center of Yeshua, of the gospels about him, and of all the other books of the New Covenant. Conversions to Christian Judaism gave way, in the wake of a swiftly expanding and apparently independent Christian church, to conversion to an autonomous Christianity whose amnesia of origin was paramount. The survival of a strong notion of Christianity's Jewish origin threatened the church's illusion of self-creation. After 70 C.E., with the collapse of Jerusalem as the base of the formative sect, the Christian movement found its converts largely among the gentiles. And though both the Hebrew Bible of the Jews and the New Covenant, which were written by, about, and for Jews, remained the Bible of the new messianic faith, by the second and third decades of the second century, Jewish messianism had been translated, in all senses, into Christianity.

---

[48] No gentiles except the centurion at the crucifixion, who first declares Yeshua God and risen. This on-the-spot conversion, after executing Yeshua, poses problems. As for Yeshua himself, his character toward gentiles is presented ambivalently by the unknown hands who composed him: While Yeshua praises one centurion as having more faith than anyone in Israel (Luke 7.9), he also speaks as one concerned solely with Jews—"I was sent only to the lost sheep of the house of Israel" (Matt. 15.24), and he embarrassingly refers to the gentiles (the non-Jews) as dogs and swine (Mark 7.27; Matt. 15.26).

OLD BIBLES OF
THE EARLY CHRISTIANS

The Bible of the early Christians remained the Jewish Bible, usually in Greek or Latin translation. In the first decades it was their sole scripture. As for the New Covenant in the church, its earliest compositions are the letters of Paul, who was executed by the Romans, probably in 62 c.e. The gospels were begun no earlier than 65 and probably after 70 c.e. The last books were completed around 150. Paul used the term "the old covenant" for the Hebrew Bible (or Old Testament), referring to the writings of the Mosaic covenant (2 Cor. 3.14). The Church Father Tertullian in the late second and third centuries already refers to the New Testament, by which he meant the gospels, the Pauline letters, and Revelation (Apocalypse). These stood out among the much larger body of Christian writings out of which a selection and canon would ultimately be determined. By the fourth century it was common in Western Europe to refer to Christian scripture as the New Testament, and, as mentioned, the main selection of twenty-seven books was allegedly made by Athanasios of Alexandria in 387 c.e., and sanctioned in Rome in 405. However, there remained six competing orderings of the books. By the beginning decades of the third century, there were many copies of scriptures that eventually formed the New Covenant. It is now virtually certain that a selection of the twenty-seven books of the New Covenant was set and published as early as 150. No codices of the earliest edition are extant, but, with changes, it served as a model for the next centuries. The role of Athanasios in determining anything truly new, which is a traditional truism, is unlikely. If his "Easter Letter" did anything, it confirmed what already was established.

As for the authors, Paul is one whose name is certain for probably seven of the thirteen letters ascribed to him. Peter may be the author of 1 Peter. The other uncertain letters have no known authorship. The gospels claim no authorship within their text, but in the second century Papias, ca. 140, suggested the names of Matthew and Mark for the books attributed to them, and Irenaeus, ca. 180, put forth Luke and John for their gospels. Acts was also linked with Luke, a friend of Paul. Luke is often called the one gentile among the Jewish evangelists. That idea is also a second-century invention.

EARLY CHRISTIANS WITHOUT A CHRISTIAN BIBLE

In his *A Historical Introduction to the New Testament,* Robert M. Grant writes that the church proclaimed Christianity without possessing the New Testament. He agrees with Helmut Koester that "the Apostolic Fathers (the earliest Christian writers outside the New Covenant) did not even make use of written gospels. Instead, they relied upon oral traditions of the same sort as those recorded by the evangelists" (25). Grant acknowledges, with unnecessary apology, the absence of a New Covenant canon:

> In dealing with the canon of the New Testament we must begin with some rather negative statements. First, the earliest Christian Bible was not, and did not, include the New Testament. Instead, it was the Old Testament, usually read in Greek, and often interpreted in the light of a number of apocalyptic documents which were not generally recognized as canonical.[49] (28)

The gospel story of a rabbi named Yeshua appeared in diverse documents (as noted, in all or part of seventeen gospels concerning Yeshua), but what served as testimony during that long period of Christianity's formation was the disputed miscellany of written document and oral tradition. Second-century Marcion,[50] marked as a gnostic heretic by all branches of later Christianity and expelled from the Church in 144, alone among the prominent messianics attempted, and failed, to exclude the Hebrew Bible[51] from Christianity. By the end of the second century, among the multitude of documents floating around, the books which now comprise the gospels already existed, and there were already disputes, particularly instigated by the figure of Mar-

---

[49] Grant is referring to the enormous pseudepigraphic scripture of the time, in particular Enoch, a Jewish apocalypse.

[50] Being accused of being a gnostic was more serious than being thought of as a Jew, since as gnosticism grew, spreading from Portugal through Europe, North Africa, the Near East and China, it was the largest and most dangerous heresy. Its last flourishing as Neo-Manichaean Cathars in the southwest France prompted the Albigensian Crusade and the establishment of the Inquisition, carried out by the Dominican order. As for Marcion, though his theistic dualism, positing a good invisible god and the evil creator god of Genesis, coincided with gnostic dualism, his message is faith, not gnosis, and with himself as the great messenger or messiah. He had little or no influence on classical Alexandrian gnosticism.

[51] Without quibbling about order and number of included books, I use "Old Testament," "Old Covenant," "Jewish Bible," "Hebrew Bible," "Hebrew Scriptures," "Tanak" (Tanakh), and "Torah" interchangeably. However, the Tanak has a different order and number of books. Torah (the Torah) is the scroll of the Five Books of Moses but is also customarily used to mean the entire Hebrew Bible. The Bible by itself, or the Christian Bible, includes the Hebrew Bible and the New Covenant. The New Covenant is also called "New Testament," "Christian scriptures," and "Greek scriptures."

cion, who, steeped in anger, rejected the Old Testament of the despised "creator God" who had trapped our spirits on this earth. Marcion did accept Paul and part of Luke, though he rejected the remaining gospels. For all his forays, Marcion was the first to attempt to formulate a canon. But despite Marcion, one book remained canon and sacred to the early Christians Jews and Christian gentiles, and that was the Torah (the Hebrew Bible), which was increasingly received in its second-century B.C.E. Septuagint Greek translation. By the time of Constantine's conversion in the early fourth century, the Torah was received in Latin translation.

NEW COVENANT, ESSENES, AND A
UNITARIAN DUAL TORAH

In their volume *Judaism in the New Testament* (London/New York: Routledge, 1993), Bruce Chilton and Jacob Neusner declare that the New Testament consists of "writings by Jews for Jews who formed a very special Israel" (9). In their essential homily they insist on the intense diversity and dissidence among the Judaisms of the period, one of which was Christianity. As we know now from the Dead Sea Scrolls, the communities at Qumran and elsewhere in southern Israel fiercely opposed the powerful Hasmonean Jews (whom Yeshua also surely opposed[52]) and saw themselves as the true "sons of light" and other

---

[52] The Hasmonean rulers were descendants of Judas Maccabeus or Yehuda the Maccabee ("the hammer") and his sons, who fought the Seleucid Antiochus Epiphanes, the Greek ruler who introduced pagan rites in the Temple at Jerusalem. With their victory in 141 B.C.E. an independent Jewish kingdom was established under the ruling dynasty of the priestly Hasmonean family, which persisted until Roman Pompey's conquest of Jerusalem in 63 B.C.E.. Yeshua, who was given a political execution as an insurrectionist, would have opposed the Hasmonean rulers, who were by then client kings of Rome. The very moment of original Hasmonean victory in 141 B.C.E. corresponded with the foundations of the Dead Sea Scroll Essene community at Qumran, who as "sons of light" angrily rejected the "sons of darkness" Hasmonean rulers in Jerusalem.

Among those who opposed Rome, the Essene opposition coincided with the militant opposition by the Zealots and the intellectual opposition by the Pharisees leaders to both Rome and their Hasmonean Jewish king. During the later major revolt against Rome by Judea and Galilee, 66–68, the Pharisees survived more intact than other Jewish sects after the Roman sack of Jerusalem and destruction of the Second Temple in 70.

The question of Jewishness of the Hasmonean kings becomes tricky and murky because of their eventual divided loyalty to foreign rulers. Herod the Great was an Idumean (considered a half-Jew) who married a Jew, Marianmne, whom he later executed along with his mother-in-law, Alexandra. His achievements were enormous with respect to new structures and lowering of taxes, and from 20 B.C.E. until his death in 4 C.E. he expanded the Second Temple in a magnificent style. His domestic life was plagued with intrigue, execution, and new alliances to descendants, and problems with Rome, which was his power source and which permitted him to consolidate his rule. When civil war broke out between Octavius and Antony (32 B.C.E.), he initially favored Antony. After Antony's defeat he cultivated Octavius's friendship.

Judaisms as representatives of the "sons of darkness." The Essenes sought an apocalyptic triumph over Jerusalem, as foretold in their *War Scroll*—the moral and religious life they would impose after conquest is seen in the *Manual of Discipline*—and the correctness alone of their Judaism is elaborated in the *Zadokite Document*. Compared to the Essenes of the Dead Sea Scrolls, the Jews who followed Yeshua, revolutionary as they were, were not extreme and not radically distinct from other centrist Judaisms.

In the Qumranic texts the Essenes have a special relation to Yeshua for the similarity of the titular designations. One is a royal figure named "son of God," but it is uncertain whether he is a Jew or an anti-god figure. To fill out the portrait of Yeshua, it is important to look at the coincidences of both titles and deeds between Essenes and Yeshua the Messiah. In *Jesus the Jew* (1981), Geza Vermes elaborates these similarities, citing a fragmentary Dead Sea Scrolls poem from the Qumran Messianic Apocalypse (4Q521), which deals with charismatic Judaism:

> . . . [the hea]vens and the earth will listen to His Messiah,
> and none therein will stray from the commandments of the holy ones.
> Seekers of the Lord, strengthen yourselves in his service!
> All you hopeful in (your) heart, will you not find the Lord in this?
> For the Lord will consider the pious, and call the righteous by name.
> Over the poor His spirit will hover and will renew the faithful with His power.
>
> And He will glorify the pious on the throne of the eternal Kingdom,
> He who liberates the captives, restores sight to the blind, straightens the b[ent].
>
> And the Lord will accomplish glorious things which have never been . . .
> For He will heal the wounded, and revive the dead and bring good news to
> the poor . . .

On this fragment, Vermes comments, "These few lines bind together the concepts of the Messiah, the Kingdom of God, healing, resurrection and the proclamation of good news to the poor, representing the same charismatic-eschatological pattern as the Gospel's announcement of victory over devil and disease" (*Jesus the Jew*, 12–13). And he cites Matthew 11.4–5, which is one of the many New Covenant passages depicting similar miracle healings and good news of resurrection for the poor. This Matthew passage derives from Isaiah 35.5,[53] bringing us back once more to the Torah:

The blind will see again and the lame walk,
The lepers are made clean and the deaf hear,
The dead are raised and the poor hear the good news.

Here, as we enter the impossible search for the historical Yeshua, we see the Essenes with parallel claims of messiahship through their "Teacher of Righteousness," who heals with his hands. There is much to associate Yeshua with in terms of precedents, and especially in recent years commentators have assigned Yeshua to many prominent groups, from Essenes and Zealots to Pharisees, and Cynics to gnostics and the Hasidim. Once Christianity takes hold, or even before, the same diversity of beliefs within the Christian fold will initiate millennia of sectarian dogma and conflict. We already see the squabbles of origin, faith, and dogma pronounced by James, Peter, and triumphant Paul. Like all Jewish factions, the leaders of the Christian Jews declared their unique authenticity. James, a conservative Jew with considerable power until his death in 66 C.E., stayed back to decree from Jerusalem; Peter felt at home, wherever he was, but demanded circumcision for all gentile converts, and allegorical Paul found his own in person and through his letters, as the inclusive missionary, for the circumcised and uncircumcised. All three founders proposed a Judaic way of life through distinctive visions and revisions of who the messiah was and what he signified. Throughout the New Covenant, the authors' scrupulous reference to verse in the authoritative Hebrew Bible marks their acceptance, however interpreted, of that covenant between God and Moses at Sinai that resulted in the Torah.

In their book *Judaism in the New Testament,* Chilton and Neusner argue for the multiplicity of Judaisms by listing, apart from the Hebrew Bible and New Covenant, "Enoch, the writings found at the Dead Sea, Josephus, Philo, the Elephantine Papyri, and the Mishnah" (*Historical Introduction,* xv). They speak of Christianity as another Judaism of antiquity, and state "the iron datum that the New Testament writers saw themselves as Israelites teaching the meaning of the Torah" (6). They express their unitarian conviction about the essence of one holy book assumed by Christians—the Hebrew Bible and New Covenant—by giving it the title "the dual Torah" (4).

---

[53] The passage in Matthew is accurately recorded from Isaiah, but Isaiah is ecstatically happy: "Then will the eyes of the blind be opened / and the ears of the deaf unstopped. / Then will the lame leap like a deer, / and the mute tongue shout for joy."

THE CREATION OF THE SEPTUAGINT

It is not feasible in a general Afterword to the gospels and Apocalypse to deal at greater length with the central matter of historicity in the New Covenant. I wish to look into the colorful tale of the translation of the Septuagint Bible, which has remained the Bible for Eastern Orthodoxy and is the source of the canonical Apocrypha. In the New Covenant, the Greek translation in the Septuagint is usually given when referring to words from the Hebrew Bible.

Apart from the versions of earlier Aramaic Targums, the first translation of the Hebrew Bible into another language is the Septuagint or Hellenistic Bible (ca. 250–175 B.C.E.), created for the Greek-speaking Jews of the diaspora in Alexandria, who by 300 B.C.E. represented perhaps a third of the city's inhabitants and may have outnumbered the Jews of Jerusalem. As mentioned, the name "Septuagint," meaning seventy, refers to the seventy-two scholars who, according to tradition, by order of King Ptolemy II Philadelphus, undertake the translation of the Hebrew Bible into Greek on the island of Pharos in the port of Alexandria. By divine coincidence, the translation is completed in seventy-two days. The story of the Septuagint translation is first contained in the *Letter of Aristeas.*

Aristeas recounts that as a gesture of goodwill, the king sends sumptuous gifts to the Temple in Jerusalem. The scholars are then sent to Alexandria, where there is an endless banquet at which both king and scholars display their wisdom in explaining Jewish ethics and theology and Greek reason and virtue, all accomplished with excessive politeness and mutual congratulations. Then the scholars are taken to Pharos and paired off into thirty-six cells. At the end of each day the work of each version is compared with the others until all the versions agree with each other, word for word. After exactly seventy-two days, the work by the seventy-two scholars is complete, "as though this coincidence had been intended" (*Aristeas,* 307). The requisite goal of a perfect translation had been achieved.

To understand this necessary miracle of translation in relation to theological and political conditions of this period, we must speak about historical background. As presented in the text, Aristeas, the author-narrator of the *Letter of Aristeas,* was an influential courtier in Ptolemy's circle and a pagan apologist for the Jews to the king himself, a main character in the work. The king is also sternly devoted to bringing forth an immaculate translation of the Jewish Bible, the first foreign religious scripture ever to be commissioned into Greek translation.

The story of the third-century Aristeas and the creation of the Septuagint was to be retold many times, and of particular interest are those retellings by the Jewish historian Josephus (37–95) and by the Neoplatonist Philo Judaeus (50? B.C.E.-C.E. 50?). However, with regard to Aristeas and his era, historical study immediately discloses the literary masks of the author, period, and genre. The author is in temporal and national disguise. Aristeas was not a third-century contemporary of the Egyptian king, and the book is not a letter but rather a *diegesis* (*narratio* in Latin) concerning, among other matters, standards and methodology in the translation of religious texts. Even the designation *letter* (*epistolis*) first appears only in a fourteenth-century manuscript, *epistolis Aristeos pros Philokratin ekphrasis* (*Aristeas,* 56). The ancient designation of the short book was simply *Aristeas to Philocrates.* The text itself is imaginative in its anachronisms, even in the early lines where the elders are described as selected from each of the six tribes (34–40); of course, by the third century B.C.E. the legendary twelve tribes as a unit had long ago disappeared from Israel.

Who was Aristeas? By abundant internal evidence in this popular book, he was an Alexandrian Jew, not of the third but more likely the second century B.C.E., arguing for harmony between Jews and Greeks, to the point of equating Yahweh and Zeus. Aristeas not only displays a Greek's love for Jewish literature, law, and ethics, but, in a political gesture, pleads for the release of Ptolemy's Jewish slaves, and persuades the king to do so as a precondition for the translation of their laws (*Aristeas,* 17–27). Aristeas, in fact, was addressing the Jewish community, and his "letter" may be thought of as a piece of internal encouragement.

If the idea of King Ptolemy commissioning the translation of the Bible for the Jews of Alexandria is a fantasy, then the logical alternative is that the Hellenized Jews commissioned the work of translation themselves. By the time of the actual composition of *Aristeas,* most if not all of the Hebrew Bible had already been rendered into the Greek Bible of the Septuagint. And the act of translation was not accomplished in seventy or seventy-two days but executed and gathered together during the course of approximately seventy-five years, from 250 to 175 B.C.E.

Here we have a famous story, to which the sacred Bible of Eastern Europe, the Septuagint, is in religious debt. Yet we discover that virtually every aspect of the story that Aristeas recounts is fiction. The story of its translation, though a parable for a Jewish cause, was, nevertheless, picked up and retold a century later by those two most famous men of the period, the historian Josephus and the philosopher Philo. In the instance of the composition of the New Covenant, the stakes were much higher than the method of translation of the

Hebrew Bible for its Alexandrian Greek-speaking Jewish community. But the story of its miraculous identical translation in a few days, like five fish feeding three thousand or five thousand of Yeshua's followers in Galilee, is beautiful but today, most often, read as allegorical truth.

HISTORY AND BEYOND

In these thoughts on historical investigation, I have raised flags of caution when looking at passages that harshly condemn a person or group. Consider the self-serving spin on a report composed half a century after an alleged event. After the questioning of events and dates, it is best to look for the universal, rather than the sectarian, in the teaching. So the Jewish philosopher Martin Buber saw the greater historic and universal faces of Yeshua when he predicted that "[o]ne day Jesus will be granted a prominent place among the teachers of the Jewish faith" (*Two Types of Faith* [New York: Harper and Row, 1961, 13]). When a Greek passage is complex, I reread, which is a great secret of reading; and when passages test credulity, I delight in the fantasy. A history of acceptance and repetition of unproven events has led me to do close reading always with the premise that the gospels are dramatic story, not arid history. And I prefer the fact that the gospels culminate as heart-rending story. Yeshua himself prefers the fantastic parable to the chronicler's argument. The historian Josephus reads almost like story, but nothing captures the fervor of the gospels. The gospels and Apocalypse go beyond interpretation of plain fact, which in any case is illusive. Paramount is the adventure of a wanderer among the deprived, healing the body, and liberating the physical and spiritual eye that explores the astronomy of cloud and mind, or drifts through neighborhoods of prodigal sons and Miryams generous with myrrh.

The scriptures tell the sorrow and pathos of the poor and the hurt. They talk to the crippled and to the blind and possessed. They move through a valley of hunger and luminosity. Parables speak the human and spiritual condition, with extraordinary beauty of word. Chapters are books of being. There is a mustard seed that drinks deep water. On each page lives a solitude of spirit. Some religious poets—the Spaniard Saint John of the Cross, who inhabited mountains of spirit and cellars of love, and the English monk Gerard Manley Hopkins, who found the mind had mountains and suffered the fell of dark— left a record of pain and transcendence that is nonsectarian and ecstatic. In like manner, these gospels and Apocalypse question the very limits of despair and interior light. And in some rooms of Jerusalem and Galilee or high in a solitary sanctuary of rocks on the northern hills, and ultimately in the broken body on the awful mound of crucifixion, there exists a night sun stronger than fact.

OLD COVENANT OR
NEW COVENANT AS IN
OLD CIRCUMCISION OR
NEW CIRCUMCISION

CIRCUMCISION IN THE HEART IN PAUL'S ROMANS

Had there been any holy scripture around when Paul was writing his epistles, he might have called the New Covenant, that later gathering of gospels, letters, and Apocalypse, "The Spiritual Circumcision." Paul argued compassionately in his letters that the old traditional covenant of his fellow Jews, which was established by the painful ceremony of the circumcision, need not be solely of the body. He advocated a new covenant, one of the spirit, which is more significant than that of the flesh. He said: "Real circumcision is a matter of the heart—it is spiritual and not literal" (Rom. 2.29). Such an interpretation left an opening to gentile converts to become messianic Jews by adopting the spirit of the rite of circumcision rather than undergoing the old rite itself. Paul's words about circumcision have usually been interpreted as a rejection of the Old Testament for a yet to be conceived or written New Testament, or a rejection of old Judaism for a new Judaism, which later, when there is scripture and a church, will, after the acknowledgment of the messiah, the Christ, be known as Christianity.

Certainly Paul was seeking to change Judaism, and among these changes one was, in disagreement with Peter, to do away with the obligation of circumcision for those who wished to join the followers of Yeshua the Messiah. His words about circumcision in the heart as well as of the flesh, in which heart and spirit prevail, also appear in Deuteronomy 10.16, Jeremiah 9.26, and Ezekiel 44.9. Paul returned to the authority of Deuteronomy precisely to show that within the Hebrew Bible there was not only the tribal obligation of a physical sign to represent a pact or covenant with God but of a spiritual sign, centered in the heart. His main source is probably a famous passage in Deuteronomy. Moses has climbed Mount Sinai a second time, and remains there forty days and forty nights, when God will write again his commandments on two tablets of stone, which earlier had been destroyed. Moses comes down and reports to Israel, his people, what the lord requires of them. Among the instructions are for a circumcision in the spirit: "Circumcise, then, the foreskin of your heart, and do not be stubborn any longer" (Deut. 10.16). This line is generally interpreted to mean that one open the mind to direct the will to God. Again in Jeremiah 9.26 we read, "Circumcise ourselves to the Lord, remove the foreskin of your heart." And once more in Ezekiel 44.9, we hear an admonishment against being "uncircumcised in heart and flesh." We see here that Paul does *not* reject Torah by contrasting his messianism to it, but goes directly to the Hebrew scriptures to show that heart and spirit are more than flesh. Indeed, with respect to circumcision, as he affirms spirit over body he also affirms that one is a Jew who in one's heart hears the voice of God.

> For a person is not a Jew who is one outwardly, nor is true circumcision something external and physical. Rather a person is a Jew who is one inwardly, and real circumcision is a matter of the heart—it is spiritual and not literal. Such a person receives praise not from others but from God.
>
> *Rom. 2.27–29*

Paul is against physical circumcision for newcomers, but he makes it perfectly clear that for a would-be convert to Judaism, the spiritual pact is essential, while the bodily sign of the pact is neither essential nor obligatory. With regard to the law, Paul breaks no law. On the contrary he finds support in the Jewish Bible for the higher place given circumcision of the heart (the spirit) over physical circumcision. But the Hebrew Bible does not take the extra step, which is to say that if the spiritual covenant is there, the physical circumcision—the covenant's external marker—can be dispensed with. Therein lies the great difference, which was to be crucial to the spread of Christianity.

Paul was a Jew, and after seeing the light on the way to Damascus, a Christian Jew. And Paul was concerned with a new covenant, which later became the name of the Greek scriptures called the New Covenant, by contrasting the spiritual circumcision in the heart in Deuteronomy, Jeremiah, and Ezekiel to the bloody rite of physical circumcision in the covenant between God and Abraham (Gen. 17.1–23), which he wanted to go beyond. God offers to reward Abraham by making him the ancestor of a multitude of nations, and many other good things. In exchange Abraham must undergo the rite of circumcision, which becomes a tribal sign of loyalty to the lord. Paul, the missionary and advocate of Yeshua in the diaspora synagogues of the Mediterranean, was convinced that the covenant with Abraham was, compared to the examples in Deuteronomy, Jeremiah, and Ezekiel, limited, brutal, and a bad marketing tool for the new Judaism.

The word for circumcision in Hebrew is *berit* (בְּרִית), "a cutting," and means not only circumcision, but, since the cutting of the circumcision was the rite confirming the covenant with God, this physical word took on a metaphorical and abstract meaning in Hebrew of "covenant." So when Paul speaks in Romans of a circumcision of the heart, he could find in the same word its cross-language levels of meaning. Knowing that in Hebrew physical circumcision and conceptual covenant reside in the same word, he can play with the Greek *peritome* (περιτομή), a cutting around, "circumcision," to ask for the dominant sense of the covenant not to be Abrahamic circumcision, the external act and sign, but the inner circumcision. But why Paul used this particular metaphor, "*berit* of the heart," for spiritual loyalty can only be deeply understood if one understands, as any Hellenized (that is, Greek-speaking) Jew would, the Hebrew equation of circumcision and spirit.[54]

The Church Fathers, picking up on Paul's notion of a spiritual circumcision as spiritual covenant, saw in Paul's argument not only a good phrase for their new scriptures, the New Covenant, but also a clearly implied rejection of the

---

[54] There is an interesting linguistic reason why *berit* took on its simultaneous meaning of "covenant." Biblical Hebrew had few abstract and conceptual words. Hence, when a conceptual word was needed, its rich denotative words for things were often upgraded to contain a conceptual meaning. Biblical Hebrew is an immediate, bold language, which carries with it a sonorous roughness and vitality. The first pages of Genesis echo with contrapuntal chant. A parallel between the bold "word as thing" in Hebrew and the "word as idea" in Greek is English words of Anglo-Saxon compared to those of Latin derivation. The Anglo-Saxon tend to be briefer, stronger, and based on image, while the Latin tends to be polysyllabic, abstract, and based on concept. In Hebrew the richness of the word *berit* is that it retains the elemental circumcision of a physical rite as well as the spiritual covenant. Both meanings sound with equal force.

To understand how circumcision works as a synecdoche, consider the word "baptism." To say that a Jewish child or an adult has been circumcised means that the person circumcised has formally become a Jew and has entered, during the ceremony, into a covenant with God, with all duties and entitlements. Equivalent to the rite of circumcision was the widespread ancient Jewish rite of baptism, as performed by John the Baptizer (Yohanan the Dipper), a Jew who lived and died before Christianity or Christian Jews existed. In 2 Kings 5.14, we read of immersion (baptism) in the river in order to be cured as by the word of God: "So he went down and immersed himself seven times in the Jordan, according to the word of the man of God; his flesh was restored like the flesh of a young boy, and he was clean." That ceremony of the baptism, meaning in Greek "to dip, as in water," later became the ceremony for formally becoming a Christian, with all duties and entitlements. It was not an unpleasant act. In the physical immediacy of being dipped in water and its covenantal symbolism of becoming a Christian, baptism became a Christian version of *berit*, with its specific physical act of the cutting of the flesh and its covenantal symbolism of becoming a Jew. As for would-be Christians who do not get baptized, or Jews and Muslims who do not get circumcised, the outlook has traditionally been grim, for here and eternity. For the Christian, it may mean an eternity in limbo. For the Jew and Muslin, God does not look on the uncircumcised as his own. Remember Genesis 17.14: "Any uncircumcised male who is not circumcised in the flesh of his foreskin shall be cut off from his people; he has broken my covenant." In every religion God is sectarian and keeps the faithful obedient to the comportment of the sect. As for women, either by neglect or ignorance of female circumcision, women were (with some notorious exceptions) exempt from genital circumcision. For the Christian woman and man, the required rite of baptism was painless and carried none of the terror of adult male circumcision for Jews and Muslims.

Old Covenant, that is, the Jewish Bible. Thereafter in languages other than Hebrew, Old Covenant became the word for the Hebrew Bible. In the Latin languages based, as noted, on Jerome's mistranslation of covenant, where covenant turned into testament, we have the New Testament and the Old Testament. That invention of Old Covenant versus New Covenant has a precedent in several later Fathers of the Church. But insofar as the words derived from Paul, the meaning was in no way a rejection of Hebrew Bible scripture but rather a reconfirmation of spiritual rites established by the Old Covenant. For Paul's physical circumcision versus spiritual circumcision is certainly not an "Old Testament Circumcision versus a New Testament circumcision." The choice was not between the authority of Hebrew and Greek scriptures (there were no Greek scriptures when Paul wrote other than his own letters), but between two ways spelled out in the Hebrew Bible.

Paul chose a spiritual way to know and make a pact with God. His words say that the true Jew is one who follows the inward meaning of circumcision. He rejects neither the Torah nor his Jewishness. His words "old" and "new" are to affirm his preferred example of virtue. As for using old and new as a powerful vehicle for rejecting the worth of the Old Testament, that was the work of later Church Fathers.

SPIRITUAL CIRCUMCISION THAT OPENS THE WAY FOR PAINLESS CONVERSION

In the first years when Christian Jews were busily proselytizing Jews and gentiles to a belief that the messiah had come to earth, died, and risen in the figure of Yeshua, a major obstacle for outsider conversion to the new sect of the Jews was the painful and dangerous ritual of the circumcision, which involved the cutting away of the foreskin. Let us look with some detail at the Abrahamic example, and how Paul, by advocating spiritual over physical proof of faith, opened the door to a rapidly expanding sect. Abraham cut a deal with God. "You shall circumcise the flesh of your foreskins, and it shall be a sign of the covenant between me and you" (Gen. 16.11).[55] The sign of the covenant inflicted by God was crucial. It sealed their agreement.

---

[55] The covenant begins in chapter 15 when in a dream Abram has a vision in which Adonai tells Abram, "Do not be afraid, Abram, I am your shield; your reward shall be very great." The name "Abraham" is explained for its similarity in Hebrew to "multitude of nations," but the roots of Abraham are *ab*, father + *raham*, exalted.

Abraham was ninety-nine when he submitted to the cutting, which provoked his unsettling laughter as he worried whether a man could father a child at his age; and he flung himself on his face and he laughed, and spoke out loud to himself, wondering whether this was a reward or a painful joke (Gen. 16.17). A year later, his son Yitzhak (Isaac) was born, and so began a line of progeny that would be the first linear family of the Jews. Appropriately, his son bore the name Yitzhak, meaning "laughter," reflecting his laughter of happiness and pain. As for Sarah, upon learning that she, at ninety, already "withered and dry," was to have a child, her first reaction was also to laugh (18.12–15).

This covenant established Abraham as the patriarchal ancestor of the Jews, the progenitor of kings, the father of his nation and of a multitude of nations. These were extraordinary rewards and protections for Abraham, a simple nomadic shepherd, owner of herds and a few slaves in his household, from perhaps the Middle Bronze Age (2000–1900 B.C.E.) or as late as the Iron Age (1200–900 B.C.E.), who could have been a historical person, or more likely an eponymous figure representing a people, Israel. In return, God, the generous landlord, demanded recognition of his sovereignty and obedience to his law. That recognition and obedience would be forever etched in the skin by circumcision of his children, the Jews, and even of foreign slaves brought into their houses. The narration of this deal between God and Abraham is fully elaborated in Genesis 17.1–14:

> And Abram was ninety-nine years old and the Lord appeared to Abram and said to him, "I am El Shaddai.[56] Walk with Me and be blameless, and I will grant My covenant between Me and you and I will multiply you very greatly." And Abram flung himself on his face, and God spoke to him, saying, "As for Me, this is My covenant with you: you shall be father to a multitude of nations. And no longer shall your name be called Abram but your name shall be Abraham, for I have made you father to a multitude of nations. And I will make you most abundantly fruitful and turn you into nations, and kings shall come forth from you. And I will establish My covenant between Me and you and your seed after you through their generations as an everlasting covenant to be God to you and to your seed after you. And I will give unto you and your seed after you the land in which you sojourn, the whole land of Canaan, as an everlasting holding, and I will be their God."

---

[56] El Shaddai is translated in the KJV and even in the modern NRSV as "God Almighty." Actually, it is a beautiful name, meaning "God of the Mountains." Robert Alter calls the translator's habit of explaining or interpreting a metaphor rather than giving a literal version "the heresy of explanation."

And God said to Abram, "As for you, you shall keep My commandment, you and your seed after you through their generations. This is My covenant which you shall keep, between Me and you and your seed after you: every male among you must be circumcised. You shall circumcise the flesh of your foreskin and it shall be the sign of the covenant between Me and you. Every eight-day-old male among you shall be circumcised through your generations, even slaves born in the household and those purchased with silver must be circumcised, and My covenant in your flesh shall be an everlasting covenant. And a male with a foreskin, who has not circumcised the flesh of his foreskin, that person shall be cut off from his folk. My covenant he has broken."

The rite was performed not only on Abraham but on his son and his household:

And Abraham was ninety-nine years old when the flesh of his foreskin was circumcised. On that very day Abraham was circumcised, and Ishmael his son, and all the men of his household, those born in the household and those purchased with silver from the foreigners, were circumcised with him.

Gen. 17.23–27

For the Christian Jews, circumcision was a dire question in those days when the new sect of messianics was establishing itself. Paul leaves the door wide open for new Christian Jews not to be circumcised. With eloquence and Talmudic logic, he argues in favor of a lofty meaning of the circumcision, the pact with God, the covenantal price for becoming a Jew and upholding the law (the commandments of Torah). Paul writes that it is worse to be circumcised and break the law than not to be circumcised yet obey the law.

In the years that Paul is writing about a mitigated and higher form of circumcision, we observe that such ideas are very much in the air. In the contemporary wisdom Gospel of Thomas, we find an extraordinary parallel that is more severe in its ridicule of physical circumcision. Yeshua is derisive, saying that the physical must yield to the spiritual. In Saying 53, he is asked about circumcision:

His followers said to him,
Is circumcision useful or not?

He answered them,
If it were useful, fathers would make their children

already circumcised from their mothers.
But the true circumcision in spirit
is worthy in every way.

Gospel of Thomas[57]

The advantage of "true circumcision in spirit" for the gentiles who would join the developing sect of Christian Jews was enormous. It meant that without going through an adult mutilation of their genital organ, they could enjoy equality of acceptance before the messianics who were born as Jews, who represented the greater body of the followers of Yeshua, including Peter and Paul, who had had their circumcision on the eighth day after their birth, hence avoiding the adult trauma of the rite.

COVENANTS AND TESTAMENTS AND THEIR NAMES OF *OLD* AND *NEW*

I have tried to convey some notion of the related meanings of "circumcision" and "covenant," and of a sign in the flesh of an everlasting covenant. As noted, the traditional translation of the Hebrew and Greek words for "covenant," *berit* and *peritome,* became erroneously in Latin *testamentum.*[58] When the Christian Bible became traditionally separated into two covenants or testaments, they took on the names of "Old Covenant" and "New Covenant," and in Western Europe, "Old Testament" and "New Testament." These two temporal signs of old and new were fashioned to distinguish two religions in a single Bible.

"Old Covenant" is a Christian Greek name for the Jewish or Hebrew Bible.

---

[57] In his *The Gospel of Thomas,* Marvin W. Meyer comments on Saying 53: "This saying critiques the value of physical circumcision and instead recommends spiritual circumcision. Compare Romans 2.25–29, as well as other passages in Paul. According to a Jewish tradition, a governor of Judea once commented to Rabbi Akiba, 'If he (that is, God) takes such pleasure in circumcision, why then does not a child come circumcised from his mother's womb?'"

[58] As covenant increasingly gains acceptance as the translation of (διαθήκη), the persistence of testament as the traditional translation of *diatheke* has prompted explanations of covenant as "an alternate translation of the Greek words (*kaine diatheke*)" (*HarperCollins Bible Dictionary,* 75). To say "alternate" suggests a choice between possible meanings. It would be better to say that "testament" is an error and "covenant" the right transfer of *diatheke* into English. Greek *diatheke* means a covenant, agreement, and can also mean "a last will and testament," but this latter possible meaning does not contain the notion of "covenant" in the Hebrew Bible. "Testament" by itself suggests not a two-way covenant, in which each party does his or her share, but a credo, a statement, or witnessing (etymological meaning) as in testimony, none of which is intended in *diatheke.* It should be noted that the Greek word διαθήκη (*diatheke*) does not have, like its Hebrew antecedent, בְּרִית (*berit*), the other meaning of circumcision, which in Greek is περιτομή (*peritome*).

The Jews did not participate in the renaming of their scripture, the Tanak or Torah or simply Bible, but in the languages they spoke they, too, in public communication have used the common appellation. In a chronological sense this appellation is accurate, for the New Testament was accepted in its final form in the late fourth century. However, while "the new" is undoubtedly appropriate for the Greek scriptures, for it followed the earlier Hebrew scriptures, the question of the epithet "old" is pragmatic but problematic.

We first encounter the actual Greek words "new covenant" (not "new testament") in Paul: "Our competence is from God, who has made us competent to be ministers of a new covenant, not of letter but of spirit; for the letter kills, but the Spirit gives life" (2 Cor. 3.6). In his letter to the Corinthians, he calls for a new covenant, but Paul did not speak of "old covenant" as a metonym to represent the larger Jewish Bible any more than was "new covenant" a metonym for future New Covenant scriptures. In no place in his letters did Paul call for new scriptures to be assembled into a Christian Bible. As a Jew who died before the gospels were composed, who sought to convince coreligionists that Yeshua was the messiah, Paul would scarcely have foreseen a new compendium of holy scripture that might be added to or replace the long-since canonized Hebrew Bible.

It was the Church Fathers Tertullian (ca. 160–230) and Origen (ca. 185–254) who were among the first to use the term "Old Covenant" for the Hebrew Bible. The earliest use of Old Covenant seems to appear in Melito, bishop of Sardis, who, according to Eusebius (*Ecclesiastical History* 4.26.12), made a list of writings of the Old Covenant, quoting Melito's letter to a certain Onesimus: "I came to the East and learned the books of the Old Covenant." This letter is dated ca. 170 c.e. We find in the New Covenant the frequent notion of witnessing and testimony or last will and testament, but the notion of witnessing or a testimony between God and his people is definitely not the primary meaning of *diatheke*.

In Western Catholic and Protestant countries, we still have the universal usage of "New Testament" as a synonym for "New Covenant." The meanings of words always change, including within a language, and especially in translation. For Christians of the Catholic and Protestant West, "New Testament" determined the name of the earlier holy scripture, which logically had to balance and also contrast with the old name for holy scripture. Hence the invention of "Old Testament" as the proper Western Christian name for the Jewish or Hebrew Bible[59]—without input from Jews about their Bible's title in its di-

---

[59] Jewish Bible and Hebrew Bible are both used for the "Old Testament." Jewish Bible implies Bible of the Jews, equivalent to "Christian scriptures" for New Covenant, and Hebrew Bible, referring to language, suggests Bible in Hebrew as opposed to "Greek scriptures" for the New Covenant.

verse translations. Jews, of course, have gone along, since public language, whatever its history, demands that in order to communicate one follows common usage.

Whether testament or covenant, either word imposes a non-Jewish title on the Jewish Bible preserved in Hebrew and Aramaic.[60] By contrast, the Quran or Koran, while pronounced and spelled differently in other languages, remains the Quran, and though schisms also exist in the Muslim world, the title of the Quran has not been an issue.

Although, as mentioned, Jews have gone along in common speech with using the term "Old Testament," this is the traditional Christian name, not the Jewish name, for their Bible. So *berit,* the source name of the Christian Bible, whether you translate it "circumcision" or "covenant," is not relevant to the diverse "right" titles of the Jewish Bible in English, in other tongues, or in Hebrew. First, it must be said that for Jews, as for Christians, the common word in English for their holy scriptures is "the Bible." Academics, to distinguish the holy scriptures of the Jews from the combined holy scriptures of Jews and Christians, speak of the Jewish Bible, the Hebrew Bible, the Law, the Scrolls. Hebrew names for the Bible are Torah (meaning "law" or "instruction") or Tanak (an acronym from initial Hebrews letters for Torah, Prophets, and Writings), or the three major divisions of Tanak: Torah (Five Books of Moses), Nevi'm (Prophets), and Kethuvim (Writings). Whatever name is given by Jews to the Bible, it is not properly the old, nor the testament, nor the covenant.

The matter of the covenant is, of course, a fundamental and deeply Jewish concept. But this Jewish concept was never used for the naming of their sacred book. In reality, "Old Testament" is little used by Christians who uneasily assumed and interpreted the Jewish Bible as their own, and who found new terms to ensure their original and unique possession of it, while at the same time expressing discomfort about their possession of an imperfect, blemished old book, with alien pre-Christian figures in it. To cite one of many commonplaces, there is "the stern God of anger and vengeance of the Old Testament" as opposed to "the God of love and compassion of the New Testament," which inexorably implies two godheads in the Christian Bible. If God is the same immutable figure in both books, then his "human" character is inferior to and other than the God described in the New Testament. Such interpretation that makes eternal God fickle of personality, changing his ways and authority with

---

[60] Some portions of Daniel and other scriptures survive and were probably written in Aramaic, which took over in later biblical times. Aramaic was the greater language of the Near East, covering much of the western Asian coast and into Mesopotamia. Eventually koine Greek replaced Aramaic in parts of this same region and elsewhere in the Seleucid (312–364 B.C.E.) and until late Byzantine periods.

the age and book, might seem irreverent, but such views have been perfectly normal. Indeed, Jack Miles, a former Jesuit, in his erudite *God: A Biography* (New York: Knopf, 1995), traces the changing nature of God in the Old Testament with respect to his relationship with man and woman. Miles is right. God's "human" personality changes from book to book. God has a minor role in the New Covenant compared to his prominence in the Hebrew Bible. In the New Covenant, Yeshua is the main figure. It is fair to say that God of the Hebrew Bible and the New Covenant appears both castigating and loving. There is God whom one appeals to in battle and God of the Ten Commandments who tells us not to kill; there is Christ militant sending sinners and unbelievers to hell and Yeshua who heals and turns the other cheek. Miles works from within scripture. What is perhaps most significant is that the relation of Christians to the Old Testament itself, as a book to be read, disparaged, discarded, or revered, changes with the century and Christian sect. The Reformation was in part fueled by new translations of the "Old Testament" into the vernacular, when the Hebrew Bible definitely rose for many Christians from damaged goods to a renewed source for information, names, and law.

ALTERING NAMES OF BIBLICAL CHARACTERS

There is an extraordinary anomaly with respect to names. While the Jews have been historically thought of, and not always as a compliment, as the authors of the Old Testament, in the Old Testament there are, in standard English editions, almost no Jews. Translation has virtually caused the magical disappearance of the Jew from the Hebrew Bible.

In the Christian Old Testament (and also in Bibles translated by Jews who accept the received Christian naming), the English term for Jew is "of the children of Israel," "an Israelite," "a Hebrew," which come to about three thousand references in *The New Strong's Exhaustive Concordance of the Bible*. To Jews, there are some ninety references. Of the ninety Old Testament references to Jews, seventy-one appear in the Book of Esther. Esther (whose name derives from the Babylonian deity Ishtar, and whose Hebrew name is Hadassah) is a heroine celebrated in the holiday of Purim. In a legend that takes place in the Persian period (400–332 B.C.E.),[61] Esther's courageous actions deliver the Jews from a pogrom (Esther 8.3–10.3). Apart from Esther, in the entire Hebrew Bible there are, in standard English translations, less than twenty references to a Jew, and no one has a name. Queen Esther is the only Jew des-

---

[61] Over the centuries the Book of Esther's place in the canon has been contested and was denounced by Luther.

ignated by name in the Christian Old Testament. Although "the children of Israel," "Israelites," and "Hebrews" abound in the Old Testament, in the New Covenant gospels there is hardly a mention of children of Israel, Israelites, or Hebrews. But the Jews have reappeared. In the New Covenant there are some two hundred references to them, designated by name or Jewish title of rabbi, ranging from John the Baptist and Yeshua to the Pharisees, high priests, and Judas.

The Jews in the Jewish Bible are Jews, whether or not they are called Israelites. But for the traditional English reader, to read Israelite for Jew provides an unnecessary distancing, suggesting that this ancient people is distinct from New Covenant Jews. As with other Hebrew epithets, Israelite comes into English through the Greek Ἰσραηλίτης (Israelites), from the Hebrew יִשְׂרְאֵלִי (yisraeli), corresponding to Israeli. Were any translation today to use a direct transliteration from Hebrew, giving us Israeli rather than Israelite, it would be clear that the Israelis and Jews are one and the same. Because of this practice of omitting the word "Jew" in the Hebrew Bible, until recently, standard reference books on the Bible speak of Jews as a people who appear in New Testament times. There are, of course, variations in presenting this information of when the Jews appear historically, but it all comes to the same, and bears no reference to history. In effect, the history of the Jews in the Hebrew Bible has been obscured. Such is the great power of names and translations of names. The Jews, whose ancient history is in the Hebrew Bible, which forms the greater part of the Christian Bible, are missing through disenfranchisement. They return as the hypocritical, plotting personalities in the Christian Jewish gospels. It is through the conscious means of translation that almost total disguisement and disenfranchisement has occurred. A Jew or Christian who reads only the English translations of the Hebrew Bible will know none of these odd illusions. For the Hebrew reader, for whom the word *Yehudim* (Jews) occurs throughout the Bible, the Jews have not lost their history.

It can be argued that the Jews had diverse appellations in the Hebrew Bible, and so no one word is appropriate. However, translation is to convey information, not etymology, and the Jews of the Old and the New Testament are the same people and should not be designated otherwise. It is enough to say that this argument for excluding the Jews from the Jewish Bible is specious. No translation of Homer suggests that Odysseus and his crew were not Greeks, though there were many words for the Greeks in ancient Greek (*Hellene,* not the tribal word *Graikos,* was the common ancient word), but in English translation and commentary there is not the slightest question that the Greeks were Greeks. So, too, the Jews were Jews.

How can it be that the Jews, by their naming, arrive strangely from nowhere in the New Covenant as inimical aliens? In the gospels, as opposed to Paul, the Jews are not clearly the Hebrews of the Psalms and prophets. They are rather the mortal enemy of Christian Jews. Yeshua ben Yosef and his immediate family, friends, and followers are ultimately spared the stain of being Jews. The Virgin Mary is not seen as a Jew. Mary in translation, church iconography, and common understanding is not seen primarily as a Jew. Therefore somewhere in the passing of information to the Christian reader and worshiper, the truth of Mary failed to get through.

I have noted that there is a linguistic effort in Greek and later translations to conceal the Jewishness of gospel heroes as shown in the earlier discussed passage "Rabbi, which translated means teacher, where are you staying?" (ῥαββί, ὃ λέγεται μεθερμηνευευον διδάσκαλε, ποῦ μένεις;) (John 1.38). Yet the Christianizing of this Semitic book about Jews is not complete. There remains the Greek word "rabbi." In the tabernacle scene, whose telling is virtually identical in the Synoptics, in Mark 9.5, the first gospel, we have *ho Petros legei to Iesou, "Rhabbi,"* (ὁ Πέτρος λέγει τῷ Ἰησοῦ· ῥαββί), "Peter says to Jesus, 'Rabbi.'" In Matthew 17.4, whose source is in part Mark, we have *ho Petros eipe to Iesou, "Kurie"* (ὁ Πέτρος εἶπεν τῷ Ἰησοῦ· κύριε), "Peter said to Jesus, 'Lord.'" In Luke 9.33, whose source is also Mark and perhaps Matthew, we have *eipen ho Petros pros ton Iesoun, "Epistata"* (εἶπεν ὁ Πέτρος πρὸς τὸν Ἰησοῦν· ἐπιστάτα), "Peter said to Jesus, 'Master.'" "Rabbi" of Mark has been changed in the later gospels to *Kyrie,* "Lord" and *Epistata,* "Master." We can think that in other instances when Yeshua is addressed as "Teacher," "Lord," or "Master" in Greek that "Rabbi" has, as in the example of the tabernacles, been changed to suppress Yeshua's Jewish title of rabbi. In the King James Version (1611) of these three passages, "Rabbi," "Lord," and "Master" are all rendered into English as "Master."

In the New King James Version (1982), however, the English text has been corrected to follow the Greek, and we have for Mark 9.5, "Peter answered and said to Jesus, 'Rabbi.'" The New King James's rendering of "Rabbi" in their English translation of Mark 9.5 happily shows the new editors' imperative not to conceal Yeshua's title.

Along with the Christian name-changing, the Jews have their ways of shaping the Hebrew Bible, which they traditionally take as a book uniquely of their authorship and history. Yet the Bible has its precursors, who turn earlier Mesopotamian figures into Jewish patriarchs and heroes. The Mesopotamian myth of the flood story in *Gilgamesh* appears in the Hebrew Bible as intrinsic to the history and origin of the Jews, though it is a reworked story from the previous millennium, whose Babylonian names have been changed into Noah and other good Hebrew names to make them appear to be the earliest Jewish patriarchs. Jews and Christians still look on mountains of Armenia for their ancestral ark when they would do better to search in the sands of present-day Iraq.

THE NEW COVENANT AND ITS PRECURSOR
AND A PARABLE FROM CHINA

One invents new names for the past so that the present can influence and re-form the past. In his masterful essay "Kafka and His Precursors," Jorge Luis Borges understood that the present shapes, influences, and even creates the past. Normally, one thinks that history creates the present and that influence travels only one way: forward. Yet Borges, a child of Kafka, influences how Kafka is seen, because he, Borges, came into being and his own prominence alters our perception of his Czech precursor. So the New Covenant influences how the Jewish Bible is seen, because the New Covenant, a child of the Jewish Bible, came into being and its own prominence alters our perception of the Jewish Bible. In a hypothetical essay, "The New Covenant and Its Precursors," one would see how later and earlier biblical works and the names they give them mutually and inexorably explore and affect each other.

So a parable on the Bible.

Jews have imagined that they live in the Torah, and have carried their Bible, in many languages, into all continents of their multiple diasporas. They took it from Ethiopia and India to London and Buenos Aires, and even to Beijing in China where in the late sixteenth century the Jesuit missionary Matteo Ricci (1552–1610)[62] was unable to persuade a delegation of the ancient community of Jews in Kaifeng, for centuries cut off from their coreligionists, that he, Bishop Ricci, who carried the word of their Bible through Asia, was not, like them, a Jew and indeed a rabbi of the Jews. He had their book. The Kaifeng Jews were by then completely Chinese in appearance and were unconcerned that the missionary had with him some additional Christian scriptures (they themselves may have had nothing after the Babylonian Captivity). Bishop Ricci, for his part, though he could not accept their request to be the rabbi for their synagogue, didn't care to persuade them of sectarian distinctions that had come to separate Jews and Christians, who were both "peoples of the book."

---

[62] The parable of the Chinese Jews and Bishop Ricci is taken from Jonathan Spence's *The Memory Palace of Matteo Ricci* (New York: Viking Penguin, 1994).

The visions of the Chinese Jews and the Italian Catholic bishop and memory master were perfectly in harmony, ecumenical, and joined in vision.

If the reader from any quarter will forgive me, there should be no worry as once in the city of Kaifeng there was no worry about two covenants, an old one and a new one.

THE CHURCH AGON BETWEEN
THE HEBREW BIBLE AND
THE NEW COVENANT
AND AN ALMOST
HAPPY RECONCILIATION

CATHOLICS AND PROTESTANTS BATTLE OVER
BIBLE TRANSLATION AND THE REEMERGENCE
OF THE HEBREW BIBLE

The rivalry between the developing Christianity and its source in Judaism comes through at every turn in the New Covenant. In *Jesus: A Revolutionary Biography* (San Francisco: HarperSan Francisco, 1994), John Dominic Crossan reviews the parallels in the birth and the circumcision scenes of John the Baptist and Yeshua, in which John reflects the best of limited figures in the Old Testament, and Yeshua the glory and salvation in the New Covenant. Crossan also compares Matthew's parallel treatment of Moses and the Pharaonic killing of the infant males to Yeshua and the Herodian killing of the infant males, as well as the worldly covenant of Moses and God at Sinai and the great spiritual covenant of Yeshua and the Father. "But once again," Crossan writes, "Matthew, like Luke, sends a strong and powerful message by his very structure. Jesus is the new and greater Moses" (15).

In the name Old Testament, "old" does not signify venerable and worthy but outmoded; and the Hebrew Bible is surpassed by the messianic fulfillment of the New Covenant. Hence, it is not surprising that in many countries, especially Spain, Italy, and Greece, the Old Testament was rarely available to the common reader and, when available, little read. The Christian Bible was, in effect, the New Covenant. With the Reformation, Protestants rediscovered the Old Testament, and the Hebrew Bible moved up a few notches in availability and esteem.

About the Bible in the Reformation, the canonized cliché is "the reformers dethroned the Pope and enthroned the Bible." By making the Bible readable in the vulgates of Western Europe, the reformers and translators into German, French, English, Italian, Spanish, Dutch, and Scandinavian permitted laypeople to read and interpret for themselves the holy scripture and by so doing removed the Bible from the exclusively privileged eyes of the clergy, whom Martin Luther called "the lords of Scripture."

In his "Address to the Nobility of the German Nation," Luther asked bitterly, why not burn our copies of the holy scripture "and content ourselves with those unlearned lords at Rome, who have the Holy Ghost within them, though in truth the Holy Ghost can dwell only in a godly heart?" In his ironic argument against the church's insistence on keeping the Hebrew Bible and Greek scriptures solely in Roman Latin, Luther even cited Abraham and Sarah as models of understanding the word of God. His reference to the Hebrew Bible alone constituted a major shift in emphasis in the difficult family dispute between the Hebrew Bible (effectively in the province of the Jews, among whom at least the males could and normally did read it daily) and the New Covenant, which was available in Latin but seldom in the vernacular languages, and consequently largely in the domain of the literate Latin-reading clergy rather than the ordinary parishioner.

Prior to the Reformation, among Christians, the Hebrew Bible was relegated so completely to the dark that its figures, beyond the primeval Adam and Eve and a few patriarchs cited in the New Covenant, were scarcely in the knowledge of parishioners at all levels of education. The Latin translation remained canon pure, while the Hebrew and Greek scriptures were deemed "corrupt originals." Yeshua throughout carried not his Aramaic/Hebrew name of *Yeshua,* nor his Greek name of *Iesous,* but his Latin name *Jesus.* With slight language variations, he still is Jesus in all countries of the West, Protestant and Catholic (but of course not in Orthodox Greece where he remains *Iesous*). In English, Yeshua bears his Latin name *Jesus* from the Saint Jerome fourth-century Vulgata. For the act of straying from the Latin Vulgata, the punishment could be death. Torture, strangulation, the axe, and fire at the stake awaited many of those audacious translators, including John Wyclif,[63] John Purvey, Etienne Dolet, and William Tyndale, who not only translated into the vernacular tongues but did so heretically from the original Hebrew and Greek texts.

With the Protestant Reformation there was a proliferation of translations made directly from the source text. As a result, the Bible entered the households and literatures of Europe and even the Puritan graveyards of New England where the presidents of Harvard and the farmers of the field carried on their grave slabs the common names of Samuel, Elihu, Ezra, and Elijah. The Hebrew Bible became so central in the education of the young that Yale Col-

---

[63] Wyclif died in his bed, but was unearthed four decades later and his bones were burned.

lege, originally a school run by the Puritan elders, not only required the study of Hebrew in its curriculum but incorporated a Greek and Hebrew logo into its full name.

TWO VIEWS OF THE JEW AMONG THE HOLY POETS

Prior to the Reformation, the New Covenant was essentially the holy scripture, and the Hebrew Bible an uncomfortable parent best left unvisited. With the audacious and dangerous translation into the vernaculars, the Hebrew Bible came back into the fold, but the deformation of its speech as the historical and religious history of the Jews was even more acute in the new translations. In Eastern Europe until the most recent times, the Hebrew Bible, for all intents and purposes, went unread except by Jews. And in the West, the Hebrew Bible was received as a guide and prophecy of the events in the New Covenant. Every page of the annotated Hebrew Bible in translation carried explanations to make it into a Christian document. So in John 12.40, to explain the disbelief by some in Yeshua's miracles, the prophet Isaiah is cited to explain this lapse, and in the next verse, 12.41, it states that Isaiah saw Yeshua's "glory and spoke of him." Thus, the Hebrew Bible became a preface to the New Covenant in which the true God appeared and which served as the main holy script which Christians would know and by which they would live. This was the price of interpretation that the Torah paid for inclusion in the Christian Bible. Yet the Hebrew Bible could not, as the angry gnostic Marcion of Sinope (2nd century C.E.) wished, be cast out completely. Although in the New Covenant the Hebrew Bible is repeatedly and overtly denigrated as spiritually inferior to the message in the Greek scriptures, it remained the law and the unique religious authority for the dissident Jewish sect of messianics who had developed around Yeshua. Without the Hebrew Bible, the new Christianity lacked a foundation for its God, its foretold savior, and the example of an old covenant which it might surpass with its new covenant.

So these two Jewish books, the Hebrew Bible and the New Covenant, were sewn together under one cloth, which is the Christian Bible. Harold Bloom speaks of the Christian appropriation of the Hebrew Bible as "an act of total usurpation," which was epitomized in the debasement of Abraham (and by direct implication Moses) and his covenant with God in Yeshua's reply to the Pharisee in John 8.58: "before Abraham was [born], I am."[64]

---

[64] See "Before Moses Was, I Am: The Original and the Belated Testaments" in *The Bible* (New York: Chelsea House, 1987), 291.

Two divergent sixteenth-century views of "usurpation" are revealed in poems by the English metaphysical poets John Donne (1573–1631) and George Herbert (1593–1633). In later life the dean of St. Paul's Cathedral in London, Donne, in his magnificent work, his nineteen "Holy Sonnets," which include "XI," not only depicts "you Jewes" as vile but as killers of "an inglorious Man," Yeshua, who by a miracle of disguise was not to be perceived as a "Jewe." More, he recalls "Jacob" in a way to make him fulfill the stereotype of the tricky, money-minded Semite. But in his penitence, Donne asserts that he, John Donne, is even worse than the Jewes, since he crucifies Yeshua daily:

Spit in my face you Jewes, and pierce my side,
Buffet, and scoffe, scoure, and crucifie mee,
For I have sinn'd, and sinn'd, and only hee,
Who could do no inquitie, hath dyed:
But by my death can not be satisfied
My sinnes, which passe the Jewes impiety:
They kill'd once an inglorious man, but I
Crucifie him daily, being now glorified.
Oh let mee then, his strange love still admire:
Kings pardon, but he bore our punishment.
And Jacob came cloth'd in vile harsh attire
But to supplant, and with gainfull intent:
God cloth'd himselfe in vile mans flesh, that so
Hee might be weake enough to so suffer woe.

George Herbert graduated from Cambridge and became a country deacon. Like Longfellow's radically sympathetic "Jewish Cemetery at Newport," which speaks of the people, referring to Newport's Spanish Jews, Herbert writes:

How came they here? What burst of Christian hate,
    What persecution, merciless and blind
Drove o'er the sea—that desert desolate—
    These Ishmaels and Hagars of mankind?
                    . . . to endure
The life of anguish and the death of fire.

Herbert speaks not only of the suffering of the Jewish people, but of their religion "purloined" by Christians. With no reservation, he also addresses the

Jews in the second person; but, the antithesis of Donne, Herbert rebukes his coreligionists for usurping Jewish words as in the baptism (a rite most famously practiced by a pre-Christian Jew, Yohanan the Baptizer), while leaving the nation to "pine and die":

The Jews
Poor nation, whose sweet sap, and juice
Our scions have purloined, and left you dry:
Whose streams we got by the Apostle's sluice,
And use in baptism, while ye pine and die.

HUGE BENEFITS FOR THE WORLD AND FOR JEWS
DUE TO THE CHRISTIAN MISPRISONING
OF THE HEBREW BIBLE

These usurpations and distortions would all seem to be travesties. I think, however, such stern judgment on the "misprisoning" of the Jewish Bibles, to use Harold Bloom's preferred word, was temporally acceptable, even though that temporary travesty persisted for nearly two thousand years. For the obstruction could not and would not be eternal, and not to understand the extraordinary benefits from the symbiotic capture of the Jewish Bible by the powerful Christian church is to be severely myopic. Of course the Jews suffered defamation and death. But consider the alternative. The Jews had created two ultimate books in the world. Had Christianity *not* appropriated the Hebrew Bible to accompany the New Covenant, it is almost a given that the Torah would, in the course of twenty centuries, have vanished into the confinement of the ghettos and become at best a significant oddity, a book like *Gilgamesh* or *The Tibetan Book of the Dead,* known by title by a few, and read by fewer. But by being preserved openly in the West, and later in the whole world by Christianity, both books penetrated every level of culture and spirit in the last two millennia. They were ripped out of Asia and presented universally, albeit in different outfits, to the people of the Earth, in translations seldom made by Jews but nevertheless magnificent. As a result of the appropriation of its Hebrew Bible, the Christian Bible presented its tales, poems, and concepts, and invented and defined huge vocabularies in most spoken languages. Joined together, the Jewish covenants became and remain, as no one would dispute, one of the most important books of the world. And this dual Bible gave not only speech and story to other languages but a sphere of thought, mood, and reference that have and continue to shape the languages of the world.

To help understand the benefits of appropriation, I offer a small travesty. Consider the Elgin marbles that reside in the British Museum today rather than on the Acropolis, taken there by Lord Elgin in 1806. They consist of a Parthenon frieze by Phidias, a caryatid, and a column from the Erechtheum. Whatever the motives, their appropriation by the English was an undeniable act of preservation, but one with grave aesthetic consequences to the statues themselves. In the 1920s, for purposes of cleanliness, the Elgin marbles were sandblasted, which removed their old patina as if they, too, like Greek gods and Greek scripture, were romanized by the alien owners. Had the English not sequestered the Elgin marbles, their survival would have been, on the basis of the survival of their companion pieces, certain. And the sandblasting was more degrading aesthetically than any weather or pollution threat in Athens. But at least the Elgin marbles have been for nearly two centuries the showpiece of classical Greek sculpture to the world, which is no mean accomplishment.

So the Hebrew Bible and its companion New Covenant have also survived with splendor, and the Hebrew Bible has been given a great worldliness by its dramatic marriage to its offspring and rival. In translation—from Latin *translatio,* "a carrying over"—that treasure which is the Bible has been carried over in the extraordinary translations of the Vulgata, of Luther, Tyndale, and the King James—and that is reward enough.

A GENTLEMAN'S AGREEMENT
IN THE GOSPELS THAT JEWS
IN THE YESHUA MOVEMENT
NOT BE PERCEIVED AS JEWS

DISAPPEARING THE JEWS FROM THE YESHUA MOVEMENT

The central religio-political quandary of the writers, editors, and copyists of the New Covenant was how to make a book about Jews into a Christian Bible. That task was imperative if Christianity was to be independent of its creators. Yet there were mighty obstacles. The characters existed before Christianity had scriptures or temples of its own name. And in the decades after Yeshua's death in 30 C.E., Peter and Paul went forth to convert other Jews and gentiles to a belief in a Jewish messiah foretold in the Hebrew Bible. These Christian Jews in the mold of Paul, dependent on the Jewish Bible and the sayings of Yeshua the Messiah, did not know who they were. They knew they were in conflict with the Jews who had not accepted Yeshua as the Jewish messiah; with Christian gnostics, who as philosophical exegetes and "heretics" saw the appeared Yeshua as a simulacrum and the creator God of Genesis as the Demiurge; and, above all, with Rome, who remained the great political enemy. The contention with Rome and its religious gods and icons is depicted especially fiercely in intertestamental scriptures of noncanonical Apocrypha and pseudepigrapha.

Pagan rulers, with their figures of high office and their idolatry, had to be buried. Indeed, the removal of Judaism from Christianity was minor compared to the three-century battle to overcome Greco-Roman religion, civilization, and political dominion. The battle was won when Constantine I shifted his capital to Constantinople and on his deathbed converted to Christianity. The general iconoclastic period (not the specific eighth- and ninth-century Byzantine debate on worshiping Christian statues and images) included the demolition of Greek and Roman statutes and temples, the razing by patriarch (later Saint) Theofilus of the Mouseion Library of Alexandria, with its 700,000 rolls, in 391 C.E. (falsely attributed to later Muslim conquest), and the closing of the academies in Alexandria and Athens. These events were symptoms of a larger fundamental world change as classical civilization gave way to the cross.

How did these early diaspora Christian Jews define themselves? Eventually, they were simply Christians. But until they got to be Christians, they had the burden of accounting for all these events that had happened to a body of Jews in Jewish Galilee and Jerusalem. So the gospels' authors had the task of blurring the Jewish identity of its pre-Christians so that later they might pass as Christians (and of demonizing those Jews who were not pre-Christians). Strictly speaking, it was impossible to make all these Jews—Yeshua, Miryam, Yosef, Yohanan the Baptizer—fully pass. Yet in practical terms, the passage to Christian honor was a monumental success. The changing of the masks was achieved despite the discomfort of hearing, in the same sentence, Yeshua addressed as rabbi while he is denouncing the Jews as children of the devil, who is called a sinner, liar, fraud, thief, and murderer (John 8.44). The incongruity would seem to sink the message, but the slander of the Jew is so constant, and the obfuscation of Jewish identity of pre-Christian so pervasive, that the traditional reader, if not the recent reader and scholar, has accepted this subversion of identity as truth. If Yeshua himself denounces the Jews as offspring of the devil, how can he himself be perceived as a Jew? Indeed, the very denunciation and hatred of the Jew serve to distance and free the accuser from Jewish identity, which is a familiar later scene in the history of the Jews. Hence, with terrible irony and consequence, the unequivocal source of historic anti-Semitism remains in a book about Herodian Temple Jews, who have various disguises to make them good or evil according to their pre-Christian or Jewish identity cards.

In summary, we witness a remarkably enduring gentleman's agreement to keep all Jews out of Christianity's mythological beginnings by changing the religion and ethnicity of Yeshua, his family, and his disciples. The anachronistic Christianization takes place in the gospels as we have them, in commentary on them—both as annotation and external texts, in scribal interpolations, in translations of the gospels, and in the resultant general perception by the public about who Yeshua and his circle were.

Some might argue that there is little deception in the text, for a careful reader can find abundant evidence that Yeshua was a Jew. Yes and no. The evidence is there and a careful reader *should* respond to it, but reading theories inform us why this text is received otherwise. Consider the pressures on a reasonable and alert reader to ignore the evidence of Jewish identity. We have gone over in detail the pattern of changing the title of rabbi to teacher, master, or lord going into and out of the Greek scriptures, and of the changing of Semitic names to Greek names and then to foreign names, such as Jesus, Mary, James, Paul, Peter, and John, which have all lost the Hebrew ring. But one might still argue that the ample evidence is there for identifying Yeshua as a Jew. True again, but by formal reader reception theory, or virtually by any sensible notion of reading, a reader-deception practice has in the past, and for the vast majority of contemporary readers today, persuaded the reader that Yeshua, Miryam, Yohanan, and the disciples are not truly Jews but early Christians whose translated names are Jesus, Mary, and John, words that come through as fine English names, with no ring or taint of Near Eastern Semitism. (The same name changes exist in other language translations of the New Covenant.) In the case of noncompetitive Greek heroes, Odysseus, Achilles, Agamemnon are not rebaptized as fine English royal names of William, Richard, and Edward. There is no need to forget the Greekness of the Greeks. But for the shadowy Jews, the reader is persuaded to suppress or forget that Semitic shade by the virulence of the anti-Jewish, demonizing speech emanating from the implied narrator as well as from Yeshua and the Jewish members of his circle.

In the subjective process of reading, there is, to begin with, a physical objective text, which comes alive only as it passes into the reader's mind, where the text's subjective transformation occurs. The reader participates in the transformation on the basis of signs inside and outside the text to receive and resolve significance. Traditionally, the extratextual element that encourages a probable reading in which Jewish identity is suppressed has come principally from Christian theology and clerical pronouncements. The most hopeful factor in altering an inevitably biased and myopic reading comes from the same extratextual sources, theologians and clergy, who are moving rapidly to a more balanced reception of the scriptures. Also, the place in the curriculum of courses or parts of courses in the Bible as literature permits an instructed reading in which religious persuasions do not deny the book an objective reception accorded to other major books. In the new school, faith and history are not in conflict. However, the full extent of the inconsistencies in the text and the overwhelming pressures on the reader to forget Yeshua as the rabbi who died on the cross (as Marc Chagall painted him in full-rabbinical attire in so many canvases) still remain largely unperceived. The correction of disguisement is real, but in its initial period.

In this translation, the restoration of biblical for Hellenized personal names is by itself a powerful marking throughout the scriptures that should signal the reader to receive the text with sensibility to the Jewish identity of the cast. Christianity is no longer a struggling religion that needs to placate the Roman Empire and to attack its parent religion in order to defend its own identity. By these restorations of the Semitic names, I would like to serve both Judaism and Christianity by highlighting the illogic of anti-Judaism in a Jewish book. I hope these versions begin to free both religions from misinformation that has led to an outmoded and unnecessary strife.

THE JESUS MOVEMENT AND THE EMERGENCE
OF A HISTORICAL YESHUA[65]

Insofar as the Hebrew Bible and New Covenant are assumed to be historical documents, they are scrutinized for their authenticity. Hence, we find the worried who complain, as Thomas Jefferson did in a letter of January 24, 1814, to John Adams, "In the New Testament there is internal evidence that parts of it have proceeded from an extraordinary man; and that other parts are of the fabric of very inferior minds. It is as easy to separate those parts, as to pick out diamonds from dunghills."

Scripture in the New Covenant is for some holy and inviolate, for others pages to be read with Jeffersonian reservations, but for devout or skeptical alike the book is constantly analyzed and interpreted. Geza Vermes construes a Yeshua who is an ascetic charismatic. While the Dead Sea Scrolls reveal a messianic figure among the Essenes at Qumran with similar messianic qualities, Vermes writes emphatically that "Jesus did not belong among the Pharisees, Essenes, Zealots or Gnostics, but was one of the holy miracle-workers of Galilee" (*Jesus the Jew*, 223). Two decades later, while still asserting that the essential Yeshua corresponds to earlier and contemporary Hasidic holy men, Vermes now moves on to describe Yeshua as one of the Pharisees, or at the very least, as one portrayed in the traditional costume of the Pharisees. In *The Changing Faces of Jesus*, he writes, "The evangelists implicitly portray Jesus as a Jew profoundly attached to the laws and customs of his people, and some of his most obvious authentic sayings confirm this picture. The gospels attest his presence in Galilean synagogues and in the Temple of Jerusalem. We are told that he had eaten the Passover just before he was arrested. His garment was like that of the Pharisees [Matt. 23.5], with the traditional tassels hanging from its edge (Matt. 9.20; Luke 8.44; Mark 6.56; Matt. 14.36; cf. Num. 15.38–40; Deut. 22.12) (208–209).

But in stressing Yeshua's Galilean nature, Vermes in no way reflects the French historian Ernest Renan's *The Life of Jesus* (1862), which treated Yeshua as a non-Semitic, Aryan Galilean from a roaming northerner tribe. We have come a long way from the once revolutionary Renan, whose perversion of Yeshua's origin was taken up by the greater Protestant Church in divinity

---

[65] See also earlier chapter on historicity.

school and pulpit in Germany during the Nazi period in order to strip the messiah of all taint of Jewishness.

In the endless search for the historical Yeshua, in addition to Jesus the Cynic, Mediterranean peasant, Hasidic charismatic, desert Essene, Pharisaic populist, and Galilean Aryan, there have been many speculations in film, theater, poetry, and novel about the real Yeshua, including Norman Mailer's syncretistic re-creation of Yeshua's everyday life and death in his *The Gospel According to the Son* (New York: Random House, 1997).

Since its beginnings, the interest in "the historical Jesus" has presented a Yeshua at odds with the biblical figure. The gospel portrayal of Yeshua as one who acquiesces to Roman administration and law is unconvincing. Beyond possible credence is his presentation in Luke as a soothsayer apologist for Titus's destruction of Jerusalem, which Luke informs us, through Yeshua's words, is the punishment the Jews deserve because of their lack of belief. The same prediction of the destruction of the Temple appears in the earlier gospels of Mark 13.1–2 and Matthew 24.1–2, but without censure of the Jews.

YESHUA AND MIRYAM SPEAKING GREEK
THAT IS A TRANSLATION OR AN INVENTION

In these preliminary observations, it is not possible to do more than raise questions about the nature of a historical Yeshua and transmission of texts. What is certain is the uncertainty of earlier held truths. For example, the curious notion of Yeshua with a Latin name Jesus, speaking Greek to a circle of Greek-speaking followers, raises questions of credulity. Then we have the question of originality of the Greek gospels. I am often asked whether I have translated the gospels from the original Greek texts. My answer is yes. Yet am I being truthful? I translate from the extant Greek texts, our earliest texts, but these "originals" are themselves, in one form or another, a translation or transmission of earlier oral or written documents. Their scripts are therefore an edition, translation, transformation—the category is secondary and complex—of earlier material. Yet no manuscript or edition of the Greek gospels has itself been called "a translation," or at the very least a text in Greek acknowledged to be derived from unknown sources that once held Yeshua's words in Aramaic.

"Translation" is a carrying of information from one place to another, inter- or intralingually. For the Greek scriptures to be deemed more than a translation, a carrying of information from an earlier to a later period adds an unfounded authority to the Greek, and deprives the texts of their plausibility as a retelling of possible events in an earlier period. The Greek texts do not contain Yeshua's

Aramaic speech, so at some point in the process of transmission there must have been a translation. However, with regard to Miryam's singing the beautiful Magnificat in Luke (1.39–55), I suspect this canticle may not be a translation from Aramaic or Hebrew but an original Greek composition written many decades after young Miryam sang.

Did I translate from the original Greek texts? Yes, but only in the sense of the earliest text in which the good news survives. What came before is hypothetical—from Q , from surviving eyewitnesses. It is better to use the word "mystery," "silence," or some noun to suggest that the enigma will remain unsolved.

THE EXACT WORD OF GOD IN TRANSLATION
AND THE ILLUSION OF THE QUIJOTE

It is largely accepted by the lay reader that in the Bible resides the exact word of God, the gospel truth as it is sometimes called, whether this truth be in Greek, Latin, or King James English. Yeshua used the parable as one of his main vehicles for conveying mysterious truths. But to find his exact words we cannot look to the gospels, unless we speak of the exact words in translation, suggesting the a = a perfectability of translation, which no one grants translation. Literary translation is a rich way of moving information, but neither literal nor free ways re-create perfectly. Imperfection is the nature of language, not a defect but a richness that keeps literatures alive as they pass through centuries and between languages. Yeshua himself, master of the parable, told tales and asked his listeners to translate each mysterious image into a living conceptual truth.

As for the truth in translation in the New Covenant, a story by Jorge Luis Borges, the modern parabolist, enlightens. In Borges's *Pierre Menard, Author of the Quijote*, Monsieur Menard has translated the opening pages of Cervantes's *Don Quijote de la Mancha* into French, which he claims as the true language of the noble Knight of the Sad Countenance. His true Quijote speaks a civilized twentieth-century French, and not the inappropriate, barbaric seventeenth-century Castilian of Quijote's Spain. Similarly, the assemblers of the Greek New Covenant have Yeshua speak late first- and second-century koine Greek, a more civilized tongue than Yeshua's Aramaic, the spoken language of the Jews. And the forty-seven marvelous King James translators of that Greek covenant have presented us the exact word of God in a civilized and memorable seventeenth-century English, which is far superior to the rudimentary demotic koine of Greek scriptures.

At each new level of translation, the new version diminishes the authority of the source text.

The failure to acknowledge a source language is not accident. Were the source language clear, this change alone would make the Jewish ethnicity of all major characters in the New Covenant perfectly clear. Harold Bloom addresses precisely this question of the language of speakers and related questions of transmission and historicity in his essay "An Interpretation." Bloom writes:

> Of the veritable text of the sayings of a historical Jesus, we have nothing. Presumably he spoke to his followers and other wayfarers in Aramaic, and except for a few phrases scattered throughout the Gospels, none of his Aramaic sayings have survived. I have wondered for some time how this could be, and wondered even more that Christian scholars have never joined in my wonder. If you believed in the divinity of Jesus, would you not wish to have preserved the actual Aramaic sayings themselves? Were they lost, still to be found in a cave somewhere in Israel? Were they never written down in the first place, so that the Greek texts were based only upon memory? For some years now, I have asked these questions whenever I have met a New Testament scholar, and I have met only blankness. Yet surely this puzzle matters. Aramaic and Greek are very different languages, and the nuances of spirituality and of wisdom do not translate readily from one into the other. Any sayings of Jesus, open or hidden, need to be regarded in this context, which ought to teach us a certain suspicion of even the most normative judgments as to authenticity, whether those judgments rise from faith or from supposedly positive scholarship. *Gospel of Thomas*[66]

Bloom wonders about the great absence, about those decades between the death of Yeshua and the Gospel of Mark: "Between Jesus and any Christianity, at least a generation of silence intervenes" (119). What happened in the most crucial initial years of Christianity's formation? Why is there no record, and from where and through whose hands come the scriptures we do have? How could the identity of a Jew, of one who will be known as man, the messiah, and God become so thoroughly confused and blurred?

As Bloom implies, there is a double vision with regard to Yeshua and the Jew throughout the New Covenant. Here we have, in translations of translations, texts in which a messianic figure, a God-Man, speaks to us in Greek

---

[66] Meyer, Marvin, *The Gospel of Thomas*, 113–114.

about himself and about his followers and condemns his enemies "the Jews" as the spawn of Satan. The double vision with regard to the Jew is the overriding paradox of the New Covenant.

SATANIZING JEWS IN JOHN AND THE OTHER GOSPELS

We see this double vision—about as clearly as double vision can be isolated and focused—in the gospel of John. The anomalies of history and myth, of spiritual mystery and elemental hate, all assemble most intensely in the Gospel of John.

Many have written about the disturbing characterization of the Jews in John, the most Jewish, most poetic, and most philosophical and mysterious of the gospels. I have tried to make sense of it, and like others I have made guesses and have been tempted to come up with a way of rendering *oi Ioudaioi*—"the Jews"—as something else in English, without violating the text. But there is no way of getting around John's epithet "the Jews."

The Satanization of the Jew in John persists. At least its context clarifies the usage, highlights the implausibility of its veracity, and annotation may invent an essential mirror in which those words, "the Jews," will not appear so sinister, and not have such sinister consequences in the religious and social history of Jews and Christians. The magnificent Gospel is attributed to John, a Greek name (Yohanan is his Jewish name), who has been identified as a Jew writing in a period before Christianity had a separate identity. His treatment of Yeshua as a Jewish prophet,[67] as a rabbi teaching in the synagogue and attending the holiday feasts of Sukkoth and Pesach (Tabernacles and Passover), is enforced by Yeshua's constant citations of earlier Jewish prophets in his sermons, all of which indicate no rupture with the Hebraic tradition. Yet, implausibly, we read in John, "His students said to him, 'Rabbi, the Jews were just now trying to stone you. . . .'" *legousin auto oi mathetai, rhabbi, nun ezitoun se lithasai oi Ioudaioi* (λέγουσιν αὐτῷ οἱ μαθηταί· ῥαββί, νῦν ἐζήτουν σε λιθάσαι οἱ Ἰουδαῖοι) (John 11.8)

The conjunction of *rabbi* and *the Jews* is an anomaly, with cross signals that befuddle the purpose of making the Jews appear abhorrent. Yet, readers are apparently not shocked to find Yeshua addressed as rabbi, and then utter words as if to suggest that he is not a rabbi of the Jews but an outsider attacking the

---

[67] George Nickelsburg comments in a letter to the author on Yeshua as a Jewish prophet: "Jesus spoke as a Jewish prophet to the Jews. However, once Christianity separated from Judaism, they took these sayings out of context and as outsiders to Judaism hurled them back to the Jews, who were the others."

Jews. And his talmidim,[68] are they not also Jews as is their rabbi? Or have they too suddenly lost their Judaism to be able to speak of "the Jews" as a people whom they and Yeshua are not, and do not represent in any way? To make further sense of this is a stretch, bringing us to the hypothetical. As they are, the gospels reflect a Christianizing of Jewish scriptures that characterizes dozens of extant second- and third-century pseudepigraphica, such as the beautiful "Jewish-Christian" gnostic scripture, the Book of Baruch.[69] In this process of converting early Jewish scripture into Christian documents, the perspective changes. The implied author speaks as a much later Christian about early events in which the Jew is normally, as in the New Covenant, depicted either as villainous or disguised, in a time warp, as a later Christian.

What is probable is that in the process of redacting whatever texts were used for John, at some point in their transmission to the present Greek form the changing of identity from Jew to non-Jew was not completed. And hence the paradox in John 11.8 of a rabbi as one who is momentarily, after the utterance of his title, rabbi not a rabbi but an unidentified non-Jew whom his opponents, the Jews, want to murder. We have two texts and two authors working against each other, and consequently Yeshua changes person. A minimal close look should alert us to foul scribal play. The attack on "the Jews" here, and about seventy times elsewhere, points to a later redaction of a text that is fashioned to appeal exclusively to gentiles as it praises those who have shed their Jewish name tag and Satanizes those it selectively identifies as the Jew.

So we see that the shaping of Yeshua and his circle as later Christians remains always uneven. Not only does Yeshua lead a rabbinical life of teaching in the synagogues and great Temple, but Yeshua as a Jew makes compelling declarations of his kinship with the Jews as the chosen, as in John 4.22, where he declares the Jews are the people of salvation: "You Shomronims worship what you do not know, for salvation is from the Jews." But then come equivocal appearances of Yeshua, where he both affirms himself as a Jew and defames the people "over there" for being Jews.

---

[68] Hebrew for "students," "disciples."

[69] The Book of Baruch, attributed to Justin, is in spirit and probably in fact the earliest extant gnostic text, though it is preserved only as a paraphrase in Hippolytos of Rome's *Refutation of All Heresies*. Robert M. Grant calls Baruch "an example of a gnosis almost purely Jewish" in *Gnosticism and Early Christianity* (New York: Columbia University Press, 1959), 19. It should be remembered that Jewish heterodoxy and gnosticism preceded Christian gnosticism, though alas, we lack texts other than in Christianized Jewish scripture such as Baruch and the evidence Gershom Scholem elaborates on in his opus magnum *Jewish Gnosticism, Merkabah Mysticism, and Talmudic Tradition* (New York: Schocken Books, 1961).

In the Temple scene (John 2.12–16), Yeshua enters with the rage of the prophets against the impious to expel the animal and coin merchants who are sullying this holiest of Jewish monuments. Is Yeshua to be taken here as an unknown alien enemy among the Jews, overturning their tables and whipping them for their sins? Or is he a devout Jew in his own Temple, admonishing his people, in violent family dispute, to reform, to clean house in order to reclaim their orthodoxy? Yet however vile the Jews are made to appear before a righteous Yeshua militant, Yeshua's reform takes place *inside* the Temple. He doesn't destroy the Temple as an *outsider* with Roman fire, nor does he urge followers to do so.

The notion of a family feud among diverse Jewish sects is essential for understanding how the angry feuds of the day, viewed later through the polemic in the gospels and after almost twenty centuries of enmity, could lead to the tragic divisions between Christians and Jews, and the massacres by Christians of Jews. The change from family feud to massacre was made possible as the historical Yeshua—*a Jew speaking as a Jew to Jews*—is altered in the interpretive gospels to be received as *a non-Jew speaking against Jews*. Concerning the many voices heard in first-century Judaism, George Nickelsburg writes: "First century Judaism was a remarkably diverse phenomenon, which could breed Pharisees, Essenes, children of Enoch, and Christians of various sorts—all of whom claimed to be faithful to their mother religion" ("Jews and Christians").[70]

YESHUA'S VILIFICATIONS OF JEWS IN THE TRADITION OF THE PROPHETS

There is nothing unusual about Jews, perceived as Jews, scourging Jews. Vituperation for sin and wrongdoing is a familiar act of self-criticism scripted in the Hebrew Bible from Genesis through the last prophets. Indeed, the Bible ends with Malachi's polemic against the priesthood, a furious assault in which he execrates the cast of priests as well as its seed. The prophet's oracle does so by assembling the Lord's words of abuse and threats from Exodus 29.14 and Leviticus 8.17 and 16.29. Nothing in the Greek scriptures outdoes the sheer wrath of his attack on corrupt authorities:

And now, O ye priests, this commandment is for you. If you will not hear, and if ye will not lay it to heart, to give glory unto my name, saith the Lord

---

[70] "Jews and Christians in the First Century: The Struggle Over Identity" in *Neotestamentica* 27(2) (1993): 365–90/1–4.5.

of Hosts, I will even send a curse upon you, and I will curse your blessings:
yea, I have cursed them already, because ye do not lay it to heart. Behold, I
will corrupt your seed, and spread dung upon your faces, even the dung of
your solemn feasts, and one shall take you away with it.

Mal. 1–3

But after the curses and threats, even the wayward priest is shown a place
within God's society, if he will listen, for he is the messenger (*malak* or angel)
of the lord:

For the priest's lips should keep knowledge, and they should seek the law at
his mouth: for he is the messenger of the Lord of hosts. But ye are departed
out of the way; ye have caused many to stumble at the law; ye have not kept
my ways, but have been partial in the law.

2.7–9

Exasperated by the priest who causes others to stumble and to violate the covenant with God, Malachi asks:

Have we not all one father? Hath not one God created us? Why do we deal
treacherously every man against his brother, by profaning the covenant of
our fathers?

2.10

The prophet tells the priests that they should not live by treachery. And he
asks for reconciliation, making clear that he, Malachi the accuser, and the offending clergy are of one family, created by the same God.

Malachi's attack is fierce. Excrement is slapped on the faces of the cursed
priests, yet no one would or could look to Malachi as a source of anti-
Semitism or Satanization of the Jew. Although the accusations are as grave as
any in John or Luke, the drama of treason occurs *within* the tribe—as it did
even in the messiah drama in the unlikely self-serving tale of a Roman execution of a Jew instigated by other Jews. Were Yeshua the Messiah truly and always perceived as Rex Judeorum and his circle truly and always perceived as
Jews throughout the texts of the messiah passion, then the Greek scriptures'
horrendous and fatal historical impact on the life and death of the Jew could
not have happened. In some other imaginary tale in which the Yeshua circles
at the Sukkoth or Passover were depicted as ordinary Jews, anti-Judaism and
the Satanization of the Jew of the historical diaspora could never have sprung
from that new covenant with God. And most tellingly, in no century after the

crucifixion of "rabbi Yeshua" could the epithet "Jew," during the bloody murder of a Jew for being a Jew, have been reasonably hurled at the victim if the would-be killer knew that his own inherited savior Yeshua was also a Jew. Cossacks, even in moments of killing, don't kill Cossacks simply because they are Cossacks.

The in-house nature of Yeshua's invective is seen by Krister Stendahl, who accounts for the heavy rhetoric of "brood of vipers" in Matthew and Luke, writing, "When such words are spoken they are spoken by a Jewish prophet for a Jewish people. Jesus identifies with his people" ("Anti-Semitism," 33). He further elaborates: "The Jesus-movement was a totally Jewish event—the gospels know of few contacts of Jesus with gentiles. Christianity begins as a Jewish reform movement, and the formative conflicts by which the Christian identity is formed are conflicts within Judaism" (32).

The characteristic attack mode against "the Jews" occurs in the episode of the Sukkoth (Festival of Booths), 7.10. Yeshua has gone up to Jerusalem for the Sukkoth feasts and he will enter the great Temple and teach there. Members of the crowd are speaking about Yeshua, for and against him. We read that "no one spoke about him openly for fear of the Jews" (7.13). Yet Jews at a Jewish festival cannot sensibly be made to whisper to each other that they must not speak openly about Yeshua, who is also a Jew, "for fear of the Jews." Although in this crudely redacted sentence the identity of the speaker and the speaker's "fearful" referents are identical—they are all Jews—by the condemnation of the referent, the reader is instructed to disassociate speaker from referent. A Jew condemns a Jew for being Jewish, and consequently the condemner ceases to be seen as a Jew. In another reversal, we have the condemnation of the Jews reinforced by having the referent Jews crying out their own self-condemnation. In the notoriously implausible street scene before Pontius Pilate, earlier discussed in the segment on historicity, the author or authors have miraculously made the Jews themselves scream out their collective guilt for the immediate moment and, prophetically, a guilt to be inherited by their children for all time in the future (Matt. 27.25).

In John and throughout the gospels, the term "the Jews" is an embracing code word for a composite enemy consisting of opponents, authorities, and unbelievers in rabbi Yeshua. Although the means of stereotyping are crude and self-contradictory, the effect is unequivocal: The Jew is Satanized. Elaine Pagels eloquently documents the Devil-making enterprise in *The Origin of Satan*. The demonization is explicit and complete in John 8.44. There Yeshua declares the children of Abraham to be the children of the devil:

You are from your father the devil
and you want to do the desires of your father.
From the beginning he was a murderer,
and he does not stand in the truth,
because there is no truth in him.
When he lies he speaks from himself,
since he is a liar and the father of lies.

It should be said that the vindictive demonization of the Jews in the Abraham and the Sukkoth scenes has less to do with the historic moment of an evangelist John or of his subjects but more with the needs of a second-century retrenchment of Christianity. As the movement became increasingly gentile, Christianity split from Judaism, the messiah was converted into the Christ, and the children of the unreconstructed Jews were converted into the children of Satan. With Yeshua's Jewish identity all but muted and dead after his crucifixion by the Romans in Jerusalem, the new Christian Fathers of the church in Rome and elsewhere could breathe independence from a Jewish parentage.

In George Nickelsburg's article, "The First Century: A Time to Rejoice and a Time to Weep," the weepers were the Jews and the rejoicers were those who, as Christian Jews and increasingly by the time of the gospels simply as Christians, rejoiced at the destruction of the Temple and Jerusalem as an act of God's justice. Nickelsburg writes:

> Once again revisionist history [the Gospels not as chronicles but as "interpretive history"] reflects the standoff between Christians and Jews at the end of the first century and reveals a startling difference in their responses to the events of the year 70. Baruch and Ezra [late noncanonical apocrypha] may attribute the destruction to sin, but their account is explicitly tempered with grief and puzzlement over the extremity of the punishment. For the evangelists, there is no pause. The Jews had it coming to them. Nor does it make any difference in the final analysis. God's redemptive activity will go on without the Temple, and God's covenantal relationship is transferred to the gentiles. There are losers, but there are winners, and the winners hardly pause to think of the losers, except with a certain satisfaction that God's justice has been enacted. (in *Religion and Theology*, Vol. 1/1 [1994]: 4–17)

However, the matter of Christianity's origins remained to plague the new sect's equanimity. The religion had its origin in these despised Suasionist Jews.

The continued existence of the Jews kept the problem alive, and so there was no end to targeting them for their Satanic ways.

CODE WORDS IN THE NEW COVENANT

Let us look carefully at the logic of a passage, typical throughout the gospels, which reveals the hand disguising the Jewishness of both Yeshua and the circle he was speaking to. The failure in completely concealing the alterations provides our clues. In John 13.33 we have:

> Children, I am with you a short while.
> You will look for me,
> and I tell you now as I said to the Jews,
> "Where I go you cannot also come."

The author of this passage has Yeshua say, "and I tell you as I said to the Jews." This verse designates three parties: the I, the you, and the Jews. Now the intimate instruction fails, because Yeshua designates the Jews as other than the I and the you, who are also Jews. If instead of saying "as I said to the Jews," Yeshua had said "as I said to other Jews or to my Jewish opponents," the phrase would have been that of a credible Jewish leader distinguishing those who were in his movement from those who were not. Then the reader could assume truthfully that Yeshua and his confidants were Jews, but that some of the Jews were antagonists and worthy of punishment. An in-house drama. But the author of the passage clearly leaps ahead to a later time when Christianity existed as a distinct group of largely non-Jewish followers and the people in this scene were gentiles rather than Jews. There, in the historical context of Yeshua's day, the words fail by being too greedy, by making Yeshua a Christian (one following himself?), not a Jew, and by making his students not Jews, and finally by designating himself and his students as belonging to some people other than the Jews. This meddling reveals that the words are not likely to be those of a historic evangelist reigning over a Jewish Passover supper in Jerusalem, but of a gentile scribe from a later time when the separation between Christian and Jew had been realized. In these ways, the authors and redactors of the gospels established a mythical identity for the founders of Christianity.

PHARISEES: WHO WERE THEY, AND WAS YESHUA
OR PAUL A PHARISEE?

As the Greek scriptures read today, there is an inexplicable shift in implied reference, which occurs when the Jews around Yeshua excoriated the Jewish priesthood, especially the Pharisees.[71] The Pharisees, meaning "separatists," were rivals of the priestly temple cult of the Sadducees. Associated with the small synagogues and the houses of prayer rather than the great Temple, they emphasized faith in the one God, with whom an individual could have, as Yeshua did, a direct relationship, without going through the formalities of the Temple. Christianity was in deep debt to the Pharisees, despite the vilification of them as "hypocritical actors" and "brood of vipers" in Matthew, for the Pharisees believed in the divine revelation of both written and oral law, and in eternal life and resurrection. They centered on the soul's immortality, which was also at the heart of Yeshua's spiritual redemption, a Platonic notion that entered Judaism and consequently Christianity during the two centuries B.C.E. of high Greek influence in Israel, which paralleled the Hasmonean struggle against and accommodation with the Greeks. It is said that the Pharisees were aloof to quotidian politics, including the revolt against the Romans in 70 C.E., in which few took part, and as a progressive sect the Pharisees held that religious ritual and practice could take place in one's own home as opposed to public synagogues and the Temple. This fact was to be of extreme significance in the survival of the Jewish tradition after the destruction of the Temple, and in the lives of the early Christians, who struggled to survive amidst enemies. They separated the worldly and spiritual spheres, and, like Yeshua, they ceded the former to Caesar in order to pursue the salvation of spiritual eternity. At the same time, other sources say that the Pharisees were not aloof but distinctly with the people in opposing Roman rule. The New Covenant is a strange book pitting Yeshua the Jew against the Pharisees, who probably shared his deviant persuasion, but whom the gospels reduce to a parody of legalistic constraints.[72]

---

[71] For discussion of slander in the Greek scriptures, see Luke T. Johnson, "The New Testament: Anti-Jewish Slander and the Conventions of Ancient Polemic," *Journal of Biblical Literature* 108 (1989): 419–441, and "Matthew's Campaign Against the Pharisees: Deploying the Devil" in Elaine Pagels' *The Origin of Satan*. For further discussion of Matthew, see Krister Stendahl, *The School of Matthew* (Uppsala: C.W.K. Gleerup, 1954).

[72] E. P. Sanders debunks the "authenticity of the charges against the Pharisees in Matt. 23" (*Jesus and Judaism* [Philadelphia: Fortress Press, 1987], 277), and develops this notion fully in *Paul and Palestinian Judaism: A Comparison of Patterns of Religion* (Philadelphia: Fortress Press, 1977) and in *Paul, the Law, and the Jewish People* (Philadelphia: Fortress Press, 1983).

Harold Bloom sees the Pharisees as the primary ally of Yeshua with regard to the belief in the resurrection, but he distinguishes between resurrection and the Platonic immortality of the soul, which he contends was the domain of Hellenistic Jews (surely Philo) and Paul and had less to do with Yeshua and the gospels. In *Omens of Millennium* (New York: Riverhead Books, 1996), Bloom writes:

> Saint Paul, like the Hellenistic Jews, seems to have absorbed Platonic notions of immortality, but there seems no Platonic influence upon Jesus himself, with his altogether Pharisaic belief in resurrection: "He is not the God of the dead but of the living." The intertestamental Jewish texts that fuse immortality and resurrection are themselves Platonized, but Jesus, despite the New Testament polemic against the Pharisees falsely argued in his name, seems less Platonized even than the Pharisees. He is in the tradition of "Yahweh alone," even if his vision of Yahweh is extraordinarily benign, at least in those passages of the gospels (and *The Gospel of Thomas*) that have the authentic aura of his voice. (158)

Burton Mack also describes the coincidences of dissent between the Jesus movement and the Pharisees. Along with the Essenes, who withdrew to Qumran near the Dead Sea, the Pharisees were opposed not only to the secular Hellenization of the Jews but also to the Hasmonean Jewish leaders. Originally, the Hasmonean family under Judas Maccabeus, who led the successful rebellion in 167–64 B.C.E. against the Greek monarchy, represented Jewish resistance to Hellenization and foreign rule; but after nearly two centuries of accommodation to Greek and Roman rulers, the Hasmonean descendants, like Herod, became puppets of their earlier adversaries. Mack writes: "The Pharisees were harsh critics of the Hasmonean establishment and, together with the priests at Qumran, they wore the Hasmoneans down" (*Who Wrote the New Testament?*, 23).

In effect, the existence of the Pharisees was an embarrassment to later Christian writers, for they were not only separatists like the early Christian Jews, but from their rank came converts—Paul claimed to be a Pharisee—to the Jesus movement.[73] Moreover, they were fiercely opposed to Roman occupation. If there is one historical reason that most contemporary scholars agree

---

[73] In *The Mythmaker: Paul and the Invention of Christianity* (San Francisco: HarperSan Francisco, 1986), Hyam Maccoby asserts that Paul was not a Pharisee, writing: "The contention of this book is that Jesus, usually represented as anything but a Pharisee, was one, while Paul, always represented as a Pharisee in his unregenerate days, never was. In the course of the argument, it will become plain why this strange reversal of the facts was brought about by the New Testament writers" (33).

upon, it is that Yeshua was executed as an seditionist, that is, a Jewish revolutionary who wanted out of the Roman occupation. But since the gospels picture Yeshua as one who accommodates the Romans—"What is of Caesar give to Caesar" (Mark 14.25) and the Roman soldiers who execute Yeshua are made the first to affirm him as innocent, God, and risen—there is also an inescapable conclusion that there is a terrible quandary of how the evangelists should treat these Romans who killed Yeshua, Paul, and all those Christian Jews, which is the concern of Apocalypse (Revelation). The Pharisees' uncomfortably similar views with the historical Yeshua executed by the Romans as a seditionist, together with their failure to accept Yeshua's divinity, could not be tolerated. The solution was to co-opt the essential position of the dissenting Pharisees and turn them from opponents of Rome to instigators and enforcers of the Romans' "unwilling" execution of Yeshua—to make the Pharisees into the establishment by demonizing them as shameless legalists, liars, and killers. In one stroke, the enemy authority was Pharisee, unbeliever, murderer, and devil.

There is also a notion among scholars that not only Yeshua's views coincided with the Pharisees (hence the special need to defame these Jews who were in spiritual harmony with Yeshua) but that Yeshua was a Pharisee.[74] Hyam Maccoby writes: "Jesus speaks and acts as a Pharisee, though the gospel editors have attempted to conceal this by representing him as opposing Pharisaism even when his sayings were most in accordance with Pharisee teaching" (*The Mythmaker*, xi). Since the Pharisees "were the centre of opposition to the Roman occupation, it was of the utmost importance to the Gospel editors to represent Jesus as having been a rebel against Jewish religion, not against the Roman occupation. The wholesale re-editing of the material in order to give a picture of conflict between Jesus and the Pharisees was thus essential" (34).

Maccoby sees the Pharisees as the center of opposition to Rome which, if Yeshua was executed for anti-Rome activities, would make them allies in the struggle. Others see the Pharisees and Yeshua as disinterested in the struggle against Rome and link them accordingly to similar positions. The evidence about the Pharisees appears in the New Covenant, in Josephus, and in rabbinic literature. The accounts are contradictory, and modern descriptions also differ widely as to their position on Rome and revolt. There is evidence, in Josephus and elsewhere, that the Pharisees strongly opposed Herod and his successors, which would imply opposition to Rome. In rabbinic literature, the Pharisees

---

[74] Geza Vermes in *The Changing Faces of Jesus* remarks that at the Passover meal Yeshua is described as wearing a Pharisee garment, "including the traditional tassels hanging from its edge." Then he notes places in the New Covenant and Hebrew Bible that describe the Pharisee attire.

are associated with the great philosophical schools of Shammai and Hillel, who were Pharisiac leaders. In the New Covenant, the Pharisees are reduced to perfidious puppets.

Ultimately, the Pharisees, who like Yeshua who was killed by Rome, had to be condemned by the authors of the gospels, who surely were writing for the survival of later Christianity amid the widespread Roman Empire. So they condemned Rome's enemies, especially the Pharisees, to appease Rome and to demonstrate their own innocence and loyalty to the Empire. But while they fiercely condemned Rome's enemies, it was unthinkable that their wrath might extend to Yeshua himself as an ememy of Rome. So Yeshua was fashioned not only as a loyal subject of Rome and enemy of the Jews but forced ungenerously into the illogical role of the most famous defender of his own executioners. Such a position was hugely unfair to Yeshua, the greatest and best-known world victim of the Roman rulers of occupied Isreal.

NEW TRANSLATIONS FORMING A CHRISTIAN BIBLE

The formidable shaping of a Christian Bible came in the unknowable beginnings. The contradictions remained, and in reading these texts, one can conjecture about the blank time of rewriting when purposeful redaction was intense, censorial eyes not there. When converting early Jews to Christianity, it was convenient to use the Septuagint Greek Bible of the Jews. Paul used the Septuagint for his apostolate and, as Lowry Nelson observes, "In the early century of proselytizing and establishing the doctrine, Greek was the prime language and Hellenized Jews the prime body of converts" (*Poetic Configurations* [University Park, PA: Pennsylvania State University Press, 1992], 118). With the later separation of Jews from the new Judaism of the Christian Jews came the need on both sides to separate the Septuagint Greek Bible of the Jews from the one of the Christians: hence, the redaction of the Septuagint for Christian usage by a series of translations, culminating in the third-century Hexapla of Origen, a polyglot version of the Hebrew Bible (named for its six columns: a Hebrew text, a Greek transliteration of it, and four Greek versions—Aquila's, Symmachus', Theodotion's, and Origen's own corrected version of the Septuagint). The Hexapla was lost with the seventh-century destruction of the library at Caesarea by the Muslims, but we do hear that in the fourth century Jerome consulted it at Caesarea for his own translation of the Vulgate. With the Romanization of the Christian movement, the Latin translation took precedence over Hebrew and Greek scripture, becoming for the Catholic Church, like the Authorized for many Protestants, the word itself.

All these transformations of identities, through scripture, corresponded to requirements for establishing by the beginning of the fifth century "a Christian epic," as Mack describes the Christian Bible, which would include both the Hebrew Bible and the Greek scriptures. As Christianity became dominant in southern Europe in the fourth century, it was increasingly important for the Greek scriptures to be a single authoritative book, no longer a disputed collection of disparate texts, but the dominant Bible within the "dual" Bible and the definitive guide to keep alive the stories of Yeshua and the apostles and to spread the word of God to the faithful and potential proselytes. The shaping of the New Covenant required that the enemies be defined, and so they were. The New Covenant also required miracles to match those in the Old Covenant. The older Bible had to fit the new one, whatever their relative status, and the exegetes found the Hebrew Bible rich in symbolism that could be seen as a source for Christian virtues and predictions of the messiah. The fitting of the two covenants together, the joining together of the authority of Moses with the apostolic writings, gave a firm and deep legitimacy to the Christian religion.

YESHUA'S CHANGING SELF

Throughout the gospels, there remain the inconsistencies and mutations of Yeshua's character during his residence on earth, within or between sentences and paragraphs, whether presented as messiah, Jew, rabbi, savior, gentile, pre-Christian, or simply alien. The schizophrenic presentation of Yeshua's Jewishness and non-Jewishness is nowhere revealed more poignantly than in the passage in John 19.40: "So they took the body of Yeshua and wrapped it in aromatic spices in linen cloths, as is the Jewish custom." John reveals that it is mandated that Yeshua be buried in the Jewish manner. Now Pilate has just washed his hands to show his innocence, his heartfelt reluctance to kill Yeshua, which will later serve him well when in some of the churches of Eastern Europe and the Near East he is canonized as St. Pontius. While Pilate appears to have made himself an acceptable gentile by washing his hands, in doing so he performs an ancient Jewish ritual. Even Pilate, in this supposedly sanitized script, is portrayed as resorting to a Jewish symbolic rite of purification. Elaine Pagels points out: "[I]n a most unlikely scene, Pilate performed a ritual that derives from Jewish law, described in the book of Deuteronomy. He washed his hands to indicate his innocence of bloodshed" (*The Origin of Satan*, 87).

After these back-and-forth passages of Yeshua's split presentation in the gospels, as Jew and abused non-Jew, the emphasis on Yeshua's Jewishness in the ritual of handling his body appears again, in John 20.16, when Mary the Magdalene first encounters Yeshua. The text has her say "Rabboni!" (which means "teacher").[75] We note, however, the inevitable and illogical cover-up in the interpolation "which means teacher" that has again been added to the text, in instructive parenthesis, to dissuade the reader from the unwelcome notion that "rabbi" actually means "rabbi," and that Yeshua is a rabbi and therefore a Jew. That a rabbi might also be a teacher does not, as some contend, excuse the intentions of the parenthesis, which is to suggest that he is not a Jewish rabbi but an unattached local teacher.

In practice, the changing of identity was accomplished by persuading the reader that Yeshua was in opposition to Jews (not to "other" Jews), to their purity laws, to their inhumane keeping of the Sabbath, to their brutish, enforcing authorities. The Jews were always *they*, not *we*. By an accumulation of convincing details in a blistering anti-Jewish message, the itinerant charismatic was disenfranchised of his Hebrew culture and ethnicity. The reader could thereby hate the Jews without hating Yeshua the Messiah. Yeshua, rather than being portrayed by the assemblers of the gospels as a God of love, is depicted as a figure who hates his fellow Jews, which can have little to do with a historic Yeshua. At this point, it is right to put this scene in a modern context. It is enough to say that Yeshua and his circle, whatever masks their writers gave them, would have fared less well in Germany between 1933 and 1945. In those days, the designation of the Jew as "vermin," found famously first in Matthew's "brood of vipers," was fixed, and even the intervention of Pope Pius XII could not have altered that designation of Yeshua's blood and racial identity, and his inevitable way to the chamber. His parents, brothers, sisters, students, and messengers would also have been picked up in trucks and sent to the death camps as Jews. In the eyes of the master race, the identity of Yeshua as one of the Jews had no way out.

SPARING GREEKS FOR EXECUTION OF SOCRATES

The Jews are the named enemy in the gospels of the Jews, which is no less insensible than having the Greeks as the named enemy in the other great death in history, the death of Socrates. The Jews at least had Romans to get them off the hook, if a literal reading of scripture is followed. While the story of the crucifixion is uncertain in all its larger facts and smaller details, the tale of the death of Socrates is certain indeed. We may not know whether Plato's reporting of Socrates' last conversations is accurate or invented. We do know that a Greek

---

[75] It means "my great teacher or master."

tribunal ordered the death of perhaps the greatest of the Greek philosophers and theologians. If the same criterion of inherited guilt by association were applied to the Greeks, then even the most generous eyes could not save the Greeks from the damnation of the ages. They had no alibis, neither Romans nor other aliens to save their people from everlasting infamy. At this, let us say there are some good turns in history. One is the surprising, blessed fact that the Greeks for their treatment of Socrates, and the Romans for theirs of Yeshua have not been condemned and vilified through the ages. There is no inheritance of alleged guilt, and there are simply and happily no takers of such profoundly mean-spirited vision.

ABANDONMENT OF YESHUA

Those who invented a Yeshua in life who was clean of Jewish stain and whose people were wicked and tainted with everlasting guilt of being a Jew were not kind to Yeshua, nor to his tribal kin, nor to their descendants. To Yeshua's people his angry creators stained their savior with a ghost of fear echoing even in the utterance of his name.

When Yeshua was on the cross as a man, desolate that his God had not saved him, he cried out, "Why have you forsaken me?" He shouted in Aramaic, his language as a Jew (not in later Christian Greek), and reproached God, asking, Why have you let Rome kill a Jew? Over the centuries his cry has not been heard.

THE EVANGELISTS
AS APOLOGISTS FOR ROME

As we have seen, in order to bring the messiah of the Jews into the church in Rome, Yeshua as Jew was blurred and essentially absolved from his religion, his ethnicity, and from his occupation as an itinerant charismatic rabbi. He was the *other*—and the other is never clarified—to be contrasted with those around him, who were identified specifically and uniformly as vile and wicked Jews. He could not be one of them. But the clergy of the Roman church still had an urgent and fierce dilemma about Rome's role in the execution of this stubbornly independent rabbi.

The clergy in Rome saw themselves as Romans and therefore as direct descendants of Pompey, who conquered Judea in 63 B.C.E. and deported large numbers of Jews as slaves to Rome; of Pontius Pilate, who ordered the centurion and his guard to execute Yeshua; of Florus and Titus, who crucified thousands of rebelling Jews, including the Christian Jews, and their entire families with extraordinary speed and efficiency. How could a Roman clergy in Rome, where messianism had taken hold, cope with the past? It did not entirely fall into historic amnesia, which is the most common way of coping with periods and events one would prefer forgotten. Its solution was to shift blame from Romans to Jews for all untoward events and, as noted, make the Roman officials the first to recognize Yeshua's earthly innocence, his God, and his own divinity as the son of God. That Roman invention of history shines as an unworthy miracle of the gospels.

The most benign explanation for the clergy's praise for its persecutors is that Rome reluctantly tolerated the expanding Christian churches, and the clerics feared that any sharp criticism of Rome with respect to the death of the messiah, any accusation of Roman deicide, would certainly lead to lethal repression.

So the gospels were shaped as an apology for Roman occupation of Israel, whose benign officials had been forced involuntarily into unpleasant acts to maintain obedience to Rome and its treasury. The evangelists were unfailing apologists for Rome. Foremost, they exonerated Rome from the death of Yeshua. They have Yeshua proclaim militantly the necessary and absolute punishment of his fellow Jews for challenging the Romans. They have Yeshua, who offers salvation, condemn the Jews for Titus's destruction of the Temple and Jerusalem four decades later. In condemning Jews, Yeshua personally exculpates Rome for the devastation of Jerusalem and its expulsion of the inhabitants, Jews and Christian Jews, into a new diaspora.

The secular moral hero of the gospels is Pontius Pilate. His ennoblement, which after his death will give him a place among the saints, is not merely an apology. He is Rome in Israel and its reasonable, humane emperor. He is certainly not a nondescript Eichmann banally following orders to kill Jews. A weak man, he kills Yeshua with a pained heart, unable to intimidate the high priests or resist the crowds in the street. He is the good bridge to Rome. Unlike Herod or his own soldiers, at no moment does Pilate participate in the maligning or mockery of Yeshua. Rather, he asks some simple questions, whose intent is to give Yeshua a way out, and then declares his distinctively personal judgment that Yeshua is innocent and states that he wants to release him. He yields only after three attempts to win his release, and then, only under the insistent pressure of the Jewish high priests and leaders, does he order him scourged and crucified. The event occurs on Friday, the day of preparation for the Passover Sabbath that will begin that evening, which makes the presence of the crowds in the street even more extraordinary. That Pilate accedes to the release of Barabbas, an insurrectionist and murderer, only emphasizes by contrast Yeshua's innocence.

Pilate's contemporaries were not so solicitous about preserving the ruler's good name. The Alexandrian Neoplatonist philosopher Philo (20 B.C.E.–C.E. 50), whose allegorical method of interpreting biblical scripture was to profoundly affect later Christian theology, wrote prolifically about Hellenistic Judaism, though without any awareness of Christian figures or events. Yeshua and his dissident Jewish sect had not, during Philo's lifetime, made a strong resonance in Alexandria, which it was later to do when it became, among other things, the initiator of Christian monasticism. Pilate, however, was known to him. In *Embassy to Gaius* (301–302), Philo "describes Pilate, whom the evangelists present as a helpless pawn, as a man of 'ruthless, stubborn and cruel disposition,' famous for, among other things, ordering 'frequent executions without trial'" (Pagels, *The Origin of Satan*, 10). As Mary Smallwood notes in *The Jews Under Roman Rule from Pompey to Diocletian* (Leiden: E. J. Brill, 1981), "At a time when the Romans in Israel were crucifying thousands of Jews for trouble making and sedition" (164), Pilate was renowned for his cruelty, venality with regard to Temple funds and other local moneys, and abundant killings. The

Roman prefect of Judea was recalled to Rome in 36 C.E. to answer for the massacre and executions of the Samaritans at Mount Gerizim.

How did Pontius Pilate become the good figure of the gospels? Mark begins the process of converting Pilate into a virtuous Roman governor and Yeshua into a non-Jewish victim of Jews. Elaine Pagels, tracing the changing portraits of Pilate through the gospels, develops in great depth the shifting of blame from Romans to Jews in the crucifixion and its resultant demonization of the Jews:

> Mark's benign portrait of Pilate increases the culpability of Jewish leaders and supports Mark's contention that Jews, not Romans, were the primary force behind Jesus' crucifixion. Throughout the following decades, as bitterness between the Jewish majority and Jesus' followers increased, the Gospels came to depict Pilate in an increasingly favorable light. As Paul Winter observes [Winter, *On the Trial of Jesus,* 88], the stern Pilate grows more mellow from Gospel to Gospel [from Mark to Matthew, from Matthew and Luke to John]. . . . The more removed from history, the more sympathetic a character he becomes. (*The Origin of Satan,* 33).

In the gospels, the evangelists demonstrate Pilate's goodness and impotence before higher forces. He is embellished as a good man, played with by evil forces. Pilate is mentioned only once more in the gospel. In his last good act he permits Yeshua's body to be taken away (Luke 23.52). The fact that the corpse was not left to rot on the cross for the vultures and dogs to pick apart and the remains thrown into a fire indicates special treatment, since part of the punishment of Roman crucifixion was the dismemberment and public humiliation of the victim. By permitting the body to be removed from the tomb, Pilate sets the stage for the discovery of the resurrection.

Apart from Yeshua and perhaps Peter, the personages in the gospels are fixed. They appear briefly, episodically, as in a travel book, and reveal little personal development. In the parables, there is perhaps more development, as in the figures of the prodigal son story, but they are a story within a story and once removed from the drama of the narration. The clear exception is Pilate. He has a crisis of conscience. He must as a Roman ruler kill in order to maintain a continuity of control, which his position requires. He is caught between loyalties to Rome and to his conscience, and sensitivity to the Jewish hierarchy and street mob. As in good theater, his order to proceed with the crucifixion establishes the tragedy. He may seem weak but not evil. And like his city of Rome, he will after his death float slowly back to the future church and be sanctified.

ROME SEEN FROM THE CATACOMBS
WHERE THE CHRISTIANS COWER

During the period when the gospels were assembled, we assume between 70 and 95 or later, neither Rome nor the Romans were viewed with pleasure. They were, as we see vividly in Revelation, the human incarnation of evil, although for obvious reasons Rome and its emperors are not mentioned by name in this wild allegory. In the Apocalypse, the Whore of Babylon may be the Roman emperor Nero or Domitian, depending on who was perceived as the worst enemy. The purpose of the apocalypses was to reveal and also conceal through allegorical disguise, thus making historical-critical analysis at best tentative.[76] Revelation surely escaped the Romanizing that characterizes the gospels. Written well after the gospels, its oddity and obscurity set it aside—it was not an early centerpiece of the emerging New Covenant—and so this revelation, including its not very veiled attack on Rome, remained intact at the heart of the poem. By the third century, when after much debate this controversial book was included in the canon, it reached us without marked political alteration of its text. It reflects its own period. The fear and fury it expresses toward the Roman emperor and his forces can hardly be reconciled with the friendliness in the synoptic gospels. John is more reserved. The catacombs of Rome, where Christian fugitives lived in terror, would not have recognized the Roman political and military figures depicted in the gospels. Their historical experience clamors against the whitewash of Roman behavior in scripture.

COINS FOR ROME

We have observed the gentle way made for Pontius Pilate to his later beatification and canonization. The goodness trickles down to his centurion, and even to the tax collectors for Rome, who took payments from farmers, city people, and the Temple. The famous scene of Yeshua and the Roman coin is normally received as a convenient separation of state and religion. It begins with the Jewish authorities who are trying to trap Yeshua by making it seem wrong to cooperate with Rome,

> "Is it right to pay the tax to Caesar or not? Should we give or not give?"
> But he saw their hypocrisy and said to them:
> "Why are you testing me?

---

[76] See Bernard McGinn's "Apocalypse" in Robert Alter and Frank Kermode, eds., *The Literary Guide to the Bible* (Cambridge, MA: Harvard University Press, 1987), 523–541.

> Bring me a denar to look at."
> They brought one. And he said to them:
>> "Whose image is this and whose name?"
> They said to him, "Caesar's."
> Yeshua said to them:
>> "The things of Caesar give to Caesar
>> and the things of God give to God."
>> (*Mark 12:14–17*)

The Pharisees remain embarrassed into silence after Yeshua's response. He has trapped them by his turn of phrase and has proven that it is not a fault to pay Rome what is Rome's.

Historically, this period was a touchy time of contention between Jew and Roman over religious matters—such as Caligula's attempt in 44–45 C.E. to set up a statue of himself in the Temple, and the tax rebellions, which Josephus reports, were ruthlessly put down. Since the scriptural position held Roman authority to be good and Jewish authority bad, especially as represented by the Pharisees (who, as noted, opposed Hellenization and Roman occupation), it was imperative to prove that tribute to Rome in the form of payment to Caesar did not interfere with tribute to God. So this passage of the coins showing Caesar's head establishes three principles: 1) Yeshua's recognition of the authority of the emperor for things of the emperor; 2) the hypocrisy of Jewish authorities who cast doubt on the authority of the emperor; and 3) that payment to the emperor does not imperil the things that are God's.

In Luke 23.2, Yeshua in captivity is accused falsely of "forbidding taxes to be paid to Caesar." Under Roman law not to pay taxes to Caesar was a crime. The gospel position here is that Yeshua is being falsely accused of opposition to Roman rule, and it affirms his goodness in going along with Roman law.

In summary, the question of paying taxes identifies the position of the parties toward the Roman occupation of Israel. One accused of disobeying Roman law (by way of not paying taxes) is a corrupting force and not a patriot to Rome. The gospels portray Yeshua as one who acquiesces to Caesar and even have him falsely accused by fellow Jews of being a revolutionary against Rome in order to show how despicable these Jews are in accusing Yeshua of having opposed Rome.

This consistent gospel picture of a Yeshua who states "The things of Caesar give to Caesar" is an unfair portrait of the charismatic rabbi who was received as the messiah. And the prevailing view by contemporary Bible historians holds that Yeshua died because he was perceived by the Romans as a political opponent with large crowds of followers, which the crucifixion of a seditionist underscores. As for the alleged poor relations with other Jews, with Temple or Sanhedrin authorities, these were Jewish matters and, as Paula Fredriksen and others note, Pilate couldn't have cared less about them.

In scripture, the Jewish tax collectors who work specifically for the Romans are fashioned in the parables and other incidents as humble and good, and in contrast to the Jewish authorities, high priests, and their scholars, who are arrogant and wicked. Such is the prevalent coloring of Jew and Roman in the gospels. In Matthew 10.3, the tax collector is Matthew. In Mark 2.13–14 and Luke 5.27–28, the same tax collector is called Levi. That Matthew and Levi are the same person (the traditional view) is unclear, and also unclear is the traditional view that the tax collector Matthew is Matthew the evangelist. While the actual names of the evangelists may be later attributions, it is very clear that the figure of a tax collector called Matthew, traditionally identified with the authorial evangelist of the same name, is portrayed not only as a good man, but good enough to be an evangelist.

THE GOOD CENTURIONS

The centurions are Roman officers who appear on two occasions in the gospels. Like the tax collectors, they are modest and virtuous. Their favorable presentation foretells the need of the later church in Rome to prepare for Yeshua's messiahship and to make Rome and Pilate, its representative in Israel, appear beneficent. The first mention of a centurion in the Synoptics is the Roman officer who implores Yeshua to heal his son who is near death. He is introduced as one "who loves our people and built our synagogue" (Luke 7.4). After Yeshua has healed the centurion's son, Yeshua praises him, for the centurion has stated that, while as a stern commander his soldiers and the slaves under his orders obey his word at once, he, before the powers of Yeshua, is unworthy to ask him to come under his roof. Yeshua is so amazed by this assertion of the centurion's humility that he says to the others, "I tell you, / I have not found such faith in Israel" (Luke 7.9). Effectively, the faith of this Roman soldier of the occupation of Israel exceeds that of any Jew, whether a follower or not of Yeshua. This hyperbole of praise for the Roman *ethnikos* ("national" or "pagan gentile") seems unfathomable and out of place, yet it corresponds accurately with the practice of making servants of Rome exemplary in their benevolence and Christian piety.

The role of the centurion, as noted, takes on a crucially dramatic role at the crucifixion. Although again unnamed, the centurion, who has just overseen the crucifixion of Yeshua by his death squad, experiences, like Saul on the way to Damascus, sudden revelation and conversion. At the instant of Yeshua's death he not only proclaims to the world Yeshua's divinity, with faith in the messiah, but presumably by doing so renounces the gods of the Romans to praise Yahweh, who is still the God of the Jews. With that event, so early in Christian history, Rome recognizes Christianity and the Christian God. In Luke, we read, "When the centurion, commander of the company of soldiers, saw what had happened, he glorified God, saying: 'Surely this was a just man'" (Luke 23.47). In Mark, the earliest gospel and in large part the source of Matthew and Luke, the praiser of Yeshua is the centurion commander of the execution who saw Yeshua breathe his last. He said, "Truly this man was the son of God." As in Luke, at this climactic moment, the evangelist author has made a Roman utter the first spoken word after Yeshua's death, and it is the praise of Christian faith, proving that even then Romans who killed Yeshua shared the later Christian conviction of Yeshua as the son of God. Matthew enlarges the scope, and his converts to Christianity include both the centurion and his troops: "When the centurion and those with him guarding Yeshua saw the earthquake and all that took place, they were terrified, and said, 'Surely he was the son of God!'" (Matt. 27.54). Only after the Romans have had their say does the narrator turn briefly to the women onlookers, who are watching from the distance. The women of Yeshua's faith, who stand there on his behalf, say nothing. Their silence is telling.

In John we find a sharply contrasting scene from that depicted in the synoptic Mark, Matthew, and Luke. There is no mention of any Roman *sur-le-champ* conversion. No centurion nor common soldier steps forward to declare his epiphany of faith in the messiah. The soldiers are merely brutal. They come to break Yeshua's legs, but, finding him already dead, "one of the soldiers stabs his side with his spear, and at once blood and water came out" (John 19.34). The omission of the pious Roman soldiers brings John's version in contention with the Synoptics. For whatever reason, John was not about to show the Roman miracle of the executioner's conversion.

TITUS AND THE STONES OF JERUSALEM

Flavius Titus, emperor of Rome 79–81, is not mentioned in the gospels. As a young man he directed the siege of Jerusalem that culminated in the piercing of the city walls and the destruction of the Temple, the heart of Jewish identity and resistance. For his conquest and the razing of Jerusalem, the Arch of Titus was built at the entrance to the Roman Forum, bearing the Latin inscription: "The Senate and the Roman people to the divine Titus, son of the divine Vespasian, and to Vespasian Augustus." And the Roman biographer Suetonius called Titus "the darling of the human race." Josephus gives us a closeup of

Titus and his soldiers during the worst days of the seige when the city was starving: "[They] caught every day five hundred Jews; nay, some days they caught more" (Josephus, "The Jewish War" in *The New Complete Works of Josephus,* trans. William Whiston [Grand Rapids, MI: Kregel, 1999], Book 5, Chapter 11, 450). "They were first whipped, and then tormented with all sorts of tortures, before they died, and were then crucified before the walls of the city" (449).

The gospels transform Yeshua into a prophet of the city's destruction, and while he weeps at the thought of its future ruin, he assigns its demise to two terrible wrongs committed by the Jews. The first offense takes place four decades after his death, which is that they will not choose the ways of peace but rebellion against Rome. The second wrong, as Luke says, is the Jews' failure to recognize Yeshua as their savior when he visited them. The Gospel of Luke, composed not earlier than 80–85 C.E., fifty years after Yeshua's death, fashioned a Yeshua who would be a rebel against the Jews of his country and scold them for their opposition to the Roman empire. Luke writes,

> If you only knew on this day those things
> creating peace! Yet now they are hidden
> from your eyes. But days will come upon you
> and your enemies will set up ramparts
> against you and encircle you and hem you in
> from all sides. They will crush you and your children,
> and not leave a stone on a stone intact in you
> since you did not know the time of your visitation.
>
> *(19.41–44)*

For Luke, the Jews' great sin is "not knowing the time of your visitation," which points to a major thesis of the gospels: The Jews brought eternal calamity upon themselves by failing to accept Yeshua.

There were clearly Jews who did and Jews who did not accept Yeshua's messiahship, but the destruction of Jerusalem, "stone upon stone," had nothing to do with such matters. It came about because of the rejection by Jews of Roman rule. This was not the first revolt against Roman or Greek rule, nor would it be the last. Centuries earlier the Maccabees had rebelled against Syro-Hellene rule, and under Judas Maccabeus recaptured Jerusalem. Hanukkah (Feast of Dedication or of the Lights) is an annual celebration of the recapturing in 167 B.C.E. of the Temple from the Syrian Antiochus IV, a Hellenizing Selucid ruler. The rebellion was prompted by Antiochus' decrees: "All Jewish customs and ceremonies were forbidden, including Sabbath and festival observance and circumcision. All Torah scrolls were to be seized and burned. All sacrifices and offering to God at the Jerusalem Temple were abolished."[77] Those who disobeyed the decrees were to be executed. The Temple became a place of worship for the Greek god Zeus Olympus, and its altar was used for sacrificing the pig on it. Antiochus called for eradication of monotheistic Judaism. Had the Jews not rebelled then against foreign rule, Judaism would surely have disappeared, which was the intention of the rulers, and without Judaism there would not have been its early sect of Christianity.

Now such rebellion by Jews against foreign rule was treason. And the disaster was not unknown to the evangelists. By the time of their writing, the prophecy had occurred. As the prophecy said, children were crushed, no stone unturned. During the reign of terror by Titus, thousands of Christian Jews, including whole families, were crucified.

It is not likely that a Yeshua of love would have wished these indiscriminate devastations upon his people, upon Christian Jews and other Jews. The detailed description of the scenes has not the quality of prophecy but of data reported to the evangelists. Hence, virtually all scholars date Mark after 70 in order to account for the author's knowledge of the Roman razing of Jerusalem. But apart from detective work on chronology, this depiction of a militant Yeshua, siding with Rome, in anger against the people of Jerusalem should be seen as a portrait wrongful to Christians at all levels of faith. It is wrongful to have the Yeshua of love and spirit call for the later Roman slaughter of his people and their condemnation to an afterlife of eternal pain. It may be best to remember that these translated scriptures are the labor of mortals—not chronicles whispered down from heaven—who record as best they can. The literal word in the gospels, especially when disturbing, is often allegorized to remove it from its surface meaning. But it may be more prudent to look for human frailty in composition, for later redaction and interpolation, and Rome an ever-present worry. In the gospels, beauty, love, spirit, and salvation may reside one page away from anger, battle, and condemnation to sulfureous Sodom and Gomorrah. The reader can choose which verses to take into the critical mind or soul.

---

[77] See, Leonard J. Greenspoon, "Between Alexandria and Antioch: Jew and Judaism in the Hellenistic Period," in *The Oxford History of the Biblical World*, ed. Michael D. Coogan (New York: Oxford University Press, 1998), 437.

TO SOFTEN THE BLOWS
BY SOFTENING
THE TRANSLATION OR
TO LET IT ALL HANG OUT

CHRISTIANIZING YESHUA

The words of a Jewish sage speaking in Aramaic to his followers were reported to others, and what he said and what happened to him became an oral memory that ended up in Greek texts by means we do not know and by authors and editors we cannot guess. The tirades against the Jews are the gospels' way of Christianizing the rabbi Yeshua. The needs of a developing religion to put its house in order made this conversion of the person of Yeshua imperative.

Concerning these questions of textual and credo history, professors of the Jesus Seminar,[78] under the theme of "the storyteller's license," say:

> We know that the evangelists not infrequently ascribed Christian words to Jesus—they made him talk like a Christian, when, in fact, he was only the precursor of the movement that was to take him as its cultic hero. They also supplied dialogue for him on many narrative occasions for which their memories could not recall an appropriate aphorism or parable. In a word, they creatively invented speech for Jesus. (*The Five Gospels*, 29)

With regard to the Christianizing of Yeshua, they write, "Christian conviction eventually overwhelms Jesus: he is made to confess what Christians had come to believe." They list how the Christianization comes about:

- Sayings and parables expressed in "Christian" language are the creation of the evangelists or their Christian predecessors.
- Sayings or parables that contrast with the language or viewpoint of the gospel in which they are embedded reflect older tradition (but not necessarily tradition that originated with Jesus).

---

[78] See Robert W. Funk and Roy W. Hoover, trans., and the Jesus Seminar, *The Five Gospels: The Search for the Authentic Words of Jesus: New Translation and Commentary* (New York: Macmillan, 1993).

- The Christian community develops apologetic statements to defend its claims and sometimes attributes such statements to Jesus. (*The Five Gospels*, 24)

SOFTEN THE BLOWS OR LET IT ALL HANG OUT?

How does a translator deal with the antipathy to Jews in the New Covenant that appears as pervasive slander? The antipathy itself may connect with a Bloomian "anxiety of influence," meaning the authorial denial and Oedipal fear of and hostility to *precursors* and *original sources.* The precursors were the Jews, and all early followers of Yeshua were messianic Jews. The original sources were Judaism and its Hebrew Bible, which the Christian Jews appropriated as their own with nominal and doctrinal changes. Harsh denial of a heritage that one cares to obliterate is common in emotional and artistic development. But how in a holy text to handle the consequences of self-anger—the donning of masks, the castigation of the original incarnation—is the uneasy problem. Hostility to women, the eternal "gender discrimination," is now routinely mitigated stylistically in most new versions of the Hebrew Bible and Greek scriptures. Can or should one also soften, in the translation, the harm of the Satanization of the Jew, which in subsequent centuries justified the thicket of oppression and slaughter?

I was tempted to follow recent versions that substitute less offensive speech for the vilifications, but then it seemed sadly correct to let the Jews take their seventy hits, and not mess with holy texts that were essentially set around 150. In a word, let the extant Greek version say what it says.

Books by Jews about Jews that invoke a fervid retribution unto death of Jews demands help in its reading in Greek as well as in its translation. How and where the help comes in, or if it should come in at all, is, apart from questions of aesthetic fidelities and semantic accuracy, the central problem in translating the Greek covenant into English.

In Introduction and Afterword, one can explain, if not explain away, the polemic. To deflect scribal interpolations and alterations, I considered making "the Jews" simply "the person" or "some people," when referring to gatherings. But in the end I came back to the need to let the Jews take those hits, and I comment in the introduction and sometimes in the annotation. To tamper with the text would, whatever the aim, carry the free license of translation into deception.

As the texts stand now, especially the beautiful and deep book of John, the message is contradictory and untenable. At least the contradictions are helpful to the observant reader to recognize a highly redacted text. It is obviously untenable that the accuser lose his identity as a Jew when accusing another Jew of being "of the Jews." That kind of denial of one's position is already castigated by Yeshua himself in the instance of his follower Peter, who in the course of one day denies being of those with Yeshua three times before the dawn cock crows. In a great irony of the New Covenant, Yeshua severely castigates Peter for denying his identity and does not forget or forgive that transgression. One must ask, Would Yeshua have also castigated his gospel biographers who, exactly like Peter's denial of himself, denied Yeshua's identity? Dostoyevsky in *The Brothers Karamatzov* poses the same matter of the identity of Yeshua in the parable of the Grand Inquisitor: Would Jesus have been arrested as an imposter had he appeared in sixteenth-century Sevilla?

The overt racism and intense anti-Judaism must remain in the text as it is. The informed reader can see the bigotry and reject the message of sectarian hatred. The abuse to the historical Yeshua himself—here turned into a man of angry bias to his own people—one can hope will eventually sink from credibility. So, unlike well-intentioned new versions, these translations leave Jews as Jews, with no euphemism, change, omission, or addition.

There is also in traditional editions of the New Covenant a problem parallel to the textual disguisement of Yeshua's identity: the scholarly annotations that anachronistically Christianize both the Hebrew Bible and the New Covenant. There is no proselytizing commentary in this edition.

GOOD-HEARTED REFORMING OF THE TEXT

What are the good-hearted reforms?

In recent years, there have been radical changes in both translation and commentary. In *The Five Gospels*, translators Robert Funk and Robert W. Hoover change the wicked "Jews" to the wicked "Judeans." This is surely done with the intention of softening the blow, yet it also raises questions. Who are the Judeans? Isn't Judean another name for Jew? And whoever they are, are not Judeans now the wicked accusers and the wicked accused, just as the Jews were made to be both the accusers and the accused in standard versions? And if the accusers are not Jews, who are they?

Most pitiful is that in their desire not to hurt the Jews, the translators have eliminated them completely, even in the annotations, where we read about "conflicts between Christians and Judeans." We are back to traditional translations of the Old Testament where the Jews also disappeared in favor of the "Israelites" and the "Hebrews." *The Five Gospels* does not resolve the central question of whether the conflict is to be considered an internal dispute between Jews or, as in traditional translations, one between good outsiders who effectively pass as non-Jews and bad rejectionist Jews. To make Jews into Judeans does not eliminate the "good outsider" versus the "bad locals" persuasion. What happens when a name changes and a people disappear is disquieting.

Another solution by the editors of the 1995 *Oxford "An Inclusive Version"* is singularly noble and, I am afraid, impossible. The editors are clearly appalled by the extant scriptures because of the described disguisements and the intrinsic hatred of the Jews. In their missionary translation they omit the words "the Jews" when those words function as an exclusively accusatory epithet. It distinguishes, on the one hand, between the term "the Jews" as a straightforward, historical way to refer to the ethnic people, of whom Yeshua was one, and, on the other, "the Jews" as "the code-word for religious people . . . who miss the revelation" (xvii). They call the Jews "opponents" or "the enemies" or "the religious authorities" or "the leaders," which they do "in order to minimize what could be perceived as a warrant for anti-Jewish bias" (xvii). Yet we soon learn who these opponents are, and they turn out to be "the most despicable" of the Jews.

Felicitations to the Oxford translators for their goodwill. They have changed the New Covenant to overcome unpleasantness, but the serious problems remain. As the Jesus Seminar directs us to hate Judeans rather than Jews, so the Oxford translators would have us hate Jewish authorities and Jewish priests and the unidentified "opponents." The changes are fishy. In making the text more friendly to some of the Jews, the editors have violated the unfriendly intention of the scriptures toward the Jews. To bowdlerize the essence of the scripture as we have it may be thought to be a form of benevolent bookburning.

One solution is to leave the text alone. It is the one followed here. When the Jews are demonized, let the Jews be called Jews. Then problems are clear, and through commentary the hatred may be seen in the context of polemical struggles of a certain time—many decades after Yeshua's life and death—and this knowledge alone diminishes the bite. The slurs appear too often but do not hold dominion and must not be allowed to do so. They are finite human blunder. They fade before the huge wonders and sundry messages of the story. And these wonders are beyond measure.

Holding dominion in the New Covenant are the beauty of the word, the compassion for the poor and hungry, the blind and the leper, the crippled and the possessed. The wisdom narration explores physical and mental suffering and offers earthly and spiritual hope. Preserved in plain Koine Greek, this supreme telling of roaming and parable is intrinsically so powerful that it survives translation with distinction in every tongue. And on each page the reader may overhear, in a reformation of openness, the solitary mystery of love.

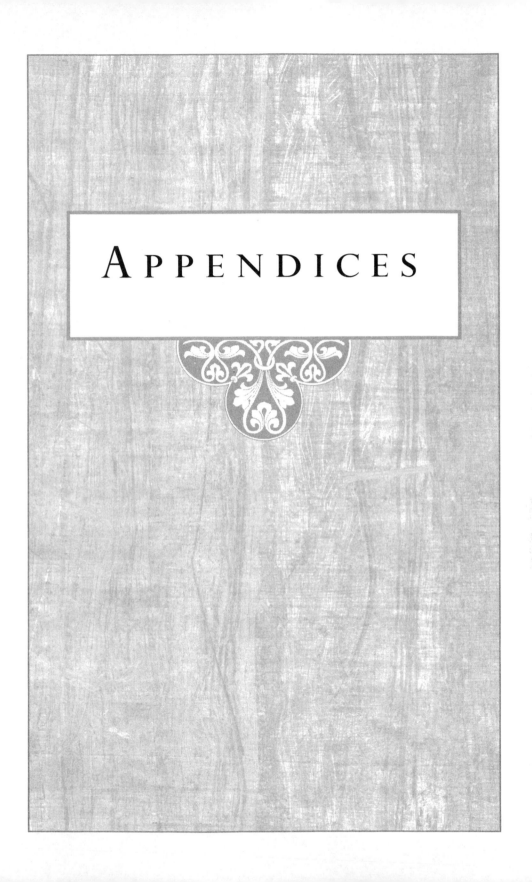

APPENDICES

NAMES OF GOD

THE NAMES OF GOD ARE THE HARDEST WORDS TO WRESTLE WITH IN THE BIBLE. THEIR CONVERSION INTO OTHER LANGUAGES RAISES AS many questions as the face of God, which no one and everyone knows. God changes names in the Hebrew Bible. He is the patristic *Elohim* of the first creation and final judgment, and, in the middle of Genesis 2.4, he is the more pervasive Lord God, *Yahweh,* who is characterized as less distant and more merciful. In the New Covenant, God is *theos,* a word taken over from classical Greek literature, where beginning with Homer and Hesiod's *Theogony, theos* designates the supreme god Zeus and the lesser gods. It is problematic how and when to replace the Greek *theos* in the New Covenant with an English word that reflects the Hebrew Bible, for one cannot choose one Hebrew name without exiling others with equal credentials as God's true epithet. But clearly the English word "God," a name loaned to us from the Germanic and Scandinavian languages, does not, as do Elohim and Yahweh, evoke the biblical creator in the Hebraic tradition. So the New Covenant is a text in search of the name of God.

God's first name we encounter as the third word in the Hebrew Genesis (reading right to left): בְּרֵאשִׁית בָּרָא אֱלֹהִים אֵת הַשָּׁמַיִם וְאֵת הָאָרֶץ (bereyshit bara elohim et ha-shamayim ve-et ha-aretz), which following the Hebrew word order in the English reads: "In the beginning | created | Elohim | the skies | and the earth." Elohim, a plural of majesty but with a singular meaning,[1] derives from *Eloah* (found mainly in Job), or from *El,* which has an independent life of its own, meaning "God" as in *El Shaddai,* "God of the Mountains," or *El Elyon,* "God Most High"; and from *El* derives Islam's *Allah.*

In the first creation story (Gen. 1–2.4), Elohim creates skies, earth, beasts, and humans, male and female, in six days. In the second creation story (Gen. 2.4),

---

[1] *Elohim* has also been taken as a singular noun whose plural form is an augmentative, rendering it something like "mighty God." There is no unanimity in accepting a "plural of majesty" for what seems to be a simple plural. In a note on this manuscript page, Professor Marvin Meyer in private correspondence to the author comments on Genesis 1.1: "I'm not really convinced by the 'plural of majesty' argument foisted on us by die-hard monotheists who cannot abide the thought of polytheism in the tradition. Hebrew religion and the whole Judeo-Christian-Islamic tradition emerged (but never fully) from polytheistic traditions. I see in Elohim's plural form the shadow of polytheism, still visible in a Yahwist or Elohist or Priestly context."

much happens all in one day: "In the day that the lord Elohim made the earth and the skies" בְּיוֹם עֲשׂוֹת יְהוָה אֱלֹהִים אֶרֶץ וְשָׁמָיִם (be-yom asot adonai elohim eretz ve-shamayim), we have not only the godhead called *Elohim* but *Adonai*, meaning "lord," and in that single day that godhead makes not only the skies and the earth but every plant of the field before it was in the earth, and dust of the ground out of which he forms a man, Adam, who has a rib destined to become Eve. Now Genesis has provided two words for God: *Elohim* and *Adonai*. Yet since the deity's secret *name*—or any *word* signifying that name—is ineffable, the true name cannot be known, written, or sounded. However, there is a way to represent God with letters that do not spell or reveal his secret name. This is the Tetragrammaton (also Tetragram), consisting of the four Hebrew consonants YHWH (*yod, he, waw* or *vav, he*), which is written יְהוָה but is normally pronounced *Adoni* (the Semitic word for "lord"). Sometimes, however, YHWH is sounded out to become *Yahweh*, and thereby becomes another surrogate name for the nameless one. And then, as in Genesis 2.4, the word for God is combined with lord, giving the epithet *Adonai Elohim* ("lord God"). We have now identified seven principal ways in English of evoking the deity: *Elohim, Adonai, Adonai Elohim,* YHWH, YHVH, *Yahweh, Yahveh.* Other less common names for God are *Baal* ("lord"), *Yah* instead of *Yahweh*, and *Meleh* ("king"), and combinations thereof. If these onomastic vicissitudes appear complicated and elusive, that is proper for the name of a spiritual God, whose reality does not descend to earthly script or voice. Finally, the surrogate name *Yahweh* has an etymological meaning too (adding another dimension for Kabbalist play), since *yahweh* is a synonym for "creator," carrying the meaning of "he brings into existence," from the Hebrew *hayâ,* "to be."

When Yeshua quotes the Hebrew Bible scripture in the Greek, his biblical citations come from the second century B.C.E. Septuagint Greek translation of the Bible for the Greek-speaking Jews of Alexandria who could no longer read the Hebrew with ease. In the Septuagint, God is *theos.* As the Hebrew names for God pass from their Semitic source into other languages, it would be appropriate to use those same traditional Hebrew names for God in the English translation from the Greek—*Elohim, Adonai,* and *Yahweh*—and were I more confident and courageous, I would have translated *theos* throughout with a Hebrew rather than a Germanic word. The difficulty is that with the Greek standing as a linguistic screen between the Hebrew and the English, one can make intelligent suppositions but not know with certainty which Hebrew name stands behind the Greek. While the Greeks may care to Hellenize the Semitic epithets for God, in English there is no reason (other than the lethargy of tradition) why the Hellenized, Romanized, and Germanized words for God do not yield to *Elohim, Adonai,* and *Yahweh* in the New Covenant.

Yahweh, which was Jehovah in the King James Version, is now used for God in many translations of the Hebrew Bible (and especially in the headings). Since it is the same God in both the Hebrew Bible and the New Covenant, why not *Yahweh* in the New Covenant? So the absence of an intermediary text, or oral or transcribed witness accounts, keeps us with *theos* (θεός), and choosing a name, particularly one name, for God in the English is also a guess. I am confident that in future translations, the decisions and the arguments for those decisions will be well made, and God in the New Covenant will sound not like a north European or a Greek but a deity bearing a Hebrew name.

The English "God" exists in Old English and is cognate with Dutch *god,* German *Gott,* Icelandic *godh,* and Goth *guth.* The epithet "God" has no more connection with the Greek or the Hebrew than "hell," which is also given to us by Germanic peoples. "Hell" comes from old Norse saga preserved in Iceland. In the Greek scriptures "hell" is *hades,* in the Hebrew Bible it is *Sheol* or *Gehenna (Gei Hinnom). Sheol* appears sixty-five times in the Hebrew Bible, the Greek word "Hades" ten times in the New Covenant, and twenty-six times in the Apocrypha. In most recent translations of the Hebrew Bible and the New Covenant, *Sheol* or *Gehenna* has replaced "hell" or "Hades." *Sheol* not only restores the Hebrew resonance but suggests the dwelling place of the dead, and *Gehenna* geographically suggests specific dark pits outside Jerusalem where the less-worthy dead dwelled in punishment, just as Hades suggests not only a history of references in Greek literature but also the extant archaic temple in Epirus, whose underground stone basement is Hades, lying less than a kilometer from the small river of the dead, the Acheron. As the Greek has its own Greek words for God, hell, and the devil, it would be similarly right for English, which is the most open language in the world to visiting words, to incorporate names of God that reflect the Hebrew Bible. About half our proper names in English, from Abraham to Elizabeth's husband Zecharias, as well as "Sabbath," "amen," and "halleluyah," are loan words that long ago entered the English from the Hebrew.

I do not know how "God" of the New Covenant should enter the English language. Each way incites positive and negative reasons for its selection. For the moment "God," the name of a northern pagan divinity, is standard English usage and for the most part is retained in this and most texts, though I suspect that *Elohim, Yahweh,* and *Adonai* will soon be calling. God has upper-case status as a name. But if it is an idea, an entity, simply a divinity, the lower case would be equally appropriate, as it was originally in all the source languages, and God may go the way of the Lord, from piety to friendly companionship. To speak about the wisdom of having the word "God" be the key sound in the Judeo-Christian tradition does not diminish the Viking and Germanic monosyllable's deep resonance when it evoked Thor, the Old Norse god of thunder, who also gave us "Thor's Day," our day of God in the middle of the week, which we keep as "Thursday."

In his translation of the Pentateuch in *The Five Books of Moses* (New York: Schocken Books, 1995), Everett Fox uses God when the name in the Hebrew is *Elohim*, and YHWH when it is the corresponding name in the Hebrew. He sometimes uses "God, YHWH" as one entity. It's not very neat, because the variables are obstinately complex. The easy solution is "God," which is a weak watering down in the English of the great sonorous words in the Hebrew. In the Catholic *The Jerusalem Bible, Yahweh* is used to represent God through most of the Hebrew Bible.

Since God's face is unseeable and his name unknowable, the best any language can offer us is a simulacrum for the visage, and various signs for the name—but not the one name that resides in mystery. Ultimately, the word "God," or whatever name some version comes up with, has minor importance. No name will lessen or increase our knowledge of God, nor inform belief in the deity's being or deny it. It is no wonder that in the Hebrew writings, God had no singular epithet. He was at once nameless, but with a secret sign that was ineffable, and so the deity took on the one name that meant itself, which was *Ha-Shem*, which means "The Name."

ORDER OF THE GOSPELS

T HE TRADITIONAL ORDER OF PRESENTING THE GOSPELS IS MAT-
THEW, MARK, LUKE, AND JOHN. THERE IS A SENSE TO THIS BECAUSE
Matthew begins with a genealogy, which, though an inartistic and tedious way
of beginning, is also a gesture indicating beginning. Whoever compiled the
genealogy, and it is almost certainly not the author of Matthew but someone
later, it is a mechanical blight on the otherwise flawlessly literary gospels. The
genealogy is followed by a presentation of the birth of Yeshua. Luke near its
beginnings also has a more complete presentation of the birth of Yeshua, and
it is third in order, so it might be argued that the gospels Matthew and Luke,
containing the two infancy narrations, should be in sequence.

John begins with another beginning, at once spiritual and dramatic: "In the
beginning was the word." Clearly John begins his gospel with a conscious parallel to the beginning of the Hebrew Bible, "In the beginning God created . . ."
So were the New Covenant to begin with the Gospel of John, it would be a
stunning opening for what became known as the Greek scriptures of the
Christian Bible. Since John is the most gnostic of the canonical gospels,
though less so than the Nag Hammadi Gospel of Thomas, to begin the New
Covenant with John would also truly represent that very strong current of
gnosticism that permeated contemporary Judaism and the history of the first
Christian Jews.

So there are reasonable arguments for diverse orders. Recently it has become a practice to present the gospels in the probable order of composition:
Mark, Matthew, Luke, and John. Since there is a consensus that the later
gospels derive in complicated and still uncertain ways from the earlier ones,
with Mark the main candidate for Matthew and Luke of the synoptic gospels,
Mark makes sense as the first book for purposes of accumulation of information. More significant is that Mark in its commanding plainness almost demands its initial place in the order of these gospels that take from each other,
and especially from Mark. Mark is raw and direct. So are the others, but they
elaborate Mark. Hence, I have followed the apparent historical sequence.

With his translation, Richmond Lattimore led the way in making Mark the
beginning.

A NOTE ON TRANSCRIPTION

FOR PURPOSES OF EASY REFERENCE TO THE ENGLISH AND GREEK TEXTS, IN THE INTRODUCTION, AFTERWORD, AND IN THE ANNOTATION, the evangelists are referred to by their traditional English names. Yeshua has largely replaced Jesus in all parts of the book, except in quotations and bibliography. The probable original proper nouns are here transliterated into English followed by their traditional spelling as they appear in other translations. In the annotation, these nouns are also given in the Greek and, when possible, in the original Aramaic and/or Hebrew.

The question of restoration is not only *what* was the probable original name, clear in most instances (with exceptions like Matthew where there are several to choose from), but what *system* to use for transcription from Aramaic and Hebrew into English. Some words, such as "Tanakh," already exist in English, but it might have been "Tanak." I chose to double the Hebrew *b* in "Shabbat," which is common practice, but to drop the *h* after *k* in "Tanak," since we do not make that consonantal distinction in English. With regard to Hebrew *bet* or *vet*, *b* or *v*, the solutions old and new are vexing. As in transcribing Greek, I prefer not to be held to reflecting source-text spelling but to reflect plain English practice. Such is especially true in transcribing Greek words, where I follow modern translators from classical Greek literature. They drop all the screens of Latin and French (as the Germans also do) when moving a word from Greek into English. So it is not latinized "Seriphus" but Greek-lettered "Serifos" for the island where Perseus flew off from in pursuit of the Medusa or it is not latinized "Alceus" but Greek "Alkaios" for the poet from Lesbos.

With respect to complexities of choice, I cite the enlightened *American Heritage Dictionary,* which explains its pauses in transcribing the word "Kabbalah." It summarizes vowel problems and the doubling of consonants in transcribing Hebrew and Arabic:

> Usage Note: There are no less than two dozen variant spellings of kabbalah, the most common of which include kabbalah, kabala, kabalah, qabalah, qabala, cabala, cabbala, kaballah, kabbala, quaballah, and qabbalah. This sort of confusion is frequently seen with Hebrew and Arabic words

borrowed into English because there exist several different systems of transliterating the Hebrew and Arabic alphabets into Roman letters. Often a more exact or scholarly transliteration, such as Qur'an, will co-exist alongside a spelling that has been heavily Anglicized (Koran). The fact that the Hebrew and Arabic alphabets do not as a rule indicate short vowels or the doubling of consonants compounds the difficulties. Spellings of kabbalah with one or two *b*'s are equally "correct," insofar as the single *b* accurately reproduces the spelling of the Hebrew, while the double *b* represents the fact that it was once pronounced with a double *b*.

GLOSSARY OF GREEK AND
BIBLICAL PROPER NAMES

Abba. Father.
Adonai. My Lord, Lord or God.
Aharon. Aaron.
Alexandros. Alexander.
Amminadav. Amminadab.
Amorah. Gomorrah.
Anan. Annas.
Andreas. Andrew.
Arpahshad. Arphaxad.
Asa. Asaph.
Avihud. Abiud.
Aviyah. Abijah.
Avraham. Abraham.
Avram. Abram.
Azur. Azor.

Baal Zevuv or Baal Zebub. Beelzebub.
Baal Zevul or Baal Zebul. Beelzebul.
Bar Abba. Barabbas.
Bartalmai. Batholomew.
Bar. Son.
Bar Yohanan. Barjona.
Bat. Daughter.
Beit Aniyah. Bethany.
Beit Hesda. Bethesda.
Beit Lehem. Bethlehem.
Beit Pagey. Bethphage.
Beit Tzaida. Bethsaida.
Beit Zaita. Bethzatha.
Ben. Son.
Benei Regesh. Boanerges.
Berekyah. Barachiah.
Bilam. Balaam.
Binyamin. Benjamin.

Caesarea Filippi. Caesarea Philippi.

Dekapolis. Decapolis.

Efesos. Ephesus.
Efrayim. Ephraim.
Einayim. Ainon. Aenon.
El. God.
Elazar. Eleazar, Lazarus.
Eli (Hebrew). My God.
Eli. Heli.
Elihud. Eliyud.
Elisheva. Elizabeth.
Eliyah. Elijah, Elias (from Greek version).
Eliyakim. Eliakim.
Elmadam. Elmadan.
Eloah. God.
Elohim. God or gods.
Eloi, Elohay (Aramaic). My God.
El Shaddai. God of the Mountains or
    The Almighty.
Enosh. Enos.
Ever. Eber.
Evyatar. Abiathar.

Fenuel. Phanuel.
Filippos. Philip.

Galil. Galilee.
Gat Shmanim, Gat Shemanim.
    Gethsemane.
Gavriel. Gabriel.
Gei Hinnom. Gehenna (hell).
Gulgulta. Golgotha.

Halfi, Halfay. Alphaeus.
Hannan. Annas.
Hannah. Anna
Hanoh. Enoch.
Har Megiddo. Armageddon.
Hesli. Esli.
Hetzron, Hestron. Hezron or Estrom.

Hevel. Abel.
Hiikiah. Hezekiah, Ezekias.
Horazim. Chorazin.
Hoshea. Hosea.

Iairos. Jairus.
Izevel. Jezebel.

Kayfa. Caiaphas.
Keainan. Cainan.
Kefa. Cephas, Peter.
Keinan. Cainan.
Kfar Nahum, Kefar Nahum. Capernaum.
Keriot. Iscariot.
Klofah. Clopas.
Korazim. Chorazim.
Korban. Corban.
Kosam. Cosam.
Kuza. Chuza.

Laodikeia. Laodicea.
Lemeh. Lemech.
Levi. Levi, Matthew.
Loukas. Luke.

Magdala (town on the Sea of Galilee).
    Mary the Magdalene
    (from Magdala).
Mahalel. Mahalaleel.
Mahat. Maath.
Malah. Melea.
Malki. Melchi.
Manah or Mana. Menna.
Markos. Mark.
Marta. Martha.
Mashiah. Messiah. Christ (in Greek
    translation).
Mattai. Matthew.
Mattan. Matthan.
Mattat. Matthat.
Mattatah. Mattatha.
Mattatiyah. Mattathias.
Meleh. Melech.
Menasheh. Manasseh.
Messiah. See Mashiah.
Metushelah. Methuselah.

Mihael. Michael.
Miryam. Mary.
Mosheh, Moshe. Moses.

Naftali. Naphtali.
Nahor. Nahot.
Naïn. Nain.
Nakdeimon. Nikodemos, Nicodemus.
Natanel or Netanel. Nathanael.
Natzeret. Nazareth.
Natzrati. Nazarene.
Nikolaos. Nicolaus.

Obev. Obeb.

Pantokrator. Pantocrator.
Parush. Pharisee.
Patmos. Patmus.
Peretz, Perets. Perez.
Pergamos. Pergamum.
Pesach, Pesah. Passover.
Pilatus. Pilate.
Pnuel. Panuel. Phanuel.
Prushim. Pharisees.

Rahav. Rahab.
Rahel. Rachel.
Ram. Aram.
Rehavan. Rehoboam, Roboam.
Reisha. Rhesa.
Reuven. Reuben.
Rut. Ruth.

Sanhedrin. Council.
Satan. Satan.
Sedom, Sdom and Amorah. Sodom and
    Gomorrah.
Shabbat, Shabat. Sabbath.
Shalem. Salim.
Shaltiel. Shealtiel.
Shaul. Saul, Paul.
Shehem. Sychar or Syhem.
Shet. Seth.
Shimi. Semein.
Shimon. Simon or Simeon.
Shimon Kefa. Simon Peter.

Shlomit. Salome.
Shlomoh, Shlomo. Solomon.
Shomron. Samaria.
Shomronim. Samaritan.
Shoshannah. Susanna.
Sukkah. Sukkoth or Tabernacle.

Taddai. Thaddeus.
Tamar. Tamar, Thamar.
Toma. Thomas.
Torah. The Torah is the Pentateuch or
   used to signify the Hebrew Bible.
Tzadok, Tsadok. Zadok or Sadducee.
Tzadokim. Sadducees.
Tzidon. Sidon.
Tzor, Tsor, Tzur, Tur. Tyre.

Uriyah. Uriah.
Uziya, Utsiya. Uzziah.

Yaakov. Jacob, James.
Yah. God.
Yahin. Achim.
Yahweh, Yahveh (the sounded four Hebrew
   vowels of the Tetragrammaton [Tetra-
   gram] for Adonai, meaning "God" or
   "Lord"). Yahweh, Yahveh, Jehovah,
   God, Lord.
YHWH, YHVH (the written four Hebrew
   vowels of the Tetragrammaton [Tetra-
   grom] for Adonai, meaning "God" or
   "Lord"). Yahweh, Yahveh, Jehovah,
   God, Lord.
Yair. Jairus.
Yannai. Jannai.
Yarden. Jordan.

Yehoniah. Yechoniah.
Yehoshafat. Jehoshaphat.
Yehuda, Yehudah. Judas, Juda, Judah, Jude.
Yehuda, Yehudah. Judea.
Yehuda man of Keriot. Judas Iscariot.
Yered. Jared.
Yeriho. Jericho.
Yerushalayim. Jerusalem.
Yeshayah. Isaiah.
Yeshua (pronounce Yeshua Yeshúa).
   Joshua, Yehoshua, Jesus.
Yeshua the Mashiah. Jesus the Messiah,
   Jesus the Christ.
Yeshua bar Yosef. Jesus son of Joseph.
Yeshua ben Yosef. Jesus son of Joseph.
Yirmiyah. Jeremiah.
Yisahar. Issachar.
Yishai. Jesse.
Yisrael. Israel.
Yisraeli. Israelite.
Yitzhak, Yitshak. Isaac.
Yodah. Joda.
Yohanan. John.
Yohanna. Joanna.
Yonah. Jonah.
Yoram. Joram, Jorim.
Yosef. Joseph.
Yoseh. Josech.
Yoshiyah. Josiah, Josias.
Yotam. Jotham.

Zakai. Zacchaeus.
Zavdai. Zebedee.
Zeharyah. Zacharias or Zechariah.
Zerubavel. Zerubbabel, Zorobabel.
Zvulun. Zebulun.

WORKS CITED AND
SELECTED BIBLIOGRAPHY

Alter, Robert. *The Art of Biblical Poetry.* New York: Basic Books, 1985.

————. *Genesis: Translation and Commentary.* New York: W.W. Norton, 1996.

————. *The David Story: Translation with Commentary of I and II Samuel.* New York: W.W. Norton, 1999.

Alter, Robert, and Frank Kermode, ed. *The Literary Guide to the Bible.* Cambridge, MA: Harvard University Press, 1967.

Aristeas to Philocrates [*Letter of Aristeas*]. Ed. and trans. Moses Hadas. New York: Harper & Brothers, 1951.

Barnstone, Willis. *The Poems of Saint John of the Cross.* Translation and Introduction. Bloomington, IN: Indiana University Press, 1967; rev. ed. New York: New Directions, 1972.

————. *The Other Bible.* San Francisco: HarperSan Francisco, 1984.

————. *Sappho and the Greek Lyric Poets.* New York: Schocken Books, 1988.

————. *The Poetics of Translation: History, Theory, Practice.* New Haven: Yale University Press, 1993.

————. *To Touch the Sky: Spiritual, Mystical and Philosophical Poems in Translation.* New York: New Directions, 1999.

————. *Apocalypse* (Revelation): A New Translation and with Introduction. New York: New Directions, 2000.

Barnstone, Willis, and Marvin Meyer, ed. *The Gnostic Bible.* Boston: Shambhala, Forthcoming.

Bloom, Harold. "Before Moses Was, I Am: The Original and the Belated Testaments." In *The Bible,* ed. and intro. Harold Bloom. New York: Chelsea House, 1987.

————. "Interpretation." In *The Gospel of Thomas. New Translation with Introduction and Notes,* by Marvin Meyer, San Francisco: HarperSan Francisco, 1992.

————. *Omens of Millennium: The Gnosis of Angels, Dreams, and Resurrection.* New York: Riverhead Books, 1996.

Borg, Marcus J. *Meeting Jesus for the First Time.* San Francisco: HarperSan Francisco, 1994.

Brown, Raymond E. *An Introduction to the New Testament.* New York: Doubleday, 1997.

Buber, Martin. *Die Chassidische Botschaft.* Heidelberg: L. Schneider, 1922.

————. *Two Types of Faith.* New York: Harper & Row, 1961.

————. *Tales of the Hasidim.* New York: Schocken Books, 1975.

Bultmann, Rudolf. *Jesus and the Word.* Trans. Louise Pettibone Smith and Erminie Huntress Lantero. New York: Scribner, 1958.

————. *The History of the Synoptic Tradition.* Trans. John Marsh. New York: Harper & Row, 1966.

Cameron, Ron. *The Other Gospels.* Philadelphia: Westminster Press, 1982.

Campbell, Joseph. *The Masks of God: Occidental Mythology.* New York: Viking Penguin, 1964; Penguin Arkana, 1991.

Charlesworth, James H. ed. *The Old Testament Pseudepigrapha*. 2 vols. Garden City, NY: Doubleday, 1983–1985.

Chilton, Bruce. *Rabbi Jesus: An Intimate Biography*. New York: Doubleday, 2000.

Chilton, Bruce, and Jacob Neusner. *Judaism in the New Testament: Practices and Beliefs*. London/New York: Routledge, 1993.

Cohen, Shaye J. D. *From the Maccabees to the Mishnah*. Philadelphia: Westminster Press, 1989.

Crossan, John Dominic. *The Essential Jesus: Original Sayings and the Earliest Images*. San Francisco: HarperSan Francisco, 1994.

———. *The Historical Jesus: A Revolutionary Biography*. San Francisco: HarperSan Francisco, 1994.

———. *Who Killed Jesus? Exposing the Roots of Anti-Semitism in the Gospel Story of the Death of Jesus*. San Francisco: HarperSan Francisco, 1996.

———. *The Birth of Christianity*. San Francisco: HarperSan Francisco, 1998.

Dickinson, Emily. *The Complete Poems of Emily Dickinson*. Ed. Thomas H. Johnson. Boston and Toronto: Little Brown and Company, 1958.

Ferry, David. *Gilgamesh: A New Rendering in English Verse*. New York: Farrar, Straus and Giroux, 1992.

Fideler, David. *Jesus Christ, Son of God: Ancient Cosmology and Early Christian Symbolism*. Wheaton, IL: Quest Books, 1993.

Fitzgerald, Robert, trans. *The Odyssey*. Garden City, NY: Doubleday, 1961.

Fitzmyer, Joseph A. *Discoveries in the Judaean Desert 19*. Oxford: Clarendon Press, 1995.

Fox, Everett. *The Five Books of Moses: A New Translation with Introduction, Commentary, and Notes*. New York: Schocken Books, 1995.

Fredriksen, Paula. *From Jesus to Christ: The Origins of the New Testament Images of Jesus*. New Haven: Yale University Press, 1988.

———. *Jesus of Nazareth, King of the Jews: A Jewish Life and the Emergence of Christianity*. New York: Knopf, 1999.

Funk, Robert W., Roy W. Hoover, trans., and the Jesus Seminar. *The Five Gospels: The Search for the Authentic Words of Jesus: New Translation and Commentary*. New York: Macmillan, 1993.

García Martínez, Florentino, ed., Wilfred G. E. Watson, trans. *The Dead Sea Scrolls Translated: The Qumran Texts in English*. 2d ed. Leiden/New Orleans: E.J. Brill/Grand Rapids, MI: W.B. Eerdmans, 1996.

Gaster, Theodor H. *The Dead Sea Scrolls in English Translation*. Translation with Introduction and Notes. New York: Doubleday Anchor, 1956.

Grant, Robert M. *Gnosticism and Early Christianity*. New York: Columbia University Press, 1959.

———. *A Historical Introduction to the New Testament*. New York: Harper & Row, 1963, New York: Simon and Schuster, 1972.

Greenspoon, Leonard J. "Between Alexandria and Antioch: Jew and Judaism in the Hellenistic Period." In *The Oxford History of the Biblical World*, ed. Michael D. Coogan. New York: Oxford University Press, 1998.

Hammond, Gerald. *The Making of the English Bible*. New York: The Philosophical Library, 1983.

Heschel, Susannah. "Transforming Jesus from Jew to Aryan: Protestant Theologies in Nazi

Germany." The Albert T. Bilgray Lecture, University of Arizona, April 1995. Alexander Jones, general ed.

Honig, Edwin. *The Poet's Other Voice: Conversation on Literary Translation.* Amherst: University of Massachusetts Press, 1985.

The Jerusalem Bible. Garden City, NJ: Doubleday, 1990.

Johnson, Luke T. "The New Testament: Anti-Jewish Slander and the Conventions of Ancient Polemic." *Journal of Biblical Literature* 108 (1989): 419–441.

Josephus. *The New Complete Works of Josephus.* Trans. William Whiston. Grand Rapids, MI: Kregel, 1999.

Kee, Howard Clark. *Jesus in History: An Approach to the Study of the Gospels.* 2d ed. New York: Harcourt Brace Jovanovich, 1977.

Klein, Charlotte. *Anti-Judaism in Christian Theology.* Trans. Edward Quinn. Philadelphia: Fortress Press, 1978.

Kloppenborg, John. *The Formation of Q: Trajectories in Ancient Wisdom Collections.* Philadelphia: Fortress Press, 1987.

———. *Q Parallels: Synopsis, Critical Notes and Concordance.* Sonoma, CA: Polebridge Press, 1988.

———*Excavating Q: The History and Setting of the Sayings Gospel.* Minneapolis: Fortress, 2000.

Koester, Helmut. *Ancient Christian Gospels: Their History and Development.* Philadelphia: Trinity Press International, 1990.

———. *Introduction to the New Testament.* Vol. I., *History, Culture, and Religion of the Hellenistic Age.* Vol. 2., *History and Literature of Early Christianity.* 2d ed. Philadelphia: Fortress Press, 1994–1996.

Kümmel, Werner Georg. *Introduction to the New Testament.* Rev. ed. Trans. from German by Howard Clark Kee. Nashville: Abingdon Press, 1975.

Lattimore, Richmond. *The Four Gospels and The Revelation: Newly Translated from the Greek.* New York: Farrar, Straus, Giroux, 1979.

Maccoby, Hyam. *The Mythmaker: Paul and the Invention of Christianity.* San Francisco: HarperSan Francisco, 1986.

Mack, Burton L. *The Lost Gospel: The Book of Q & Christian Origins.* San Francisco: HarperSan Francisco, 1993.

———. *Who Wrote the New Testament?: The Making of the Christian Myth.* San Francisco: HarperSan Francisco, 1995.

Mailer, Norman. *The Gospel According to the Son.* New York: Random House, 1997.

McGrath, Alister E. *In the Beginning: The Story of the King James Bible.* New York: Doubleday, 2001.

Meeks, Wayne. *The First Urban Christians: The Social World of the Apostle Paul.* New Haven: Yale University Press, 1983.

Metzger, Bruce M. *The Early Versions of the New Testament: Their Origin, Transmission, and Limitations.* Oxford: Clarendon Press, 1977.

———. *The Text of the New Testament: Its Transmission, Corruption, and Restoration.* New York: Oxford University Press, 1992.

Meyer, Marvin. *The Gospel of Thomas. New Translation with Introduction and Notes.* Interpretation by Harold Bloom. San Francisco: HarperSan Francisco, 1992.

———. *The Unknown Sayings of Jesus.* San Francisco: HarperSan Francisco, 1998.

Miles, Jack. *God: A Biography.* New York: Knopf, 1995.

Miller, Robert J., ed., *The Complete Gospels: Annotated Scholars Version.* Sonoma, CA: Polebridge Press, 1992–1994.

Nelson, Jr., Lowry. *Poetic Configurations.* University Park, PA: Pennsylvania State University Press, 1992.

New Testament and Psalms. New York: Oxford University Press, 1995.

Nicholls, William. *Christian Anti-Semitism: A History of Hate.* Northvale, NJ/London: Jason Aronson, 1995.

Nickelsburg, George W. E. "The Genre and Function of the Markan Passion Narrative." *Harvard Theological Review* 73 (1980): 153–184.

———. "Revealed Wisdom as a Criterion for Inclusion and Exclusion: From Jewish Sectarianism to Early Christianity." In *To See Ourselves as Others See Us: Christians, Jews, "Others" in Late Antiquity,* ed. Jacob Neusner and Ernest S. Frerichs. Chico, CA: Scholars Press, 1985.

———. "Jews and Christians in the First Century: The Struggle Over Identity." *Neotestamentica* 27(2) (1993): 365–390.

———. "The First Century: A Time to Rejoice and a Time to Weep." *Religion and Theology* 1(1) (1994): 4–17.

Pagels, Elaine. *The Gnostic Gospels.* New York: Random House, 1979.

———. *Adam, Eve, and the Serpent.* New York: Vintage, 1988.

———. *The Origin of Satan.* New York: Vintage, 1995.

Pearson, Birger A. "The Gospel according to the 'Jesus Seminar': On Some Recent Trends in Gospel Research." In *The Emergence of the Christian Religion: Essays on Early Christianity.* Harrisburg, PA: Trinity Press International, 1997.

Petersen, Norman R. *The Gospel of John and the Sociology of Light: Language and the Characterization in the Fourth Gospel.* Valley Forge: Trinity Press International, 1993.

Philo. *Embassy to Gaius.* In *Philo.* Loeb edition. Vol. 10. Trans. F. H. Colson. London: Heinemann, 1962.

Pines, Shlomo. *An Arabic Version of the Testimonium Flavianum and Its Implications.* Jerusalem: The Israel Academy of Sciences and Humanities, 1971.

Pinsky, Robert, trans. *The Inferno of Dante.* Foreword by John Freccero. New York: Farrar, Straus and Giroux, 1994.

Price, Reynolds. *Three Gospels.* New York: Scribners, 1996.

Robinson, James M., ed. *The Nag Hammadi Library.* San Francisco: Harper & Row, 1977.

Robinson, James M., Paul Hoffman, and John S. Kloppenborg, ed. *The Critical Edition of Q.* Minneapolis: Fortress Press, 2000.

Sanders, E. P. *Paul and Palestinian Judaism: A Comparison of Patterns of Religion.* Philadelphia: Fortress Press, 1977.

———. *Paul, the Law, and the Jewish People.* Philadelphia: Fortress Press, 1983.

———. *Jesus and Judaism.* Philadelphia: Fortress Press, 1987.

———. "Jesus Christ." In *Eerdman's Dictionary of the Bible,* ed. David Noel Freedman. Grand Rapids, MI/ Cambridge, UK: William B. Eerdman's Publishing Co., 2000.

Scholem, Gershom. *Jewish Gnosticism, Merkabah Mysticism, and Talmudic Tradition.* New York: Schocken Books, 1961.

———. *Sabbatai Sevi: The Mystical Messiah, 1626–1676.* Princeton: Princeton University Press, 1973.

———. *Origins of the Kaballah.* Princeton University Press, 1987.

Schonfield, Hugh J. *The Original New Testament.* Trans. and Intro. San Francisco: Harper & Row, 1985.

Schweitzer, Albert. *The Quest of the Historical Jesus.* Intro. James M. Robinson, trans. W. Montgomery of *Von Reimarus zur Wrede* (1906). New York: Macmillan, 1968.

Sidney, Sir Philip. *The Psalms of Sir Philip Sidney and the Countess of Pembroke.* Ed. J. C. A. Rathmell. Garden City, NY: Doubleday, 1963.

Spence, Jonathan. *Memory Palace of Matteo Ricci.* New York: Viking Penguin, 1994.

Spong, John Shelby. *Liberating the Gospels: Reading the Bible with Jewish Eyes: Freeing Jesus from 2,000 Years of Misunderstanding.* San Francisco: HarperSan Francisco, 1996.

Smallwood, Mary. *The Jews Under Roman Rule from Pompey to Diocletian.* Leiden: E. J. Brill, 1981.

Stanton, Graham. *Gospel Truth? New Light on Jesus and the Gospels.* London: HarperCollins, 1995.

Stendahl, Krister. *The School of Matthew.* Uppsala: C.W.K. Gleerup, 1954.

———. "Anti-Semitism." In *The Oxford Companion to the Bible,* ed. Bruce M. Metzger and Michael D. Coogan. New York: Oxford University Press, 1993.

Stern, M. "The History of Judea Under Roman Rule." In *A History of the Jewish People,* ed. H. H. Ben-Sasson. Cambridge, MA: Harvard University Press, 1976.

Streeter, Burnett Hillman. *The Four Gospels: A Study of Origins.* London: Macmillan, 1930.

Strong, James. *The New Strong's Exhaustive Concordance of the Bible.* Nashville: Thomas Nelson, 1999.

Trobisch, David. *The First Edition of the New Testament.* New York: Oxford University Press, 2000.

Tyndale, William. "The Obedience of a Christian Man" (1522). In *The Work of William Tyndale.* Ed. and intro. G. E. Duffield. Preface by F. F. Bruce. Philadelphia: Fortress Press, 1965.

———. *Tyndale's New Testament,* trans. William Tyndale and ed. David Daniell. New Haven: Yale University Press, 1989.

Vermes, Geza. *Jesus the Jew.* Philadelphia: Fortress Press, 1981.

———. *The Complete Dead Sea Scrolls in English.* Trans. and Ed. from the Hebrew and Aramaic. London Allen Lane/The Penguin Press, 1997.

———. *The Changing Faces of Jesus.* New York: Viking Compass, 2000.

Wilson, A. N. *Jesus: A Life.* New York: Ballantine Books, 1993.

Wilson, Ian. *The Evidence.* Washington, DC: Regnery Publishing Inc., 2000.

Winter, Paul. *On the Trial of Jesus.* Rev. and ed. T. A. Burkill and Geza Vermes. Berlin/New York: De Gruter, 1974.

GREEK TEXTS

The Greek New Testament, ed. Kurt Aland and Barbara Aland. Stuttgart, Germany: Deutsche Bibelgesellshaft: United Bible Societies, 1993.

Greek-English New Testament, ed. Eberhard Nestle, Erwin Nestle, Kurt Aland, and Barbara Aland. 7th ed. Under the title *Novum Testamentum Graece.* Includes parallel texts of 2d ed. of Revised Standard Version. Stuttgart, Germany: Deutsche Bibelgesellshaft, 1993.

Brown, Robert K., and Philip W. Comfort, trans. J. D. Douglas, ed. *The New Interlinear New Testament with The New Revised Standard Version. The Greek New Testament,* United Bible Societies' Fourth Corrected Edition (same text as the *Novum Testamentum Graece,* 26th edition) originally ed. Eberhard and Erwin Nestle; reed. Kurt Aland, Matthew Black, Carlo M. Martini, Bruce M. Metzger, and Allen Wilgren. Wheaton, IL: Tyndale House Publications, 1990.